Marketing text in the world?

Answer:
Experience. Leadership. Innovation.

Marketing: The Core

5/e

Roger A. Kerin
Southern Methodist University

Steven W. Hartley
University of Denver

William Rudelius
University of Minnesota

The McGraw·Hill Companies

**McGraw-Hill
Irwin**

MARKETING: THE CORE, FIFTH EDITION

Published by McGraw-Hill/Irwin, a business unit of The McGraw-Hill Companies, Inc., 1221 Avenue of the Americas, New York, NY, 10020. Copyright © 2013 by The McGraw-Hill Companies, Inc. All rights reserved. Printed in the United States of America. Previous editions © 2011, 2009, and 2007. No part of this publication may be reproduced or distributed in any form or by any means, or stored in a database or retrieval system, without the prior written consent of The McGraw-Hill Companies, Inc., including, but not limited to, in any network or other electronic storage or transmission, or broadcast for distance learning.

Some ancillaries, including electronic and print components, may not be available to customers outside the United States.

This book is printed on acid-free paper.

1 2 3 4 5 6 7 8 9 0 DOW/DOW 1 0 9 8 7 6 5 4 3 2

ISBN   978-0-07-802892-2
MHID   0-07-802892-2

Senior Vice President, Products & Markets: *Kurt L. Strand*
Vice President, General Manager, Products & Markets: *Brent Gordon*
Vice President, Content Production & Technology Services: *Kimberly Meriwether David*
Managing Director: *Paul Ducham*
Executive Brand Manager: *Sankha Basu*
Executive Director of Development: *Ann Torbert*
Development Editor: *Gina Huck Siegert*
Development Editor: *Sean M. Pankuch*
Marketing Manager: *Donielle Xu*
Lead Project Manager: *Christine A. Vaughan*
Senior Buyer: *Carol A. Bielski*
Lead Designer: *Matthew Baldwin*
Cover Image: *© Getty Images*
Senior Content Licensing Specialist: *Jeremy Cheshareck*
Photo Researcher: *Mike Hruby*
Senior Media Project Manager: *Susan Lombardi*
Media Project Manager: *Joyce J. Chappetto*
Typeface: *10.5/12 Times Roman*
Compositor: *Aptara® Inc.*
Printer: *R. R. Donnelley*

All credits appearing on page or at the end of the book are considered to be an extension of the copyright page.

Library of Congress Cataloging-in-Publication Data

Kerin, Roger A.
  Marketing : the core / Roger A. Kerin, Steven W. Hartley, William Rudelius.—5th ed.
    p. cm.
  Includes index.
  ISBN-13: 978-0-07-802892-2 (alk. paper)
  ISBN-10: 0-07-802892-2 (alk. paper)
  1. Marketing. I. Hartley, Steven William. II. Rudelius, William. III. Title.
HF5415.K452 2013
658.8—dc23
                              2012030984

The Internet addresses listed in the text were accurate at the time of publication. The inclusion of a website does not indicate an endorsement by the authors or McGraw-Hill, and McGraw-Hill does not guarantee the accuracy of the information presented at these sites.

A MESSAGE FROM THE AUTHORS

Times change. Yet the more times change, the more important the constants of success become. In our textbooks and supplements, we have channeled our efforts into three competitive "points of difference": Experience, Leadership, and Innovation.

Experience. Collectively, we have taught more than 50,000 students, managers, and instructors in a dozen countries, often using one of our 18 international editions that appear in 10 languages. From these classrooms we've discovered that a "learn-by-doing" approach, based on extended, high-involvement examples and real-life marketing decisions, works best. In addition, we've learned to integrate the most important new content and technologies such as our new Chapter 16 on social media, and our online teaching/learning tool—*Connect Marketing*. Our students and their employers often tell us that a well-written marketing plan in a student's portfolio is an asset in today's competitive job interviews, so we've developed text elements that facilitate having students write marketing plans when smaller class sizes permit. In both the textbook and instructor's manual, we provide detailed guidelines and insights for instructors and students.

Leadership. The popularity of our text in the United States and around the globe is the result, in part, of our efforts to play a leadership role in the development of new principles and practices and the use of new learning pedagogies. For example, we're at the forefront of the coverage of ethics, technology, and now social media in the marketing discipline. Some other examples include:

- *LearnSmart within* Connect. This exciting McGraw-Hill technology improves student learning while enabling instructors to monitor and measure performance continuously.
- *Marketing dashboards.* Marketing managers are trying to mine the oceans of data using marketing dashboards, a boxed feature in many of the chapters.
- *Job preparation.* We believe having students "do marketing" in textbook examples, marketing plans, and in-class activities—such as our SWOT analysis to "market yourself"—increases their job placement chances.

Innovation. Our textbooks and supplements seek to serve the needs of students of all learning styles. To help instructors and students achieve this, our innovations include:

- *Quick response (QR) codes.* Each chapter in this edition has several QR codes, allowing a student's smartphone (or tablet device) scanner to link to relevant TV ads and video extensions of the textbook.
- *Marketing2Go app.* This smartphone app connects students to the 5th edition using familiar technology to offer interesting and convenient access to our materials.
- *Video cases.* Introduced in our first edition, these cases have brought real-life marketing problems into the classroom. Our new videos include Groupon, Trek, Toyota, Mary Kay, Mountain Dew, Carmex, and Bitter Girls.
- *Instructor's Survival Kit.* The props and product samples let students see and hold the actual products discussed in our in-class activities.
- *Visual test items.* Our research shows that two-thirds of marketing students skim or ignore a textbook's tables and graphs. These visual test items use a series of questions to assess and reward student understanding of such figures.

We are excited to have this opportunity to share our interests with you. Welcome to our 5th edition of *Marketing: The Core!*

Roger A. Kerin
Steven W. Hartley
William Rudelius

Preface

Marketing: The Core uses a unique, innovative, and effective pedagogical approach developed by the authors through the integration of their combined classroom alternative and consulting experiences. The elements of this approach have been the foundation for each edition of *Marketing: The Core* and serve as the core of the text and its supplements as they evolve and adapt to changes in student learning styles, the growth of the marketing discipline, and the development of new instructional technologies. The distinctive features of the approach are illustrated below:

High Engagement Style
Easy-to-read, high-involvement, interactive writing style that engages students through active learning techniques.

Rigorous Framework
A pedagogy based on the use of Learning Objectives, Learning Reviews, Learning Objectives Reviews, Applying Marketing Knowledge, and supportive student supplements.

Personalized Marketing
A vivid and accurate description of businesses, marketing professionals, and entrepreneurs—through cases, exercises, and testimonials—that allows students to personalize marketing and identify possible career interests.

Marketing: The Core, 5/e
Pedagogical Approach

Traditional and Contemporary Coverage
Comprehensive and integrated coverage of traditional and contemporary concepts.

Marketing Decision Making
The use of extended examples, cases, and videos involving marketing professionals making marketing decisions.

Integrated Technology
The use of powerful technical resources and learning solutions, such as *Connect*, LearnSmart, media-enhanced PowerPoints, and QR codes.

The goal of the 5th edition of *Marketing: The Core* is to create an exceptional experience for today's students and instructors of marketing. The development of *Marketing: The Core* was based on a rigorous process of assessment, and the outcome of the process is a text and package of learning tools that are based on *experience*, *leadership*, and *innovation* in marketing education.

EXPERIENCE

The author team brings extraordinary experience to the development of their text. For example, they have benefited from the feedback of many users of previous editions of *Marketing: The Core*—a group that now exceeds more than one million students! In addition, the authors are experienced instructors who, in their combined careers, have taught more than 50,000 students, using many teaching styles, tools, and technologies. Finally, as researchers and consultants, the authors have worked with many of the world's leading companies.

Social Media Marketing Chapter 16: Extensive Coverage of the Newest Marketing Environment

This edition features a dedicated chapter for social media marketing. This new environment is rapidly changing and constantly growing. The authors cover the building blocks of social media marketing and provide thorough, relevant content to your students. The authors discuss major social media platforms like Facebook, Twitter, LinkedIn, and YouTube. They explain how they do marketing and how companies can use those outlets for marketing purposes. Also discussed in Chapter 16 are methods of measuring a company's success with social media marketing. This new chapter represents the authors' commitment to keeping your students informed and on the cutting-edge of marketing.

Connect Marketing

This McGraw-Hill product has allowed the author team to develop a comprehensive online resource to enable students to learn faster, study more efficiently, and increase knowledge retention.

Connect Marketing provides features like:

- Book-specific interactive assignments
- Simple assignment management for instructors
- Immediate feedback for students
- eBook access
- Library and Study Center
- Powerful filtering and reporting function

Marketing Plan Activities in *Connect*

Included in this edition are auto-graded *Connect* Interactive Applications based on the marketing plan approach presented in Appendix A, and the Building Your Marketing Plan exercises at the end of each chapter. These activities are built to help students understand the pieces of a marketing plan and how the concepts of the text tie in to those portions. If you are a professor who assigns the marketing plan as a semester-long project, use these activities to supplement your marketing plan coverage—allowing students to reinforce the concepts before developing their own plan. If you are a professor who simply does not have the time to grade full marketing plans from each and every student, use these activities to replace the marketing plan project and students can leave your class better prepared for a career in marketing.

LEADERSHIP

The first text to integrate new content areas such as ethics, technology, interactive marketing, marketing dashboards and metrics, and social media.

The first custom-made videos to accompany a marketing text.

The first teaching package to utilize active learning approaches in the text and the instructor resources.

These are just a few examples that illustrate how the Kerin author team has played a leadership role in the development and delivery of marketing pedagogy. This book is recognized as the market leader in the United States and Canada and continues to introduce new, leading-edge principles and practices to students and instructors around the world.

Social Media Integration throughout the Learning Package

More than just a new, dedicated social media marketing chapter, this new edition goes above and beyond to integrate social media marketing in all aspects of learning.

- Use our *Marketing2Go* app to design a marketing piece and tweet it out to your professor and followers.
- Scan a QR code and jump to a Dr Pepper ad on YouTube.
- Instructors can visit kerin.tv/blog to get great ideas for in-class activities and discussions relevant to current events.
- Students can react to the Marketing Question of the Day on Twitter and respond with the #QotD hashtag.

This edition of *Marketing: The Core* not only delivers the content via social media, but also allows you to respond to it the same way.

Marketing Dashboards Interactive Applications

A staple of the Kerin franchise, our Using Marketing Dashboards feature in the text delivers common marketing metrics to students in a nonthreatening, digestible way. We have taken these fan favorites and developed *Connect* activities around them. These activities allow students to follow the path of learn it, practice it, apply it. Students are introduced to the metric, allowed to practice it, and then asked to apply that metric and make a real-life business decision based on the dashboard of that metric and information.

LearnSmart within *Connect*

LearnSmart is an adaptive learning system designed to help students learn faster, study more efficiently, and retain more knowledge for greater success. LearnSmart adaptively assesses students' skill levels to determine which topics students have mastered and which require further practice. Then it delivers customized learning content based on the students' strengths and weaknesses. The result: Students learn faster and more efficiently because they get the help they need, right when they need it—instead of getting stuck on lessons or being continually frustrated with stalled progress.

INNOVATION

To secure *Marketing: The Core's* position in the marketplace, the author team consistently creates innovative pedagogical tools that encourage interaction and match students' learning styles. The authors keep their fingers on the pulse of technology and education to bring real innovation to their text package.

QR Codes: 21st Century Marketing for Your Book

These little codes are becoming more and more preva-lent. Companies are using them on direct mail pieces, in-store displays, catalogs, etc. *Marketing: The Core,* 5/e is joining the QR party. These codes bring the text to life with ads and videos to tie the concepts of the book to companies and media to which students relate. These videos allow us to keep the text even more current. We can point students to the most recent, exciting media—

QR 2–4
IBM Video Case

keeping the text relevant to each student. Please use our mobile app, *Marketing2Go,* to access QR code links found throughout the book. If you don't have access to a smartphone or tablet device, go to www.kerin.tv to find the links through your computer.

Marketing2Go: Connecting Students with the Content

Marketing2Go further connects students to the 5th edition. The application contains functions that allow students to both practice exercises from the text and also create QR codes and marketing materials (from templates) to be shared through multiple social media outlets.

Marketing2Go is yet another example of the commitment to innovation by the author team and provides students with relevant content in the palms of their hands.

Marketing2Go contains a QR-code reader so when students come across one of these black and white squares in the book, they can use the app to scan in and unveil the ad or video to which it is linked.

Marketing2Go also gives access to the newly redesigned Using Marketing Dashboard activities. These activities in the app allow students to practice the metrics and generation of useful marketing dashboards discussed in the Using Marketing Dashboard boxes in the text.

Marketing2Go allows students to view the @KerinMarketing Twitter feed and respond to the Marketing Question of the Day. They will be able to view other responses to the question with the hashtag #QotD.

Students can access a 10-question quiz for each chapter through *Marketing2Go*. These questions act as a refresher and quality assessment of the main objectives of that specific chapter.

Through *Marketing2Go*, students can create their own QR codes and marketing materials using these codes. Everything from an invitation to a campus event to a business card with a code to a résumé website, students can create well-designed marketing material in a matter of minutes.

www.kerinmarketing.com: Keeping Up-to-Date and Engaged

The Kerin Marketing blog (see www.kerinmarketing.com) provides current news articles about important and interesting events in marketing. Students can search with key words, review the article archives, and exchange comments with other readers. The site also provides access to the course videos and links to the Online Learning Center (OLC).

New and Revised Content

Chapter 1—New Coverage of Customer Value Proposition and New Examples, Including Facebook and Trader Joe's. 3M's innovation process is described in the chapter-opening example and the end-of-chapter case with updates about the success of its third-generation Post-it® Flag Highlighter. New examples such as Facebook, Trader Joe's, the Terrafugia Transition flying car, and the Louvre have been added, and a new discussion of customer value propositions is included in the section on the four Ps.

Chapter 2—New Coverage of Social Entrepreneurship, Marketing Dashboards, and a New Case on IBM's Smarter Planet Strategy. Social entrepreneurship examples from Teach For America, Sight-Life, and Hand-in-Hand are presented in the new Making Responsible Decisions box. A new marketing dashboard illustrates state-of-the-art visualization graphics and describes important dashboard design issues. Chapter 2 also has a new video case on IBM's "Smarter Planet" strategy, focusing on how businesses can use information to be more efficient, productive, and responsive.

Chapter 3—Integration of Content on the Marketing Environment, Ethical Behavior, and Social Responsibility and a New Video Case on Toyota's Green Car Initiatives. Chapters 3 and 4 of the previous edition have been combined in this edition. The many environmental factors that led to the extraordinary growth of Facebook are described in the opening example. Discussions of changes related to environmental forces, ethics, and sustainable development are also included. In addition, a new end-of-chapter video case—Toyota: Building Cleaner, Greener Cars—describes the car manufacturer's strategic partnership to provide national parks such as Yellowstone, the Everglades, and Yosemite with hybrid vehicles to reduce noise and emissions in the parks.

Chapter 4—New Examples of Consumer Behavior Concepts. The Chapter 4 discussion of alternative evaluation is updated with the latest information about smartphones such as Apple, BlackBerry, and HTC. New purchase decision behaviors such as the use of price comparison smartphone apps are also discussed. Other new examples include Post cereal advertising, which links the product to health benefits; Advil's advertising, which facilitates cognitive learning; and Colgate's efforts to change attitudes about toothpaste by adding new attributes to the product. Chapter 4 also includes a new video case about Groupon and how the company's "group coupons" influence consumer purchase decisions.

Chapter 5—Updated Coverage of Supplier Diversity and New Video Case. Chapter 5 includes a new video case—Trek: Building Better Bikes through Organizational Buying—which describes how Trek evaluates suppliers on quality, delivery, price, and environmental impact. The case also describes how Trek's attention to environmental impact is leading to an approach it calls "Eco Buying."

Chapter 6—New Material on Dell's Global Growth, World Trade Flows, and Cultural Influence on Advertising. Chapter 6 includes an updated chapter-opening example featuring Dell's global initiative to begin sales and distribution of low-cost notebook, laptop, and desktop personal computers in India. In addition, Chapter 6 includes new examples of cultural influences on Microsoft advertising. The consumer income and purchasing power section also describes the launch of a new Levi Strauss brand, Denizen, in China.

Chapter 7—New Coverage of Marketing Metrics for Social Media and the Explosion of Internet Data Mining. A new section on social media as a method of collecting primary data has been added to Chapter 7. In addition, a new Using Marketing Dashboards box introduces several social media metrics, including conversation velocity, share of voice, and sentiment, and describes their use at Carmex. Chapter 7 also provides an updated section about data mining on social networks and a new video case about marketing research at Carmex.

Chapter 8—New Market-Product Grid Example, and New Product Differentiation, Cannibalization, and Competition Discussions. The Chapter 8 section on Using Market Product Grids includes a new example and figure about types of sleepers and pillows! The chapter also includes a new discussion about product differentiation and its potential impact on quality and cost. The section on segmentation trade-offs now discusses the possibility of cannibalization at Walmart. Finally, a new discussion on competition has been added to Step 5: Take Marketing Actions to Reach Target Markets.

Chapter 9—New Examples of Product Failures, New Marketing Matters Box, New Test Market Discussion. Chapter 9 has many new examples of new product failures including Colgate Kitchen Entrees and Life Savers soda. Updated coverage of industrial design at professional R&D laboratories such as IDEO has been added. A new, comprehensive discussion of Stage 6: Market Testing has also been added.

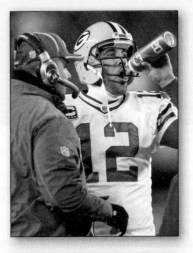

Chapter 10—Updated Examples and New Mary Kay Video Case. Gatorade's new products—Gatorade Prime, Gatorade Perform, and Gatorade Recover—are discussed in the updated opening example for Chapter 10. New Dr Pepper advertising is used to illustrate brand personality traits. In addition, a new video case about building the Mary Kay brand in India has been added to the chapter!

Chapter 11—New Coverage of Vizio's Value Pricing, Amazon's Penetration Pricing, and New Dashboard. Chapter 11 opens with an updated description of VIZIO's use of pricing to help it become the fastest growing HDTV company in the United States. The chapter also includes a new Using Marketing Dashboards box about the brand price premium of Red Bull related to competitive brands Rockstar and Monster.

Chapter 12—New Examples of Exclusive Distribution and Disintermediation. Chapter 12 includes new discussion of exclusive distribution agreements at Saks and disintermediation at American Airlines. The video case on Amazon has been updated to illustrate the company's extraordinary logistics and supply chain management expertise.

Chapter 13—Introduction of Location Services, Green Retailing, Shopper Marketing, and Integration of Wholesaling. The chapter-opening example for Chapter 13 describes location-based social networking services, such as foursquare, which allow retailers to personalize their offerings to potential customers. New coverage of the trend toward green retailing is now included in a Making Responsible Decisions box describing retailer practices, their new requirements for suppliers, and assistance provided by the U.S. Green Retail Association. The concept of shopper marketing has been added to the discussion of retailing strategy. Finally, a discussion of wholesaling has been integrated into the chapter.

Chapter 14—Introduction of the "Twitterverse," Updated Coverage of Mobile Marketing, New Material on "Do Not Track" Legislation, and a New Video Case on Mountain Dew. Chapter 14 begins with a discussion of the use of Twitter as a means of engaging consumers today. In addition, the Marketing Matters box presents an updated discussion of the use of mobile marketing as part of integrated marketing communications campaigns designed to reach "digital natives." The Geico campaign developed by *Advertising Age* magazine's Media Agency of the Year, Horizon, is discussed as an example of the trend toward IMC. A new Making Responsible Decisions box discusses the general issue of online privacy and the implications of proposed "Do-Not-Track" legislation. The chapter ends with a new video case about the "Dewmocracy" campaign, which utilized social media as part of its IMC program to develop a new Mountain Dew flavor.

Chapter 15—New Advertising and Sales Promotion Examples and Content. A new chapter-opening example about the trend toward OTV (online TV) has been added to Chapter 15. Examples of the new capability such as Hulu, YouTube channels, and Netflix, are discussed. New examples of advertising include Red Bull's Valentine's Day ad, the U.S. Army's "Army Strong," campaign, and a Dorito's Super Bowl ad. Media changes such as TV and cable program "tagging," the growth of infomercials, the specialization of magazines, and the shift to online versions of traditional newspapers are discussed. In addition, new examples of sales promotions such as Groupon's daily coupon services have been added.

Chapter 16—New Chapter on Social Media Marketing! Chapter 16 addresses the incredible growth and impact of social media on the marketing discipline. The chapter discusses the broad range of social media from Facebook and Pinterest, to YouTube and LinkedIn, to World of Warcraft and Second Life. Chapter 16 also covers how marketing managers can use social media in developing their marketing strategies and offers specific examples with Facebook, Twitter, LinkedIn, and YouTube. The chapter discusses how to measure the results of social media programs and gives many examples of some of the best mobile apps. The video case is about the Facebook launch of a brand for teenage girls called Bitter Girls.

Chapter 17—New Chapter Opening Example and Updated Description of Salesperson Time Allocations. Chapter 17 opens with a new example about today's sales professional. The example describes Lindsey Smith, a sales representative for GE Healthcare, and the four pillars of her selling approach: creating value, building trust, emphasizing competitive advantage, and providing solutions. An updated description of salesperson time allocations has been added to the section on order-getting salespeople. In addition, new material about the influence of Anne Mulcahy on Xerox Corporation is included in the video case.

Chapter 18—Updated Examples and Descriptions of the Interactive Marketing Environment. Chapter 18 includes an updated description of Seven Cycles's use of its interactive, multilanguage website to become the world's largest custom bicycle frame builder. The example describes online collaboration, customization, and feedback elements of the site. Updated information about total online retail sales and sales by product category through 2015 is also presented. A new discussion about behavioral targeting is included in the Why Consumers Shop and Buy Online section.

Appendix B—New and Updated Career Information. Appendix B, "Planning a Career in Marketing," has been updated to include new salary information, job descriptions for positions such as social media marketing manager, résumé preparation, job search techniques, and interview skills.

Organization

The 5th edition of *Marketing: The Core* is divided into four parts. Part 1, *"Initiating the Marketing Process,"* looks first at what marketing is and how it creates customer value and customer relationships (Chapter 1). Then Chapter 2 provides an overview of the strategic marketing process that occurs in an organization—which provides a framework for the text. Appendix A provides a sample marketing plan as a reference for students. Chapter 3 analyzes the five major environmental factors in our changing marketing environment and provides a framework for including ethical and social responsibility considerations in marketing decisions.

Part 2, *"Understanding Buyers and Markets,"* first describes, in Chapter 4, how individual consumers reach buying decisions. Next, Chapter 5 looks at organizational buyers and markets and how they make purchase decisions. And finally, in Chapter 6, the dynamics of world trade and the influence of cultural diversity on global marketing practices are explored.

In Part 3, *"Targeting Marketing Opportunities,"* the marketing research function and how information about prospective consumers is linked to marketing strategy and decisions is discussed in Chapter 7. The process of segmenting and targeting markets and positioning products appears in Chapter 8.

Part 4, *"Satisfying Marketing Opportunities,"* covers the marketing mix elements. The product element is divided into the natural chronological sequence of first developing new products and services (Chapter 9) and then managing the existing products, services, and brands (Chapter 10). In Chapter 11, pricing is covered in terms of the way organizations set prices. Two chapters address the place (distribution) aspects of marketing: "Managing Marketing Channels and Supply Chains" (Chapter 12), and "Retailing and Wholesaling" (Chapter 13). Chapter 14 discusses integrated marketing communications and direct marketing. The primary forms of mass market communication—advertising, sales promotion, and public relations—are covered in Chapter 15. Social media are covered in Chapter 16 as a separate chapter to reflect their growing importance in the marketing discipline. Personal selling and sales management are covered in Chapter 17. Chapter 18 describes how interactive and multichannel marketing influences customer value and the customer experience through context, content, community, customization, connectivity, and commerce.

The book closes with Appendix B, "Planning a Career in Marketing," which discusses marketing jobs and how to get them. In addition, a detailed Glossary, Learning Review Answers, and three indexes (name, company/product, and subject) complete the book.

Engaging Features

Chapter-opening vignettes introduce students to chapter concepts by using an exciting company as an example. Students are immediately engaged while learning about real-world companies.

Marketing Matters boxes highlight real-world examples of customer value creation and delivery and entrepreneurship that give students further insight into the practical world of marketing.

Marketing Matters > > > > > customer value

The Global Teenager—A Market of 2 Billion Voracious Consumers with $250 Billion to Spend

The "global teenager" market consists of 2 billion 13- to 19-year-olds in Europe, North and South America, and industrialized nations of Asia and the Pacific Rim who have experienced intense exposure to television (MTV broadcasts in 169 countries in 28 languages), movies, travel, the Internet, and global advertising by companies such as Apple, Sony, Nike, and Coca-Cola. The similarities among teens across these countries are greater than their differences. For example, a global study of middle-class teenagers' rooms in 25 industrialized countries indicated it was difficult, if not impossible, to tell whether the rooms were in Los Angeles, Mexico City, Tokyo, Rio de Janeiro, Sydney, or Paris. Why? Teens spend $250 billion annually for a common gallery of products: Nintendo video games, Tommy Hilfiger apparel, Levi's blue

jeans, Nike and Adidas athletic shoes, Swatch watches, Apple iPods, Benetton apparel, and Cover Girl cosmetics (shown in the photo).

Teenagers around the world appreciate fashion and music and desire novelty and trendier designs and images. They also acknowledge an Americanization of fashion and culture based on another study of 6,500 teens in 26 countries. When asked what country had the most influence on their attitudes and purchase behavior, 54 percent of teens from the United States, 87 percent of those from Latin America, 80 percent of the Europeans, and 80 percent of those from Asia named the United States. This phenomenon has not gone unnoticed by parents. As one parent in India said, "Now the young dress, talk, and eat like Americans."

Making Responsible Decisions boxes focus on social responsibility, sustainability, and ethics. These boxes provide exciting, current examples of how companies approach these subjects in their marketing strategy.

Making Responsible Decisions > > > > > > > ethics

Global Ethics and Global Economics—The Case of Protectionism

World trade benefits from free and fair trade among nations. Nevertheless, governments of many countries continue to use tariffs and quotas to protect their various domestic industries. Why? Protectionism earns profits for domestic producers and tariff revenue for the government. There is a cost, however. Protectionist policies cost Japanese consumers between $75 billion and $110 billion annually. U.S. consumers pay about $70 billion each year in higher prices because of tariffs and other protective restrictions.

Sugar and textile import quotas in the United States, automobile and banana import tariffs in Euro... and automobile

tire import tariffs in the United States, beer import tariffs in Canada, and rice import tariffs in Japan protect domestic industries but also interfere with world trade for these products. Regional trade agreements, such as those found in the provisions of the European Union and the North American Free Trade Agreement, may also pose a situation whereby member nations can obtain preferential treatment in quotas and tariffs but nonmember nations cannot.

Protectionism, in its many forms, raises an interesting global ethical question. Is protectionism, no matter how applied, an ethical practice?

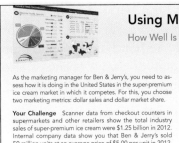

Using Marketing Dashboards

How Well Is Ben & Jerry's Doing?

As the marketing manager for Ben & Jerry's, you need to assess how it is doing in the United States in the super-premium ice cream market in which it competes. For this, you choose two marketing metrics: dollar sales and dollar market share.

Your Challenge Scanner data from checkout counters in supermarkets and other retailers show the total industry sales of super-premium ice cream were $1.25 billion in 2012. Internal company data show you that Ben & Jerry's sold 50 million units at an average price of $5.00 per unit in 2012. A "unit" in super-premium ice cream is one pint.

Using Marketing Dashboards boxes help students apply common marketing metrics to typical decisions faced by marketing managers.

Building Your Marketing Plan is an end-of-chapter feature that requires students to go through the practical application of creating their own marketing plan.

building your marketing plan

To do a consumer analysis for the product—the good, service, or idea—in your marketing plan:

1 Identify the consumers who are most likely to buy your product—the primary target market—in terms of (a) their demographic characteristics and (b) any other kind of characteristics you believe are important.

2 Describe (a) the main points of difference of your product for this group and (b) what problem they help

solve for the consumer, in terms of the first stage in the consumer purchase decision process in Figure 4–1.

3 Identify the one or two key influences for each of the four outside boxes in Figure 4–4: (a) marketing mix, (b) psychological, (c) sociocultural, and (d) situational influences.

This consumer analysis will provide the foundation for the marketing mix actions you develop later in your plan.

INSTRUCTOR RESOURCES

Instructor's Manual

The Instructor's Manual (IM) to accompany *Marketing: The Core* is an all-inclusive resource designed to make an instructor's preparation for teaching much easier. The Instructor's Manual lists the resources available to instructors: (1) PowerPoint slide references to selected figures and images; (2) Learning Objectives and Key Terms; (3) detailed Lecture Notes that identify where QR codes and In-Class Activities (ICAs) can be discussed; and (4) comprehensive Teaching Notes for the end-of-chapter video cases. A separate In-Class Activities Guide is located in the *Instructor's Survival Kit* (ISK) box, which contains the ICAs that link to sample products in the ISK box to make marketing come to life in the classroom.

FIGURE 9-1 **Market segmentation links market needs to an organization's marketing program through marketing mix actions**

Visual Test Items

We offer more than 5,000 test questions categorized by topic and Bloom's Levels of Learning (knowledge, comprehension, or application) and correlated to the Learning Objectives, level of difficulty (easy, medium, and hard), and AACSB's Assurance of Learning Standards to assist instructors in developing their exams. There are also a number of visual test items in the test bank that include images and figures from the book itself to assess student learning.

EZ Test Online

Our comprehensive bank of test questions is provided in several formats for simple use by any instructor in any setting. Our test bank is available through a computerized test bank powered by McGraw-Hill's flexible electronic testing software program EZ Test Online (www.eztestonline.com). EZ Test Online allows you to create paper and online tests or quizzes in this easy-to-use program! Imagine being able to create and access your test or quiz anywhere, at any time, without installing the testing software. Now, with EZ Test Online, instructors can select questions from multiple McGraw-Hill test banks or author their own, and then either print the test for paper distribution or give it online. It also allows you to export your tests for use in WebCT, Blackboard, PageOut, and Apple's iQuiz.

PowerPoint Presentations

The PowerPoint presentations feature slides that can be used and personalized by instructors to help present concepts to students efficiently. The Online Learning Center contains media-rich PowerPoint presentations that contain links to website addresses and QR codes to make an engaging and interesting classroom lecture.

to get, Secondly, where the owner of a trademark has spent energy, time, and money in presenting to the public the product, he is protected in this investment from misappropriation in pirates and cheats.

3-1   LANHAM ACT   KNOWLEDGE

The *Lanham Act* (1946)
a.   prevents someone from using a trademark on a non-competing product.
b.   provides for registration of a company's trademarks.
c.   protects only the consumer.
d.   allows a company to secure rights to a name before actual use.
e.   facilitates the protection of U.S. trademark rights throughout the world.

Answer: b   **Page:** 83   **LO:** 6   **LL:** 1   **AACSB:** 3
Rationale: Text term definition—*Lanham Act*

3-2   REGULATORY FORCES - PRODUCT RELATED   COMPREHENSION

The *Lanham Act* cannot protect the rights to a trademark if
a.   the company is accused of violating the Sherman Antitrust Act.
b.   the product patent is less than 17 years old.
c.   the name or symbol has become generic.
d.   the statute of limitations has run out.
e.   the government refuses to enforce violations.

Answer: c   **Page:** 83   **LO:** 6   **LL:** 2   **AACSB:** 3
Rationale: A company can lose its trademark if it becomes generic, which means that it has become merely a commonly used descriptive word for the product, such as elevator and aspirin.

New and Revised Video Cases

A unique series of 18 contemporary marketing video cases is available on DVD and at www.kerin.tv. Each video case corresponds with chapter-specific topics and the end-of-chapter case in the text. The video cases feature a variety of organizations and provide balanced coverage of services, consumer products, small businesses, *Fortune* 500 firms, and business-to-business examples. The 5th edition package includes new videos featuring IBM, Toyota, Groupon, Trek, Carmex, Mountain Dew, Bitter Girls, and Mary Kay.

Instructor Newsletter and Blog

The Instructor Newsletter has been developed for adopters of *Marketing: The Core*. This newsletter is devoted to providing innovative resources to help improve student learning, offer timely marketing examples, and make class preparation easier. The newsletter includes links to video clips from *Bloomberg Businessweek* and other sources, synopses of articles with in-class discussion questions, teaching tips, and discussion of pedagogical features of *Marketing: The Core*. The newsletter is offered eight times during the academic year and is available through e-mail, on our website, http://core.kerin.tv, and on our blog, www.kerinmarketing.com.

Instructor's Survival Kit (ISK)

The Instructor's Survival Kit contains product samples for use in the classroom to illustrate marketing concepts and encourage student involvement and learning, often with teams working on a task for 5 to 15 minutes in class. Today's students are more likely to learn and be motivated by active participative experiences than by classic classroom lecture and discussion. *Marketing: The Core* utilizes product samples from both large and small firms that will interest today's students. When appropriate, sample print and TV ads and other videos are included in the PowerPoint presentations located on the ICA CD in the ISK box.

Less Managing. More Teaching. Greater Learning.

McGraw-Hill *Connect Marketing* is an online assignment and assessment solution that connects students with the tools and resources they'll need to achieve success. McGraw-Hill *Connect Marketing* helps prepare students for their future by enabling faster learning, more efficient studying, and higher retention of knowledge.

Connect Interactive Applications

Engaging students beyond simply reading and recall, students practice key concepts by applying them with these textbook specific interactive exercises in every chapter.

Critical thinking makes for a higher level of learning. Each interactive application is followed up by a series of concept checks to reinforce key topics and further increase student understanding. Students walk away from interactive applications with more practice and better understanding than simply reading the chapter. All interactive applications are automatically scored and entered into the instructor gradebook.

Video Cases

These cases give students the opportunity to watch case videos and answer questions as they go.

Drag & Drop

These exercises reinforce concepts of the chapter in a smooth, interactive way.

Decision Generators

These specific, real-world scenarios require students to make real business decisions.

Case Analysis

These exercises encourage students to read a case and answer close-ended questions to demonstrate writing and critical-thinking skills.

McGraw-Hill *Connect Plus Marketing*

McGraw-Hill reinvents the textbook learning experience for the modern student with *Connect Plus Marketing*. A seamless integration of an eBook and *Connect Marketing*, *Connect Plus Marketing* provides all of the *Connect Marketing* features plus the following:

- An integrated eBook, allowing for anytime, anywhere access to the textbook.
- Dynamic links between the problems or questions you assign to your students and the location in the eBook where that problem or question is covered.
- A powerful search function to pinpoint and connect key concepts in a snap.

In short, *Connect Marketing* offers you and your students powerful tools and features that optimize your time and energies, enabling you to focus on course content, teaching, and student learning. *Connect Marketing* also offers a wealth of content resources for both instructors and students. This state-of-the-art, thoroughly tested system supports you in preparing students for the world that awaits. For more information about *Connect*, go to www.mcgrawhillconnect.com, or contact your local McGraw-Hill sales representative.

Assurance of Learning Ready

Many educational institutions today are focused on the notion of *assurance of learning*, an important element of some accreditation standards. *Marketing: The Core* is designed specifically to support your assurance of learning initiatives with a simple, yet powerful solution. Each test bank question for *Marketing: The Core* maps to a specific chapter learning outcome/objective listed in the text. You can use our test bank software, EZ Test and EZ Test Online, or in *Connect Marketing* to easily query for learning outcomes/objectives that directly relate to the learning objectives for your course. You can then use the reporting features of EZ Test to aggregate student results in a similar fashion, making the collection and presentation of assurance of learning data simple and easy.

AACSB Statement

The McGraw-Hill Companies is a proud corporate member of AACSB International. Understanding the importance and value of AACSB accreditation, *Marketing: The Core*, 5e, recognizes the curricula guidelines detailed in the AACSB Assurance of Learning Standards for business accreditation by connecting selected questions in the test bank to six of the thirteen general knowledge and skill guidelines in the AACSB standards. The statements contained in *Marketing: The Core*, 5e, are provided only as a guide for the users of this textbook. The AACSB leaves content coverage and assessment within the purview of individual schools, the mission of the school, and the faculty. While *Marketing: The Core*, 5e, and the teaching package make no claim of any specific AACSB qualification or evaluation, we have within *Marketing: The Core*, 5e, labeled selected questions according to the six general knowledge and skills areas.

McGraw-Hill Customer Care Contact Information

At McGraw-Hill, we understand that getting the most from new technology can be challenging. That's why our services don't stop after you purchase our products. You can e-mail our product specialists 24 hours a day to get product training online. Or you can search our knowledge bank of Frequently Asked Questions on our support website. For Customer Support, call 800-331-5094, e-mail mhsupport@mcgraw-hill.com, or visit www.mhhe.com/support. One of our technical support analysts will be able to assist you in a timely fashion.

Acknowledgments

To ensure continuous improvement of our textbook and supplements we have utilized an extensive review and development process for each of our past editions. Building on that history, the development process for the 5th edition of *Marketing: The Core*, included several phases of evaluation and a variety of stakeholder audiences (e.g., students, instructors, etc.).

Reviewers who were vital in the changes that were made to the fifth edition and its supplements include:

Wendy Achey
Northampton Community College

Chris Anicich
California State University-Fullerton

Godwin Ariguzo
University of Massachusetts-Dartmouth

Tim Aurand
Northern Illinois University

Suman Basuroy
University of Oklahoma

Connie Bateman
University of North Dakota

Leta Beard
University of Washington

Cathleen Behan
Northern Virginia Community College

John Benavidez
University of New Mexico

Ellen Benowitz
Mercer County Community College

Karen Berger
Pace University

Abhi Biswas
University of Texas-Dallas

John Brandon
Ashland University

Glen Brodowsky
California State University-San Marcos

Catherine Campbell
University of Maryland-University College

Gary Carson
Rice University

Tom Castle
Mount Mercy University

Erin Cavusgil
Baker College-Flint

Kirti Celly
California State University-Dominguez Hills

Donald Chang
Metro State College of Denver

Janet Ciccarelli
Herkimer County Community College

Reid Claxton
East Carolina University

Debbie Coleman
Miami University

Mayukh Dass
Texas Tech University

Beth Deinert
Southeast Community College

Frances Depaul
Westmoreland County Community College

Casey Donoho
California State University-Chico

Ron Dougherty
Davidson County Community College

Diane Dowdell
Saint Mary's University

Paul Dowling
University of Utah

Laura Dwyer
Rochester Institute of Technology

Rita Dynan
La Salle University

Alexander Edsel
University of Texas-Dallas

Kellie Emrich
Cuyahoga Community College

David Erickson
Lakeland College

Phyllis Fein
SUNY-Westchester Community College

John Finlayson
Creighton University

Kasia Firlej
Purdue University-Calumet

Michael Fowler
Brookdale Community College

Tracy Fulce
Oakton Community College

Bashar Gammoh
University of Toledo

James Gaubert
Clemson University

Larry Goldstein
Iona College

Karen Gore
Ivy Tech Community College

Stacia Gray
University of Central Oklahoma

Mike Hagan
University of Houston-Clear Lake

Julie Haworth
University of Texas-Dallas

Bryan Hayes
Mississippi College

Yi He
California State University-East Bay

Adrienne Hinds
George Mason University

Fred Hurvitz
Penn State University

Paul Jackson
Ferris State University

Cydney Johnson
Morrisville State College

Katie Kemp
Middle Tennessee State University

Joe Kim
Rider University

Brian Kinard
University of North Carolina-Wilmington

Martyn Kingston
University of Utah-Salt Lake City

Chiranjeev Kohli
California State University-Fullerton

Christopher Kondo
California State University-Fullerton

David Kuhlmeier
Valdosta State University

Jane Lang
East Carolina University

Cecil Leaonard
Bristol Community College

Cindy Leverenz
Blackhawk Technical College

Jay Lipe
University of Minnesota

Jason Little
Jackson State University

Jun Ma
Indiana University-Purdue University-Fort Wayne

Cesar Maloles
California State University-East Bay

James Marco
Wake Technical Community College

Larry Marks
Kent State University

Maria McConnell
Lorain County Community College

Roger McIntyre
East Carolina University

Jane McKay-Nesbitt
Bryant University

Havva Jale Meric
East Carolina University

Matt Meuter
California State University-Chico

Fekri Meziou
Augsburg College

Jennie Mitchell
Northern Arizona University

Rex Moody
University of Colorado

Robert Morris
Florida State University at Jacksonville

Farrokh Moshiri
University of California-Riverside

Gordon Mosley
Troy University

James Muncy
Valdosta State University

Suzanne Murray
Wilkes University

Paul Myer
University of Maine

Edwin Nelson
Westmoreland County Community College

Jennifer Nelson
California State University-Chico

Eric Newman
California State University-San Bernardino

Yue Pan
University of Dayton

Anil Pandya
Northeastern Illinois University

Vladimir Pashkevich
Marymount Manhattan College

Thomas Passero
Owens Community College

Bill Peterson
University of Texas-Austin

Chuck Pickett
Washington State University-Vancouver

Susie Pryor
Washburn University

Abe Qastin
Lakeland College

Kristen Regine
Johnson & Wales University

Timothy Reisenwitz
Valdosta State University

Alicia Revely
Cincinnati State Community College

Kim Richmond
Saint Joseph's University

Sandra Robertson
Thomas Nelson Community College

Bruce Robertson
San Francisco State University

Dennis Rosen
University of Kansas

Kathryn Schifferle
California State University-Chico

Mary Schramm
Quinnipiac University

Roberta Schultz
Western Michigan University-Grand Rapids

Kim Sebastiano
Cleveland State University

Lisa Simon
California Polytechnic State University

Kimberly Smith
County College of Morris

Julie Sneath
University of South Alabama

Gonca Soysal
University of Texas-Dallas

Pat Spirou
Southern New Hampshire University

Martin St. John
Westmoreland County Community College

Angela Stanton
Radford University

Susan Stanix
Delaware County Community College

John Striebich
Monroe Community College

Andrei Strijnev
University of Texas-Dallas

Randy Stuart
Kennesaw State University

Steve Taylor
Illinois State University

Scott Thorne
Southeast Missouri State University

Hsin-Min Tong
Radford University

Dan Toy
California State University-Chico

Sue Umashankar
University of Arizona

Ann Veeck
Western Michigan University-Kalamazoo

Bronis Verhage
Georgia State University

Judy Wagner
East Carolina University

Joan Williams
Northeastern State University

Kathleen Williamson
University of Houston-Clear Lake

Lauren Wright
California State University-Chico

Lan Wu
California State University-East Bay

Srdan Zdravkovic
Saint Louis University

James Zemanek
East Carolina University

Christopher Ziemnowicz
University of North Carolina-Pembroke

Lisa Zingaro
Oakton Community College

The preceding section demonstrates the amount of feedback and developmental input that went into this project, and we are deeply grateful to the numerous people who have shared their ideas with us. Reviewing a book or supplement takes an incredible amount of energy and attention. We are glad so many of our colleagues took the time to do it. Their comments have inspired us to do our best.

Reviewers who contributed to the first four editions of this book include:

Nadia J. Abgrab
Kerri Acheson
Roy Adler
Praveen Aggarwal
Christie Amato
Linda Anglin

Ismet Anitsal
William D. Ash
Corinne Asher
Gerard Athaide
April Atwood
Andy Aylesworth

Patricia Baconride
Ainsworth Bailey
Siva Balasubramanian
A. Diane Barlar
James H. Barnes
Karen Becker-Olsen

Frederick J. Beier
Thom J. Belich
Joseph Belonax
Jill Bernaciak
Thomas M. Bertsch
Parimal Bhagat

Carol Bienstock
Kevin W. Bittle
Brian Bittner
Chris Black
Christopher P. Blocker
Jeff Blodgett
Nancy Bloom
Charles Bodkin
Larry Borgen
Koren Borges
Nancy Boykin
Thomas Brashear
Martin Bressler
Elten Briggs
Bruce Brown
William Brown
William G. Browne
Kendrick W. Brunson
Judy Bulin
David J. Burns
Alan Bush
John Buzza
Stephen Calcich
Nate Calloway
William J. Carner
Larry Carter
Gerald O. Cavallo
Carmina Cavazos
S. Tamer Cavusgil
Bruce Chadbourne
S. Choi Chan
Joel Chilsen
Sang Choe
Kay Chomic
Melissa Clark
Alfred Cole
Mark Collins
Howard Combs
Clare Comm
Clark Compton
Mary Conran
Cristanna Cook
Sherry Cook
John Coppelt
John Cox
Scott Cragin
Donna Crane

Ken Crocker
Jane Cromartie
Joe Cronin
Linda Crosby
James Cross
Lowell E. Crow
Brent Cunningham
John H. Cunningham
Bill Curtis
Bob Dahlstrom
Richard M. Dailey
Dan Darrow
Neel Das
Hugh Daubek
Clay Daughtrey
Martin Decatur
Francis DeFea
Joseph Defilippe
Linda M. Delene
Tino DeMarco
Jobie Devinney-Walsh
Alan Dick
Irene Dickey
Paul Dion
William B. Dodds
James H. Donnelly
Shanmugasundaram
Doraiswamy
Michael Dore
Michael Drafke
Darrin C. Duber-Smith
Lawrence Duke
Bob Dwyer
Eddie V. Easley
Eric Ecklund
Roger W. Egerton
Steven Engel
Barbara Evans
Ken Fairweather
Bagher Fardanesh
Larry Feick
Lori Feldman
Kevin Feldt
Karen Flaherty
Theresa Flaherty
Elizabeth R. Flynn
Leisa Flynn

Charles Ford
Renee Foster
Judy Foxman
Donald Fuller
Stan Garfunkel
Stephen Garrott
Roland Gau
Glen Gelderloos
Susan Geringer
David Gerth
James Ginther
Susan Godar
Dan Goebel
Marc Goldberg
Leslie A. Goldgehn
Kenneth Goodenday
Robert Gorman
Darrell Goudge
James Gould
Kimberly Grantham
Nancy Grassilli
Barnett Greenberg
James L. Grimm
Pamela Grimm
Pola B. Gupta
Amy Handlin
Richard Hansen
Donald V. Harper
Dotty Harpool
Lynn Harris
Robert C. Harris
Ernan Haruvy
Santhi Harvey
Ron Hasty
James A. Henley, Jr.
Ken Herbst
Jonathan Hibbard
Richard M. Hill
Nathan Himelstein
Donald Hoffer
Al Holden
Fred Honerkamp
Donna M. Hope
Kristine Hovsepian
Jarrett Hudnal
Mike Hyman
Rajesh Iyer

Donald R. Jackson
Kenneth Jameson
David Jamison
Deb Jansky
Jianfeng Jiang
James C. Johnson
Wesley Johnston
Keith Jones
Robert Jones
Mary Joyce
Jacqueline Karen
Janice Karlen
Sudhir Karunakaran
Rajiv Kashyap
Herbert Katzenstein
Philip Kearney
George Kelley
Ram Kesaran
Roy Klages
John Kohn
Douglas Kornemann
Kathleen Krentler
Terry Kroeten
Anand Kuman
Nanda Kumar
Michelle Kunz
Ann T. Kuzma
John Kuzma
Priscilla LaBarbera
Duncan G. LaBay
Christine Lai
Jay Lambe
Tim Landry
Irene Lange
Richard Lapidus
Donald Larson
Ron Larson
Ed Laube
J. Ford Laumer
Debra Laverie
Marilyn Lavin
Gary Law
Robert Lawson
Wilton Lelund
Karen LeMasters
Richard C. Leventhal
Leonard Lindenmuth

Natasha Lindsey
Ann Little
Eldon L. Little
Yong Liu
Yunchuan Liu
Ritu Lohtia
James Lollar
Paul Londrigan
Lynn Loudenback
Ann Lucht
Harold Lucius
Mike Luckett
Robert Luke
Michael R. Luthy
Richard J. Lutz
Marton L. Macchiete
Rhonda Mack
Patricia Manninen
Kenneth Maricle
Tom Marshall
Elena Martinez
James Maskulka
Carolyn Massiah
Tamara Masters
Charla Mathwick
Michael Mayo
James McAlexander
Peter J. McClure
Phyllis McGinnis
Jim McHugh
Gary F. McKinnon
Ed McLaughlin
Jo Ann McManamy
Kristy McManus
Bob McMillen
Samuel E. McNeely
Lee Meadow
Sanjay S. Mehta
James Meszaros
George Miaoulis
Ronald Michaels
Herbert A. Miller
Stephen W. Miller
Soon Hong Min
Theodore Mitchell
Steven Moff
Kim Montney

Melissa Moore
Linda Morable
Fred Morgan
William Motz
Rene Mueller
Donald F. Mulvihill
James Munch
Jeanne Munger
Linda Munilla
Bill Murphy
Brian Murray
Janet Murray
Keith Murray
Joseph Myslivec
Sunder Narayanan
Nancy Nentl
Bob Newberry
Donald G. Norris
Carl Obermiller
Dave Olson
Lois Olson
James Olver
Ben Oumlil
Notis Pagiavlas
Allan Palmer
Dennis Pappas
June E. Parr
Philip Parron
David Terry Paul
Richard Penn
John Penrose
William Pertula
Michael Peters
Susan Peterson
Linda Pettijohn
Renee Pfeifer-Luckett
Bruce Pilling
William S. Piper
Stephen Pirog
Robert Pitts
Gary Poorman
Vonda Powell
Carmen Powers
Joe Puzi
Edna Ragins
Priyali Rajagopal
Daniel Rajaratnam

James P. Rakowski
Rosemary Ramsey
Barbar Ribbens
William Rice
Cathie Rich-Duval
Joe Ricks
Heikki Rinne
Linda Rochford
William Rodgers
Christopher Roe
Jean Romeo
Teri Root
Tom Rossi
Vicki Rostedt
Heidi Rottier
Larry Rottmeyer
Robert Rouwenhorst
Robert W. Ruekert
Maria Sanella
Charles Schewe
Starr F. Schlobohm
Lisa M. Sciulli
Stan Scott
Eberhard Seheuling
Harold S. Sekiguchi
Doris M. Shaw
Eric Shaw
Ken Shaw
Dan Sherrel
Philip Shum
Susan Sieloff
Rob Simon
Bob E. Smiley
Allen Smith
David Smith
Ruth Ann Smith
Sandra Smith
Norman Smothers
James V. Spiers
Craig Stacey
Miriam B. Stamps
Cheryl Stansfield
Joe Stasio
Tom Stevenson
Kathleen Stuenkel
Scott Swan
Ric Sweeney

Michael Swenson
Robert Swerdlow
Vincent P Taiani
Clint Tankersley
Ruth Taylor
Andrew Thacker
Tom Thompson
Fred Trawick
Thomas L. Trittipo
Gary Tucker
Ottilia Voegtli
Jeff von Freymann
Gerald Waddle
Randall E. Wade
Blaise Waguespack, Jr.
Harlan Wallingford
Joann Wayman
Mark Weber
Don Weinrauch
Robert S. Welsh
Ron Weston
Michelle Wetherbee
Sheila Wexler
Max White
Alan Whitebread
James Wilkins
Erin Wilkinson
Janice Williams
Kaylene Williams
Robert Williams
Jerrry W. Wilson
Joseph Wisenblit
Robert Witherspoon
Kim Wong
Van R. Wood
Wendy Wood
Letty Workman
William R. Wynd
Donna Yancey
Poh-Lin Yeoh
Mark Young
Sandra Young
Gail M. Zank
Leon Zurawicki

Special thanks are due to Erin Steffes of Towson University who has taken on the responsibility of developing our *Connect Marketing* offering. Her diligence and attention to detail have created an exceptional digital component to our package which truly enhances the student learning experience. We are thrilled to have her on our team!

Our long-time collaborator, Michael Vessey, led our efforts on the Instructor's Manual, In-Class Activities, and the Instructor's Survival Kit. In addition, he provided cases, research assistance, and many special images. Michael is an exceptional education and learning consultant who brings an extraordinary familiarity with marketing and contemporary pedagogies to our project.

Thanks are also due to many other colleagues who contributed to the text, cases, and supplements. They include: Linda Rochford of the University of Minnesota-Duluth; Kevin Upton of the University of Minnesota-Twin Cities; Nancy Nentl of Metropolitan State University; David Brennan of the University of St. Thomas; Leslie Kendrik of Johns Hopkins University; Lau Geok Theng of the National University of Singapore; and Leigh McAlister of the University of Texas at Austin. Tia Quinlan-Wilder led the production of the Test Bank. In addition, Michael Vessey, Kim Ballard, Lydia MacKenzie, Paul Sandholm, Daryl Natz, Jacob Cotten, Alan Bail, Lisa Vessey, Steven Rudelius, and Thomas Rudelius also provided assistance with the Test Bank. Rick Armstrong of Armstrong Photography, Nick Kaufman and Michelle Morgan of NKP Media, Bruce McLean of World Class Communication Technologies, Paul Fagan of Fagan Productions, Dan Hundley and George Heck of Token Media, Martin Walter of White Room Digital, Scott Bolin of Bolin Marketing, Dan Stephenson of the Philadelphia Phillies, and Andrew Schones of Pure Imagination produced the videos. In addition, Nancy Harrower of Concordia University has taken on the responsibility for our newsletter and blog (www.kerinmarketing.com).

Many businesspeople also provided substantial assistance by making available information that appears in the text, videos, and supplements—much of it for the first time in college materials. Thanks are due to David Ford and Don Rylander of Ford Consulting Group; Mark Rehborg of Tony's Pizza; Vivian Callaway, Sandy Proctor, and Anna Stoesz of General Mills; David Windorski, Tom Barnidge, and Erica Scheibel of 3M; Nicholas Skally, Jeremy Stonier, and Joe Olivas of Prince Sports; David Montgomery, David Buck, and Bonnie Clark of the Philadelphia Phillies; Ian Wolfman of imc²; Brian Niccol of Pizza Hut; Stan Jacot of ConAgra Snack Foods; Kim Nagele of JCPenney, Inc.; Charles Besio of the Sewell Automotive Group, Inc.; Lindsey Smith of GE Healthcare; Sheryl Adkins-Green of Mary Kay, Inc.; Mattison Crowe of Seven Cycles, Inc.; Jeff Gerst, Holly Matson, Nick Naumann, and Dane Hartzell of Bolin Marketing; Jennifer Katz, Amanda Axvig, and Brian Stucky of AOI Marketing; and Nelson Ng from Dundas Data Visualization, Inc.

Staff support from the Southern Methodist University, the University of Denver, and the University of Minnesota was essential. We gratefully acknowledge the help of Wanda Hanson, Jeanne Milazzo, Candi Duke, Gloria Valdez, and Jill Johnson for their many contributions.

Checking countless details related to layout, graphics, clear writing, and last minute changes to ensure timely examples is essential for a sound and accurate textbook. This also involves coordinating activities of authors, designers, editors, compositors, and production specialists. Christine Vaughan, our Lead Project Manager, of McGraw-Hill/Irwin's production staff and editorial consultant, Gina Huck Siegert of Imaginative Solutions, Inc., provided the necessary oversight and hand-holding for us, while retaining a refreshing sense of humor, often under tight deadlines. Thank you again.

Finally, we acknowledge the professional efforts of the McGraw-Hill/Irwin staff. Completion of our book and its many supplements required the attention and commitment of many editorial, production, marketing, and research personnel. Our Burr Ridge-based team included Paul Ducham, Sankha Basu, Sean Pankuch, Matt Baldwin, Carol Bielski, Jeremy Cheshareck, Joyce Chappetto, Sue Lombardi, Donielle Xu, Liz Steiner, and many others. In addition we relied on Michael Hruby for constant attention regarding photo elements of the text. Handling the countless details of our text, supplement, and support technologies has become an incredibly complex challenge. We thank all these people for their efforts!

Roger A. Kerin
Steven W. Hartley
William Rudelius

BRIEF CONTENTS

DETAILED CONTENTS

Part 1   Initiating the Marketing Process

**3   UNDERSTANDING THE MARKETING
ENVIRONMENT, ETHICAL BEHAVIOR, AND
SOCIAL RESPONSIBILITY   59**

Part 2

Understanding Buyers and Markets

Part 3

Targeting Marketing Opportunities

Part 4   Satisfying Marketing Opportunities

Marketing: The Core

- "To contribute to human welfare by application of biomedical engineering in the research, design, manufacture, and sale of instruments or appliances that alleviate pain, restore health, and extend life."

People see this "rising figure" mural in the headquarters of a world-class...

This inspiration and focus appear in the mission statements of both business firms and nonprofit organizations:

- Southwest Airlines: To be dedicated "to the highest quality of Customer Service delivered with a sense of warmth, friendliness, individual pride, and Company Spirit."
- American Red Cross: "To provide relief to victims of disaster and help prevent, prepare for, and respond to emergencies."

Each statement exhibits the qualities of a good mission: a clear, challenging, and compelling picture of an envisioned future.

Recently, many organizations have added a social element to their mission statements to reflect an ideal

In the first half of the 20th cen...

Creating Customer Relationships and Value through Marketing

1

LEARNING OBJECTIVES

After reading this chapter you should be able to:

LO1 Define marketing and identify the diverse factors influencing marketing activities.

LO2 Explain how marketing discovers and satisfies consumer needs.

LO3 Distinguish between marketing mix factors and environmental forces.

LO4 Explain how organizations build strong customer relationships and customer value through marketing.

LO5 Describe how today's customer relationship era differs from prior eras.

DISCOVERING HOW COLLEGE STUDENTS STUDY HELPS LAUNCH A NEW PRODUCT AT 3M

"How do college students really study?" asked David Windorski, a 3M inventor, in trying to develop a new product.

Specifically, how do they read their textbooks, take class notes, write term papers, and prepare for exams? After finding the answers, he needed to convert this knowledge into a product that actually helps students improve their studying. Finally, Windorski and 3M had to manufacture and market this product using 3M's world-class adhesive technology.

Sound simple? Perhaps. But David Windorski invested several years of his life creating an actual product students could use.[1] This process of discovering and satisfying consumer needs is the essence of how organizations such as 3M create genuine customer value through effective marketing. David Windorski's invention got a personal testimonial from host Oprah Winfrey on her TV show. More on this later.[2]

Discovering Student Study Needs

As an inventor of Post-it® brand products, David Windorski's main job is to design new products. He gets creative "thinking time" under 3M's "15 Percent Rule," during which inventors can use up to 15 percent of their time to do initially unfunded research that might lead to marketable 3M products. Windorski and a team of four college students observed and questioned dozens of students about how they studied.

Windorski describes what college students were telling him about their study habits that might lead to a new Post-it® product:

> It's kind of natural to highlight a passage in the textbook or notes and then mark it with a Post-it® Note or Post-it® Flag of some kind. So it's reasonable to put Post-it® products together with a highlighter to have two functions in one.

Satisfying Student Study Needs

In designing a marketable product for students, Windorski used wood blocks and modeling clay (see insert on opposite page) to mock up a number of nonworking models that showed him how the product would feel.

His search for the 2-in-1 highlighter plus Post-it® Flags then produced working models that students could actually use to give him feedback. Windorski had taken some giant steps in trying not only to discover students' needs for his product but also to satisfy those needs with a practical, useful product. Later in the chapter we'll see what products resulted from his innovative thinking and the initial marketing plan that 3M used to launch his products.

WHAT IS MARKETING?

The good news is that you are already a marketing expert! You perform many marketing activities and make marketing-related decisions every day. For example, would you sell more Samsung SmartTV 65-inch 3D LED HDTVs at $5,399 or $999 each? You answered $999, right? So your experience in shopping gives you some expertise in marketing. As a consumer, you've been involved in thousands of marketing decisions, but mostly on the buying and not the selling side. But to test your expertise, answer the "marketing expert" questions posed in Figure 1–1. You'll find the answers within the next several pages.

The bad news is, good marketing isn't always easy. That's why every year thousands of new products fail in the marketplace and then quietly slide into oblivion. Examples of new products that vary from spectacular successes to dismal failures appear throughout the textbook.

Marketing and Your Career

Marketing affects all individuals, all organizations, all industries, and all countries. This book seeks to teach you marketing concepts, often by having you actually "do marketing"—by putting you in the shoes of a marketing manager facing actual marketing decisions. The book also shows marketing's many applications and how it affects

The chief executive officer (second from left) of the world's largest social media company and his key executives sometimes spend their free time playing pool or paintball.

our lives. This knowledge should make you a better consumer, enable you to be a more informed citizen, and help you in your career planning.

Perhaps your future will involve doing sales and marketing for a large organization. Working for a well-known company—Apple, Ford, Facebook, or eBay—can be personally satisfying and financially rewarding, and you may gain special respect from your friends.

Small businesses also offer marketing careers. Small businesses are the source of the majority of new U.S. jobs. So you might become your own boss by being an entrepreneur and starting your own business.

In February 2004, a 19-year-old college sophomore from Harvard University started his own small web service business from his dorm room. He billed it as "an online directory that connects people through social networks at colleges." That student, of course, was Mark Zuckerberg.[3] The success of the Facebook launch defies comprehension. Zuckerberg's new Thefacebook.com website signed up 900 Harvard students in the four days after it appeared in early 2004 and by the second week, there were almost 5,000 members. Unlike Facebook, not every Internet start-up reaches almost a billion users a few years after its launch. In fact, more than half of all new businesses fail within five years of their launch.

FIGURE 1–1
The see-if-you're-really-a-marketing-expert test.

Answer the questions below. The correct answers are given later in the chapter.

1. True or false. You can now buy a flying car for about $279,000 that takes off or lands at most airports, has a safety parachute, drives on any roadway, gets 35 mpg, and can fill up at most gasoline stations.

2. True or false. The 60-year lifetime value of a loyal Kleenex customer is $994.

3. To be socially responsible, 3M puts what recycled material into its very successful ScotchBrite® Never Rust™ soap pads? (*a*) aluminum cans, (*b*) steel-belted tires, (*c*) plastic bottles, (*d*) computer screens.

Marketing: Delivering Benefits to the Organization, Its Stakeholders, and Society

marketing
The activity for creating and delivering offerings that benefit the organization, its stakeholders, and society.

The American Marketing Association represents marketing professionals. Combining its 2004 and 2007 definitions, "**marketing** is the activity for creating, communicating, delivering, and exchanging offerings that benefit its customers, the organization, its stakeholders, and society at large."[4] This definition shows marketing is far more than simply advertising or personal selling. It stresses the need to deliver genuine benefits in the offerings of goods, services, and ideas marketed to customers. Also, note that the organization doing the marketing, the stakeholders affected (such as customers, employees, suppliers, and shareholders), and society should all benefit.

To serve both buyers and sellers, marketing seeks (1) to discover the needs and wants of prospective customers and (2) to satisfy them. These prospective customers include both individuals, buying for themselves and their households, and organizations, buying for their own use (such as manufacturers) or for resale (such as wholesalers and retailers). The key to achieving these two objectives is the idea of **exchange**, which is the trade of things of value between a buyer and a seller so that each is better off after the trade.[5]

exchange
The trade of things of value between a buyer and a seller so that each is better off.

The Diverse Factors Influencing Marketing Activities

Although an organization's marketing activity focuses on assessing and satisfying consumer needs, countless other people, groups, and forces interact to shape the nature of its activities (see Figure 1–2). Foremost is the organization itself, whose mission and objectives determine what business it is in and what goals it seeks. Within the organization, management is responsible for establishing these goals. The marketing department works closely with a network of other departments and employees to help provide the customer-satisfying products required for the organization to survive and prosper.

FIGURE 1–2
A marketing department relates to many people, organizations, and forces. Note that the marketing department both *shapes* and *is shaped by* its relationship with these internal and external groups.

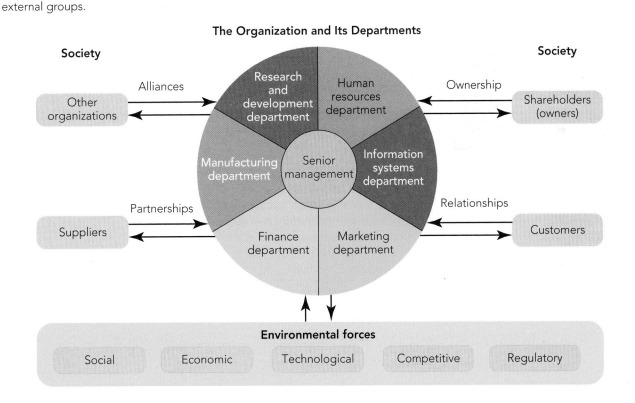

Figure 1–2 also shows the key people, groups, and forces outside the organization that influence its marketing activities. The marketing department is responsible for facilitating relationships, partnerships, and alliances with the organization's customers, its shareholders (or often representatives of groups served by a nonprofit organization), its suppliers, and other organizations. Environmental forces involving social, economic, technological, competitive, and regulatory considerations also shape an organization's marketing activities. Finally, an organization's marketing decisions are affected by and, in turn, often have an important impact on society as a whole.

The organization must strike a balance among the sometimes differing interests of these individuals and groups. For example, it is not possible to simultaneously provide the lowest-priced and highest-quality products to customers and pay the highest prices to suppliers, the highest wages to employees, and the maximum dividends to shareholders.

What Is Needed for Marketing to Occur

For marketing to occur, at least four factors are required: (1) two or more parties (individuals or organizations) with unsatisfied needs, (2) a desire and ability on their part to be satisfied, (3) a way for the parties to communicate, and (4) something to exchange.

Two or More Parties with Unsatisfied Needs Suppose you've developed an unmet need—a desire for information about late-breaking celebrity news—but you don't yet know that *People* magazine exists. Also unknown to you is that several copies of *People* are sitting on the magazine rack at your nearest bookstore, waiting to be purchased. This is an example of two parties with unmet needs: you, desiring celebrity-related information, and your bookstore owner, needing someone to buy a copy of *People* magazine.

Marketing doesn't happen in a vacuum. The text describes the four factors needed, say, to buy a *People* magazine.

Desire and Ability to Satisfy These Needs Both you and the bookstore owner want to satisfy these unmet needs. Furthermore, you have the money to buy the item and the time to get to the bookstore. The store's owner has not only the desire to sell *People* but also the ability to do so since it's stocked on the shelves.

A Way for the Parties to Communicate The marketing transaction of buying a copy of *People* will never occur unless you know the product exists and its location. Similarly, the store owner won't stock the magazine unless there's a market of potential buyers nearby. When you receive a free sample in the mail or see the magazine on display in the bookstore, this communications barrier between you (the buyer) and your bookstore (the seller) is overcome.

Something to Exchange Marketing occurs when the transaction takes place and both the buyer and seller exchange something of value. In this case, you exchange your money for the bookstore's magazine. Both you and the bookstore have gained something and also given up something, but you are both better off because you have each satisfied your unmet needs. You have the opportunity to read *People*, but you gave up some money; the store gave up the magazine but received money, which enables it to remain in business. This exchange process and, of course, the ethical and legal foundations of exchange are central to marketing.

learning review

1. What is marketing?

2. Marketing focuses on _____ and _____ consumer needs.

3. What four factors are needed for marketing to occur?

HOW MARKETING DISCOVERS AND SATISFIES CONSUMER NEEDS

LO2

The importance of discovering and satisfying consumer needs in order to develop and offer successful products is so critical to understanding marketing that we look at each of these two steps in detail next. Let's start by asking you to analyze the three products below.

For these three products, identify (1) what benefits the product provides buyers and (2) what factors or "showstoppers" might doom the product in the marketplace. Answers are discussed in the text.

Vanilla-mint-flavored toothpaste in an aerosol container

A flying car— available in 2013!

A mid-calorie diet cola

To access this QR code link, see the instructions on page xi of the preface.

QR 1–1
Terrafugia
Transition
Video

Discovering Consumer Needs

The first objective in marketing is discovering the needs of prospective customers. But these prospective customers may not always know or be able to describe what they need and want. When Apple built its first Apple II personal computer and started a new industry, consumers didn't really know what the benefits would be. So they had to be educated about how to use personal computers. In contrast, Bell, a U.S. bicycle helmet maker, listened to its customers, collected hundreds of their ideas, and put several into its new products.[6] This is where effective marketing research, the topic of Chapter 7, can help.

The Challenge: Meeting Consumer Needs with New Products

New-product experts generally estimate that up to 94 percent of the more than 40,000 new consumable products (food, beverage, health, beauty, and other household and pet products) introduced in the United States annually "don't succeed in the long run."[7] Robert M. McMath, who has studied more than 110,000 of these new-product launches, has two key suggestions: (1) focus on what the customer benefit is, and (2) learn from the past.[8]

The solution to preventing product failures seems embarrassingly obvious. First, find out what consumers need and want. Second, produce what they need and want, and don't produce what they don't need and want. The three products shown above illustrate just how difficult it is to achieve new-product success, a topic covered in more detail in Chapter 9.

Without reading further, think about the potential benefits to customers and possible "showstoppers"—factors that might doom the product—for each of the three products pictured. Some of the products may come out of your past, and others may be on your horizon. Here's a quick analysis of the three products:

- *Dr. Care Toothpaste.* After extensive research, Dr. Care family toothpaste in its aerosol container was introduced more than two decades ago. The vanilla-mint-flavored product's benefits were advertised as being easy to use and sanitary. Pretend for a minute that you are five years old and left alone in the bathroom to brush your teeth using your Dr. Care toothpaste. Hmm! Apparently, surprised parents were not enthusiastic about the bathroom wall paintings sprayed by their future Rembrandts—a showstopper that doomed this creative product.[9]

- *Terrafugia Transition.* In 2013, Terrafugia plans to introduce the Transition®, the world's first combination personal airplane and car. The Transition's flexibility allows it to land at most of the 5,200 general aviation airports in the United States. As a car, it can fold its wings, making it drivable on a roadway—from highways to residential streets! The Transition comes with a safety parachute and has a 23-gallon tank that can be filled at most gasoline stations. The proposed cost? About $279,000; you can reserve one for just a $10,000 deposit (see question 1, Figure 1–1). Potential showstoppers: The price and a potential buyer's concern that a vehicle bumped in a fender bender on a road might not be something to fly around in.[10]

- *Pepsi Next.* In early 2012, PepsiCo launched a new cola brand—Pepsi Next. It is "tastefully" sweetened with a combination of high fructose corn sugar and three artificial sweeteners, resulting in a soft drink that has 60 calories—60 percent less than regular Pepsi-Cola. Pepsi Next will battle for market share in the mid-calorie segment of soft drinkers who want both taste and low calories. Pepsi's taste tests for Pepsi Next, conducted in 2011, exceeded the firm's expectations. A potential showstopper: In the past, mid-calorie soft drinks Pepsi XL (1995), Pepsi Edge (2004), and Coca-Cola C2 (2004) all failed as "transition" sodas from regular to diet. Will Pepsi Next be next? As always, you'll be the judge![11]

Firms spend billions of dollars annually on marketing and technical research that significantly reduces, but doesn't eliminate, new-product failure. So meeting the changing needs of consumers is a continuing challenge for firms around the world.

Consumer Needs and Consumer Wants   Should marketing try to satisfy consumer needs or consumer wants? Marketing tries to do both. Heated debates rage over this question, fueled by the definitions of needs and wants and the amount of freedom given to prospective customers to make their own buying decisions.

A *need* occurs when a person feels deprived of basic necessities such as food, clothing, and shelter. A *want* is a need that is shaped by a person's knowledge, culture, and personality. So if you feel hungry, you have developed a basic need and desire to eat something. Let's say you then want to eat an apple or a microwave snack because, based on your past experience, you know these will satisfy your hunger need. Effective marketing, in the form of creating an awareness of good products at convenient locations, can clearly shape a person's wants.

Certainly, marketing tries to influence what we buy. A question then arises: At what point do we want government and society to step in to protect consumers? Most consumers would say they want government to protect us from harmful drugs and unsafe cars but not from candy bars and soft drinks. To protect college students, should government restrict their use of credit cards?[12] Such questions have no clear-cut answers, which is why legal and social issues are central to marketing. Because even psychologists and economists still debate the exact meanings of *need* and *want*, we shall use the terms interchangeably throughout the book.

As shown in the left side of Figure 1–3, discovering needs involves looking carefully at prospective customers, whether they are children buying M&Ms candy, college students buying highlighters, or firms buying Xerox color copiers. A principal activity of a firm's marketing department is to scrutinize its consumers to understand what they need and want and the forces that shape those needs and wants.

What a Market Is   Potential consumers make up a **market**, which is people with both the desire and the ability to buy a specific offering. All markets ultimately are people. Even when we say a firm bought a Xerox copier, we mean one or several people in the firm decided to buy it. People who are aware of their unmet needs may have the desire to buy the product, but that alone isn't sufficient. People must also have the ability to buy, such as the authority, time, and money. People may even "buy" an idea that results in an action, such as having their blood pressure checked annually or turning down their thermostat to save energy.

QR 1–2
Pepsi Next Ad

Studying late at night for an exam and being hungry, you decide to microwave a bag of Hot Pockets Snackers bite-sized sandwiches. Is this a need or want? The text discusses the role of marketing in influencing decisions like this.

market
People with both the desire and the ability to buy a specific offering.

FIGURE 1–3

Marketing seeks first to discover consumer needs through extensive research. It then seeks to satisfy those needs by successfully implementing a marketing program possessing the right combination of the marketing mix—the four Ps.

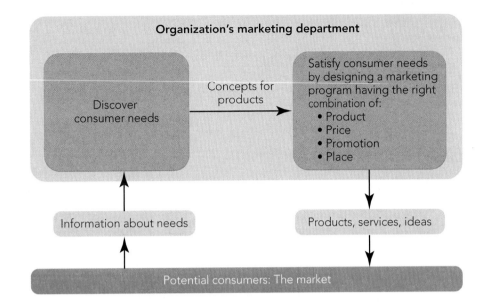

Satisfying Consumer Needs

Marketing doesn't stop with the discovery of consumer needs. Because the organization obviously can't satisfy all consumer needs, it must concentrate its efforts on certain needs of a specific group of potential consumers. This is the **target market**—one or more specific groups of potential consumers toward which an organization directs its marketing program.

The Four Ps: Controllable Marketing Mix Factors Having selected its target market consumers, the firm must take steps to satisfy their needs, as shown in the right side of Figure 1–3. Someone in the organization's marketing department, often the marketing manager, must develop a complete marketing program to reach consumers by using a combination of four tools, often called "the four Ps"—a useful shorthand reference to them first published by Professor E. Jerome McCarthy:[13]

- *Product.* A good, service, or idea to satisfy the consumer's needs.
- *Price.* What is exchanged for the product.
- *Promotion.* A means of communication between the seller and buyer.
- *Place.* A means of getting the product to the consumer.

We'll define each of the four Ps more carefully later in the book, but for now it's important to remember that they are the elements of the **marketing mix**. These four elements are the controllable factors—product, price, promotion, and place—that can be used by the marketing manager to solve a marketing problem. For example, when a company puts a product on sale, it is changing one element of the marketing mix—namely, the price. The marketing mix elements are called *controllable factors* because they are under the control of the marketing department in an organization.

Designing an effective marketing mix also conveys to potential buyers a clear **customer value proposition**, which is a cluster of benefits that an organization promises customers to satisfy their needs. For example, Walmart's customer value proposition can be described as "everyday low prices for a broad range of products that are always in stock in convenient locations." Michelin's customer value proposition can be summed up as "providing safety-conscious parents greater security in tires at a premium price."[14]

The Uncontrollable, Environmental Forces While marketers can control their marketing mix factors, there are forces that are mostly beyond their control (see Figure 1–2). These are the **environmental forces** in a marketing decision, those involving social, economic, technological, competitive, and regulatory forces. Examples are

---

target market
One or more specific groups of potential consumers toward which an organization directs its marketing program.

marketing mix
The controllable factors—product, price, promotion, and place—that the marketing manager can use to solve a marketing problem.

customer value proposition
A cluster of benefits that an organization promises customers to satisfy their needs.

environmental forces
The uncontrollable social, economic, technological, competitive, and regulatory forces that affect the results of a marketing decision.

what consumers themselves want and need, changing technology, the state of the economy in terms of whether it is expanding or contracting, actions that competitors take, and government restrictions. Covered in detail in Chapter 3, these five forces may serve as accelerators or brakes on marketing, sometimes expanding an organization's marketing opportunities while at other times restricting them.

THE MARKETING PROGRAM: HOW CUSTOMER RELATIONSHIPS ARE BUILT

LO4

An organization's marketing program connects it with its customers. To clarify this link, we will first discuss the critically important concepts of customer value, customer relationships, and relationship marketing. Then we will illustrate these concepts using 3M's marketing program for its new Post-it® products for students.

Customer Value and Customer Relationships

Intense competition in today's fast-paced domestic and global markets has caused massive restructuring of many American industries and businesses. American managers are seeking ways to achieve success in this new, more intense level of global competition.

This has prompted many successful U.S. firms to focus on "customer value." That firms gain loyal customers by providing unique value is the essence of successful marketing. What is new, however, is a more careful attempt at understanding how a firm's customers perceive value and then actually creating and delivering that value.[15] For our purposes, **customer value** is the unique combination of benefits received by targeted buyers that includes quality, convenience, on-time delivery, and both before-sale and after-sale service at a specific price. Loyal, satisfied customers are likely to repurchase more over time.[16] Firms now actually try to place a dollar value on the purchases of loyal, satisfied customers during their lifetimes. For example, loyal Kleenex customers average 6.7 boxes a year, about $994 over 60 years in today's dollars (see question 2, Figure 1–1).[17]

Research suggests that firms cannot succeed by being all things to all people. Instead, firms must find ways to build long-term customer relationships to provide unique value that they alone can deliver to targeted markets. Many successful firms have chosen to deliver outstanding customer value with one of three value strategies: best price, best product, or best service.[18]

customer value

Buyers' benefits, including quality, convenience, on-time delivery, and before- and after-sale service at a specific price.

Southwest Airlines, Starbucks, and Home Depot provide customer value using three very different approaches. For their strategies, see the text.

10

Companies such as Walmart, Southwest Airlines, and Costco have all been successful offering consumers the best price. Other companies, such as Starbucks, Nike, and Johnson & Johnson, claim to provide the best products on the market. Finally, companies such as Marriott, Lands' End, and Home Depot deliver value by providing exceptional service.

Relationship Marketing and the Marketing Program

A firm achieves meaningful customer relationships by creating connections with its customers through careful coordination of the product, its price, the way it's promoted, and how it's placed.

Relationship Marketing: Easy to Understand, Hard to Do The hallmark of developing and maintaining effective customer relationships is today called **relationship marketing**, which links the organization to its individual customers, employees, suppliers, and other partners for their mutual long-term benefit. In terms of selling a product, relationship marketing involves a personal, ongoing relationship between the organization and its individual customers that begins before and continues after the sale.[19]

Huge manufacturers find this rigorous standard of relationship marketing difficult to achieve. Today's information technology, along with cutting-edge manufacturing and marketing processes, has led to tailoring products or services to the tastes of individual customers in high volumes at a relatively low cost. So you can place an Internet order for all the components of an Apple iMac and have it delivered in four or five days—in a configuration tailored to your unique wants. But with today's Internet purchases, you will probably have difficulty achieving the same personal, tender-loving care connection that you once had with your neighborhood computer store, bookstore, or other local retailer.[20]

relationship marketing

Linking the organization to its individual customers, employees, suppliers, and other partners for their mutual long-term benefit.

The Marketing Program

Effective relationship marketing strategies help marketing managers discover what prospective customers need. They must translate this information into some concepts for products the firm might develop (see Figure 1–3). These concepts must then be converted into a tangible **marketing program**—a plan that integrates the marketing mix to provide a good, service, or idea to prospective buyers. These prospects then react to the offering favorably (by buying) or unfavorably (by not buying), and the process is repeated. As shown in Figure 1–3, in an effective organization this process is continuous: Consumer needs trigger product concepts that are translated into actual products that stimulate further discovery of consumer needs.

marketing program

A plan that integrates the marketing mix to provide a good, service, or idea to prospective buyers.

learning review

4. An organization can't satisfy the needs of all consumers, so it must focus on one or more subgroups, which are its _____.

5. What are the four marketing mix elements that make up the organization's marketing program?

6. What are environmental forces?

3M's Strategy and Marketing Program to Help Students Study

To see some specifics of an actual marketing program, let's return to our earlier example of 3M inventor David Windorski and his search for a way to combine felt-tip highlighters and 3M's Post-it® Notes or Post-it® Flags to help college students in their studying.

3M's initial product line of Post-it® Flag Highlighters and Post-it® Flag Pens includes variations in color and line widths.

Moving from Ideas to a Marketable Highlighter Product

After working on 15 or 20 wood and clay models, Windorski concluded he had to build a highlighter product that would dispense Post-it® Flags because the Post-it® Notes were simply too large to put inside the barrel of a highlighter.

Hundreds of the initial highlighter prototypes with Post-it® Flags inside were produced and given to students—and also office workers—to get their reactions. This research showed users wanted a convenient, reliable cover to protect the Post-it® Flags in the highlighter. So Windorski's rotating cover for the Post-it® Flags was born.

Adding the Post-it® Flag Pen

Most of David Windorski's initial design energies under 3M's 15 Percent Rule had gone into his Post-it® Flag Highlighter research and development. But Windorski also considered other related products. Many people in offices need immediate access to Post-it® Flags while writing with pens. Students are a potential market for this product, too, but probably a smaller market segment than office workers.

A Marketing Program for the Post-it® Flag Highlighter and Pen

After several years of research, development, and production engineering, 3M introduced its new products. Figure 1–4 outlines the strategies for each of the four marketing mix elements in 3M's program to market its Post-it® Flag Highlighters and Post-it® Flag Pens. Although similar, we can compare the marketing program for each of the two products:

- *Post-it® Flag Highlighter.* The target market is mainly college students, so 3M's initial challenge was to build student awareness of a product that they didn't know existed. The company used a mix of print ads in college newspapers and a

FIGURE 1–4
Marketing programs for the launch of two Post-it® brand products targeted at two customer market segments.

MARKETING PROGRAM ACTIVITY TO REACH:

MARKETING MIX ELEMENT	COLLEGE STUDENT SEGMENT	OFFICE WORKER SEGMENT	RATIONALE FOR MARKETING PROGRAM ACTIVITY
Product strategy	Offer Post-it® Flag Highlighter to help college students in their studying	Offer Post-it® Flag Pen to help office workers in their day-to-day work activities	Listen carefully to the needs and wants of potential customer segments to use 3M technology to introduce a useful, innovative product
Price strategy	Seek retail price of about $3.99 to $4.99 for a single Post-it® Flag Highlighter or $5.99 to $7.99 for a three-pack	Seek retail price of about $3.99 to $4.99 for a single Post-it® Flag Pen; wholesale prices are less	Set prices that provide genuine value to the customer segment being targeted
Promotion strategy	Run limited promotion with a TV ad and some ads in college newspapers and then rely on student word-of-mouth messages	Run limited promotion among distributors to get them to stock the product	Increase awareness among potential users who have never heard of this new, innovative 3M product
Place strategy	Distribute Post-it® Flag Highlighters through college bookstores, office supply stores, and mass merchandisers	Distribute Post-it® Flag Pens through office wholesalers and retailers and mass merchandisers	Make it easy for prospective buyers to buy at convenient retail outlets (both products) or to get at work (Post-it® Flag Pens only)

TV ad and then relied on word-of-mouth advertising—students telling their friends how great the product is. Gaining distribution in college bookstores and having attractive packaging was also critical. Plus, 3M charged a price to distributors that it hoped would give a reasonable bookstore price to students and an acceptable profit to distributors and 3M.

- *Post-it® Flag Pen.* The primary target market is people working in offices. But some students are potential customers, so 3M gained distribution in some college bookstores of Post-it® Flag Pens, too. But the Post-it® Flag Pens are mainly business products—bought by the purchasing department in an organization and stocked as office supplies for employees to use. So the marketing program in Figure 1–4 reflects the different distribution or "place" strategies for the two products.

How well did these new 3M products do in the marketplace? They have done so well that 3M bestowed a prestigious award on David Windorski and his team. In what must be considered any inventor's dream come true, Oprah Winfrey flew David Windorski to Chicago to appear on her TV show and thank him in person. She told Windorski and her audience that the Post-it® Flag Highlighter is changing the way she does things at home and at work—especially in going through potential books she might recommend for her book club. "David, I know you never thought this would happen when you were in your 3M lab . . . but I want you to take a bow before America for the invention of this . . . (highlighter). It's the most incredible invention," she said.[21]

Welcome to the third generation of Post-it® Flag Highlighters: the 3-in-1 Post-it® Flag Pen and Highlighter. The cap contains the Post-it® flags.

Extending the Product Line

The success of these two products has also led Windorski to design a second generation of Post-it® Flag Highlighters and Pens *without* the rotating cover to make it easier to insert replacement flags. The new tapered design is also easier for students to hold and use.

The success of the second generation of Post-it® Flag Highlighters, in turn, has spawned a family of related products. One is a line of Post-it® Flag Pens with yellow, pink, or blue inks, available individually or in a three-pack.

Is it too much trouble when you're studying to grab for a 3M Post-it® Flag, then a highlighter, and then your pen? You're in luck! New to the family of 3M products is the latest generation of David Windorski's innovations: A 3-in-1 combination that has a highlighter on one end, a pen on the other, and 3M Post-it® Flags on top, as shown in the photo.

HOW MARKETING BECAME SO IMPORTANT

LO5

To understand why marketing is a driving force in the modern global economy, let us look at (1) the evolution of the market orientation, (2) ethics and social responsibility in marketing, and (3) the breadth and depth of marketing activities.

Evolution of the Market Orientation

Many American manufacturers have experienced four distinct stages in the life of their firms.[22] The first stage, the *production era,* covers the early years of the United States up until the 1920s. Goods were scarce and buyers were willing to accept virtually any goods that were available and make do with them.[23] In the *sales era* from the 1920s to the 1960s, manufacturers found they could produce more goods than buyers could consume. Competition grew. Firms hired more salespeople to find new buyers. This sales era continued into the 1960s for many American firms.

Starting in the late 1950s, marketing became the motivating force among many American firms and the *marketing concept era* dawned. The **marketing concept** is the idea that an organization should (1) strive to satisfy the needs of consumers (2) while

marketing concept
The idea that an organization should strive to satisfy the needs of consumers while also trying to achieve the organization's goals.

also trying to achieve the organization's goals. General Electric probably launched the marketing concept and its focus on consumers when its 1952 annual report stated: "The concept introduces . . . marketing . . . at the beginning rather than the end of the production cycle and integrates marketing into each phase of the business."[24]

Firms such as General Electric, Facebook, and Marriott have achieved great success by putting huge effort into implementing the marketing concept, giving their firms what has been called a *market orientation*. An organization that has a **market orientation** focuses its efforts on (1) continuously collecting information about customers' needs, (2) sharing this information across departments, and (3) using it to create customer value.[25] The result is today's *customer relationship era*, in which firms seek continuously to satisfy the high expectations of customers.

This focus on customers has led to *customer relationship management (CRM)*, the process of identifying prospective buyers, understanding them intimately, and developing favorable long-term perceptions of the organization and its offerings so that buyers will choose them in the marketplace.[26] This requires the commitment of managers and employees throughout the organization.[27]

The foundation of customer relationship management is really *customer experience*, which is the internal response that customers have to all aspects of an organization and its offering. This internal response includes both the direct and indirect contacts of the customer with the company. Direct contacts include the customer's contacts with the seller through buying, using, and obtaining service. Indirect contacts most often involve unplanned "touches" with the company through word-of-mouth comments from other customers, reviewers, and news reports.

In terms of outstanding customer experience, Trader Joe's is high on the list and was named "America's hottest retailer" by *Fortune* magazine in 2010.[28] What makes the customer experience and loyalty of shoppers at Trader Joe's unique? The reasons include:

- Setting low prices, made possible by offering its own brands rather than well-known national ones.
- Offering unusual, affordable products not available from other retailers, like Thai lime-and-chili cashews.
- Providing rare employee "engagement" to help customers, like actually walking them to where the roasted chestnuts are—rather than saying "aisle five."

This commitment to providing a *real* customer experience, rather than just paying lip service to it, is what gives Trader Joe's its *Fortune* rating.[29]

market orientation

Focusing organizational efforts to collect and use information about customers' needs to create customer value.

Fortune magazine recently named Trader Joe's its "hottest retailer." This reflects the company's focus on providing a great customer experience—from the low prices on its own brands (shown here) to an employee walking a customer personally to the roasted chestnuts rather than just saying "aisle five."

Ethics and Social Responsibility: Balancing Interests of Groups

Today, the standards of marketing practice have shifted from an emphasis on producers' interests to consumers' interests. Organizations increasingly consider the social and environmental consequences of their actions for all parties.

Ethics Many marketing issues are not specifically addressed by existing laws and regulations. Should information about a firm's customers be sold to other organizations? Should consumers be on their own to assess the safety of a product? These questions raise difficult ethical issues. Many companies, industries, and professional associations have developed codes of ethics to assist managers.

Social Responsibility While many ethical issues involve only the buyer and seller, others involve society as a whole. A manufacturer dumping toxic wastes into streams has an impact on the environment and society. This example illustrates the issue of social responsibility, the idea that individuals and organizations are accountable to a larger society. The well-being of society at large should be recognized in an

societal marketing concept

The view that organizations should satisfy the needs of consumers in a way that also provides for society's well-being.

organization's marketing decisions. In fact, some marketing experts stress the **societal marketing concept**, the view that an organization should discover and satisfy the needs of its consumers in a way that also provides for society's well-being.[30] For example, Scotchbrite® Never Rust™ soap pads from 3M—which are made from recycled plastic bottles—are more expensive than competitors' products (SOS and Brillo) but superior because they don't rust or scratch (see question 3, Figure 1–1).

The Breadth and Depth of Marketing

Strategies in marketing art museums include planning new "satellite" museums like this one for the Louvre in Abu Dhabi.

Marketing today affects every person and organization. To understand this, let's analyze (1) who markets, (2) what is marketed, (3) who buys and uses what is marketed, (4) who benefits from these marketing activities, and (5) how they benefit.

Who Markets?   Every organization markets. It's obvious that business firms involved in manufacturing (Heinz), retailing (Trader Joe's), and providing services (Marriott) market their offerings. And nonprofit organizations such as your local hospital, your college, places (cities, states, countries), and even special causes (Race for the Cure) also engage in marketing. Finally, individuals such as political candidates often use marketing to gain voter attention and preference.[31]

What Is Marketed?   Goods, services, and ideas are marketed. *Goods* are physical objects, such as toothpaste, cameras, or computers, that satisfy consumer needs. *Services* are intangible items such as airline trips, financial advice, or art museums. *Ideas* are thoughts about concepts, actions, or causes.

product

A good, service, or idea consisting of a bundle of tangible and intangible attributes that satisfies consumers' needs and is received in exchange for money or something else of value.

In this book, goods, services, and ideas are all considered "products" that are marketed. So a **product** is a good, service, or idea consisting of a bundle of tangible and intangible attributes that satisfies consumers' needs and is received in exchange for money or something else of value.

Services like those offered by art museums, hospitals, and sports teams are relying more heavily on effective marketing. For example, financial pressures have caused art museums to innovate to market their unique services—the viewing of artworks by visitors—to increase revenues. This often involves levels of rare creativity unthinkable several decades ago.

This creativity ranges from establishing a global brand identity by launching overseas museums to offering sit-at-home video tours. France's Louvre, home to the *Mona Lisa* painting, is developing a new satellite museum in Abu Dhabi housed in an architecturally space-age building.[32] Russia's world-class 1,000-room State Hermitage Museum wanted to find a way to market itself to potential first-time visitors. So it partnered with IBM to let you take a "virtual tour" of its exhibits while watching on your iPad and relaxing. To be a "virtual tourist," go to www.hermitagemuseum.org and click on the "Virtual Visit" link.

QR 1–4
Hermitage
Tour Video

Ideas are most often marketed by nonprofit organizations or the government. So the Nature Conservancy markets the cause of protecting the environment. Charities market the idea that it's worthwhile for you to donate your time or money. And state governments in Arizona and Florida market taking a warm, sunny winter vacation in their states.

ultimate consumers

The people who use the products and services purchased for a household.

organizational buyers

Manufacturers, wholesalers, retailers, and government agencies that buy products and services for their own use or for resale.

Who Buys and Uses What Is Marketed?   Both individuals and organizations buy and use goods and services that are marketed. **Ultimate consumers** are the people—whether 80 years or eight months old—who use the products and services purchased for a household. In contrast, **organizational buyers** are those manufacturers, wholesalers, retailers, and government agencies that buy products and services for their

15

Cultivate fresh ideas and help them take root.

Live, learn, and work with a community overseas. Be a Volunteer.
peacecorps.gov

Effective marketing can benefit society like marketing the idea of volunteering for the Peace Corps.

utility
The benefits or customer value received by users of the product.

own use or for resale. Although the terms *consumers, buyers,* and *customers* are sometimes used for both ultimate consumers and organizations, there is no consistency on this. In this book you will be able to tell from the example whether the buyers are ultimate consumers, organizations, or both.

Who Benefits?   In our free-enterprise society there are three specific groups that benefit from effective marketing: consumers who buy, organizations that sell, and society as a whole. True competition between products and services in the marketplace ensures that consumers can find value from the best products, the lowest prices, or exceptional service. Providing choices leads to the consumer satisfaction and quality of life that we expect from our economic system.

Organizations that provide need-satisfying products with effective marketing programs—for example, Target, IBM, and Avon—have blossomed. But competition creates problems for ineffective competitors, such as eToys and hundreds of other dot-com businesses that failed a decade ago.

Finally, effective marketing benefits society.[33] It enhances competition, which both improves the quality of products and services and lowers their prices. This makes countries more competitive in world markets and provides jobs and a higher standard of living for their citizens.

How Do Consumers Benefit?   Marketing creates **utility**, the benefits or customer value received by users of the product. This utility is the result of the marketing exchange process and the way society benefits from marketing. There are four different utilities: form, place, time, and possession. The production of the product or service constitutes *form utility. Place utility* means having the offering available where consumers need it, whereas *time utility* means having it available when needed. *Possession utility* is the value of making an item easy to purchase through the provision of credit cards or financial arrangements. Marketing creates its utilities by bridging space (place utility) and hours (time utility) to provide products (form utility) for consumers to own and use (possession utility).

| learning review | **7.** What are the two key characteristics of the marketing concept? |
| | **8.** What is the difference between ultimate consumers and organizational buyers? |

LEARNING OBJECTIVES REVIEW

LO1   *Define marketing and identify the diverse factors influencing marketing activities.*
Marketing is an organizational function and a set of processes for creating, communicating, and delivering value to customers and for managing customer relationships in ways that benefit the organization and its stakeholders. This definition relates to two primary goals of marketing: (*a*) discovering the needs of prospective customers and (*b*) satisfying them. Achieving these two goals also involves the four marketing mix factors largely controlled by the organization and the five environmental forces that are generally outside its control.

LO2   *Explain how marketing discovers and satisfies consumer needs.*
The first objective in marketing is discovering the needs and wants of consumers who are prospective buyers and customers.

This is not easy because consumers may not always know or be able to describe what they need and want. A need occurs when a person feels deprived of basic necessities such as food, clothing, and shelter. A want is a need that is shaped by a person's knowledge, culture, and personality. Effective marketing can clearly shape a person's wants and tries to influence what he or she buys. The second objective in marketing is satisfying the needs of targeted consumers. Because an organization obviously can't satisfy all consumer needs, it must concentrate its efforts on certain needs of a specific group of potential consumers or target market—one or more specific groups of potential consumers toward which an organization directs its marketing program. Having selected its target market consumers, the organization then takes action to satisfy their needs by developing a unique marketing program to reach them.

LO3 *Distinguish between marketing mix factors and environmental forces.*

Four elements in a marketing program designed to satisfy customer needs are product, price, promotion, and place. These elements are called the marketing mix, the four Ps, or the controllable variables because they are under the general control of the marketing department. Environmental forces, also called uncontrollable variables, are largely beyond the organization's control. These include social, economic, technological, competitive, and regulatory forces.

LO4 *Explain how organizations build strong customer relationships and customer value through marketing.*

The essence of successful marketing is to provide sufficient value to gain loyal, long-term customers. Customer value is the unique combination of benefits received by targeted buyers that usually includes quality, price, convenience, on-time delivery, and both before-sale and after-sale service. Marketers do this by using one of three value strategies: best price, best product, or best service.

LO5 *Describe how today's customer relationship era differs from prior eras.*

U.S. business history is divided into four overlapping periods: the production era, the sales era, the marketing concept era, and the current customer relationship era. The production era covers the period up until the 1920s, when buyers were willing to accept virtually any goods that were available. The central notion was that products would sell themselves. The sales era lasted from the 1920s to the 1960s. Manufacturers found they could produce more goods than buyers could consume, and competition grew, so the solution was to hire more salespeople to find new buyers. In the late 1950s, the marketing concept era dawned when organizations adopted a strong market orientation and integrated marketing into each phase of their business. In today's customer relationship era, organizations seek continuously to satisfy the high expectations of customers—an aggressive extension of the marketing concept era.

FOCUSING ON KEY TERMS

customer value p. 10
customer value proposition p. 9
environmental forces p. 9
exchange p. 5
market p. 8
market orientation p. 14

marketing p. 5
marketing concept p. 13
marketing mix p. 9
marketing program p. 11
organizational buyers p. 15
product p. 15

relationship marketing p. 11
societal marketing concept p. 15
target market p. 9
ultimate consumers p. 15
utility p. 16

APPLYING MARKETING KNOWLEDGE

1 What consumer wants (or benefits) are met by the following products or services? (*a*) Carnation Instant Breakfast, (*b*) Adidas running shoes, (*c*) Hertz Rent-A-Car, and (*d*) television home shopping programs.

2 Each of the four products, services, or programs in question 1 has substitutes. Respective examples are (*a*) a ham and egg breakfast, (*b*) regular tennis shoes, (*c*) taking a bus, and (*d*) a department store. What consumer benefits might these substitutes have in each case that some consumers might value more highly than those mentioned in question 1?

3 What are the characteristics (e.g., age, income, education) of the target market customers for the following products or services? (*a*) *National Geographic* magazine, (*b*) *People* magazine, (*c*) New York Giants football team, and (*d*) the U.S. Open tennis tournament.

4 A college in a metropolitan area wishes to increase its evening-school offerings of business-related courses such as marketing, accounting, finance, and management. Who are the target market customers (students) for these courses?

5 What actions involving the four marketing mix elements might be used to reach the target market in question 4?

6 What environmental forces (uncontrollable variables) must the college in question 4 consider in designing its marketing program?

7 Does a firm have the right to "create" wants and try to persuade consumers to buy goods and services they didn't know about earlier? What are examples of "good" and "bad" want creation? Who should decide what is good and what is bad?

building your marketing plan

If your instructor assigns a marketing plan for your class, don't make a face and complain about the work—for two special reasons. First, you will get insights into trying to actually "do marketing" that often go beyond what you can get by simply reading the textbook. Second, thousands of graduating students every year get their first job by showing prospective employers a "portfolio" of samples of their written work from college—often a marketing plan if they have one. This can work for you.

This "Building Your Marketing Plan" section at the end of each chapter suggests ways to improve and focus your marketing plan. You will use the sample marketing plan in Appendix A (following Chapter 2) as a guide, and this section after each chapter will help you apply those Appendix A ideas to your own marketing plan.

The first step in writing a good marketing plan is to have a business or product that enthuses you and for which you can get detailed information, so you can avoid glittering generalities. We offer these additional bits of advice in selecting a topic:

- *Do* pick a topic that has personal interest for you—a family business, a business or product you or a friend might want to launch, or a student organization needing marketing help.

- *Do not* pick a topic that is so large it can't be covered adequately or so abstract it will lack specifics.

1 Now to get you started on your marketing plan, list four or five possible topics and compare these with the criteria your instructor suggests and those shown above. Think hard, because your decision will be with you all term and may influence the quality of the resulting marketing plan you show to a prospective employer.

2 When you have selected your marketing plan topic, whether the plan is for an actual business, a possible business, or a student organization, write the "company description" in your plan, as shown in Appendix A.

---

video case 1   3M's Post-it® Flag Highlighter: Extending the Concept!

QR 1–5
3M Flag
Highlighters
Video Case

"I didn't go out to students and ask, 'What are your needs, or what are your wants?' " 3M inventor David Windorski explains to a class of college students. "And even if I did ask, they probably wouldn't say, 'Put flags inside a highlighter.' "

So Windorski turned the classic textbook approach to marketing on its head.

That classic approach—as you saw earlier in Chapter 1—says to start with needs and wants of potential customers and then develop the product. But sometimes new-product development runs in the opposite direction: Start with a new product idea—such as personal computers—and then see if there is a market. This is really what Windorski did, using a lot of marketing research along the way after he developed the concept of the Post-it® Flag Highlighter.

EARLY MARKETING RESEARCH

During this new-product development process, Windorski and 3M did a lot of marketing research on students. For example, students were asked to dump the contents of their backpacks on the table and to explain what they carried around and then to react to some early highlighter models. Also, several times six or seven students were interviewed together and observed by 3M researchers from behind a one-way mirror—the focus group technique discussed in Chapter 8. Other students were interviewed individually.

Windorski's early models were nonworking clay ones. These nonworking models told him how the innovative highlighters would feel to students eventually using the real ones. When early working models of the Post-it® Flag Highlighter finally existed, several hundred were produced and given to students to use for a month. Their reactions were captured on a questionnaire.

THE NEW-PRODUCT LAUNCH

After the initial marketing research and dozens of technical tests in 3M laboratories, David Windorski's new 3M highlighter product was ready to be manufactured and marketed.

Here's a snapshot of the pre-launch issues that were solved before the product could be introduced:

- *Technical issues.* Can we generate a computer-aided database for injection molded parts? What tolerances do we need? The 3M highlighter is really a technological marvel. For the parts on the highlighter to work, tolerances must be several thousandths of an inch—less than the thickness of a piece of paper.

- *Manufacturing issues.* Where should the product be manufactured? Because 3M chose a company outside the United States, precise translations of critical technical specifications were needed. Windorski spent time in the factory working with engineers and manufacturing specialists there to ensure that 3M's precise production standards would be achieved.

- *Product issues.* What should the brand name be for the new highlighter product? Marketing research and many meetings gave the answer: "The Post-it® Flag Highlighter." How many to a package? What color(s)? What should the packaging look like in order to (1) display the product well at retail and (2) communicate its points of difference effectively?

- *Price issues.* With many competing highlighters, what should the price be for 3M's premium highlighter that will provide 3M adequate profit? Should the suggested retail price be the same in college bookstores, mass merchandisers (Walmart, Target), and office supply stores (Office Max, Office Depot)?

- *Promotion issues.* How can 3M tell students the product exists? Might office workers want it and use it? Should there be print ads, TV ads, and point-of-sale displays explaining the product?

- *Place (distribution) issues.* With the limited shelf space in college bookstores and other outlets, how can 3M persuade retailers to stock its new product?

THE MARKETING PROGRAM TODAY AND TOMORROW

The highlighter turned out to be more popular than 3M expected. The company often hears from end users how much they like the product.

So what can 3M do for an encore to build on the product's initial success? This involves taking great care to introduce product extensions to attract new customers while still retaining its solid foundation of loyal existing customers. Also, 3M's products have to appeal not only to the ultimate consumers but also to retailers who want new items to display in high-traffic areas.

Product and packaging decisions for the Post-it® Flag Highlighter reflect this innovative focus. In terms of product extensions, David Windorski designed new Post-it® Flag Highlighters and Pens that are easier to hold and that have the flags permanently accessible without twisting. As to packaging, it's critical that it (1) communicates the flags-plus-highlighter idea, (2) be attractive, and (3) achieves both goals with the fewest words.

Innovation at 3M never stops. An example is the recently introduced 3-in-1 combination that contains a highlighter, a pen, and 3M Post-it® Flags (see photo on page 13).

At 3M, promotion budgets are limited because it relies heavily on its technology for a competitive advantage. This also applies to the Post-it® Flag Highlighter. So you probably have never seen a print or TV ad for it. Yet potential student buyers, the product's main target market, must be made aware that it exists. So 3M searches continually for simple, effective promotions to alert students about this product.

Great technology is meaningless unless the product is available where potential buyers can purchase it. Unlike college bookstores that exist largely to serve students, mass merchandisers and office supply stores track, measure, and

seek to maximize the profit of every square foot of selling space. So 3M must convince these retail chains that selling space devoted to its highlighter line will be more profitable than stocking competing products. The challenge for 3M: finding ways to make the Post-it® Flag Highlighter prominent on shelves of college bookstores and retail chains.

If the Post-it® Flag Highlighter is doing well in the United States, why not try to sell it around the world? But even here 3M faces critical questions: Which countries will be the best markets? What highlighter colors and packaging work best in each country? How do we physically get the product to these markets in a timely and cost-efficient manner?

David Windorski also invented another product for students based on 3M's adhesive technology: restickable 3- by 5-inch note cards. Their point of difference: They stick to surfaces for brainstorming sessions or notebooks when you want them to and slide across each other *without sticking* when you want them to do that. Asked by students how it's possible, Windorski just smiles.

Questions

1 (a) How did 3M's David Windorski get ideas from college students to help him in designing the final commercial version of the Post-it® Flag Highlighter? (b) How were these ideas important to the success of the product?

2 What (a) special advantages and (b) potential problems did 3M have in introducing a new highlighter-with-flags product for college students?

3 Visit your college bookstore before you answer. (a) Where would you display the Post-it® Flag Highlighter in a college bookstore, and (b) how can the display increase student awareness of the product?

4 In what ways might 3M try to promote its Post-it® Flag Highlighter and make students more aware of the product?

5 What are the (a) special opportunities and (b) potential challenges for 3M in taking its Post-it® Flag Highlighter into international markets? (c) On which countries should 3M focus its marketing efforts?

Ben & Jerry's Mission

Ben & Jerry's is founded on & dedicated to a sustainable corporate concept of linked prosperity. Our mission consists of 3 interrelated parts:

SOCIAL mission

To operate the Company in a way that actively recognizes the central role that business plays in society by initiating innovative ways to improve the quality of life locally, nationally and internationally.

PRODUCT mission

To make, distribute and sell the finest quality all natural ice cream and euphoric concoctions with a continued commitment to incorporating wholesome, natural ingredients and promoting business practices that respect the Earth and the Environment.

ECONOMIC mission

To operate the Company on a sustainable financial basis of profitable growth, increasing value for our stakeholders and expanding opportunities for development and career growth for our employees.

Underlying the Mission is the determination to seek new & creative ways of addressing all 3 parts, while holding a deep respect for individuals inside & outside the company, & for the communities of which they are a part.

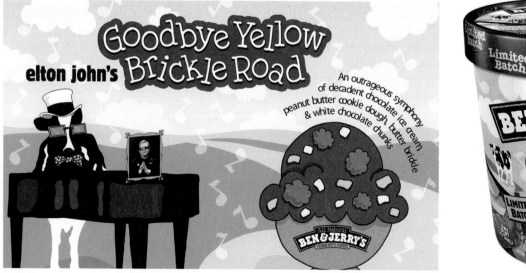

elton john's **Goodbye Yellow Brickle Road**

An outrageous symphony of decadent chocolate ice cream, peanut butter cookie dough, butter brickle & white chocolate chunks

Developing Successful Marketing and Organizational Strategies

2

LEARNING OBJECTIVES

After reading this chapter you should be able to:

 LO1 Describe two kinds of organizations and the three levels of strategy in them.

LO2 Describe how core values, mission, organizational culture, business, and goals are important to organizations.

LO3 Explain why managers use marketing dashboards and marketing metrics.

LO4 Discuss how an organization assesses where it is now and where it seeks to be.

LO5 Explain the three steps of the planning phase of the strategic marketing process.

 LO6 Describe the elements of the implementation and evaluation phases of the strategic marketing process.

WANT TO BE AN ENTREPRENEUR? GET AN "A" IN A CORRESPONDENCE COURSE IN ICE CREAM MAKING!

The two founding entrepreneurs of Ben & Jerry's have successfully implemented some highly creative marketing and organizational strategies over the years. For example:

- *Caring Dairy.* They buy their milk and cream from a cooperative that guarantees their supplies are bovine growth hormone free.

- *PartnerShops.* Their "social entrepreneurship" PartnerShop programs enable community-based nonprofit organizations to own and operate ScoopShops that help employ at-risk youth and young adults to better their lives.

- *Fair Trade.* They believe that "people should get their fair share of the pie." To that end, they practice Fair Trade–certified sourcing of key ingredients—cocoa, coffee, and vanilla—for their deliciously unique flavors like Bonnaroo Buzz. These items are purchased from producers in developing countries who practice sustainable farming techniques.

- *AIDS Prevention and Care.* They developed a limited edition "Goodbye Yellow Brickle Road" ice cream in partnership with Sir Elton John to help his worldwide AIDS Foundation. The name is a play on one of his most popular song titles. The flavor is "an outrageous symphony of decadent chocolate ice cream, peanut butter cookie dough, butterbrickle, and white chocolate chunks."

This creative, funky business is Ben & Jerry's Homemade Holdings, Inc., which links its mission statement to social causes designed to improve humanity, as shown on the opposite page.

Their business started in 1978 when long-time friends Ben Cohen and Jerry Greenfield headed north to Vermont to start an ice cream parlor in a renovated gas station. Buoyed with enthusiasm, $12,000 in borrowed and saved money, and ideas from a $5 Penn State correspondence course in ice cream making, Ben and Jerry were off and scooping.[1] Today, Ben & Jerry's is owned by Unilever, which is the market leader in the global ice cream industry—one that is expected to reach $68 billion by 2015.[2] While customers love Ben & Jerry's rich premium ice cream, many buy its products to support its social mission.

Chapter 2 describes how organizations set goals to give an overall direction to their organizational and marketing strategies. The marketing department of an organization converts these strategies into plans that must be implemented and then evaluated.

TODAY'S ORGANIZATIONS

LO1

In studying today's visionary organizations, it is important to recognize (1) the kinds of organizations that exist, (2) what strategy is, and (3) how this strategy relates to the three levels of structure found in many large organizations.

Kinds of Organizations

An *organization* is a legal entity that consists of people who share a common mission. They develop *offerings* (products, services, or ideas) that create value for both the organization and its customers by satisfying their needs and wants.[3] Today's organizations can be divided into business firms and non-profit organizations.

A *business firm* is a privately owned organization such as Target, Nike, or Hyundai that serves its customers to earn a profit so that it can survive. **Profit** is the money left after a business firm's total expenses are subtracted from its total revenues and is the reward for the risk it undertakes in marketing its offerings.

In contrast, a *nonprofit organization* is a nongovernmental organization that serves its customers but does not have profit as an organizational goal. Instead, its goals may be operational efficiency or client satisfaction. Regardless, it also must receive sufficient funds above its expenses to continue operations. Social entrepreneurs, like Teach For America, SightLife, and Hand in Hand International described in the Making Responsible Decisions box, seek to solve the practical needs of society and are usually structured as nonprofit organizations.[4] For simplicity in the rest of the book, the terms *firm, company, corporation,* and *organization* are used interchangeably to cover both business and nonprofit operations.

Organizations that develop similar offerings create an *industry,* such as the computer industry or the automobile industry.[5] As a result, organizations make strategic decisions that reflect the dynamics of the industry to create a compelling and sustainable advantage for their offerings relative to those of competitors to achieve a superior level of performance.[6] Much of an organization's marketing strategy is having a clear understanding of the industry within which it competes.

Hyundai is an example of a business firm, a privately owned organization that serves customers to earn a profit.

profit

The reward to a business firm for the risk it undertakes in marketing its offerings.

strategy

An organization's long-term course of action that delivers a unique customer experience while achieving its goals.

What Is Strategy?

An organization has limited human, financial, technological, and other resources available to produce and market its offerings—it can't be all things to all people! Every organization must develop strategies to help focus and direct its efforts to accomplish its goals. However, the definition of strategy has been the subject of debate among management and marketing theorists. For our purpose, **strategy** is an organization's long-term course of action designed to deliver a unique customer experience while achieving its goals.[7] All organizations set a strategic direction. And marketing helps to both set this direction and move the organization there.

Structure of Today's Organizations

Large organizations are extremely complex. They usually consist of three organizational levels whose strategies are linked to marketing, as shown in Figure 2–1.

Corporate Level The *corporate level* is where top management directs overall strategy for the entire organization. "Top management" usually means the board of directors and senior management officers with a variety of skills and experiences that are invaluable in establishing overall strategy.

The president or chief executive officer (CEO) is the highest ranking officer in the organization and is usually a member of its board of directors. This person must possess

QR 2–1
Teach For
America Video

Using Social Entrepreneurship to Help People

What do Teach For America, SightLife, and Hand in Hand International have in common?

The answer: They are all "social entrepreneurs" that are actively practicing—you guessed it!—social entrepreneurship. In a nutshell, social entrepreneurship applies innovative approaches to organize, create, and manage a venture to solve the practical needs of society. They usually are nonprofit organizations and focus on issues facing people who lack the financial or political means to solve their own problems. Let's look at the three social entrepreneurs mentioned above, models of creative nonprofit organizations.

TEACHFORAMERICA

Teach For America

Launched by college senior Wendy Kopp, Teach For America is the national corps of outstanding recent college graduates who commit to teach for two years in urban and rural public schools and become lifelong leaders in expanding educational opportunity. In fall 2011, 9,300 corps members taught in 43 regions across the country, while nearly 24,000 Teach For America alumni continue working from inside and outside the field of education for the fundamental changes necessary to ensure educational excellence and equity.

SightLife

The mission of SightLife is incredibly clear and specific: "To end cornea blindness." Cornea blindness, affecting 10 million people globally, can be cured by transplanting a donated, healthy cornea to replace a diseased one. Seattle-based SightLife finds cornea donors and prepares the tissues for surgery. Seeking to create 900 eye banks around the world, SightLife recruited Tim Schottman to lead the effort. He had been part of the global strategy team at Starbucks that often opened six or seven stores in a day. Schottman's reaction to the SightLife challenge was, "Ah, only 900—that's not that hard."

Hand in Hand International

Using a technique called microfinance, Hand in Hand provides small loans (about $125) to women in India, South Africa, and Afghanistan who want to start and operate a small business. A Hand in Hand self-help group reaches out to the poorest, least educated, would-be businesswomen and teaches them first the basics (reading, writing, and arithmetic) and then the skills needed to operate a business. Percy Barnevik, the founder of Hand in Hand, says he wanted to "gift" his knowledge, abilities, and passion as a retired CEO to improve society's quality of life.

leadership skills and expertise ranging from overseeing the organization's daily operations to spearheading strategy planning efforts that may determine its very survival.

In recent years many large firms have changed the title of the head of marketing from vice president of marketing to chief marketing officer (CMO). These CMOs have an increasingly important role in top management because of their ability to think

FIGURE 2–1
The board of directors oversees the three levels of strategy in organizations: corporate, strategic business unit, and functional.

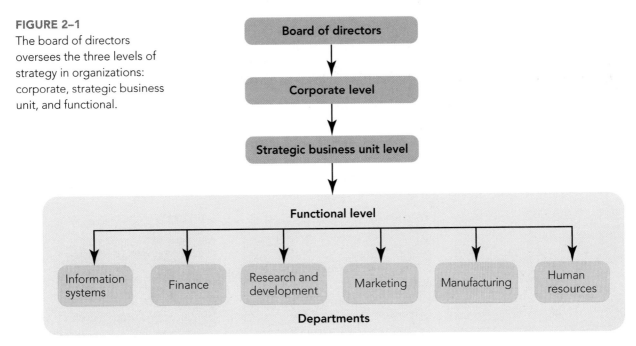

Prada manages a portfolio or group of businesses—including perfume, leather goods, and luggage—each of which may be viewed as a strategic business unit (SBU).

strategically. Most bring multi-industry backgrounds, cross-functional management expertise, analytical skills, and intuitive marketing insights to their job.[8]

Strategic Business Unit Level   Some multimarket, multiproduct firms, such as Prada and Johnson & Johnson, manage a portfolio or group of businesses. Each group is a *strategic business unit (SBU)*, which is a subsidiary, division, or unit of an organization that markets a set of related offerings to a clearly defined group of customers. At the *strategic business unit level*, managers set a more specific strategic direction for their businesses to exploit value-creating opportunities. For less complex firms with a single business focus, such as Ben & Jerry's, the corporate and business unit levels may merge.

Functional Level   Each strategic business unit has a *functional level*, where groups of specialists actually create value for the organization. The term *department* generally refers to these specialized functions such as marketing and finance (see Figure 2–1). At the functional level, the organization's strategic direction becomes its most specific and focused. Just as there is a hierarchy of levels within an organization, there is a hierarchy of strategic directions set by managers at each level.

A key role of the marketing department is to look outward by listening to customers, developing offerings, and implementing marketing program activities. When developing marketing programs for new or improved offerings, an organization's senior management may form *cross-functional teams*. These consist of a small number of people from different departments who are mutually accountable to accomplish a task or a common set of performance goals. Sometimes these teams will have representatives from outside the organization, such as suppliers or customers, to assist them.

---

learning review

1. What is the difference between a business firm and a nonprofit organization?

2. What are examples of a functional level in an organization?

STRATEGY IN VISIONARY ORGANIZATIONS

LO2

FIGURE 2–2

Today's visionary organization uses key elements to
(1) establish a foundation and
(2) set a direction using
(3) strategies that enable it to develop and market its offerings successfully.

To be successful, today's organizations must be forward looking. They must both anticipate future events and respond quickly and effectively. A visionary organization must specify its foundation (why does it exist?), set a direction (what will it do?), and formulate strategies (how will it do it?) as shown in Figure 2–2.[9]

Organizational Foundation: Why Does It Exist?

An organization's foundation is its philosophical reason for being—why it exists. Successful visionary organizations use this foundation to guide and inspire their employees through three elements: core values, mission, and organizational culture.

Organizational foundation (why)		Organizational direction (what)		Organizational strategies (how)	

• Core values
• Mission (vision)
• Organizational culture
	+	• Business
		• Goals (objectives)
		  ○ Long-term
		  ○ Short-term
			=	• By level
				  ○ Corporate
				  ○ SBU
				  ○ Functional
					• By offering
					  ○ Product
					  ○ Service
					  ○ Idea

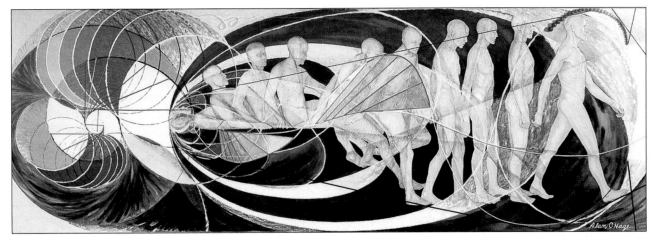

People see this "rising figure" mural in the headquarters of a world-class corporation. What does it signify? What does it say to employees? To others? For some insights and why it is important, see the text.

core values
The fundamental, passionate, and enduring principles that guide an organization.

mission
A statement or vision of an organization's function in society.

QR 2–2
Medtronic
Video

Core Values   An organization's **core values** are the fundamental, passionate, and enduring principles that guide its conduct over time.[10] A firm's founders or senior management develop these core values, which are consistent with their essential beliefs and character.[11] They capture the firm's heart and soul and serve to inspire and motivate its *stakeholders*—employees, shareholders, board of directors, suppliers, distributors, creditors, unions, government, local communities, and customers. Core values also are timeless and guide the organization's conduct. To be effective, an organization's core values must be communicated to and supported by its top management and employees; if not, they are just hollow words.[12]

Mission   By understanding its core values, an organization can take steps to define its **mission**, a statement of the organization's function in society that often identifies its customers, markets, products, and technologies. Often used interchangeably with *vision*, a *mission statement* should be clear, concise, meaningful, inspirational, and long-term.[13]

Medtronic is a world leader in producing heart pacemakers and other electrical stimulation devices to treat diabetes, Parkinson's disease, and chronic back pain.[14] Medtronic almost died in infancy when it was trying to raise start-up capital. A world-renowned consulting company surveyed doctors and "concluded there was no foreseeable market for pacemakers."[15] Earl Bakken, its founder, wrote this mission statement for Medtronic when it was launched a half century ago (and which today remains virtually unchanged):

> To contribute to human welfare by application of biomedical engineering in the research, design, manufacture, and sale of instruments or appliances that alleviate pain, restore health, and extend life.

Similar inspiration and focus appear in the mission statements of both business firms and nonprofit organizations:

- Southwest Airlines: To be dedicated "to the highest quality of Customer Service delivered with a sense of warmth, friendliness, individual pride, and Company Spirit."
- American Red Cross: "To provide relief to victims of disaster and help prevent, prepare for, and respond to emergencies."

Each statement exhibits the qualities of a good mission: a clear, challenging, and compelling picture of an envisioned future.

Recently, many organizations have added a social element to their mission statements to reflect an ideal that is morally right and worthwhile. This is what Ben & Jerry's social mission statement shows in the chapter opener. Stakeholders, particularly customers, employees, and now society, are asking organizations to be exceptional citizens by providing long-term value while solving society's problems.

In the first half of the 20th century, what "business" did railroad executives believe they were in? The text reveals their disastrous error.

organizational culture
The set of values, ideas, attitudes, and behavioral norms that is learned and shared among the members of an organization.

business
The underlying industry or market sector of an organization's offering.

Organizational Culture An organization must connect with all of its stakeholders. Thus, an important corporate-level marketing function is communicating its core values and mission to them. Medtronic has a "rising figure" wall mural at its headquarters. The firm also presents every new employee with a medallion depicting this "rising figure" on one side and the company's mission statement on the other. And each December, several patients describe to a large employee holiday celebration how Medtronic devices have changed their lives.[16] These activities send clear messages to employees and other stakeholders about Medtronic's **organizational culture**, the set of values, ideas, attitudes, and norms of behavior that is learned and shared among the members of an organization.

Organizational Direction: What Will It Do?

As shown in Figure 2–2, the organization's foundation enables it to set a direction in terms of (1) the "business" it is in and (2) its specific goals.

Business A **business** describes the clear, broad, underlying industry or market sector of an organization's offering. To help define its business, an organization looks at the set of organizations that sell similar offerings—those that are in direct competition with each other—such as "the ice cream business." The organization can then begin to answer the questions, "What do we do?" or "What business are we in?"

Professor Theodore Levitt saw that 20th century American railroads defined their business too narrowly, proclaiming, "We are in the railroad business!" This myopic focus caused them to lose sight of who their customers were and what they needed. So railroads failed to develop strategies to compete with airlines, barges, pipelines, and trucks. As a result, many railroads merged or went bankrupt. Railroads should have realized they were in "the transportation business."[17]

With today's increased global competition, many organizations are rethinking their *business model*, the strategies an organization develops to provide value to the customers it serves. Technological innovation is often the trigger for this business model change. American newspapers are looking for a new business model as former subscribers get their news online.[18] Bookstore retailer Barnes & Noble, too, is rethinking its business model as e-book readers like Amazon's Kindle and Apple's iPad appear.[19]

The Marketing Matters box describes how Netflix founder and Chief Executive Officer Reed Hastings got the idea for his start-up. His business model is changing continuously to reflect the way Internet breakthroughs are able to stream movies more conveniently to a consumer's TV set, game console, or iPad.[20] But new competitors to Netflix are all around—such as Redbox, Amazon, and Apple's streamed movies. Will there be a new business model for Netflix? Stay tuned.

goals (objectives)
Targets of performance to be achieved, often by a specific time.

Goals **Goals** or **objectives** (terms used interchangeably in this book) are statements of an accomplishment of a task to be achieved, often by a specific time. For example, Netflix might set a goal of being the top provider of online movies by 2014. Goals convert an organization's mission and business into long- and short-term performance targets. Business firms can pursue several different types of goals:

- *Profit.* Most firms seek to maximize profits—to get as high a financial return on their investments (ROI) as possible.
- *Sales* (dollars or units). If profits are acceptable, a firm may elect to maintain or increase its sales even though profits may not be maximized.
- *Market share.* **Market share** is the ratio of sales revenue of the firm to the total sales revenue of all firms in the industry, including the firm itself.
- *Quality.* A firm may offer the highest quality, as Medtronic does with its implantable medical devices.
- *Customer satisfaction.* Customers are the reason the organization exists, so their perceptions and actions are of vital importance. Satisfaction can be measured with surveys or by the number of customer complaints an organization receives.

market share
Ratio of a firm's sales to the total sales of all firms in the industry.

Marketing Matters > > > > entrepreneurship

The Netflix Launch and Its Continually Changing Business Model!

If in 1997 a customer had been charged a late fee of $40 for a VHS tape of *Apollo 13,* what might she or he have done? Maybe just grumble and pay it?

In the case of Reed Hastings, he was embarrassed, apparently paid the $40 late fee, and—this is where he's different—got to thinking that there's a big market out there. "So I started to investigate the idea of how to create a movie-rental business by mail," he told a *Fortune* magazine reviewer.

The Original Business Model

"Early on, the first concept we launched was rental by mail, but it wasn't subscription based so it worked more like Blockbuster," says Hastings, the founder and chief executive officer of Netflix. It wasn't very popular. So in 1999, he relaunched his idea with a new business model—as a subscription service, pretty much the mail business you see today. "We named the company Netflix, not DVDs by Mail because we knew that eventually we would deliver movies directly over the Internet," Hastings says.

Netflix's Changing Business Model

The Netflix DVDs-by-mail model delivered movies on DVD to customers for a fixed monthly fee—and drove Blockbuster to seek Chapter 11 bankruptcy protection. But the Netflix business model changed over eight months in 2008: from "Watch Now," enabling subscribers to watch any of 1,000 streaming movies on a PC, to partnering with TiVo, Xbox, and others to enable their systems to let you see one of about 12,000 movies on your television.

The movie distribution channel has also expanded with web-ready TVs like Sony's Bravia, game consoles like Xbox 360, and new entrants like Apple's iPad.

With Netflix breaking a series of technology barriers, its "any movie, any time" business is just around the corner. In mid-2011, Netflix introduced controversial new pricing options: DVD only, streaming only, or both. Then in late-2011, when customer reaction exploded, Reed Hastings canceled the plan to separate Netflix's DVD-by-mail business from its movie streaming service. Change is a constant in the Netflix business model.

Netflix is altering its "business model" to respond to changing consumer demand and technologies. See the text and Marketing Matters box for the reasons behind these changes at Netflix.

- *Employee welfare.* A firm may recognize the critical importance of its employees by stating its goal of providing them with good employment opportunities and working conditions.
- *Social responsibility.* Firms may seek to balance the conflicting goals of stakeholders to promote their overall welfare, even at the expense of profits.

Nonprofit organizations (such as museums and hospitals) also have goals, such as to serve consumers as efficiently as possible. Similarly, government agencies set goals that seek to serve the public good.

Organizational Strategies: How Will It Do It?

As shown in Figure 2–2, the organizational foundation sets the "why" of organizations and the organizational direction sets the "what." To convert these into actual results, the organizational strategies are concerned with the "how." These organizational strategies vary in at least two ways, depending on (1) a strategy's level in the organization and (2) the offerings an organization provides to its customers.

Variation by Level   Moving down an organization involves creating increasingly specific, detailed strategies and plans. For example, at the corporate level, top managers may struggle with writing a meaningful mission statement; while at the functional level, the issue is whether Joan or Adam makes tomorrow's sales call.

Variation by Offering   Organizational strategies also vary by the organization's offering. The strategy will be far different when marketing a very tangible physical product (a Medtronic heart pacemaker), a service (a Southwest Airlines flight), or an idea (a donation to the American Red Cross).

---

learning review

3. What is the meaning of an organization's mission?

4. What is the difference between an organization's business and its goals?

Tracking Strategic Performance with Marketing Dashboards

Although marketing managers can set strategic directions for their organizations, how do they know if they are making progress in getting there? One answer is to measure performance by using marketing dashboards.

marketing dashboard
The visual computer display of essential marketing information.

Car Dashboards and Marketing Dashboards   A **marketing dashboard** is the visual computer display of the essential information related to achieving a marketing objective.[21] Often, active hyperlinks provide further detail. An example is when a chief marketing officer (CMO) wants to see daily what the effect of a new TV advertising campaign is on a product's sales.[22]

The idea of a marketing dashboard really comes from the display of information found on a car's dashboard. On a car's dashboard we glance at the fuel gauge and take action when our gas is getting low. With a marketing dashboard, a marketing manager glances at a graph or table and makes a decision whether to take action or to analyze the problem further.[23]

marketing metric
A measure of the value or trend of a marketing activity or result.

Dashboards, Metrics, and Plans   The marketing dashboard of Sonatica, a hypothetical hardware and software firm, appears in Figure 2–3. It shows graphic displays of key performance indicators linked to its product lines.[24] Each display in a marketing dashboard shows a **marketing metric**, which is a measure of the quantitative value or trend of a marketing activity or result.[25] The choice of which marketing metrics to display is critical for a busy marketing manager, who can be overwhelmed with irrelevant data.[26]

Today's marketers use *data visualization,* which presents information about an organization's marketing metrics graphically so marketers can quickly (1) spot deviations from plans and (2) take corrective actions.[27] The Sonatica marketing dashboard in Figure 2–3 uses data visualization tools like graphs and a map to provide a snapshot of how parts of its business are performing as of December 2012:

FIGURE 2–3
An effective marketing dashboard, like this one from Sonatica, a hypothetical hardware and software firm, helps managers assess a business situation at a glance.

- *Website Traffic Sources.* The color-coded perimeter of the pie chart shows the three main sources of website traffic (referral sites at 47 percent, search engines

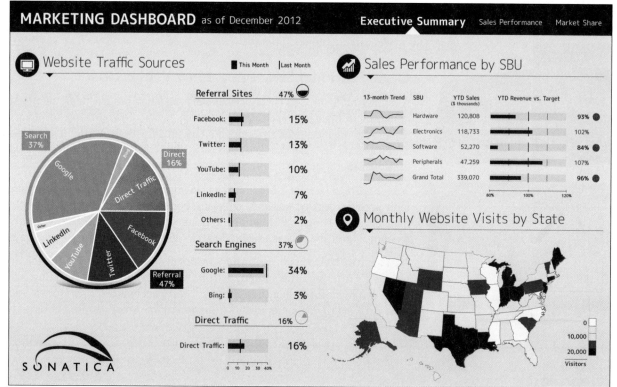

Source: Dundas Data Visualization, Inc.

Using Marketing Dashboards

How Well Is Ben & Jerry's Doing?

As the marketing manager for Ben & Jerry's, you need to assess how it is doing in the United States in the super-premium ice cream market in which it competes. For this, you choose two marketing metrics: dollar sales and dollar market share.

Your Challenge   Scanner data from checkout counters in supermarkets and other retailers show the total industry sales of super-premium ice cream were $1.25 billion in 2012. Internal company data show you that Ben & Jerry's sold 50 million units at an average price of $5.00 per unit in 2012. A "unit" in super-premium ice cream is one pint.

Your Findings   Dollar sales and dollar market share can be calculated for 2012 using simple formulas and displayed on the Ben & Jerry's marketing dashboard as follows:

$$\text{Dollar sales (\$)} = \text{Average price} \times \text{Quantity sold}$$
$$= \$5.00 \times 50 \text{ million units}$$
$$= \$250 \text{ million}$$

$$\text{Dollar market share (\%)} = \frac{\text{Ben \& Jerry's sales (\$)}}{\text{Total industry sales (\$)}}$$
$$= \frac{\$250 \text{ million}}{\$1.25 \text{ billion}}$$
$$= 0.20 \text{ or } 20\%$$

Your dashboard displays show that from 2011 to 2012 dollar sales increased from $240 million to $250 million and that dollar market share grew from 18.4 to 20.0 percent.

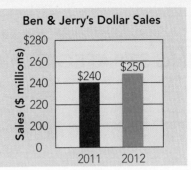

Ben & Jerry's Dollar Sales

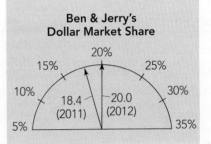

Ben & Jerry's Dollar Market Share

Your Action   The results need to be compared with the goals established for these metrics. In addition, they should be compared with previous years' results to see if the trends are increasing, flat, or decreasing. This will lead to appropriate actions.

at 37 percent, and direct traffic at 16 percent), with each of eight specific sources represented as one slice in the pie. Of the 47 percent of traffic coming from referral sites, the horizontal *bullet graphs* to the right show that Sonatica's Facebook visits comprise 15 percent of total website traffic, up from a month ago (as shown by the vertical line).

- *Sales Performance by SBU.* The *spark lines* (the wavy lines in the far left column) show the 13-month trends of Sonatica's strategic business units (SBUs). For example, the trends in electronics and peripherals are generally up, causing their sales to exceed their YTD (year to date) targets. Conversely, both software and hardware sales failed to meet YTD targets, a problem quickly noted by a marketing manager seeing the red "warning" circles in their rows at the far right. This suggests immediate corrective actions for the software and hardware SBUs.
- *Monthly Website Visits by State.* The U.S. map shows that the darker the state, the greater the number of website visits for the current month. For example, Texas has close to 20,000 visits per month, while Illinois has none.

The Ben & Jerry's dashboard in the Using Marketing Dashboards box shows how the two widely used marketing metrics of dollar sales and dollar market share can help the company assess its growth performance from 2011 to 2012. The Using Marketing Dashboard boxes in later chapters highlight other key marketing metrics and how they lead to actions.

marketing plan

A road map for the marketing activities of an organization for a specified future time period.

Most organizations tie the marketing metrics they track in their marketing dashboards to the quantitative objectives established in their **marketing plan**, which is a road map for the marketing activities of an organization for a specified future time period, such as one year or five years. The planning phase of the strategic marketing process (discussed later in this chapter) usually results in a marketing plan that sets the direction for the marketing activities of an organization. Appendix A at the end of this chapter provides guidelines for writing a marketing plan.

SETTING STRATEGIC DIRECTIONS

LO4

To set a strategic direction, an organization needs to answer two difficult questions: (1) Where are we now? and (2) Where do we want to go?

A Look Around: Where Are We Now?

Asking an organization where it is at the present time involves identifying its competencies, customers, and competitors.

Lands' End's unconditional guarantee for its products highlights its focus on customers.

Competencies Senior managers must ask the question: What do we do best? The answer involves an assessment of the organization's core *competencies,* which are its special capabilities—the skills, technologies, and resources—that distinguish it from other organizations and provide customer value. Exploiting these competencies can lead to success.[28]

Medtronic's competencies include world-class technology, training, and service that respond to life-threatening medical needs. *Bloomberg Businessweek* magazine has called Medtronic "the standard setter for quality."[29] Competencies should be distinctive enough to provide a *competitive advantage,* a unique strength relative to competitors that provides superior returns, often based on quality, time, cost, or innovation.[30]

Customers Ben & Jerry's customers are ice cream and frozen yogurt eaters who have different preferences (form, flavor, health, and convenience). Medtronic's customers are cardiologists and heart surgeons who serve patients. Lands' End communicates a remarkable commitment about its customer experience and product quality with these unconditional words:

Guaranteed. Period.®

The Lands' End website points out that this guarantee has always been an unconditional one. It reads: "If you're not satisfied with any item, simply return it to us at any time for an exchange or refund of its purchase price." But to get the message across more clearly to its customers, it created the two-word guarantee. The point is that Lands' End's strategy must provide genuine value to customers to ensure that they have a satisfying experience.[31]

Competitors In today's global marketplace, the distinctions among competitors are increasingly blurred. Lands' End started as a catalog retailer. But today, Lands' End competes with not only other clothing catalog retailers but also traditional department stores, mass merchandisers, and specialty shops. Even well-known clothing brands such as Liz Claiborne now have their own chain stores. Although only some of the clothing in any of these stores directly competes with Lands' End offerings, all these retailers have websites to sell their offerings over the Internet. This means there's a lot of competition out there.

Growth Strategies: Where Do We Want to Go?

Knowing where the organization is at the present time enables managers to set a direction for the firm and allocate resources to move in that direction. Two techniques to aid managers with these decisions are (1) business portfolio analysis and (2) diversification analysis.

business portfolio analysis

A technique that managers use to quantify performance measures and growth targets of their firms' strategic business units.

Business Portfolio Analysis The Boston Consulting Group (BCG), a nationally known management consulting firm, has developed **business portfolio analysis**. It is a technique that managers use to quantify performance measures and growth targets to analyze their firms' strategic business units (SBUs) as though they were a collection of separate investments.[32] The purpose of the tool is to determine the appeal of each SBU or offering and then determine the amount of cash each should receive.

The BCG business portfolio analysis requires an organization to locate the position of each of its SBUs on a growth-share matrix (see Figure 2–4). The vertical axis is the *market growth rate*, which is the annual rate of growth of the SBU's industry. The horizontal axis is the *relative market share*, defined as the sales of the SBU divided by the sales of the largest firm in the industry. A relative market share of $10\times$ (at the left end of the scale) means that the SBU has 10 times the share of its largest competitor, whereas a share of $0.1\times$ (at the right end of the scale) means it has only 10 percent of the share of its largest competitor.

The BCG has given specific names and descriptions to the four resulting quadrants in its growth-share matrix based on the amount of cash they generate for or require from the organization:

- *Cash cows* are SBUs that generate large amounts of cash, far more than they can use. They have dominant shares of slow-growth markets and provide cash to cover the organization's overhead and to invest in other SBUs.
- *Stars* are SBUs with a high share of high-growth markets that may need extra cash to finance their own rapid future growth. When their growth slows, they are likely to become cash cows.

FIGURE 2–4
Boston Consulting Group business portfolio analysis for Kodak's consumer-related SBUs with relative sales as they appeared in 2003 (solid red circles). The arrows show where the SBUs appeared headed in 2012.

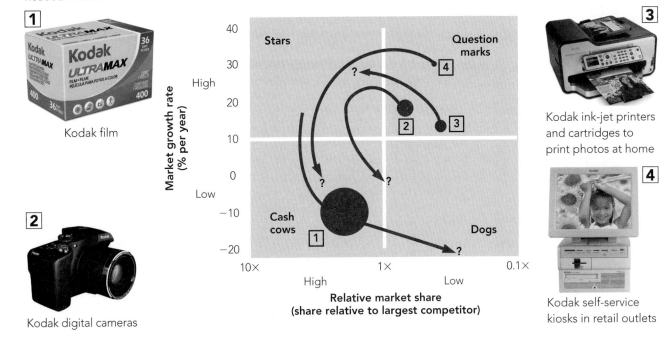

1 Kodak film

2 Kodak digital cameras

3 Kodak ink-jet printers and cartridges to print photos at home

4 Kodak self-service kiosks in retail outlets

- *Question marks* are SBUs with a low share of high-growth markets. They require large injections of cash just to maintain their market share, much less increase it. The name implies management's dilemma for these SBUs: choosing the right ones to invest in and phasing out the rest.
- *Dogs* are SBUs with low shares of slow-growth markets. Although they may generate enough cash to sustain themselves, they do not hold the promise of ever becoming real winners for the organization. Dropping SBUs that are dogs may be required, except when relationships with other SBUs, competitive considerations, or potential strategic alliances exist.[33]

An organization's SBUs often start as question marks and go counterclockwise around Figure 2–4 to become stars, then cash cows, and finally dogs. Because an organization has limited influence on the market growth rate, its main alternative is to try to change its relative market share. To do this, management decides what future role each SBU should have and either injects or removes cash from it.

While most examples in this book highlight successful companies and strategies, tragic failures also provide important lessons. A look at Kodak over the past decade shows how new technologies and changing consumer tastes can dramatically impact an iconic brand.

Founded in 1880, Kodak had 90 percent of film and 85 percent of camera sales in the United States by 1976.[34] In the early 1990s, Kodak was regularly rated as one of the five most valuable global brands. Until 2000, Kodak relied on its traditional film for the bulk of its revenues and profits because of the billions of photos taken with film cameras each year. It reaped huge profits on repeat business from traditional film sales and *not* on camera purchases. This is often called the "razor and blade strategy," a phrase resulting from the idea that a company (like Gillette) can lose money selling one product (its Fusion razors) because of the huge profits it makes from the repeated sales of a related product (its razor blade cartridges).

Four Kodak SBUs (see the solid red circles in Figure 2–4) are shown as they may have appeared in 2003 and serve as an example of BCG analysis. The area of each solid red circle in Figure 2–4 is roughly proportional to each SBU's 2003 sales revenue. The arrows show where the four SBUs were headed from 2003 to 2012. Here's a quick snapshot of what happened to each Kodak SBU from 2003 to 2012:

1. *Kodak film.* An $8 billion *cash cow* in 2003, Kodak's film sales were its biggest single source of revenue. In a free fall because of the explosive growth of digital cameras, Kodak film sales dropped to $500 million in 2009, moving it from being a *cash cow* to a *dog*. By 2012, film sales virtually disappeared.
2. *Kodak digital cameras.* Kodak invented the digital camera in 1975—but did not exploit the technology, fearing it would cannibalize sales from its film business. However, Kodak became the market leader in the United States in 2005, its digital cameras becoming a *cash cow*. With the arrival of smartphones, sales fell dramatically by 2012 and its digital cameras approached being a *dog*.[35]
3. *Kodak ink-jet printers and cartridges to print digital photos at home.* Starting strong in the late 2000s, this market has soured as online photo sharing has grown. At the end of 2011, the 845 million Facebook users uploaded more than 250 million photos *per day* to its website! So the use of Kodak ink-jet photo printers to print hard copies of photos has declined since 2009. Yet, Kodak believes that this *question mark* SBU can grow significantly due to its strong market position and technologies.[36]
4. *Kodak self-service kiosks in retail outlets.* Kodak and Fujifilm photo kiosks allow photo enthusiasts to take the images from their digital camera or smartphone and then store, share, manipulate, and print these images. Today, about 100,000 Kodak Picture kiosks are located in retail outlets. But images are increasingly being stored and shared on Facebook or just the capture device, making Kodak's kiosks a potential *question mark* or *dog* if these trends continue.[37]

How can Ben & Jerry's develop new products and social responsibility programs that contribute to its mission? The text describes how the strategic marketing process and its SWOT analysis can help.

FIGURE 2–5

Four market-product
strategies: alternative ways
to expand sales revenues
for Ben & Jerry's using
diversification analysis.

MARKETS	PRODUCTS	
	Current	New
Current	**Market penetration** Selling more Ben & Jerry's super-premium ice cream to Americans	**Product development** Selling a new product such as children's clothing under the Ben & Jerry's brand to Americans
New	**Market development** Selling Ben & Jerry's super-premium ice cream to Brazilians for the first time	**Diversification** Selling a new product such as children's clothing under the Ben & Jerry's brand to Brazilians for the first time

In January 2012, Kodak filed for bankruptcy protection, a victim of its inability to recognize consumer trends and implement new technologies to respond to them. The firm announced that it was "phasing out" its digital cameras, picture frames, and pocket video cameras by the middle of 2012 due in large part to the growth of smartphones. The clear message for marketing strategists: Know *when* to change your business model and *do* it!

diversification analysis
A technique a firm uses to search for growth opportunities from among current and new products and markets.

Diversification Analysis **Diversification analysis** is a technique that helps a firm search for growth opportunities from among current and new markets as well as current and new products.[38] For any market, there is both a current product (what the firm now sells) and a new product (what the firm might sell in the future). And for any product there is both a current market (the firm's existing customers) and a new market (the firm's potential customers). As Ben & Jerry's seeks to increase sales revenues, it considers all four market-product strategies shown in Figure 2–5:

QR 2–3
B&J's Bonnaroo
Buzz Ad

- *Market penetration* is a marketing strategy to increase sales of current products in current markets, such as selling more Ben & Jerry's Bonnaroo Buzz Fair Trade-sourced ice cream to U.S. consumers. There is no change in either the basic product line or the markets served. Increased sales are generated by selling either more ice cream (through better promotion or distribution) *or* the same amount of ice cream at a higher price to its current customers.
- *Market development* is a marketing strategy to sell current products to new markets. For Ben & Jerry's, Brazil is an attractive new market. There is good news and bad news for this strategy: As household incomes of Brazilians increase, consumers can buy more ice cream; however, the Ben & Jerry's brand may be unknown to Brazilian consumers.
- *Product development* is a marketing strategy of selling new products to current markets. Ben & Jerry's could leverage its brand by selling children's clothing in the United States. This strategy is risky because Americans may not see the company's expertise in ice cream as extending to children's clothing.
- *Diversification* is a marketing strategy of developing new products and selling them in new markets. This is a potentially high-risk strategy for Ben & Jerry's if it decides to try to sell Ben & Jerry's branded clothing in Brazil. Why? Because the firm has neither previous production nor marketing experience on which to draw in marketing clothing to Brazilian consumers.

learning review

5. What is the difference between a marketing dashboard and a marketing metric?

6. What is business portfolio analysis?

7. Explain the four market-product strategies in diversification analysis.

THE STRATEGIC MARKETING PROCESS

After an organization assesses where it is and where it wants to go, other questions emerge, such as:

1. How do we allocate our resources to get where we want to go?
2. How do we convert our plans into actions?
3. How do our results compare with our plans, and do deviations require new plans?

To answer these questions, an organization uses the **strategic marketing process**, whereby an organization allocates its marketing mix resources to reach its target markets. This process is divided into three phases: planning, implementation, and evaluation, as shown in Figure 2–6.

The Planning Phase of the Strategic Marketing Process

Figure 2–6 shows the three steps in the planning phase of the strategic marketing process: (1) situation (SWOT) analysis, (2) market-product focus and goal setting, and (3) the marketing program.

Step 1: Situation (SWOT) Analysis The essence of **situation analysis** is taking stock of where the firm or product has been recently, where it is now, and where it is headed in terms of the organization's marketing plans and the external forces and trends affecting it. An effective summary of a situation analysis is a **SWOT analysis**, an acronym describing an organization's appraisal of its internal **S**trengths and **W**eaknesses and its external **O**pportunities and **T**hreats.

The SWOT analysis is based on an exhaustive study of four areas that form the foundation upon which the firm builds its marketing program:

- Identify trends in the organization's industry.
- Analyze the organization's competitors.
- Assess the organization itself.
- Research the organization's present and prospective customers.

strategic marketing process

An approach whereby an organization allocates its marketing mix resources to reach its target markets.

situation analysis

Taking stock of where a firm or product has been recently, where it is now, and where it is headed.

SWOT analysis

An acronym describing an organization's appraisal of its internal strengths and weaknesses and its external opportunities and threats.

FIGURE 2–6

The strategic marketing process has three vital phases: planning, implementation, and evaluation. The figure also shows where these phases are discussed in the text.

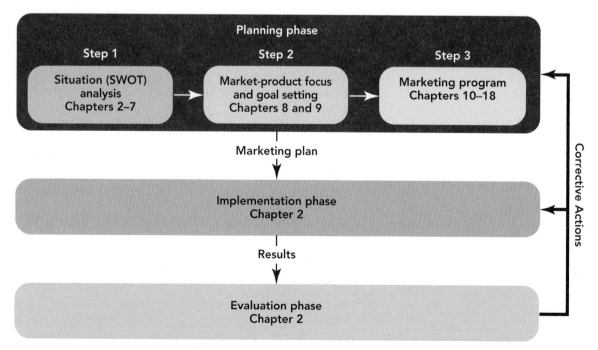

FIGURE 2–7
Ben & Jerry's: a SWOT
analysis to keep it growing.
The picture painted in this
SWOT analysis is the basis for
management actions.

LOCATION OF FACTOR	TYPE OF FACTOR	
	Favorable	Unfavorable
Internal	**Strengths** • Prestigious, well-known brand name among U.S. consumers • Complements Unilever's other ice cream brands • Recognized for its social mission, values, and actions	**Weaknesses** • B&J's social responsibility actions could reduce focus • Experienced managers needed to help growth • Modest sales growth and profits in recent years
External	**Opportunities** • Growing demand for quality ice cream in overseas markets • Increasing U.S. demand for 100-calorie novelties such as cones and bars • Many U.S. firms successfully use product and brand extensions	**Threats** • B&J customers read nutritional labels and are concerned with sugary and fatty desserts • Competes with General Mills and Nestlé brands • Increasing competition in international markets

Assume you are responsible for doing the SWOT analysis for Unilever, Ben & Jerry's parent company shown in Figure 2–7. Note that the SWOT table has four cells formed by the combination of internal versus external factors (the rows) and favorable versus unfavorable factors (the columns) that identify Ben & Jerry's strengths, weaknesses, opportunities, and threats.

The task is to translate the results of the SWOT analysis into specific actions that will help the firm grow. The ultimate goal is to identify the *critical* strategy-related factors that impact the firm and then build on vital strengths, correct glaring weaknesses, exploit significant opportunities, and avoid disaster-laden threats.

The Ben & Jerry's SWOT analysis in Figure 2–7 can be the basis for these kinds of specific actions. An action in each of the four cells might be:

- *Build on a strength.* Find specific efficiencies in distribution with Unilever's existing ice cream brands.
- *Correct a weakness.* Recruit experienced managers from other consumer product firms to help stimulate growth.
- *Exploit an opportunity.* Develop new product lines of low-fat, low-carb frozen yogurts and sorbets to respond to consumer health concerns.
- *Avoid a disaster-laden threat.* Focus on less risky international markets, such as Canada and Mexico.

Step 2: Market-Product Focus and Goal Setting   Determining which products will be directed toward which customers (step 2 of the planning phase in Figure 2–6) is essential for developing an effective marketing program (step 3). This decision is often based on **market segmentation**, which involves aggregating prospective buyers into groups, or segments, that (1) have common needs and (2) will respond similarly to a marketing action. This enables an organization to focus specific marketing programs on its target market segments.

In the case of Medtronic, executives researched a potential new market in Asia by talking extensively with doctors in India and China. These doctors wanted an affordable pacemaker that was reliable and easy to implant. So Medtronic developed and marketed a new product, the Champion heart pacemaker, directed at their needs.

market segmentation
The sorting of potential buyers into groups that have common needs and will respond similarly to a marketing action.

Goal setting involves specifying measurable marketing objectives to be achieved. For example, the goal may be to introduce Medtronic's Champion pacemaker in Asia. Let's examine Medtronic's five-year plan to reach the "affordable and reliable" pacemaker segment that results in its marketing program:[39]

- *Set marketing and product goals.* Chances of new-product success are increased by specifying both market and product goals. Based on their market research, Medtronic executives set the following goal: Market its pacemaker within three years, manufactured in China for the Asian market.
- *Select target markets.* The Champion pacemaker will be targeted at cardiologists and heart surgery clinics in India, China, and other Asian countries.
- *Find points of difference.* **Points of difference** are those characteristics of a product that make it superior to competitive substitutes. Just as a competitive advantage is a unique strength of an entire organization compared to its competitors, points of difference are unique characteristics of one of its products that make it superior to competitive products it faces in the marketplace. For the Champion pacemaker, the key points of difference are high quality, long life, reliability, ease of use, and low cost.
- *Position the product.* The pacemaker will be "positioned" in cardiologists' and patients' minds as a medical device that is high quality and reliable with a long, nine-year life. The name Champion was selected after testing acceptable names among doctors in India, China, Pakistan, Singapore, and Malaysia.

So step 2 in the planning phase of the strategic marketing process—deciding which products will be directed toward which customers—is the foundation for step 3, developing the marketing program.

Step 3: Marketing Program   Activities in step 2 tell the marketing manager which customers to target and which customer needs the firm's product offerings can satisfy—the *who* and *what* aspects of the strategic marketing process. The *how* aspect—step 3 in the planning phase—involves developing the program's marketing mix (the four Ps) and its budget. Figure 2–8 shows that each marketing mix element is combined to provide a cohesive marketing program. The five-year

points of difference

Those characteristics of a product that make it superior to competitive substitutes.

FIGURE 2–8
The four Ps elements of the marketing mix must be blended to produce a cohesive marketing program.

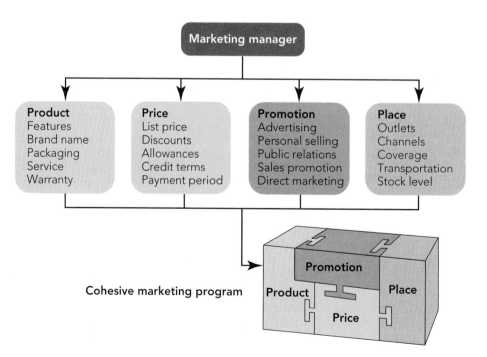

The Champion: Medtronic's high-quality, long-life, low-cost heart pacemaker for Asian market segments.

marketing plan of Medtronic's Champion pacemaker includes these marketing mix activities:

- *Product strategy.* Offer a Champion brand heart pacemaker with features needed by Asian patients.
- *Price strategy.* Manufacture the Champion to control costs so that it can be priced below $1,000 (in U.S. dollars)—an affordable price for Asian markets.
- *Promotion strategy.* Introduce the Champion at medical conventions across Asia to demonstrate its many beneficial features.
- *Place (distribution) strategy.* Search out, utilize, and train reputable medical device distributors across Asia to call on cardiologists and medical clinics.

Putting this marketing program into effect requires that the firm commit time and money to it in the form of a sales forecast (see Chapter 7) and budget that must be approved by top management.

<table>
<tr><td>learning review</td><td>8. What are the three steps of the planning phase of the strategic marketing process?

9. What are points of difference and why are they important?</td></tr>
</table>

The Implementation Phase of the Strategic Marketing Process

As shown in Figure 2–6, the result of the tens or hundreds of hours spent in the planning phase of the strategic marketing process is the firm's marketing plan. Implementation, the second phase of the strategic marketing process, involves carrying out the marketing plan that emerges from the planning phase. If the firm cannot put the marketing plan into effect—in the implementation phase—the planning phase was a waste of time.

There are four components of the implementation phase: (1) obtaining resources, (2) designing the marketing organization, (3) defining precise tasks, responsibilities, and deadlines, and (4) actually executing the marketing program designed in the planning phase.

Obtaining Resources   A key task in the implementation phase of the strategic marketing process is finding adequate people and financial resources to deliver the marketing program successfully. Start-up firms often obtain this financing by selling stock or obtaining venture capital. Marketing managers in existing organizations obtain these resources by getting top management to divert profits from BCG stars or cash cows.

Designing the Marketing Organization   A marketing program needs a marketing organization to implement it. Figure 2–9 on the next page shows the organization chart of a typical manufacturing firm, giving some details of the marketing department's structure. Four managers of marketing activities are shown to report to the vice president of marketing or chief marketing officer. Several regional sales managers and an international sales manager may report to the manager of sales. The product or brand managers and their subordinates help plan, implement, and evaluate the marketing plans for their offerings. However, the entire marketing organization is responsible for converting these marketing plans into reality.

Defining Precise Tasks, Responsibilities, and Deadlines   Successful implementation requires that team members know the tasks for which they are responsible and the deadline for completing them. To implement the thousands of tasks on a new aircraft design, Lockheed Martin typically holds weekly program meetings. The outcome of each of these meeting is an *action item list,* an aid to implementing a marketing plan consisting of four columns: (1) the task, (2) the person responsible for completing that task, (3) the date to finish the task, and (4) what is to be delivered. Within hours of completing a program meeting, the action item list is circulated to those attending. This then serves as the starting agenda for the next meeting. Meeting minutes are viewed as secondary

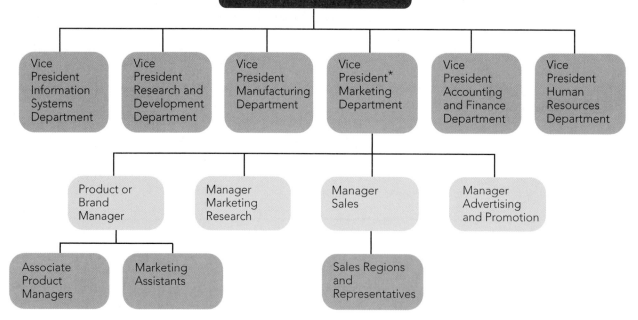

President/Chief Executive Officer

| Vice President Information Systems Department | Vice President Research and Development Department | Vice President Manufacturing Department | Vice President* Marketing Department | Vice President Accounting and Finance Department | Vice President Human Resources Department |

Product or Brand Manager | Manager Marketing Research | Manager Sales | Manager Advertising and Promotion

Associate Product Managers | Marketing Assistants

Sales Regions and Representatives

*Called chief marketing officer (CMO) in many corporations.

FIGURE 2–9

Organization of a typical manufacturing firm, showing a breakdown of the marketing department.

and backward looking. Action item lists are forward looking, clarify the targets, and put strong pressure on people to achieve their designated tasks by the deadline.

Suppose, for example, that you and two friends undertake a term project on the problem. "How can the college increase attendance at its performing arts concerts?" The instructor says the term project must involve a mail survey of a sample of students, and the written report with the survey results must be submitted by the end of the 11-week quarter. To begin, you identify all the project tasks and then estimate the time required to complete each one. To complete it in 11 weeks, your team must plan which activities can be done concurrently to save time.

Scheduling activities can be done efficiently with a *Gantt chart*, which is a graph of a program schedule. Figure 2–10 shows a Gantt chart—invented by Henry L. Gantt—

FIGURE 2–10

This Gantt chart shows how three students can schedule tasks to complete a term project on time. Software programs, such as Microsoft Project, simplify the task of developing a program schedule or Gantt chart.

Task description	Students involved in task	Week of quarter 1 2 3 4 5 6 7 8 9 10 11
1. Construct and test a rough-draft questionnaire for clarity (in person, not by mail) on friends	A	
2. Type and copy the final questionnarie	C	
3. Randomly select the names of 200 students from the school directory	A	
4. Address and stamp envelopes; mail questionnaires	C	
5. Collect returned questionnaires	B	
6. Tabulate and analyze data from returned questionnaires	B	
7. Write final report	A, B, C	
8. Type and submit final report	C	

KEY: ▲ Planned completion date ▢ Planned period of work   Current date
△ Actual completion date ▢ Actual period of work

38

used to schedule the class project, demonstrating how the concurrent work on several tasks enables the students to finish the project on time. The key to project scheduling is to distinguish tasks that *must* be done sequentially from those that *can* be concurrently.

Executing the Marketing Program   Marketing plans are meaningless without effective execution of those plans. This requires attention to detail for both marketing strategies and marketing tactics. A **marketing strategy** is the means by which a marketing goal is to be achieved, usually characterized by a specified target market and a marketing program to reach it. The term implies both the end sought (target market) and the means to achieve it (marketing program).

To implement a marketing program successfully, hundreds of detailed decisions are often required. These decisions, called **marketing tactics**, are detailed day-to-day operational decisions essential to the overall success of marketing strategies. Writing ads and setting prices for new product lines are examples of marketing tactics.

The Evaluation Phase of the Strategic Marketing Process

The evaluation phase of the strategic marketing process seeks to keep the marketing program moving in the direction set for it (see Figure 2–6). Accomplishing this requires the marketing manager to (1) compare the results of the marketing program with the goals in the written plans to identify deviations and (2) act on these deviations—correcting negative deviations and exploiting positive ones.

Comparing Results with Plans to Identify Deviations   Suppose you are on a Kodak task force in 2003 responsible for making plans through 2012. You observe that Kodak's sales revenues from 1998 through 2003, or line AB in Figure 2–11, exhibit a very flat trend. Extending the 1998–2003 trend to 2012 along line BC shows very flat sales revenues, a totally unacceptable, no-growth strategy.

Kodak's growth target of 6 percent annually, the line BD in Figure 2–10, would give sales revenues of $16 billion in 2006 and $24 billion in 2012. This reveals a wedge-shaped shaded gap in the figure. Planners call this the *planning gap*, the difference between the projection of the path to reach a new goal (line BD) and the projection of the path of the results of a plan already in place (line BC).

The ultimate purpose of the firm's marketing program is to "fill in" this planning gap—in the case of your Kodak task force, to move its future sales revenue line from the no-growth line BC up to the challenging target of line BD. But poor performance can result in actual sales revenues (line BE) being far less than the targeted levels, the actual situation Kodak has faced continuously in the years since 2003. This is the essence of evaluation: comparing actual results with goals set.

---

marketing strategy
The means by which a marketing goal is to be achieved.

marketing tactics
Detailed day-to-day operational decisions essential to the overall success of marketing strategies.

Kodak's PLAYSPORT pocket video camera can upload its videos to YouTube. Sadly, in 2012 the line was being sold off as part of Kodak's bankruptcy actions.

FIGURE 2–11
The evaluation phase of the strategic marketing process requires that the organization compare actual results with goals to identify and act on deviations to fill in its "planning gap." The text describes how Kodak is working to fill in its planning gap.

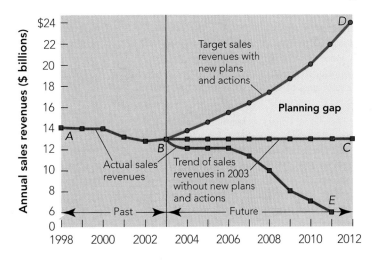

In this example, the Kodak task force in 2003 used trend extrapolation to project the historic trend through 2012. But as shown by the discrepancy between line BC (the trend extrapolation) and line BE (Kodak's actual annual sales revenues), serious forecasting problems can occur. In this case, Kodak failed to anticipate the drastic effect that digital technology would have on sales of its film and film cameras. This challenge for Kodak highlights the difficulties in making long-range projections in industries in which technology and consumer tastes are changing rapidly.

Acting on Deviations   When evaluation shows that actual performance has failed to meet expectations, managers need to take corrective actions. In response to the negative and positive deviations from targets, your Kodak task force might have considered the following in, say, 2005 when problems in meeting sales revenues targets became apparent:

- *Exploiting a positive deviation.* With Kodak's new line of digital cameras becoming #1 in the U.S. market in 2005, Kodak might have tried to move quickly to offer these new products to international customers.
- *Correcting a negative deviation.* If initial international sales of the new digital cameras failed to achieve planned targets, Kodak might have reconsidered its pricing or distribution strategies.

Sadly, as we saw earlier in the business portfolio analysis of four Kodak product lines, between 2003 and 2012 Kodak never found a new Boston Consulting Group star or cash cow. It needed one to fill in its planning gap and to replace the huge vacuum left by Kodak's disappearing film sales that had been its cash cow for generations.

---

learning review

10. What is the implementation phase of the strategic marketing process?

11. How do the goals set for a marketing program in the planning phase relate to the evaluation phase of the strategic marketing process?

LEARNING OBJECTIVES REVIEW

LO1   *Describe two kinds of organizations and the three levels of strategy in them.*
An organization is a legal entity of people who share a common mission. There are two kinds. One is a business firm that is a privately owned organization that serves its customers to earn a profit so that it can survive. The other is a nonprofit, nongovernmental organization that serves its customers but does not have profit as a goal. Most large business firms and nonprofit organizations are divided into three levels of strategy: (*a*) the corporate level, where top management directs overall strategy for the entire organization; (*b*) the strategic business unit level, where managers set a more specific strategic direction for their businesses to exploit value-creating opportunities; and (*c*) the functional level, where groups of specialists actually create value for the organization.

LO2   *Describe how core values, mission, organizational culture, business, and goals are important to organizations.*
Organizations exist to accomplish something for someone. To give organizations direction and focus, they continuously assess their core values, mission, organizational culture, business, and goals. Today's organizations specify their foundation, set a direction, and formulate strategies—the "why," "what," and "how" factors, respectively. Core values are the organization's fundamental, passionate, and enduring principles that guide its conduct over time—what Enron forgot when it lost sight of its responsibilities to its stakeholders. The organization's mission is a statement of its function in society, often identifying its customers, markets, products, and technologies. Organizational culture is a set of values, ideas, attitudes, and norms of behavior that is learned and shared among the members of an organization. To answer the question, "What business are we in?" an organization defines its "business"—the clear, broad, underlying industry category or market sector of its offering. Finally, the organization's goals (or objectives) are statements of an accomplishment of a task to be achieved, often by a specific time.

LO3   *Explain why managers use marketing dashboards and marketing metrics.*
Marketing managers use marketing dashboards to visually display on a single computer screen the essential information required to make a decision to take an action or further analyze a problem. This information consists of key performance measures of a product category, such as sales or market share, and is known as a marketing metric, which is a measure of the quantitative value or trend of a marketing activity or result. Most organizations tie their marketing metrics to the quantitative objectives established in their marketing plan, which is a road map for the marketing activities of an organization for a specified future time period, such as one year or five years.

LO4 *Discuss how an organization assesses where it is now and where it seeks to be.*

Managers of an organization ask two key questions to set a strategic direction. The first question, "Where are we now?" requires an organization to (*a*) reevaluate its competencies to ensure that its special capabilities still provide a competitive advantage; (*b*) assess its present and prospective customers to ensure they have a satisfying customer experience—the central goal of marketing today; and (*c*) analyze its current and potential competitors from a global perspective to determine whether it needs to redefine its business.

The second question, "Where do we want to go?" requires an organization to set a specific direction and allocate resources to move it in that direction. Business portfolio and diversification analyses help an organization do this. Managers use business portfolio analysis to assess the organization's strategic business units (SBUs), product lines, or individual products as though they were a collection of separate investments (cash cows, stars, question marks, and dogs) to determine the amount of cash each should receive. Diversification analysis is a tool that helps managers use one or a combination of four strategies to increase revenues: market penetration (selling more of an existing product to existing markets); market development (selling an existing product to new markets); product development (selling a new product to existing markets); and diversification (selling new products to new markets).

LO5 *Explain the three steps of the planning phase of the strategic marketing process.*

An organization uses the strategic marketing process to allocate its marketing mix resources to reach its target markets. This process is divided into three phases: planning, implementation, and evaluation. The planning phase consists of (*a*) a situation (SWOT) analysis, which involves taking stock of where the firm or product has been recently, where it is now, and where it is headed. This assessment focuses on the organization's internal factors (strengths and weaknesses) and the external forces and trends affecting it (opportunities and threats); (*b*) a market-product focus through market segmentation (grouping buyers into segments with common needs and similar responses to marketing programs) and goal setting, which in part requires creating points of difference (those characteristics of a product that make it superior to competitive substitutes); and (*c*) a marketing program that specifies the budget and activities (marketing strategies and tactics) for each marketing mix element.

LO6 *Describe the elements of the implementation and evaluation phases of the strategic marketing process.*

The implementation phase of the strategic marketing process carries out the marketing plan that emerges from the planning phase. It has four key elements: (*a*) obtaining resources; (*b*) designing the marketing organization to perform product management, marketing research, sales, and advertising and promotion activities; (*c*) developing schedules to identify the tasks that need to be done, the time that is allocated to each one, the people responsible for each task, and the deadlines for each task—often with an action item list and Gantt chart; and (*d*) executing the marketing strategies, which are the means by which marketing goals are to be achieved, and their associated marketing tactics, which are the detailed day-to-day operational decisions essential to the overall success of a firm's marketing strategies. These are the marketing program actions a firm takes to achieve the goals set forth in its marketing plan.

The evaluation phase of the strategic marketing process seeks to keep the marketing program moving in the direction that was established in the marketing plan. This requires the marketing manager to compare the results from the marketing program with the marketing plan's goals to (*a*) identify deviations or "planning gaps" and (*b*) take corrective actions to exploit positive deviations or correct negative ones.

FOCUSING ON KEY TERMS

business p. 26
business portfolio analysis p. 31
core values p. 25
diversification analysis p. 33
goals (objectives) p. 26
market segmentation p. 35
market share p. 26

marketing dashboard p. 28
marketing metric p. 28
marketing plan p. 30
marketing strategy p. 39
marketing tactics p. 39
mission p. 25
objectives (goals) p. 26

organizational culture p. 26
points of difference p. 36
profit p. 22
situation analysis p. 34
strategic marketing process p. 34
strategy p. 22
SWOT analysis p. 34

APPLYING MARKETING KNOWLEDGE

1 (*a*) Using Medtronic as an example, explain how a mission statement gives it a strategic direction. (*b*) Create a mission statement for your own career.

2 What competencies best describe (*a*) your college or university and (*b*) your favorite restaurant?

3 Why does a product often start as a question mark and then move counterclockwise around the BCG's growth-share matrix shown in Figure 2–4?

4 Select one strength, one weakness, one opportunity, and one threat from the Ben & Jerry's SWOT analysis shown in Figure 2–7. Suggest an action that a B&J marketing manager might take to address each factor.

5 What is the main result of each of the three phases of the strategic marketing process? (*a*) planning, (*b*) implementation, and (*c*) evaluation.

6 The goal-setting step in the planning phase of the strategic marketing process sets quantified objectives for use in the evaluation phase. What does a manager do if measured results fail to meet objectives? Exceed objectives?

1 Read Appendix A, "Building an Effective Marketing Plan." Then write a 600-word executive summary for the Paradise Kitchens marketing plan using the numbered headings shown in the plan. When you have completed the draft of your own marketing plan, write a 600-word executive summary to go in the front of your own marketing plan.

2 Using Chapter 2 and Appendix A as guides, focus your marketing plan by (a) writing your mission statement in 25 words or less, (b) listing three nonfinancial goals and three financial goals, (c) writing your competitive advantage in 35 words or less, and (d) creating a SWOT analysis table.

3 Draw a simple organization chart for your organization.

video case 2 IBM: Using Strategy to Build a "Smarter Planet"

QR 2–4
IBM Video
Case

"'Smarter Planet' is not an advertising campaign, it's not even a marketing campaign, it is a business strategy," explains Ann Rubin, vice president of Advertising at IBM.

The "Smarter Planet" strategy is based on the idea that the next major revolution in the global marketplace will be the instrumentation and integration of the world's processes and infrastructures, generating unprecedented amounts of data. The data captured and analyzed in industries such as banking, energy, health care, and retailing will allow IBM to help businesses be more efficient, productive, and responsive.

THE COMPANY

Founded in 1911, IBM has a history of innovation and focus on customers. The blue covers on its computers, blue letters in the IBM logo, and dark blue suits worn by IBM salespeople led to the now popular company nickname, "Big Blue." Today, it has over 400,000 employees in more than 200 countries. *Forbes* magazine ranks IBM as the fourth most valuable brand in the world. The company is a leading developer of new business technologies, receiving more than 5,000 patents each year. Some of its well-known inventions include the automated teller machine (ATM), the hard disk drive, the magnetic stripe card, relational databases, and the Universal Product Code (UPC). In addition, IBM recently gained attention for its artificial intelligence program called Watson, which challenged two *Jeopardy!* game show champions, and won!

VALUES, MISSION, AND STRATEGY

Recently, IBM initiated a project to facilitate online discussions of key business issues among 50,000 employees to identify common themes and perspectives. According to Sam Palmisano, current CEO of IBM, "We needed to affirm IBM's reason for being, what sets the company apart, and what should drive our actions as individual IBMers." The results were three underlying values of IBM's business practices: (1) dedication to every client's success, (2) innovation that matters—for our company and for the world, and (3) trust and personal responsibility in all relationships. These values now come to life at IBM in its "policies, procedures, and daily operations," explains Palmisano.

IBM's core values also help to define its mission, or its general function in society. In clear, concise, inspirational language IBM's mission statement is:

- At IBM, we strive to lead in the invention, development and manufacture of the industry's most advanced information technologies, including computer systems, software, storage systems, and microelectronics.
- We translate these advanced technologies into value for our customers through our professional solutions, services, and consulting businesses worldwide.

The mission, and the values it represents, helps define the organizational culture at IBM. Executives, managers, and all employees create the culture through the strategies they select and the detailed plans for accomplishing them.

IBM's strategies are based on its assessment of fundamental changes in the business environment. First, IBM sees global changes such as fewer trade barriers, the growth of developing economies, and increasing access to the World Wide Web. These changes necessitate a new type of corporation that IBM calls the "globally integrated enterprise." Second, IBM foresees a new model of computing that includes computational capability in phones, cameras, cars, and other appliances and allows economic, social, and physical systems to be connected. This connectivity creates a "smarter planet." Finally, IBM predicts a growing demand for custom-made technological solutions that help organizations measure and achieve specific outcomes.

As a result, IBM began to shift from commodity-based businesses such as PCs and hard disk drives, to "customizable" businesses such as software and services. The change in IBM was so substantial that it has described its plan in a document called the *2015 Road Map*. The Map describes four strategic opportunities: (1) growth markets such as China, India, Brazil, and Africa, (2) business analytics and optimization, (3) cloud and smarter computing, and (4) the connected, "smarter" planet. These opportunities suggest a strategy that delivers value through business and IT innovation to selected industries with an integrated enterprise. The overarching strategy that highlights IBM's capabilities is called "Building a Smarter Planet."

BUILDING A SMARTER PLANET

The Smarter Planet initiative is designed for clients who value IBM's industry and process expertise, systems integration capability, and research capacity. A smarter planet, while global by definition, happens on the industry level. It is driven by forward-thinking organizations that share a common outlook: they see change as an opportunity, and they act on possibilities, not just react to problems.

Smarter business for a Smarter Planet.

What 3 million lines of code means to a piece of luggage.

John Kennedy, vice president of Marketing, explains, "'A Smarter Planet' actually surfaced from observing what was happening in our clients. They were looking to take the vast amount of data that was being generated inside their companies and looking to better understand it." To IBM "smart" solutions have three characteristics. They are instrumented, they are intelligent, and they are interconnected. Millions of digital devices, now connected through the Internet, produce data that can be turned into knowledge through advanced computational power. IBM believes that this knowledge can help reduce costs, cut waste, improve efficiency, and increase productivity for companies, industries, and cities.

Since introducing the Smarter Planet strategy, IBM has collaborated with more than 600 organizations around the globe. The success of the strategy is evident in the broad range of industries where "smart" solutions are being implemented. They include banking; communications; electronics, automotive and aerospace; energy and utilities; government; health care; insurance; oil and gas; retailing; and transportation. Each industry has reported a variety of applications.

In a study of 439 cities, for example, smart solutions such as ramp metering, signal coordination, and accident management reduced travel delays by more than 700,000 annually, saving each city $15 million. A study by the U.S. Department of Energy found that consumers with smart electric meters cut their power usage and saved 10 percent on their power bills. Retailers who implemented smart systems to analyze buying behavior, merchandise assortment, and demand were able to cut supply chain costs by 30 percent, reduce inventory levels by 25 percent, and increase sales by 10 percent.

THE BUILDING A SMARTER PLANET MARKETING PLAN

Marketing and communications professionals at IBM have developed the marketing plan for IBM's "Smarter Planet" strategy. The general goal is to describe the company's view of the next era of information technology and its impact on business and society. The execution of the plan includes messaging from Palmisano, an advertising campaign, an Internet presence, and public relations communications. In addition, IBM measures and tracks the performance of the marketing activities.

The importance of the Smarter Planet strategy was first communicated through a message from the top. Palmisano prepared a "Letter from the Chairman" for the annual report. His message was a powerful statement. Smarter Planet, according to Palmisano, "is not a metaphor. It describes the infusion of intelligence into the way the world actually works."

IBM also used a print and television advertising campaign to add detail to Palmisano's message. The ads focused on the ability to improve the world now, with IBM's help. "I think what's different about Smarter Planet," says Ann Rubin, "is that it was not inward facing, it was looking out at what the world needed. We felt like we could go out there and influence the world for the better."

IBM recently celebrated its 100th anniversary! Its record of success is testimony to the resilience of a business model that encourages long-term strategies that can say "Welcome to a Smarter Planet."

Questions

1 What is IBM's "Smarter Planet" business strategy? How does this strategy relate to IBM's mission and values?
2 Conduct a SWOT analysis for IBM's Smarter Planet initiative. What are the relevant trends to consider for the next three to five years?
3 How can IBM communicate its strategy to companies, cities, and governments?
4 What are the benefits of the Smarter Planet initiative to *(a)* society and *(b)* IBM?
5 How should IBM measure the results of the Smarter Planet strategy?

A Building an Effective Marketing Plan

"New ideas are a dime a dozen," observes Arthur R. Kydd, "and so are new products and new technologies." Kydd should know. As chief executive officer of St. Croix Venture Partners, he and his firm have provided the seed money and venture capital to launch more than 60 start-up firms in the last 30 years. Today, those firms have more than 5,000 employees. Kydd explains:

> I get 200 to 300 marketing and business plans a year to look at, and St. Croix provides start-up financing for only two or three. What sets a potentially successful idea, product, or technology apart from all the rest is markets and marketing. If you have a real product with a distinctive point of difference that satisfies the needs of customers, you may have a winner. And you get a real feel for this in a well-written marketing or business plan.[1]

This appendix (1) describes what marketing and business plans are, including the purposes and guidelines in writing effective plans, and (2) provides a sample marketing plan.

MARKETING PLANS AND BUSINESS PLANS

After explaining the meanings, purposes, and audiences of marketing plans and business plans, this section describes some writing guidelines for them and what external funders often look for in successful plans.

Meanings, Purposes, and Audiences

A marketing plan is a road map for the marketing activities of an organization for a specified future time period, such as one year or five years.[2] No single "generic" marketing plan applies to all organizations and all situations. Rather, the specific format for a marketing plan for an organization depends on the following:

- *The target audience and purpose.* Elements included in a particular marketing plan depend heavily on (1) who the audience is and (2) what its purpose is. A marketing plan for an internal audience seeks to point the direction for future marketing activities and is sent to all individuals in the organization who must

implement the plan or who will be affected by it. If the plan is directed to an external audience, such as friends, banks, venture capitalists, or potential investors for the purpose of raising capital, it has the additional function of being an important sales document. In this case, it contains elements such as the strategic plan/focus, organization, structure, and biographies of key personnel that would rarely appear in an internal marketing plan. Also, the financial information is far more detailed when the plan is used to raise outside capital. The elements of a marketing plan for each of these two audiences are compared in Figure A–1.

- *The kind and complexity of the organization.* A small neighborhood restaurant has a somewhat different marketing plan than Medtronic, which serves international markets. The restaurant's plan would be relatively simple and directed at serving customers in a local market. In Medtronic's case, because there is a hierarchy of marketing plans, various levels of detail would be used—such as the entire organization, the strategic business unit, or the product/product line.

- *The industry.* Both the restaurant serving a local market and Medtronic, selling heart pacemakers globally, analyze competition. However, their geographic thrusts are far different, as are the complexities of their offerings and, hence, the time periods likely to be covered by their plans. A one-year marketing plan may be adequate for the restaurant, but Medtronic may need a five-year planning horizon because product-development cycles for complex, new medical devices may be three or four years.

In contrast to a *marketing plan*, a **business plan** is a road map for the entire organization for a specified future period of time, such as one year or five years.[3] A key difference between a marketing plan and a business plan is that the business plan contains details on the research and development (R&D)/operations/manufacturing activities of the organization. Even for a manufacturing business, the marketing plan is probably 60 or 70 percent of the entire business plan. For firms like a small restaurant or an auto repair shop, their marketing and business plans are

Element of the plan	Marketing plan		Business plan	
	For internal audience (to direct the firm)	For external audience (to raise capital)	For internal audience (to direct the firm)	For external audience (to raise capital)
1. Executive summary	✓	✓	✓	✓
2. Description of company		✓		✓
3. Strategic plan/focus		✓		✓
4. Situation analysis	✓	✓	✓	✓
5. Market-product focus	✓	✓	✓	✓
6. Marketing program strategy and tactics	✓	✓	✓	✓
7. R&D and operations program			✓	✓
8. Financial projections	✓	✓	✓	✓
9. Organization structure		✓		✓
10. Implementation plan	✓	✓	✓	✓
11. Evaluation	✓		✓	
Appendix A: Biographies of key personnel		✓		✓
Appendix B, etc.: Details on other topics	✓	✓	✓	✓

FIGURE A–1

Elements in typical marketing and business plans targeted at different audiences.

virtually identical. The elements of a business plan typically targeted at internal and external audiences appear in the two right-hand columns in Figure A–1.

The Most-Asked Questions by Outside Audiences

Lenders and prospective investors reading a business or marketing plan that is used to seek new capital are probably the toughest audiences to satisfy. Their most-asked questions include the following:

1. Is the business or marketing idea valid?
2. Is there something unique or distinctive about the product or service that separates it from substitutes and competitors?
3. Is there a clear market for the product or service?
4. Are the financial projections realistic and healthy?
5. Are the key management and technical personnel capable, and do they have a track record in the industry in which they must compete?
6. Does the plan clearly describe how those providing capital will get their money back and make a profit?

Rhonda Abrams, author of *The Successful Business Plan,* observes, "Although you may spend five months preparing your plan, the cold, hard fact is that an investor or lender can dismiss it in less than five minutes. If you don't make a positive impression in those critical first five minutes, your plan will be rejected."[4] While her comments apply to plans seeking to raise capital, the first five questions listed above apply equally well to plans for internal audiences.

Writing and Style Suggestions

There are no magic one-size-fits-all guidelines for writing successful marketing and business plans. Still, the following writing and style guidelines generally apply:[5]

- Use a direct, professional writing style. Use appropriate business terms without jargon. Present and future tenses with active voice ("I will write an effective marketing plan") are generally better than past tense and passive voice ("An effective marketing plan was written by me").
- Be positive and specific to convey potential success. At the same time, avoid superlatives ("terrific," "wonderful"). Specifics are better than glittering generalities.

- Use numbers for impact, justifying projections with reasonable quantitative assumptions, where possible.
- Use bullet points for succinctness and emphasis. As with the list you are reading, bullets enable key points to be highlighted effectively.
- Use A-level (the first level) and B-level (the second level) headings under the numbered section headings to help readers make easy transitions from one topic to another. This also forces the writer to organize the plan more carefully. Use these headings liberally, at least one every 200 to 300 words.
- Use visuals where appropriate. Photos, illustrations, graphs, and charts enable massive amounts of information to be presented succinctly.
- Shoot for a plan 15 to 35 pages in length, not including financial projections and appendixes. An uncomplicated small business may require only 15 pages, while a high-technology start-up may require more than 35 pages.
- Use care in layout, design, and presentation. Laser printers give a more professional look than ink-jet printers do. Use 11- or 12-point type (you are now reading 10.5-point type) in the text. Use a serif type (with "feet," like that you are reading now) in the text because it is easier to read, and sans serif (without "feet") in graphs and charts like Figure A–1. A bound report with a nice cover and a clear title page adds professionalism.

These guidelines are used, where possible, in the sample marketing plan that follows.

SAMPLE FIVE-YEAR MARKETING PLAN FOR PARADISE KITCHENS, INC.

To help interpret the marketing plan for Paradise Kitchens, Inc., that follows, we will describe the company and suggest some guidelines in interpreting the plan.

Background on Paradise Kitchens, Inc.

With a degree in chemical engineering, Randall F. Peters spent 15 years working for General Foods and Pillsbury with a number of diverse responsibilities: plant operations, R&D, restaurant operations, and new business development. His wife, Leah, with degrees in both molecular cellular biology and food science, held various Pillsbury executive positions in new category development, packaged goods, and restaurant R&D. In the company's start-up years, Paradise Kitchens survived on the savings of Randy and Leah, the co-founders. With their backgrounds, they decided Randy should serve as president and CEO of Paradise Kitchens, and Leah should focus on R&D and corporate strategy.

Interpreting the Marketing Plan

The marketing plan on the next pages, based on an actual Paradise Kitchens plan, is directed at an external audience (see Figure A–1). To protect proprietary information about the company, some details and dates have been altered, but the basic logic of the plan has been kept.

Notes in the margins next to the Paradise Kitchens plan fall into two categories:

1. *Substantive notes* are in blue boxes. These notes elaborate on the significance of an element in the marketing plan and are keyed to chapter references in this textbook.
2. *Writing style, format, and layout notes* are in red boxes and explain the editorial or visual rationale for the element.

A word of encouragement: Writing an effective marketing plan is hard but also challenging and satisfying work. Dozens of the authors' students have used effective marketing plans they wrote for class in their interviewing portfolio to show prospective employers what they could do and to help them get their first job.

Color-Coding Legend

Blue boxes explain significance of marketing plan elements.	Red boxes give writing style, format, and layout guidelines.

The Table of Contents provides quick access to the topics in the plan, usually organized by section and subsection headings.

Seen by many experts as the single most important element in the plan, the two-page Executive Summary "sells" the plan to readers through its clarity and brevity. For space reasons, it is not shown here, but the Building Your Marketing Plan exercise at the end of Chapter 2 asks the reader to write an Executive Summary for this plan.

The Company Description highlights the recent history and recent successes of the organization.

The Strategic Focus and Plan sets the strategic direction for the entire organization, a direction with which proposed actions of the marketing plan must be consistent. This section is not included in all marketing plans. See Chapter 2.

The qualitative Mission statement focuses the activities of Paradise Kitchens for the stakeholder groups to be served. See Chapter 2.

FIVE-YEAR MARKETING PLAN
Paradise Kitchens,® Inc.

Table of Contents

1. Executive Summary

2. Company Description

Paradise Kitchens®, Inc., was started by cofounders Randall F. Peters and Leah E. Peters to develop and market Howlin' Coyote® Chili, a unique line of single serve and microwavable Southwestern/Mexican style frozen chili products. The Howlin' Coyote line of chili was first introduced into the Minneapolis–St. Paul market and expanded to Denver two years later and Phoenix two years after that.

To the Company's knowledge, Howlin' Coyote is the only premium-quality, authentic Southwestern/Mexican style, frozen chili sold in U.S. grocery stores. Its high quality has gained fast, widespread acceptance in these markets. In fact, same-store sales doubled in the last year for which data are available. The Company believes the Howlin' Coyote brand can be extended to other categories of Southwestern/Mexican food products, such as tacos, enchiladas, and burritos.

Paradise Kitchens believes its high-quality, high-price strategy has proven successful. This marketing plan outlines how the Company will extend its geographic coverage from 3 markets to 20 markets by the year 2016.

3. Strategic Focus and Plan

This section covers three aspects of corporate strategy that influence the marketing plan: (1) the mission, (2) goals, and (3) core competency/sustainable competitive advantage of Paradise Kitchens.

Mission

The mission of Paradise Kitchens is to market lines of high-quality Southwestern/Mexican food products at premium prices that satisfy consumers in this fast-growing food segment while providing challenging career opportunities for employees and above-average returns to stockholders.

Goals

For the coming five years Paradise Kitchens seeks to achieve the following goals:

- Nonfinancial goals
    1. To retain its present image as the highest-quality line of Southwestern/Mexican products in the food categories in which it competes.
    2. To enter 17 new metropolitan markets.
    3. To achieve national distribution in two convenience store or supermarket chains by 2012 and five by 2013.
    4. To add a new product line every third year.
    5. To be among the top five chili lines—regardless of packaging (frozen or canned)—in one-third of the metro markets in which it competes by 2013 and two-thirds by 2015.
- Financial goals
    1. To obtain a real (inflation-adjusted) growth in earnings per share of 8 percent per year over time.
    2. To obtain a return on equity of at least 20 percent.
    3. To have a public stock offering by the year 2013.

Core Competency and Sustainable Competitive Advantage

In terms of core competency, Paradise Kitchens seeks to achieve a unique ability to (1) provide distinctive, high-quality chilies and related products using Southwestern/Mexican recipes that appeal to and excite contemporary tastes for these products and (2) deliver these products to the customer's table using effective manufacturing and distribution systems that maintain the Company's quality standards.

To translate these core competencies into a sustainable competitive advantage, the Company will work closely with key suppliers and distributors to build the relationships and alliances necessary to satisfy the high taste standards of our customers.

To help achieve national distribution through chains, Paradise Kitchens introduced this point-of-purchase ad that adheres statically to the glass door of the freezer case.

To improve readability, each numbered section usually starts on a new page. (This is not done in this plan to save space.)

The Situation Analysis is a snapshot to answer the question, "Where are we now?" See Chapter 2.

The SWOT analysis identifies strengths, weaknesses, opportunities, and threats to provide a solid foundation as a springboard to identify subsequent actions in the marketing plan. See Chapter 2.

Each long table, graph, or photo is given a figure number and title. It then appears as soon as possible after the first reference in the text, accommodating necessary page breaks. This also avoids breaking long tables like this one in the middle. Short tables or graphs are often inserted in the text without figure numbers because they don't cause serious problems with page breaks.

Effective tables seek to summarize a large amount of information in a short amount of space.

4. Situation Analysis

This situation analysis starts with a snapshot of the current environment in which Paradise Kitchens finds itself by providing a brief SWOT (strengths, weaknesses, opportunities, threats) analysis. After this overview, the analysis probes ever-finer levels of detail: industry, competitors, company, and consumers.

SWOT Analysis

Figure 1 shows the internal and external factors affecting the market opportunities for Paradise Kitchens. Stated briefly, this SWOT analysis highlights the great strides taken by the company since its products first appeared on grocers' shelves.

Figure 1.   SWOT Analysis for Paradise Kitchens

Internal Factors	Strengths	Weaknesses
Management	Experienced and entrepreneurial management and board	Small size can restrict options
Offerings	Unique, high-quality, high-price products	Many lower-quality, lower-price competitors
Marketing	Distribution in three markets with excellent acceptance	No national awareness or distribution; restricted shelf space in the freezer section
Personnel	Good workforce, though small; little turnover	Big gap if key employee leaves
Finance	Excellent growth in sales revenues	Limited resources may restrict growth opportunities when compared to giant competitors
Manufacturing	Sole supplier ensures high quality	Lack economies of scale of huge competitors
R&D	Continuing efforts to ensure quality in delivered products	Lack of canning and microwavable food processing expertise

External Factors	Opportunities	Threats
Consumer/Social	Upscale market, likely to be stable; Southwestern/Mexican food category is fast-growing segment due to growth in Hispanic American population and desire for spicier foods	Premium price may limit access to mass markets; consumers value a strong brand name
Competitive	Distinctive name and packaging in its markets	Not patentable; competitors can attempt to duplicate product; others better able to pay slotting fees
Technological	Technical breakthroughs enable smaller food producers to achieve many economies available to large competitors	Competitors have gained economies in canning and microwavable food processing
Economic	Consumer income is high; convenience important to U.S. households	More households "eating out," and bringing prepared take-out into home
Legal/Regulatory	High U.S. Food & Drug Administration standards eliminate fly-by-night competitors	Mergers among large competitors being approved by government

In the Company's favor internally are its strengths of an experienced management team and board of directors, excellent acceptance of its lines in the three metropolitan markets in which it competes, and a strong manufacturing and distribution system to serve these limited markets. Favorable external factors (opportunities) include the increasing appeal of Southwestern/Mexican foods, the strength of the upscale market for the Company's products, and food-processing technological breakthroughs that make it easier for smaller food producers to compete.

Among unfavorable factors, the main weakness is the limited size of Paradise Kitchens relative to its competitors in terms of the depth of the management team, available financial resources, and national awareness and distribution of product lines. Threats include the danger that the Company's premium prices may limit access to mass markets and competition from the "eating-out" and "take-out" markets.

Industry Analysis: Trends in Frozen and Mexican Foods

Frozen Foods. According to *Grocery Headquarters*, consumers are flocking to the frozen food section of grocery retailers. The reasons: hectic lifestyles demanding increased convenience and an abundance of new, tastier, and nutritious products.[6] By 2007, the latest year for which data are available, total sales of frozen food in supermarkets, drugstores, and mass merchandisers, such as Target and Costco (excluding Walmart), reached $29 billion. Prepared frozen meals, which are defined as meals or entrees that are frozen and require minimal preparation, accounted for $8.1 billion, or 26 percent of the total frozen food market.

Sales of Mexican entrees totaled $506 million in 2007.[7] Heavy consumers of frozen meals, those who eat five or more meals every two weeks, tend to be kids, teens, and adults 35–44 years old.[8]

Mexican Foods. Currently, Mexican foods such as burritos, enchiladas, and tacos are used in two-thirds of American households. These trends reflect a generally more favorable attitude on the part of all Americans toward spicy foods that include red chili peppers. The growing Hispanic population in the United States, about 48 million and almost $978 billion in purchasing power in 2009, partly explains the increasing demand for Mexican food. This Hispanic purchasing power is projected to be over $1.3 trillion in 2014.[9]

Competitor Analysis: The Chili Market

The chili market represents over $500 million in annual sales. On average, consumers buy five to six servings annually, according to the NPD Group. The products fall primarily into two groups: canned chili (75 percent of sales) and dry chili (25 percent of sales).

This page uses a "block" style and does *not* indent each paragraph, although an extra space separates each paragraph. Compare this page with page 50, which has indented paragraphs. Most readers find indented paragraphs in marketing plans and long reports are easier to follow.

The Company Analysis provides details of the company's strengths and marketing strategies that will enable it to achieve the mission and goals identified earlier. See Chapters 2 and 7.

The higher-level "A heading" of Customer Analysis has a more dominant typeface and position than the lower-level "B heading" of Customer Characteristics. These headings introduce the reader to the sequence and level of topics covered. The organization of this textbook uses this kind of structure and headings.

Satisfying customers and providing genuine value to them is why organizations exist in a market economy. This section addresses the questions "Who are the customers for Paradise Kitchens's products?" See Chapters 4, 5, 6, 7, and 8.

Bluntly put, the major disadvantage of the segment's dominant product, canned chili, is that it does not taste very good. A taste test described in an issue of *Consumer Reports* magazine ranked 26 canned chili products "poor" to "fair" in overall sensory quality. The study concluded, "Chili doesn't have to be hot to be good. But really good chili, hot or mild, doesn't come out of a can."

Company Analysis

The husband-and-wife team that co-founded Paradise Kitchens, Inc., has 44 years of experience between them in the food-processing business. Both have played key roles in the management of the Pillsbury Company. They are being advised by a highly seasoned group of business professionals, who have extensive understanding of the requirements for new-product development.

The Company now uses a single outside producer with which it works closely to maintain the consistently high quality required in its products. The greater volume has increased production efficiencies, resulting in a steady decrease in the cost of goods sold.

Customer Analysis

In terms of customer analysis, this section describes (1) the characteristics of customers expected to buy Howlin' Coyote products and (2) health and nutrition concerns of Americans today.

Customer Characteristics. Demographically, chili products in general are purchased by consumers representing a broad range of socioeconomic backgrounds. Howlin' Coyote chili is purchased chiefly by consumers who have achieved higher levels of education and whose income is $50,000 and higher. These consumers represent 50 percent of canned and dry mix chili users.

The household buying Howlin' Coyote has one to three people in it. Among married couples, Howlin' Coyote is predominantly bought by households in which both spouses work. While women are a majority of the buyers, single men represent a significant segment.

Because the chili offers a quick way to make a tasty meal, the product's biggest users tend to be those most pressed for time. Howlin' Coyote's premium pricing also means that its purchasers are skewed toward the higher end of the income range. Buyers range in age from 25 to 54 and often live in the western United States, where spicy foods are more readily eaten.

The five Howlin' Coyote entrees offer a quick, tasty meal with high-quality ingredients.

Health and Nutrition Concerns. Coverage of food issues in the U.S. media is often erratic and occasionally alarmist. Because Americans are concerned about their diets, studies from organizations of widely varying credibility frequently receive significant attention from the major news organizations. For instance, a study of fat levels of movie popcorn was reported in all the major media. Similarly, studies on the healthfulness of Mexican food have received prominent play in print and broadcast reports. The high caloric levels of much Mexican and Southwestern-style food have been widely reported and often exaggerated. Some Mexican frozen-food competitors, such as Don Miguel, Mission Foods, Ruiz Foods, and Jose Ole, plan to offer or have recently offered more "carb-friendly" and "fat-friendly" products in response to this concern.

Howlin' Coyote is already lower in calories, fat, and sodium than its competitors, and those qualities are not currently being stressed in its promotions. Instead, in the space and time available for promotions, Howlin' Coyote's taste, convenience, and flexibility are stressed.

5. Market-Product Focus

This section describes the five-year marketing and product objectives for Paradise Kitchens and the target markets, points of difference, and positioning of its lines of Howlin' Coyote chilies.

Marketing and Product Objectives

Howlin' Coyote's marketing intent is to take full advantage of its brand potential while building a base from which other revenue sources can be mined—both in and out of the retail grocery business. These are detailed in four areas below:

- Current markets. Current markets will be grown by expanding brand and flavor distribution at the retail level. In addition, same-store sales will be grown by increasing consumer awareness and repeat purchases, thereby leading to the more efficient broker/warehouse distribution channel.

- New markets. By the end of Year 5, the chili, salsa, burrito, and enchilada business will be expanded to a total of 20 metropolitan areas, which represent 53 percent of the 38 major U.S. metropolitan markets. This will represent 70 percent of U.S. food store sales.

- Food service. Food service sales will include chili products and smothering sauces. Sales are expected to reach $693,000 by the end of Year 3 and $1.5 million by the end of Year 5.

- New products. Howlin' Coyote's brand presence will be expanded at the retail

A heading should be spaced closer to the text that follows (and that it describes) than the preceding section to avoid confusion for the reader. This rule is not followed for the Target Markets heading, which now unfortunately appears to "float" between the preceding and following paragraphs.

This section identifies the specific niches or target markets toward which the company's products are directed. When appropriate and when space permits, this section often includes a market-product grid. See Chapter 8.

An organization cannot grow by offering only "me-too products." The greatest single factor in a new product's failure is the lack of significant "points of difference" that set it apart from competitors' substitutes. This section makes these points of difference explicit. See Chapter 9.

A positioning strategy helps communicate the company's unique points of difference of its products to prospective customers in a simple, clear way. This section describes this positioning. See Chapters 8 and 9.

level through the addition of new products in the frozen-foods section. This will be accomplished through new-product concept screening in Year 1 to identify new potential products. These products will be brought to market in Years 2 and 3.

Target Markets

The primary target market for Howlin' Coyote products is households with one to three people, where often both adults work, with individual income typically above $50,000 per year. These households contain more experienced, adventurous consumers of Southwestern/Mexican food and want premium quality products.

To help buyers see the many different uses for Howlin' Coyote chili, recipes are even printed on the *inside* of the packages.

Points of Difference

The "points of difference"—characteristics that make Howlin' Coyote chilies unique relative to competitors—fall into three important areas:

- Unique taste and convenience. No known competitor offers a high-quality, "authentic" frozen chili in a range of flavors. And no existing chili has the same combination of quick preparation and home-style taste that Howlin' Coyote does.
- Taste trends. The American palate is increasingly intrigued by hot spices. In response to this trend, Howlin' Coyote brands offer more "kick" than most other prepared chilies.
- Premium packaging. Howlin' Coyote's packaging graphics convey the unique, high-quality product contained inside and the product's nontraditional positioning.

Positioning

In the past chili products have been either convenient or tasty, but not both. Howlin' Coyote pairs these two desirable characteristics to obtain a positioning in consumers' minds as very high-quality "authentic Southwestern/Mexican tasting" chilies that can be prepared easily and quickly.

Everything that has gone before in the marketing plan sets the stage for the marketing mix actions—the four Ps—covered in the marketing program. See Chapters 9 through 18.

This section describes in detail three key elements of the company's product strategy: the product line, its quality and how this is achieved, and its "cutting edge" packaging. See Chapters 9 and 10.

This Price Strategy section makes the company's price point very clear, along with its price position relative to potential substitutes. When appropriate and when space permits, this section might contain a break-even analysis. See Chapter 11.

This "introductory overview" sentence tells the reader the topics covered in the section—in this case in-store demonstrations, recipes, and cents-off coupons. While this sentence may be omitted in short memos or plans, it helps readers see where the text is leading. These sentences are used throughout this plan. This textbook also generally utilizes these introductory overview sentences to aid your comprehension.

6. Marketing Program

The four marketing mix elements of the Howlin' Coyote chili marketing program are detailed below. Note that "chile" is the vegetable and "chili" is the dish.

Product Strategy

After first summarizing the product line, the approach to product quality and packaging is covered.

Product Line. Howlin' Coyote chili, retailing for $3.99 for an 11-ounce serving, is available in five flavors. The five are Green Chile Chili, Red Chile Chili, Beef and Black Bean Chili, Chicken Chunk Chili, and Mean Bean Chili.

Unique Product Quality. The flavoring systems of the Howlin' Coyote chilies are proprietary. The products' tastiness is due to extra care lavished upon the ingredients during production. The ingredients used are of unusually high quality. Meats are low-fat cuts and are fresh, not frozen, to preserve cell structure and moistness. Chilies are fire-roasted for fresher taste. Tomatoes and vegetables are select quality. No preservatives or artificial flavors are used.

Packaging. Reflecting the "cutting edge" marketing strategy of its producers, Howlin' Coyote bucks conventional wisdom in packaging. It avoids placing predictable photographs of the product on its containers. Instead, Howlin' Coyote's package shows a Southwestern motif that communicates the product's out-of-the-ordinary positioning.

The Southwestern motif makes Howlin' Coyote's packages stand out in a supermarket's freezer case.

Price Strategy

Howlin' Coyote Chili is, at $3.99 for an 11-ounce package, priced comparably to the other frozen offerings and higher than the canned and dried chili varieties. However, the significant taste advantages it has over canned chilies and the convenience advantages over dried chilies justify this pricing strategy.

Promotion Strategy

Key promotion programs feature in-store demonstrations, recipes, and cents-off coupons.

Elements of the Promotion Strategy are highlighted in terms of the three key promotional activities the company is emphasizing: in-store demonstrations, recipes, and cents-off coupons. For space reasons the company's online strategies are not shown in the plan. See Chapters 14, 15, and 16.

Another bulleted list adds many details for the reader, including methods of gaining customer awareness, trial, and repeat purchases as Howlin' Coyote enters new metropolitan areas.

The Place Strategy is described here in terms of both (1) the present method and (2) the new one to be used when the increased sales volume makes it feasible. See Chapters 12 and 13.

All the marketing mix decisions covered in the just-described marketing program have both revenue and expense effects. These are summarized in this section of the marketing plan.

Note that this section contains no introductory overview sentence. While the sentence is not essential, many readers prefer to see it to avoid the abrupt start with Past Sales Revenues.

In-Store Demonstrations. In-store demonstrations enable consumers to try Howlin' Coyote products and discover their unique qualities. Demos will be conducted regularly in all markets to increase awareness and trial purchases.

Recipes. Because the products' flexibility of use is a key selling point, recipes are offered to consumers to stimulate use. The recipes are given at all in-store demonstrations, on the back of packages, through a mail-in recipe book offer, and in coupons sent by direct-mail or freestanding inserts.

Cents-Off Coupons. To generate trial and repeat-purchase of Howlin' Coyote products, coupons are distributed in four ways:

- In Sunday newspaper inserts. These inserts are widely read and help generate awareness.
- In-pack coupons. Each box of Howlin' Coyote chili will contain coupons for $1 off two more packages of the chili. These coupons will be included for the first three months the product is shipped to a new market. Doing so encourages repeat purchases by new users.
- Direct-mail chili coupons. Those households that fit the Howlin' Coyote demographics described previously will be mailed coupons.
- In-store demonstrations. Coupons will be passed out at in-store demonstrations to give an additional incentive to purchase.

Place (Distribution) Strategy

Howlin' Coyote is distributed in its present markets through a food distributor. The distributor buys the product, warehouses it, and then resells and delivers it to grocery retailers on a store-by-store basis. As sales grow, we will shift to a more efficient system using a broker who sells the products to retail chains and grocery wholesalers.

Sunday newspaper inserts encourage consumer trial and provide recipes to show how Howlin' Coyote chili can be used in summer meals.

7. Financial Data and Projections

Past Sales Revenues

Historically, Howlin' Coyote has had a steady increase in sales revenues since its introduction in 2003. In 2007, sales jumped spectacularly, due largely to new promotion strategies. Sales have continued to rise, but at a less dramatic rate. Sales revenues appear in Figure 2.

Five-Year Projections

Five-year financial projections for Paradise Kitchens appear below. These projections reflect the continuing growth in number of cases sold (with eight packages of Howlin' Coyote chili per case).

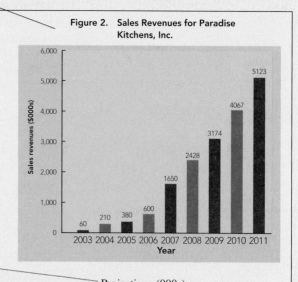

Figure 2. Sales Revenues for Paradise Kitchens, Inc.

Financial Element	Actual 2011	Projections (000s)				
		Year 1 2012	Year 2 2013	Year 3 2014	Year 4 2015	Year 5 2016
Cases sold (000s)	353	684	889	1,249	1,499	1,799
Net sales ($000s)	$5,123	$9,913	$12,884	$18,111	$21,733	$26,080
Gross profit ($000s)	$2,545	$4,820	$ 6,527	$ 8,831	$10,597	$12,717
Operating profit ($000s)	$ 339	$ 985	$ 2,906	$ 2,805	$ 3,366	$ 4,039

8. Organization

Paradise Kitchens's present organization appears in Figure 3. It shows the four people reporting to the President. Below this level are both the full-time and part-time employees of the Company.

Figure 3. The Paradise Kitchens Organization

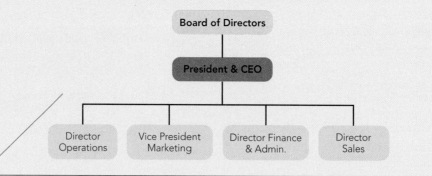

The Implementation Plan shows how the company will turn plans into results. Charts are often used to set deadlines and assign responsibilities for the many tactical marketing decisions needed to enter a new market.

At present, Paradise Kitchens operates with full-time employees in only essential positions. It now augments its full-time staff with key advisors, consultants, and subcontractors. As the firm grows, people with special expertise will be added to the staff.

9. Implementation Plan

Introducing Howlin' Coyote chilies to 17 new metropolitan markets is a complex task and requires that creative promotional activities gain consumer awareness and initial trial. Counting the three existing metropolitan markets in which Paradise Kitchens competes, by 2016 it will be in 20 metropolitan markets or 53 percent of the top 38 U.S. metropolitan markets. The anticipated rollout schedule to enter these metropolitan markets appears in Figure 4.

Figure 4.   Rollout Schedule to Enter New U.S. Markets

Year	New Markets Added Each Year	Cumulative Markets	Cumulative Percentage of 38 Major U.S. Markets
Today (2011)	2	5	16
Year 1 (2012)	3	8	21
Year 2 (2013)	4	12	29
Year 3 (2014)	2	14	37
Year 4 (2015)	3	17	45
Year 5 (2016)	3	20	53

The essence of Evaluation is comparing actual sales with the targeted values set in the plan and taking appropriate actions. Note that the section briefly describes a contingency plan for alternative actions, depending on how successful the entry into a new market turns out to be.

The diverse regional tastes in chili will be monitored carefully to assess whether minor modifications may be required in the chili recipes. As the rollout to new metropolitan areas continues, Paradise Kitchens will assess manufacturing and distribution trade-offs. This is important in determining whether to start new production with selected high-quality regional contract packers.

10. Evaluation

Monthly sales targets in cases have been set for Howlin' Coyote chili for each metropolitan area. Actual case sales will be compared with these targets and tactical marketing programs modified to reflect the unique sets of factors in each metropolitan area.

Appendix A. Biographical Sketches of Key Personnel

Appendix B. Detailed Financial Projections

Various appendixes may appear at the end of the plan, depending on the purpose and audience for them. For example, résumés of key personnel or detailed financial spreadsheets often appear in appendixes. For space reasons these are not shown here.

Understanding the Marketing Environment, Ethical Behavior, and Social Responsibility

3

WHAT IS THE WORLD'S THIRD LARGEST NATION? THE SOCIAL NATION CREATED BY FACEBOOK!

When Mark Zuckerberg launched Facebook he had no idea that today the almost one billion-member "social nation" he created would be smaller than only China and India.

How did Facebook grow so quickly? The marketing environment changed! Let's take a look at how environmental forces influenced Facebook:

Facebook and the Influence of Environmental Forces
There are many forces that influenced Facebook:

- *Social forces* changed as people became increasingly interested in the social aspects of the Internet. They wanted tools for obtaining information, offering opinions, and interacting with friends.

- *Economic forces* also influenced the demand for Facebook as the cost of wireless connectivity, Internet service, and smartphones rapidly declined and made social networking affordable for consumers around the world.

- *Technological advances* in data storage, server speed, and programming software made social networks fast and convenient. When Sixdegrees, a social network that preceded Facebook, offered its service, technology could not allow users to post or tag photos—a very popular element of the social network today.

- *Competitive forces* by companies such as Friendster, Collegester, and MySpace provided many alternatives and a rush to expand. Today, Google and Facebook are becoming fierce competitors for the role of society's depository of information.

- *Legal and regulatory forces* also affected Facebook. The company obtained rights to the name, developed privacy guidelines, and settled a claim that some of the ideas behind Facebook had come from other students.

The result of these forces was a unique network that quickly connected the world. You and most of your friends are probably already part of a social network, and possibly the largest nation in the world![1] Chapter 17 provides additional discussion on social networks and social media.

Many businesses operate in environments where important forces change. Anticipating and responding to changes often means the difference between marketing success and failure. This chapter describes how the marketing environment has changed in the past and how it is likely to change in the future.

ENVIRONMENTAL SCANNING

LO1

environmental scanning
The process of acquiring information on events outside the organization to identify and interpret potential trends.

Changes in the marketing environment are a source of opportunities and threats to be managed. The process of continually acquiring information on events occurring outside the organization to identify and interpret potential trends is called **environmental scanning**. Environmental trends typically arise from five sources: social, economic, technological, competitive, and regulatory forces. As shown in Figure 3–1 and described later in this chapter, these forces affect the marketing activities of a firm in numerous ways.

An Environmental Scan of Today's Marketplace

What trends might affect marketing in the future? A firm conducting an environmental scan of the marketplace might uncover key trends such as the growth of social networks, the increasing economic impact of Asia, the expanding availability of mobile apps, the growing importance of customer-generated content as a competitive advantage, and the growth of online privacy regulation.[2] These trends affect consumers and the businesses and organizations that serve them. Trends such as these are described in the following discussion of the five environmental forces.

SOCIAL FORCES

LO2

social forces
The demographic characteristics and the culture of the population.

demographics
Description of a population according to characteristics such as age, gender, ethnicity, income, and occupation.

The **social forces** of the environment include the demographic characteristics and the culture of the population. Changes in these forces can have a dramatic impact on marketing strategy.

Demographics

Describing a population according to selected characteristics such as age, gender, ethnicity, income, and occupation is referred to as **demographics**. Three key demographic characteristics include a population profile, a description of generational cohorts, and a description of racial and ethnic diversity.

The Population at a Glance   The most recent estimates indicate there are 6.9 billion people in the world today, and the population is likely to grow to 9.5 billion

FIGURE 3–1
Environmental forces affect the organization, as well as its suppliers and customers.

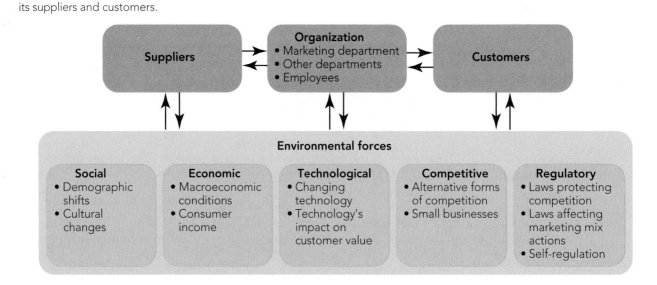

by 2050. While this growth has led to the term *population explosion*, the increases have not occurred worldwide; they are primarily in the developing countries of Africa, Asia, and Latin America. In fact, India is predicted to have the world's largest population in 2050 with 1.69 billion people, and China will be a close second with 1.31 billion people. Another important global trend is the shifting age structure of the world population. Worldwide, the number of people 60 years and older is expected to more than triple in the coming decades and reach 2 billion by 2050.[3]

Studies of the demographic characteristics of the U.S. population suggest several important trends. Generally, the population is becoming larger, older, and more diverse. The 2010 Census reported that the resident population of the United States was 308 million people. If current trends in life expectancy, birthrates, and immigration continue, by 2030 the U.S. population will exceed 373 million people.[4]

Generational Cohorts   A major reason for the graying of America is that the 76 million baby boomers—the generation of children born between 1946 and 1964—are growing older. **Baby boomers** are retiring at a rate of 10,000 every 24 hours, and they will all be 65 or older by 2030.[5]

The baby boom cohort is followed by **Generation X**, which includes the 15 percent of the population born between 1965 and 1976. This period is also known as the *baby bust*, because the number of children born each year was declining. This is a generation of consumers who are self-reliant, supportive of racial and ethnic diversity, and better educated than any previous generation. They also have become the largest segment of business travelers.[6]

The generational cohort labeled **Generation Y**, or *millennials*, includes the 72 million Americans born between 1977 and 1994. This was a period of increasing births, which resulted from baby boomers having children, and it is often referred to as the *echo-boom* or *baby boomlet*. Generation Y exerts influence on music, sports, computers, video games, and all forms of communication and networking. The Making Responsible Decisions box on the next page describes how millennials' interest in sustainability is influencing colleges, graduate schools, and employers.[7]

Racial and Ethnic Diversity   Another notable demographic characteristic of the U.S. population is its changing racial and ethnic composition. Approximately one in three U.S. residents belongs to the following racial or ethnic groups: African American,

baby boomers
The generation of children born between 1946 and 1964.

Generation X
Members of the U.S. population born between 1965 and 1976.

Generation Y
The 72 million Americans born between 1977 and 1994.

Which generational cohorts are these three advertisers trying to reach?

Millennials Are Going to Change the World!

QR 3–1
Net Impact
Video

Millennials are determined to make a difference in the world and, by doing so, make the world a better place. They are idealistic and eager to get started, particularly when it comes to environmental sustainability, which millennials believe is part of what it means to be socially responsible. The group includes students in college and graduate school and many early career employees. In different ways each group is making its voice heard.

There are approximately 17 million undergraduate millennials who expect sustainable campus communities that include LEED (Leadership in Energy and Environmental Design)-certified housing, campus transit systems, and recycling programs. Graduate students are looking for programs with sustainability electives, case studies, and potential for involvement with organizations such as Net Impact

NET IMPACT

(www.netimpact.org), a nonprofit for students who want to "use business to improve the world." Early career employees want "green" jobs such as social responsibility officer, environmental consultant, and sustainability database specialist at companies that are eco-conscious and advocate good citizenry.

Sara Hochman is a typical example. She was interested in environmental issues in college, and her first job was as an environmental consultant. To make a bigger impact on her clients, she decided she "needed to beef up my business skills," so she enrolled in graduate school at the University of Chicago where she could take an elective on renewable energy and join the Energy Club.

Have you made similar choices or decisions based on your interest and concern about sustainability? What will the world look like after the millennials have made their changes? It is difficult to predict. As experts Peter Leyden and Ruy Teixeira advise, however, we should, "Hang on for the ride!"

Native American or Alaska Native, Asian American, or Native Hawaiian or Pacific Islander. While the growing size of these groups has been identified through new Census data, their economic impact on the marketplace is also very noticeable. By 2015, Hispanics, African Americans, and Asian Americans will spend $1.5 trillion, $1.2 trillion, and $775 billion each year, respectively. To adapt to this new marketplace, many companies are developing **multicultural marketing** programs, which are combinations of the marketing mix that reflect the unique attitudes, ancestry, communication preferences, and lifestyles of different races and ethnic groups.[8]

multicultural marketing
Marketing programs that reflect unique aspects of different races.

Culture

A second social force, **culture**, incorporates the set of values, ideas, and attitudes that are learned and shared among the members of a group. Because many of the elements of culture influence consumer buying patterns, monitoring national and global cultural trends is important for marketing. Cross-cultural analysis needed for global marketing is discussed in Chapter 6.

Culture includes values that may differ over time and between countries. During the 1970s, a list of values in the United States included achievement, work, efficiency, and material comfort. Today, commonly held values include personal control, continuous change, equality, individualism, self-help, competition, future orientation, and action. These values are useful in understanding most current behaviors of U.S. consumers, particularly when they are compared to values in other countries. Contrasting values outside the United States, for example, include belief in fate, the importance of tradition, a focus on group welfare, and acceptance of birthright.

An increasingly important value for consumers in the United States and around the globe is sustainability and preservation of the environment. Concern for the environment is one reason consumers are buying hybrid gas-electric automobiles, such as the

culture
The set of values, ideas, and attitudes that is learned and shared among the members of a group.

Toyota Prius and the Chevy Volt, and electric vehicles, such as the Nissan Leaf. Companies also are changing their business practices to respond to trends in consumer values. Walmart has set ambitious goals to cut energy use by buying more local products, reducing packaging, and switching to renewable power. The company recently installed wind turbines on parking lot light poles in several test stores. Recent research also indicates that consumers are committed to brands with a strong link to social action. For example, Brita's "Filter for Good" campaign asks consumers to take a pledge to reduce their plastic bottle waste.[9]

---

learning review

1. Describe three generational cohorts.

2. Why are many companies developing multicultural marketing programs?

3. How are important values such as sustainability reflected in the marketplace today?

ECONOMIC FORCES

LO3

The second component of the environmental scan, the **economy**, pertains to the income, expenditures, and resources that affect the cost of running a business and household. We'll consider two aspects of these economic forces: a macroeconomic view of the marketplace and a microeconomic perspective of consumer income.

economy

Pertains to the income and resources that affect the cost of running a business or household.

Macroeconomic Conditions

Of particular concern at the macroeconomic level is the performance of the economy based on indicators such as GDP (gross domestic product), unemployment, and price changes (inflation or deflation). In an inflationary economy, the cost to produce and buy products and services escalates as prices increase. From a marketing standpoint, if prices rise faster than consumer incomes, the number of items consumers can buy decreases. This relationship is evident in the cost of a college education. The National Center for Public Policy and Higher Education reports that since 1980 college tuition and fees have increased 440 percent while family income rose less than 150 percent. The share of family income required to pay for tuition at public four-year colleges has risen from 12 percent in 1980 to 24 percent today.[10]

Periods of declining economic activity are referred to as recessions. During recessions, businesses decrease production, unemployment rises, and many consumers have less money to spend. The U.S. economy experienced recessions from 1973–75, 1981–82, 1990–91, and in 2001. Most recently, a recessionary period began in 2007 and ended in 2009, becoming the longest in recent history.[11]

Consumer Income

The microeconomic trends in terms of consumer income are also important issues for marketers. Having a product that meets the needs of consumers may be of little value if they are unable to purchase it. A consumer's ability to buy is related to income, which consists of gross, disposable, and discretionary components.

Gross Income   The total amount of money made in one year by a person, household, or family unit is referred to as *gross income* (or "money income" at the Census Bureau). While the typical U.S. household earned only about $8,700 of income in 1970, it earned about $49,445 in 2010. When gross income is adjusted for inflation, however, income of that typical U.S. household was relatively stable. In fact, inflation-adjusted income has only varied between $42,527 and $53,252 since 1968. Approximately 54 percent of U.S. households have an annual income between $25,000 and $99,999.[12] Are you from a typical household?

Disposable Income   The second income component, *disposable income*, is the money a consumer has left after paying taxes to use for necessities such as food, housing, clothing, and transportation. Thus, if taxes rise or fall faster than income, consumers are likely to have more or less disposable income. Similarly, dramatic changes in prices of products can require spending adjustments. In recent years, for example, as the price of gasoline increased, consumers found themselves adjusting their spending in other categories. In addition, the decline in home prices has had a psychological impact on consumers, who tend to spend more when they feel their net worth is rising and postpone purchases when it declines. During a recessionary period, spending, debt, and use of credit all decline. The recent downturn has led many consumers to switch from premium brands to lower-priced brands.[13]

Discretionary Income   The third component of income is *discretionary income*, the money that remains after paying for taxes and necessities. Discretionary income is used for luxury items such as a Cunard cruise. An obvious problem in defining discretionary versus disposable income is determining what is a luxury and what is a necessity.

The Department of Labor monitors consumer expenditures through its annual Consumer Expenditure Survey. In 2009, consumers spent about 13 percent of their income on food, 34 percent on housing, and 3.5 percent on clothes. While an additional 22 percent is often spent on transportation and health care, the remainder is generally viewed as discretionary. The percentage of income spent on food and housing typically declines as income increases, which can provide an increase in discretionary income. Discretionary expenditures also can be increased by reducing savings. The Bureau of Labor Statistics observed that during the 1990s and early 2000s the savings rate declined to zero. That trend was reversed in 2008 when the government issued stimulus checks designed to improve the economy and consumers saved the money rather than spent it. Recent data on consumer expenditures indicate that the savings rate has now risen to approximately 6 percent.[14]

As consumers' discretionary income increases, so does the opportunity to indulge in the luxurious leisure travel marketed by Cunard.

Cunard Cruise Line
www.cunard.com

TECHNOLOGICAL FORCES

technology
Inventions from applied science or engineering research.

Our society is in a period of dramatic technological change. **Technology**, the third environmental force, refers to inventions or innovations from applied science or engineering research. Each new wave of technological innovation can replace existing products and companies. Do you recognize the items pictured below and what they may replace?

Technology of Tomorrow

Technological change is the result of research, so it is difficult to predict. Some of the most dramatic technological changes occurring now, however, include the following:

- Social networks are evolving into social platforms that provide functionality, community, and identity well beyond the value provided by traditional corporate websites.
- "Natural user interfaces" are utilizing gesture, touch, and voice to change the way we interact with and control computers and complicated machines.
- Green technologies such as SmartGrid infrastructure, online energy management, and consumer-generated energy (e.g., home wind turbines) are gaining widespread acceptance among American consumers.
- Biotechnology is being used to develop genetically modified crops to create enough food for a growing world population.

Some of these trends in technology are already seen in today's marketplace. Facebook, for example, enables users to log into other online communities using their Facebook identity through Facebook Connect. Microsoft has pioneered natural user interface use with its 3D image capture technology called Kinect. Google has developed Power-Meter, a free energy monitoring tool that allows consumers to view their home energy consumption from anywhere online. Other technologies, such as tablet computers, online meeting services, and satellite communicators, are likely to replace or become substitutes for existing products and services such as magazines, business travel, and even wireless service.[15]

Technological change leads to new products. What products might be replaced by these innovations?

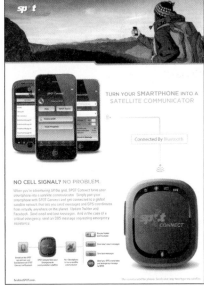

Technology's Impact on Customer Value

Advances in technology have important effects on marketing. First, the cost of technology is plummeting, causing the customer value assessment of technology-based products to focus on other dimensions such as quality, service, and relationships. *PC Magazine* publishes an article titled, "The Best Free Software," each year to tell readers about companies that give their software away, with the expectation that advertising or upgrade purchases will generate revenue. A similar approach is used by many U.S. cellular telephone vendors, who charge little for the telephone if the purchase leads to a long-term telephone service contract.[16]

Technology also provides value through the development of new products. Recent examples that have generated extraordinary consumer interest include Amazon's Kindle, Nintendo's Wii Sports video game, and Discovery Communications 3D television channel, 3net. A new version of Apple's iPad also has received attention from many consumers. The new product provides a high-resolution display, a camera that faces the user, and compatibility with 90,000 software programs, utilities, and apps. Other new products likely to be available soon include injectable health monitors that send glucose, oxygen, and other clinical information to a wristwatch-like monitor and robots that use artificial intelligence to master specific tasks.[17]

marketspace

An information- and communication-based electronic exchange environment occupied by digitized offerings.

The transformative power of technology may be best illustrated by the rapid growth of the **marketspace**, an information- and communication-based electronic exchange environment mostly occupied by sophisticated computer and telecommunication technologies and digitized offerings. Any activity that uses some form of electronic communication in the inventory, exchange, advertisement, distribution, and payment of goods and services is often called *electronic commerce*. Network technologies are now used for everything from filing expense reports, to monitoring daily sales, to sharing information with employees, to communicating instantly with suppliers.

COMPETITIVE FORCES

competition

Alternative firms that could provide a product to satisfy a specific market's needs.

The fourth component of the environmental scan, **competition**, refers to the alternative firms that could provide a product to satisfy a specific market's needs. There are various forms of competition, and each company must consider its present and potential competitors in designing its marketing strategy.

Alternative Forms of Competition

LO5

Four basic forms of competition exist. They fall on a continuum from pure competition to monopolistic competition to oligopoly to pure monopoly.

At one end of the continuum is *pure competition*, in which there are many sellers and they each have a similar product. Companies that deal in commodities common to agribusiness (for example, wheat, rice, and grain) often are in a pure competition position in which distribution (in the sense of shipping products) is important but other elements of marketing have little impact.

In the second point on the continuum, *monopolistic competition*, many sellers compete with substitutable products within a price range. For example, if the price of coffee rises too much, consumers may switch to tea. Coupons or sales are frequently used marketing tactics.

Oligopoly, a common industry structure, occurs when a few companies control the majority of industry sales. The wireless telephone industry, for example, is dominated by AT&T, Verizon, and Sprint-Nextel, which have 123, 92, and 48 million subscribers, respectively. Similarly, the entertainment industry in the United States is dominated by Viacom, Disney, and Time Warner, and the major firms in the U.S. defense contractor industry are Boeing, Northrup Grumman, and Lockheed Martin. Critics of oligopolies suggest that because there are few sellers, price competition among firms is not desirable because it leads to reduced profits for all producers.[18]

The final point on the continuum, *pure monopoly*, occurs when only one firm sells the product. Monopolies are common for producers of goods considered essential to a community: water, electricity, and cable service. Typically, marketing plays a small role in a monopolistic setting because it is regulated by the state or federal government. Government control usually seeks to ensure price protection for the buyer, although deregulation in recent years has encouraged price competition in the electricity market. Concern that Microsoft's 86 percent share of the PC operating system market was a monopoly led to lawsuits and consent decrees from the U.S. Justice Department and investigations and fines from the European Union. Because Google's market share of the online search market exceeds 65 percent, the CEO of Google recently asked for guidelines to avoid similar investigations.[19]

Small Businesses as Competitors

While large companies provide familiar examples of the forms and components of competition, small businesses make up the majority of the competitive landscape for most businesses. Consider that there are approximately 27.5 million small businesses in the United States, which employ half of all private sector employees. In addition, small businesses generate 65 percent of all new jobs annually and 50 percent of the gross domestic product (GDP). Research has shown a strong correlation between national economic growth and the level of new small business activity in previous years.[20]

---

learning review

4. What is the difference between a consumer's disposable and discretionary income?

5. How does technology impact customer value?

6. In pure competition there are a _____ number of sellers.

REGULATORY FORCES

LO6

regulation
Restrictions that state and federal laws place on business.

For any organization, the marketing and broader business decisions are constrained, directed, and influenced by regulatory forces. **Regulation** consists of restrictions state and federal laws place on business with regard to the conduct of its activities. Regulation exists to protect companies as well as consumers. Federal and state regulation seeks to ensure competition and fair business practices. For consumers, the focus of regulation is to protect them from unfair trade practices and ensure their safety.

Protecting Competition

Major federal legislation has been passed to encourage competition, which is deemed desirable because it permits the consumer to determine which competitor will succeed and which will fail. The first such law was the *Sherman Antitrust Act* (1890). Lobbying by farmers in the Midwest against fixed railroad shipping prices led to the passage of this act, which forbids (1) contracts, combinations, or conspiracies in restraint of trade and (2) actual monopolies or attempts to monopolize any part of trade or commerce. Because of vague wording and government inactivity, however, there was only one successful case against a company in the nine years after the act became law, and the Sherman Act was supplemented with the *Clayton Act* (1914). This act forbids certain actions that are likely to lessen competition, although no actual harm has yet occurred.

In the 1930s, the federal government had to act again to ensure fair competition. During that time, large chain stores appeared, such as the Great Atlantic & Pacific Tea Company (A&P). Small businesses were threatened, and they lobbied for the *Robinson-Patman Act* (1936). This act makes it unlawful to discriminate in prices charged to different purchasers of the same product, where the effect may substantially lessen competition or help to create a monopoly.

Protecting Producers and Consumers

Various federal laws are intended to protect the company while others are intended to protect the consumer. In some cases the laws are designed to protect both.

A company, for example, can protect its competitive position with the patent law, which gives inventors of new and novel products the right to exclude others from making, using, or selling products that infringe on the patented invention. The federal copyright law is another way for a company to protect its competitive position. The copyright law gives the author of a literary, dramatic, musical, or artistic work the exclusive right to print, perform, or otherwise copy that work. Copyright is secured automatically when the work is created. Digital technology has necessitated additional copyright legislation, called the *Digital Millennium Copyright Act* (1998), to improve the protection of copyrighted digital products.[21]

Federal laws also protect consumers. Various laws address each of the four elements of the marketing mix. Product requirements, for example, are specified in laws such as the *Child Protection Act* (1966), the *Nutritional Labeling and Education Act* (1990), and the *Consumer Product Safety Act* (1972), which established the Consumer Product Safety Commission. Many of these laws came about because of **consumerism**, a grassroots movement started in the 1960s to increase the influence, power, and rights of consumers in dealing with institutions.

Laws also address pricing, distribution, and promotion. The *FTC Act of 1914*, for example, established the Federal Trade Commission (FTC) to monitor unfair business practices. The FTC has the power to (1) issue cease and desist orders and (2) order corrective advertising. In issuing a cease and desist order, the FTC orders a company to stop practices the commission considers unfair. With corrective advertising, the FTC can require a company to spend money on advertising to correct previous misleading promotion. Other laws, such as the *Deceptive Mail Prevention and*

consumerism

A movement started to increase the influence, power, and rights of consumers in dealing with institutions.

QR 3–2
FTC Video

These products are identified by protected trademarks. Are any of these trademarks in danger of becoming generic?

Companies must meet certain requirements before they can display this logo on their websites.

Better Business Bureau
www.bbbonline.com

self-regulation
An alternative to government control, whereby an industry attempts to police itself.

Enforcement Act (1999), the *Telephone Consumer Protection Act* (1991), and the *Controlling the Assault of Non-Solicited Pornography and Marketing* (*CAN-SPAM*) *Act* (2004), are designed to guide the use of direct mail, telemarketing, e-mail solicitations, and other forms of promotion.[22]

An example of a law that protects producers and consumers is the *Lanham Act* (1946), which provides for the registration of trademarks. Registration under the Lanham Act provides important advantages to a trademark owner but it does not confer ownership. A company can lose its trademark if it becomes generic, which means that it has come to be a common, descriptive word for the product. Coca-Cola, Whopper, and Xerox are registered trademarks, and competitors cannot use these names. Aspirin and escalator, however, are former trademarks that are now generic terms in the United States and can be used by anyone. Consumers benefit from trademarks because it allows them to correctly identify products they want to purchase.[23]

Control through Self-Regulation

An alternative to government regulation is **self-regulation**, where an industry attempts to police itself. The major television networks, for example, have used self-regulation to set their own guidelines for TV ads for children's toys. There are two problems with self-regulation, however: noncompliance by members and enforcement. In addition, if attempts at self-regulation are too strong, they may violate the Robinson-Patman Act. The best-known self-regulatory group is the Better Business Bureau (BBB). This agency is a voluntary alliance of companies whose goal is to help maintain fair practices. Although the BBB has no legal power, it does try to use "moral suasion" to get members to comply with its standards.

There is a distinction between laws, which are society's values that are enforceable in courts, and ethics, which deal with personal and moral principles and values. The following sections discuss ethical behavior and social responsibility in marketing.

learning review

7. The _____ Act was punitive toward monopolies, whereas the _____ Act was preventive.

8. The Federal Trade Commission (FTC) monitors _____.

9. How does the Better Business Bureau encourage companies to follow its standards for commerce?

UNDERSTANDING ETHICAL MARKETING BEHAVIOR

ethics
The moral principles and values that govern the actions and decisions of an individual or a group.

Ethics are the moral principles and values that govern the actions and decisions of an individual or group.[24] They serve as guidelines on how to act rightly and justly when faced with moral dilemmas. Researchers have identified numerous factors that influence ethical marketing behavior.[25] Figure 3–2 on the next page presents a framework that shows these factors and their relationships.

Societal Culture and Norms

As described previously, *culture* refers to the set of values, ideas, and attitudes that are learned and shared among the members of a group. Culture also serves as a socializing force that dictates what is morally right and just. This means that moral standards are relative to particular societies.[26] These standards often reflect the laws and regulations that affect social and economic behavior, which can create ethical dilemmas. Companies

FIGURE 3–2
A framework for understanding
ethical behavior. Each of these
influences has an effect on
ethical marketing behavior, as
described in the text.

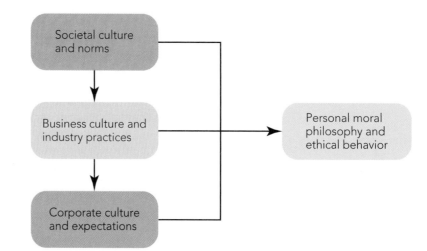

that compete in the global marketplace recognize this fact. Consider UPS, the world's largest package delivery company operating in more than 200 countries and territories worldwide.[27] According to the company's global compliance and ethics coordinator, "Although languages and cultures around the world may be different, we do not change our ethical standards at UPS. Our ethics program is global in nature." Not surprisingly, UPS is consistently ranked among the world's most ethical companies.

Business Culture and Industry Practices

Societal culture provides a foundation for understanding moral behavior in business activities. *Business cultures* "comprise the effective rules of the game, the boundaries between competitive and unethical behavior, [and] the codes of conduct in business dealings."[28] Consumers have witnessed instances where business cultures in the financial (inside trading), insurance (deceptive sales practices), and defense (bribery) industries went awry. Business culture affects ethical conduct both in the exchange relationship between sellers and buyers and in the competitive behavior among sellers.

Ethics of Exchange   The exchange process is central to the marketing concept. Ethical exchanges between sellers and buyers should result in both parties being better off after a transaction.

Before the 1960s, the legal concept of *caveat emptor*—let the buyer beware—was pervasive in the American business culture. In 1962, President John F. Kennedy outlined a **Consumer Bill of Rights** that codified the ethics of exchange between buyers and sellers. These were the right (1) to safety, (2) to be informed, (3) to choose, and (4) to be heard. Consumers expect and often demand that these rights be protected, as have American businesses.

Ethics of Competition   Business culture also affects ethical behavior in competition. Two kinds of unethical behavior are most common: (1) economic espionage and (2) bribery.

Economic espionage is the clandestine collection of trade secrets or proprietary information about a company's competitors. This practice is illegal and unethical and carries serious criminal penalties for the offending individual or business. Espionage activities include illegal trespassing, theft, fraud, misrepresentation, wiretapping, the search of a competitor's trash, and violations of written and implicit employment agreements with noncompete clauses. More than half of the largest firms in the United States have uncovered espionage in some form, costing them $300 billion annually in lost sales.[29] Read the Making Responsible Decisions box to learn how Pepsi-Cola responded to an offer to obtain confidential information about its archrival's marketing plans.[30]

The second form of unethical competitive behavior is giving and receiving bribes and kickbacks. Bribes and kickbacks are often disguised as gifts, consultant fees, and

Consumer Bill of Rights
Codified the ethics of exchange between buyers and sellers, including rights to safety, to be informed, to choose, and to be heard.

Making Responsible Decisions > > > > > > > ethics

Corporate Conscience in the Cola War

Suppose you are a senior executive at Pepsi-Cola and that a Coca-Cola employee offers to sell you the marketing plan and sample for a new Coke product at a modest price. Would you buy it knowing Pepsi-Cola could gain a significant competitive edge in the cola war?

When this question was posed in an online survey of marketing and advertising executives, 67 percent said they would buy the plan and product sample if there were no repercussions. What did Pepsi-Cola do when this offer actually occurred? The company immediately contacted Coca-Cola, which contacted the FBI. An undercover FBI agent paid the employee $30,000 in cash stuffed in a Girl Scout cookie box as a down payment and later arrested the employee and accomplices. When asked about the inci-

dent, a Pepsi-Cola spokesperson said: "We only did what any responsible company would do. Competition must be tough, but must always be fair and legal."

Why did the 33 percent of respondents in the online survey say they would decline the offer? Most said they would prefer competing ethically so they could sleep at night. According to a senior advertising agency executive who would decline the offer: "Repercussions go beyond potential espionage charges. As long as we have a conscience, there are repercussions."

So what happened to the Coca-Cola employee and her accomplices? She was sentenced to eight years in prison and ordered to pay $40,000 in restitution. Her accomplices were each sentenced to five years in prison.

favors. This practice is more common in business-to-business and government marketing than in consumer marketing. In general, bribery is most evident in industries experiencing intense competition and in countries in the earlier stages of economic development. According to a United Nations study, 15 percent of all companies in industrialized countries have to pay bribes to win or retain business. In Asia, this figure is 40 percent. In Eastern Europe, 60 percent of all companies must pay bribes to do business. A recent poll of senior executives engaged in global marketing revealed that Somalia was the most likely country to engage in bribery to win or retain business. Denmark, New Zealand, and Singapore were the least likely.[31]

Corporate Culture and Expectations

A third influence on ethical practices is corporate culture. *Corporate culture* is the set of values, ideas, and attitudes that is learned and shared among the members of an organization. The culture of a company demonstrates itself in the dress ("We don't wear ties"), sayings ("The IBM Way"), and manner of work (team efforts) of employees. Culture is also apparent in the expectations for ethical behavior present in formal codes of ethics and the ethical actions of top management and co-workers.

code of ethics

A formal statement of ethical principles and rules of conduct.

Codes of Ethics   A **code of ethics** is a formal statement of ethical principles and rules of conduct. It is estimated that 86 percent of U.S. companies have some sort of ethics code and one of every four large companies has corporate ethics officers. Ethics codes typically address contributions to government officials and political parties, customer and supplier relations, conflicts of interest, and accurate recordkeeping.

Ethical Behavior of Top Management and Co-Workers   One reason for violating ethics codes rests in the perceived behavior of top management and co-workers.[32] Observing peers and top management and gauging responses to unethical behavior play an important role in individual actions. A study of business executives reported that 40 percent had been implicitly or explicitly rewarded for engaging in ethically troubling behavior. About 31 percent of those who refused to engage in unethical behavior were penalized, through either outright punishment or a diminished

What does 3M's Scotchgard have to do with ethics, social responsibility, and a $200 million loss in annual sales? Read the text to find out.

moral idealism
A personal moral philosophy that considers certain individual rights or duties as universal, regardless of the outcome.

utilitarianism
A personal moral philosophy that focuses on the "greatest good for the greatest number."

status in the company.[33] Clearly, ethical dilemmas can bring personal and professional conflict. For this reason, numerous states have laws protecting *whistle-blowers*, employees who report unethical or illegal actions of their employers.

Your Personal Moral Philosophy and Ethical Behavior

Ultimately, ethical choices are based on the personal moral philosophy of the decision maker. Moral philosophy is learned through the process of socialization with friends and family and by formal education. It is also influenced by the societal, business, and corporate culture in which a person finds him- or herself. Two prominent personal moral philosophies have direct bearing on marketing practice: (1) moral idealism and (2) utilitarianism.

Moral Idealism   **Moral idealism** is a personal moral philosophy that considers certain individual rights or duties as universal, regardless of the outcome. This philosophy exists in the Consumer Bill of Rights and is favored by moral philosophers and consumer interest groups. For example, the right to know applies to probable defects in an automobile that relate to safety.

This philosophy also applies to ethical duties. A fundamental ethical duty is to do no harm. Adherence to this duty prompted the recent decision by 3M executives to phase out production of a chemical 3M had manufactured for nearly 40 years. The substance, used in far-ranging products from pet food bags, candy wrappers, carpeting, and 3M's popular Scotchgard fabric protector, had no known harmful health or environmental effect. However, the company discovered that the chemical appeared in minuscule amounts in humans and animals around the world and accumulated in tissue. Believing that the substance could be possibly harmful in large doses, 3M voluntarily stopped its production, resulting in a $200 million loss in annual sales.[34]

Utilitarianism   An alternative perspective on moral philosophy is **utilitarianism**, which is a personal moral philosophy that focuses on "the greatest good for the greatest number" by assessing the costs and benefits of the consequences of ethical behavior. If the benefits exceed the costs, then the behavior is ethical. If not, then the behavior is unethical. This philosophy underlies the economic tenets of capitalism and, not surprisingly, is embraced by many business executives and students.[35]

learning review	10. What rights are included in the Consumer Bill of Rights?
	11. Economic espionage includes what kinds of activities?
	12. What is meant by moral idealism?

UNDERSTANDING SOCIAL RESPONSIBILITY IN MARKETING

social responsibility
The idea that organizations are part of a larger society and are accountable to that society for their actions.

As we saw in Chapter 1, the societal marketing concept stresses marketing's social responsibility by not only satisfying the needs of consumers but also providing for society's welfare. **Social responsibility** means that organizations are part of a larger society and are accountable to that society for their actions. Like ethics, agreement on the nature and scope of social responsibility is often difficult to come by, given the diversity of values present in different societal, business, and corporate cultures.

Three Concepts of Social Responsibility

There are three concepts of social responsibility: (1) profit responsibility, (2) stakeholder responsibility, and (3) societal responsibility.

Profit Responsibility *Profit responsibility* holds that companies have a simple duty: to maximize profits for their owners or stockholders. This view is expressed by Nobel Laureate Milton Friedman, who said, "There is one and only one social responsibility of business—to use its resources and engage in activities designed to increase its profits so long as it stays within the rules of the game, which is to say, engages in open and free competition without deception or fraud."[36]

Stakeholder Responsibility Criticism of the profit view has led to a broader concept of social responsibility. *Stakeholder responsibility* focuses on the obligations an organization has to those who can affect achievement of its objectives. These constituencies include consumers, employees, suppliers, and distributors. Source Perrier S.A., the supplier of Perrier bottled water, exercised this responsibility when it recalled 160 million bottles of water in 120 countries after traces of a toxic chemical were found in 13 bottles. The recall cost the company $35 million, and the profit from $40 million in lost sales. Even though the chemical level was not harmful to humans, Source Perrier's president believed he acted in the best interests of the firm's consumers, distributors, and employees by removing "the least doubt, as minimal as it might be, to weigh on the image of the quality and purity of our product"—which it did.[37]

Societal Responsibility An even broader concept of social responsibility has emerged in recent years. *Societal responsibility* refers to obligations that organizations have (1) to the preservation of the ecological environment and (2) to the general public. Today, emphasis is placed on the *triple-bottom line*—recognition of the need for organizations to improve the state of people, the planet, and profit simultaneously if they are to achieve sustainable, long-term growth.[38] Growing interest in green marketing, cause marketing, social audits, and sustainable development reflects this recognition.

Green marketing—marketing efforts to produce, promote, and reclaim environmentally sensitive products—takes many forms.[39] At 3M, product development opportunities emanate both from consumer research and its "Pollution Prevention Pays" program. This program solicits employee suggestions on how to reduce pollution and recycle materials. Since 1975, this program has generated over 8,000 3P projects that eliminated more than 3 billion pounds of air, water, and solid-waste pollutants from the environment. Xerox's "Design for the Environment" program focuses on ways to make its equipment recyclable and remanufacturable. Today, 100 percent of Xerox-designed products are remanufacturable. This effort has kept more than 2.3 billion pounds of equipment from being discarded in U.S. landfills.

Socially responsible efforts on behalf of the general public are becoming more common. A formal practice is **cause marketing**, which occurs when the charitable contributions of a firm are tied directly to the customer revenues produced through the promotion of one of its products.[40] This definition distinguishes cause marketing from a firm's standard charitable contributions, which are outright donations. For example, Procter & Gamble raises funds for the Special Olympics when consumers purchase selected company products, and MasterCard International links usage of its card with fund-raising for institutions that combat cancer, heart disease, child abuse, drug abuse, and muscular dystrophy. Barnes & Noble promotes literacy, and Coca-Cola sponsors local Boys and Girls Clubs. Avon Products, Inc., focuses on different issues in different countries, including breast cancer, domestic violence, and disaster relief, among many others.

Cause marketing programs incorporate all three concepts of social responsibility by addressing public concerns and satisfying customer needs. They can also enhance corporate sales and profits as described in the Marketing Matters box on the next page.[41]

---

green marketing
Marketing efforts to produce, promote, and reclaim environmentally sensitive products.

cause marketing
Tying the charitable contributions of a firm directly to sales produced through the promotion of one of its products.

QR 3–3
Häagen-Dazs
Video

Avon Products, Inc., successfully employs cause marketing programs in the fight against breast cancer.

Avon Products, Inc.
www.avon.com

Marketing Matters > > > > > customer value

Will Consumers Switch Brands for a Cause? Yes, If . . .

American Express Company pioneered cause marketing when it sponsored the renovation of the Statue of Liberty. This effort raised $1.7 million for the renovation, increased card usage among cardholders, and attracted new cardholders. In 2001, U.S. companies raised more than $5 billion for causes they champion. It is estimated that cause marketing raised over $10 billion in 2011.

Cause marketing benefits companies as well as causes. Research indicates that 85 percent of U.S. consumers say they have a more favorable

opinion of companies that support causes they care about. Also, 80 percent of consumers say they will switch to a brand or retailer that supports a good cause if the price and quality of brands or retailers are equal. In short, cause marketing may be a valued point of difference for brands and companies, all other things being equal.

For more information, including news, links, and case studies, visit the Cause Marketing Forum website at www.causemarketingforum .com.

Sustainable Development: Doing Well by Doing Good

Sustainable development involves conducting business in a way that protects the natural environment while making economic progress. Ecologically responsible initiatives such as green marketing represent one such initiative. Recent initiatives related to working conditions at offshore manufacturing sites that produce goods for U.S. companies focus on quality-of-life issues. Public opinion surveys show that 90 percent of U.S. citizens are concerned about working conditions under which products are made in Asia and Latin America. Companies such as Reebok, Nike, Liz Claiborne, Levi Strauss, and Mattel have responded by imposing codes of conduct to reduce harsh or abusive working conditions at offshore manufacturing facilities.[42] Reebok, for example, now monitors production of its sporting apparel and equipment to ensure that no child labor is used in making its products.

Companies that evidence societal responsibility have been rewarded for their efforts. Research has shown that these companies (1) benefit from favorable word of mouth among consumers and (2) typically outperform less responsible companies in terms of financial performance.[43]

---

learning review

13. What is meant by social responsibility?

14. Marketing efforts to produce, promote, and reclaim environmentally sensitive products are called _____.

15. What is sustainable development?

LEARNING OBJECTIVES REVIEW

LO1 *Explain the purpose of environmental scanning.*
Environmental scanning is the process of continually acquiring information on events occurring outside the organization to identify and interpret potential trends. Environmental trends typically arise from five sources: social, economic, technological, competitive, and regulatory forces. A firm conducting an environmental scan of the marketplace might uncover key trends such as the growth of social networks, the increasing economic impact of Asia, and many others.

LO2 *Describe social forces such as demographics and culture.*
The social forces of the environment include the demographic characteristics and the culture of the population. Three key

demographic characteristics include a population profile, a description of generational cohorts (baby boomers, Generation X, and Generation Y), and a description of racial and ethnic diversity. Culture incorporates the set of values, ideas, and attitudes that is learned and shared among the members of a group.

LO3 *Discuss how economic forces affect marketing.*
Two aspects of economic forces include macroeconomic conditions related to the marketplace and microeconomic factors such as consumer income. Indicators of marketplace conditions include GDP, unemployment, and price changes (inflation or deflation). Consumer income has gross, disposable, and discretionary

components. The state of the economy and changes in income can influence consumers' ability to buy products and services.

LO4 *Describe how technological changes can affect marketing.* Technological innovations can replace existing products and services. Changes in technology can also have an impact on customer value by reducing the cost of products, improving the quality of products, and providing new products that were not previously feasible. Electronic commerce is transforming how companies do business.

LO5 *Discuss the forms of competition that exist in a market.* There are four forms of competition: pure competition, monopolistic competition, oligopoly, and monopoly. While large companies are often used as examples of marketplace competitors, there are 27.5 million small businesses in the United States that have a significant impact on the economy.

LO6 *Explain how regulatory forces ensure competition and protect producers and consumers.* Regulation exists to protect companies and consumers. Legislation that ensures a competitive marketplace includes the Sherman Antitrust Act. Companies can protect their competitive position with patent and copyright laws. Consumers are protected by laws that address each of the four elements of the marketing mix. Laws such as the Lanham Act, which provides for the registration of trademarks, benefit both companies and consumers. Self-regulation through organizations such as the Better Business Bureau provides an alternative to federal and state regulation.

LO7 *Identify factors that influence ethical and unethical marketing decisions.* Four factors presented in Figure 3–2 influence ethical marketing behavior. They are: societal culture and norms, business culture and industry practices, corporate culture and expectations, and personal moral philosophy and ethical behavior.

LO8 *Describe the different concepts of social responsibility.* Social responsibility means that organizations are part of a larger society and are accountable to that society for their actions. There are three concepts of social responsibility, profit responsibility, stakeholder responsibility, and societal responsibility.

FOCUSING ON KEY TERMS

baby boomers p. 61
cause marketing p. 73
code of ethics p. 71
competition p. 66
Consumer Bill of Rights p. 70
consumerism p. 68
culture p. 62
demographics p. 60

economy p. 63
environmental scanning p. 60
ethics p. 69
Generation X p. 61
Generation Y p. 61
green marketing p. 73
marketspace p. 66
moral idealism p. 72

multicultural marketing p. 62
regulation p. 67
self-regulation p. 69
social forces p. 60
social responsibility p. 72
technology p. 65
utilitarianism p. 72

APPLYING MARKETING KNOWLEDGE

1 For many years Gerber has manufactured baby food in small, single-sized containers. In conducting an environmental scan, identify three trends or factors that might significantly affect this company's future business, and then propose how Gerber might respond to these changes.

2 Describe the new features you would add to an automobile designed for consumers in the 55+ age group. In what magazines would you advertise to appeal to this target market?

3 New technologies are continuously improving and replacing existing products. Although technological change is often difficult to predict, suggest how the following companies and products might be affected by the Internet and digital technologies: (*a*) Kodak cameras and film, (*b*) American Airlines, and (*c*) the Metropolitan Museum of Art.

4 Why would Xerox be concerned about its name becoming generic?

5 Develop a Code of Ethics for a new online vitamin store. Does your code address advertising? Privacy? Use by children?

6 Compare and contrast moral idealism and utilitarianism as alternative personal moral philosophies.

7 How would you evaluate Milton Friedman's view of the social responsibility of a firm?

building your marketing plan

Your marketing plan will include a situation analysis based on internal and external factors that are likely to affect your marketing program, and an assessment of the affect of your plan on potential stakeholders.

1 To summarize information about external factors, create a table and identify three trends related to each of the five forces (social, economic, technological, competitive, and regulatory) that relate to your product or service.

2 When your table is complete, describe how each of the trends represents an opportunity or a threat for your business.

3 Identify what, if any, ethical and social responsibility issues might arise for each type of stakeholder.

QR 3–4
Toyota Video
Case

"Toyota's mission is to become the most respected and admired car company in America," explains Jana Hartline, manager of environmental communications at Toyota. To accomplish this, Jana and her colleagues at Toyota are working toward a future where a wide range of innovative vehicles, fuel technologies, and partnerships converge to create an economically vibrant, mobile society in harmony with the environment. It's a challenge Jana finds exciting and the result is cleaner, greener cars!

THE COMPANY

Kiichiro Toyoda began research on gasoline-powered engines in 1930. By 1935 he had developed passenger car prototypes, and in 1957 he introduced the "Toyopet" in the United States. The Toyopet was not successful and was discontinued. In 1965, however, the Corona was introduced, and it was followed by the Corolla in 1968. The Corolla went on to become the best-selling passenger car in the world, with 27 million purchased in more than 140 countries!

Today, Toyota is the world's largest automobile manufacturer. The company is ranked the eighth largest corporation by *Fortune* magazine. The company's core principle is "to contribute to society and the economy by producing high-quality products and services." Its success is often attributed to a business philosophy referred to as "The Toyota Way."

The Toyota Way is used to (1) improve processes and products, (2) build trust, and (3) empower individuals and teams. There are two values that act as pillars of The Toyota Way. They are continuous improvement and respect for people. According to Jana Hartline, the two values are "integrated into everything that we do on a daily basis," creating "a unique corporate environment."

As the company has grown it has also sought a larger role in society. Toyota created the Toyota USA Foundation with a $10 million endowment and a mission to make Toyota a leading corporate citizen. Combining The Toyota Way with its corporate philanthropy has been very successful. Toyota believes that the foundation of its success involves a constant spirit of challenge and enthusiasm for new ideas. For example, Toyota's environmental vision includes the concept of sustainable mobility.

ENVIRONMENTAL VISION AND THE PRIUS

To make its environmental vision actionable, Toyota developed a five-year Environmental Action Plan. The plan is structured around five key areas:

- Energy and Climate Change
- Recycling and Resource Management
- Air Quality
- Environmental Management
- Cooperation with Society

For each area Toyota creates goals and measurable targets based on a life-cycle view of vehicles: from design, to manufacturing, to sales and distribution, to use, and finally to how the vehicle is recycled at end-of-life. One of its top goals has been to develop advanced vehicle technologies to complement traditional automobile technologies.

Ed LaRocque, national manager of vehicle marketing, describes how Toyota started one of these initiatives:

In the early 90s Toyota developed what we called the G21 vision. The goal of the G21 plan was to bring a vehicle to market that represented a great value, and had great environmental benefits, not just in Japan but globally.

The concept was eventually introduced as the Prius, a hybrid vehicle with a gasoline engine and an electric motor combination called the Hybrid Synergy Drive. The car received an EPA-estimated mileage rating of 50 mpg. Initially the Prius was attractive to very eco-conscious consumers but met with some resistance from the press and the general population. The cars were fuel efficient, but they were not attractive. Since the first introduction, Toyota has made changes and introduced two new generations of the Prius to help it become the world's most-popular hybrid and the winner of the Kelley Blue Book 2010 Top 10 Green Car award.

Toyota's development of new technologies such as the Hybrid Synergy Drive helped it recognize the implications for the entire mobility system. A strategy for sustainable mobility affects not only new technologies and vehicles, but also new energy sources, new transportation systems, and the many partnerships of involved stakeholders. Advertising for the Prius emphasizes this point, claiming the car provides "Harmony between man, nature, and machine." In the long-term, however, this strategy will not be successful if consumers are not aware of or knowledgeable about advanced technologies. To increase awareness and knowledge Toyota specified the development of partnerships as a goal.

STRATEGIC PARTNERSHIPS

Toyota believes that partnerships with relevant organizations help increase awareness of its technologies and products. These programs are designed to educate people so they can reduce their environmental footprint. One of these programs, for example, is *Together Green*—a $20 million, five-year alliance with Audubon to fund projects, train leaders, and offer volunteer opportunities. Similarly, Toyota has partnered with the World Wildlife Fund to establish hybrid energy systems, oil recycling programs, and renewable energy outreach campaigns. The exposure from these programs is often much more effective than other communication options. Mary Nickerson, national manager of advanced technology, explains: "we [have] used partnerships with the American Lung Association, with the Electric Drive Transportation Association, Environmental Media Association, and the national parks to help touch many more millions of people than we ever could have done with a traditional advertising campaign."

Toyota recently announced a grant of $5 million and 25 Toyota vehicles in support of U.S. National Parks. Parks included in this grant and other Toyota partnerships are Yellowstone National Park, Great Smoky Mountains National Park, Everglades National Park, Yosemite National Park, the Grand Canyon, the Santa Monica National Recreation Area, and the Golden Gate Bridge Foundation. The national parks partnership offers an opportunity to enhance the experiences of visitors through education and hybrid vehicle use (park employees use the donated Toyota vehicles to reduce noise and emissions in the parks).

Generally, the goal of the national parks partnership program is to make a personal connection with park visitors about Toyota's hybrid vehicles when they are in a natural setting in which they are receptive to receiving a message about sustainable mobility. The message implies important links: "Green" Vehicles > Cleaner Air > Preservation of Parks

In addition, Toyota believes that the programs have other benefits, including:

- Strengthening Toyota's image as an environmental leader among automakers
- Communicating a message of environmental stewardship
- Building awareness of the Prius and other Toyota hybrids
- Educating park visitors on the benefits of advanced vehicle technology

Research by Toyota indicates that the program is working. A recent corporate image study indicated that among four leading automakers (Toyota, Honda, Ford, GM), Toyota was rated highest on dimensions such as "Leader in High MPG," "Leader in Technology Development," "Environmentally Friendly Vehicles," and "Wins Environmental Awards."

THE FUTURE

Figure 1 shows the results of a survey of consumer interests and their response to the question, "Who should take the lead in addressing environmental issues?" The results suggest that in the future consumers will expect businesses to be proactive about the environment and sustainability.

For Toyota, a focus on sustainability will mean considering the environmental, social, and economic consequences of the auto business, continuously working to reduce the negative and increasing the positive impacts of its activities and decisions. The increasing importance of sustainability will challenge Toyota to look at these impacts from all stages of the vehicle life cycle. It will also encourage Toyota's managers to consider the opinions of many stakeholders such as consumers, regulators, local communities, and nongovernmental organizations.

The recent concerns about Toyota vehicle product quality that led to the recall of 16 million vehicles have hurt Toyota's reputation. In the future, all activities, including the partnership strategy and the national parks program, will determine if Toyota can become "the most respected car company in the world."

Questions

1 How does Toyota's approach to social responsibility relate to the three concepts of social responsibility described in the text (profit responsibility, stakeholder responsibility, and societal responsibility)?
2 How does Toyota's view of sustainable mobility contribute to the company's overall mission?
3 Has Toyota's National Parks project been a success? What indicators suggest that the project has had an impact?
4 What future activities would you suggest for Toyota as it strives to improve its reputation?

FIGURE 1
Who should take the lead in addressing environmental issues?

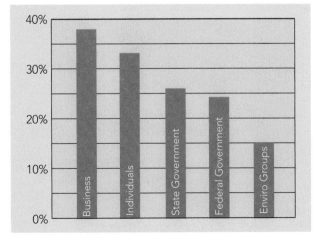

Understanding Consumer Behavior

4

LEARNING OBJECTIVES

After reading this chapter you should be able to:

LO1 Describe the stages in the consumer purchase decision process.

LO2 Distinguish among three variations of the consumer purchase decision process: routine, limited, and extended problem solving.

LO3 Identify major psychological influences on consumer behavior.

LO4 Identify major sociocultural influences on consumer behavior.

ENLIGHTENED CARMAKERS KNOW WHAT CUSTOM(H)ERS VALUE

Who buys 60 percent of new cars? Who influences 80 percent of new-car buying decisions? Women. Yes, women.

Women are a driving force in the U.S. automobile industry. Enlightened carmakers have hired women designers, engineers, and marketing executives to better understand and satisfy this valuable car buyer and influencer. What have they learned? While car price and quality are important, women and men think and feel differently about key elements of the new-car buying decision process and experience.

- *The sense of styling.* Women and men care about styling. For men, styling is more about a car's exterior lines and accents. Women are more interested in interior design and finishes. Designs that fit their proportions, provide good visibility, offer ample storage space, and make for effortless parking are particularly important.

- *The need for speed.* Both sexes want speed, but for different reasons. Men think about how many seconds it takes to get from zero to 60 miles per hour. Women want to feel secure that the car has enough acceleration to outrun an 18-wheeler trying to pass them on a freeway entrance ramp.

- *The substance of safety.* Safety for men is about features that help avoid an accident, such as antilock brakes and responsive steering. For women, safety is about features that help to survive an accident, including passenger airbags and reinforced side panels.

- *The shopping experience.* The new-car-buying experience differs between men and women. Generally, men decide upfront what car they want and set out alone to find it. By contrast, women approach it as an intelligence-gathering expedition. Referred to as *CROPing*, women shoppers look for *CR*edible *OP*inions. They actively seek information and postpone a purchase decision until all options have been evaluated. Women frequently visit auto-buying websites, read car-comparison articles, and scan car advertisements. Still, recommendations of friends and relatives matter most. Women typically shop three dealerships before making a purchase decision—one more than men.

Carmakers have learned that women, more than men, dislike the car-buying experience and specifically, the experience of dealing with car salespeople. In particular, women dread the price negotiations that are often involved in buying a new car. Not surprisingly, about half of women car buyers take a man with them to finalize the terms of sale.[1]

This chapter examines **consumer behavior**, the actions a person takes in purchasing and using products and services, including the mental and social processes that come before and after these actions. This chapter shows how the behavioral sciences help answer questions such as why people choose one product or brand over another, how they make these choices, and how companies use this knowledge to provide value to consumers.

CONSUMER PURCHASE DECISION PROCESS AND EXPERIENCE

Behind the visible act of making a purchase lies an important decision process and consumer experience that must be investigated. The stages a buyer passes through in making choices about which products and services to buy is the **purchase decision process**. This process has the five stages shown in Figure 4–1: (1) problem recognition, (2) information search, (3) alternative evaluation, (4) purchase decision, and (5) postpurchase behavior.

Problem Recognition: Perceiving a Need

Problem recognition, the initial step in the purchase decision, is perceiving a difference between a person's ideal and actual situations big enough to trigger a decision.[2] This can be as simple as finding an empty milk carton in the refrigerator; noting, as a first-year college student, that your high school clothes are not in the style that other students are wearing; or realizing that your notebook computer may not be working properly.

In marketing, advertisements or salespeople can activate a consumer's decision process by showing the shortcomings of competing (or currently owned) products. For instance, an advertisement for a new generation smartphone could stimulate problem recognition because it emphasizes "maximum use from one device."

Information Search: Seeking Value

After recognizing a problem, a consumer begins to search for information, the next stage in the purchase decision process. First, you may scan your memory for previous experiences with products or brands.[3] This action is called *internal search*. For frequently purchased products such as shampoo and conditioner, this may be enough.

Or a consumer may undertake an *external search* for information.[4] This is needed when past experience or knowledge is insufficient, the risk of making a wrong purchase decision is high, and the cost of gathering information is low. The primary sources of external information are (1) *personal sources*, such as relatives and friends whom the consumer trusts; (2) *public sources*, including various product-rating organizations such as *Consumer Reports*, government agencies, and TV "consumer programs"; and (3) *marketer-dominated sources*, such as information from sellers including advertising, company websites, salespeople, and point-of-purchase displays in stores.

FIGURE 4–1

The purchase decision process consists of five stages.

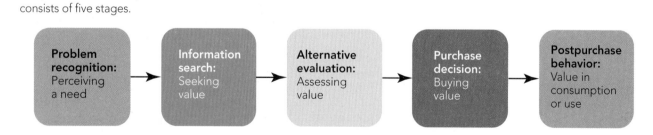

BRAND	MODEL	PRICE	DISPLAY	VOICE QUALITY	MESSAGING	WEB BROWSING	BATTERY LIFE
Apple	iPhone 4S	$200	Excellent	Good	Very Good	Excellent	Very Good
BlackBerry	Torch 9810	50	Very Good	Good	Excellent	Excellent	Good
HTC	HD7S	100	Excellent	Good	Very Good	Very Good	Fair
LG	Quantum	50	Very Good	Good	Very Good	Very Good	Good
Motorola	Atrix 4G	100	Excellent	Good	Very Good	Excellent	Excellent
Samsung	Galaxy S II	200	Excellent	Good	Excellent	Excellent	Excellent

Rating: ● Excellent ◓ Very Good ○ Good ◒ Fair ⬤ Poor

FIGURE 4–2

Consumer Reports.org provides an evaluation of smartphones for consumers. Source: *Consumer Reports.org*, Smartphone Ratings, November 2011. This excerpted list of smartphones is ONLY for AT&T customers. These smartphones are listed alphabetically and not in the order of their Ratings.

Consumer Reports

www.consumerreports.org

Suppose you are thinking about buying a new smartphone. You will probably tap several of these information sources: friends and relatives, advertisements, brand and company websites, and stores carrying these phones (for demonstrations). You might study the comparative evaluation of selected smartphones appearing in *Consumer Reports*, a portion of which appears in Figure 4–2.[5]

Alternative Evaluation: Assessing Value

The information search stage clarifies the problem for the consumer by (1) suggesting criteria to use for the purchase, (2) yielding brand names that might meet the criteria, and (3) developing consumer value perceptions. Given only the information shown in Figure 4–2, which selection criteria would you use in buying a smartphone? Would you use price, display, voice quality, messaging, web browsing, battery life, or some other combination of these or other criteria?

For some of you, the information provided may be inadequate because it does not contain all the factors you might consider when evaluating smartphones. These factors are a consumer's *evaluative criteria*, which represent both the objective attributes of a brand (such as display) and the subjective ones (such as prestige) you use to compare different products and brands.[6] Firms try to identify and capitalize on both types of criteria to create the best value for the money paid by you and other consumers. These criteria are often displayed in advertisements.

Consumers often have several criteria for evaluating brands. Knowing this, companies seek to identify the most important evaluative criteria that consumers use when judging brands. For example, among the evaluative criteria shown in the columns of Figure 4–2, suppose you use three in considering smartphones: (1) a retail price of $200 or less, (2) very good or excellent messaging capability, and (3) very good or excellent battery life. These criteria establish the brands in your *consideration set*—the group of brands that you would consider from among all the brands of which you are aware in the product class.[7] Your evaluative criteria result in three brands and their respective models (the Apple iPhone 4S, the Motorola Atrix 4G, and the Samsung Galaxy S II) in your consideration set. If these alternatives are unsatisfactory, you can change your evaluative criteria to create a different consideration set of brands and models. For example, you might decide that display is important and compare alternatives based on that evaluative criterion as well.

Purchase Decision: Buying Value

Having examined the alternatives in the consideration set, you are almost ready to make a purchase decision. Two choices remain: (1) from whom to buy and (2) when to buy. For a product like a smartphone, the information search process probably involved visiting retail stores, seeing different brands advertised on television and newspapers, and viewing a smartphone on a seller's website. The choice of which seller to buy from will depend on such considerations as the terms of sale, your past experience buying from the seller, and the return policy. Often a purchase decision involves a simultaneous evaluation of both product attributes and seller characteristics. For example, you might choose the second-most preferred smartphone brand at a store or website with a liberal refund and return policy versus the most preferred brand with more conservative policies.

Deciding when to buy is determined by a number of factors. For instance, you might buy sooner if one of your preferred brands is on sale or its manufacturer offers a rebate. Other factors such as the store atmosphere, pleasantness or ease of the shopping experience, salesperson assistance, time pressure, and financial circumstances could also affect whether a purchase decision is made now or postponed.[8]

Use of the Internet to gather information, evaluate alternatives, and make buying decisions adds a technological dimension to the consumer purchase decision process and buying experience. For example, 45 percent of consumers with price comparison smartphone apps routinely compare prices for identical products across different sellers at the point of purchase prior to making a purchase decision.[9]

Postpurchase Behavior: Value in Consumption or Use

After buying a product, the consumer compares it with his or her expectations and is either satisfied or dissatisfied. If the consumer is dissatisfied, marketers must determine whether the product was deficient or consumer expectations were too high. Product deficiency may require a design change. If expectations are too high, perhaps the company's advertising or the salesperson oversold the product's features and benefits.

Sensitivity to a customer's consumption or use experience is extremely important in a consumer's value perception. For example, research on telephone services provided by Sprint and AT&T indicates that satisfaction or dissatisfaction affects consumer value perceptions.[10] Studies show that satisfaction or dissatisfaction affects consumer communications and repeat-purchase behavior. Satisfied buyers tell three other people about their experience. Dissatisfied buyers complain to nine people.[11] Satisfied buyers also tend to buy from the same seller each time a purchase occasion arises. The financial impact of repeat-purchase behavior is signficant, as described in the Marketing Matters box.[12]

Firms such as General Electric (GE), Johnson & Johnson, Coca-Cola, and British Airways focus attention on postpurchase behavior to maximize customer satisfaction and retention. These firms, among many others, now provide toll-free telephone numbers, offer liberalized return and refund policies, and engage in extensive staff training to handle complaints, answer questions, record suggestions, and solve consumer problems. For example, GE has a database that stores 750,000 answers regarding about 8,500 of its models in

A satisfactory or unsatisfactory consumption or use experience is an important factor in postpurchase behavior. Marketer attention to this stage can pay huge dividends as described in the text.

Marketing Matters > > > > > customer value

The Value of a Satisfied Customer to the Company

Customer satisfaction and experience underlie the marketing concept. But how much is a satisfied customer worth?

This question has prompted firms to calculate the financial value of a satisfied customer over time. Frito-Lay, for example, estimates that the average loyal consumer in the Southwestern United States eats 21 pounds of snack chips a year. At a price of $2.50 a pound, this customer spends $52.50 annually on the company's snacks such as Lays and Ruffles potato chips, Doritos and Tostitos tortilla chips, and Fritos corn chips. Exxon estimates that a loyal customer will spend $500 annually for its branded gasoline, not including candy, snacks, oil, or repair services purchased at its gasoline stations. Kimberly-Clark reports that a loyal customer will buy 6.7 boxes of its Kleenex tissues each year and will spend $994 on facial tissues over 60 years, in today's dollars.

These calculations have focused marketer attention on the buying experience, customer satisfaction, and retention. Ford Motor Company set a target of increasing customer retention—the percentage of Ford owners whose next car is also a Ford—from 60 percent to 80 percent. Why? Ford executives say that each additional percentage point is worth a staggering $100 million in profits.

This calculation is not unique to Ford. Research shows that a 5 percent improvement in customer retention can increase a company's profits by 70 to 80 percent.

It takes 12 muscles to smile or 3 simple ingredients.

Just potatoes, all natural oil & a dash of salt.

Happiness *is* simple

Lay's Classic

120 product lines to handle 3 million calls annually. Such efforts produce positive postpurchase communications among consumers and foster relationship building between sellers and buyers.

Often a consumer is faced with highly attractive alternatives, such as an Apple, Motorola, or Samsung smartphone. If you choose the Apple, you might think, "Should I have purchased the Motorola or Samsung?" This feeling of postpurchase psychological tension or anxiety is called *cognitive dissonance*. To alleviate it, consumers often attempt to applaud themselves for making the right choice. So after your purchase, you may seek information to confirm your choice by asking friends questions like, "Don't you like my new phone?" or by reading ads of the brand you chose. You might even look for negative features about the brands you didn't buy and decide that the Motorola and Samsung headsets don't feel right. Firms often use ads or follow-up calls from salespeople in this postpurchase behavior stage to assure buyers that they made the right decision. For many years, Buick ran an advertising campaign with the message, "Aren't you really glad you bought a Buick?"

Consumer Involvement and Problem-Solving Variations

involvement

The personal, social, and economic significance of a purchase to the consumer.

Sometimes consumers don't engage in the five-stage purchase decision process. Instead, they skip or minimize one or more stages depending on the level of **involvement**, the personal, social, and economic significance of the purchase to the consumer.[13] High-involvement purchase occasions typically have at least one of three characteristics: The item to be purchased (1) is expensive, (2) can have serious personal consequences, or (3) could reflect on one's social image. For these occasions,

	HIGH ◄ CONSUMER INVOLVEMENT ► LOW		
CHARACTERISTICS OF THE CONSUMER PURCHASE DECISION PROCESS	EXTENDED PROBLEM SOLVING	LIMITED PROBLEM SOLVING	ROUTINE PROBLEM SOLVING
Number of brands examined	Many	Several	One
Number of sellers considered	Many	Several	Few
Number of product attributes evaluated	Many	Moderate	One
Number of external information sources used	Many	Few	None
Time spent searching	Considerable	Little	Minimal

FIGURE 4–3

Comparison of problem-solving variations: extended problem solving, limited problem solving, and routine problem solving.

consumers engage in extensive information search, consider many product attributes and brands, form attitudes, and participate in word-of-mouth communication. Low-involvement purchases, such as toothpaste and soap, barely involve most of us, but audio and video systems and automobiles are very involving.

There are three general variations in the consumer purchase decision process based on consumer involvement and product knowledge. Figure 4–3 shows some of the important differences between the three problem-solving variations.

Extended Problem Solving In extended problem solving, each of the five stages of the consumer purchase decision process is used and considerable time and effort are devoted to the search for external information and the identification and evaluation of alternatives. Several brands are in the consideration set, and these are evaluated on many attributes. Extended problem solving exists in high-involvement purchase situations for items such as automobiles and audio systems.

Limited Problem Solving In limited problem solving, consumers typically seek some information or rely on a friend to help them evaluate alternatives. Several brands might be evaluated using a moderate number of attributes. Limited problem solving might be used in choosing a toaster, a restaurant for lunch, and other purchase situations in which the consumer has little time or effort to spend.

Routine Problem Solving For products such as table salt and milk, consumers recognize a problem, make a decision, and spend little effort seeking external information and evaluating alternatives. The purchase process for such items is virtually a habit and typifies low-involvement decision making. Routine problem solving is typically the case for low-priced, frequently purchased products.

Involvement and Marketing Strategy Low and high consumer involvement have important implications for marketing strategy. If a company markets a low-involvement product and its brand is a market leader, attention is placed on (1) maintaining product quality, (2) avoiding stockout situations so that buyers don't substitute a competing brand, and (3) repetitive advertising messages that reinforce a consumer's knowledge or assure buyers they made the right choice. Market

What does this ad for Post Grape-Nuts, Post Shredded Wheat, and Post Raisin Bran whole grain cereals have to do with getting these products into a consumer's consideration set? Read the text to find out.

challengers have a different task. They must break buying habits by using free samples, coupons, and rebates to encourage trial of their brand. Advertising messages will focus on getting their brand into a consumer's consideration set. For example, Campbell's V8 vegetable juice advertising message—"I could have had a V8!"—is targeted at consumers who routinely purchase fruit juices and soft drinks. Marketers can also link their brand attributes with high-involvement issues. Post Cereals does this by linking consumption of its whole grain cereals with improved heart health and protection against major diseases.

Marketers of high-involvement products know that their consumers constantly seek and process information about objective and subjective brand attributes, form evaluative criteria, rate product attributes in various brands, and combine these ratings for an overall brand evaluation—like that described in the smartphone purchase decision. Market leaders ply consumers with product information through advertising and personal selling and use social media to create online experiences for their company or brand. Market challengers capitalize on this behavior through comparative advertising that focuses on existing product attributes and often introduce novel evaluative criteria for judging competing brands. Challengers also benefit from Internet search engines such as Microsoft Bing and Google that assist buyers of high-involvement products.

Situational Influences

Often the purchase situation will affect the purchase decision process. Five *situational influences* have an impact on the purchase decision process: (1) the purchase task, (2) social surroundings, (3) physical surroundings, (4) temporal effects, and (5) antecedent states.[14] The purchase task is the reason for engaging in the decision. The search for information and the evaluation of alternatives may differ depending on whether the purchase is a gift, which often involves social visibility, or for the buyer's own use. Social surroundings, including the other people present when a purchase decision is made, may also affect what is purchased. Consumers accompanied by children buy about 40 percent more items than consumers shopping by themselves. Physical surroundings such as decor, music, and crowding in retail stores may alter how purchase decisions are made. Temporal effects such as time of day or the amount of time available will influence where consumers have breakfast and lunch and what is ordered. Finally, antecedent states, which include the consumer's mood or the amount of cash on hand, can influence purchase behavior and choice. For example, consumers with credit cards purchase more than those with cash or debit cards.

Figure 4–4 on the next page shows the many influences that affect the consumer purchase decision process. The decision to buy a product also involves important psychological and sociocultural influences. These two influences are covered in the remainder of this chapter. Marketing mix influences are described later in Part 4 of the book.

learning review

1. What is the first stage in the consumer purchase decision process?

2. The brands a consumer considers buying out of the set of brands in a product class of which the consumer is aware are collectively called the _____.

3. What is the term for postpurchase anxiety?

FIGURE 4–4
Influences on the consumer
purchase decision process
come from both internal and
external sources.

Marketing mix influences
- Product
- Price
- Promotion
- Place

Psychological influences
- Motivation and personality
- Perception
- Learning
- Values, beliefs, and attitudes
- Lifestyle

Consumer purchase decision process
Problem recognition
Information search
Alternative evaluation
Purchase decision
Postpurchase behavior

Sociocultural influences
- Personal influence
- Reference groups
- Family
- Culture and subculture

Situational influences
- Purchase task
- Social surroundings
- Physical surroundings
- Temporal effects
- Antecedent states

PSYCHOLOGICAL INFLUENCES ON CONSUMER BEHAVIOR

LO3

Psychology helps marketers understand why and how consumers behave as they do. In particular, psychological concepts such as motivation and personality; perception; learning; values, beliefs, and attitudes; and lifestyle are useful for interpreting buying processes and directing marketing efforts.

Motivation and Personality

Motivation and personality are two familiar psychological concepts that have specific meanings and marketing implications. These concepts are closely related and are used to explain why people do some things and not others.

motivation

The energizing force that stimulates behavior to satisfy a need.

Motivation   **Motivation** is the energizing force that stimulates behavior to satisfy a need. Because consumer needs are the focus of the marketing concept, marketers try to arouse these needs.

An individual's needs are boundless. People possess physiological needs for basics such as water, shelter, and food. They also have learned needs, including self-esteem, achievement, and affection. Psychologists point out that these needs may be hierarchical; that is, once physiological needs are met, people seek to satisfy their learned needs.

FIGURE 4–5

The hierarchy of needs is based on the idea that motivation comes from a need. If a need is met, it's no longer a motivator, so a higher-level need becomes the motivator. Higher-level needs demand support of lower-level needs.

QR 4–1
Match.com
Video

Self-actualization needs:
Self-fulfillment

Personal needs:
Status, respect, prestige

Social needs:
Friendship, belonging, love

Safety needs:
Freedom from harm, financial security

Physiological needs:
Food, water, shelter, oxygen

Figure 4–5 shows one need hierarchy and classification scheme that contains five need classes.[15] *Physiological needs* are basic to survival and must be satisfied first. A Red Lobster advertisement featuring a seafood salad attempts to activate the need for food. *Safety needs* involve self-preservation as well as physical and financial well-being. Smoke detector and burglar alarm manufacturers focus on these needs, as do insurance companies and retirement plan advisors. *Social needs* are concerned with love and friendship. Dating services, such as Match.com and eHarmony, and fragrance companies try to arouse these needs. *Personal needs* include the need for achievement, status, prestige, and self-respect. The American Express Centurian Card and Brooks Brothers Clothiers appeal to these needs. Sometimes firms try to arouse multiple needs to stimulate problem recognition. Michelin has combined safety with parental love to promote tire replacement for automobiles. *Self-actualization needs* involve personal fulfillment. For example, a long-running U.S. Army recruiting program invited enlistees to "Be all you can be."

personality

A person's consistent behaviors or responses to recurring situations.

Personality While motivation is the energizing force that makes consumer behavior purposeful, a consumer's personality guides and directs behavior. **Personality** refers to a person's consistent behaviors or responses to recurring situations.

Although many personality theories exist, most identify key traits—enduring characteristics within a person or in his or her relationships with others. Such traits include assertiveness, extroversion, compliance, dominance, and aggression, among others. These traits are inherited or formed at an early age and change little over the years. Research suggests that compliant people prefer known brand names and use more mouthwash and toilet soaps. Aggressive types use razors, not electric shavers, apply more cologne and aftershave lotions, and purchase signature goods such as Gucci, Yves St. Laurent, and Donna Karan as an indicator of status.[16]

These personality characteristics are often revealed in a person's *self-concept*, which is the way people see themselves and the way they believe others see them. Marketers recognize that people have an actual self-concept and an ideal self-concept. The actual self refers to how people actually see themselves. The ideal self describes how people would like to see themselves. These two self-images are reflected in the products and brands a person buys, including automobiles, home appliances and furnishings, magazines, consumer electronics, clothing, grooming and leisure products, and frequently, the stores in which a person shops. The importance of self-concept is summed up by a senior marketing executive at Lenovo, a global supplier of notebook computers: "The notebook market is getting more like cars. The car you drive reflects you, and notebooks are becoming a form of self-expression as well."[17]

The Ethics of Subliminal Messages

For over 50 years, the topic of subliminal perception and the presence of subliminal messages and images embedded in commercial communications have sparked heated debate.

The Federal Communications Commission has denounced subliminal messages as deceptive. Still, consumers spend $50 million a year for subliminal messages designed to help them raise their self-esteem, stop compulsive buying, quit smoking, or lose weight. Almost two-thirds of U.S. consumers think subliminal messages are present in commercial communications; about half are firmly convinced that this practice can cause them to buy things they don't want.

Subliminal messages are not illegal in the United States, however, and marketers are often criticized for pursuing opportunities to create these messages in both electronic and print media. A book by August Bullock, *The Secret Sales Pitch*, is devoted to this topic. Bullock identifies images and advertisements that he claims contain subliminal messages and describes techniques that can be used for conveying these messages. Do you "see" the subliminal message that is embedded in the book's cover?

Do you believe that a marketer's attempts to implant subliminal messages in electronic and print media are a deceptive practice and unethical, regardless of their intent?

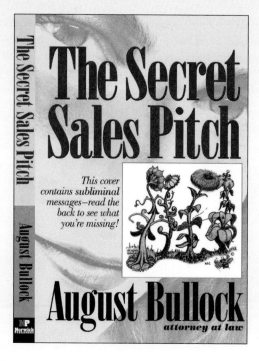

Perception

perception

The process by which a person selects, organizes, and interprets information to create a meaningful picture of the world.

One person sees a Cadillac as a mark of achievement; another sees it as ostentatious. This is the result of **perception**—the process by which an individual selects, organizes, and interprets information to create a meaningful picture of the world.

Selective Perception Because the average consumer operates in a complex environment, the human brain attempts to organize and interpret information with a process called *selective perception*, a filtering of exposure, comprehension, and retention. *Selective exposure* occurs when people pay attention to messages that are consistent with their attitudes and beliefs and ignore messages that are inconsistent. Selective exposure often occurs in the postpurchase stage of the consumer decision process, when consumers read advertisements for the brand they just bought. It also occurs when a need exists—you are more likely to "see" a McDonald's advertisement when you are hungry rather than after you have eaten a pizza.

Selective comprehension involves interpreting information so that it is consistent with your attitudes and beliefs. A marketer's failure to understand this can have disastrous results. For example, Toro introduced a small, lightweight snowblower called the Snow Pup. Even though the product worked, sales failed to meet expectations. Why? Toro later found out that consumers perceived the name to mean that Snow Pup was a toy or too light to do any serious snow removal. When the product was renamed Snow Master, sales increased sharply.[18]

Selective retention means that consumers do not remember all the information they see, read, or hear, even minutes after exposure to it. This affects the internal and external information search stage of the purchase decision process. This is why furniture and automobile retailers often give consumers product brochures to take home with them when they leave the showroom.

Because perception plays an important role in consumer behavior, it is not surprising that the topic of subliminal perception is a popular item for discussion. *Subliminal perception* means that you see or hear messages without being aware of them. The presence and effect of subliminal perception on behavior is a hotly debated issue, with more popular appeal than scientific support. Indeed, evidence suggests that such messages have limited effects on behavior.[19] If these messages did influence behavior, would their use be an ethical practice? (See the Making Responsible Decisions box.)[20]

Perceived Risk Perception plays a major role in the perceived risk in purchasing a product or service. **Perceived risk** represents the anxiety felt because the consumer cannot anticipate the outcomes of a purchase but believes there may be negative consequences. Examples of possible negative consequences are the size of the financial outlay required to buy the product (can I afford $500 for those skis?), the risk of physical harm (is bungee jumping safe?), and the performance of the product (will the whitening toothpaste work?). A more abstract form is psychosocial (what will my friends say about my tattoo?). Perceived risk affects a consumer's information search, because the greater the perceived risk, the more extensive the external search stage is likely to be.

Recognizing the importance of perceived risk, companies develop strategies to reduce the consumer's perceived risk and encourage purchases. These strategies and examples of firms using them include the following:

- *Obtaining seals of approval:* The Good Housekeeping seal for Fresh Step cat litter.
- *Securing endorsements from influential people:* Endorsements for Promise soft spread from 9 out of 10 cardiologists.

perceived risk
The anxiety felt when a consumer cannot anticipate possible negative outcomes of a purchase.

Why does Clorox tout the Good Housekeeping seal for its Fresh Step cat litter? Why does Mary Kay, Inc., offer a free sample of its Velocity brand fragrance through its website? The answers appear in the text.

The Clorox Company
www.freshstep.com

Mary Kay, Inc.
www.marykay.com

- *Providing free trials of the product:* Samples of Mary Kay's Velocity fragrance.
- *Giving extensive usage instructions:* Clairol hair coloring products.
- *Providing warranties and guarantees:* Kia Motors's 10-year, 100,000-mile warranty.

Learning

Much consumer behavior is learned. Consumers learn which information sources to consult for information about products and services, which evaluative criteria to use when assessing alternatives, and, more generally, how to make purchase decisions. **Learning** refers to those behaviors that result from (1) repeated experience and (2) reasoning.

Behavioral Learning
Behavioral learning is the process of developing automatic responses to a situation built up through repeated exposure to it. Four variables are central to how consumers learn from repeated experience: drive, cue, response, and reinforcement. A *drive* is a need that moves an individual to action. Drives, such as hunger, might be represented by motives. A *cue* is a stimulus or symbol perceived by consumers. A *response* is the action taken by a consumer to satisfy the drive. *Reinforcement* is the reward. Being hungry (drive), a consumer sees a cue (a billboard), takes action (buys a sandwich), and receives a reward (it tastes great!).

Marketers use two concepts from behavioral learning theory. *Stimulus generalization* occurs when a response elicited by one stimulus (cue) is generalized to another stimulus. Using the same brand name for different products is an application of this concept, such as Tylenol Cold & Flu and Tylenol P.M. *Stimulus discrimination* refers to a person's ability to perceive differences in stimuli. Consumers' tendency to perceive all light beers as being alike led to Budweiser Light commercials that distinguished between many types of "light beers" and Bud Light.

Cognitive Learning
Consumers also learn through thinking, reasoning, and mental problem solving without direct experience. This type of learning, called *cognitive learning*, involves making connections between two or more ideas or simply observing the outcomes of others' behaviors and adjusting your own accordingly. Firms also influence this type of learning. Through repetition in advertising, messages such as "Advil is a pain reliever" attempt to link a brand (Advil) and an idea (pain reliever) by showing someone using the brand and finding relief.

Brand Loyalty
Learning is also important to marketers because it relates to habit formation—the basis of routine problem solving. Furthermore, there is a close link between habits and **brand loyalty**, which is a favorable attitude toward and consistent purchase of a single brand over time. Brand loyalty results from the positive reinforcement of previous actions. A consumer reduces risk and saves time by consistently purchasing the same brand of shampoo and has favorable results—healthy, shining hair. There is evidence of brand loyalty in many commonly purchased products in the United States and the global marketplace. However, the incidence of brand loyalty appears to be declining in North America, Western Europe, and Japan.[21]

Values, Beliefs, and Attitudes

Values, beliefs, and attitudes play a central role in consumer decision making and related marketing actions.

learning
Behaviors that result from repeated experience and reasoning.

How does this advertisement for Advil that features the active lifestyle of women apply to cognitive learning? Read the text to find out.

Advil
www.advil.com

brand loyalty
A favorable attitude toward and consistent purchase of a single brand over time.

Attitudes toward Colgate Total toothpaste and Hellmann's Real Mayonnaise were successfully changed by these ads. How? Read the text to find out how marketers can change consumer attitudes toward products and brands.

Colgate-Palmolive
www.colgate.com

Hellmann's
www.hellmanns.com

attitude
A tendency to respond to something in a consistently favorable or unfavorable way.

beliefs
A consumer's perception of how a product or brand performs.

Attitude Formation   An **attitude** is a "learned predisposition to respond to an object or class of objects in a consistently favorable or unfavorable way."[22] Attitudes are shaped by our values and beliefs, which are learned. Values vary by level of specificity. We speak of American core values, including material well-being and humanitarianism. We also have personal values, such as thriftiness and ambition. Marketers are concerned with both but focus mostly on personal values. Personal values affect attitudes by influencing the importance assigned to specific product attributes. Suppose thriftiness is one of your personal values. When you evaluate cars, fuel economy (a product attribute) becomes important. If you believe a specific car brand has this attribute, you are likely to have a favorable attitude toward it.

Beliefs also play a part in attitude formation. **Beliefs** are a consumer's subjective perception of how a product or brand performs on different attributes. Beliefs are based on personal experience, advertising, and discussions with other people. Beliefs about product attributes are important because, along with personal values, they create the favorable or unfavorable attitude the consumer has toward certain products, services, and brands.

Attitude Change   Marketers use three approaches to try to change consumer attitudes toward products and brands, as shown in the following examples.[23]

1. *Changing beliefs about the extent to which a brand has certain attributes.* To allay mothers' concerns about ingredients in its mayonnaise, Hellmann's successfully communicated the product's high Omega 3 content, which is essential to human health.
2. *Changing the perceived importance of attributes.* Pepsi-Cola made freshness an important product attribute when it stamped freshness dates on its cans. Before

doing so, few consumers considered cola freshness an issue. After Pepsi spent about $25 million on advertising and promotion, a consumer survey found that 61 percent of cola drinkers believed freshness dating was an important attribute.

3. *Adding new attributes to the product.* Colgate-Palmolive included a new antibacterial ingredient, tricloson, in its Colgate Total Toothpaste and spent $100 million marketing the brand. The result? Colgate Total Toothpaste is now a billion-dollar-plus global brand.

Consumer Lifestyle

Lifestyle is a mode of living that is identified by how people spend their time and resources, what they consider important in their environment, and what they think of themselves and the world around them. The analysis of consumer lifestyles, called *psychographics*, provides insights into consumer needs and wants. Lifestyle analysis has proven useful in segmenting and targeting consumers for new and existing products and services (see Chapter 8).

Psychographics, the practice of combining psychology, lifestyle, and demographics, is often used to uncover consumer motivations for buying and using products and services. A prominent psychographic system is VALS from Strategic Business Insights (SBI).[24] The VALS system identifies eight consumer segments based on (1) their primary motivation for buying and having certain products and services and (2) their resources.

According to SBI researchers, consumers are motivated to buy products and services and seek experiences that give shape, substance, and satisfaction to their lives. But not all consumers are alike. Consumers are inspired by one of three primary motivations—ideals, achievement, and self-expression—that give meaning to their self or the world and govern their activities. The different levels of resources enhance or constrain a person's expression of his or her primary motivation. A person's resources include psychological, physical, demographic, and material capacities such as income, self-confidence, and risk-taking.

The VALS system seeks to explain why and how consumers make purchase decisions.

- *Ideals-motivated groups.* Consumers motivated by ideals are guided by knowledge and principle. *Thinkers* are mature, reflective, and well-educated people who value order, knowledge, and responsibility. They are practical consumers and deliberate information-seekers who value durability and functionality in products over styling and newness. *Believers*, with fewer resources, are conservative, conventional people with concrete beliefs based on traditional, established codes: family, religion, community, and the nation. They choose familiar products and brands, favor American-made products, and are generally brand loyal.

- *Achievement-motivated groups.* Consumers motivated by achievement look for products and services that demonstrate success to their peers or to a peer group they aspire to. *Achievers* have a busy, goal-directed lifestyle and a deep commitment to career and family. Image is important to them. They favor established, prestige products and services and are interested in time-saving devices given their hectic schedules. *Strivers* are trendy, fun-loving, and less self-confident than Achievers. They also have lower levels of education and household income. Money defines success for them. They favor stylish products and are as impulsive as their financial circumstances permit.

- *Self-expression-motivated groups.* Consumers motivated by self-expression desire social or physical activity, variety, and risk. *Experiencers* are young, enthusiastic, and impulsive consumers who become excited about new possibilities but are equally quick to cool. They savor the new, the offbeat, and the risky. Their energy

The VALS classification system places consumers with abundant resources—psychological, physical, and material means and capacities—near the top of the chart and those with minimal resources near the bottom. The chart segments consumers by their basis for decision making: ideals, achievement, or self-expression. The boxes intersect to indicate that some categories may be considered together. For instance, a marketer may categorize Thinkers and Believers together. Do you want to know your VALS profile? If you do, respond to the questions on the VALS survey at www.strategicbusinessinsight.com. Simply click "VALS." You will receive your profile in real time.

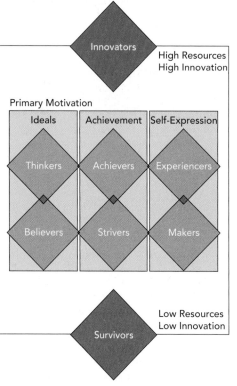

finds an outlet in exercise, sports, outdoor recreation, and social activities. Much of their income is spent on fashion items, entertainment, and socializing and particularly on looking good and having the latest things. *Makers*, with fewer resources, express themselves and experience the world by working on it—raising children or fixing a car. They are practical people who have constructive skills, value self-sufficiency, and are unimpressed by material possessions except those with a practical or functional purpose.

- *High- and low-resource groups.* Two segments stand apart. *Innovators* are successful, sophisticated, take-charge people with high self-esteem and abundant resources of all kinds. Image is important to them, not as evidence of power or status, but as an expression of cultivated tastes, independence, and character. They are receptive to new ideas and technologies. Their lives are characterized by variety. *Survivors*, with the least resources of any segment, focus on meeting basic needs (safety and security) rather than fulfilling desires. They represent a modest market for most products and services and are loyal to favorite brands, especially if they can be purchased at a discount.

Each of these segments exhibits unique media preferences. Experiencers and Strivers are the most likely to visit Internet chat rooms. Innovators, Thinkers, and Achievers tend to read business and news magazines such as *Fortune* and *Time*. Makers read automotive magazines. Believers are the heaviest readers of *Reader's Digest*. GeoVALS™ estimates the percentage of each VALS group by zip code.

---

learning review

4. The problem with the Toro Snow Pup was an example of selective _____.

5. What three attitude-change approaches are most common?

6. What does *lifestyle* mean?

SOCIOCULTURAL INFLUENCES ON CONSUMER BEHAVIOR

Sociocultural influences, which evolve from a consumer's formal and informal relationships with other people, also exert a significant impact on consumer behavior. These involve personal influence, reference groups, family influence, culture, and subculture.

Personal Influence

A consumer's purchases are often influenced by the views, opinions, or behaviors of others. Two aspects of personal influence are very important to marketing: opinion leadership and word-of-mouth activity.

opinion leaders
Individuals who have social influence over others.

Opinion Leadership   Individuals who exert direct or indirect social influence over others are called **opinion leaders**. Opinion leaders are considered to be knowledgeable about or users of particular products and services, so their opinions influence others' choices.[25] Opinion leadership is widespread in the purchase of cars and trucks, entertainment, clothing and accessories, club membership, consumer electronics, vacation locations, food, and financial investments. A study by *Popular Mechanics* magazine identified 18 million opinion leaders who influence the purchases of some 85 million consumers for do-it-yourself products.

About 10 percent of U.S. adults are opinion leaders. Identifying, reaching, and influencing opinion leaders is a major challenge for companies. Some firms use

Firms use actors or athletes as spokespersons to represent their products, such as Leonardo DiCaprio and Maria Sharapova for TAG Heuer watches.

TAG Heuer
www.tagheuer.com

actors or sports figures as spokespersons to represent their products, such as actor Leonardo DiCaprio and tennis player Maria Sharapova for TAG Heuer watches. Others promote their products in media believed to reach opinion leaders. Still others use more direct approaches. For example, a carmaker recently invited influential community leaders and business executives to test-drive its new models. Some 6,000 accepted the offer, and 98 percent said they would recommend their tested car. The company estimated that the number of favorable recommendations totaled 32,000.

word of mouth
People influencing each other in personal conversations.

Word of Mouth The influencing of people during conversations is called **word of mouth**. Word of mouth is the most powerful and authentic information source for consumers because it typically involves friends viewed as trustworthy. According to a recent study, 67 percent of U.S. consumer product sales are directly based on word-of-mouth activity among friends, family, and colleagues.[26]

The power of personal influence has prompted firms to promote positive and retard negative word of mouth. For instance, "teaser" advertising campaigns are run in advance of new-product introductions to stimulate conversations. Other techniques such as advertising slogans, music, and humor also heighten positive word of mouth. Many commercials shown during the Super Bowl are created expressly to initiate conversations about the advertisements and featured product or service the next day. Increasingly, companies recruit and deploy people to produce *buzz*—popularity created by consumer word of mouth. Read the Marketing Matters box to learn how this is done by BzzAgent.[27] The video shows the BzzAgent campaign for Dove hair care products.

QR 4–2
Dove Video

On the other hand, rumors about Kmart (snake eggs in clothing), Taco Bell (beef content in taco meat filling), Corona Extra beer (contamination), and Snickers candy bars in Russia (a cause of diabetes) have resulted in negative word of mouth, none of which was based on fact. Overcoming or neutralizing negative word of mouth is difficult and costly. However, supplying factual information, providing toll-free numbers for consumers to call the company, and giving appropriate product demonstrations have proven helpful.

The power of word of mouth is magnified by the Internet through online forums, blogs, social media, and websites. In fact, companies use special software to monitor online messages and find out what consumers are saying about their products, services, and brands. They have found that 30 percent of people spreading negative information have never owned or used the product, service, or brand![28]

94

Marketing Matters > > > > > customer value

BzzAgent—The Buzz Experience

Have you recently heard about a new product, movie, website, book, or restaurant from someone you know . . . or a complete stranger? If so, you may have had a word-of-mouth experience.

Marketers recognize the power of word of mouth. The challenge has been to harness that power. BzzAgent Inc. does just that. Its worldwide volunteer army of over 800,000 natural-born talkers channel their chatter toward products and services they deem authentically worth talking about. "Our goal is to capture honest word of mouth," says David Balter, BzzAgent's founder, "and to build a network that turns passionate customers into brand evangelists."

BzzAgent's method is simple. Once a client signs on with BzzAgent, the company searches its "agent" database for those who match the demographic and psychographic profile of the target market for a client's offering. Agents then can sign up for a buzz campaign and receive a sample product and a training manual for buzz-creating strategies. Each time an agent completes an activity, he or she is expected to file an online report describing the nature of the buzz and its effectiveness. BzzAgent

coaches respond with encouragement and feedback on additional techniques.

Agents keep the products they promote. They also earn points redeemable for books, CDs, and other items by filing detailed reports. Who are the agents? About 65 percent are older than 25, 70 percent are women, and two are *Fortune* 500 CEOs. All are gregarious and genuinely like the product or service, otherwise they wouldn't participate in the buzz campaign.

Estée Lauder, Monster.com, Anheuser-Busch, Penguin Books, Lee, Michelin, Wrigley, Arby's, Nestlé, Hershey Foods, and Volkswagen have used BzzAgent. But BzzAgent's buzz isn't cheap, and not everything is buzz worthy. Deploying 1,000 agents on a 12-week campaign can cost a company $95,000, exclusive of product samples. BzzAgent researches a product or service before committing to a campaign and rejects about 80 percent of the companies that seek its service. It also refuses campaigns for politicians, religious groups, and certain products, such as firearms. Interested in BzzAgent? Visit its website at www.bzzagent.com.

Reference Groups

reference groups
People to whom an individual looks as a basis for self-appraisal or as a source of personal standards.

Reference groups are people to whom an individual looks as a basis for self-appraisal or as a source of personal standards. Reference groups affect consumer purchases because they influence the information, attitudes, and aspiration levels that help set a consumer's standards. For example, one of the first questions one asks others when planning to attend a social occasion is, "What are you going to wear?" Reference groups influence the purchase of luxury products but not necessities—reference groups exert a strong influence on the brand chosen when its use or consumption is highly visible to others.

Consumers have many reference groups, but three groups have clear marketing implications. A *membership group* is one to which a person actually belongs, including fraternities and sororities, social clubs, and the family. Such groups are easily identifiable and are targeted by firms selling insurance, insignia products, and charter vacations. An *aspiration group* is one that a person wishes to be a member of or wishes to be identified with, such as a professional society. Firms frequently rely on spokespeople or settings associated with their target market's aspiration group in their advertising. A *dissociative group* is one that a person wishes to maintain a distance from because of differences in values or behaviors.

Family Influence

Family influences on consumer behavior result from three sources: consumer socialization, passage through the family life cycle, and decision making within the family or household.

Consumer Socialization   The process by which people acquire the skills, knowledge, and attitudes necessary to function as consumers is called *consumer socialization.*[29] Children learn how to purchase (1) by interacting with adults in purchase situations and (2) through their own purchasing and product usage experiences. Research shows that children evidence brand preferences at age two, and these preferences often last a lifetime. This knowledge prompted the licensing of the well-known Craftsman brand name to MGA Entertainment for its children's line of My First Craftsman power tools. Other examples of products designed to attract younger consumers include Time Inc.'s *Sports Illustrated for Kids* and Yahoo! Kids and Kids Only, offered by Yahoo! and America Online, respectively, which offer special areas where young audiences can view a separate children's menu.

Family Life Cycle   Consumers act and purchase differently as they go through life. The **family life cycle** concept describes the distinct phases that a family progresses through from formation to retirement, each phase bringing with it identifiable purchasing behaviors.[30] Figure 4–6 illustrates the traditional progression as well as contemporary variations of the family life cycle. Today, the *traditional family*—married couple with children younger than 18 years—constitutes just 21 percent of all U.S. households. The remaining 78 percent of U.S. households include single parents; unmarried couples; divorced, never-married, or widowed individuals; and older married couples whose children no longer live at home.

Young singles' buying preferences are for nondurable items, including prepared foods, clothing, personal care products, and entertainment. They represent a target market for recreational travel, automobile, and consumer electronics firms. Young married couples without children are typically more affluent than young singles because usually both spouses are employed. These couples exhibit preferences for furniture, housewares, and gift items for each other. Young marrieds with children are driven by the needs of their children. They make up a sizable market for life insurance, various children's products, and home furnishings. Single parents with children are the least financially secure of households

family life cycle

A family's progression from formation to retirement, each phase bringing with it distinct purchasing behaviors.

FIGURE 4–6

Modern family life cycle stages and flows. Can you identify people you know in different stages? Do they follow the purchase patterns described in the text?

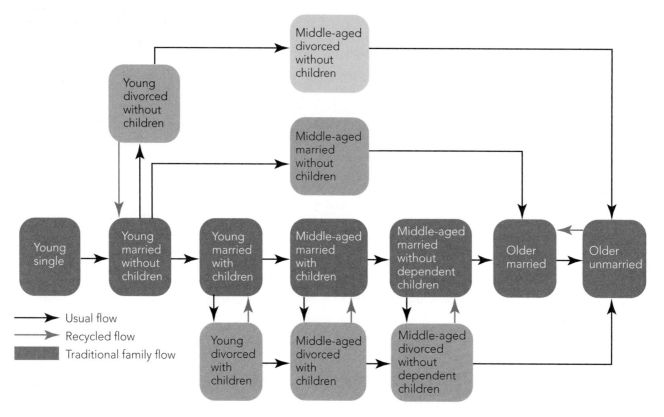

with children. Their buying preferences are often affected by a limited economic status and tend toward convenience foods, child care services, and personal care items.

Middle-aged married couples with children are typically better off financially than their younger counterparts. They are a significant market for leisure products and home improvement items. Middle-aged couples without children typically have a large amount of discretionary income. These couples buy better home furnishings, status automobiles, and financial services. Persons in the last two phases—older married and older unmarried—make up a sizable market for prescription drugs, medical services, vacation trips, and gifts for younger relatives.

Family Decision Making A third influence in the decision-making process occurs within the family.[31] Two decision-making styles exist: spouse-dominant and joint decision making. With a joint decision-making style, most decisions are made by both husband and wife. Spouse-dominant decisions are those for which either the husband or the wife is mostly responsible. Research indicates that wives tend to have more say when purchasing groceries, children's toys, clothing, and medicines. Husbands tend to be more influential in home and car maintenance purchases. Joint decision making is common for cars, vacations, houses, home appliances and electronics, family finances, and medical care. As a rule, joint decision making increases with the education of the spouses.

Roles of individual family members in the purchase process are another element of family decision making. Five roles exist: (1) information gatherer, (2) influencer, (3) decision maker, (4) purchaser, and (5) user. Family members assume different roles for different products and services. This knowledge is important to firms. For example, 89 percent of wives either influence or make outright purchases of men's clothing. Even though women are often the grocery decision maker, they are not necessarily the purchaser. Today, 51 percent of men are the primary grocery shopper in their household.

Increasingly, preteens and teenagers are the information gatherers, influencers, decision makers, and purchasers of products and services for the family, given the prevalence of working parents and single-parent households. The market for products bought by or for preteens and teenagers surpasses $200 billion annually. These figures help explain why, for example, Nabisco, Johnson & Johnson, Hewlett-Packard, Apple, Kellogg,

Today, 51 percent of men are primary grocery shoppers in their households. Marketers that supply the $560 billion retail food industries are now adjusting store layouts and shelf placements to cater to men.

P&G, Nike, Sony, and Oscar Mayer, among countless other companies, spend more than $70 billion annually in electronic and print media that reach preteens and teens.

Culture and Subculture

As described in Chapter 3, *culture* refers to the set of values, ideas, and attitudes that are learned and shared among the members of a group. Thus, we often refer to the American culture, the Latin American culture, or the Japanese culture. Cultural underpinnings of American buying patterns were described in Chapter 3; Chapter 7 will explore the role of culture in global marketing.

Subgroups within the larger, or national, culture with unique values, ideas, and attitudes are referred to as **subcultures**. Various subcultures exist within the American culture. The three largest racial/ethnic subcultures in the United States are Hispanics, African Americans, and Asian Americans. Collectively, they are expected to account for one in four U.S. consumers and to spend about $3.6 trillion for goods and services in 2015.[32] Each group exhibits sophisticated social and cultural behaviors that affect buying patterns, which provides the basis for multicultural marketing programs described in Chapter 3.

Hispanic Buying Patterns

Hispanics represent the largest racial/ethnic subculture in the United States in terms of population and spending power. About 50 percent of Hispanics in the United States are immigrants, and the majority are under the age of 25. One-third of Hispanics are younger than 18.

Research on Hispanic buying practices has uncovered several consistent patterns:[33]

1. Hispanics are quality and brand conscious. They are willing to pay a premium price for premium quality and are often brand loyal.
2. Hispanics prefer buying American-made products, especially those offered by firms that cater to Hispanic needs.
3. Hispanic buying preferences are strongly influenced by family and peers.
4. Hispanics consider advertising a credible product information source, and U.S. firms spend more than $6 billion annually on advertising to Hispanics.
5. Convenience is not an important product attribute to Hispanic homemakers with respect to food preparation or consumption, nor is low caffeine in coffee and soft drinks, low fat in dairy products, or low cholesterol in packaged foods.

Despite some consistent buying patterns, marketing to Hispanics has proven to be a challenge for two reasons. First, the Hispanic subculture is diverse and composed of Mexicans, Puerto Ricans, Cubans, and others of Central and South American ancestry. Cultural differences among these nationalities often affect product preferences. For example, Campbell Soup Company sells its Casera line of soups, beans, and sauces using different recipes to appeal to Puerto Ricans on the East Coast and Mexicans in the Southwest. Second, a language barrier exists, and commercial messages are frequently misinterpreted when translated into Spanish. Volkswagen learned this lesson when the Spanish translation of its "Drivers Wanted" slogan suggested "Chauffeurs Wanted." The Spanish slogan was changed to "*Agarra calle*," a slang expression that can be loosely translated as "Let's hit the road."

Sensitivity to the unique needs of Hispanics by firms has paid huge dividends. For example, Metropolitan Life Insurance is the largest insurer of Hispanics. Goya Foods dominates the market for ethnic food products sold to Hispanics. Best Foods's Mazola Corn Oil captures two-thirds of the Hispanic market for this product category. Time, Inc., has more than 750,000 subscribers to its *People en Español*.

African American Buying Patterns

African Americans have the second-largest spending power of the three racial/ethnic subcultures in the United States. Consumer research on African American buying patterns has focused on

subcultures
Subgroups within the larger, or national, culture with unique values, ideas, and attitudes.

Why does Best Foods advertise its Mazola Corn Oil in Spanish? Read the text for the answer.

Mazola Corn Oil
www.mazola.com

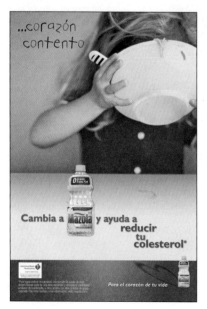

African American women represent a large market for health and beauty products. Cosmetics companies such as Maybelline actively seek to serve this market.

Maybelline
www.maybelline.com

similarities and differences with Caucasians. When socioeconomic status differences between African Americans and Caucasians are removed, there are more similarities than points of difference. Differences in buying patterns are greater within the African American subculture, due to levels of socioeconomic status, than between African Americans and Caucasians of similar status.

Even though similarities outweigh differences, there are consumption patterns that do differ between African Americans and Caucasians.[34] For example, African Americans spend far more than Caucasians on boy's clothing, rental goods, and audio equipment. Adult African Americans are twice as likely to own a pager and spend twice as much for online services, on a per capita basis, than Caucasians. African American women spend three times more on health and beauty products than Caucasian women. Furthermore, the typical African American family is five years younger than the typical Caucasian family. This factor alone accounts for some of the observed differences in preferences for clothing, music, shelter, cars, and many other products, services, and activities. Finally, it must be emphasized that, historically, African Americans have been deprived of employment and educational opportunities in the United States. Both factors have resulted in income disparities between African Americans and Caucasians, which influence purchase behavior.

Recent research indicates that while African Americans are price conscious, they are strongly motivated by quality and choice. They respond more to products such as apparel and cosmetics and advertising that appeal to their African American pride and heritage as well as address their ethnic features and needs regardless of socioeconomic status.

Asian American Buying Patterns   About 70 percent of Asian Americans are immigrants. Most are under the age of 30.

The Asian subculture is composed of Chinese, Japanese, Filipinos, Koreans, Asian Indians, people from Southeast Asia, and Pacific Islanders. The diversity of the Asian subculture is so great that generalizations about buying patterns of this group are difficult to make.[35] Consumer research on Asian Americans suggests that individuals and families can be divided into two groups. *Assimilated* Asian Americans are conversant in English, highly educated, hold professional and managerial positions, and exhibit buying patterns very much like the typical American consumer. *Nonassimilated* Asian Americans are recent immigrants who still cling to their native languages and customs.

The diversity of Asian Americans evident in language, customs, and tastes requires marketers to be sensitive to different Asian nationalities. For example, Anheuser-Busch's agricultural products division sells eight varieties of California-grown rice, each with a different Asian label to cover a range of nationalities and tastes. The company's advertising also addresses the preferences of Chinese, Japanese, and Koreans for different kinds of rice bowls. McDonald's actively markets to Asian Americans. According to a company executive, "We recognize diversity in this market. We try to make our messages in the language they prefer to see them."

Studies show that the Asian American subculture as a whole is characterized by hard work, strong family ties, appreciation for education, and median family incomes exceeding those of any other ethnic group. This subculture is also the most entrepreneurial in the United States, as evidenced by the number of Asian-owned businesses. These qualities led Metropolitan Life Insurance to identify Asian Americans as a target for insurance following the company's success in marketing to Hispanics.

learning review

7. What are the two primary forms of personal influence?

8. Marketers are concerned with which types of reference groups?

9. What two challenges must marketers overcome when marketing to Hispanics?

LEARNING OBJECTIVES REVIEW

LO1 *Describe the stages in the consumer purchase decision process.*

The consumer purchase decision process consists of five stages. They are problem recognition, information search, alternative evaluation, purchase decision, and postpurchase behavior. Problem recognition is perceiving a difference between a person's ideal and actual situation big enough to trigger a decision. Information search involves remembering previous purchase experiences (internal search) and external search behavior such as seeking information from other sources. Alternative evaluation clarifies the problem for the consumer by (*a*) suggesting the evaluative criteria to use for the purchase, (*b*) yielding brand names that might meet the criteria, and (*c*) developing consumer value perceptions. The purchase decision involves the choice of an alternative, including from whom to buy and when to buy. Postpurchase behavior involves the comparison of the chosen alternative with a consumer's expectations, which leads to satisfaction or dissatisfaction and subsequent purchase behavior.

LO2 *Distinguish among three variations of the consumer purchase decision process: routine, limited, and extended problem solving.*

Consumers don't always engage in the five-stage purchase decision process. Instead, they skip or minimize one or more stages depending on the level of involvement—the personal, social, and economic significance of the purchase. For low-involvement purchase occasions, consumers engage in routine problem solving. They recognize a problem, make a decision, and spend little effort seeking external information and evaluating alternatives. For high-involvement purchase occasions, each of the five stages of the consumer purchase decision process is used and considerable time and effort are devoted to the search for external information and the identification and evaluation of alternatives. With limited problem solving, consumers typically seek some information or rely on a friend to help them evaluate alternatives.

LO3 *Identify major psychological influences on consumer behavior.*

Psychology helps marketers understand why and how consumers behave as they do. In particular, psychological concepts such as motivation and personality, perception, learning, values, beliefs and attitudes, and lifestyle are useful for interpreting buying processes. Motivation is the energizing force that stimulates behavior to satisfy a need. Personality refers to a person's consistent behaviors or responses to recurring situations. Perception is the process by which an individual selects, organizes, and interprets information to create a meaningful picture of the world. Consumers filter information through selective exposure, comprehension, and retention.

Much consumer behavior is learned. Learning refers to those behaviors that result from (*a*) repeated experience and (*b*) reasoning. Brand loyalty results from learning. Values, beliefs, and attitudes are also learned and influence how consumers evaluate products, services, and brands. A more general concept is lifestyle. Lifestyle, also called psychographics, combines psychology and demographics and focuses on how people spend their time and resources, what they consider important in their environment, and what they think of themselves and the world around them.

LO4 *Identify major sociocultural influences on consumer behavior.*

Sociocultural influences, which evolve from a consumer's formal and informal relationships with other people, also affect consumer behavior. These involve personal influence, reference groups, the family, culture, and subculture. Opinion leadership and word-of-mouth behavior are two major sources of personal influence on consumer behavior. Reference groups are people to whom an individual looks as a basis for self-approval or as a source of personal standards. Family influences on consumer behavior result from three sources: consumer socialization, passage through the family life cycle, and decision making within the family or household. Finally, a person's culture and subculture have been shown to influence product preferences and buying patterns.

FOCUSING ON KEY TERMS

attitude p. 91
beliefs p. 91
brand loyalty p. 90
consumer behavior p. 80
family life cycle p. 96
involvement p. 83

learning p. 90
motivation p. 86
opinion leaders p. 93
perceived risk p. 89
perception p. 88
personality p. 87

purchase decision process p. 80
reference groups p. 95
subcultures p. 98
word of mouth p. 94

APPLYING MARKETING KNOWLEDGE

1 Review Figure 4–2, which shows the smartphone attributes identified by *Consumer Reports*. Which attributes are important to you? What other attributes might you consider? Which brand would you prefer?

2 Suppose research at Panasonic reveals that prospective buyers are anxious about buying high-definition television sets. What strategies might you recommend to the company to reduce consumer anxiety?

3 Assign one or more levels of the hierarchy of needs and the motives described in Figure 4–5 to the following products: (*a*) life insurance, (*b*) cosmetics, (*c*) *The Wall Street Journal*, and (*d*) hamburgers.

4 With which stage in the family life cycle would the purchase of the following products and services be most closely identified? (*a*) bedroom furniture, (*b*) life insurance, (*c*) a Caribbean cruise, (*d*) a house mortgage, and (*e*) children's toys.

To do a consumer analysis for the product—the good, service, or idea—in your marketing plan:

1 Identify the consumers who are most likely to buy your product—the primary target market—in terms of (*a*) their demographic characteristics and (*b*) any other kind of characteristics you believe are important.

2 Describe (*a*) the main points of difference of your product for this group and (*b*) what problem they help solve for the consumer, in terms of the first stage in the consumer purchase decision process in Figure 4–1.

3 Identify the one or two key influences for each of the four outside boxes in Figure 4–4: (*a*) marketing mix, (*b*) psychological, (*c*) sociocultural, and (*d*) situational influences.

This consumer analysis will provide the foundation for the marketing mix actions you develop later in your plan.

video case 4   Groupon: Helping Consumers with Purchase Decisions

**QR 4–4
Groupon Video
Case**

University of Chicago graduate student Andrew Mason was in a rut. "There's so much to do in Chicago," he explains, "but I found myself going to the same movie theaters and restaurants."

To help people like him try new places, Mason started a website that offered coupons to large groups. He reasoned that people would try something new if the price was low enough, and that businesses would offer low prices if they knew they could sell a large quantity. The result was Groupon, a company that offers "group coupons" in deal-of-the-day offerings for local or national businesses. Consumers love the concept, buying everything from restaurant certificates, to yoga lessons, to tickets to a museum exhibit. "We think the Internet has the potential to change the way people discover and buy from local businesses," says Mason.

THE COMPANY AND GROUPON CONCEPT

Mason started with a website called ThePoint.org, which was designed to organize campaigns, protests, boycotts, and fund-raising drives for important social issues. ThePoint was not successful but it provided the concept of making offers that are only carried out if enough people commit to participate in them. With that idea Mason launched Groupon in October 2008 with a two-pizzas-for-the-price-of-one offer at the Motel Bar, located in the same building where ThePoint rented space. The concept quickly grew in Chicago and Groupon expanded into other U.S. cities, and then into other countries. Today Groupon is available in 375 American cities and 40 countries, and its subscriber base has grown from 400 in 2008 to 60 million today. According to *Forbes* magazine, Groupon is the fastest growing company in history.

Part of Groupon's success is the simplicity of its business model—offer subscribers at least one deal in their city each day. The unique aspect of the concept is that a certain number of people need to buy into the offer before the coupon discount is valid. Approximately 95 percent of Groupon offers "tip," or reach the number of buyers required by the merchant. Once the minimum number is met, Groupon and the merchant split the revenue. For example, a yoga studio might offer a $100 membership for $50 if 200 people participate in the offer. Once 200 consumers have indicated interest, the deal "tips" and Groupon and the yoga studio each receive 50 percent of the revenue. Everyone wins. Consumers receive an exceptional value, the merchant obtains new customers without any advertising cost, and Groupon generates revenue for creating value in the marketplace.

Many of the deals have generated extraordinary demand. The Joffrey Ballet, for example, sold 2,338 season subscriptions, doubling its subscriber base in one day! Similarly, consumers purchased 445,000 Groupons offering $50 worth of merchandise for $25 at the Gap, and 6,561 tickets to a King Tut exhibit in New York's Times Square for half price at $18 apiece. The most popular offering so far was a $25 ticket for an architectural boat tour in Chicago for $12. Groupon sold 19,822 tickets in eight hours! The company's attention to customer satisfaction ensures success stories like these. "We have a policy called 'The Groupon Promise' that any customer can return a Groupon, no questions asked—even if they used it—if they feel like Groupon has let them down," explains Mason. Groupon's success has attracted many more merchants than it can accommodate. In fact, only about 12 percent of all merchants that contact Groupon are selected to offer a deal.

In addition to the deal-of-the-day offerings, Groupon has several other services. First, it is testing a concept called Groupon Stores which allows merchants to create their own deals and send them out to their own audience. This allows more merchants to participate on a regular

basis. Second, the company has recently introduced a mobile service called Groupon Now. To use the service, consumers log in to the app on their smartphone and select one of two options: "I'm Hungry" or "I'm Bored." The phone then transmits its location to the Groupon servers and displays a list of nearby deals at restaurants or entertainment venues. The Groupon Now offerings represent a combination of Yellow Pages advertising and newspaper coupons for price-conscious consumers.

Groupon's growth is evident in some amazing numbers. The company now sends more than 900 deals each day, occupies six floors of the former Montgomery Ward headquarters in Chicago, and employs more than 5,900 people. In addition, Groupon has created a market of consumer deal hunters and an industry of more than 500 competitive deal services. The competitors include LevelUp, Tippr, Bloomspot, Scoutmob, BuyWithMe, Yelp, and OpenTable. In addition, Google Offers, Facebook Deals, Yahoo! Deals, and Amazon's LivingSocial are all recently launched deal services.

USING COUPONS TO INFLUENCE CONSUMERS' BUYING BEHAVIOR

"Part of the reason that Groupon has grown as quickly as it has is because we really understand consumer behavior," explains Julie Mossler, public relations and consumer marketing manager at Groupon. Generally, Groupon consumers follow the same purchase decision process common to many consumer purchases. The first stage, problem recognition, may be triggered by an e-mail or an appointment to have lunch with friends. Groupon deal-of-the-day e-mail messages, for example, often present consumers with an opportunity to do something they wouldn't ordinarily do—take sky-diving lessons or subscribe to the ballet. Groupon Now presents real-time offers on smartphone apps in response to an immediate need in a specific location. While the two types of offers generate different types of purchases, they both begin the purchase process.

The second stage, information search, may simply be a review of previous experiences with the merchant making the offer, online comparisons with competitors, or discussions with friends on Facebook or Twitter. In fact, the collective buying aspect of Groupon encourages subscribers to share promotions with family and friends to increase the chances of reaching the required number of buyers.

In the alternative evaluation stage many Groupon customers focus on price as the most important evaluative criteria, although other aspects such as quantity or time restrictions may be considered. The Groupon Now offers, for example, may only be valid on specific days or during short windows of time. Piece Brewery & Pizzeria in Chicago used Groupon Now to sell a $30 coupon for $20 valid only during its slow periods—11 A.M. to 3 P.M. Tuesday through Thursday.

The fourth stage, the purchase decision, is made online and then confirmed when the deals tip. Bo Hurd, national sales manager at Groupon, believes that the purchase stage is unique for Groupon users. He explains, "the fact that [consumers] have put money on the line. . . is driving them from the online piece, to the computers. . . to do something, to try something." Finally, after the purchase consumers compare their experience with their expectations to determine if they are satisfied or dissatisfied.

Psychological, sociocultural, and situational factors also influence Groupon users' purchase behavior. The recession has increased the importance of personal values such as thriftiness, so deal-prone people who were attracted to websites such as Gilt in fashion and Woot in consumer electronics are also attracted to Groupon. The typical Groupon user is an 18- to 34-year old woman with an average income of about $70,000. This is significant because this group's affinity to social media enables the use of Groupon, which depends on e-mail and smartphone apps to reach its customers. Specific situations such as planning entertainment activities, finding a close restaurant for lunch, or buying a gift are also common to Groupon users. As Groupon has learned more about its subscribers, it has begun personalizing the deals they see. The company uses variables such as gender, location of residence or office, and buying history to match deals with the customers. This process provides offers that are more likely to be of interest to consumers and allows Groupon to serve more merchants.

GROUPON CHALLENGES

As popular as Groupon has become, it does face three challenges. The first challenge is related to the use of coupons. Some consumers buy the coupons but never use them, eventually leaving them dissatisfied and unlikely to use Groupon again. Some consumers use the coupons but do not become regular customers. Because of the deep discounts used to sell the Groupons, most of the deals are not profitable for the merchants, so they are dissatisfied if the Groupon users do not make repeat purchases. David Perlman, owner of the Essex restaurant in New York City, for example, offered deals on Groupon and OpenTable, selling 1,500 and 1,000 coupons, respectively. Now he is comparing the diners each deal brought in to determine which group has generated more repeat customers. Some merchants are also concerned that frequent discounting could discourage customers from ever making purchases without a discount.

Another challenge facing Groupon is managing its growth. The company has expanded into Europe, Latin America, Asia, and Russia by acquiring local daily deal services. For example, in Europe it purchased CityDeal, in Russia it purchased Darberry, and in Japan it purchased Qpod. It also acquired sites with customer bases in Hong Kong, Singapore, Taiwan, and the Philippines. As a result, Groupon currently has more subscribers abroad than in the United States, although more deals are still sold in the United States. As Groupon continues to grow, it anticipates that it must develop a comprehensive understanding of the differences in international buying behaviors.

Finally, Groupon faces an extraordinary level of competition. Part of the problem is that the daily deal technology is not very sophisticated and the model is easy to copy. Manufacturers, large retailers, and small businesses are all trying the concept. ConAgra has offered a group coupon deal for its Healthy Choice brand through a Facebook app, Walmart launched its own deals app called Crowdsaver, and some businesses use recently developed plug-and-play software that helps build deals into their websites. Mason hopes that Groupon Now is one answer to this challenge because it is much more difficult to replicate. "We have always been thinking about how to solve these fundamental problems of our model. We have known since very early on that some form of real-time deal optimization is where this had to go," he explains.

Groupon's success is the result of a simple and effective business model and an insightful understanding of consumer behavior. In the future, Groupon's strategies will require continued attention to understanding consumers around the globe. Mossler explains: "Groupon has been heralded as the fastest growing company of all time, and the reason for that is because we have solved this unsolvable problem, which is how do you engage with local customers. The model really works anywhere as long as you adapt for local communities."

Questions

1 How has an understanding of consumer behavior helped Groupon grow from 400 subscribers in Chicago in 2008 to 60 million subscribers in 40 countries today?

2 What is the Groupon Promise? How does the Groupon Promise affect a consumer's perceived risk and cognitive dissonance?

3 Describe the five-stage purchase decision process for a typical Groupon user.

4 What are possible psychological and sociological influences on the Groupon consumer purchase decision process?

5 What challenges does Groupon face in the future? What actions would you recommend related to each challenge?

jcpenney

little**red**book

our **ABSOLUTE LOWEST**
prices on spring's hot trends!

earn
double
points
for jcp rewards
see details on flap

34⁹⁹
floral dress,
inside flap

Understanding Organizations as Customers

5

LEARNING OBJECTIVES

After reading this chapter you should be able to:

LO1 Distinguish among industrial, reseller, and government organizational markets.

LO2 Describe the key characteristics of organizational buying that make it different from consumer buying.

LO3 Explain how buying centers and buying situations influence organizational purchasing.

LO4 Recognize the importance and nature of online buying in organizational markets.

BUYING PUBLICATION PAPER IS A SERIOUS MARKETING RESPONSIBILITY AT JCPENNEY

Kim Nagele views paper differently than most people do. As the senior sourcing manager at JCPMedia, he and a team of purchasing professionals buy more than 200,000 tons of publication paper annually at a cost of hundreds of millions of dollars.

JCPMedia is the print and paper purchasing arm for JCPenney, the third-largest retailer in the United States. Paper is serious business at JCPMedia, which buys publication paper for JCPenney newspaper inserts and direct-mail pieces. Some 10 companies from around the world—including Verso Paper in the United States; Catalyst Paper, Inc., in Canada; Norske Skog in Norway; and UPM-Kymmene, Inc., in Finland—supply paper to JCPMedia.

"The choice of paper and suppliers is also a significant marketing decision given the sizable revenue and expense consequences," notes Gary Pats, marketing production and support director at JCPenney. Not surprisingly, JCPMedia paper buyers work closely with JCPenney marketing personnel and within budget constraints to ensure that the right quality and quantity of publication paper is purchased at the right price point for merchandise featured in the millions of newspaper inserts and direct-mail pieces distributed every year.

In addition to paper quality and price, buyers formally evaluate paper supplier capabilities, often by extended visits to supplier facilities. These include a supplier's capacity to deliver on-time selected grades of paper from specialty items to magazine papers, the availability of specific types of paper to meet printing deadlines, and formal programs focused on the life cycle of paper products. For example, a supplier's forestry management and sustainability practices are considered in the JCPMedia buying process.[1]

The next time you thumb through a JCPenney newspaper insert or direct-mail piece, take a moment to notice the paper. Considerable effort and attention was given to its selection and purchase decision by Gary Pats, Kim Nagele, and JCPMedia paper buyers.

Purchasing paper for JCPMedia is one example of organizational buying. This chapter examines the different types of organizational buyers; key characteristics of organizational buying, including online buying; buying situations; unique aspects of the organizational buying process; and some typical buying procedures and decisions in today's organizational markets.

THE NATURE AND SIZE OF ORGANIZATIONAL MARKETS

LO1

business marketing
The marketing of products and services to firms, governments, or not-for-profit organizations.

organizational buyers
Manufacturers, wholesalers, retailers, and government agencies that buy products and services for their own use or for resale.

Understanding organizational markets and buying behavior is a necessary prerequisite for effective business marketing. **Business marketing** is the marketing of products and services to companies, governments, or not-for-profit organizations for use in the creation of goods and services that they can produce and market to others. Because over half of all U.S. business school graduates take jobs in firms that engage in business marketing, it is important to understand the characteristics of organizational buyers and their buying behavior.

Organizational buyers are those manufacturers, wholesalers, retailers, and government agencies that buy products and services for their own use or for resale. For example, these organizations buy computers and telephone services for their own use. However, manufacturers buy raw materials and parts that they reprocess into the finished products they sell. Wholesalers and retailers resell the products they buy without reprocessing them.

Organizational buyers include all buyers in a nation except ultimate consumers. These organizational buyers purchase and lease large volumes of capital equipment, raw materials, manufactured parts, supplies, and business services. In fact, because they often buy raw materials and parts, process them, and sell the upgraded product several times before it is purchased by the final organizational buyer or ultimate consumer, the total annual purchases of organizational buyers are far greater than those of ultimate consumers. IBM alone buys nearly $48 billion in products and services each year for its own use or resale.[2]

Organizational buyers are divided into three markets: (1) industrial, (2) reseller, and (3) government.[3] Each market is described next.

Industrial Markets

There are about 7.7 million firms in the industrial, or business, market. These *industrial firms* in some way reprocess a product or service they buy before selling it again to the next buyer. This is certainly true of Corning, Inc., which transforms an exotic blend of materials to create optical fiber capable of carrying much of the telephone traffic in the United States on a single strand. It is also true (if you stretch your imagination) of a firm selling services, such as a bank that takes money from its depositors, reprocesses it, and "sells" it as loans to borrowers.

The importance of services in the United States today is emphasized by the composition of industrial markets. Companies that primarily sell physical goods (manufacturers; mining; construction; and farms, timber, and fisheries) represent 25 percent of all the industrial firms. The services market sells diverse services such as legal advice, auto repair, and dry cleaning. Along with finance, insurance, and real estate businesses, and transportation, communication, public utility firms, and not-for-profit organizations, service companies represent 75 percent of all industrial firms. Because of the size and importance of service companies and not-for-profit organizations (such as the American Red Cross), services marketing is discussed in detail in Chapter 10.

Reseller Markets

Wholesalers and retailers that buy physical products and resell them again without any reprocessing are *resellers*. In the United States there are about 1.5 million retailers and 435,000 wholesalers. In Chapters 12 and 13 you will see how manufacturers use wholesalers and retailers in their distribution ("place") strategies as channels through which their products reach ultimate consumers. In this chapter, we look at these resellers mainly as organizational buyers in terms of (1) how they make their own buying decisions and (2) which products they choose to carry.

The Orion lunar spacecraft to be designed, developed, tested, and evaluated by Lockheed Martin Corp. is an example of a purchase by a government unit, namely the National Aeronautics and Space Administration (NASA). Read the text to find out how much NASA will pay for the Orion lunar spacecraft prior to its launch in 2016.

Lockheed Martin Corporation
www.lockheedmartin.com

QR 5–1
NASA Video

Government Markets

Government units are the federal, state, and local agencies that buy products and services for the constituents they serve. There are about 89,500 of these government units in the United States. These purchases include the $10.5 billion the National Aeronautics and Space Administration (NASA) intends to pay to Lockheed Martin to develop and produce the Orion lunar spacecraft scheduled for launch in 2016 as well as lesser amounts spent by local school and sanitation districts.[4]

MEASURING DOMESTIC AND GLOBAL INDUSTRIAL, RESELLER, AND GOVERNMENT MARKETS

North American Industry Classification System (NAICS)

Provides common industry definitions for Canada, Mexico, and the United States.

The measurement of industrial, reseller, and government markets is an important first step for a firm interested in gauging the size of one, two, or all three of these markets in the United States and around the world. This task has been made easier with the **North American Industry Classification System (NAICS)**.[5] The NAICS provides common industry definitions for Canada, Mexico, and the United States, which makes it easier to measure economic activity in the three member countries of the North American Free Trade Agreement (NAFTA). The NAICS replaced the Standard Industrial Classification (SIC) system, a version of which has been in place for more than 50 years in the three NAFTA member countries. The SIC neither permitted comparability across countries nor accurately measured new or emerging industries. Furthermore, the NAICS is consistent with the International Standard Industrial Classification of All Economic Activities, published by the United Nations, to facilitate measurement of global economic activity.

The NAICS groups economic activity to permit studies of market share, demand for products and services, import competition in domestic markets, and similar studies. It designates industries with a numerical code in a defined structure. A six-digit coding system is used. The first two digits designate a sector of the economy, the third digit designates a subsector, and the fourth digit represents an industry group. The fifth digit designates a specific industry and is the most detailed level at which comparable data are available for Canada, Mexico, and the United States. The sixth digit designates individual country-level national industries. Figure 5–1 on the next page shows a breakdown within the information industries sector (code 51) to illustrate the classification scheme.

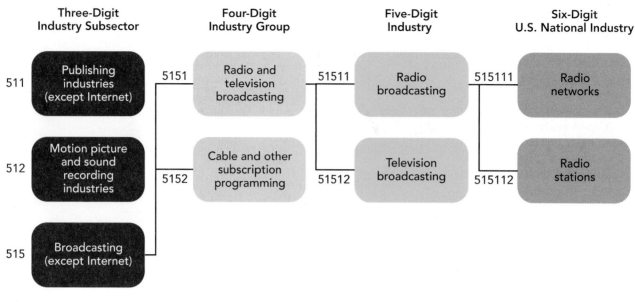

Three-Digit Industry Subsector	Four-Digit Industry Group	Five-Digit Industry	Six-Digit U.S. National Industry
511 Publishing industries (except Internet)	5151 Radio and television broadcasting	51511 Radio broadcasting	515111 Radio networks
512 Motion picture and sound recording industries	5152 Cable and other subscription programming	51512 Television broadcasting	515112 Radio stations
515 Broadcasting (except Internet)			

FIGURE 5–1

NAICS breakdown for the information industries sector: NAICS code 51 (abbreviated).

The NAICS permits a firm to find the NAICS codes of its present customers and then obtain NAICS-coded lists for similar firms. Also, it is possible to monitor NAICS categories to determine the growth in various sectors and industries to identify promising marketing opportunities. However, the NAICS has an important limitation. Five-digit national industry codes are not available for all three countries because the respective governments will not reveal data when too few organizations exist in a category.

---

learning review

1. What are the three main types of organizational buyers?

2. What is the North American Industry Classification System (NAICS)?

CHARACTERISTICS OF ORGANIZATIONAL BUYING

LO2

Organizations are different from individuals, so buying for an organization is different from buying for yourself or your family. In both cases the objective in making the purchase is to solve the buyer's problem—to satisfy a need or want. But unique objectives and policies of an organization put special constraints on how it makes buying decisions. Understanding the characteristics of organizational buying is essential in designing effective marketing programs to reach these buyers. Key characteristics of organizational buying are listed in Figure 5–2 and discussed next.[6]

Demand Characteristics

derived demand

The demand for industrial products and services is driven by demand for consumer products and services.

Consumer demand for products and services is affected by their price and availability and by consumers' personal tastes and discretionary income. By comparison, industrial demand is derived. **Derived demand** means that the demand for industrial products and services is driven by, or derived from, demand for consumer products and services. For example, the demand for Weyerhaeuser's pulp and paper products is based on consumer demand for newspapers, FedEx packages, and disposable diapers. Derived demand is based on expectations of future consumer demand. For instance, Whirlpool buys parts for its washers and dryers in anticipation of consumer demand, which is affected by the replacement cycle for these products and by consumer income.

Market characteristics	• Demand for industrial products and services is derived. • Few customers typically exist, and their purchase orders are large.
Product or service characteristics	• Products or services are technical in nature and purchased on the basis of specifications. • Many of the goods purchased are raw and semifinished. • Heavy emphasis is placed on delivery time, technical assistance, and postsale service.
Buying process characteristics	• Technically qualified and professional buyers follow established purchasing policies and procedures. • Buying objectives and criteria are typically spelled out, as are procedures for evaluating sellers and their products or services. • There are multiple buying influences, and multiple parties participate in purchase decisions. • There are reciprocal arrangements, and negotiation between buyers and sellers is commonplace. • Online buying over the Internet is widespread.
Marketing mix characteristics	• Direct selling to organizational buyers is the rule, and distribution is very important. • Advertising and other forms of promotion are technical in nature. • Price is often negotiated, evaluated as part of broader seller and product or service qualities, and frequently affected by quantity discounts.

FIGURE 5–2

Key characteristics and dimensions of organizational buying behavior.

Size of the Order or Purchase

The size of the purchase involved in organizational buying is typically much larger than that in consumer buying. The dollar value of a single purchase made by an organization often runs into thousands or millions of dollars. For example, Siemens Energy & Automation's Airport Logistics Division was awarded a $28 million contract to build a baggage handling and security system for JetBlue Airways's terminal at John F. Kennedy International Airport.[7]

With so much money at stake, most organizations place constraints on their buyers in the form of purchasing policies or procedures. Buyers must often get competitive bids from at least three prospective suppliers when the order is above a specific amount, such as $5,000. When the order is above an even higher amount, such as $50,000, it may require the review and approval of a vice president or even the president of the company. Knowing how order size affects buying practices is important in determining who participates in the purchase decision and makes the final decision, and the length of time required to arrive at a purchase agreement.

Number of Potential Buyers

Firms selling consumer products or services often try to reach thousands or millions of individuals or households. For example, your local supermarket or bank probably serves thousands of people. Kellogg tries to reach 80 million North American households with its breakfast cereals and probably succeeds in selling to a third or half of these in any given year. Firms selling to organizations are often restricted to far fewer buyers. Gulfstream Aerospace Corporation can sell its business jets to a few thousand organizations throughout the world, and Goodyear sells its original equipment tires to fewer than 10 car manufacturers.

Organizational Buying Objectives

Organizations buy products and services for one main reason: to help them achieve their objectives. For business firms the buying objective is usually to increase profits through reducing costs or increasing revenues. For example, 7-Eleven buys automated inventory systems to increase the number of products that can be sold through its convenience stores and to keep them fresh. Nissan Motor Company switched its advertising agency because it expects the new agency to devise a more effective ad campaign to help it sell more cars and increase revenues. To improve executive decision making, many firms buy advanced computer systems to process data. The objectives of nonprofit firms and government agencies are usually to meet the needs of the groups they serve.

Many companies today have broadened their buying objectives to include an emphasis on buying from minority- and women-owned suppliers and vendors. Companies such as Pitney Bowes, PepsiCo, Coors, and JCPenney report that sales, profits, and customer satisfaction have increased because of their minority- and women-owned supplier and vendor initiatives.[8] Other companies include environmental initiatives. For example, Lowe's and Home Depot no longer purchase lumber from companies that harvest timber from the world's endangered forests. Successful business marketers recognize that understanding buying objectives is a necessary first step in marketing to organizations.

Organizational Buying Criteria

In making a purchase, the buying organization must weigh key buying criteria that apply to the potential supplier and what it wants to sell. *Organizational buying criteria* are the objective attributes of the supplier's products and services and the capabilities of the supplier itself. These criteria serve the same purpose as the evaluative criteria used by consumers and described in Chapter 4. The most commonly used criteria are (1) price, (2) ability to meet the quality specifications required for the item, (3) ability to meet required delivery schedules, (4) technical capability, (5) warranties and claim policies in the event of poor performance, (6) past performance on previous contracts, and (7) production facilities and capacity.[9] Suppliers that meet or exceed these criteria create customer value.

As a practical example, Figure 5–3 shows the actual buying criteria employed by organizational buyers when choosing among machine vision system products and suppliers, as well as the frequency with which these criteria are used. Interestingly, of the various selection criteria listed, a machine vision system's price is among the least frequently mentioned.[10]

FIGURE 5–3

Product and supplier selection criteria for buying machine vision equipment for product inspection emphasize factors other than price. This is not surprising. Product inspection uncovers potential problems when consumers consume or use a product, such as unfilled or improperly sealed packages and foreign substances in containers.

An optic component in a larger machine vision system for soft drink cans.

Percentage of machine vision buyers citing individual selection criteria.

Criterion	Percentage
Performance	80%
Technical support	68%
Ease of use	67%
Ease of setup	63%
Complete solution (including software)	60%
Ruggedness	56%
Customization ability	53%
Price	48%
Integration expertise	42%
Full tool set	42%
Speed	38%

Marketing Matters > > > > > customer value

Harley-Davidson's Supplier Collaboration Creates Customer Value . . . and a Great Ride

It's nice to be admired. Harley-Davidson's well-deserved reputation for innovation, product quality, and talented management and employees has made it a perennial member of *Fortune* magazine's list of "America's Most Admired Companies."

Harley-Davidson is also respected by suppliers for the way it collaborates with them in product design. According to a company spokesperson: "We involve our suppliers as much as possible in future products, new-product development, and get them working with us." Emphasis is placed on quality benchmarks, cost control, delivery schedules, and technological innovation as well as building mutually beneficial, long-term relationships. Face-to-face communication is encouraged, and many suppliers have personnel stationed at Harley-Davidson's Product Development Center.

The relationship between Harley-Davidson and Milsco Manufacturing is a case in point. Milsco has been the sole source of original equipment motorcycle seats and a major supplier of aftermarket parts and accessories, such as saddlebags, for Harley-Davidson since 1934. Milsco engineers and designers work closely with their Harley counterparts in the design of each year's new products.

The notion of a mutually beneficial relationship is expressed by Milsco's manager of industrial design: "Harley-Davidson refers to us as stakeholders, someone who can win or lose from a successful or failed program. We all share responsibility toward one another." He also notes that Harley-Davidson is not Milsco's only customer. It is simply the customer that he most respects.

Many organizational buyers today are transforming their buying criteria into specific requirements that are communicated to prospective suppliers. This practice, called *supplier development*, involves the deliberate effort by organizational buyers to build relationships that shape suppliers' products, services, and capabilities to fit a buyer's needs and those of its customers. Consider Deere & Company, the maker of John Deere farm, construction, and lawn-care equipment. Deere employs supplier-development engineers who work full-time with the company's suppliers to improve their efficiency and quality and reduce their costs. According to a Deere senior executive, "Their quality, delivery, and costs are, after all, our quality, delivery, and costs."[11] Read the Marketing Matters box to learn how Harley-Davidson emphasizes supplier collaboration in its product design.[12]

Buyer–Seller Relationships and Supply Partnerships

Another distinction between organizational and consumer buying behavior lies in the nature of the relationship between organizational buyers and suppliers. Specifically, organizational buying is more likely to involve complex negotiations concerning delivery schedules, price, technical specifications, warranties, and claim policies. These negotiations also can last for an extended period. This was the case when the Lawrence Livermore National Laboratory acquired two IBM supercomputers—each with capacity to perform 360 trillion mathematical operations per second—at a cost of $290 million.[13]

Reciprocal arrangements also exist in organizational buying. *Reciprocity* is an industrial buying practice in which two organizations agree to purchase each other's products and services. The U.S. Justice Department disapproves of reciprocal buying because it restricts the normal operation of the free market. However, the practice exists and can limit the flexibility of organizational buyers in choosing alternative suppliers.

Long-term contracts are also prevalent.[14] For instance, Kraft Foods, Inc., is spending $1.7 billion over seven years for global information technology services provided

Sustainable Procurement for Sustainable Growth

Manufacturers, retailers, wholesalers, and governmental agencies are increasingly sensitive to how their buying decisions affect the environment. Concerns about the depletion of natural resources; air, water, and soil pollution; and the social consequences of economic activity have given rise to the concept of sustainable procurement. Sustainable procurement aims to integrate environmental considerations into all stages of an organization's buying process with the goal of reducing the negative impact on human health and the physical environment.

Starbucks is a pioneer and worldwide leader in sustainable procurement. The company's attention to quality coffee extends to its coffee growers located in more than 20 countries. This means that Starbucks pays coffee farmers a fair price for the beans; that the coffee is grown in an ecologically

sound manner; and that Starbucks invests in the farming communities where its coffees are produced. In this way, Starbucks focuses on the sustainable growth of its suppliers.

---

by Electronic Data Systems. Hewlett-Packard has a 10-year, $3 billion contract to manage Procter & Gamble's information technology in 160 countries.

QR 5–2
Starbucks
Sustainability
Video

In some cases, buyer–seller relationships evolve into supply partnerships.[15] A *supply partnership* exists when a buyer and its supplier adopt mutually beneficial objectives, policies, and procedures for the purpose of lowering the cost or increasing the value of products and services delivered to the ultimate consumer. Intel, a manufacturer of microprocessors and the "computer inside" of most personal computers, is an example. Intel supports its suppliers by offering them quality management programs and by investing in supplier equipment that produces fewer product defects and boosts supplier productivity. Suppliers, in turn, provide Intel with consistent high-quality products at a lower cost for its customers, the makers of personal computers, and finally you, the ultimate customer.

Retailers, too, have forged partnerships with their suppliers. Walmart has such a relationship with Procter & Gamble for ordering and replenishing P&G's products in its stores. By using computerized cash register scanning equipment and direct electronic linkages to P&G, Walmart can tell P&G what merchandise is needed, along with how much, when, and to which store to deliver it on a daily basis.

Supply partnerships often include provisions for what is called *sustainable procurement*. This buying practice is described in the Making Responsible Decisions box.[16]

THE ORGANIZATIONAL BUYING PROCESS AND THE BUYING CENTER

organizational buying behavior

The process by which organizations determine the need for products and then choose among alternative suppliers.

Organizational buyers, like consumers, engage in a decision process when selecting products and services. **Organizational buying behavior** is the decision-making process that organizations use to establish the need for products and services and identify, evaluate, and choose among alternative brands and suppliers. There are important similarities and differences between the two decision-making processes. To better understand the nature of organizational buying behavior, we first compare it with consumer buying behavior. We then describe a unique feature of organizational buying—the buying center.

Stages in the Organizational Buying Process

As shown in Figure 5–4, the five stages a student might use in buying a smartphone also apply to organizational purchases. However, comparing the two smartphone columns in

STAGE IN THE BUYING DECISION PROCESS	CONSUMER PURCHASE: SMARTPHONE FOR A STUDENT	ORGANIZATIONAL PURCHASE: EARBUD HEADSET FOR A SMARTPHONE
Problem recognition	Student doesn't like the features of the smartphone now owned and desires a new one.	Marketing research and sales departments observe that competitors are improving the earbud headsets for their smartphones. The firm decides to improve the earbud headsets on its own new models, which will be purchased from an outside supplier.
Information search	Student uses past experience, that of friends, ads, the Internet, and *Consumer Reports* to collect information and uncover alternatives.	Design and production engineers draft specifications for earbud headsets. The purchasing department identifies suppliers of earbud headsets.
Alternative evaluation	Alternative smartphones are evaluated on the basis of important attributes desired in a phone, and several stores are visited.	Purchasing and engineering personnel visit with suppliers and assess (1) facilities, (2) capacity, (3) quality control, and (4) financial status. They drop any suppliers not satisfactory on these factors.
Purchase decision	A specific brand of smartphone is selected, the price is paid, and the student leaves the store.	They use (1) quality, (2) price, (3) delivery, and (4) technical capability as key buying criteria to select a supplier. Then they negotiate terms and award a contract.
Postpurchase behavior	Student reevaluates the purchase decision, and may return the phone to the store if it is unsatisfactory.	They evaluate suppliers using a formal vendor rating system and notify a supplier if the earbud headsets do not meet their quality standard. If the problem is not corrected, they drop the firm as a future supplier.

FIGURE 5–4

Comparing the stages in a consumer and organizational purchase decision process.

Figure 5–4 reveals some key differences. For example, when a manufacturer buys an earbud headset for its units from a supplier, more individuals are involved, supplier capability becomes more important, and the postpurchase evaluation behavior is more formal. The earbud headset buying decision process is typical of the steps made by organizational buyers.

The Buying Center: A Cross-Functional Group

For routine purchases with a small dollar value, a single buyer or purchasing manager often makes the purchase decision alone. In many instances, however, several people in the organization participate in the buying process. The individuals in this group, called a **buying center**, share common goals, risks, and knowledge important to a purchase decision. For most large multistore chain resellers, such as Sears, 7-Eleven convenience stores, Target, or Safeway, the buying center is highly formalized and is called a *buying committee*. However, most industrial firms or government units use informal groups of people or call meetings to arrive at buying decisions.

The importance of the buying center requires that a firm marketing to many industrial firms and government units understand the structure, the technical and business functions represented, and the behavior of these groups.[17] Four questions provide guidance in understanding the buying center in these organizations: (1) Which individuals are in the buying center for the product or service? (2) What is the relative influence of each member of the group? (3) What are the buying criteria of each member? and (4) How does each member of the group perceive our firm, our products and services, and our salespeople?

buying center
The group of people in an organization that participates in the buying process.

Effective marketing to organizations requires an understanding of buying centers and their role in purchase decisions.

People in the Buying Center The composition of the buying center in a given organization depends on the specific item being bought. Although a buyer or purchasing manager is almost always a member of the buying center, individuals from other functional areas are included, depending on what is to be purchased. In buying a million-dollar machine tool, the president (because of the size of the purchase) and the production vice president or manager would probably be members. For key components to be included in a final manufactured product, a cross-functional group of individuals from research and development (R&D), engineering, and quality control are likely to be added. For new word-processing equipment, experienced secretaries who will use the equipment would be members. Still, a major question in penetrating the buying center is finding and reaching the people who will initiate, influence, and actually make the buying decision.

Roles in the Buying Center Researchers have identified five specific roles that an individual in a buying center can play.[18] In some purchases the same person may perform two or more of these roles.

- *Users* are the people in the organization who actually use the product or service, such as a secretary who will use a new word processor.
- *Influencers* affect the buying decision, usually by helping define the specifications for what is bought. The information technology manager would be a key influencer in the purchase of a new mainframe computer.
- *Buyers* have formal authority and responsibility to select the supplier and negotiate the terms of the contract. Kim Nagele performs this role as senior sourcing manager at JCPMedia, as described in the chapter opening example.
- *Deciders* have the formal or informal power to select or approve the supplier that receives the contract. In routine orders the decider is usually the buyer or purchasing manager; in important technical purchases it is more likely to be someone from R&D, engineering, or quality control. The decider for a key component being incorporated in a final manufactured product might be any of these three people.
- *Gatekeepers* control the flow of information in the buying center. Purchasing personnel, technical experts, and secretaries can all keep salespeople or information from reaching people performing the other four roles.

Buying Situations and the Buying Center The number of people in the buying center largely depends on the specific buying situation. Researchers who have studied organizational buying identify three types of buying situations, called **buy classes**. These buy classes vary from the routine reorder, or *straight rebuy*, to the completely new purchase, termed *new buy*. In between these extremes is the *modified rebuy*. Figure 5–5 summarizes how buy classes affect buying center tendencies in different ways.[19] Some examples will clarify the differences.[20]

- *New buy.* Here the organization is a first-time buyer of the product or service. This involves greater potential risks in the purchase, so the buying center is enlarged to include all those who have a stake in the new buy. Procter & Gamble's purchase of a multimillion-dollar fiber-optic network from Corning, Inc., for its corporate offices in Cincinnati, represented a new buy.[21]
- *Straight rebuy.* Here the buyer or purchasing manager reorders an existing product or service from the list of acceptable suppliers, probably without even checking with users or influencers from the engineering, production, or quality control departments. Office supplies and maintenance services are usually obtained as straight rebuys.

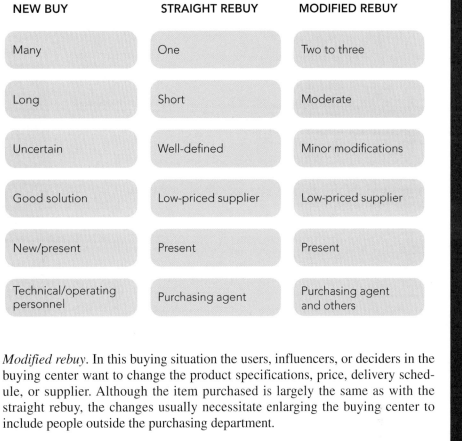

BUYING CENTER DIMENSION	BUY-CLASS SITUATION		
	NEW BUY	STRAIGHT REBUY	MODIFIED REBUY
People involved	Many	One	Two to three
Decision time	Long	Short	Moderate
Problem definition	Uncertain	Well-defined	Minor modifications
Buying objective	Good solution	Low-priced supplier	Low-priced supplier
Suppliers considered	New/present	Present	Present
Buying influence	Technical/operating personnel	Purchasing agent	Purchasing agent and others

FIGURE 5–5

The buying situation affects buying center behavior in different ways. Understanding these differences can pay huge dividends for companies that market to organizations.

- *Modified rebuy.* In this buying situation the users, influencers, or deciders in the buying center want to change the product specifications, price, delivery schedule, or supplier. Although the item purchased is largely the same as with the straight rebuy, the changes usually necessitate enlarging the buying center to include people outside the purchasing department.

---

learning review

3. What one department is almost always represented by a person in the buying center?

4. What are the three types of buying situations or buy classes?

ONLINE BUYING IN ORGANIZATIONAL MARKETS

LO4

Organizational buying behavior and business marketing continues to evolve with the application of Internet technology. Organizations dwarf consumers in terms of online transactions made, average transaction size, and overall purchase volume. In fact, organizational buyers account for about 80 percent of the global dollar value of all online transactions.

Prominence of Online Buying in Organizational Markets

Online buying in organizational markets is prominent for three major reasons.[22] First, organizational buyers depend heavily on timely supplier information that describes product availability, technical specifications, application uses, price, and delivery schedules. This information can be conveyed quickly via Internet technology. Second, this technology has been shown to substantially reduce buyer order processing costs. At General Electric, online buying has cut the cost of a transaction from $50 to $100 per purchase, to about $5. Third, business marketers have found that Internet technology can reduce marketing costs, particularly sales and advertising expense, and broaden their potential customer base for many types of products and services.

For these reasons, online buying is popular in all three kinds of organizational markets. For example, airlines electronically order over $400 million in spare parts from the Boeing Company each year. Customers of W. W. Grainger, a large U.S. wholesaler of maintenance, repair, and operating supplies, buy more than $425 million worth of these products annually online. Supply and service purchases totaling $650 million each year are made online by the Los Angeles County government.

E-Marketplaces: Virtual Organizational Markets

e-marketplaces

Online trading communities that bring together buyers and supplier organizations.

A significant development in organizational buying has been the creation of online trading communities, called **e-marketplaces**, that bring together buyers and supplier organizations. These online communities go by a variety of names, including business-to-business (B2B) exchanges and e-hubs, and make possible the real-time exchange of information, money, products, and services.

E-marketplaces can be independent trading communities or private exchanges. Independent e-marketplaces act as a neutral third party and provide an Internet technology trading platform and a centralized market that enable exchanges between buyers and sellers. They charge a fee for their service and exist in settings that have one or more of the following features: (1) thousands of geographically dispersed buyers and sellers, (2) volatile prices caused by demand and supply fluctuations, (3) time sensitivity due to perishable offerings and changing technologies, and (4) easily comparable offerings between a variety of sellers.

Examples of independent e-marketplaces include PlasticsNet (plastics), Hospital Network.com (health care supplies and equipment), and Textile Web (garment and apparel products). Small business buyers and sellers, in particular, benefit from independent e-marketplaces. These e-marketplaces offer them an economical way to expand their customer base and reduce the cost of products and services. To serve entrepreneurs and the

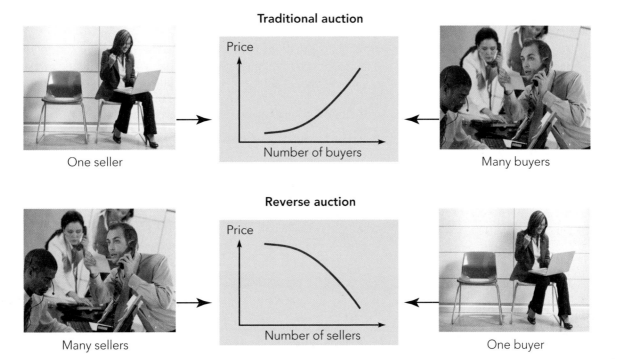

Traditional auction

One seller → [Price vs. Number of buyers] ← Many buyers

Reverse auction

Many sellers → [Price vs. Number of sellers] ← One buyer

FIGURE 5–6

Buyer and seller participants and price behavior differ by type of online auction. As an organizational buyer, would you prefer to participate in a traditional auction or a reverse auction?

QR 5–3
Agentrics
Video

traditional auction

Occurs when a seller puts an item up for sale and would-be buyers bid in competition with each other.

reverse auction

Occurs when a buyer communicates a need for something and would-be suppliers bid in competition with each other.

small business market in the United States, eBay launched eBayBusiness. Read the Marketing Matters box to learn more about this independent trading community.[23]

Large companies tend to favor private exchanges that link them with their network of qualified suppliers and customers. Private exchanges focus on streamlining a company's purchase transactions with its suppliers and customers. Like independent e-marketplaces, they provide a technology trading platform and central market for buyer–seller interactions. They are not a neutral third party, however, but represent the interests of their owners. For example, Agentrics is an international business-to-business private exchange. It connects more than 250 retail customers with 80,000 suppliers. Its members include Best Buy, Campbell Soup, Costco, Radio Shack, Safeway, Target, Tesco, and Walgreens.[24] The Global Healthcare Exchange engages in the buying and selling of health care products for over 3,900 hospitals and more than 300 health care suppliers, such as Abbott Laboratories, GE Medical Systems, Johnson & Johnson, Medtronic USA, and McKesson Corporation in North America.[25]

Online Auctions in Organizational Markets

Online auctions have grown in popularity among organizational buyers and business marketers. Many e-marketplaces offer this service. Two general types of auctions are common: (1) a traditional auction and (2) a reverse auction.[26] Figure 5–6 shows how buyer and seller participants and price behavior differ by type of auction. Let's look at each auction type more closely to understand the implications of each for buyers and sellers.

In a **traditional auction** a seller puts an item up for sale and would-be buyers are invited to bid in competition with each other. As more would-be buyers become involved, there is an upward pressure on bid prices. Why? Bidding is sequential. Prospective buyers observe the bids of others and decide whether or not to increase the bid price. The auction ends when a single bidder remains and "wins" the item with its highest price. Traditional auctions are often used to dispose of excess merchandise. For example, Dell, Inc., sells surplus, refurbished, or closeout computer merchandise at its www.dellauction.com website.

A reverse auction works in the opposite direction from a traditional auction. In a **reverse auction**, a buyer communicates a need for a product or service and would-be suppliers are invited to bid in competition with each other. As more would-be suppliers become involved, there is a downward pressure on bid prices for the buyer's business. Why? Like traditional auctions, bidding is sequential and prospective suppliers observe the bids of others and decide whether or not to decrease the bid price. The auction ends when a single bidder remains and "wins" the business with its lowest price. Reverse auctions benefit organizational buyers by reducing the cost of their purchases. As an example, United Technologies Corp. estimates that it has saved $600 million on the purchase of $6 billion in supplies using online reverse auctions.[27]

learning review

5. What are e-marketplaces?

6. In general, which type of online auction creates upward pressure on bid prices and which type creates downward pressure on bid prices?

LEARNING OBJECTIVES REVIEW

LO1 *Distinguish among industrial, reseller, and government organizational markets.*

There are three different organizational markets: industrial, reseller, and government. Industrial firms in some way reprocess a product or service they buy before selling it to the next buyer. Resellers—wholesalers and retailers—buy physical products and resell them again without any reprocessing. Government agencies, at the federal, state, and local levels, buy goods and services for the constituents they serve. The North American Industry Classification System (NAICS) provides common industry definitions for Canada, Mexico, and the United States, which facilitates the measurement of economic activity for these three organizational markets.

LO2 *Describe the key characteristics of organizational buying that make it different from consumer buying.*

Seven major characteristics of organizational buying make it different from consumer buying. These include demand characteristics, the size of the order or purchase, the number of potential buyers, buying objectives, buying criteria, buyer–seller relationships and supply partnerships, and multiple buying influences within organizations. The organizational buying process itself is more formalized, more individuals are involved, supplier capability is more important, and the postpurchase evaluation behavior often includes performance of the supplier and the item purchased. Figure 5–4 details how the purchase decision process differs between a consumer and an organization. The example in Figure 5–3 describing the purchase of a machine vision system by an industrial firm illustrates the organizational buying process in greater depth.

LO3 *Explain how buying centers and buying situations influence organizational purchasing.*

Buying centers and buying situations have an important influence on organizational purchasing. A buying center consists of a group of individuals who share common goals, risks, and knowledge important to a purchase decision. A buyer or purchasing manager is almost always a member of a buying center. However, other individuals may affect organizational purchasing due to their unique roles in a purchase decision. Five specific roles that a person may play in a buying center include users, influencers, buyers, deciders, and gatekeepers. The specific buying situation will influence the number of people and the different roles played in a buying center. For a routine reorder of an item—a straight rebuy situation—a purchasing manager or buyer will typically act alone in making a purchasing decision. When an organization is a first-time purchaser of a product or service—a new buy situation—a buying center is enlarged and all five roles in a buying center often emerge. A modified rebuy buying situation lies between these two extremes.

LO4 *Recognize the importance and nature of online buying in organizational markets.*

Organizations dwarf consumers in terms of online transactions made and purchase volume. Online buying in organizational markets is popular for three reasons. First, organizational buyers depend on timely supplier information that describes product availability, technical specifications, application uses, price, and delivery schedules. This information can be conveyed quickly via Internet technology. Second, this technology substantially reduces buyer order processing costs. Third, business marketers have found that Internet technology can reduce marketing costs, particularly sales and advertising expense, and broaden their customer base. Two developments in online buying have been the creation of e-marketplaces and online auctions. E-marketplaces provide a technology trading platform and a centralized market for buyer–seller transactions and make possible the real-time exchange of information, money, products, and services. These e-marketplaces can be independent trading communities, such as PlasticsNet, or private exchanges, such as the Global Healthcare Exchange. Online traditional and reverse auctions represent a second major development. With traditional auctions, the highest-priced bidder "wins." Conversely, the lowest-priced bidder "wins" with reverse auctions.

FOCUSING ON KEY TERMS

business marketing p. 106
buy classes p. 114
buying center p. 113
derived demand p. 108

e-marketplaces p. 116
North American Industry Classification System (NAICS) p. 107
organizational buyers p. 106

organizational buying behavior p. 112
reverse auction p. 117
traditional auction p. 117

APPLYING MARKETING KNOWLEDGE

1 Describe the major differences among industrial firms, resellers, and government units in the United States.

2 List and discuss the key characteristics of organizational buying that make it different from consumer buying.

3 What is a buying center? Describe the roles assumed by people in a buying center and what useful questions should be raised to guide any analysis of the structure and behavior of a buying center.

4 A firm that is marketing multimillion-dollar wastewater treatment systems to cities has been unable to sell a new type of system. This setback has occurred even though the firm's systems are cheaper than competitive systems and meet U.S. Environmental Protection Agency (EPA) specifications. To date, the firm's marketing efforts have been directed to city purchasing departments and the various state EPAs to get on approved bidder's lists. Talks with city-employed personnel have indicated that the new system is very different from current systems and therefore city sanitary and sewer department engineers, directors of these two departments, and city council members are unfamiliar with the workings of the system. Consulting engineers, hired by cities to work on the engineering and design features of these systems and paid on a percentage of system cost, are also reluctant to favor the new system. (*a*) What roles do the various individuals play in the purchase process for a wastewater treatment system? (*b*) How could the firm improve the marketing effort behind its new system?

building your marketing plan

Your marketing plan may need an estimate of the size of the market potential or industry potential (see Chapter 8) for a particular product market in which you compete. Use these steps:

1 Define the product market precisely, such as ice cream.

2 Visit the NAICS website at www.census.gov.

3 Click "NAICS" and enter a keyword that describes your product market (e.g., ice cream).

4 Follow the instructions to find the specific NAICS code for your product market and the economic census data that detail the dollar sales and provide the estimate of market or industry potential.

video case 5   Trek: Building Better Bikes through Organizational Buying

QR 5–4 Trek Video Case

"Let me tell you a little bit about the history of Trek," says Mark Joslyn, vice president of human resources at Trek Bicycle Corporation. "It's a fantastic story," he continues proudly, "It's a story about a business that started in response to a market opportunity." That opportunity was to build bicycles with the highest-quality frames. In fact, Trek's mission was simple: "Build the best bikes in the world." To do this Trek needed to find the best raw materials from the best vendors. Michael Leighton, a Trek product manager, explains, "Our relationship with our vendors is incredibly important, and one of our recipes for success!"

THE COMPANY

Trek Bicycle was founded in 1976 by Richard Burke and Bevill Hogg. With just five employees they began manufacturing bicycles in a Wisconsin barn. From the beginning they targeted the high-quality, prestige segment of the bicycle market, using only the best materials and components for their bicycles. The first year they manufactured 900 custom-made bicycles which sold quickly.

Soon, Trek exceeded its manufacturing capacity. It built a new 26,000-square-foot factory and corporate headquarters to help meet growing demand.

Trek's focus on quality meant that it was very sensitive to the materials used to manufacture the bicycles. The first models, for example, used hand-brazed steel for the frames. Then, borrowing ideas from the aerospace industry, Trek soon began making frames out of bonded aluminum. Following on the success of its aluminum bicycles, Trek began manufacturing bicycles out of carbon fiber. The idea was to be "at the front of technology," explains Joslyn.

The company also expanded its product line. Its first bikes were designed to compete directly with Japanese and Italian bicycles, and included road racing models. In 1983 Trek manufactured its first mountain bike. In 1990 Trek developed a new category of bicycle—called a multitrack—that combined the speed of road bikes with the ruggedness of mountain bikes. The company also began manufacturing children's bikes, tandem bikes, BMX bikes, and models used by police departments and the U.S. Secret Service. In addition, it added a line of cycling apparel called Trek Wear and cycling accessories such as helmets. Recently, Trek also undertook an Eco Design initiative to build bicycles and parts that are "green" in

terms of the environmental impact of manufacturing them, how long they last, and how they can be recycled. To accommodate these production demands, Trek expanded its facilities two more times.

In 1997, Trek became a sponsor of American cyclist Lance Armstrong. In 1999, riding a Trek bicycle, Armstrong won his first Tour de France racing competition, and subsequently went on to win the race in seven consecutive years. As Trek's popularity increased, it began to expand outside of the United States. For example, the company acquired a Swiss bicycle company called Villiger and the oldest bicycle company in Germany, Diamant. It also expanded into China, opening two stores and signing deals with 20 Chinese distributors.

Today, Trek is one of the leading manufacturers of bicycles and cycling products, with more than $600 million in sales and 2,000 employees. Trek's products are now marketed through 1,700 dealers in North America and wholly owned subsidiaries in seven countries, and through distributors in 80 other countries. Its brands include Trek, Gary Fisher, Bontrager, and Klein. As a global company, Trek's mission has evolved also, and today the mission is to "help the world use the bicycle as a simple solution to complex problems." Trek employees believe that the bicycle is the most efficient form of human transportation and that it can combat climate change, ease urban congestion, and build human fitness. Their motto: "We believe in bikes." Mark Joslyn explains:

> In the world today we are faced with a number of challenges. We are faced with congestion, issues with mobility, issues with the environment, and quite frankly, issues with health. We believe that the bicycle is a simple solution to all of those things. We are clearly an alternative to other forms of transportation and that's evident in the way that people are embracing cycling not just for recreation but also for

transportation. And more and more, particularly in the United States, we are seeing people move to the bike as a way to get around and get to the places they need to ultimately get their life done.

ORGANIZATIONAL BUYING AT TREK

Trek's success at accomplishing its mission is the result of many important business practices, including its organizational buying process. The process begins when managers specify types of materials such as carbon fiber, component parts such as wheels and shifters, and finishing materials such as paint and decals needed to produce a Trek product. In addition, they specify quality requirements, sizing standards, and likely delivery schedules. According to Leighton, once the requirements are known, the next step is to "go to our buying center and say 'can you help us find this piece?'"

The buying center is the group of individuals who are responsible for finding the best suppliers and vendors for the organization's purchases. At Trek the buying center consists of a purchasing manager, buyers who identify domestic and international sources of materials and components, and representatives from research and development, production, and quality control. The communication between the product managers and the buying center is important. "I work very closely with our buying centers to ensure that we're partnering with vendors who can supply reliable quality, and they are actually the ones who, with our quality control team, go in and say 'yes this vendor is building product to the quality that meets Trek's standards,' and they also negotiate the pricing. Our buying center domestically is a relatively small team of people and they are focused on specific components."

When potential suppliers are identified, they are evaluated on four criteria—quality, delivery capabilities, price, and environmental impact of their production process. This allows Trek to compare alternative suppliers and to select the best match for Trek and its customers. Once a business is selected as a Trek supplier, it is continuously evaluated on elements of the four criteria. For example, current suppliers might receive scores on the number of defects in a large quantity of supplies, whether just-in-time orders made their deadlines, if target prices were maintained, and if recycled packaging was used. At Trek the tool that is used to record information about potential and existing suppliers is called a "white paper." Michael Leighton describes how they work: "Our buying center is tasked with developing what we call white papers. It's a sheet that managers can look at that shows issues and benefits related to working with these people." Every effort is made to develop long-term relationships with suppliers so that they become partners with Trek. These partnerships mean that Trek's success also contributes to the partner's success.

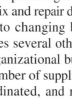

Trek's product managers and the buying center are involved in three types of organizational purchases. First, new buys are purchases that are made for the first time. Second, modified rebuys involve changing some aspect of a previously ordered product. Finally, straight rebuys are reorders of existing products from the list of acceptable suppliers. Leighton offers examples of each type of purchase at Trek:

> So, [for] a new buy, we work with our buying centers to find new products, something we've never done before whether it's a new saddle with a new material or a new technology that goes into the frame that damps vibration or gives a better ride. Another case might be electric bikes—maybe we are putting a motor in a bike, that's a new thing, so our buying center will help us go find those vendors. A modified rebuy is basically a saddle with a little bit different material but we are sharing some components of it, so the existing components of the saddle [are the same] . . . the cover is new, so it's a little bit different, but it's just the evolution of the product. A straight rebuy is looking at our strategic vision for the component further on down the line where we are just buying the same component and the volume goes up. We look at how can we make this a better business; can we save some money or can we make it more worth our while to keep buying the same product rather than buying something new.

While each of the types of purchases may occur frequently at Trek, the criteria that are used to select or evaluate a vendor may vary by the type of purchase and the type of product, making the buying process a dynamic challenge for managers.

ECO BUYING AND THE FUTURE AT TREK

One of Trek's criteria for evaluating existing and potential vendors is their environmental impact. Joslyn says it well: "We evaluate our vendors on many criteria including, increasingly, the elements that we would consider to be the 'green' part of their offering." For example, Trek recently selected a supplier that (1) owned a quarry for extracting material, (2) used its own manufacturing facilities, and (3) used natural gas instead of coal in its production process. This was appealing to Trek because it suggested that the supplier had a "thorough understanding" of the impact of the product on the environment from start to finish.

Trek's organizational buying reflects the growing importance of its "Eco" perspective. Its bikes are becoming "smarter" as it adds electric-assist components to help them become a practical transportation alternative. Its bikes are also becoming "greener" as more low-impact materials and components are used and as packaging size and weight are reduced. Trek is also addressing the issue of recycling by building the bikes to last longer, using its dealers to help recycle tires and tubes, and funding a nonprofit organization called Dream Bikes to teach youth to fix and repair donated bikes.

In addition to changing bikes and the way it makes them, Trek faces several other challenges as it strives to improve its organizational buying process. For example, the growing number of suppliers and vendors necessitates constant, coordinated, and real-time communication to ensure that all components are available when they are needed. In addition, changes in consumer interests and in economic conditions means that Trek must anticipate fluctuations in demand and make appropriate changes in order sizes and delivery dates. As Mark Joslyn explains, "Everything we do all the time can and should be improved. So the search for ideas inside of our business and outside of our business, always looking for ways that we can improve and bring new technology and new solutions to the marketplace, is just a core of who we are."

Questions

1 What is the role of the buying center at Trek? Who is likely to comprise the buying center in the decision to select a new supplier at Trek?

2 What selection criteria does Trek utilize when it selects a new supplier or evaluates an existing supplier?

3 How has Trek's interest in the environmental impact of its business influenced its organizational buying process?

4 Provide an example of each of the three buying situations—straight rebuy, modified rebuy, and new buy—at Trek.

Understanding and Reaching Global Consumers and Markets

6

LEARNING OBJECTIVES

After reading this chapter you should be able to:

LO1 Identify the major trends that have influenced world trade and global marketing.

LO2 Identify the environmental forces that shape global marketing efforts.

LO3 Name and describe the alternative approaches companies use to enter global markets.

LO4 Explain the distinction between standardization and customization when companies craft worldwide marketing programs.

HOW DELL, INC., BUILT A BILLION-DOLLAR BUSINESS IN INDIA

Why did Dell, Inc., embark on a bold global growth initiative in 2007? Simply put, "Our success was going to be largely dependent on our ability to expand globally," acknowledged Steve Felice, former president of Dell Asia-Pacific and Japan.

Dell's global initiative focused on emerging economies in Asia, Africa, and Latin America. Compared with mature economies in North America and Western Europe, emerging economies offered significant growth potential, according to Michael Dell, Dell's founder and chief executive officer. Today, India is one of the fastest-growing markets for Dell, Inc., and posts annual sales approaching $2 billion.

Dell's global initiative included a bold departure from its prior product development practices and sales, services, and distribution strategy. Prior to its global initiative, Dell designed products for global requirements and distributed the same product globally. The company now designs low-cost notebook, laptop, and desktop personal computers for customers in China, India, and other emerging economies.

Dell's signature direct sales, service, and distribution strategy also changed. The company built its U.S. business with telephone- and Internet-based sales without retailers. In emerging economies and India, however, customers prefer to see, touch, and use a personal computer before they buy. In response, Dell used individual sales affiliates who reached out to customers in person and gave them a first-hand product experience at their doorstep. At the same time, Dell opened 38 exclusive stores across India and joined hands with Indian chain retailers such as Croma and eZone for a shop-in-a-shop counter for its products. Dell backed this hybrid retail model with extended onsite service (technicians coming to individuals' homes) in 650 cities for retail and small business customers as well.

Advertising followed, with Dell opting for real-life entrepreneurs to endorse its products. The "Take Your Own Path" advertising campaign, shown on the facing page, proved to be highly effective. Dell's success in India illustrates the importance of understanding global customers and reaching them by adapting to their needs.[1]

This chapter describes today's complex and dynamic global marketing environment. It begins with a description of a borderless economic world. Attention is then focused on prominent cultural, economic, and political-regulatory factors that present both an opportunity and a challenge for global marketers. Four major global market entry strategies are then detailed. Finally, the task of designing, implementing, and evaluating worldwide marketing programs for companies such as Dell, Inc., is described.

MARKETING IN A BORDERLESS ECONOMIC WORLD

The dollar value of world trade has more than doubled in the past decade, despite the recent recession. Manufactured products and commodities account for 75 percent of world trade. Service industries, including telecommunications, transportation, insurance, education, banking, and tourism, represent the other 25 percent of world trade. Four trends have significantly affected world trade and global marketing:

> Trend 1: Decline of economic protectionism by individual countries.
>
> Trend 2: Rise of economic integration and free trade among nations.
>
> Trend 3: Global competition among global companies for global consumers.
>
> Trend 4: Emergence of a networked global marketspace.

Decline of Economic Protectionism

protectionism

The practice of shielding one or more industries within a country's economy from foreign competition through the use of tariffs or quotas.

tariff

A government tax on goods or services entering a country, primarily serving to raise prices on imports.

Protectionism is the practice of shielding one or more industries within a country's economy from foreign competition, usually through the use of tariffs or quotas. The economic argument for protectionism is that it preserves jobs, protects a nation's political security, discourages economic dependency on other countries, and encourages the development of domestic industries. Read the Making Responsible Decisions box and decide for yourself if protectionism has an ethical dimension.

A **tariff** is a tax on goods or services entering a country. Because a tariff raises the price of an imported product, tariffs give a price advantage to domestic products competing in the same market. The effect of tariffs on world trade and consumer prices is substantial.[2] Consider U.S. rice exports to Japan. The U.S. Rice Millers' Association claims that if the Japanese rice market were opened to imports by lowering tariffs, lower prices would save Japanese consumers $6 billion annually, and the United States would gain a large share of the Japanese rice market. Similarly, tariffs imposed on bananas by Western European countries cost consumers $2 billion a year, and U.S. consumers pay $5 billion annually for tarriffs on imported shoes.

quota

A restriction placed on the amount of a product allowed to enter or leave a country.

A **quota** is a restriction placed on the amount of a product allowed to enter or leave a country. By limiting the supply of foreign products, an import quota helps domestic industries retain a certain percentage of the domestic market. For consumers, however, the limited supply may mean higher prices for domestic products. The best-known quota concerns the limits of foreign automobile sales in many countries. Less visible quotas apply to the importation of mushrooms, heavy motorcycles, textiles, color TVs, and sugar. For example, U.S. sugar import quotas have existed for over 70 years and preserve about half of the U.S. sugar market for domestic producers. American consumers pay almost $3 billion annually in extra food costs because of this quota.

World Trade Organization

Institution that sets rules governing trade between its members through a panel of trade experts.

Both tariffs and quotas discourage world trade (see Figure 6–1). As a result, the major industrialized nations of the world formed the **World Trade Organization** (WTO) in 1995 to address a broad array of world trade issues. The 153 member countries of the WTO, which includes the United States, account for more than 97 percent of world trade.[3] The WTO sets rules governing trade between its members through panels of trade experts who decide on trade disputes between members and issue binding decisions. The WTO reviews more than 200 disputes each year.

Rise of Economic Integration

In recent years, a number of countries with similar economic goals have formed transnational trade groups or signed trade agreements for the purpose of promoting free trade among member nations and enhancing their individual economies. Two of the best-known examples are the European Union (or simply EU) and the North American Free Trade Agreement (NAFTA).

Making Responsible Decisions > > > > > > > > > > ethics

Global Ethics and Global Economics—The Case of Protectionism

World trade benefits from free and fair trade among nations. Nevertheless, governments of many countries continue to use tariffs and quotas to protect their various domestic industries. Why? Protectionism earns profits for domestic producers and tariff revenue for the government. There is a cost, however. Protectionist policies cost Japanese consumers between $75 billion and $110 billion annually. U.S. consumers pay about $70 billion each year in higher prices because of tariffs and other protective restrictions.

Sugar and textile import quotas in the United States, automobile and banana import tariffs in European countries, shoe and automobile

tire import tariffs in the United States, beer import tariffs in Canada, and rice import tariffs in Japan protect domestic industries but also interfere with world trade for these products. Regional trade agreements, such as those found in the provisions of the European Union and the North American Free Trade Agreement, may also pose a situation whereby member nations can obtain preferential treatment in quotas and tariffs but nonmember nations cannot.

Protectionism, in its many forms, raises an interesting global ethical question. Is protectionism, no matter how applied, an ethical practice?

European Union The European Union consists of 27 member countries that have eliminated most barriers to the free flow of goods, services, capital, and labor across their borders (see Figure 6–2 on the next page).[4] This single market houses more than 500 million consumers with a combined gross domestic product larger than that of the United States. In addition, 17 countries have adopted a common currency called the *euro*. Adoption of the euro has been a boon to electronic commerce in the EU by eliminating the need to continually monitor currency exchange rates.

The EU creates abundant marketing opportunities because firms no longer find it necessary to market their products and services on a nation-by-nation basis. Rather, pan-European marketing strategies are possible due to greater uniformity in product

FIGURE 6–1

How does protectionism affect world trade? Protectionism hinders world trade through tariff and quota policies of individual countries. Tariffs increase prices and quotas limit supply.

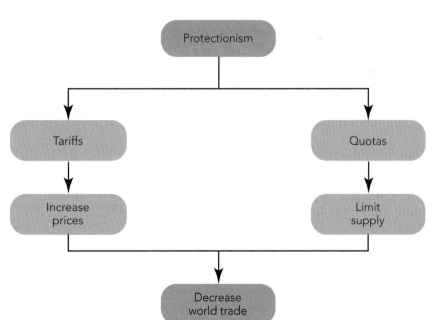

FIGURE 6–2
The European Union in
mid-2012 consists of
27 countries with more than
500 million consumers.

European Union
www.europa.eu.int

and packaging standards; fewer regulatory restrictions on transportation, advertising, and promotion imposed by countries; and the removal of most tariffs that affect pricing practices. For example, Colgate-Palmolive Company now markets its Colgate toothpaste with one formula and package across EU countries at one price. Black & Decker—the maker of electrical hand tools, appliances, and other consumer products—now produces 8, not 20, motor sizes for the European market, resulting in production and marketing cost savings. These practices were previously impossible with different government and trade regulations. Europeanwide distribution from fewer locations is also feasible given open borders. French tire maker Michelin has closed 180 of its European distribution centers and now uses just 20 to serve all EU countries.

North American Free Trade Agreement   The North American Free Trade Agreement (NAFTA) lifted many trade barriers between Canada, Mexico, and the United States and created a marketplace with more than 450 million consumers.[5] NAFTA has stimulated trade flows among member nations as well as cross-border retailing, manufacturing, and investment. For example, NAFTA paved the way for Walmart to move to Mexico, Target to move to Canada, and Mexican supermarket giant Gigante to move into the United States. Whirlpool Corporation's Canadian subsidiary stopped making washing machines in Canada and moved that operation to Ohio. Whirlpool then shifted the production of kitchen ranges and compact dryers to Canada. Ford invested $60 million in its Mexico City manufacturing plant to produce smaller cars and light trucks for global sales.

A New Reality: Global Competition among Global Companies for Global Consumers

The emergence of a largely borderless economic world has created a new reality for marketers of all shapes and sizes. Today, world trade is driven by global competition among global companies for global consumers.

Global Competition **Global competition** exists when firms originate, produce, and market their products and services worldwide. The automobile, pharmaceutical, apparel, electronics, aerospace, and telecommunication fields represent well-known industries with sellers and buyers on every continent. Other industries that are increasingly global in scope include soft drinks, cosmetics, ready-to-eat cereals, snack chips, and retailing.

Global competition broadens the competitive landscape for marketers. The familiar "cola war" waged by Pepsi-Cola and Coca-Cola in the United States has been repeated around the world, including in India, China, and Argentina. Procter & Gamble's Pampers and Kimberly-Clark's Huggies have taken their disposable diaper rivalry from the United States to Western Europe. Boeing and Europe's Airbus vie for lucrative commercial aircraft contracts on virtually every continent.

Global Companies Three types of companies populate and compete in the global marketplace: (1) international firms, (2) multinational firms, and (3) transnational firms.[6] All three employ people in different countries, and many have administrative, marketing, and manufacturing operations (often called *divisions* or *subsidiaries*) around the world. However, a firm's orientation toward and strategy for global markets and marketing defines the type of company it is or attempts to be.

An *international firm* engages in trade and marketing in different countries as an extension of the marketing strategy in its home country. Generally, these firms market their existing products and services in other countries the same way they do in their home country. Avon, for example, successfully distributes its product line through direct selling in Asia, Europe, and South America, employing virtually the same marketing strategy used in the United States.

Pepsi-Cola, now available in about 160 countries and territories, accounts for a quarter of all soft drinks sold internationally. This Brazilian ad—"How to make jeans last 10 years"—features the popular Diet Pepsi brand targeted at weight-conscious consumers.

PepsiCo, Inc.
www.pepsico.com

A *multinational firm* views the world as consisting of unique parts and markets to each part differently. Multinationals use a **multidomestic marketing strategy**, which means that they have as many different product variations, brand names, and advertising programs as countries in which they do business. For example, Lever Europe, a division of Unilever, markets its fabric softener known as Snuggle in the United States in 10 European countries under seven brand names, including Kuschelweich in Germany, Coccolino in Italy, and Mimosin in France. These products have different packages, different advertising programs, and occasionally different formulas. Procter & Gamble markets Mr. Clean, its popular multipurpose cleaner, in North America and Asia. But you won't necessarily find the Mr. Clean brand in other parts of the world. In many Latin American countries, Mr. Clean is Mastro Limpio. Mr. Clean is Mr. Proper in most parts of Europe, Africa, and the Middle East.

A *transnational firm* views the world as one market and emphasizes cultural similarities across countries or universal consumer needs and wants more than differences. Transnational marketers employ a **global marketing strategy**—the practice of standardizing marketing activities when there are cultural similarities and adapting them when cultures differ. This approach benefits marketers by allowing them to realize economies of scale from their production and marketing activities.

Global marketing strategies are popular among many business-to-business marketers such as Caterpillar and Komatsu (heavy construction equipment) and Texas Instruments, Intel, and Hitachi (semiconductors). Consumer goods marketers such as Timex, Seiko, and Swatch (watches), Coca-Cola and Pepsi-Cola (cola soft drinks), Mattel and Lego (children's toys), Nike and Adidas (athletic shoes), Gillette (personal care products), L'Oréal and Shiseido (cosmetics), and McDonald's and Kentucky Fried Chicken (quick-service restaurants) successfully execute this strategy.

Each of these companies markets a **global brand**—a brand marketed under the same name in multiple countries with similar and centrally coordinated marketing programs.[7] Global brands have the same product formulation or service concept, deliver the same benefits to consumers, and use consistent advertising across multiple countries and cultures. This isn't to say that global brands are not sometimes tailored to specific cultures or countries. However, adaptation is used only when necessary to better connect the brand to consumers in different markets.

Consider McDonald's.[8] This global marketer has adapted its proven formula of "food, fun, and families" across 119 countries on six continents. Although the Golden Arches and Ronald McDonald appear worldwide, McDonald's tailors other aspects of its marketing program. It serves beer in Germany, wine in France, and coconut, mango, and tropical mint shakes in Hong Kong. Hamburgers are made with different meat and spices in Japan, Thailand, India, and the Philippines. But McDonald's world-famous french fry is standardized. Its french fry in Beijing, China, tastes like the one in Paris, France, which tastes like the one in your neighborhood.

Global Consumers Global competition among global companies often focuses on the identification and pursuit of global consumers as described in the Marketing Matters box.[9] **Global consumers** consist of consumer groups living in many countries or regions of the world who have similar needs or seek similar features and benefits from products or services. Evidence suggests the presence of a global middle-income class, a youth market, and an elite segment, each consuming or using a common assortment of products and services, regardless of geographic location.

A variety of companies have capitalized on the global consumer. Whirlpool, Sony, and IKEA have benefited from the growing global middle-income class desire for kitchen appliances, consumer electronics, and home furnishings, respectively. Levi Strauss, Nike, Adidas, Coca-Cola, and Apple have tapped the global youth market. DeBeers, Chanel, Gucci, Rolls-Royce, and Sotheby's and Christie's, the world's largest fine art and antique auction houses, cater to the elite segment for luxury goods worldwide.

Marketing Matters > > > > > customer value

The Global Teenager—A Market of 2 Billion Voracious Consumers with $250 Billion to Spend

The "global teenager" market consists of 2 billion 13- to 19-year-olds in Europe, North and South America, and industrialized nations of Asia and the Pacific Rim who have experienced intense exposure to television (MTV broadcasts in 169 countries in 28 languages), movies, travel, the Internet, and global advertising by companies such as Apple, Sony, Nike, and Coca-Cola. The similarities among teens across these countries are greater than their differences. For example, a global study of middle-class teenagers' rooms in 25 industrialized countries indicated it was difficult, if not impossible, to tell whether the rooms were in Los Angeles, Mexico City, Tokyo, Rio de Janeiro, Sydney, or Paris. Why? Teens spend $250 billion annually for a common gallery of products: Nintendo video games, Tommy Hilfiger apparel, Levi's blue

jeans, Nike and Adidas athletic shoes, Swatch watches, Apple iPods, Benetton apparel, and Cover Girl cosmetics (shown in the photo).

Teenagers around the world appreciate fashion and music and desire novelty and trendier designs and images. They also acknowledge an Americanization of fashion and culture based on another study of 6,500 teens in 26 countries. When asked what country had the most influence on their attitudes and purchase behavior, 54 percent of teens from the United States, 87 percent of those from Latin America, 80 percent of the Europeans, and 80 percent of those from Asia named the United States. This phenomenon has not gone unnoticed by parents. As one parent in India said, "Now the youngsters dress, talk, and eat like Americans."

Emergence of a Networked Global Marketspace

The use of Internet technology as a tool for exchanging goods, services, and information on a global scale is the fourth trend affecting world trade. Almost 3 billion businesses, educational institutions, government agencies, and households worldwide are expected to have Internet access by 2015. The broad reach of this technology suggests that its potential for promoting world trade is huge.

The promise of a networked global marketspace is that it enables the exchange of goods, services, and information from companies *anywhere* to customers *anywhere* at *any time* and at a lower cost. This promise has become a reality for buyers and sellers in industrialized countries that possess the telecommunications infrastructure necessary to support Internet technology.

Marketers recognize that the networked global marketspace offers unprecedented access to prospective buyers on every continent. Companies that have successfully

Sweden's IKEA is capitalizing on the home-improvement trend sweeping through China. The home-furnishings retailer is courting young Chinese consumers who are eagerly updating their housing with modern, colorful but inexpensive furniture. IKEA entered China in 1998. The company expects to have at least 18 stores open in China by 2015.

IKEA
www.ikea.com

Nestlé is an innovator in customizing website content and communicating with consumers in their native languages. The website shown here is for Hungary.

Nestlé Company
www.nestle.com

capitalized on this access manage multiple country and language websites that customize content and communicate with consumers in their native tongue. Nestlé, the world's largest packaged food manufacturer, coffee roaster, and chocolate maker, is a case in point. The company operates 65 individual country websites in more than 20 languages that span five continents.

---

learning review

1. What is protectionism?

2. The North American Free Trade Agreement was designed to promote free trade among which countries?

3. What is the difference between a multidomestic marketing strategy and a global marketing strategy?

A GLOBAL ENVIRONMENTAL SCAN

Global companies conduct continuing environmental scans of the five sets of environmental factors described earlier in Figure 3–1 (social, economic, technological, competitive, and regulatory forces). This section focuses on three kinds of uncontrollable environmental variables—cultural, economic, and political-regulatory—that affect global marketing practices in strikingly different ways than those in domestic markets.

Cultural Diversity

cross-cultural analysis
The study of similarities and differences among consumers in two or more nations or societies.

values
A society's personally or socially preferable modes of conduct or states of existence that tend to persist over time.

Marketers must be sensitive to the cultural underpinnings of different societies if they are to initiate and consummate mutually beneficial exchange relationships with global consumers. A necessary step in this process is **cross-cultural analysis**, which involves the study of similarities and differences among consumers in two or more nations or societies.[10] A thorough cross-cultural analysis involves an understanding of and an appreciation for the values, customs, symbols, and language of other societies.

Values A society's **values** represent personally or socially preferable modes of conduct or states of existence that tend to persist over time. Understanding and

Chicken Maharaja Mac™

I'M THE KING OF GOOD TASTE!!!

McDonald's sells its popular Maharaja Mac in India. Read the text to discover its ingredients.

customs

Norms and expectations about the way people do things in a specific country.

Foreign Corrupt Practices Act (1977)

A law that makes it a crime for U.S. corporations to bribe an official of a foreign government or political party to obtain or retain business.

cultural symbols

Things that represent ideas or concepts in a specific culture.

Cultural symbols evoke deep feelings. What cultural lesson did Coca-Cola executives learn when they used the Eiffel Tower and the Parthenon in a global advertising campaign? Read the text to find the answer.

working with these aspects of a society are important factors in global marketing. For example,

- McDonald's does not sell beef hamburgers in its restaurants in India because the cow is considered sacred by almost 85 percent of the population. Instead, McDonald's sells the Maharaja Mac: two all-chicken patties, special sauce, lettuce, cheese, pickles, onions on a sesame-seed bun.
- Germans have not been overly receptive to the use of credit cards such as Visa or MasterCard and installment debt to purchase goods and services. Indeed, the German word for debt, *Schuld*, is the same as the German word for guilt.

Cultural values become apparent in the personal values of individuals that affect their attitudes and beliefs and the importance assigned to specific behaviors and attributes of goods and services. These personal values affect consumption-specific values, such as the use of installment debt by Germans, and product-specific values, such as the importance assigned to credit card interest rates.

Customs **Customs** refer to the normal and expected ways of doing things in a specific country. Clearly customs can vary significantly from country to country. Some customs may seem unusual to Americans. Consider, for example, that in France, men wear more than twice the number of cosmetics than women do and that Japanese women give Japanese men chocolates on Valentine's Day.

The custom of giving token business gifts is popular in many countries where they are expected and accepted. However, bribes, kickbacks, and payoffs offered to entice someone to commit an illegal or improper act on behalf of the giver for economic gain is considered corrupt in any culture. The prevalence of bribery in global marketing has led to an agreement among the world's major exporting nations to make bribery of foreign government officials a criminal offense. This agreement is patterned after the **Foreign Corrupt Practices Act (1977)**, as amended by the *International Anti-Dumping and Fair Competition Act* (1998). These acts make it a crime for U.S. corporations to bribe an official of a foreign government or political party to obtain or retain business in a foreign country. For example, the German engineering company Siemens AG paid an $800 million fine for $1 billion in alleged bribes of government officials around the globe.[11]

Cultural Symbols **Cultural symbols** are things that represent ideas and concepts. Symbols and symbolism play an important role in cross-cultural analysis because different cultures attach different meanings to things. By cleverly using cultural symbols, global marketers can tie positive symbolism to their products,

services, and brands to enhance their attractiveness to consumers. However, improper use of symbols can spell disaster. A culturally sensitive global marketer will know that:[12]

- North Americans are superstitious about the number 13, and Japanese feel the same way about the number 4. *Shi*, the Japanese word for four, is also the word for death. Knowing this, Tiffany & Company sells its fine glassware and china in sets of five, not four, in Japan.
- "Thumbs-up" is a positive sign in the United States. However, in Russia and Poland, this gesture has an offensive meaning when the palm of the hand is shown, as AT&T learned. The company reversed the gesture depicted in ads, showing the back of the hand, not the palm.

Cultural symbols evoke deep feelings. Consider how executives at Coca-Cola Company's Italian office learned this lesson. In a series of advertisements directed at Italian vacationers, the Eiffel Tower, the Empire State Building, and the Tower of Pisa were turned into the familiar Coca-Cola bottle. However, when the white marble columns in the Parthenon that crowns the Acropolis in Athens were turned into Coca-Cola bottles, the Greeks were outraged. Greeks refer to the Acropolis as the "holy rock," and a government official said the Parthenon is an "international symbol of excellence" and that "whoever insults the Parthenon insults international culture." Coca-Cola apologized for the ad.[13]

Language   Global marketers should know not only the native tongues of countries in which they market their products and services but also the nuances and idioms of a language. Even though about 100 official languages exist in the world, anthropologists estimate that at least 3,000 different languages are spoken. There are 20 official languages spoken in the European Union, and Canada has two official languages (English and French). Seventeen major languages are spoken in India alone.

Microsoft operates in over 100 countries and more often than not speaks to its customers in their own language. Its "I'm a PC, and Windows 7 was my idea" copy theme uses the same imagery around the world but has been translated and adapted for markets outside the United States. For example, the French version says, "I said I wanted a more intuitive PC, and there it is, more intuitive. No one can refuse me anything." Why? "I'm a PC" doesn't make much sense outside the United States. Read the text to learn how language affects global marketing.

Microsoft Corporation
www.microsoft.com

What does the Nestlé Kit Kat bar have to do with academic achievement in Japan? Read the text to find out.

Nestlé Company
www.nestle.com

---

back translation
Retranslating a word or phrase back into the original language using a different interpreter to catch errors.

QR 6–2
Nestlé Japan
Video

The Coca-Cola Company has made a huge financial investment in bottling and distribution facilities in Russia.

The Coca-Cola Company
www.thecoca-colacompany
.com

English, French, and Spanish are the principal languages used in global diplomacy and commerce. However, the best language to use to communicate with consumers is their own, as any seasoned global marketer will attest to. Unintended meanings of brand names and messages have ranged from the absurd to the obscene:

- When the advertising agency responsible for launching Procter & Gamble's successful Pert shampoo in Canada realized that the name means "lost" in French, it substituted the brand name Pret, which means "ready."
- The Vicks brand name common in the United States is German slang for sexual intimacy; therefore, Vicks is called Wicks in Germany.

Experienced global marketers use **back translation**, where a translated word or phrase is retranslated into the original language by a different interpreter to catch errors. For example, IBM's first Japanese translation of its "Solution for a small planet" advertising message yielded "Answers that make people smaller." The error was corrected. Nevertheless, unintended translations can produce favorable results. Consider Kit Kat bars marketed by Nestlé worldwide. Kit Kat is pronounced "kitto katsu" in Japanese, which roughly translates to "Surely win." Japanese teens eat Kit Kat bars for good luck, particularly when taking crucial school exams.[14]

Economic Considerations

Global marketing is also affected by economic considerations. Therefore, a scan of the global marketplace should include (1) an assessment of the economic infrastructure in these countries, (2) measurement of consumer income in different countries, and (3) recognition of a country's currency exchange rates.

Economic Infrastructure The *economic infrastructure*—a country's communications, transportation, financial, and distribution systems—is a critical consideration in determining whether to try to market to a country's consumers and organizations. Parts of the infrastructure that North Americans or Western Europeans take for granted can be huge problems elsewhere—not only in developing nations but even in Eastern Europe, the Indian subcontinent, and China, where such an infrastructure is assumed to be in place. For example, PepsiCo has invested $1.5 billion in transportation, manufacturing, and distribution systems in China and India since 2010.

The communication infrastructures in these countries also differ. This infrastructure includes telecommunication systems and networks in use, such as telephones, cable television, broadcast radio and television, computer, satellite, and wireless telephone. In general, the communication infrastructure in many developing countries is limited or antiquated compared with that of developed countries.

Even the financial and legal system can cause problems. Formal operating procedures among financial institutions and the notion of private property is still limited. As a consequence, it is estimated that two-thirds of the commercial transactions in Russia involve nonmonetary forms of payment. The legal red tape involved in obtaining titles to buildings and land for manufacturing, wholesaling, and retailing operations also has been a huge problem. Still, the Coca-Cola Company plans to invest $1 billion by 2015 for bottling facilities in Russia, and Frito-Lay spent $60 million to build a plant outside Moscow to make Lay's potato chips.

Consumer Income and Purchasing Power A global marketer selling consumer goods must also consider what the average per capita or household income is among a country's consumers and how the income is distributed to determine a nation's purchasing power. Per capita income varies greatly between nations. Average yearly per capita income in EU countries is about $33,000 and is less than $500 in some developing countries such as Liberia. A country's income distribution is important because it gives a more reliable picture of a country's purchasing power. Generally, as the proportion of middle-income households in a country increases, the greater a nation's purchasing capability tends to be.

Seasoned global marketers recognize that people in developing countries often have government subsidies for food, housing, and health care that supplement their income. So people with seemingly low incomes are actually promising customers for a variety of products. For instance, a consumer in South Asia earning the equivalent of $250 per year can afford Gillette razors. When that consumer's income rises to $1,000, a Sony television becomes affordable, and a new Volkswagen or Nissan can be bought with an annual income of $10,000. In developing countries of Eastern Europe, a $1,000 annual income makes a refrigerator affordable, and $2,000 brings an automatic washer within reach—good news for Whirlpool, the world's leading manufacturer and marketer of major home appliances.

Efforts to raise household incomes in developing countries is evident in the popularity of microfinance. **Microfinance** is the practice of offering small, collateral-free loans to

microfinance

The practice of offering small, collateral-free loans to individuals who otherwise would not have access to the capital necessary to begin small businesses or other income-generating activities.

Levi Strauss & Co. launched its Denizen brand jeans in China in late 2010. Created for teens and young adults in emerging markets who cannot afford Levi-branded jeans, Denizen will eventually be sold worldwide, primarily in developing countries in Latin America and Africa.

Levi Strauss & Co.
www.levistrauss.com

QR 6–3
Denizen Video

Hindustan Lever's Project Shakti initiative in India has resulted in over 45,000 women entrepreneurs selling Lever products in 135,000 villages—with more to come.

Unilever
www.unilever .com

currency exchange rate
The price of one country's currency expressed in terms of another country's currency.

individuals who otherwise would not have access to the capital necessary to begin small businesses or other income-generating activities. An example of microfinance is found in Hindustan Lever's Project Shakti initiative in India. The company realized it could not sell to the rural poor in India unless it found ways to distribute its products such as soap, shampoos, and laundry detergents. Lever provided start-up loans to women to buy stocks of products to sell to local villagers. Today, over 45,000 women entrepreneurs sell Lever products to 600,000 Indian consumers in 135,000 villages in India. Equally important, these women now have a source of income, whereas before they had nothing.[15]

Income growth in developing countries of Asia, Latin America, and Eastern Europe is expected to stimulate world trade. The number of consumers in these countries earning the equivalent of $10,000 per year is expected to surpass the number of consumers in the United States, Japan, and Western Europe combined by 2015. By one estimate, half of the world's population has now achieved "middle-class" status.[16] For this reason, developing countries represent a prominent marketing opportunity for global companies.

Currency Exchange Rates A **currency exchange rate** is the price of one country's currency expressed in terms of another country's currency. As economic conditions change, so can the exchange rate between countries. One day the U.S. dollar may be worth 121.7 Japanese yen or 1.5 Swiss francs. But the next day it may be worth 120.5 Japanese yen or 1.3 Swiss francs.

Fluctuations in exchange rates among the world's currencies can affect everyone from international tourists to global companies. For example, when the U.S. dollar is "strong" against the euro, it takes fewer dollars to purchase goods in the EU. As a result, more U.S. tourists will travel to Europe. This is great news for Europe's travel industry, but bad news for European consumers who want to buy U.S. goods, as they will have to pay more for them. And they may choose not to buy. Mattel learned this lesson the hard way in the late 1990s. The company was unable to sell its popular Holiday Barbie doll and accessories in many international markets because they were too expensive. Why? Barbie prices, expressed in U.S. dollars, were set without regard for how they would translate into other currencies and were too high for many foreign buyers.[17]

Political-Regulatory Climate

The political and regulatory climate for marketing in a country or region of the world means not only identifying the current climate but determining how long a favorable or unfavorable climate will last. An assessment of a country or regional political-regulatory climate includes an analysis of its political stability and trade regulations.

Political Stability Trade among nations or regions depends on political stability. Billions of dollars have been lost in the Middle East and Africa as a result of internal political strife, terrorism, and war. Losses such as these encourage careful selection of politically stable countries and regions of the world for trade.

Political stability in a country is affected by numerous factors, including a government's orientation toward foreign companies and trade with other countries. These factors combine to create a political climate that is favorable or unfavorable for marketing and financial investment in a country or region of the world.

Trade Regulations Countries have rules that govern business practices within their borders. These rules often serve as trade barriers.[18] For example, Japan has some 11,000 trade regulations. Japanese car safety rules effectively require all automobile replacement parts to be Japanese and not American or European; public health rules make it illegal to sell aspirin or cold medicine without a pharmacist present. The Malaysian government has regulations stating that "advertisements must not project or promote an excessively aspirational lifestyle," Greece bans toy advertising, Sweden outlaws all advertisements to children, and Saudi Arabia bans Mattel's Barbie dolls because they are a symbol of Western decadence.

learning review

4. Cross-cultural analysis involves the study of _____.

5. When foreign currencies can buy more U.S. dollars, are U.S. products more or less expensive for a foreign consumer?

COMPARING GLOBAL MARKET-ENTRY STRATEGIES

Once a company has decided to enter the global marketplace, it must select a means of market entry. Four general options exist: (1) exporting, (2) licensing, (3) joint venture, and (4) direct investment.[19] As Figure 6–3 demonstrates, the amount of financial commitment, risk, marketing control, and profit potential increases as the firm moves from exporting to direct investment.

Exporting

exporting

Producing goods in one country and selling them in another country.

Exporting is producing goods in one country and selling them in another country. This entry option allows a company to make the least number of changes in terms of its product, its organization, and even its corporate goals. Host countries usually do not like this practice because it provides less local employment than under alternative means of entry.

Indirect exporting is when a firm sells its domestically produced goods in a foreign country through an intermediary. It has the least amount of commitment and risk but will probably return the least profit. Indirect exporting is ideal for a company that has no overseas contacts but wants to market abroad. The intermediary is often a distributer that has the marketing know-how and resources necessary for the effort to succeed.

FIGURE 6–3

A firm's profit potential and control over marketing activities increase as it moves from exporting to direct investment as a global market-entry strategy. But so does a firm's financial commitment and risk. Firms often engage in exporting, licensing, and joint ventures before pursuing a direct investment strategy.

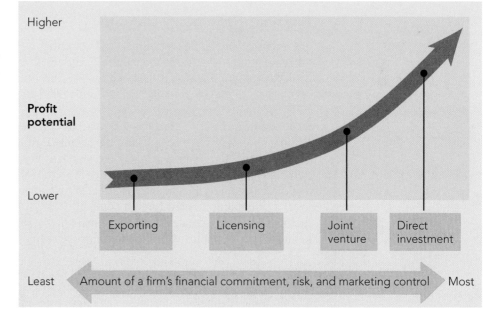

How does a medium-sized U.S. cosmetics firm sell 1.5 million tubes of lipstick in Japan annually? Fran Wilson Creative Cosmetics can attribute its success to a top-quality product, effective advertising, and a novel export marketing program. The firm's Moodmatcher lip coloring comes in green, orange, silver, black, and six other hues that change to a shade of pink, coral, or red, depending on a woman's chemistry when it's applied.

The company does not sell to department stores. According to a company spokesperson, "Shiseido and Kanebo (two large Japanese cosmetics firms) keep all the other Japanese or import brands out of the major department stores." Rather, the company sells its Moodmatcher lipstick through a network of Japanese distributors that reach Japan's 40,000 beauty salons.

The result? The company, with its savvy Japanese distributors, accounted for 20 percent of the lipsticks exported annually to Japan by U.S. cosmetics companies.

Fran Wilson Creative Cosmetics uses an indirect exporting approach to sell its products in Japan. Read the Marketing Matters box to find out how this innovative marketer and its Japanese distributors sell 20 percent of the lipsticks exported to Japan by U.S. cosmetics companies.[20]

Direct exporting is when a firm sells its domestically produced goods in a foreign country without intermediaries. Most companies become involved in direct exporting when they believe their volume of sales will be sufficiently large and easy to obtain so that they do not require intermediaries. For example, the exporter may be approached by foreign buyers that are willing to contract for a large volume of purchases. Direct exporting involves more risk for the company than indirect exporting but also opens the door to increased profits. The Boeing Company applies a direct exporting approach. Boeing is the world's largest aerospace company and the largest U.S. exporter.

Even though exporting is commonly employed by large firms, it is the prominent global market-entry strategy among small- and medium-sized companies. For example, 60 percent of U.S. firms exporting products have fewer than 100 employees. These firms account for about 33 percent of total U.S. merchandise exports.[21]

Licensing

Under *licensing*, a company offers the right to a trademark, patent, trade secret, or other similarly valued item of intellectual property in return for a royalty or a fee. The advantages to the company granting the license are low risk and a capital-free entry into a foreign country. The licensee gains information that allows it to start with a competitive advantage, and the foreign country gains employment by having the product manufactured locally. For instance, Yoplait yogurt is licensed from Sodima, a French cooperative, by General Mills for sales in the United States.

There are some serious drawbacks to this mode of entry, however. The licensor forgoes control of its product and reduces the potential profits gained from it. In addition, while the relationship lasts, the licensor may be creating its own competition. Some

Strauss Group's joint venture with PepsiCo markets Frito-Lay's Cheetos, Ruffles, Doritos, and other snacks in Israel.

Strauss Group
www.strauss-group.com

Nestlé has made a sizable direct investment in ice cream manufacturing in China to produce its global brands such as Drumstick. Nestlé operates 26 factories in China.

Nestlé Company
www.nestle.com

licensees are able to modify the product somehow and enter the market with product and marketing knowledge gained at the expense of the company that got them started. To offset this disadvantage, many companies strive to stay innovative so that the licensee remains dependent on them for improvements and successful operation. Finally, should the licensee prove to be a poor choice, the name or reputation of the company may be harmed.

A variation of licensing is *franchising*. Franchising is one of the fastest-growing market-entry strategies. More than 75,000 franchises of U.S. firms are located in countries throughout the world. Franchises include soft-drink, motel, retailing, fast-food, and car rental operations and a variety of business services. McDonald's is a premier global franchiser. With some 18,500 units outside the United States, about 66 percent of McDonald's sales come from non-U.S. operations.[22]

Joint Venture

When a foreign company and a local firm invest together to create a local business, it is called a **joint venture**. These two companies share the ownership, control, and profits of the new company. For example, the Strauss Group has a joint venture with PepsiCo to market Frito-Lay's Cheetos, Ruffles, Doritos, and other snacks in Israel.[23]

The advantages of this option are twofold. First, one company may not have the necessary financial, physical, or managerial resources to enter a foreign market alone. The joint venture between Ericsson, a Swedish telecommunications firm, and CGCT, a French switch maker, enabled them together to beat out AT&T for a $100 million French contract. Ericsson's money and technology combined with CGCT's knowledge of the French market helped them to win the contract that neither of them could have won alone. Second, a government may require or strongly encourage a joint venture before it allows a foreign company to enter its market. For example, in China, international giants such as Procter & Gamble, Starbucks, and General Motors operate wholly or in part through joint ventures.

The disadvantages arise when the two companies disagree about policies or courses of action for their joint venture or when governmental bureaucracy bogs down the effort. For example, U.S. firms often prefer to reinvest earnings gained, whereas some foreign companies may want to spend those earnings. Or a U.S. firm may want to return profits earned to the United States, while the local firm or its government may oppose this—a problem faced by many potential joint ventures in Eastern Europe, Russia, Latin America, and South Asia.

Direct Investment

The biggest commitment a company can make when entering the global market is *direct investment*, which entails a domestic firm actually investing in and owning a foreign subsidiary or division. Examples of direct investment are Nissan's Smyrna, Tennessee, plant that produces pickup trucks and the Mercedes-Benz factory in Vance, Alabama, that makes the M-class sports utility vehicle. Many U.S.-based global companies also use this mode of entry. Reebok entered Russia by creating a subsidiary known as Reebok Russia.

For many companies, direct investment often follows one of the other three market-entry strategies.[24] For example, both FedEx and UPS entered China through joint ventures with Chinese companies. Each subsequently purchased the interests of its partner and converted the Chinese operations into a division.

The advantages to direct investment include cost savings, better understanding of local market conditions, and fewer local restrictions. Firms entering foreign markets using direct investment believe that these advantages outweigh the financial commitments and risks involved.

learning review

6. What mode of entry could a company follow if it has no previous experience in global marketing?

7. How does licensing differ from a joint venture?

CRAFTING A WORLDWIDE MARKETING PROGRAM

The choice of a market-entry strategy is a necessary first step for a marketer when joining the community of global companies. The next step involves the challenging task of planning, implementing, and evaluating marketing programs worldwide.

Successful global marketers standardize global marketing programs whenever possible and customize them wherever necessary. The extent of standardization and customization is often rooted in a careful global environment scan supplemented with judgment based on experience and marketing research.

Product and Promotion Strategies

Global companies have five strategies for matching products and their promotion efforts to global markets. As Figure 6–4 shows, the strategies focus on whether a company extends or adapts its product and promotion message for consumers in different countries and cultures.

FIGURE 6–4

Five product and promotion strategies for global marketing exist based on whether a company extends or adapts its product and promotion message for consumers in different countries and cultures. Read the text to learn how different companies employ these strategies.

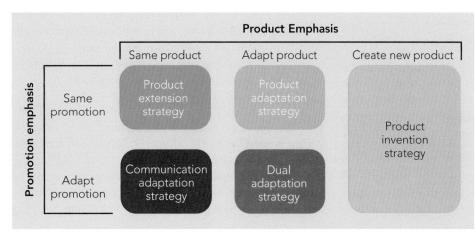

A product may be sold globally in one of three ways: (1) in the same form as in its home market, (2) with some adaptations, or (3) as a totally new product:[25]

1. *Product extension.* Selling virtually the same product in other countries is a product extension strategy. It works well for products such as Coca-Cola, Gillette razors, Wrigley's gum, Sony consumer electronics, Harley-Davidson motorcycles, Nike apparel and shoes, and Apple iPhones. As a general rule, product extension seems to work best when the consumer target market for the product is alike across countries and cultures—that is, consumers share the same desires, needs, and uses for the product.

2. *Product adaptation.* Changing a product in some way to make it more appropriate for a country's climate or consumer preferences is a product adaptation strategy. Exxon sells different gasoline blends based on each country's climate. Frito-Lay produces and markets its potato chips in Russia, but don't expect them to taste like the chips eaten in North America. Russians prefer dairy, meat, and seafood-flavored potato chips. Likewise, Gerber baby food comes in different varieties in different countries. Vegetable and rabbit meat is a favorite in Poland. Freeze-dried sardines and rice is popular in Japan. Maybelline's makeup is adapted to local skin types and weather across the globe, including an Asia-specific mascara that doesn't run during the rainy season.

3. *Product invention.* Alternatively, companies can invent totally new products designed to satisfy common needs across countries. Black & Decker did this with its Snake Light flexible flashlight. Created to address a global need for portable lighting, the product became a best seller in North America, Europe, Latin America, and Australia and is the most successful new product developed by Black & Decker. Similarly, Whirlpool developed a compact, automatic clothes washer specifically for households in developing countries with annual household incomes of $2,000. Called Ideale, the washer features bright colors because washers are often placed in home living areas, not hidden in laundry rooms (which don't exist in many homes in developing countries).

An identical promotion message is often used for the product extension and product adaptation strategies around the world. Gillette uses the same global message for its men's toiletries: "Gillette, the Best a Man Can Get." Even though Exxon adapts its gasoline blends for different countries based on climate, the promotion message is unchanged: "Put a Tiger in Your Tank."

Global companies may also adapt their promotion message. For instance, the same product may be sold in many countries but advertised differently. As an example, L'Oréal, a French health and beauty products marketer, introduced its Golden Beauty brand of sun care products through its Helena Rubenstein subsidiary in Western Europe with a *communication adaptation strategy*. Recognizing that cultural and buying motive differences related to skin care and tanning exist, Golden Beauty advertising features dark tanning for northern Europeans, skin protection to avoid wrinkles among Latin Europeans, and beautiful skin for Europeans living along the Mediterranean Sea, even though the products are the same.

QR 6–4
Nescafé China
Video

Other companies use a *dual adaptation strategy* by modifying both their products and promotion messages. Nestlé does this with Nescafé coffee. Nescafé is marketed using different coffee blends and promotional campaigns to match consumer preferences in different countries. For example, Nescafé, the world's largest brand of coffee, generally emphasizes the taste, aroma, and warmth of shared moments in its advertising around the world. However, Nescafé is advertised in Thailand as a way to relax from the pressures of daily life.

These examples illustrate the simple rule applied by global companies: Standardize product and promotion strategies whenever possible and customize them wherever necessary. This is the art of global marketing.[26]

Gillette delivers the same global message whenever possible as shown in the Gillette for Women Venus ads from the United States, Mexico, and France.

The Gillette Company

www.gillette.com

Distribution Strategy

Distribution is of critical importance in global marketing. The availability and quality of retailers and wholesalers as well as transportation, communication, and warehousing facilities are often determined by a country's stage of economic development. Figure 6–5 outlines the channel through which a product manufactured in one country must travel to reach its destination in another country. The first step involves the seller; its headquarters is the starting point and is responsible for the successful distribution to the ultimate consumer.

The next step is the channel between two nations, moving the product from one country to another. Intermediaries that can handle this responsibility include resident buyers in a foreign country, independent merchant wholesalers who buy and sell the product, or agents who bring buyers and sellers together.

Once the product is in the foreign nation, that country's distribution channels take over. These channels can be very long or surprisingly short, depending on the product line. In Japan, fresh fish go through three intermediaries before getting to a retail outlet. Conversely, shoes only go through one intermediary.

Pricing Strategy

Global companies also face many challenges in determining a pricing strategy as part of their worldwide marketing effort. Individual countries, even those with free trade agreements, may impose considerable competitive, political, and legal constraints on the pricing latitude of global companies. For example, antitrust authorities in Germany limited Walmart from selling some items below cost to lure shoppers. As a result, Walmart was unable to compete against German discount stores. This, and other factors, led Walmart to leave Germany in 2006 following eight years without a profit.[27]

FIGURE 6–5
Channels of distribution in global marketing are often long and complex.

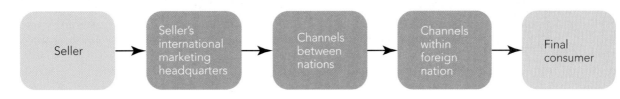

Pricing too low or too high can have dire consequences. When prices appear too low in one country, companies can be charged with dumping, a practice subject to severe penalties and fines. *Dumping* is when a firm sells a product in a foreign country below its domestic price or below its actual cost. A trade dispute involving U.S. apple growers and Mexico is a case in point. Mexican trade officials claimed that U.S. growers were selling their red and golden delicious apples in Mexico below the actual cost of production. They imposed a 101 percent tariff on U.S. apples, and a severe drop in U.S. apple exports to Mexico resulted. Subsequent negotiations set a floor on the price of U.S. apples sold to Mexico.[28]

When companies price their products very high in some countries but competitively in others, they face a gray market problem. A *gray market*, also called *parallel importing*, is a situation where products are sold through unauthorized channels of distribution.[29] A gray market comes about when individuals buy products in a lower-priced country from a manufacturer's authorized retailer, ship them to higher-priced countries, and then sell them below the manufacturer's suggested retail price through unauthorized retailers. Many well-known products have been sold through gray markets, including Seiko watches, Chanel perfume, and Mercedes-Benz cars. Parallel importing is legal in the United States. It is illegal in the European Union.

---

learning review

8. Products may be sold globally in three ways. What are they?

9. What is dumping?

LEARNING OBJECTIVES REVIEW

LO1 *Identify the major trends that have influenced world trade and global marketing.*

Four major trends have influenced the landscape of global marketing in the past decade. First, there has been a decline of economic protectionism by individual countries, leading to a reduction in tariffs and quotas. Second, there is growing economic integration and free trade among nations, reflected in the creation of the European Union and the North American Free Trade Agreement. Third, there exists global competition among global companies for global consumers, resulting in firms adopting global marketing strategies and promoting global brands. And finally, a networked global marketspace has emerged using Internet technology as a tool for exchanging goods, services, and information on a global scale.

LO2 *Identify the environmental forces that shape global marketing efforts.*

Three major environmental forces shape global marketing efforts. First, there are cultural forces, including values, customs, cultural symbols, and language. Economic forces also shape global marketing efforts. These include a country's stage of economic development and economic infrastructure, consumer income and purchasing power, and currency exchange rates. Finally, political-regulatory forces in a country or region of the world create a favorable or unfavorable climate for global marketing efforts.

LO3 *Name and describe the alternative approaches companies use to enter global markets.*

Companies have four alternative approaches for entering global markets. These are exporting, licensing, joint venture, and direct investment. Exporting involves producing goods in one country and selling them in another country. Under licensing, a company offers the right to a trademark, patent, trade secret, or similarly valued item of intellectual property in return for a royalty or fee. In a joint venture, a foreign company and a local firm invest together to create a local business. Direct investment entails a domestic firm actually investing in and owning a foreign subsidiary or division.

LO4 *Explain the distinction between standardization and customization when companies craft worldwide marketing programs.*

Companies distinguish between standardization and customization when crafting worldwide marketing programs. Standardization means that all elements of the marketing program are the same across countries and cultures. Customization means that one or more elements of the marketing program are adapted to meet the needs or preferences of consumers in a particular country or culture. Global marketers apply a simple rule when crafting worldwide marketing programs: Standardize marketing programs whenever possible and customize them wherever necessary.

FOCUSING ON KEY TERMS

APPLYING MARKETING KNOWLEDGE

1 Explain what is meant by this statement: "Quotas are a hidden tax on consumers, whereas tariffs are a more obvious one."

2 How successful would a television commercial in Japan be if it featured a husband surprising his wife in her dressing area on Valentine's Day with a small box of chocolates containing four candies? Explain.

3 As a novice in global marketing, which global market-entry strategy would you be likely to start with? Why? What other alternatives are available for a global market entry?

4 Coca-Cola is sold worldwide. In some countries, Coca-Cola owns the bottling facilities; in others, it has signed contracts with licensees or it relies on joint ventures. When selecting a licensee in each country, what factors should Coca-Cola consider?

building your marketing plan

Does your marketing plan involve reaching global customers outside the United States? If the answer is no, read no further and do not include a global element in your plan. If the answer is yes, try to identify the following:

1 What features of your product are especially important to potential customers?

2 In which countries these potential customers live?

3 What special marketing issues are involved in trying to reach them?

Answers to these questions will help in developing more detailed marketing mix strategies described in later chapters.

video case 6 CNS Breathe Right Strips: Going Global

QR 6–5
Breathe Right Video Case

"It's naive to treat 'international' as one big market—particularly within OTC," explains Marti Morfitt, president and CEO of CNS, the company that manufactures Breathe Right® nasal strips. "There are many discrete, unique markets, and local expertise is needed to understand the dynamics within each and address them effectively."

"OTC" refers to over-the-counter medical products such as aspirin or cough syrup that customers can buy without a doctor's prescription. Breathe Right nasal strips qualify as an OTC product. But that doesn't mean there isn't a lot of technology and medical science behind it.

Breathe Right nasal strips are innovative adhesive strips with patented dual flex bars inside. When attached to the nose, they gently lift and hold open nasal passages, making it easier to breathe. Breathe Right strips are used for a variety of reasons, all to help breathe better through the nose: athletes hoping to play their best (particularly when wearing mouth guards); snorers (and their spouses) hoping for a quiet night's sleep; and allergy, sinusitis, and cold sufferers looking for drug-free relief from nasal congestion.

HOW IT ALL BEGAN

Breathe Right strips were invented by Bruce Johnson, a chronic nasal congestion sufferer. At times Johnson put straws or paper clips in his nose at night to keep his nasal passages open. He eventually came up with a prototype for Breathe Right strips. He brought his invention to CNS, Inc., which recognized its market potential. CNS took the strips to the Food and Drug Administration for approval of claims for relief of snoring and nasal congestion.

CNS, a small company, had a limited marketing budget. However, it got a big public relations break when Jerry Rice, the wide receiver for the San Francisco 49ers, wore a Breathe Right strip on national TV and scored two touchdowns during the 49ers' 1995 Super Bowl victory. Demand for the strips soared.

"What really helped sales of Breathe Right strips was that CNS had done a very effective job of getting press kits in the hands of news and sports media," says Morfitt. "When people on television asked, 'What is that funny looking thing on his nose?' the reporters could talk about how the strip was an effective consumer product for everyone. And a $1.4 million business turned into a $45 million business in just one year."

THE DECISION TO GO GLOBAL

As awareness and trial in the United States was building, CNS began to get inquiries from people in other countries asking where they could buy strips. In 1995 CNS decided to take advantage of global interest and introduce Breathe Right strips internationally.

What countries did CNS choose to enter with its Breathe Right strips? "Countries we focus on are those with a large OTC market, high per-capita spending in the OTC market, and future prospects for growth," says Kevin McKenna, vice president for international at CNS. All these factors relate to market size. "But the real key to success in a market is a local partner that is entrepreneurial and has an ability to execute in terms of achieving distribution and sales."

IMPORTANCE OF LOCAL PARTNERS

Dynamic world market changes in the past 30 years have influenced opportunities for global sales of Breathe Right strips. Key trends include increased availability of OTC products formerly available only by prescription; and a global push toward self-care, spurred by the increasing cost of health and medical care. Additionally, OTC products have extended beyond the traditional boundary of the pharmacy and into grocery and other channels; and the role of the pharmacist has expanded from that of medical professional to one that includes selling and marketing OTC products to consumers.

At the same time, changes were taking place within CNS. When Morfitt joined CNS in 1998, she began pulling together a new management group with extensive experience in marketing consumer packaged goods, both in the United States and abroad. CNS began seeking "hungry" international partners who would bring greater localized market expertise and direct-selling capabilities than past partners. Morfitt also wanted partners with demonstrated entrepreneurial spirit to match that of the new management team.

The company's partner in Italy, BluFarm Group, uses its local knowledge and direct-selling skills to partner with pharmacists to teach them how to increase sales of Breathe Right strips in their stores. In Italy, as throughout much of Europe, OTC products such as antacids, aspirin, and nasal strips are typically placed behind pharmacy counters and therefore not visible to customers. The only way to sell a product is for a customer to ask for it by name. BluFarm Group recognized the importance of in-store advertising and sales execution to build awareness and created point-of-sale materials such as window and counter displays to let customers know that Breathe Right strips were available in the store. "BluFarm's ability to capture consumers' awareness of Breathe Right strips as they walk in the retailer's door has beneficial results for CNS, BluFarm, pharmacists, and consumers," says McKenna.

"Working with an experienced local partner helps overcome surprises in global markets," says Nick Naumann, senior marketing communications manager at CNS. One surprise: universal product codes (UPC) on packaging aren't "universal"—they are used only in the United States and Canada. "Different forms of those codes in other countries can take a few weeks to six months or more of government review to obtain," he says.

Even the same packaging colors don't work around the globe. Research with U.S. consumers revealed they wanted darker packaging to suggest the strips' use at night by snorers and those with stuffed noses. " 'Too grim and negative' Asian and European consumers told us," says Naumann. Breathe Right strips in those countries have a lighter, airier look than in the United States to convey the open feeling one gets from the nasal strips.

MANAGING GLOBAL GROWTH

Today, Breathe Right strips are sold in more than 25 countries. To ensure the Breathe Right brand continues to meet growth expectations, CNS now uses a three-stage approach to penetrate and develop new markets:

- Stage 1: Explore/test the concept.
  —Use screening criteria to identify high-potential markets.
  —Identify potential partners.
  —Validate concept with research.
  —Develop strategy and launch test market.

- Stage 2: Establish the product.
  —Penetrate the marketplace.
  —Refine messages for local market.
  —Evaluate partnership and marketing strategies.

- Stage 3: Manage the product.
  —Achieve sustainability/profitability.
  —Exploit new product and new use opportunities.

Overall, this approach starts with what works in the United States and extends it into new markets, paying

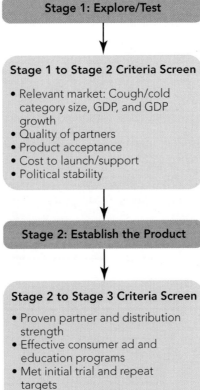

close attention to local needs and customs. Throughout the three stages CNS conducts market research and makes financial projections.

As shown in the figure, at each stage of the market development process, performance must be met for the product to enter the next stage. Once success with Breathe Right nasal strips is established in a country, the groundwork is laid and international partners have the ability to introduce other Breathe Right products.

LOOKING FORWARD

"We believe the Breathe Right brand has great potential, both domestically and around the world," says Morfitt. "Growth will come both from further expansion of Breathe Right nasal strips and from other drug-free, better-breathing line extensions."

Questions

1 What are the advantages and disadvantages for CNS taking Breathe Right strips into international markets?

2 What are the advantages to CNS of (*a*) using its three-stage process to enter new global markets and (*b*) having specific criteria to move through the stages?

3 Using the CNS criteria, with what you know, which countries should have highest priority for CNS?

4 Which single segment of potential Breathe Right strip users would you target to enter new markets?

5 Which marketing mix variables should CNS emphasize the most to succeed in a global arena? Why?

Marketing Research: From Customer Insights to Actions

LEARNING OBJECTIVES

After reading this chapter you should be able to:

 LO1 Identify the reason for conducting marketing research.

LO2 Describe the five-step marketing research approach that leads to marketing actions.

LO3 Explain how marketing uses secondary and primary data.

 LO4 Discuss the uses of observations, questionnaires, panels, experiments, and newer data collection methods.

LO5 Explain how information technology and data mining lead to marketing actions.

  LO6 Describe three approaches to developing a company's sales forecast.

HOW TEST SCREENINGS AND TRACKING STUDIES REDUCE MOVIE RISKS

The Hunger Games, Harry Potter and the Deathly Hallows: Part 2, and Avatar are movies that their studios count on for huge profits.[1] But what can these studios do to try to reduce the costly risks of a movie's box-office failure?

What's in a Movie Name?

Fixing bad names for movies—like *Rope Burns* and *Shoeless Joe*—can turn potential disasters into hugely successful blockbusters. Don't remember seeing these movies? Well, test screenings—a form of marketing research—found that moviegoers like you had problems with these titles. Here's what happened:

- *Rope Burns* became *Million Dollar Baby* because audiences didn't like the original name. The movie won the 2005 Academy Award™ for Best Picture and starred Hilary Swank as a woman boxer and Clint Eastwood as her trainer.

- Shown frequently on television now, *Shoeless Joe* became the baseball classic *Field of Dreams* because audiences thought Kevin Costner might be playing a homeless person.

Filmmakers want movie titles that are concise, grab attention, capture the essence of the film, and have no legal restrictions to reduce risk to the studio—the same factors that make a good brand name.[2]

The Risks of Today's (and Tomorrow's) Blockbuster Movies

Bad titles, poor scripts, temperamental stars, costly special effects, and several blockbuster movies released at the same time are just a few of the nightmares studios face. Studios try to reduce their risk by developing appealing sequels, like those created for *Harry Potter, Shrek,* and *Batman.* And you guessed it: *The Hunger Games* will also have a sequel in 2013.

With a typical film costing over $100 million to produce and market,[3] studios also try to reduce their risks by:

- *Conducting test screenings.* In test screenings, 300 to 400 prospective moviegoers are recruited to attend a "sneak preview" of a film before its release.[4] After viewing the movie, the audience fills out an exhaustive survey to critique its title, plot, characters, music, and ending to identify improvements to make in the final edit.[5]

QR 7–1
The Hunger
Games Movie
Video

- *Using tracking studies.* Immediately before an upcoming film's release, studios will ask prospective moviegoers in the target audience three key questions: (1) Are you aware of the film? (2) Are you interested in seeing the film? and (3) Will you see the film this weekend?[6] Studios use these data to forecast the movie's opening weekend box office sales and, if necessary, run last-minute ads to promote the film.

Converting Marketing Research Results into Actions

Director James Cameron even had to produce a short "mini" test screening of a 3D segment of *Avatar* to convince four Twentieth Century Fox executives to fund his movie. *Avatar* became #1 in all-time worldwide gross ticket sales.[7]

These examples show how marketing research leads to decisive marketing actions, the main topic of this chapter. Also, marketing research is often used to help a firm develop its sales forecasts, the final topic of this chapter.

THE ROLE OF MARKETING RESEARCH

LO1

Let's (1) look at what marketing research is, (2) identify some difficulties with it, and (3) describe the five steps marketers use to conduct it.

What Is Marketing Research?

marketing research
The process of collecting and analyzing information in order to recommend actions.

Marketing research is the process of defining a marketing problem and opportunity, systematically collecting and analyzing information, and recommending actions.[8] Although imperfect, marketers conduct marketing research to reduce the risk of and thereby improve marketing decisions.

The Challenges in Doing Good Marketing Research

Whatever the marketing issue involved—whether discovering consumer tastes or setting the right price—good marketing research is challenging. For example:

- Suppose your firm is developing a new product never before seen by consumers. Will consumers really know whether they are likely to buy a product that they have never thought about before?
- Imagine if you, as a consumer, were asked about your personal hygiene habits. Even though you know the answers, will you reveal them? When personal or status questions are involved, will people give honest answers?
- Will consumers' actual purchase behavior match their stated interest or intentions? Will they buy the same brand they say they will?

Marketing research must overcome these difficulties and obtain the information needed so that marketers can make reasonable estimates about what consumers want and will buy.

Five-Step Marketing Research Approach

LO2

A *decision* is a conscious choice from among two or more alternatives. All of us make many such decisions daily. At work we choose from alternative ways to accomplish an assigned task. At college we choose from alternative courses. As consumers we choose from alternative brands. No magic formula guarantees correct decisions.

Managers and researchers have tried to improve the outcomes of decisions by using more formal, structured approaches to *decision making,* the act of consciously choosing from among alternatives. The systematic marketing research approach used to

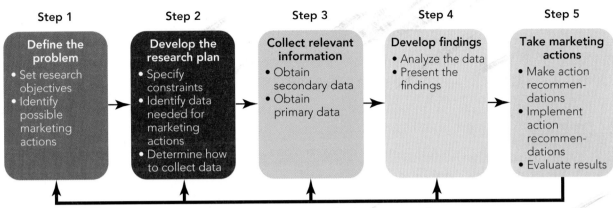

Step 1	Step 2	Step 3	Step 4	Step 5
Define the problem • Set research objectives • Identify possible marketing actions	**Develop the research plan** • Specify constraints • Identify data needed for marketing actions • Determine how to collect data	**Collect relevant information** • Obtain secondary data • Obtain primary data	**Develop findings** • Analyze the data • Present the findings	**Take marketing actions** • Make action recommen-dations • Implement action recommen-dations • Evaluate results

Feedback to learn lessons for future research

FIGURE 7–1

Five-step marketing research approach leading to marketing actions. Lessons learned from past research mistakes are fed back to improve each of the steps.

collect information to improve marketing decisions and actions described in this chapter uses five steps and is shown in Figure 7–1. Although the five-step approach described here focuses on marketing decisions, it provides a systematic checklist for making both business and personal decisions.

STEP 1: DEFINE THE PROBLEM

For how Fisher-Price conducts marketing research by observing young children who can't read, see the text.

Every marketing problem faces its own research challenges. For example, toy designers at Fisher-Price conduct marketing research to discover how children play, how they learn, and what they like to play with.[9] As part of its marketing research, Fisher-Price invites children to play at its state-licensed nursery school in East Aurora, New York. From behind one-way mirrors, toy designers and marketing researchers watch the children use—and abuse—toys, which helps the firm develop better products. This is an example of using observational data, discussed later in the chapter.

The original model of a classic Fisher-Price toy, the Chatter Telephone™, was simply a wooden phone with a dial that rang a bell. However, observers noted that the children kept grabbing the receiver like a handle to pull the phone along behind them, so a designer added wheels, a noisemaker, and eyes that bobbed up and down.

A careful look at Fisher-Price's toy marketing research shows the two key elements of defining a problem: setting the research objectives and identifying possible marketing actions.

Set the Research Objectives

Research objectives are specific, measurable goals the decision maker—in this case, an executive at Fisher-Price—seeks to achieve in conducting the marketing research. For Fisher-Price, the immediate research objective was to decide whether to market the old or new telephone design.

Identify Possible Marketing Actions

measures of success

Criteria or standards used in evaluating proposed solutions to a problem.

Effective decision makers develop specific **measures of success**, which are criteria or standards used in evaluating proposed solutions to the problem. Different research outcomes—based on the measure of success—lead to different marketing actions. For the Fisher-Price problem, if a measure of success were the total time children spent

The wheels, noisemaker, and bobbing eyes on Fisher-Price's hugely successful Chatter Telephone resulted from careful marketing research on children.

playing with each of the two telephone designs, the results of observing them would lead to clear-cut actions as follows:

Measure of Success: Playtime	Possible Marketing Action
• Children spent more time playing with old design.	• Continue with old design; don't introduce new design.
• Children spent more time playing with new design.	• Introduce new design; drop old design.

One test of whether marketing research should be done is if different outcomes will lead to different marketing actions. If all the research outcomes lead to the same action—such as top management sticking with the older design regardless of what the observed children liked—the research is useless and a waste of money. In this case, research results showed that kids liked the new design, so Fisher-Price introduced its noisemaking pull-toy Chatter Telephone, which became a toy classic and has sold millions.

Marketing researchers know that defining a problem is an incredibly difficult task. If the objectives are too broad, the problem may not be researchable. If they are too narrow, the value of the research results may be seriously lessened. This is why marketing researchers spend so much time defining a marketing problem precisely and writing a formal proposal that describes the research to be done.[10]

STEP 2: DEVELOP THE RESEARCH PLAN

The second step in the marketing research process requires that the researcher (1) specify the constraints on the marketing research activity, (2) identify the data needed for marketing actions, and (3) determine how to collect the data.

Specify Constraints

constraints

Restrictions placed on potential solutions to a problem.

The **constraints** in a decision are the restrictions placed on potential solutions to a problem. Examples include the limitations on the time and money available to solve the problem. Thus, Fisher-Price might set two constraints on its decision to select either the old or new version of the Chatter Telephone: The decision must be made in 10 weeks and no research budget is available beyond that needed for collecting data in its nursery school.

Identify Data Needed for Marketing Actions

Often marketing research studies wind up collecting a lot of data that are interesting but irrelevant for marketing decisions that result in marketing actions. In the Fisher-Price Chatter Telephone case, it might be nice to know the children's favorite colors, whether they like wood or plastic toys better, and so on. In fact, knowing answers to these questions might result in later modifications of the toy, but right now the problem is to select one of two toy designs. So this study must focus on collecting data that will help managers make a clear choice between the two telephone designs.

Determine How to Collect Data

Determining how to collect useful marketing research data is often as important as actually collecting the data—step 3 in the process, which is discussed later. Two key elements in deciding how to collect the data are (1) concepts and (2) methods.

Concepts In the world of marketing, *concepts* are ideas about products or services. To find out about consumer reaction to a potential new product, marketing researchers frequently develop a *new-product concept*, that is, a picture or verbal description of a product or service the firm might offer for sale. For example, Fisher-Price's addition of a noisemaker, wheels, and eyes to the basic design of its Chatter Telephone made the toy more fun for children and increased sales.

Methods *Methods* are the approaches that can be used to collect data to solve all or part of a problem. For example, if you were the marketing researcher at Fisher-Price responsible for the Chatter Telephone, you would face a number of methods issues in developing your research plan, including the following:

- Can we actually ask three- or four-year-olds meaningful questions that they can answer about their liking or disliking the two designs of toys?
- Are we better off not asking them questions but simply observing their behavior in playing with the two designs of toys?
- If we simply observe the children's playing behavior, how can we do this in a way to get the best information without biasing the results?

How can you find and use the methods that other marketing researchers have found successful? Information on useful methods is available in tradebooks, textbooks, and handbooks that relate to marketing and marketing research. Some periodicals and technical journals, such as the *Journal of Marketing* and the *Journal of Marketing Research*, both published by the American Marketing Association, summarize methods and techniques valuable in addressing marketing problems.

Special methods vital to marketing are (1) sampling and (2) statistical inference. For example, marketing researchers often use *sampling* by selecting a group of distributors, customers, or prospects, asking them questions, and treating their answers as typical of all those in whom they are interested. They may then use *statistical inference* to generalize the results from the sample to much larger groups of distributors, customers, or prospects to help decide on marketing actions.

---

learning review

1. What is marketing research?
2. What is the five-step marketing research approach?
3. What are constraints, as they apply to developing a research plan?

STEP 3: COLLECT RELEVANT INFORMATION

Collecting enough relevant information to make a rational, informed marketing decision sometimes simply means using your knowledge to decide immediately. At other times it entails collecting an enormous amount of information at great expense.

Figure 7–2 on the next page shows how the different kinds of marketing information fit together. **Data**, the facts and figures related to the problem, are divided into two main parts: secondary data and primary data. **Secondary data** are facts and figures that have already been recorded prior to the project at hand. As shown in Figure 7–2, secondary data are divided into two parts—internal and external secondary data—depending on whether the data come from inside or outside the organization needing the research. **Primary data** are facts and figures that are newly collected for the project. Figure 7–2 shows that primary data can be divided into observational data, questionnaire data, and other sources of data.

Secondary Data: Internal

The internal records of a company generally offer the most easily accessible marketing information. These internal sources of secondary data may be divided into two related parts: (1) marketing inputs and (2) marketing outcomes.

Marketing input data relate to the effort expended to make sales. These range from sales and advertising budgets and expenditures to salespeople's call reports. The call reports describe the number of sales calls per day, who was visited, and what was discussed.

data
The facts and figures related to a problem.

secondary data
Facts and figures that have already been recorded prior to the project at hand.

primary data
Facts and figures that are newly collected for a project.

FIGURE 7–2

Types of marketing information. Researchers must choose carefully among these to get the best results, considering time and cost constraints.

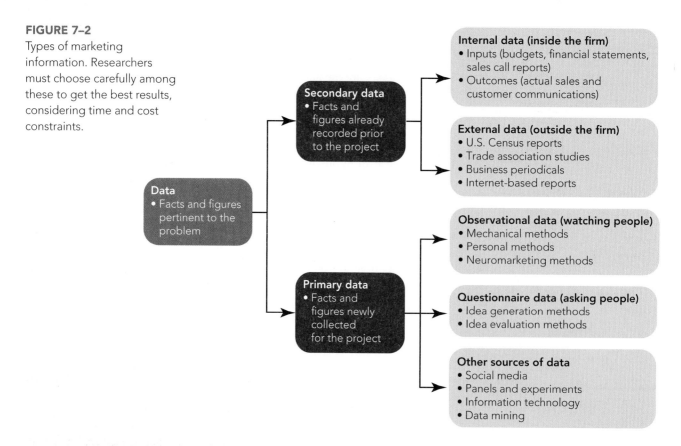

Data
• Facts and figures pertinent to the problem

Secondary data
• Facts and figures already recorded prior to the project

Internal data (inside the firm)
• Inputs (budgets, financial statements, sales call reports)
• Outcomes (actual sales and customer communications)

External data (outside the firm)
• U.S. Census reports
• Trade association studies
• Business periodicals
• Internet-based reports

Primary data
• Facts and figures newly collected for the project

Observational data (watching people)
• Mechanical methods
• Personal methods
• Neuromarketing methods

Questionnaire data (asking people)
• Idea generation methods
• Idea evaluation methods

Other sources of data
• Social media
• Panels and experiments
• Information technology
• Data mining

Scanner data at supermarket checkout counters provide valuable information for marketing decisions.

QR 7–2
Census 2010
Video

Marketing outcome data relate to the results of the marketing efforts. These involve billing records on shipments from the accounting department and include sales and repeat sales, often broken down by sales representative, industry, and geographic region. In addition, communications from customers—e-mails, phone calls, and letters—can reveal both complaints and what is working well.[11]

Secondary Data: External

Published data from outside the organization are external secondary data. The U.S. Census Bureau publishes a variety of useful reports. Best known is the Census 2010, which is the most recent count of the U.S. population that occurs every 10 years. Recently, the Census Bureau began collecting data annually from a smaller number of people through the American Community Survey. Both surveys contain detailed information on American households, such as the number of people per household and their age, sex, race/ethnic background, income, occupation, and education. Marketers use these data to identify characteristics and trends of ultimate consumers.

The Census Bureau also publishes the Economic Census, which is conducted every five years. These reports are vital to business firms selling products and services to organizations. The 2007 Economic Census contains data on the number and sales of establishments in the United States that produce a product or service based on its geography (states, counties, zip codes, etc.), industry sector (manufacturing, retail trade, etc.), and North American Industry Classification System (NAICS) code.

Several market research companies pay households and businesses to record all their purchases using a paper or electronic diary. Such *syndicated panel* data economically answer questions that require consistent data collection over time, such as, How many times did our customers buy our products this year compared to last year? Examples of syndicated panels that provide a standard set of data on a regular basis are

Marketing Matters >>>>>>>> technology

Online Databases and Internet Resources Useful to Marketers

Information contained in online databases available via the Internet consists of indexes to articles in periodicals and statistical or financial data on markets, products, and organizations that are accessed either directly or via Internet search engines or portals through keyword searches.

Statistical and financial data on markets, products, and organizations include:

- *The Wall Street Journal* (www.wsj.com), CNBC (www.cnbc.com), and *Fox Business News* (www.foxbusiness.com) provide up-to-the-minute business news and video clips about companies, industries, and trends that affect the marketing environment.
- STAT-USA (www.stat-usa.gov) and the Census Bureau (www.census.gov) of the U.S. Department of Commerce provide information on U.S. business, economic, and trade activity collected by the federal government.

Portals and search engines include:

- USA.gov (www.usa.gov) is the portal to all U.S. government websites. Users click on links to browse by topic or enter keywords for specific searches.
- Google (www.google.com) is the most popular portal to the entire Internet. Users enter keywords for specific searches and then click on results of interest.

Some of these websites are accessible only if your educational institution has paid a subscription fee. Check with your institution's website.

---

the Nielsen Media Research's TV ratings and the J. D. Power's automotive quality and customer satisfaction surveys.

Some data services provide comprehensive information on household demographics and lifestyle, product purchases, TV viewing behavior, and responses to coupon and free-sample promotions. Their advantage is that a single firm can collect, analyze, interrelate, and present all this information. For consumer product firms such as Procter & Gamble, sales data from various channels are critical to allocate scarce marketing resources. As a result, they use services such as SymphonyIRIGroup's InfoScan and Nielsen's Scantrack to collect product sales and coupon/free-sample redemptions that have been scanned at the checkout counters of supermarket, drug, convenience, and mass merchandise retailers.

Finally, trade associations, universities, and business periodicals provide detailed data of value to market researchers and planners. These data are now available online via the Internet and can be identified and located using a search engine such as Google or Bing. The Marketing Matters box provides examples.

Advantages and Disadvantages of Secondary Data

A general rule among marketing people is to obtain secondary data first and then collect primary data. Two important advantages of secondary data are (1) the tremendous time savings because the data have already been collected and published or exist internally and (2) the low cost, such as free or inexpensive Census reports. Furthermore, a greater level of detail is often available through secondary data, especially U.S. Census Bureau data.

However, these advantages must be weighed against some significant disadvantages. First, the secondary data may be out of date, especially if they are U.S. Census data collected only every 5 or 10 years. Second, the definitions or categories might not be quite right for a researcher's project. For example, the age groupings or product categories might be wrong for the project. Also, because the data have been collected for another purpose, they may not be specific enough for the project. In such cases it may be necessary to collect primary data.

learning review

4. What is the difference between secondary and primary data?

5. What are some advantages and disadvantages of secondary data?

Primary Data: Watching People

LO4

observational data

Facts and figures obtained by watching, either mechanically or in person, how people behave.

Observing people and asking them questions are the two principal ways to collect new or primary data for a marketing study. Facts and figures obtained by watching, either mechanically or in person, how people actually behave is the way marketing researchers collect **observational data**. Observational data can be collected by mechanical (including electronic), personal, or neuromarketing methods.

Mechanical Methods   National TV ratings, such as those of Nielsen Media Research shown in Figure 7–3, are an example of mechanical observational data collected by a "people meter." The device measures what channel and program is tuned and who is watching. The people meter is a box that (1) is attached to TV sets, VCRs, DVRs (digital video recorders), cable boxes, and satellite dishes in more than 9,000 households across the country; (2) has a remote that operates the meter when a viewer begins and finishes watching a TV program; and (3) stores and then transmits the viewing information each night to Nielsen Media Research. Data are also collected on TV viewing using less sophisticated meters or TV diaries (a paper-pencil measurement system).

In early 2012, Nielsen introduced "cross-platform television ratings," which combine Nielsen's existing TV ratings with its new online campaign ratings. These ratings include consumer viewing of TV programs seen not only on regular TV but also that are streamed through the Internet on devices like PCs, smart phones, tablets, and video game consoles.[12]

On the basis of all these observational data, Nielsen Media Research then calculates the rating and share of each TV program. With 114.7 million TV households in the United States, a single rating point equals 1 percent, or 1,147,000 TV households.[13] For TV viewing, a share point is the percentage of TV sets in use tuned to a particular program. Because TV and cable networks sell over $61 billion annually in advertising and set advertising rates to advertisers on the basis of those data, precision in the Nielsen data is critical.[14]

A change of 1 percentage point in a rating can mean gaining or losing millions of dollars in advertising revenues because advertisers pay rates on the basis of the size of the audience for a TV program. So as Figure 7–3 shows, we might expect to pay more for a 30-second TV ad on *NCIS* than one on *The Mentalist*. Broadcast and cable networks may change the time slot or even cancel a TV program if its ratings are consistently poor and advertisers are unwilling to pay a rate based on a higher guaranteed rating.

Nielsen people meters give each family member a "personal viewing button" that the TV viewer pushes to make the Nielsen TV ratings possible.

FIGURE 7–3

Nielsen Television Index Ranking Report for network TV prime-time households for the week ending May 20, 2012. The difference of a few share points in Nielsen TV ratings affects the cost of a TV ad on a show and even whether the show remains on the air.

Rank	Program	Network	No. of Viewers (millions)	Rating	Share
1	*NCIS*	CBS	19.1	12.0	20
2	*American Idol—Wednesday*	FOX	17.7	10.5	17
3	*American Idol—Thursday*	FOX	16.4	9.8	17
4	*Dancing with the Stars*	ABC	15.8	10.2	16
5	*NCIS: Los Angeles*	CBS	15.2	9.6	15
6	*Criminal Minds*	CBS	13.7	8.5	14
7	*CBS Sunday Movie Special*	CBS	13.5	8.3	13
8	*Dancing with the Stars—Results*	ABC	13.2	8.8	13
9	*The Mentalist*	CBS	13.1	8.2	14
10	*Person of Interest*	CBS	12.9	8.3	13

Source: Nielsen © 2012. Prime time Broadcast Total Viewership for the week ending May 20, 2012. Viewing estimates include live viewing and DVR playback on the same day, defined as 3 A.M. to 3 P.M. Rank is based on the number of U.S. viewers from Nielsen Media Research's National People Meter Sample. "Number of viewers" in the table is the millions of U.S. viewers projected from the People Meter Sample.

What determines if *American Idol* stays on the air? For the importance of the TV "ratings game," see the text.

But TV advertisers today have a special problem: With about three out of four TV viewers skipping ads with TiVo or channel surfing during commercials, how many people are actually seeing their TV ad? Now services such as Nielsen Media Research and Media Check offer advertisers minute-by-minute measurement of how many viewers stay tuned during commercials. Recently, TiVo also expanded its service to allow TV advertisers to see how many and what kind of users are watching their commercials.[15] The viewership data in Figure 7–3 include not only live TV but also programs recorded on DVRs. With these more precise measures of who is likely to see a TV ad, buying TV ads is becoming more scientific.[16]

Personal Methods Observational data can take some strange twists. Jennifer Voitle, a laid-off investment bank employee with four advanced degrees, responded to an Internet ad and found a new career: *mystery shopper*. Companies pay mystery shoppers to check on the quality and pricing of their products and the integrity of and customer service provided by their employees. Jennifer gets paid to travel to exotic hotels, eat at restaurants, play golf, test-drive new cars, shop for clothes, and play arcade games. But her role posing as a customer gives her client unique marketing research information that can be obtained in no other way. Says Jennifer, "Can you believe they call this work?"[17]

Watching consumers in person or recording them are two other observational approaches. For example, Procter & Gamble watches women do their laundry, clean the floor, put on makeup, and so on because they comprise 80 percent of its customers! And Gillette records consumers brushing their teeth in their own bathrooms to see how they really brush—not just how they say they brush. The new-product result: Gillette's Oral-B CrossAction toothbrush.[18]

Ethnographic research is a specialized observational approach in which trained observers seek to discover subtle behavioral and emotional reactions as consumers encounter products in their "natural use environment," such as in their home or car.[19] Recently, Kraft launched Deli Creations, which are sandwiches made with its Oscar Mayer meats, Kraft cheeses, and Grey Poupon mustard, after spending several months with consumers in their kitchens. Kraft discovered that consumers wanted complete, ready-to-serve meals that are easy to prepare—and it had the products to create them.[20]

Is this *really* marketing research? A mystery shopper at work.

Personal observation is both useful and flexible, but it can be costly and unreliable when different observers report different conclusions when watching the same event. And while observation can reveal *what* people do, it cannot easily determine *why* they do it. This is the principal reason for using neuromarketing and questionnaires, our next topics.

Neuromarketing Methods Global brand expert Martin Lindstrom believes that most traditional marketing research—like focus groups and surveys—is wasted because consumers' feelings toward products and brands reside deep within the subconscious part of their brains. Lindstrom used brain scanning to analyze the buying processes of more than 2,000 participants. Lindstrom merged neuroscience—the study of the brain—with marketing! His controversial findings using "neuromarketing" are summarized in his breakthrough book *Buyology*.[21]

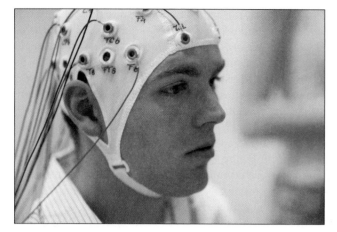

"Neuromarketing" often uses a cap with dozens of sensors to measure brain waves to try to understand consumers better. For some changes made by Campbell Soup Company based on neuromarketing, see the text.

questionnaire data
Facts and figures obtained by asking people about their attitudes, awareness, intentions, and behaviors.

Based on the results of neuromarketing studies, Campbell Soup Company recently changed the labels of most of its soup cans. Some of the changes: Steam now rises from more vibrant images of soup; the "unemotional spoons" have disappeared; and the script logo is smaller and has been moved to the bottom of the can.[22]

Primary Data: Asking People

How many dozens of times have you filled out some kind of a questionnaire? Maybe a short survey at school or a telephone or e-mail survey to see if you are pleased with the service you received. Asking consumers questions and recording their answers is the second principal way of gathering information.

We can divide this primary data collection task into (1) idea generation methods and (2) idea evaluation methods, although they sometimes overlap and each has a number of special techniques.[23] Each survey method results in valuable **questionnaire data**, which are facts and figures obtained by asking people about their attitudes, awareness, intentions, and behaviors.

Idea Generation Methods—Coming Up with Ideas In the past the most common way of collecting questionnaire data to generate ideas was through an *individual interview*, which involves a single researcher asking questions of one respondent. This approach has many advantages, such as being able to probe for additional ideas using follow-up questions to a respondent's initial answers, but it is very expensive. Later in the chapter we'll discuss some alternatives.

General Mills sought ideas about why Hamburger Helper didn't fare well when introduced. Initial instructions called for cooking a half-pound of hamburger separately from the noodles or potatoes, which were later mixed with the hamburger. So General Mills researchers used a special kind of individual interview called *depth interviews* in which researchers ask lengthy, free-flowing kinds of questions to probe for underlying ideas and feelings. These depth interviews showed consumers (1) didn't think it contained enough meat and (2) didn't want the hassle of cooking in two different pots. The Hamburger Helper product manager changed the recipe to call for a full pound of meat and to allow users to prepare it in one dish, leading to product success.

Focus groups are informal sessions of 6 to 10 past, present, or prospective customers in which a discussion leader, or moderator, asks their opinions about the firm's and its competitors' products, how they use these products, and special needs they have that these products don't address. Often recorded and conducted in special interviewing rooms with a one-way mirror, these groups enable marketing researchers and managers to hear and watch consumer reactions. The informality and peer support in an effective focus group help uncover ideas that are often difficult to obtain with individual interviews. For example, 3M heard consumers complain in eight focus groups that standard steel wool pads scratched their expensive cookware. This led to 3M's internationally successful Scotch-Brite Never Scratch soap pad.[24]

Finding "the next big thing" for consumers has caused marketing researchers to turn to some less traditional techniques. For example, "fuzzy front end" methods attempt early identification of elusive consumer tastes or trends. Trend Hunter is a firm that seeks to anticipate and track "the evolution of cool." Trend hunting (or watching) is the practice of identifying "emerging shifts in social behavior," which are driven by changes in pop culture that can lead to new products. Trend Hunter has identified over 150,000 "micro-trends" through its global network of 102,000 members and features several of these trends on its daily Trend Hunter TV broadcast via its website (see www.trendhunter.com/tv).[25]

QR 7–3
Trend Hunter
Video

Idea Evaluation Methods—Testing an Idea In idea evaluation, the marketing researcher tries to test ideas discovered earlier to help the marketing manager recommend marketing actions. Idea evaluation methods often involve conventional questionnaires using personal, mail, telephone, fax, and online (e-mail or Internet) surveys of a large sample of past, present, or prospective consumers. In choosing among them, the marketing researcher balances the cost of the particular method against the expected quality of the information and speed with which it can be obtained.

Personal interview surveys enable the interviewer to be flexible in asking probing questions or getting reactions to visual materials but are very costly. Mail surveys are usually biased because those most likely to respond have had especially positive or negative experiences with the product or brand. While telephone interviews allow flexibility, unhappy respondents may hang up on the interviewer, even with the efficiency of computer-assisted telephone interviewing (CATI).

Wendy's does marketing research continuously to discover changing customer wants.

Increasingly, marketing researchers have begun to use online (e-mail and Internet) surveys to collect primary data. The reason: Most consumers have an Internet connection and an e-mail account. Marketers can embed a survey in an e-mail sent to targeted respondents. When they open the e-mail, consumers can either see the survey or click on a link to access it from a website. Marketers can also ask consumers to complete a "pop up" survey in a separate window when they access an organization's website. Many organizations use this method to have consumers assess their products and services or evaluate the design and usability of their websites.

The advantages of online surveys are that the cost is relatively minimal and the turnaround time from data collection to report presentation is much quicker than the traditional methods discussed earlier. However, online surveys have serious drawbacks: Some consumers may view e-mail surveys as "junk" or "spam" and may either choose to not receive them (if they have a "spam blocker") or purposely or inadvertently delete them, unopened. For Internet surveys, some consumers have a "pop-up blocker" that prohibits a browser from opening a separate window that contains the survey; thus, they may not be able to participate in the research. For both e-mail and Internet surveys, consumers can complete the survey multiple times, creating a significant bias in the results. This is especially true for online panels. In response, research firms, such as MarketTools which markets Zoomerang, have developed sampling technology to prohibit this practice.[26]

The foundation of all research using questionnaires is developing precise questions that get clear, unambiguous answers from respondents.[27] Figure 7–4 on the next two pages shows a number of formats for questions taken from a Wendy's survey that assessed fast-food restaurant preferences among present and prospective consumers.

Question 1 is an example of an *open-ended question*, which allows respondents to express opinions, ideas, or behaviors in their own words without being forced to choose among alternatives that have been predetermined by a marketing researcher. This information is invaluable to marketers because it captures the "voice" of respondents, which is useful in understanding consumer behavior, identifying product benefits, or developing advertising messages.

In contrast, *closed-end* or *fixed alternative questions* require respondents to select one or more response options from a set of predetermined choices. Question 2 is an example of a *dichotomous question*, the simplest form of a fixed alternative question that allows only a "yes" or "no" response.

A fixed alternative question with three or more choices uses a *scale*. Question 5 is an example of a question that uses a *semantic differential scale*, a five-point scale in which the opposite ends have one- or two-word adjectives that have opposite meanings. For example, depending on the respondent's opinion regarding the cleanliness of Wendy's restaurants, he or she would check the left-hand space on the scale, the right-hand space, or one of the three other intervening points. Question 6 uses a *Likert scale*, in which the respondent indicates the extent to which he or she agrees or disagrees with a statement.

1. What things are most important to you when you decide to eat out and go to a fast-food restaurant?

_____

_____

_____

2. Have you eaten at a fast-food restaurant in the past month?

☐ Yes   ☐ No

3. If you answered yes to question 2, how often do you eat fast food?

☐ Once a week   ☐ 2 to 3 times a month   ☐ Once a month or less

4. How important is it to you that a fast-food restaurant satisfies you on the following characteristics? [Check the box that describes your feelings for each item listed.]

CHARACTERISTIC	VERY IMPORTANT	SOMEWHAT IMPORTANT	IMPORTANT	UNIMPORTANT	SOMEWHAT UNIMPORTANT	VERY UNIMPORTANT
• Taste of food	☐	☐	☐	☐	☐	☐
• Cleanliness	☐	☐	☐	☐	☐	☐
• Price	☐	☐	☐	☐	☐	☐
• Variety of menu	☐	☐	☐	☐	☐	☐

5. For each of the characteristics listed below, check the space on the scale that describes how you feel about Wendy's. Mark an X on only **one** of the five spaces for each item listed.

CHARACTERISTIC	CHECK THE SPACE THAT DESCRIBES THE DEGREE TO WHICH WENDY'S IS . . .						
• Taste of food	Tasty	____	____	____	____	____	Not tasty
• Cleanliness	Clean	____	____	____	____	____	Dirty
• Price	Inexpensive	____	____	____	____	____	Expensive
• Variety of menu	Broad	____	____	____	____	____	Narrow

FIGURE 7–4

To obtain the most valuable information from consumers, this Wendy's survey utilizes four different kinds of questions discussed in the text *(continued on the next page)*.

The questionnaire in Figure 7–4 provides valuable information to the marketing researcher at Wendy's. Questions 1 to 8 inform him or her about the respondent's likes and dislikes in eating out, frequency of eating out at fast-food restaurants generally and at Wendy's specifically, and sources of information used in making decisions about fast-food restaurants. Question 9 gives details about the respondent's personal or household characteristics, which can be used in trying to segment the fast-food market, a topic discussed in Chapter 9.

Marketing research questions must be worded precisely so that all respondents interpret the same question similarly. For example, in a question asking whether you eat at fast-food restaurants regularly, the word *regularly* is ambiguous. Two people might answer "yes" to the question, but one might mean "once a day" while the other means "once or twice a month." However, each of these interpretations suggests that dramatically different marketing actions be directed to these two prospective consumers.

The high cost of using personal interviews in homes has increased the use of *mall intercept interviews*, which are personal interviews of consumers visiting shopping

6. Check one box that describes your agreement or disagreement with each statement listed below:

STATEMENT	STRONGLY AGREE	AGREE	DON'T KNOW	DISAGREE	STRONGLY DISAGREE
• Adults like to take their families to fast-food restaurants	☐	☐	☐	☐	☐
• Our children have a say in where the family chooses to eat	☐	☐	☐	☐	☐

7. How important are each of the following sources of information to you when selecting a fast-food restaurant at which to eat? [Check one box for each source listed.]

SOURCE OF INFORMATION	VERY IMPORTANT	SOMEWHAT IMPORTANT	NOT AT ALL IMPORTANT
• Television	☐	☐	☐
• Newspapers	☐	☐	☐
• Radio	☐	☐	☐
• Billboards	☐	☐	☐
• Internet/social networks	☐	☐	☐

8. How often do you eat out at each of the following fast-food restaurants? [Check one box for each source listed.]

RESTAURANT	ONCE A WEEK OR MORE	2 TO 3 TIMES A MONTH	ONCE A MONTH OR LESS
• Burger King	☐	☐	☐
• McDonald's	☐	☐	☐
• Wendy's	☐	☐	☐

9. Please answer the following questions about you and your household. [Check only one for each item.]

a. What is your gender? ☐ Male ☐ Female

b. What is your marital status? ☐ Single ☐ Married ☐ Other (widowed, divorced, etc.)

c. How many children under age 18 live in your home? ☐ 0 ☐ 1 ☐ 2 ☐ 3 or more

d. What is your age? ☐ Under 25 ☐ 25–44 ☐ 45 or older

e. What is your total annual individual or household income?
☐ Less than $15,000 ☐ $15,000–49,000 ☐ Over $49,000

FIGURE 7–4 (continued)

centers. These face-to-face interviews reduce the cost of personal visits to consumers in their homes while providing the flexibility to show respondents visual cues such as ads or actual product samples. However, a critical disadvantage of mall intercept interviews is that the people interviewed may not be representative of the consumers targeted, giving a biased result.

Electronic technology has revolutionized traditional concepts of interviews or surveys. Today, respondents can walk up to a kiosk in a shopping center, read questions off a screen, and key their answers into a computer on a touch screen. Fully automated telephone interviews exist in which respondents key their replies on a touch-tone telephone.

Primary Data: Other Sources

Three other methods of collecting primary data exist that overlap somewhat with the methods just discussed. These involve using (1) social media, (2) panels and experiments, (3) information technology, and (4) data mining.

Using Marketing Dashboards

Are the Carmex Social Media Programs Working Well?

As a marketing consultant to Carmex, you've just been asked to assess its social media activities for its lip balm product line.

Carmex has recently launched new social media programs and promotions to tell U.S. consumers more about its line of lip balm products. These include Facebook and Twitter contests to allow Carmex likers and followers to win free samples by connecting with Carmex. A creative "Carmex Kiss" widget allows users to upload their photo and to send an animated kiss to a friend.

Your Challenge   To assess how the Carmex social media programs are doing, you choose these five metrics: (1) Carmex conversation velocity—total Carmex mentions on the Internet; (2) Facebook likers—the number of Facebook users in a time period who have liked Carmex's Facebook brand page; (3) Twitter followers—the number of Twitter users in a time period who follow Carmex's Twitter feed; (4) Carmex share of voice—Carmex mentions on the Internet as a percentage of mentions of all major lip balm brands; and (5) Carmex sentiment—the percentage of Internet Carmex share-of-voice mentions that are (a) positive, (b) neutral, or (c) negative.

Your Findings   Analyzing the marketing dashboard here, you reach these conclusions. First, the number of both Facebook likers and Twitter followers for Carmex is up significantly for 2012 compared to 2011; this is good news. Second, the Carmex share of voice of 35 percent is good, certainly relative to the 48 percent for the #1 brand Chapstick. But especially favorable is Carmex's 12 percent increase in share of voice compared to a year ago. Third, the Carmex sentiment dashboard shows 80 percent of the mentions are positive, and only 5 percent are negative. Even more significant is that positive mentions are up 23 percent over last year.

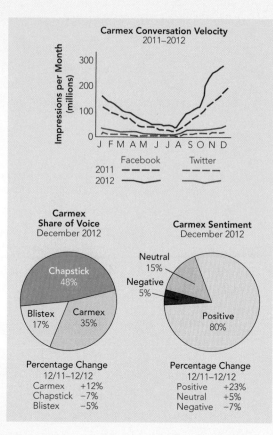

Your Actions   You conclude that Carmex's social media initiatives are doing well. Your next step is to probe deeper into the data to see which ones—such as free samples or the Carmex Kiss—have been especially effective in triggering the positive results and build on these successes in the future.

Carmex lip balms are packaged in jars, sticks, and squeezable tubes and are offered in a variety of flavors.

Social Media   Facebook, Twitter, and other social media are revolutionizing not only the way people connect with each other but also the way today's products are advertised and sold. As a result, new kinds of marketing research are required. These must reflect the more direct connections of advertisers with present and prospective buyers, the speed and sheer volume of customer feedback data, and the new marketing metrics and measures of success of social media promotions.

Carma Laboratories, Inc., the maker of Carmex lip balm, is a third generation, family-owned business with a history of accessibility to customers. In fact, founder Alfred Woelbing personally responded to every letter he received from customers. Today, Carma Labs relies on social media programs to help promote its products.[28]

Carmex lip balm is meant to reduce cold sore symptoms and soothe dry and chapped lips. It is packaged in jars, sticks, and squeezable tubes. The U.S. Carmex product line includes original, strawberry, lime twist, vanilla, and cherry flavors. Although Carmex lip balm sales trend behind Chapstick and Blistex, Carmex consumers tend to be loyalists—true zealots.

Carmex's home page topics range from its Carmex Kiss widget to its family history. For how it uses social media marketing research, see the Using Marketing Dashboards box.

To discover how Walmart used test markets to help develop its internationally successful supercenters, see the text.

One opportunity for Carmex (mycarmex.com) is to conduct marketing research using social media listening tools to understand the nature of online lip balm conversations. Lip balm is a seasonal product, with both sales and online activity peaking during the cough–cold season of November through March.

The Using Marketing Dashboards box shows how Carmex uses marketing metrics to assess its social media programs for its line of products. Data have been modified to protect proprietary information.

Carmex uses several social media metrics, such as *conversation velocity, share of voice,* and *sentiment.*[29] These metrics are tracked by electronic search engines that comb the Internet for consumers' behaviors and "brand mentions" to calculate share of voice and determine whether these brand mentions appear to be "positive," "neutral," or "negative" in order to calculate "sentiment." Widely used Facebook metrics are the number of *fans, likers,* or *likes,* which are measures of Facebook users opting in to a brand's messages and liking the brand.

Marketing researchers increasingly want to glean information from sites to "mine" their raw consumer-generated content in real time. However, when relying on this consumer-generated content, the sample of individuals from whom this content is gleaned may not be statistically representative of the marketplace.[30]

Panels and Experiments Two special ways that observations and questionnaires are sometimes used are panels and experiments.

Marketing researchers often want to know if consumers change their behavior over time, so they take successive measurements of the same people. A *panel* is a sample of consumers or stores from which researchers take a series of measurements. For example, the NPD Group collects data about consumer purchases such as apparel, food, and electronics from its Online Panel, which consists of nearly 2 million individuals worldwide. So a firm like General Mills can count the frequency of consumer purchases to measure switching behavior from one brand of its breakfast cereal (Wheaties) to another (Cheerios) or to a competitor's brand (Kellogg's Special K). A disadvantage of panels is that the marketing research firm needs to recruit new members continually to replace those who drop out. These new recruits must match the characteristics of those they replace to keep the panel representative of the marketplace.

An *experiment* involves obtaining data by manipulating factors under tightly controlled conditions to test cause and effect. The interest is in whether changing one of the independent variables (a cause) will change the behavior of the dependent variable that is studied (the result). In marketing experiments, the independent variables of interest—sometimes called the marketing *drivers*—are often one or more of the marketing mix elements, such as a product's features, price, or promotion (like advertising messages or coupons). The ideal dependent variable usually is a change in the purchases (incremental unit or dollar sales) of individuals, households, or organizations. For example, food companies often use *test markets,* which offer a product for sale in a small geographic area to help evaluate potential marketing actions. In 1988, Walmart opened three experimental stand-alone supercenters to gauge consumer acceptance before deciding to open others. Today, Walmart operates over 3,000 supercenters around the world.

A potential difficulty with experiments is that outside factors (such as actions of competitors) can distort the results of an experiment and affect the dependent variable (such as sales). A researcher's task is to identify the effect of the marketing variable of interest on the dependent variable when the effects of outside factors in an experiment might hide it.

information technology
Involves operating computer networks that can store and process data.

Information Technology **Information technology** involves operating computer networks that can store and process data. Today information technology can extract hidden information from large databases such as those containing retail sales collected through barcode scanners at checkout counters and households' product purchases and TV viewing behavior.

Figure 7–5 shows how marketers use information technology, data, models, and queries to obtain results that lead to marketing actions.

Today's marketing managers can be drowned in an ocean of data; they need to adopt strategies for dealing with complex, changing views of the competition, the market, and the consumer. The Internet and PC power help make sense out of this vast amount of information. The marketer's task is to convert it into useful information that will lead to marketing actions.[31]

As shown at the top of Figure 7–5, marketers use information technology that consists of computers linked together through sophisticated communication networks to access and retrieve data from internal and external sources. These data sources are stored, organized, and managed in databases. Collectively, these databases form a *data warehouse*.

As shown at the bottom of Figure 7–5, marketers use computers to query the databases in the data warehouse with marketing questions. These questions go through statistical models that organize and manipulate the data to analyze and identify the relationships that exist. The results are then presented using tables and graphics for easier interpretation. When querying a database, marketers can use *sensitivity analysis* to ask "what if" questions to determine how hypothetical changes in product or brand *drivers*—the factors that influence the buying decisions of a household or organization—can affect sales.

FIGURE 7–5
How marketing researchers and managers use information technology to turn information into action.

Information technology: Computers and communication networks

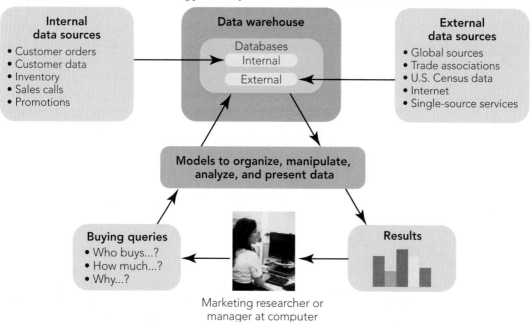

Marketing researcher or manager at computer

At 10 P.M., what is this man likely to buy besides these diapers? For the curious answer that data mining gives, see the text.

Traditional marketing research typically involves identifying possible drivers and then collecting data. For example, we might collect data to test the hypothesis that increasing couponing (the driver) during spring will increase trials by first-time buyers (the result).

Data Mining   In contrast, *data mining* is the extraction of hidden predictive information from large databases to find statistical links between consumer purchasing patterns and marketing actions. Some of these are common sense: Since many consumers buy peanut butter and grape jelly together, why not run a joint promotion between Skippy peanut butter and Welch's grape jelly? But would you have expected that men buying diapers in the evening sometimes buy a six-pack of beer as well? Supermarkets discovered this when they mined checkout data from scanners. So they placed diapers and beer near each other, then placed potato chips between them—and increased sales on all three items! On the near horizon is RFID (radio frequency identification) technology using "smart tags" on the diapers and beer to tell whether they wind up in the same shopping bag.

Data mining related to the Internet and social media is exploding. In 2012, companies are expected to spend $840 million for online data, double the 2009 amount. This increased investment in data mining also includes a greater focus on the more than $2 billion spent annually on social media advertising. And the cost to an advertiser for that one bit of special information about you? Two-fifths of a cent.[32]

Advantages and Disadvantages of Primary Data

Compared with secondary data, primary data have the advantages of being more flexible and more specific to the problem being studied. The main disadvantages are that primary data are usually far more costly and time-consuming to collect than secondary data.

learning review

6. What is the difference between observational and questionnaire data?

7. Which type of survey provides the greatest flexibility for asking probing questions: mail, telephone, or personal interview?

8. What is the difference between a panel and an experiment?

STEP 4: DEVELOP FINDINGS

LO5

Mark Twain once observed, "Collecting data is like collecting garbage. You've got to know what you're going to do with the stuff before you collect it." Thus, marketing data and information have little more value than garbage unless they are analyzed carefully and translated into logical findings, which is step 4 in the marketing research approach.[33]

Analyze the Data

Schwan Food Company produces 3 million frozen pizzas a day under brand names that include Tony's and Red Baron. Let's see how Teré Carral, the marketing manager for the Tony's brand, might address a market segment question in early 2013. We will use hypothetical data to protect Tony's proprietary information.

Teré is concerned about the limited growth in the Tony's brand over the past four years. She hires a consultant to collect and analyze data to explain what's going on with her brand and to recommend ways to improve its growth. Teré asks the consultant to put together a proposal that includes the answers to two key questions:

1. How are Tony's sales doing on a household basis? For example, are fewer households buying Tony's pizzas, or is each household buying fewer Tony's? Or both?
2. What factors might be contributing to Tony's very flat sales over the past four years?

Facts uncovered by the consultant are vital. For example, is the average household consuming more or less Tony's pizza than in previous years? Is Tony's flat sales performance related to a specific factor? With answers to these questions Teré can take actions to address the issues in the coming year.

Present the Findings

Findings should be clear and understandable from the way the data are presented. Managers are responsible for *actions*. Often it means delivering the results in clear pictures and, if possible, in a single page.

The consultant gives Teré the answers to her questions using the marketing dashboards in Figure 7–6, a creative way to present findings graphically. Let's look over Teré's shoulder as she interprets these findings:

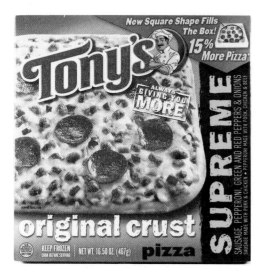

How are sales doing? To see how marketers at Tony's Pizza assessed this question and the results, read the text.

- Figure 7–6A, Annual Sales—This shows the annual growth of the Tony's Pizza brand is stable but virtually flat from 2009 through 2012.
- Figure 7–6B, Average Annual Sales per Household—Look closely at this graph. At first glance, it seems like sales in 2012 are *half* what they were in 2009, right? But be careful to read the numbers on the vertical axis. They show that household purchases of Tony's have been steadily declining over the past four years, from an average of 3.4 pizzas per household in 2009 to 3.1 pizzas per household in 2012. (Significant, but hardly a 50 percent drop.) Now the question is, if Tony's annual sales are stable, yet the average individual household is buying fewer Tony's pizzas, what's going on? The answer is, more households are buying pizzas—it's just that each household is buying fewer Tony's pizzas. That households aren't choosing Tony's is a genuine source of concern. But again, here's a classic example of a marketing problem representing a marketing opportunity. The number of households buying pizza is *growing*, and that's good news for Tony's.
- Figure 7–6C, Average Annual Sales per Household, by Household Size—This chart starts to show a source of the problem: Even though average sales of pizza to households with only one or two people are stable, households with three or four people and those with five or more are declining in average annual pizza consumption. Which households tend to have more than two people? Answer: Households *with children*. Therefore, we should look more closely at the pizza-buying behavior of households with children.
- Figure 7–6D, Average Annual Sales per Household, by Age of Children in the Household—The real problem that emerges is the serious decline in average consumption in the households with younger children, especially in households with children in the 6-to-12-year-old age group.

Identifying a sales problem in households with children 6 to 12 years old is an important discovery, as Tony's sales are declining in a market segment that is known to be one of the heaviest in buying pizzas.

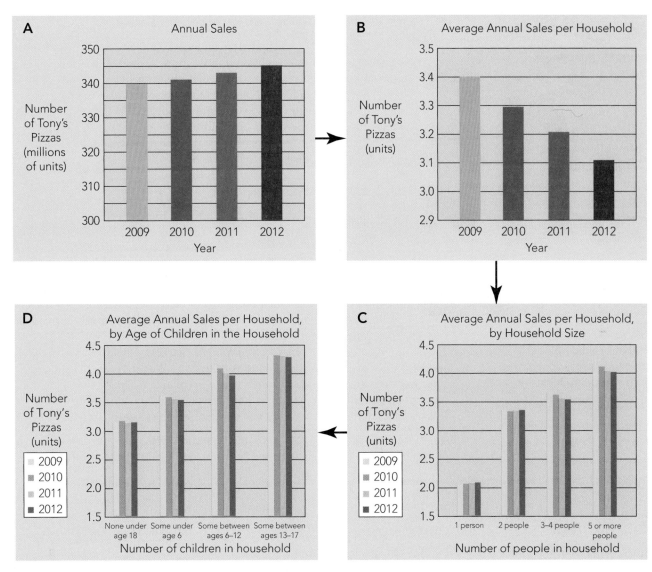

FIGURE 7–6

These marketing dashboards present findings to Tony's marketing manager that will lead to recommendations and actions.

Source: Teré Carral, Tony's Pizza.

STEP 5: TAKE MARKETING ACTIONS

Effective marketing research doesn't stop with findings and recommendations—someone has to identify the marketing actions, put them into effect, and monitor how the decisions turn out, which is the essence of step 5.

Make Action Recommendations

Teré Carral, the marketing manager for Tony's Pizza, meets with her team to convert the market research findings into specific marketing recommendations with a clear objective: Target households with children ages 6 to 12 to reverse the trend among this segment and gain strength in one of the most important segments in the frozen pizza category. Her recommendation is to develop:

- An advertising campaign that will target children 6 to 12 years old.
- A monthly promotion calendar with this age group target in mind.
- A special event program reaching children 6 to 12 years old.

Implement the Action Recommendations

As her first marketing action, Teré undertakes advertising research to develop ads that appeal to children in the 6-to-12-year-old age group and their families. The research shows that children like colorful ads with funny, friendly characters. She gives these research results to her advertising agency, which develops several sample ads for her review. Teré selects three that are tested on children to identify the most appealing one, which is then used in her next advertising campaign for Tony's Pizza. This is the ad shown to the left.

Evaluate the Results

Evaluating results is a continuing way of life for effective marketing managers. There are really two aspects of this evaluation process:

* *Evaluating the decision itself.* This involves monitoring the marketplace to determine if action is necessary in the future. For Teré, is her new ad successful in appealing to 6-to-12-year-old children and their families? Are sales increasing to this target segment? The success of this strategy suggests Teré should add more follow-up ads with colorful, funny, friendly characters.

* *Evaluating the decision process used.* Was the marketing research and analysis used to develop the recommendations effective? Was it flawed? Could it be improved for similar situations in the future? Teré and her marketing team must be vigilant in looking for ways to improve the analysis and results—to learn lessons that might apply to future marketing research efforts at Tony's.

Marketing research at Tony's Pizza helped develop this colorful, friendly ad targeted at families with children in the 6-to-12-year-old age group.

Again, systematic analysis does not guarantee success. But, as in the case of Tony's Pizza, it can improve a firm's success rate for its marketing decisions.

---

learning review

9. How does data mining differ from traditional marketing research?
10. In the marketing research for Tony's Pizza, what is an example of (*a*) a finding and (*b*) a marketing action?

SALES FORECASTING TECHNIQUES

sales forecast
The total sales of a product that a firm expects to sell during a specified time period under specified conditions.

Forecasting or estimating potential sales is often a key goal in a marketing research study. Good sales forecasts are important for a firm as it schedules production. The term **sales forecast** refers to the total sales of a product that a firm expects to sell during a specified time period under specified environmental conditions and its own marketing efforts. For example, Betty Crocker might develop a sales forecast of 4 million cases of cake mix for U.S. consumers in 2013, assuming consumers' dessert preferences remain constant and competitors don't change prices.

Three main sales forecasting techniques are often used: (1) judgments of the decision maker, (2) surveys of knowledgeable groups, and (3) statistical methods.

Judgments of the Decision Maker

Probably 99 percent of all sales forecasts are simply the judgment of the person who must act on the results of the forecast—the individual decision maker. *A direct forecast* involves estimating the value to be forecast without any intervening steps. Examples appear daily: How many quarts of milk should I buy? How much money should I get out of the ATM?

How might a marketing manager at New Balance forecast for its Minimus running shoe sales through 2015? Read the text to find out.

A *lost-horse forecast* involves starting with the last known value of the item being forecast, listing the factors that could affect the forecast, assessing whether they have a positive or negative impact, and making the final forecast. The technique gets its name from how you'd find a lost horse: go to where it was last seen, put yourself in its shoes, consider those factors that could affect where you might go (to the pond if you're thirsty, the hayfield if you're hungry, and so on), and go there.

For example, New Balance recently introduced its Minimus, shoes that are 50 percent lighter than other lightweight shoes. Its unique features are designed to make running easier and limit foot injuries. Suppose a New Balance marketing manager in early 2013 needs to make a sales forecast through 2015. She would take the known value of 2012 sales and list positive factors (good acceptance of its high-tech designs, great publicity) and the negative factors (the economic recession, competition from established name brands) to arrive at the final series of sales forecasts.[34]

Surveys of Knowledgeable Groups

If you wonder what your firm's sales will be next year, ask people who are likely to know something about future sales. Two common groups that are surveyed to develop sales forecasts are prospective buyers and the firm's salesforce.

A *survey of buyers' intentions forecast* involves asking prospective customers if they are likely to buy the product during some future time period. For industrial products with few prospective buyers, this can be effective. There are only a few hundred customers in the entire world for Boeing's large airplanes, so Boeing surveys them to develop its sales forecasts and production schedules.

A *salesforce survey forecast* involves asking the firm's salespeople to estimate sales during a coming period. Because these people are in contact with customers and are likely to know what customers like and dislike, there is logic to this approach. However, salespeople can be unreliable forecasters—painting too rosy a picture if they are enthusiastic about a new product or too grim a forecast if their sales quota and future compensation are based on it.

Statistical Methods

The best-known statistical method of forecasting is *trend extrapolation*, which involves extending a pattern observed in past data into the future. When the pattern is described with a straight line, it is *linear trend extrapolation*. Suppose that in early 2000 you were a sales forecaster for the Xerox Corporation and had actual sales data running from 1988 to 1999 (see Figure 7–7). Using linear trend extrapolation, you

FIGURE 7–7
Linear trend extrapolation of sales revenues at Xerox, made at the start of 2000.

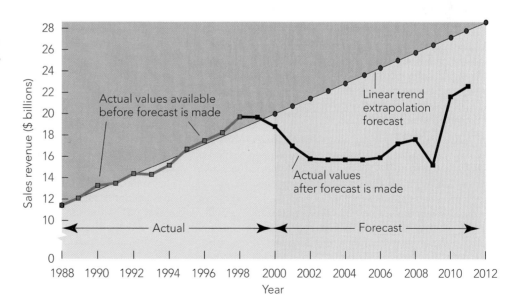

draw a line to fit the past sales data and project it into the future to give the forecast values shown for 2000 to 2012.

If in 2012 you want to compare your forecasts with actual results, you are in for a surprise—illustrating the strength and weakness of trend extrapolation. Trend extrapolation assumes that the underlying relationships in the past will continue into the future, which is the basis of the method's key strength: simplicity. If this assumption proves correct, you have an accurate forecast. However, if this proves wrong, the forecast is likely to be wrong. In this case, your forecasts from 2000 through 2011 were too high, as shown in Figure 7–7, largely because of fierce competition in the photocopying industry. The spike in 2010 sales revenues is mainly due to new acquisitions.

---

learning review

11. What are the three kinds of sales forecasting techniques?

12. How do you make a lost-horse forecast?

LEARNING OBJECTIVES REVIEW

LO1 *Identify the reason for conducting marketing research.*
To be successful, products must meet the wants and needs of potential customers. So marketing research reduces risk by providing the vital information to help marketing managers understand those wants and needs and translate them into marketing actions.

LO2 *Describe the five-step marketing research approach that leads to marketing actions.*
Marketing researchers engage in a five-step decision-making process to collect information that will improve marketing decisions. The first step is to define the problem, which requires setting the research objectives and identifying possible marketing actions. The second step is to develop the research plan, which involves specifying the constraints, identifying data needed for marketing decisions, and determining how to collect the data. The third step is to collect the relevant information, which includes considering pertinent secondary data (both internal and external) and primary data (by observing and questioning consumers) as well as using information technology and data mining to trigger marketing actions. The fourth step is to develop findings from the marketing research data collected. This involves analyzing the data and presenting the findings of the research. The fifth and last step is to take marketing actions, which involves making and implementing the action recommendations.

LO3 *Explain how marketing uses secondary and primary data.*
Secondary data have already been recorded prior to the start of the project and consist of two parts: (*a*) internal secondary data, which originate from within the organization, such as sales reports and customer comments, and (*b*) external secondary data, which are created by other organizations, such as the U.S. Census Bureau (which provides data on the country's population, manufacturers, retailers, and so on) or business and trade publications (which provide data on industry trends, market size, etc.). Primary data are collected specifically for the project and are obtained by either observing or questioning people.

LO4 *Discuss the uses of observations, questionnaires, panels, experiments, and newer data collection methods.*
Marketing researchers observe people in various ways, such as electronically using Nielsen people meters to measure TV viewing behavior or personally using mystery shoppers or ethnographic techniques. A recent electronic innovation is neuromarketing—using high-tech brain scanning to record the responses of a consumer's brain to marketing stimuli like packages or TV ads. Questionnaires involve asking people questions (*a*) in person using interviews or focus groups or (*b*) via a questionnaire using a telephone, fax, print, e-mail, or Internet survey. Panels involve a sample of consumers or stores that are repeatedly measured through time to see if their behaviors change. Experiments, such as test markets, involve measuring the effect of marketing variables such as price or advertising on sales. Collecting data from social networks like Facebook or Twitter is increasingly important because users can share their opinions about products and services with countless "friends" around the globe.

LO5 *Explain how information technology and data mining lead to marketing actions.*
Today's marketing managers are often overloaded with data—from internal sales and customer data to external data on TV viewing habits or grocery purchases from the scanner data at checkout counters. Information technology enables this massive amount of marketing data to be stored, accessed, and processed. The resulting databases can be queried using data mining to find statistical relationships useful for marketing decisions and actions.

LO6 *Describe three approaches to developing a company's sales forecast.*

One approach uses the subjective judgments of the decision maker, such as direct or lost-horse forecasts. A direct forecast involves estimating the value to be forecast without any intervening steps. A lost-horse forecast starts with the last known value of the item being forecast, and then lists the factors that could affect the forecast, assesses whether they have a positive or negative impact, and makes the final forecast. Surveys of knowledgeable groups, a second method, involve obtaining information such as the intentions of potential buyers or estimates provided by the salesforce. Statistical methods involving extending a pattern observed in past data into the future are a third approach. The best-known statistical method is linear trend extrapolation.

FOCUSING ON KEY TERMS

constraints p. 150
data p. 151
information technology p. 162
marketing research p. 148

measures of success p. 149
observational data p. 154
primary data p. 151
questionnaire data p. 156

sales forecast p. 166
secondary data p. 151

APPLYING MARKETING KNOWLEDGE

1 Suppose your dean of admissions is considering surveying high school seniors about their perceptions of your school to design better informational brochures for them. What are the advantages and disadvantages of doing (*a*) telephone interviews and (*b*) an Internet survey of seniors requesting information about the school?

2 Wisk detergent decides to run a test market to see the effect of coupons and in-store advertising on sales. The index of sales is as follows:

Element in Test Market	Weeks before Coupon	Week of Coupon	Week after Coupon
Without in-store ads	100	144	108
With in-store ads	100	268	203

What are your conclusions and recommendations?

3 Suppose Fisher-Price wants to run a simple experiment to evaluate a proposed Chatter Telephone design. It has two different groups of children on which to run its experiment for one week each. The first group has the old toy telephone, whereas the second group is exposed to the newly designed pull toy with wheels, a noisemaker, and bobbing eyes. The dependent variable is the average number of minutes during the two-hour play period that one of the children is playing with the toy, and the results are as follows:

Element in Experiment	First Group	Second Group
Independent variable	Old design	New design
Dependent variable	13 minutes	62 minutes

Should Fisher-Price introduce the new design? Why?

4 Nielsen Media Research obtains ratings of local TV stations in small markets by having households fill out diary questionnaires. These give information on (*a*) who is watching TV and (*b*) the program being watched. What are the limitations of this questionnaire method?

5 The format in which information is presented is often vital. (*a*) If you were a harried marketing manager and queried your information system, would you rather see the results in tables or charts and graphs? (*b*) What are one or two strengths and weaknesses of each format?

6 (*a*) Why might a marketing researcher prefer to use secondary data rather than primary data in a study? (*b*) Why might the reverse be true?

7 Which of the following variables would linear trend extrapolation be more accurate for? (*a*) Annual population of the United States or (*b*) annual sales of cars produced in the United States by Ford. Why?

building your marketing plan

To help you collect the most useful data for your marketing plan, develop a three-column table:

1 In column 1, list the information you would ideally like to have to fill holes in your marketing plan.
2 In column 2, identify the source for each bit of information in column 1, such as an Internet search, talking to prospective customers, looking at internal data, and so forth.
3 In column 3, set a priority on information you will have time to spend collecting by ranking each item: 1 = most important; 2 = next most important, and so forth.

"What makes social media 'social' is its give and take," says Jeff Gerst of Bolin Marketing, who manages the Carmex® social media properties. By "give" Gerst is referring to the feedback consumers send on social media; "take" is what they receive—such as news and coupons. "For Carmex, Facebook isn't just a way to share coupons or the latest product news, but it is also a marketing research resource. We have instantaneous access to the opinions of our consumers."

"While some people think of social media as 'free,' that is not true. However, almost everything in social media can be faster and cheaper than in the offline world," adds Dane Hartzell, general manager of Bolin Digital. "Many platforms have been prebuilt and we marketers only need to modify them slightly."

CARMEX AND ITS PRODUCT LINE

Although Carmex has been making lip balm since 1937, only in the last five years has it made serious efforts to stress growth and become more competitive. For example, Carmex has:

- Extended its lip balm products into new flavors and varieties.
- Expanded into nearly 40 international markets.
- Developed the Carmex Moisture Plus line of premium lip balms for women.
- Launched a line of skin care products, its first venture outside of lip care.

Carmex has used social media tools in developing all of these initiatives, but the focus of this case is how Carmex might use Facebook marketing research to grow its lip balm varieties in the United States.

FACEBOOK MARKETING RESEARCH: TWO KEY METRICS

"We have three potential new flavors and we can only put two into quantitative testing," explains Jeff Gerst to his team. "So we have two goals in doing marketing research

on this. One is to use Facebook to help us determine which two flavors we should move forward with. The second goal is to drive our Facebook metrics."

The two key Facebook metrics the Carmex marketing team has chosen to help narrow the flavor choices from three to two are "likes" and "engagement." "Likes" are the number of new "likers" to the brand's Facebook Page. This metric measures the size of the brand's Facebook audience. In contrast, "engagement" measures how active its Facebook audience is with Carmex. Any time a liker posts a comment on the Carmex Wall, likes its status, or replies to one of its posts, the engagement level increases.

The easiest way for Carmex to grow the number of "likes" on its Facebook Page is through contests and promotions. If it gives away prizes, people will be drawn to its site and its likes will increase. However, these people may not actually be fans of the Carmex product so at the end of the promotion, they may "unlike" Carmex or they may remain fans but not engage with the Carmex Page at all.

"One of the biggest challenges facing Facebook Community Managers for brands is how to grow your likes without hurting the level of engagement," says Holly Matson, director of experience planning at Bolin Marketing.

"Depending on how we go about conducting the research," Gerst adds, "we can drive engagement with our existing Facebook community, we can use this as an opportunity to grow our Facebook community or, potentially, we could do both." The benefits of this Carmex Facebook strategy are two-fold: (1) narrowing the number of flavors to be researched from three to two and (2) enhancing the connections with the Carmex Facebook community.

FIGURE 1

Facebook Open-Ended Poll Question

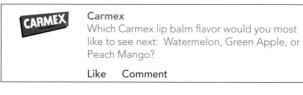

FIGURE 2

Facebook Fixed-Alternative Poll Question

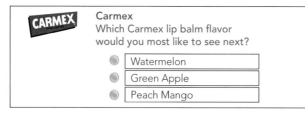

HOW THE METRICS MIGHT BE USED

Carmex's Facebook activity can benefit (1) by using a poll to increase engagement, (2) by launching a contest to increase the number of likers, and (3) by trying to increase both engagement and likers through combining a poll with a contest.

The "Engagement" Strategy: Use a Poll

Let's look at two ways to use the engagement strategy showing actual Facebook screens. First, Carmex can post a somewhat open-ended question on its Facebook Wall, such as, "Which Carmex lip balm flavor would you most like to see next: Watermelon, Green Apple, or Peach Mango?" (Figure 1). However, consumers are less likely to respond to a question if they have to type in a response and have their name attached to it.

Alternatively, Carmex can post the same question on its Wall as a fixed-alternative poll question (Figure 2). Then consumers need only to click on a flavor to vote; this is quick, anonymous, and will drive more people to vote, where more votes means more engagement. Within five minutes Carmex will have several dozen votes and, by the end of a business day, Carmex can very easily have over 500 responses.

In this scenario, the consumers are content because they are able to engage with a brand they like and have their opinions heard. Carmex is content because it has engaged hundreds of its fans on its Facebook Page, and it gains results that are very helpful in deciding which flavors to put into testing. This scenario gets an answer quickly and drives fan engagement with existing fans but does not drive new likers to the Carmex Facebook Page.

The "Likes" Strategy: Use a Contest

If Carmex wants to grow the size of its Facebook community, which means the number of its brand page "likes," it can adopt a different strategy. Carmex can announce a contest where if consumers "like" Carmex on Facebook and share a comment, they will be entered to win three limited-edition flavors. The chance to win limited-edition flavors is exciting to Carmex enthusiasts, and a contest like this will draw new consumers to the page. Carmex can ask the winners to review the limited edition flavors and see if there is a consensus on which flavors should move on to quantitative testing. Setting up

a contest, developing official rules, promoting the contest through Facebook ads, and fulfilling a contest can be costly and time-consuming.

The Combined Strategy: Use Poll and Contest

Carmex can also choose to layer these two strategies into a combined strategy where it runs the limited-edition flavor contest to promote new likes and meanwhile posts the poll question on its Facebook Wall to drive engagement.

REACHING A DECISION

Figure 3 shows the potential results from the three Facebook strategies being considered—the poll only, the contest only, or both strategies together. Assume the Carmex marketing team has sought your help in selecting a strategy and needs your answers to the questions below.

FIGURE 3

Potential Results from Three Possible Facebook Strategies

FACEBOOK STRATEGY	POTENTIAL IMPACT ON...		
	Increased "Engagement"	Increased "Likes"	Cost
Poll Only	High	Low	Low
Contest Only	Low	High	Moderate
Poll + Contest	High	High	Moderate to High

☐ Favorable   ☐ Neutral   ☐ Unfavorable

Questions

1 What are the advantages and disadvantages for the Carmex marketing team in collecting data to narrow the flavor choices from three to two using (*a*) an online survey of a cross-section of Internet households or (*b*) an online survey of Carmex Facebook likers?

2 (*a*) On a Facebook brand page, what are "engagement" and "likes" really measuring? (*b*) For Carmex, which is more important and why?

3 (*a*) What evokes consumers' "engagement" on a brand page on Facebook? (*b*) What attracts consumers to "like" a brand page on Facebook?

4 (*a*) What are the advantages of using a fixed-alternative poll question on Facebook? (*b*) When do you think it would be better to use an open-ended question?

5 (*a*) If you had a limited budget and two weeks to decide which two flavors to put into quantitative testing, would you choose a "poll only" or a "contest only" strategy? Why? (*b*) If you had a sizable budget and two months to make the same decision, which scenario would you choose? Why?

Market Segmentation, Targeting, and Positioning

8

LEARNING OBJECTIVES

After reading this chapter you should be able to:

 LO1 Explain what market segmentation is and when to use it.

LO2 Identify the five steps involved in segmenting and targeting markets.

LO3 Recognize the bases used to segment consumer and organizational (business) markets.

LO4 Develop a market-product grid to identify a target market and recommend resulting actions.

LO5 Explain how marketing managers position products in the marketplace.

ZAPPOS.COM'S "WOW" = SEGMENTS + SERVICE

Tony Hsieh (opposite page) showed signs of being an entrepreneur early in life. He's now chief executive officer (CEO) of online retailer Zappos.com, now owned by Amazon.com. The company name is derived from the Spanish word *zapatos*, which means shoes.

In college, Hsieh sold pizzas out of his dorm room. Alfred Lin bought pizzas from Hsieh and then sold them by the slice to other students. Lin is now Hsieh's chief financial officer.[1]

A Clear Market Segmentation Strategy

Hsieh, Lin, and founder Nick Swinmurn have given Zappos.com a clear, specific market segmentation strategy: Offer a huge selection of shoes to people who will buy them online. Recently Zappos.com has added lines of clothes, accessories, beauty aids, and housewares. This focus on the segment of online buyers generates over $1 billion in sales annually.[2]

Pamela Leo, a New Jersey customer, says, "With Zappos I can try the shoes in the comfort of my own home. . . . It's fabulous."[3] Zappos.com also provides free shipping both ways and offers more than 1,000 brands to customers.

Delivering WOW Customer Service

Asked about Zappos.com, Hsieh says, "We try to spend most of our time on stuff that will improve customer-service levels."[4] This customer-service obsession for its market segment of online customers means that all new Zappos.com employees—whether the chief financial officer or the children's footwear buyer—go through four weeks of customer-loyalty training. Hsieh offers $2,000 to anyone completing the training who wants to leave Zappos.com. The theory: If you take the money and run, you're not right for Zappos.com. Few take the money!

Ten "core values" are the foundation for the Zappos.com culture, brand, and business strategies. Some examples:[5]

#1. Deliver WOW through service. This focus on exemplary customer service encompasses all 10 core values.

#3. Create fun and a little weirdness. In a Zappos.com day, cowbells ring, parades appear, and modified-blaster gunfights arise (opposite page).

#6. Build open and honest relationships with communication. Employees are told to say what they think.

The other Zappos.com core values appear on its website: www.zappos.com. Tony Hsieh's strategy on core values and customer service appears on Twitter, where he has more than 1.8 million followers.[6]

The Zappos.com strategy illustrates successful market segmentation and targeting, the first topics in Chapter 8. The chapter ends with the topic of positioning the organization, product, or brand.

WHY SEGMENT MARKETS?

LO1

A business firm segments its markets so it can respond more effectively to the wants of groups of potential buyers and thus increase its sales and profits. Not-for-profit organizations also segment the clients they serve to satisfy client needs more effectively while achieving the organization's goals. Let's describe (1) what market segmentation is and (2) when to segment markets, sometimes using the Zappos.com segmentation strategy as an example.

What Market Segmentation Means

market segmentation

Aggregates potential buyers into groups that have common needs and will respond similarly to a marketing action.

market segments

The relatively homogeneous groups of prospective buyers that result from the market segmentation process.

product differentiation

The strategy of using different marketing mix activities to help consumers perceive a product as being different and better than competing products.

People have different needs and wants, even though it would be easier for marketers if they didn't. **Market segmentation** involves aggregating prospective buyers into groups that (1) have common needs and (2) will respond similarly to a marketing action. **Market segments** are the relatively homogeneous groups of prospective buyers that result from the market segmentation process. Each market segment consists of people who are relatively similar to each other in terms of their consumption behavior.

The existence of different market segments has caused firms to use a marketing strategy of **product differentiation**. This strategy involves a firm using different marketing mix activities, such as product features and advertising, to help consumers perceive the product as being different and better than competing products. The perceived differences may involve physical features, such as size or color, or nonphysical ones, such as image or price.

Segmentation: Linking Needs to Actions   The process of segmenting a market and selecting specific segments as targets is the link between the various buyers' needs and the organization's marketing program, as shown in Figure 8–1. Market segmentation is only a means to an end: It leads to tangible marketing actions that can increase sales and profitability.

Market segmentation first stresses the importance of grouping people or organizations in a market according to the similarity of their needs and the benefits they are looking for in making a purchase. Second, such needs and benefits must be related to specific marketing actions that the organization can take, such as a new product or special promotion.

The Zappos.com Segmentation Strategy   The Zappos.com target customer segment originally consisted of people who wanted to (1) have a wide selection of shoes, (2) shop online in the convenience of their own homes, and (3) receive quick delivery and free returns. Zappos's actions include offering a huge inventory of shoes using an online selling strategy and providing overnight delivery. These actions have enabled Zappos.com to create a positive customer experience and generate repeat purchases. Zappos's success in selling footwear has enabled it to add lines of clothing, handbags, and sunglasses to reach new segments of buyers.

QR 8–1
Zappos Lady
Gaga Video

FIGURE 8–1

Market segmentation links market needs to an organization's marketing program—its specific marketing mix actions designed to satisfy those needs.

Identify market needs

Benefits in terms of:
- Product features
- Expense
- Quality
- Savings in time and convenience

Link needs to actions

Take steps to segment and target markets

Execute marketing program actions

A marketing mix in terms of:
- Product
- Price
- Promotion
- Place (distribution)

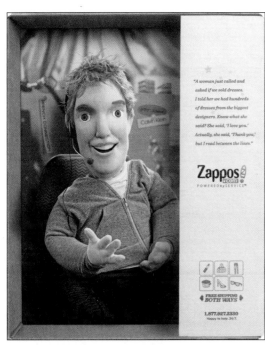

Zappos.com is reaching buyer segments beyond shoes with its edgy, attention-getting ads and WOW service.

market-product grid

A framework relating the segments of a market to products or marketing actions of the firm.

With over 8 million customers and 5,000 calls daily to Zappos's service center, its executives believe the speed with which a customer receives an online purchase plays a big role in gaining repeat customers.[7] The company continues to stress this point of difference of providing the absolute best service among online sellers.

Using Market Product Grids   How do you sleep—on your side, your back, or your stomach? These are really the key market segments of sleepers. Sleep researchers have discovered that you'll probably get a better night's sleep if you have the right firmness of pillow under your head. So we can develop the market-product grid shown in Figure 8–2.[8]

A **market-product grid** is a framework to relate the market segments of potential buyers to products offered or potential marketing actions. The market-product grid in Figure 8–2 shows the different market segments for bed pillows—the side, back, and stomach sleepers—in the horizontal rows. The product offerings—the pillows—appear in the vertical columns and are based on three different pillow firmnesses.

Market research reveals the size of each sleeper segment, as shown by both the percentages and circles in Figure 8–2. This tells pillow manufacturers the relative importance of each of the three market segments when they schedule production. It also emphasizes the importance of the firm pillow product targeted at the side sleeper market segment. As Figure 8–2 shows, this segment is almost three times the size of the other two combined. Therefore, meeting the needs of this market segment with the right quality pillow is especially important.

When and How to Segment Markets

One-size-fits-all mass markets—like that for Tide laundry detergent 40 years ago—no longer exist. The marketing officer at Procter & Gamble, which markets Tide, says, "Every one of our brands is targeted." As the size of the middle-income market has shrunk in the recent recession, P&G has a new segmentation strategy: Offer different products to reach (1) high-income and (2) low-income families.[9]

A business goes to the trouble and expense of segmenting its markets when it expects that this will increase its sales, profit, and return on investment. When expenses are greater than the potentially increased sales from segmentation, a firm should not attempt to segment its market. Three specific segmentation strategies that illustrate this point are (1) one product and multiple market segments, (2) multiple products and multiple market segments, and (3) segments of one, or mass customization.

FIGURE 8–2
This market-product grid shows the kind of sleeper that is targeted for each of the bed pillows with a different firmness. The percentages and sizes of the circles show how dominant side sleepers are, who need firm pillows.

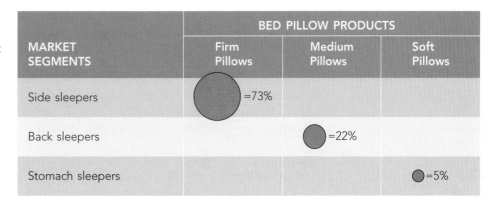

MARKET SEGMENTS	BED PILLOW PRODUCTS		
	Firm Pillows	Medium Pillows	Soft Pillows
Side sleepers	=73%		
Back sleepers		=22%	
Stomach sleepers			=5%

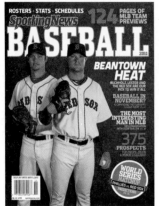

These *different* covers for the *same* magazine issue show a very effective market segmentation strategy. For which strategy it is and why it works, see the text.

One Product and Multiple Market Segments When an organization produces only a single product or service and attempts to sell it to two or more market segments, it avoids the extra costs of developing and producing additional versions of the product. In this case, the incremental costs of taking the product into new market segments are typically those of a separate promotional campaign or a new channel of distribution.

Magazines and books are single products frequently directed at two or more distinct market segments. The *Sporting News Baseball Yearbook* used 16 different covers featuring a baseball star from each of its regions in the United States. Harry Potter's phenomenal seven-book success is based on both author J. K. Rowling's fiction-writing wizardry and her publisher's creativity in marketing to preteen, teen, and adult segments of readers around the world. More than 450 million Harry Potter books, audio books, and e-books have been sold in 67 languages.[10] In the United States, the books were often at the top of *The New York Times* fiction best-seller list—for adults. Although separate covers for magazines or separate advertisements for books are expensive, these expenses are minor compared with the costs of producing multiple versions of magazines or books for several different market segments.

Multiple Products and Multiple Market Segments Ford's different lines of cars, SUVs, and pickup trucks are each targeted at a different type of customer—examples of multiple products aimed at multiple market segments. Producing these different vehicles is clearly more expensive than producing only a single vehicle. But this strategy is very effective *if* it meets customers' needs better, doesn't reduce quality or increase price, and adds to Ford's sales revenues and profits.

Unfortunately, this product differentiation strategy in the auto industry has a huge potential downside: The proliferation of different models and options can reduce quality and raise prices—especially in relation to foreign imports. Perhaps the extreme was in 1982, when the Ford Thunderbird had exactly 69,120 options compared with 32 (including colors) on the 1982 Honda Accord.[11]

Three decades later Ford is relearning its models and options lessons. Its current successful turnaround is partly related to a reduction in the number of frames, engines, and brands offered. As a result, Ford has reduced its number of models from 97 to 36 and sold off the Jaguar, Land Rover, and Volvo brands. Although there are fewer choices, Ford's simplified product line provides two benefits to consumers: (1) lower prices through producing a higher volume of fewer models and (2) higher quality because of the ability to debug fewer basic designs.[12]

Segments of One: Mass Customization American marketers are rediscovering today what their ancestors running the corner general store knew a century ago: Each customer has unique needs and wants and desires special tender loving care. Economies of scale in manufacturing and marketing during the past century made mass-produced goods so affordable that most customers were willing to compromise their individual tastes and settle for standardized products. Today's Internet ordering and flexible manufacturing and marketing processes have made *mass customization* possible, which means tailoring goods or services to the tastes of individual customers on a high-volume scale.

Mass customization is the next step beyond *build-to-order* (BTO), manufacturing a product only when there is an order from a customer. Apple uses BTO systems that trim work-in-progress inventories and shorten delivery times to customers. To do this, Apple restricts its computer manufacturing line to only a few basic models that can be assembled in four minutes. This gives customers a good choice with quick delivery. But even this system falls a bit short of total mass customization because customers do not have an unlimited number of features from which to choose.

The Segmentation Trade-Off: Synergies versus Cannibalization   The key to successful product differentiation and market segmentation strategies is finding the ideal balance between satisfying a customer's individual wants and achieving *organizational synergy*, the increased customer value achieved through performing organizational functions such as marketing or manufacturing more efficiently. The "increased customer value" can take many forms: more products, improved quality of existing products, lower prices, easier access to products through improved distribution, and so on. So the ultimate criterion for an organization's marketing success is that customers should be better off as a result of the increased synergies.

The organization should also achieve increased revenues and profits from the product differentiation and market segmentation strategies it uses. When the increased customer value involves adding new products or a new chain of stores, the product differentiation–market segmentation trade-off raises a critical issue: Are the new products or new chain simply stealing customers and sales from the older, existing ones? This is known as *cannibalization*.

Marketers increasingly emphasize a two-tier, "Tiffany/Walmart" strategy. Many firms now offer different variations of the same basic offering to high-end and low-end segments. Gap's Banana Republic chain sells blue jeans for $58, whereas Old Navy stores sell a slightly different version for $22.

Unfortunately, the lines between customer segments can often blur and lead to problems, such as the Ann Taylor flagship store competing with its LOFT outlets. The flagship Ann Taylor chain targets "successful, relatively affluent, fashion-conscious women" while its sister Ann Taylor LOFT chain targets "value-conscious women who want a casual lifestyle at work and home." The LOFT stores wound up stealing sales from the Ann Taylor chain. The result: More than 100 stores from both chains were recently closed.[13] Both chains are now aggressively targeting their customers by stressing online sales and opening new factory outlet stores.

Walmart is now operating 10 stores to test the concept of "Walmart Express," stores that are one-tenth the size of its supercenters and will sell groceries. These smaller stores are intended to compete with the dollar chains and bare-bones outlets (like Germany's Aldi supermarket chain), which are stealing U.S. Walmart customers and causing lagging sales. Will its own Tiffany/Walmart strategy—or perhaps "Walmart/Aldi strategy"—prove successful or simply be another case of cannibalization?[14]

Ann Taylor Stores Corporation's LOFT chain tries to reach younger and value-conscious women with a casual lifestyle while its flagship Ann Taylor chain targets more sophisticated and relatively affluent women. For the potential dangers of this two-segment strategy, see the text.

learning review

1. Market segmentation involves aggregating prospective buyers into groups that have two key characteristics. What are they?

2. In terms of market segments and products, what are the three market segmentation strategies?

STEPS IN SEGMENTING AND TARGETING MARKETS

LO2

Figure 8–3 identifies the five-step process used to segment a market and select the target segments on which an organization wants to focus. Segmenting a market requires both detailed analysis and large doses of common sense and managerial judgment. So market segmentation is both science and art!

For the purposes of our discussion, assume that you have just purchased a Wendy's restaurant. Your Wendy's is located next to a large urban university, one that offers both day and evening classes. Your restaurant offers the basic Wendy's fare: hamburgers, chicken and deli sandwiches, salads, french fries, and Frosty desserts. Even though you are part of a chain that has some restrictions on menu and décor, you are free to set your hours of business and to develop local advertising. How can market segmentation help? In the sections that follow, you will apply the five-step process for segmenting and targeting markets to arrive at marketing actions for your Wendy's restaurant.

Step 1: Group Potential Buyers into Segments

It's not always a good idea to segment a market. Grouping potential buyers into meaningful segments involves meeting some specific criteria that answer the questions, "Would segmentation be worth doing?" and "Is it possible?" If so, a marketer must find specific variables that can be used to create these various segments.

Criteria to Use in Forming the Segments
A marketing manager should develop market segments that meet five essential criteria:[15]

- *Simplicity and cost-effectiveness of assigning potential buyers to segments.* A marketing manager must be able to put a market segmentation plan into effect. This means identifying the characteristics of potential buyers in a market and then cost-effectively assigning them to a segment.
- *Potential for increased profit.* The best segmentation approach is the one that maximizes the opportunity for future profit and return on investment (ROI). If this potential is maximized without segmentation, don't segment. For nonprofit organizations, the criterion is the potential for serving clients more effectively.
- *Similarity of needs of potential buyers within a segment.* Potential buyers within a segment should be similar in terms of common needs that, in turn, lead to a common marketing action, such as product features sought or advertising media used.
- *Difference of needs of buyers among segments.* If the needs of the various segments aren't very different, combine them into fewer segments. A different segment usually requires a different marketing action that, in turn, means greater costs. If increased sales don't offset extra costs, combine segments and reduce the number of marketing actions.
- *Potential of a marketing action to reach a segment.* Reaching a segment requires a simple but effective marketing action. If no such action exists, don't segment.

FIGURE 8–3

The five key steps in segmenting and targeting markets link the market needs of customers to the organization's marketing program.

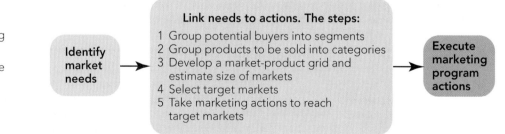

Identify market needs

Link needs to actions. The steps:
1. Group potential buyers into segments
2. Group products to be sold into categories
3. Develop a market-product grid and estimate size of markets
4. Select target markets
5. Take marketing actions to reach target markets

Execute marketing program actions

Who are your target customers? What are they like? Where do they live? How can you reach them?

These questions are answered by Nielsen Claritas, whose Nielsen PRIZM® consumer segmentation system classifies every household into one of 66 demographically and behaviorally distinct neighborhood segments to identify lifestyles and purchase behavior within a defined geographic market area, such as zip code or household. Many organizations today use these neighborhood segments, especially with social media.

Want to know what your neighborhood is like? Go to www.mybestsegments.com and click the "You Are Where You Live" image. Then, type in your zip code (and security code) to find out what the most common segments are in your neighborhood.

For a description of these segments, click the "Segment Look-Up" tab. Is this your "flock"? What specific product or service organizations might be interested in targeting these segments?

LO3

This appliance includes everything from a small refrigerator, freezer, and microwave oven to a charging station for laptops and mobile phones. To which market segment might this appeal? The answer appears in the text.

Ways to Segment Consumer Markets   Four general bases of segmentation can be used to segment U.S. consumer markets. These four segmentation bases are (1) *geographic segmentation*, which is based on where prospective customers live or work (region, city size); (2) *demographic segmentation*, which is based on some objective physical (gender, race), measurable (age, income), or other classification attribute (birth era, occupation) of prospective customers; (3) *psychographic segmentation*, which is based on some subjective mental or emotional attributes (personality), aspirations (lifestyle), or needs of prospective customers; and (4) *behavioral segmentation*, which is based on some observable actions or attitudes by prospective customers—such as where they buy, what benefits they seek, how frequently they buy, and why they buy. Some examples are:

- *Geographic segmentation: Region.* Campbell Soup Company found that its canned nacho cheese sauce, which could be heated and poured directly onto nacho chips, was too spicy for Americans in the East and not spicy enough for those in the West and Southwest. The result: Campbell's plants in Texas and California produced a hotter nacho cheese sauce than that produced in the other plants to serve their regions better.
- *Demographic segmentation: Household size.* More than half of all U.S. households are made up of only one or two persons, so Campbell packages meals with only one or two servings for this market segment.
- *Psychographic segmentation: Lifestyle.* Nielsen Claritas's lifestyle segmentation is based on the belief that "birds of a feather flock together." Thus, people of similar lifestyles tend to live near one another, have similar interests, and buy similar offerings. This is of great value to marketers. The Nielsen PRIZM classifies every household in the United States into one of 66 unique market segments. See the Marketing Matters box for a profile of where you live.
- *Behavioral segmentation: Product features.* Understanding what features are important to different customers is a useful way to segment markets because it can lead directly to specific marketing actions, such as a new product, an ad campaign, or a distribution system. For example, college dorm residents frequently want to keep and prepare their own food to save money or have a late-night snack. However, their dorm rooms are often woefully short of space. MicroFridge understands this and markets a combination microwave, refrigerator, freezer, and charging station appliance targeted to these students.

CHAPTER 8   MARKET SEGMENTATION, TARGETING, AND POSITIONING

- *Behavioral segmentation: Usage rate.* **Usage rate** is the quantity consumed or patronage—store visits—during a specific period. It varies significantly among different customer groups. Airlines have developed frequent-flier programs to encourage passengers to use the same airline repeatedly to create loyal customers. This technique, sometimes called *frequency marketing*, focuses on usage rate. One key conclusion emerges about usage: In market segmentation studies, some measurement of usage by, or sales obtained from, various segments is central to the analysis.

The Aberdeen Group recently analyzed which segmentation bases were used by the 20 percent most profitable organizations of the 220 surveyed. From highest to lowest, these were the segmentation bases they used:

- Geographic bases—88 percent.
- Behavioral bases—65 percent.
- Demographic bases—53 percent.
- Psychographic bases—43 percent.

The top 20 percent often use more than one of these bases in their market segmentation studies, plus measures such as purchase histories and usage rates of customers.[16]

Experian Simmons continuously surveys over 25,000 adults each year to obtain quarterly, projectable usage rate data from the U.S. national population for more than 500 consumer product categories and 8,000+ brands. Its purpose is to discover how the products and services they buy and the media they use relate to their behavioral, psychographic, and demographic characteristics.[17]

Usage rate is sometimes referred to in terms of the **80/20 rule**, a concept that suggests 80 percent of a firm's sales are obtained from 20 percent of its customers. The percentages in the 80/20 rule are not exactly 80 percent and 20 percent but they suggest that a small fraction of customers provides most of a firm's sales.

Patronage of Fast-Food Restaurants   As part of its survey, Experian Simmons asked adults which fast-food restaurant(s) was (1) the sole or only restaurant, (2) the primary one, or (3) one of several secondary ones they patronized. As a Wendy's restaurant owner, the information depicted in Figure 8–4 should give you some ideas in developing a marketing program for your local market. For example, the Wendy's bar graph in Figure 8–4 shows

FIGURE 8–4

Comparison of various kinds of users and nonusers for Wendy's, Burger King, and McDonald's fast-food restaurants. This table gives Wendy's restaurants a snapshot of its customers compared to those of its major competitors.

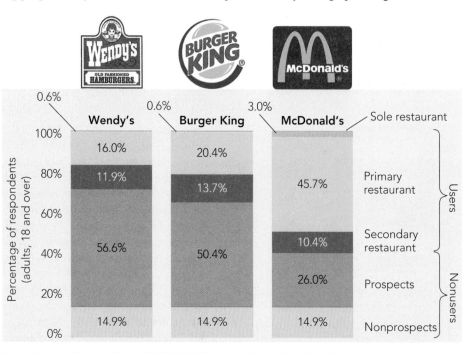

Source: Experian Simmons Winter 2012 NHCS Full-Year Adult Survey 12 OneViewSM Crosstabulation Report © Experian Simmons 2012.

that your sole (0.6 percent) and primary (16.0 percent) user segments are somewhat behind Burger King and far behind McDonald's. Thus, your challenge is to look at these two competitors and devise a marketing program to win customers from them.

The nonusers part of the Wendy's bar graph in Figure 8–4 also provides ideas. It shows that 14.9 percent of adult Americans don't go to fast-food restaurants in a typical month and are really nonprospects—unlikely to ever patronize any fast-food restaurant. However, 56.6 percent of nonusers are prospects who may be worth a targeted marketing program. These adults use the product category (fast food) but do not yet patronize Wendy's. New menu items or promotional strategies may succeed in converting these prospects into users that patronize Wendy's.

Variables to Use in Forming Segments for Wendy's To analyze your Wendy's customers, you need to identify which variables to use to segment them. Because the restaurant is located near a large urban university, the most logical starting point for segmentation is really behavioral: Are the prospective customers students or nonstudents?

To segment the students, you could try a variety of (1) geographic variables, such as city or zip code, (2) demographic variables, such as gender, age, year in school, or college major, or (3) psychographic variables, such as personality or needs. But none of these variables really meets the five criteria listed previously—particularly, the fifth criterion about leading to a doable marketing action to reach the various segments. The bases of segmentation for the "students" segment really combines two variables: (1) where students live and (2) when they are on campus. This results in four "student" segments:

- Students living in dormitories (university residence halls, sororities, fraternities).
- Students living near the university in apartments.
- Day commuter students living outside the area.
- Night commuter students living outside the area.

The three main segments of "nonstudents" include:

- Faculty and staff members who work at the university.
- People who live in the area but aren't connected with the university.
- People who work in the area but aren't connected with the university.

People in each of these nonstudent segments aren't quite as similar as those in the student segments, which makes them harder to reach with a marketing program or action. Think about (1) whether the needs of all these segments are different and (2) how various advertising media can be used to reach these groups effectively.

Ways to Segment Organizational (Business) Markets A number of variables can be used to segment organizational (business) markets. For example, a product manager at Xerox responsible for its new line of multifunction (MFP) color printers might use these segmentation bases and corresponding variables:

- *Geographic segmentation: Statistical area.* Firms located in a metropolitan statistical area might receive a personal sales call, whereas those in a micropolitan statistical area might be contacted by telephone.
- *Demographic segmentation: NAICS code.* Firms categorized by the North American Industry Classification System code as manufacturers that deal with customers throughout the world might have different document printing needs than retailers or lawyers serving local customers.
- *Demographic segmentation: Number of employees.* The size of the firm is related to the volume of digital documents produced, so firms with varying numbers of employees might be specific target markets for different Xerox copier systems.
- *Behavioral segmentation: Usage rate.* Similar to this segmentation variable for consumer markets, features are often of major importance in organizational markets. So Xerox can target organizations needing fast printing, copying, and scanning in color—the benefits and features emphasized in the ad for its Xerox Color WorkCentre 7775 MFP (multi-functional printer) system.

What variables might Xerox use to segment organizational markets to respond to a firm's color-copying problems? For the possible answer and related marketing actions, see the text.

PRACTICAL COLOR

Our color prints run on just pennies a page. Our tracking software increases the mileage you get out of color. Our total satisfaction guarantee* protects your investment. Xerox Color. It makes business sense.

XEROX.

xerox.com/freqcolor

Technology | Document Management | Consulting Services

3. The process of segmenting and targeting markets is a bridge between which two marketing activities?

4. What is the difference between the demographic and behavioral bases of market segmentation?

QR 8–2
Dave's Hot 'n Juicy Ad

Step 2: Group Products to Be Sold into Categories

What does your Wendy's restaurant sell? Of course you are selling individual products such as Frostys, hamburgers, and fries. But for marketing purposes you're really selling combinations of individual products that become a "meal." This distinction is critical, so let's discuss both (1) individual Wendy's products and (2) groupings of Wendy's products.

Individual Wendy's Products   When Dave Thomas founded Wendy's in 1969, he offered only four basic items: "Hot 'n juicy" hamburgers, Frosty Dairy Desserts (Frostys), french fries, and soft drinks. Since then, Wendy's has introduced many new products and innovations to compete for customers' fast-food dollars. Some of these are shown in Figure 8–5. New products include salads, low trans fat chicken sandwiches, and natural-cut fries with sea salt. But there are also nonproduct innovations to increase consumer convenience like drive-thru services and E-Pay to enable credit card purchases.

Figure 8–5 also shows that each product or innovation is not targeted equally to all market segments based on gender, needs, or university affiliation. The cells in Figure 8–5 labeled "P" represent Wendy's primary target market segments when it introduced each product or innovation. The boxes labeled "S" represent the secondary target

FIGURE 8–5

Wendy's new products and other innovations target specific market segments based on a customer's gender, needs, or university affiliation.

MARKET SEGMENT		PRODUCT OR INNOVATION								
GENERAL	GROUP WITH NEED	HOT 'N JUICY HAMBURGER (1969)	DRIVE THRU (1970)	99¢ SUPER VALUE MEALS (1989)	SALAD SENSATIONS (2002)	E-PAY (2003)	LOW TRANS FAT CHICKEN SANDWICHES (2006)	BREAKFAST SANDWICHES (2007)	NATURAL CUT FRIES WITH SEA SALT (2010)	DAVE'S HOT 'N JUICY HAMBURGERS (2011)
GENDER	Male	P	P	P	S	P	S	P	P	P
	Female				P	P	P			
NEEDS	Price/Value			P	S					
	Health Conscious				P		P			
	Convenience	S	P		S	P		P		S
	Meat Lovers	P		S			S		S	P
UNIVERSITY AFFILIATION	Affiliated (students, faculty, staff)	P	S	P	P	P	P	S		P
	Nonaffiliated (residents, workers)	S	P	S	S	S	S	P		S

Key: P = Primary market   S = Secondary market

market segments that also bought these products or used these innovations. In some cases, Wendy's discovered that large numbers of people in a segment not originally targeted for a particular product or innovation bought or used it anyway.

Groupings of Wendy's Products: Meals Finding a means of grouping the products a firm sells into meaningful categories is as important as grouping customers into segments. If the firm has only one product or service, this isn't a problem. But when it has many, these must be grouped in some way so buyers can relate to them. This is why department stores and supermarkets are organized into product groups, with the departments or aisles containing related merchandise. Likewise, manufacturers organize products into groupings in the catalogs they send to customers.

What are the product groupings for your Wendy's restaurant? It could be the item purchased, such as hamburgers, salads, a Frosty, and french fries. This is where judgment—the qualitative aspect of marketing—comes in. Customers really buy an eating experience—a meal occasion that satisfies a need at a particular time of day. So the product groupings that make the most marketing sense are the five "meals" based on the time of day consumers buy them: breakfast, lunch, between-meal snack, dinner, and after-dinner snack. These groupings are more closely related to the way purchases are actually made and permit you to market the entire meal, not just your individual items such as french fries or hamburgers.

Step 3: Develop a Market-Product Grid and Estimate the Size of Markets

As noted earlier in the chapter, a market-product grid is a framework to relate the market segments of potential buyers to products offered or potential marketing actions by an organization. In a complete market-product grid analysis, each cell in the grid can show the estimated market size of a given product sold to a specific market segment. Let's first look at forming a market-product grid for your Wendy's restaurant and then estimate market sizes.

Forming a Market-Product Grid for Wendy's Developing a market-product grid means identifying and labeling the markets (or horizontal rows) and product groupings (or vertical columns), as shown in Figure 8–6. From our earlier discussion we've chosen to divide the market segments into students versus nonstudents, with

FIGURE 8–6
A market–product grid for your Wendy's fast-food restaurant next to an urban university. The numbers in the grid show the estimated size of the market in each cell, which leads to selecting the shaded target market.

MARKET SEGMENTS	PRODUCTS: MEALS				
	Breakfast	Lunch	Between-Meal Snack	Dinner	After-Dinner Snack
Student					
Dormitory	0	1	3	0	3
Apartment	1	3	3	1	1
Day commuter	0	3	2	1	0
Night commuter	0	0	1	3	2
Nonstudent					
Faculty or staff	0	3	1	1	0
Live in area	0	1	2	2	1
Work in area	1	3	0	1	0

Key: 3 = Large market; 2 = Medium market; 1 = Small market; 0 = No market.

Wendy's has been aggressive in introducing new menu items to appeal to customers—such as making its classic cheeseburger thicker and offering new premium toppings.

subdivisions of each. The columns—or "products"—are really the meals (or eating occasions) customers enjoy at the restaurant.

Estimating Market Sizes for Wendy's Now the size of the market in each cell (the unique market-product combination) of the market-product grid must be estimated. For your Wendy's restaurant, this involves estimating the sales of each kind of meal expected to be sold to each student and nonstudent market segment.

The market size estimates in Figure 8–6 vary from a large market ("3") to no market at all ("0") for each cell in the market-product grid. These may be simple guesstimates if you don't have the time or money to conduct formal marketing research (as discussed in Chapter 7). But even such crude estimates of the size of specific markets using a market-product grid are helpful in determining which target market segments to select and which product groupings to offer.

Step 4: Select Target Markets

A firm must take care to choose its target market segments carefully. If it picks too narrow a set of segments, it may fail to reach the volume of sales and profits it needs. If it selects too broad a set of segments, it may spread its marketing efforts so thin that the extra expense exceeds the increased sales and profits.

Criteria to Use in Selecting the Target Segments Two kinds of criteria in the market segmentation process are those used to (1) divide the market into segments (discussed earlier) and (2) actually pick the target segments. Even experienced marketing executives often confuse them. Five criteria can be used to select the target segments for your Wendy's restaurant:

- *Market size.* The estimated size of the market in the segment is an important factor in deciding whether it's worth going after. There is really no market for breakfasts among dormitory students with meal plans (Figure 8–6), so you should not devote any marketing effort toward reaching this tiny segment.
- *Expected growth.* Although the size of the market in the segment may be small now, perhaps it is growing significantly or is expected to grow in the future. Sales of fast-food meals eaten outside the restaurants are projected to exceed those eaten inside. And Wendy's has been shown to be the fast-food leader in average time to serve a drive-thru order—faster than McDonald's. This speed and convenience is potentially very important to night commuters in adult education programs.
- *Competitive position.* Is there a lot of competition in the segment now or is there likely to be in the future? The less the competition, the more attractive the segment is. For example, if the college dormitories announce a new policy of "no meals on weekends," this segment is suddenly more promising for your restaurant. Wendy's recently introduced the E-Pay pay-by-credit-card service at its restaurants to keep up with a similar service at McDonald's.
- *Cost of reaching the segment.* A segment that is inaccessible to a firm's marketing actions should not be pursued. For example, the few nonstudents who live in the area may not be reachable with ads in newspapers or other media. As a result, you should not waste money trying to advertise to them.
- *Compatibility with the organization's objectives and resources.* If your Wendy's restaurant doesn't yet have the cooking equipment to make breakfasts and has a policy against spending more money on restaurant equipment, then don't try to reach the breakfast segment. As is often the case in marketing decisions, a particular segment may appear attractive according to some criteria and very unattractive according to others.

Choose the Wendy's Segments Ultimately, a marketing executive has to use these criteria to choose the segments for special marketing efforts. As shown in Figure 8–6, let's assume you've written off the breakfast product grouping for two reasons: It's too small a market and it's incompatible with your objectives and resources. In terms of competitive position and cost of reaching the segment, you focus on the four student segments and *not* the three nonstudent segments (although you're certainly not going to turn their business away!). This combination of market-product segments—your target market—is shaded in Figure 8–6.

Step 5: Take Marketing Actions to Reach Target Markets

The purpose of developing a market-product grid is to trigger marketing actions to increase sales and profits. This means that someone must develop and execute an action plan in the form of a marketing program.

Your Immediate Wendy's Segmentation Strategy With your Wendy's restaurant you've already reached one significant decision: There is a limited market for breakfast, so you won't open for business until 10:30 A.M. In fact, Wendy's first attempt at a breakfast menu was a disaster and was discontinued in 1986. However, that strategy has changed yet again, with its new "fresh made breakfast" menu now being offered in select locations.

Another essential decision is where and what meals to advertise to reach specific market segments. An ad in the student newspaper could reach all the student segments, but it might be too expensive. If you choose three segments for special attention (Figure 8–7), advertising actions to reach them might include:

- *Day commuters* (an entire market segment). Run ads inside commuter buses and put flyers under the windshield wipers of cars in parking lots used by day commuters. These ads and flyers promote all the meals at your restaurant to a single segment of students, a horizontal cut through the market-product grid.

FIGURE 8–7

Advertising actions to market various meals to a range of possible market segments of students.

MARKET SEGMENTS	PRODUCTS: MEALS			
	Lunch	Between-Meal Snack	Dinner	After-Dinner Snack
Dormitory students	1	3	0	3
Apartment students	3	3	1	1
Day commuter students	3	2	1	0
Night commuter students	0	1	3	2

Ads in buses; flyers under windshield wipers of cars in parking lots

Ad campaign: "Ten percent off all purchases between 2:00 and 4:30 P.M. during winter quarter"

Ad on flyer under windshield wipers of cars in night parking lots: "Free Frosty with this coupon when you buy a drive-thru meal between 5:00 and 8:00 P.M."

Key: 3 = Large market; 2 = Medium market; 1 = Small market; 0 = No market.

- *Between-meal snacks* (directed to all four student markets). To promote eating during this downtime for your restaurant, offer "Ten percent off all purchases between 2:00 and 4:30 P.M. during winter quarter." This ad promotes a single meal to all four student segments, a vertical cut through the market-product grid.
- *Dinners to night commuters.* The most focused of all three campaigns, this promotes a single meal to the single segment of night commuter students. The campaign uses flyers placed under the windshield wipers of cars in night parking lots. To encourage eating dinner at Wendy's, offer a free Frosty with the coupon when the person buys a meal between 5 and 8 P.M. using the drive-thru window.

Depending on how your advertising actions work, you can repeat, modify, or drop them and design new campaigns for other segments you deem are worth the effort. This advertising example is just a small piece of a complete marketing program for your Wendy's restaurant.

There's always plenty of competition in the hamburger business. Five Guys Burgers and Fries has grown to almost 1,000 outlets in the past decade.

Keeping an Eye on Competition   Other competitors are not sitting still, so in running your Wendy's you must be aware of their strategies. McDonald's, with many of its locations offering free Wi-Fi, is aggressively marketing its "garden" snack wraps, McCafe coffee beverages, oatmeal, and high-margin fruit smoothies.[18] Burger King has won awards for its "Subservient Chicken" and "Whopper Sacrifice" social media campaigns and is upgrading its outlets and broadening its breakfast menu.[19]

Even new hamburger chains are popping up. In 1986, a Virginia husband-and-wife team started the Five Guys Burgers and Fries hamburger restaurant and 15 years later had only five restaurants in the Washington, D.C., area. But from 2003 to 2012, Five Guys exploded, with more than 1,000 locations nationwide and 1,500 new restaurants planned. Some of its points of difference: Simple menu and décor, modest prices, only fresh ground beef (none frozen), and a trans-fat-free menu (cooking with peanut oil). But who's keeping track? The Big Three of McDonald's, Burger King, and Wendy's certainly are. All three are responding aggressively to reach the new "fast-casual" market segment that wants healthier food at lower prices in sit-down restaurants.[20]

What about the nonhamburger chains? Many are now selling food items and trying to gain market share from the Big Three. These include convenience store chains like 7-Eleven, coffee shops like Starbucks, smoothie outlets like Jamba Juice, and gas stations with prepared and reheatable packaged food.[21]

Future Strategies for Your Wendy's Restaurant   Changing customer tastes and competition mean you must alter your strategies when necessary. This involves looking at (1) what Wendy's headquarters is doing, (2) what competitors are doing, and (3) what might be changing in the area served by your restaurant.

Wendy's recently introduced aggressive new marketing programs that include:[22]

- Targeting 25-to-49-year-old customers, not just 18-to-24-year-old ones.
- Positioning Wendy's as a lower-cost fast-food chain.
- Offering improved menu items like natural-cut fries with sea salt in 2010, Dave's Hot 'n Juicy hamburgers in 2011, and a thicker classic cheeseburger with new premium toppings and a spicy guacamole chicken club sandwich in 2012.
- Introducing four new salad varieties, featuring 11 different greens and apples, pecans, and asiago cheese.

The Wendy's strategy has been remarkably successful. Zagat's Fast-Food Survey recently rated it #1 on a number of key criteria among "mega" fast-food chains.[23]

Marketing Matters > > > > > > > technology

Apple's Segmentation Strategy—Camp Runamok No Longer

Camp Runamok was the nickname given to Apple in the early 1980s because the innovative company had no coherent series of product lines directed at identifiable market segments. Today, Apple has targeted its various lines of Macintosh computers at specific market segments, as shown in the accompanying market-product grid.

Because the market-product grid shifts as a firm's strategy changes, the one here is based on Apple's product lines in mid-2012. The grid suggests the market segmentation strategy Apple is using to compete in the digital age.

MARKETS		COMPUTER PRODUCTS				
SECTOR	SEGMENT	Mac Pro	MacBook Pro	iMac	MacBook Air	Mac Mini
CONSUMER	Individuals		✓	✓	✓	✓
	Small/home office		✓	✓	✓	
	Students			✓	✓	✓
	Teachers		✓	✓		
PROFESSIONAL	Medium/large business	✓	✓	✓	✓	✓
	Creative	✓	✓	✓		
	College faculty		✓	✓	✓	
	College staff			✓	✓	

How has Apple moved from its 1977 Apple II to today's iMac? The Marketing Matters box provides insights.

QR 8–3
Apple's 1984 Super Bowl Ad

With these corporate Wendy's plans and new actions from competitors, maybe you'd better rethink your market segmentation decisions on hours of operation. Also, if new businesses have moved into your area, what about a new strategy to reach people that work in the area? Or a new promotion for the night owls and early birds—the 12 A.M. to 5 A.M. customers.

Apple's Ever-Changing Segmentation Strategy Steve Jobs and Steve Wozniak didn't realize they were developing today's multibillion-dollar PC industry when they invented the Apple I in a garage on April Fool's Day in 1976. However, when the Apple II was displayed at a computer trade show in 1977, consumers loved it and Apple Computer was born. Typical of young companies, Apple focused on its products and had little concern for its markets. Its creative, young engineers were often likened to "Boy Scouts without adult supervision."[24] Yet in 1984 the new Apple Macintosh revolutionized computers, and its 1984 Super Bowl TV ad is generally recognized as the best TV ad in history.

In 1997, Steve Jobs detailed his vision for a reincarnated Apple by describing a new market segmentation strategy that he called the "Apple Product Matrix." This strategy consisted of developing two general types of computers (desktops and portables) targeted at two market segments—the consumer and professional sectors.

In most segmentation situations, a single product does not fit into an exclusive market niche. Rather, product lines and market segments overlap. So Apple's market segmentation strategy enables it to offer different products to meet the needs of different market segments, as shown in the Marketing Matters box.

Market-Product Synergies: A Balancing Act

Recognizing opportunities for key synergies—that is, efficiencies—is vital to success in selecting target market segments and making marketing decisions. Market-product grids illustrate where such synergies can be found. How? Let's consider Apple's market-product grid in the Marketing Matters box on the previous page and examine the difference between marketing synergies and product synergies shown there.

- *Marketing synergies.* Running horizontally across the grid, each row represents an opportunity for efficiency in terms of a market segment. Were Apple to focus on just one group of consumers, such as the medium/large business segment, its marketing efforts could be streamlined. Apple would not have to spend time learning about the buying habits of students or college faculty. So it could probably create a single ad to reach the medium/large business target segment (the yellow row), highlighting the only products they'd need to worry about developing: the Mac Pro, the MacBook Pro, the iMac, and the MacBook Air. Although clearly not Apple's strategy today, new firms often focus only on a single customer segment.
- *Product synergies.* Running vertically down the market-product grid, each column represents an opportunity for efficiency in research and development (R&D) and production. If Apple wanted to simplify its product line, reduce R&D and production expenses, and manufacture only one computer, which might it choose? Based on the market-product grid, Apple might do well to focus on the iMac (the orange column), because every segment purchases it.

Marketing synergies often come at the expense of product synergies because a single customer segment will likely require a variety of products, each of which will have to be designed and manufactured. The company saves money on marketing but spends more on production. Conversely, if product synergies are emphasized, marketing will have to address the concerns of a wide variety of consumers, which costs more time and money. Marketing managers responsible for developing a company's product line must balance both product and marketing synergies as they try to increase the company's profits.

---

learning review

5. What factor is estimated or measured for each of the cells in a market-product grid?

6. What are some criteria used to decide which segments to choose for targets?

7. How are marketing and product synergies different in a market-product grid?

POSITIONING THE PRODUCT

LO5

When a company introduces a new product, a decision critical to its long-term success is how prospective buyers view it in relation to those products offered by its competitors. **Product positioning** refers to the place a product occupies in consumers' minds based on important attributes relative to competitive products. By understanding where consumers see a company's product or brand today, a marketing manager can seek to change its future position in their minds. This requires **product repositioning**, *changing* the place a product occupies in a consumer's mind relative to competitive products.

Two Approaches to Product Positioning

Marketers follow two main approaches to positioning a new product in the market. *Head-to-head positioning* involves competing directly with competitors on similar product attributes in the same target market. Using this strategy, Dollar Rent A Car competes directly with Avis and Hertz.

product positioning
The place a product occupies in consumers' minds based on important features relative to competitive products.

product repositioning
Changing the place a product occupies in consumers' minds relative to competitive products.

More "zip" for chocolate milk? The text and Figure 8–8 describe how American dairies have successfully repositioned chocolate milk to appeal to adults.

Differentiation positioning involves seeking a less-competitive, smaller market niche in which to locate a brand. McDonald's tried to appeal to the health-conscious segment with its low-fat McLean Deluxe hamburger to avoid competing directly with Wendy's and Burger King. But this item was eventually dropped from the menu.

Writing a Positioning Statement

Marketing managers often convert their positioning ideas for the offering into a succinct written positioning statement. The positioning statement is used not only internally within the marketing department, but also for others, outside it, such as research and development engineers or advertising agencies.[25] Here is the Volvo positioning statement for the North American market:

> For upscale American families who desire a carefree driving experience, Volvo is a premium-priced automobile that offers the utmost in safety and dependability.

This focuses Volvo's North American marketing strategy, so Volvo advertising almost always mentions safety and dependability.

Product Positioning Using Perceptual Maps

A key to positioning a product or brand effectively is discovering the perceptions in the minds of potential customers by taking four steps:

1. Identify the important attributes for a product or brand class.
2. Discover how target customers rate competing products or brands with respect to these attributes.
3. Discover where the company's product or brand is on these attributes in the minds of potential customers.
4. Reposition the company's product or brand in the minds of potential customers.

As shown in Figure 8–8, from these data it is possible to develop a **perceptual map**, a means of displaying in two dimensions the location of products or brands in the minds of consumers. This enables a manager to see how consumers perceive competing products or brands, as well as the firm's own product or brand.

perceptual map
A means of displaying the position of products or brands in consumers' minds.

FIGURE 8–8
The strategy American dairies are using to reposition chocolate milk to reach adults: Have adults view chocolate milk as both more nutritional and more "adult."

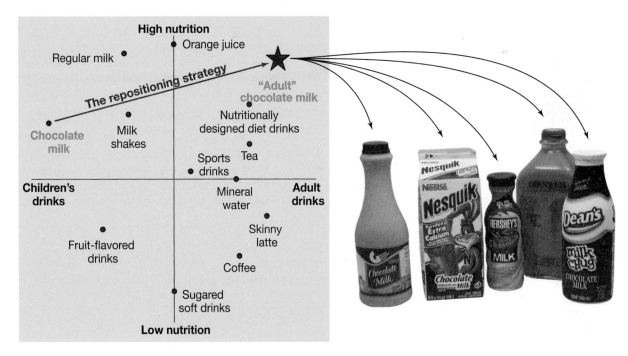

A Perceptual Map to Reposition Chocolate Milk for Adults

Recently, U.S. dairies decided to reposition chocolate milk in the minds of American adults to increase its sales. This is how dairies repositioned chocolate milk for American adults using the four steps listed on the previous page:

1. *Identify the important attributes (or scales) for adult drinks.* Research reveals the key attributes adults use to judge various drinks are (*a*) low versus high nutrition and (*b*) children's drinks versus adult drinks, as shown by the two axes in Figure 8–8.

2. *Discover how adults see various competing drinks.* Locate various adult drinks on these axes, as shown in Figure 8–8.

3. *Discover how adults see chocolate milk.* Figure 8–8 shows adults see chocolate milk as moderately nutritious (on the vertical axis) but as mainly a child's drink (on the horizontal axis).

4. *Reposition chocolate milk to make it more appealing to adults.* What actions did U.S. dairies take to increase sales? They repositioned chocolate milk to the location of the star shown in the perceptual map in Figure 8–8.

The dairies' arguments are nutritionally powerful. For women, chocolate milk provides calcium, critically important in female diets. And dieters get a more filling, nutritious beverage than with a soft drink for about the same calories. The result: Chocolate milk sales increased dramatically, much of it because of adult consumption.[26] Part of this is due to giving chocolate milk "nutritional respectability" for adults, but another part is due to the innovative packaging that enables many new chocolate milk containers to fit in a car's cup holders.

---

learning review

8. What is the difference between product positioning and product repositioning?

9. Why do marketers use perceptual maps in product positioning decisions?

LEARNING OBJECTIVES REVIEW

LO1 *Explain what market segmentation is and when to use it.*
Market segmentation involves aggregating prospective buyers into groups that (*a*) have common needs and (*b*) will respond similarly to a marketing action. Organizations go to the expense of segmenting their markets when it increases their sales, profits, and ability to serve customers better.

LO2 *Identify the five steps involved in segmenting and targeting markets.*
Step 1 is to group potential buyers into segments. Buyers within a segment should have similar characteristics to each other and respond similarly to marketing actions like a new product or a lower price. Step 2 involves putting related products to be sold into meaningful groups. In step 3, organizations develop a market-product grid with estimated sizes of markets in each of the market-product cells of the resulting table. Step 4 involves selecting the target market segments on which the organization should focus. Step 5 involves taking marketing mix actions—often in the form of a marketing program—to reach the target market segments.

LO3 *Recognize the bases used to segment consumer and organizational (business) markets.*
Bases used to segment consumer markets include geographic, demographic, psychographic, and behavioral ones. Organizational markets use the same bases except for psychographic ones.

LO4 *Develop a market-product grid to identify a target market and recommend resulting actions.*
Organizations use five key criteria to segment markets, whose groupings appear in the rows of the market-product grid. Groups of related products appear in the columns. After estimating the size of the market in each cell in the grid, they select the target market segments on which to focus. They then identify marketing mix actions—often in a marketing program—to reach the target market most efficiently.

LO5 *Explain how marketing managers position products in the marketplace.*
Marketing managers often locate competing products on two-dimensional perceptual maps to visualize the products in the minds of consumers. They then try to position new products or reposition existing products in this space to attain maximum sales and profits.

FOCUSING ON KEY TERMS

80/20 rule p. 180
market-product grid p. 175
market segmentation p. 174

market segments p. 174
perceptual map p. 189
product differentiation p. 174

product positioning p. 188
product repositioning p. 188
usage rate p. 180

APPLYING MARKETING KNOWLEDGE

1 What variables might be used to segment these consumer markets? (*a*) lawn mowers, (*b*) frozen dinners, (*c*) dry breakfast cereals, and (*d*) soft drinks.

2 What variables might be used to segment these industrial markets? (*a*) industrial sweepers, (*b*) photocopiers, (*c*) computerized production control systems, and (*d*) car rental agencies.

3 In Figure 8–6, the dormitory market segment includes students living in college-owned residence halls, sororities, and fraternities. What market needs are common to these students that justify combining them into a single segment in studying the market for your Wendy's restaurant?

4 You may disagree with the estimates of market size given for the rows in the market-product grid in Figure 8–6. Estimate the market size, and give a brief justification for these market segments: (*a*) dormitory students, (*b*) day commuters, and (*c*) people who work in the area.

5 Suppose you want to increase revenues for your fast-food restaurant even further. Referring to Figure 8–7, what advertising actions might you take to increase revenues from (*a*) dormitory students, (*b*) dinners, and (*c*) after-dinner snacks consumed by night commuters?

6 Locate these drinks on the perceptual map in Figure 8–8: (*a*) cappuccino, (*b*) beer, and (*c*) soy milk.

building your marketing plan

Your marketing plan (*a*) needs a market-product grid to focus your marketing efforts and also (*b*) leads to a forecast of sales for the company. Use these steps:

1 Define the market segments (the rows in your grid) using the bases of segmentation used to segment consumer and organizational markets.

2 Define the groupings of related products (the columns in your grid).

3 Form your grid and estimate the size of the market in each market-product cell.

4 Select the target market segments on which to focus your efforts with your marketing program.

5 Use the information and the lost-horse forecasting technique to make a sales forecast (company forecast).

6 Draft your positioning statement.

video case 8 Prince Sports, Inc.: Tennis Racquets for Every Segment

QR 8–4
Prince Sports
Video Case

"Over the last decade we've seen a dramatic change in the media to reach consumers," says Linda Glassel, vice president of sports marketing and brand image of Prince Sports, Inc.

PRINCE SPORTS IN TODAY'S CHANGING WORLD

"Today—particularly in reaching younger consumers—we're now focusing so much more on social marketing and social networks, be it Facebook, Twitter, or internationally with Hi5, Bebo, and Orkut," she adds.

Linda Glassel's comments are a snapshot look at what Prince Sports faces in the changing world of tennis in the 21st century.

Prince Sports is a racquet sports company whose portfolio of brands includes Prince (tennis, squash, and badminton), Ektelon (racquetball), and Viking (platform/paddle tennis). Its complete line of tennis products alone is astounding: more than 150 racquet models; more than 50 tennis strings; over 50 footwear models; and countless types of bags, apparel, and other accessories.

Prince prides itself on its history of innovation in tennis—including inventing the first "oversize" and "longbody" racquets, the first "synthetic gut" tennis string, and the first "Natural Foot Shape" tennis shoe. Its challenge today is to continue to innovate to meet the needs of all levels of tennis players.

"One favorable thing for Prince these days is the dramatic growth in tennis participation—higher than it's been in many years," says Nick Skally (center in the photo on page 192), senior marketing manager. A recent study by the Sporting Goods Manufacturers Association confirms this point: Tennis participation in the United States was up 43 percent—the fastest growing traditional individual sport in the country.

TAMING TECHNOLOGY TO MEET PLAYERS' NEEDS

Every tennis player wants the same thing: to play better. But they don't all have the same skills, or the same ability to swing a racquet fast. So adult tennis players fall very broadly into three groups, each with special needs:

- *Those with shorter, slower strokes.* They want maximum power in a lightweight frame.
- *Those with moderate to full strokes.* They want the perfect blend of power and control.
- *Those with longer, faster strokes.* They want greater control with less power.

To satisfy all these needs in one racquet is a big order.

"When we design tennis racquets, it involves an extensive amount of market research on players at all levels," explains Tyler Herring, global business director for performance tennis racquets. Prince's research led it to introduce its breakthrough O^3 technology. "Our O^3 technology solved an inherent contradiction between racquet speed and

sweet spot," he says. Never before had a racquet been designed that simultaneously delivers faster racquet speed with a dramatically increased "sweet spot." The "sweet spot" in a racquet is the middle of the frame that gives the most power and consistency when hitting. Recently, Prince introduced its latest evolution of the O^3 platform called EXO^3. Its newly patented design suspends the string bed from the racquet frame—thereby increasing the sweet spot by up to 83 percent while reducing frame vibration up to 50 percent.

SEGMENTING THE TENNIS MARKET

"The three primary market segments for our tennis racquets are our performance line, our recreational line, and our junior line," says Herring. He explains that within each of these segments Prince makes difficult design trade-offs to balance (1) the price a player is willing to pay, (2) what playing features (speed versus spin, sweet spot versus control, and so on) they want, and (3) what technology can be built into the racquet for the price point.

Within each of these three primary market segments, there are at least two subsegments—sometimes overlapping! Figure 1 gives an overview of Prince's market segmentation strategy and identifies sample racquet models. The three right-hand columns show the design variations of length, unstrung weight, and head size. The table shows the complexities Prince faces in converting its technology into a racquet with physical features that satisfy players' needs.

DISTRIBUTION AND PROMOTION STRATEGIES

"Prince has a number of different distribution channels—from mass merchants like Walmart and Target, to sporting goods chains, to smaller specialty tennis shops," says Nick Skally. For the large chains Prince contributes co-op advertising for its in-store circulars, point-of-purchase displays, in-store signage, consumer brochures, and even "space planograms" to help the retailer plan the layout of Prince products in its tennis area. Prince aids for small tennis specialty shops include a supply of demo racquets, detailed catalogs, posters, racquet and string guides, merchandising fixtures, and hardware, such as racquet hooks and footwear shelves, in addition to other items. Prince also provides these shops with "player standees," which are corregated life-size cutouts of professional tennis players.

Prince reaches tennis players directly through its website (www.princetennis.com), which gives product information, tennis tips, and the latest tennis news. Besides using social networks like Facebook and Twitter, Prince runs ads in regional and national tennis publications and develops advertising campaigns for online sites and broadcast outlets.

In addition to its in-store activities, advertising, and online marketing, Prince invests heavily in its Teaching Pro program. These sponsored teaching pros receive all the latest product information, demo racquets, and equipment from Prince, so they can truly be Prince ambassadors in their community. Aside from their regular lessons, instructors and teaching professionals hold local "Prince Demo events" around the country to give potential

FIGURE 1
Prince targets racquets at specific market segments

Market Segments				Product Features in Racquet		
Main Segments	**Subsegments**	**Segment Characteristics (Skill level, age)**	**Brand Name**	**Length (Inches)**	**Unstrung Weight (Ounces)**	**Head Size (Sq. In.)**
Performance	Precision	For touring professional players wanting great feel, control, and spin	EXO³ Ignite 95	27.0	11.8	95
	Thunder	For competitive players wanting a bigger sweet spot and added power	EXO³ Red 95	27.25	9.9	105
Recreational	Small head size	Players looking for a forgiving racquet with added control	AirO Lightning MP	27.0	9.9	100
	Larger head size	Players looking for a larger sweet spot and added power	AirO Maria Lite OS	27.0	9.7	110
Junior	More experienced young players	Ages 8 to 15; somewhat shorter and lighter racquets than high school adult players	AirO Team Maria 23	23.0	8.1	100
	Beginner	Ages 5 to 11; much shorter and lighter racquets; tennis balls with 50% to 75% less speed for young beginners	Air Team Maria 19	19.0	7.1	82

customers a hands-on opportunity to see and try various Prince racquets, strings, and grips.

Prince also sponsors over 100 professional tennis players who appear in marquee events such as the four Grand Slam tournaments (Wimbledon and the Australian, French, and U.S. Opens). TV viewers can watch Russia's Maria Sharapova walk onto a tennis court carrying a Prince racquet bag or France's Gael Monfils hit a service ace using his Prince racquet.

Where is Prince headed in the 21st century? "As a marketer, one of the biggest challenges is staying ahead of the curve," says Glassel. And she stresses, "It's learning, it's studying, it's talking to people who understand where the market is going."

Questions

1 In the 21st century what trends in the environmental forces (social, economic, technological, competitive,

and regulatory) (*a*) work for and (*b*) work against success for Prince Sports in the tennis industry?

2 Because sales of Prince Sports in tennis-related products depends heavily on growth of the tennis industry, what marketing activities might it use in the United States to promote tennis playing?

3 What promotional activities might Prince use to reach (*a*) recreational players and (*b*) junior players?

4 What might Prince do to help it gain distribution and sales in (*a*) mass merchandisers like Target and Walmart and (*b*) specialty tennis shops?

5 In reaching global markets outside the United States (*a*) what are some criteria that Prince should use to select countries in which to market aggressively, (*b*) what three or four countries meet these criteria best, and (*c*) what are some marketing actions Prince might use to reach these markets?

iCloud

Stores your content and
wirelessly pushes it to all your devices

Developing New Products and Services

9

LEARNING OBJECTIVES

After reading this chapter you should be able to:

LO1 Recognize the terms that pertain to products and services.

LO2 Identify the ways to classify consumer and business products and services.

LO3 Describe four unique elements of services.

LO4 Explain the significance of "newness" and "consumer learning" in terms of new products and services.

LO5 Describe the factors affecting the success or failure of a new product or service.

LO6 Explain the purposes of each step of the new-product process.

QR 9–1
Apple
iPad Ad

APPLE'S NEW-PRODUCT INNOVATION MACHINE

The stage in front of an auditorium is empty except for a chair, a table, and a huge screen with a large white logo. Then, in walks a legend ready for his magic show in his black mock turtleneck, jeans, and gray New Balance sneakers.

Apple's Innovation Machine

The legend, of course, is Steve Jobs (opposite page), co-founder and former chairman of the board of Apple, Inc., who died in October 2011. *Advertising Age* anointed Steve Jobs as Marketer of the Decade. *Fortune* rated Apple as the world's most-admired company while *Bloomberg Businessweek* has perennially identified Apple as the world's most innovative company. The magic shows Jobs orchestrated over the years introduced many of Apple's market-changing innovations, such as the:

- Apple II—the first commercial personal computer (1977).

- Macintosh—the first personal computer with a mouse and a graphical user interface (1984).

- iPod—the first commercially successful MP3 digital music player (2001).

- iPhone—the world's best multitouch mobile phone and media player (2007).

- MacBook Air—the extremely thin laptop that uses a solid state drive instead of a hard disk (2008).

- iPad—the thin, tablet-shaped device, now with the dazzling Retina Display color screen, that enables users to read books, newspapers, and magazines and access an array of "apps" such as video games (2010).

Steve Jobs's innovations revolutionized six industries: personal computers, animated movies, music, phones, tablet computing, and digital publishing.[1]

iCloud: Where the Digital Lifestyle Is Heading

Because many consumers now use multiple devices (smartphones like iPhone, PCs like iMac, and tablet devices like iPad), all of them need a way to share the music, photos, videos, files, and apps that reside on any one device. Enter iCloud (opposite page), "Which will now be the center of your digital life," as Steve Jobs explained in mid-2011. "iCloud stores all your content and wirelessly pushes any changes or purchases from one device automatically [up to the 'cloud' and then] down to all your other devices. Consumers won't have to worry about syncing their devices any longer to transfer their data. With iCloud, it will just work!"[2] Welcome to *cloud computing*, which involves moving the data and processing tasks normally hosted on your own personal computer onto a remote data center server accessible by the Internet.[3]

As the previous timeline of Apple's innovation shows, the life of an organization depends on how it conceives, produces, and markets *new* products (goods, services, and ideas), the topic of this chapter. Chapter 10 discusses the process of managing *existing* products, services, and brands.

WHAT ARE PRODUCTS AND SERVICES?

The essence of marketing is in developing products and services to meet buyer needs. A **product** is a good, service, or idea consisting of a bundle of tangible and intangible attributes that satisfies consumers' needs and is received in exchange for money or something else of value. Let's look more carefully at the meanings of goods, services, and ideas.

A Look at Goods, Services, and Ideas

product
A good, service, or idea consisting of tangible and intangible features that satisfies consumers' needs and is received in exchange for money or something else of value.

A *good* has tangible attributes that a consumer's five senses can perceive. For example, Apple's iPad can be touched and its features can be seen and heard. A good also may have intangible attributes consisting of its delivery or warranties and embody more abstract concepts, such as becoming healthier or wealthier. Goods also can be divided into nondurable goods and durable goods. A *nondurable* good is an item consumed in one or a few uses, such as food products and fuel. A *durable* good is one that usually lasts over many uses, such as appliances, cars, and mobile phones. This classification method also provides direction for marketing actions. For example, nondurable goods, such as Wrigley's gum, rely heavily on consumer advertising. In contrast, costly durable goods, such as cars, generally emphasize personal selling.

Services are intangible activities or benefits that an organization provides to satisfy consumers' needs in exchange for money or something else of value. Services have become a significant part of the U.S. economy, exceeding 40 percent of its gross domestic product. Hence, a product may be the breakfast cereal you eat, whereas a service may be a tax return an accountant fills out for you.

services
Intangible activities or benefits that an organization provides to satisfy consumers' needs in exchange for money or something else of value.

Finally, in marketing, an *idea* is a thought that leads to a product or action, such as a concept for a new invention or getting people out to vote.

Throughout this book, *product* generally includes not only physical goods but services and ideas as well. When *product* is used in its narrower meaning of "goods," it should be clear from the example or sentence.

Classifying Products

Two broad categories of products widely used in marketing relate to the type of user. **Consumer products** are products purchased by the ultimate consumer, whereas **business products** (also called *B2B products* or *industrial products*) are products organizations buy that assist in providing other products for resale. But some products can be considered both consumer and business items. For example, an Apple iMac computer can be sold to consumers for personal use or to business firms for office use. Each classification results in different marketing actions. Viewed as a consumer product, the iMac would be sold through Apple's retail stores or directly from its website. As a business product, an Apple salesperson might contact a firm's purchasing department directly and offer discounts for multiple purchases.

consumer products
Products purchased by the ultimate consumer.

business products
Products organizations buy that assist directly or indirectly in providing other products for resale.

Consumer Products The four types of consumer products shown in Figure 9–1 differ in terms of (1) the effort the consumer spends on the decision, (2) the attributes used in making the purchase decision, and (3) the frequency of purchase. *Convenience*

BASIS OF COMPARISON	CONVENIENCE PRODUCT	SHOPPING PRODUCT	SPECIALTY PRODUCT	UNSOUGHT PRODUCT
Product	Toothpaste, cake mix, hand soap, ATM cash withdrawal	Cameras, TVs, briefcases, airline tickets	Rolls-Royce cars, Rolex watches, heart surgery	Burial insurance, thesaurus
Price	Relatively inexpensive	Fairly expensive	Usually very expensive	Varies
Place (distribution)	Widespread; many outlets	Large number of selective outlets	Very limited	Often limited
Promotion	Price, availability, and awareness stressed	Differentiation from competitors stressed	Uniqueness of brand and status stressed	Awareness is essential
Brand loyalty of consumers	Aware of brand but will accept substitutes	Prefer specific brands but will accept substitutes	Very brand loyal; will not accept substitutes	Will accept substitutes
Purchase behavior of consumers	Frequent purchases; little time and effort spent shopping	Infrequent purchases; needs much comparison shopping time	Infrequent purchases; needs extensive search and decision time	Very infrequent purchases; some comparison shopping

FIGURE 9–1

How a consumer product is classified significantly affects which products consumers buy and the marketing strategies used.

products are items that the consumer purchases frequently, conveniently, and with a minimum of shopping effort. *Shopping products* are items for which the consumer compares several alternatives on criteria such as price, quality, or style. *Specialty products* are items that the consumer makes a special effort to search out and buy. *Unsought products* are items that the consumer does not know about or knows about but does not initially want.

Figure 9–1 shows how each type of consumer product stresses different marketing mix actions, degrees of brand loyalty, and shopping effort. But how a consumer product is classified depends on the individual. One woman may view a camera as a shopping product and visit several stores before deciding on a brand, whereas her friend may view a camera as a specialty product and make a special effort to buy only a Nikon.

Business Products A major characteristic of business products is that their sales are often the result of *derived demand*; that is, sales of business products frequently result (or are derived) from the sale of consumer products. For example, as consumer demand for Ford cars (a consumer product) increases, the company may increase its demand for paint spraying equipment (a business product).

Business products may be classified as components or support products. *Components* are items that become part of the final product. These include raw materials such as lumber, as well as assemblies such as a Ford car engine. *Support products* are items used to assist in producing other products and services. These include:

- *Installations*, such as buildings and fixed equipment.
- *Accessory equipment*, such as tools and office equipment.
- *Supplies*, such as stationery, paper clips, and brooms.
- *Industrial services*, such as maintenance, repair, and legal services.

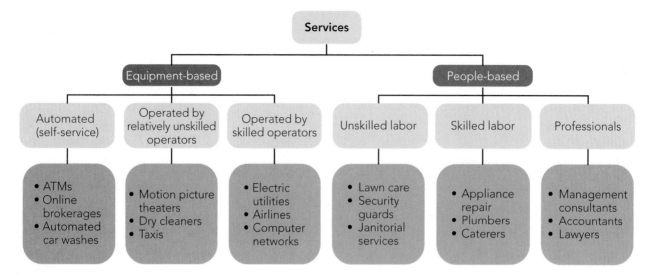

```
                                    Services

          Equipment-based                              People-based

   Automated    Operated by    Operated by    Unskilled labor   Skilled labor   Professionals
   (self-service) relatively    skilled
                 unskilled      operators
                 operators
```

Automated (self-service)	Operated by relatively unskilled operators	Operated by skilled operators	Unskilled labor	Skilled labor	Professionals
• ATMs • Online brokerages • Automated car washes	• Motion picture theaters • Dry cleaners • Taxis	• Electric utilities • Airlines • Computer networks	• Lawn care • Security guards • Janitorial services	• Appliance repair • Plumbers • Caterers	• Management consultants • Accountants • Lawyers

FIGURE 9–2

Services can be classified as equipment-based or people-based.

Strategies to market business products reflect both the complexities of the product involved (paper clips versus computer-machine tools) and the buy-class situations discussed in Chapter 5.

Classifying Services

Services can be classified according to whether they are delivered by (1) people or equipment, (2) business firms or nonprofit organizations, or (3) government agencies. Organizations in each of these categories often use significantly different kinds of market-mix strategies to promote their services.

Delivery by People or Equipment Figure 9–2 shows the great diversity of organizations that offer services. People-based professional services include those offered by advertising agencies or medical doctors. Sears utilizes skilled labor to offer appliance repair services. Broadview Security uses relatively unskilled labor to provide its security guard services. The quality of all these people-based services can vary significantly depending on the abilities of the person delivering the service.

Figure 9–2 also suggests that equipment-based services do not have the marketing concern of inconsistent quality because employees do not have direct contact when providing the service to consumers. Instead, consumers receive these automated services without interacting with any service employees, such as doing self check-in at Southwest Airlines, watching a movie at a local theater, or using Schwab's online stock trading.[4]

American Red Cross

Delivery by Business Firms or Nonprofit Organizations As discussed in Chapter 2, privately owned firms must make profits to survive, while nonprofit organizations seek to satisfy clients and be efficient. The kinds of services each offers affect their marketing activities. Recently, many nonprofit organizations, such as The American Red Cross, have used marketing to improve their communications and better serve those in need.

Delivery by Government Agencies Governments at the federal, state, and local levels provide a broad range of services. These organizations also have adopted many marketing practices used by business firms. For example, the United States Postal Service's "Easy Come. Easy Go" marketing campaign is designed to allow it to compete better with UPS, FedEx, DHL, and foreign postal services for global package delivery business.

The Uniqueness of Services

Four unique elements distinguish services from goods. These are *intangibility, inconsistency, inseparability,* and *inventory*—referred to as the **four I's of services**.

Intangibility   Being intangible, services can't be touched or seen before the purchase decision. Instead, services tend to be a performance rather than an object, which makes them much more difficult for consumers to evaluate. To help consumers assess and compare services, marketers try to make them tangible or show the benefits of using the service.

four I's of services
The four unique elements that distinguish services from goods: intangibility, inconsistency, inseparability, and inventory.

Inconsistency   Services depend on the people who provide them. As a result, their quality varies with each person's capabilities and day-to-day job performance. Inconsistency is more of a problem in services than it is with tangible goods. Tangible products can be good or bad in terms of quality, but with modern production lines, their quality will at least be consistent. On the other hand, the Philadelphia Phillies baseball team may have great hitting and pitching one day and the next day lose by 10 runs. Organizations attempt to reduce inconsistency through standardization and training.

Inseparability   Inseparability means that the consumer cannot distinguish the service provider from the service itself. For example, the quality of large lectures at your university or college may be excellent, but if you don't get your questions answered, find the counseling services poor, or do not receive adequate library assistance, you may not be satisfied with the entire educational experience delivered. Therefore, you probably won't separate your perception of the "educational experience"—the service itself—from all the people delivering the educational services for that institution.

Inventory   Many goods have inventory handling costs that relate to their storage, perishability, and movement. With services, these costs are more subjective and are related to **idle production capacity**, which is when the service provider is available but there is no demand for the service. For a service, inventory cost involves paying the service provider along with any needed equipment. If a physician is paid to see patients but no one schedules an appointment, the idle physician's salary must be paid regardless of whether the service was performed. In service businesses that pay employees a commission, such as a part-time clerk at Sears, the sales clerk's work hours can be reduced to lower Sears's idle production capacity.

idle production capacity
When the service provider is available but there is no demand for the service.

Today, many businesses find it useful to distinguish between their core product—either a good or a service—and supplementary services. U.S. Bank has both a core service (a checking account) and supplementary services, such as deposit assistance, parking, drive-throughs, and ATMs. Supplementary services often allow service providers to differentiate their offerings from those of competitors to add value for consumers.

The text describes how the broad Little Remedies product line benefits both consumers and retailers.

Assessing Service Quality

Once a consumer tries a service, how is it evaluated? Primarily by comparing expectations about a service offering to the actual experience a consumer has with the service.[5] Differences between the consumer's expectations and his or her actual experiences are identified through *gap analysis*. This analysis asks consumers to assess their expectations and experiences on dimensions of service quality such as those illustrated in Figure 9–3 on the next page for airline customers.[6] Expectations are influenced by word-of-mouth communications, personal needs, past experiences, and promotional activities, while actual experiences

DIMENSION	DEFINITION	EXAMPLES OF QUESTIONS AIRLINE CUSTOMERS MIGHT ASK
Reliability	Ability to perform the promised service dependably and accurately	Is my flight on time?
Tangibility	Appearance of physical facilities, equipment, personnel, and communication materials	Are the gate, the plane, and the baggage area clean?
Responsiveness	Willingness to help customers and provide prompt service	Are the flight attendants willing to answer my questions?
Assurance	Knowledge and courtesy of employees and their ability to convey trust and confidence	Are the ticket counter attendants, flight attendants, and pilots knowledgeable about their jobs?
Empathy	Caring, individualized attention provided to customers	Do the employees determine if I have special seating, meal, baggage, transfer, or rebooking needs?

FIGURE 9–3

The five dimensions related to the quality of a service are illustrated with questions airline customers might ask.

are determined by the way an organization delivers its service.[7] What if someone is dissatisfied and complains? Recent studies suggest that customers who experience a "service failure" will increase their satisfaction if the service provider makes a sincere attempt to address the complaint.[8]

Product Items, Product Lines, and Product Mixes

Most organizations offer a range of products and services to consumers. A **product item** is a specific product that has a unique brand, size, or price. For example, Ultra Downy softener for clothes comes in several different sizes. Each size is a separate *stock keeping unit* (SKU), which is a unique identification number that defines an item for ordering or inventory purposes.

A **product line** is a group of product or service items that are closely related because they satisfy a class of needs, are used together, are sold to the same customer group, are distributed through the same outlets, or fall within a given price range. Nike's product lines include shoes and clothing, whereas the Mayo Clinic's service lines consist of inpatient hospital care and outpatient physician services. Each product line has its own marketing strategy.

The Little Remedies product line consists of more than a dozen nonprescription medicines for infants and young children sold in a family of creative packages. A broad product line enables both consumers and retailers to simplify their buying decisions. If a family has a good experience with one Little Remedies product, it might buy another one in the line. And an extensive line enables Little Remedies to obtain distribution chains such as Babies "Я" Us and Walmart, avoiding the need for retailers to deal with many different suppliers.

Many firms offer a **product mix**, which consists of all of the product lines offered by an organization. For example, Cray Inc. has a small product mix of five supercomputer lines that are sold mostly to governments and large businesses. Procter & Gamble, however, has a large product mix that includes product lines such as beauty and grooming (Crest toothpaste and Gillette razors) and household care (Tide detergent and Pampers diapers).

product item

A specific product that has a unique brand, size, or price.

product line

A group of products that are closely related because they are similar in terms of consumer needs and uses, market segments, sales outlets, or prices.

QR 9–2
Little Remedies
Ad

product mix

All the product lines offered by a company.

learning review

1. What are the four main types of consumer products?

2. What are the 4 I's of services?

3. What is the difference between a product line and a product mix?

NEW PRODUCTS AND WHY THEY SUCCEED OR FAIL

LO4

New products are the lifeblood of a company and keep it growing, but the financial risks can be large. Before discussing how new products reach the market, we'll begin by looking at *what* a new product is.

What Is a New Product?

The term *new* is difficult to define. Is Sony's PlayStation Move *new* when there was already a PlayStation 3?[9] Is Nintendo's Wii *new* when its Game-Cube launch goes back to 2001? What does *new* mean for new-product marketing? Newness from several points of view are discussed next.

Newness Compared with Existing Products If a product is functionally different from existing products, it can be defined as new. Sometimes this newness is revolutionary and creates a whole new industry, as in the case of the Apple II computer. At other times more features are added to an existing product to try to appeal to more customers. And as microprocessors now appear everywhere from computers to appliances, consumers' lives get far more complicated. This proliferation of extra features—sometimes called "feature bloat"—overwhelms many consumers. The Marketing Matters box on the next page describes how founder Robert Stephens and his Geek Squad are working to address the rise of feature bloat.[10]

Newness from the Consumer's Perspective A second way to define new products is in terms of their effects on consumption. This approach classifies new products according to the degree of learning required by the consumer, as shown in Figure 9–4.

Sony must take care in launching its "new" PlayStation Move, when a PlayStation 3 exists already.

FIGURE 9–4

The degree of "newness" in a new product affects the amount of learning effort consumers must exert to use the product and the resulting marketing strategy.

	← LOW Degree of New Consumer Learning Needed HIGH →		
BASIS OF COMPARISON	**CONTINUOUS INNOVATION**	**DYNAMICALLY CONTINUOUS INNOVATION**	**DISCONTINUOUS INNOVATION**
Definition	Requires no new learning by consumers	Disrupts consumer's normal routine but does not require totally new learning	Requires new learning and consumption patterns by consumers
Examples	New improved shaver, detergent, and toothpaste	Electric toothbrush, compact disk player, and automatic flash unit for cameras	Wireless router, digital video recorder, and electric car
Marketing strategy	Gain consumer awareness and wide distribution	Advertise points of difference and benefits to consumers	Educate consumers through product trial and personal selling

Feature Bloat: Geek Squad to the Rescue!

Adding more features to a product to satisfy more consumers seems like a no-brainer strategy for success.

Feature Bloat

In fact, most marketing research with potential buyers of a product done *before* they buy shows they say they *do want* more features in the product. It's when the new product gets home that the "feature bloat" problems occur—often overwhelming the consumer with mind-boggling complexity.

Computers pose a special problem for homeowners because there's no in-house technical assistance like that existing in large organizations. Also, to drive down prices of home computers, usually little customer support service is available. Ever call the manufacturer's toll-free "help" line? One survey showed that 29 percent of the help-line callers wound up swearing at the customer service representative and 21 percent just screamed.

The Geek Squad to the Rescue

Computer feature bloat has given rise to what TV's *60 Minutes* says is "the multibillion-dollar service industry populated by the very people who used to be shunned in the high-school cafeteria: Geeks like Robert Stephens!"

More than a decade ago he turned his geekiness into the Geek Squad—a group of technically savvy people who can fix almost any computer problem. "There's usually some frantic customer at the door pointing to some device in the corner that will not obey," Stephens explains.

"The biggest complaint about tech support people is rude, egotistical behavior," says Stephens. So he launched the Geek Squad to show some friendly humility by having team members work their wizardry while:

1. Showing genuine concern to customers.
2. Dressing in geeky white shirts, black clip-on ties, and white socks, a "uniform" borrowed from NASA engineers.
3. Driving to customer homes or offices in black-and-white VW "geekmobiles."

Do customers appreciate the 6,000-person Geek Squad, now owned by Best Buy? Robert Stephens answers by explaining, "People will say, 'They saved me . . . they saved my data.'" This includes countless college students working on their papers or theses with data lost somewhere in their computers—"data they promised themselves they'd back up next week."

For how the kind of innovation present in this ketchup bottle affects the marketing strategy, see the text.

With a *continuous innovation*, consumers don't need to learn new behaviors. Toothpaste manufacturers can add new attributes or features like "whitens teeth" or "removes plaque" when they introduce a new or improved product. But the extra features in the new toothpaste do not require buyers to learn new tooth-brushing behaviors, so it is a continuous innovation. The benefit of this simple innovation is that effective marketing mainly depends on generating awareness, so there is no need to reeducate customers.

With a *dynamically continuous innovation*, only minor changes in behavior are required. Heinz launched its EZ Squirt Ketchup in an array of unlikely hues—from green and orange to pink and teal—with kid-friendly squeeze bottles and nozzles.[11] Encouraging kids to write their names on hot dogs or draw dinosaurs on burgers as they use this new product requires only minor behavioral changes. So the marketing strategy here is to educate prospective buyers on the product's benefits, advantages, and proper use.

A *discontinuous innovation* involves making the consumer learn entirely new consumption patterns to use the product. Have you bought a wireless router for your computer? Congratulations if you installed it yourself! Recently, one-third of those bought at Best Buy were returned because they were too complicated to set up—the problem with a discontinuous innovation. So marketing efforts for discontinuous innovations usually involve not only gaining initial consumer awareness but also educating consumers on both the benefits and proper use of the innovative product, activities that can cost millions of dollars—and maybe require Geek Squad help.

The text describes the potential benefits and dangers of an incremental innovation such as Purina's Elegant Medleys, its restaurant-inspired food for cats.

Newness in Legal Terms The U.S. Federal Trade Commission (FTC) advises that the term *new* be limited to use with a product up to six months after it enters regular distribution. The difficulty with this suggestion is in the interpretation of the term *regular distribution*.

Newness from the Organization's Perspective Successful organizations view newness and innovation in their products at three levels. The lowest level, which usually involves the least risk, is a product line extension. This is an incremental improvement of an existing product line the company already sells. For example, Purina added its "new" line of Elegant Medleys, a "restaurant-inspired food for cats," to its existing line of 50 varieties of its Fancy Feast gourmet cat food. This has the potential benefit of adding new customers but the twin dangers of increasing expenses and cannibalizing its existing line.

At the next level is (1) a significant jump in innovation or technology or (2) a brand extension involving putting an established brand name on a new product in an unfamiliar market. In the first case, the significant jump in technology might be when a cellphone manufacturer offers new smartphones or a film camera producer offers digital cameras.

The second case—using an existing brand name to introduce a new product into an unfamiliar market—looks deceptively easy for companies with a powerful, national brand name. Colgate thought so. It puts its brand name on a line of frozen dinners called Colgate's Kitchen Entrees. The product line died quickly. A marketing expert calls this "one of the most bizarre brand extensions ever," observing that the Colgate brand name, which is strongly linked to toothpaste in people's minds, does not exactly get their "taste buds tingling."[12]

The third and highest level of innovation involves a radical invention, a truly revolutionary new product. Apple's Apple II, the first "personal computer," and its iPad are examples of radical inventions.

Effective new-product development in large firms exists at all three levels.

Why Products and Services Succeed or Fail

We all know the giant product and service successes—such as Apple's iPhone, Google, and CNN. Yet the thousands of product failures every year that slide quietly into oblivion cost American businesses billions of dollars. Ideally, a new product or service needs a precise *protocol*, a statement that, before product development begins, identifies (1) a well-defined target market; (2) specific customers' needs, wants, and preferences; and (3) what the product will be and do to satisfy consumers.

New-product success or failure? For the special problems these two products faced, see the text.

Research reveals how difficult it is to produce a single commercially successful new product, especially among consumer packaged goods (CPG) that appear on supermarket shelves one month and are gone forever a few months later. Most American families buy the same 150 items over and over again—making it difficult to gain buyers for new products. So less than 3 percent of new consumer packaged goods exceed first-year sales of $50 million—the benchmark of a successful CPG launch.[13]

To learn marketing lessons and convert potential failures to successes, we can analyze why new products fail and then study several failures in detail. As we go through the new-product process later in the chapter, we can identify ways such failures might have been avoided—admitting that hindsight is clearer than foresight.

Marketing Reasons for New-Product Failures Both marketing and nonmarketing factors contribute to new-product failures. Using the research results from several studies on new-product success and failure, we can identify critical marketing factors—which sometimes overlap—that often separate new-product winners and losers:[14]

1. *Insignificant point of difference.*   Research shows that a distinctive point of difference is the single most important factor for a new product to defeat competitive ones—having superior characteristics that deliver unique benefits to the user. In the mid-1990s, General Mills launched Fingos, a sweetened cereal flake about the size of a corn chip with a $34 million promotional budget. Consumers were supposed to snack on them dry, but they didn't.[15] The point of difference was not important enough to get consumers to stop eating competing snacks such as popcorn and potato chips.

2. *No economical access to buyers.* Grocery products provide an example of this factor. Today's mega-supermarkets carry more than 30,000 different SKUs. With about 20,000 new consumer packaged goods (food, beverage, health and beauty aids, household, and pet items) introduced globally each month, the cost to gain access to retailer shelf space is huge. Because shelf space is judged in terms of sales per square foot, Thirsty Dog! (a zesty beef-flavored, vitamin-enriched, mineral-loaded, lightly carbonated bottled water for your dog) must displace an existing product on the supermarket shelves, a difficult task with the high sales-per-square-foot demands of these stores. Thirsty Dog! failed to generate enough sales to meet these requirements.

3. *Incomplete market and product protocol before product development starts.* Without this protocol, firms try to design a vague product for a phantom market. Developed by Kimberly-Clark, Avert Virucidal tissues contained vitamin C derivatives scientifically designed to kill cold and flu germs when users sneezed, coughed, or blew their noses into them. The product failed in test marketing. People didn't believe the claims and were frightened by the "cidal" in the brand name, which they connected to words like *suicidal*. A big part of Avert's failure was its lack of a product protocol that clearly defined how it would satisfy consumer wants and needs.[16]

4. *Not satisfying customer needs on critical factors.* Overlapping somewhat with point 1, this factor stresses that problems on one or two critical factors can kill the product, even though the general quality is high. For example, the Japanese, like the British, drive on the left side of the road. Until 1996, U.S. carmakers sent Japan few right-hand-drive cars—unlike German carmakers, which exported right-hand-drive models in several of their brands.

5. *Bad timing.* This results when a product is introduced too soon, too late, or when consumer tastes are shifting dramatically. Bad timing gives new-product managers nightmares. Microsoft, for example, introduced its Zune player a few years after Apple launched its iPod and other competitors offered their new MP3 players.

6. *Poor product quality.* This factor often results when a product is not thoroughly tested. The costs to an organization for poor quality can be staggering and include the labor, materials, and other expenses to fix the problem—not to mention the lost sales, profits, and market share that usually result. In early 2007, with a $500 million promotional budget, Microsoft launched its Windows

Lessons from new-product failures: Why might consumers choose not to buy a tissue to kill cold and flu germs . . .

... or a spray to get rid of scary creatures from a child's bedroom? Answers appear in the text.

Vista to replace its successful predecessor Windows XP. But the Vista software had so many quality problems with compatibility and performance, even Microsoft's most loyal users revolted. Today its problems would be highlighted even faster as Facebook and Twitter users post their complaints.[17]

7. *Too little market attractiveness.* The ideal is a large target market with high growth and real buyer need. But often the target market is too small or competitive to warrant the huge expenses necessary to reach it. OUT! International's Hey! There's A Monster In My Room spray was designed to rid scary creatures from a kid's bedroom and had a bubble-gum fragrance. While a creative and cute product, the brand name probably kept the kids awake at night more than their fear of the monsters because it implied the monster was still hiding in the bedroom. Also, was this a real market?

8. *Poor execution of the marketing mix: brand name, package, price, promotion, distribution.* Somewhere in the marketing mix there can be a showstopper that kills the product. Introduced by Gunderson & Rosario, Inc., Garlic Cake was supposed to be served as an hors d'oeuvre with sweet breads, spreads, and meats, but somehow the company forgot to tell this to potential consumers. Garlic Cake died because consumers were left to wonder just what a Garlic Cake is and when on earth a person would want to eat it.

Simple marketing research should have revealed the problems in these new-product disasters. Developing successful new products may sometimes involve luck, but more often it involves having a product that really meets a need and has significant points of difference over competitive products.

What Were They Thinking? Organizational Problems in New-Product Failures
A number of other organizational problems can cause new-product disasters. Key ones—some of which overlap—include:

1. *Not really listening to the "voice of the consumer."* Product managers may believe they "know better" than their customers or feel they "can't afford" the valuable marketing research that could uncover problems.

2. *Skipping stages in the new-product process.* Although details may vary, the seven-stage new-product process discussed in the next section is a sequence used in some form by most large organizations. Skipping a stage often leads to disaster.

3. *Pushing a poorly conceived product into the market to generate quick revenue.* Today's marketing managers are under incredible pressure from top management to meet quarterly revenue targets. This focus on speed often results in overlooking the network of services needed to support the physical product.[18]

4. *Encountering "groupthink" in task force and committee meetings.* Someone in the new-product planning meeting knows or suspects the product concept is a dumb idea. But that person is afraid to speak up for fear of being cast as a "negative thinker" and "not a team player" and then being ostracized from real participation in the group. Do you think someone on the Life Savers new-product team suspected a Life Savers soda wasn't a good idea but was afraid to speak up?[19] In the same way, a strong public commitment to a new product by its key advocate may make it difficult to kill the product even when new negative information comes to light.[20]

5. *Not learning critical takeaway lessons from past failures.* The easiest lessons are from "intelligent failures"—ones that happen early in the new-product process. At this point these failures are less expensive and immediately give better understanding of customers' wants and needs.

6. *Avoiding the "NIH problem."* A great idea is a great idea, regardless of its source. Yet in the bureaucracy that can occur in large organizations, ideas from outside often get rejected simply because they come from outside—what has been termed the "not-invented-here (NIH) problem."

Many of these organizational problems contribute to the eight marketing reasons for new-product failures described earlier.

Introduce a Life Savers soda? The text asks if "groupthink" played a part in this new-product decision.

Using Marketing Dashboards

Which States Are Underperforming?

In 2009, you started your own company to sell a nutritious, high-energy snack you developed. It is now January 2013. As a marketer, you ask yourself, "How well is my business growing?"

Your Challenge   The snack is sold in all 50 states. Your goal is 10 percent annual growth. To begin 2013, you want to quickly solve any sales problems that occurred during 2012. You know that states whose sales are stagnant or in decline are offset by those with greater than 10 percent growth.

Studying a table of the sales and percent change versus a year ago in each of the 50 states would work but be very time-consuming. A good graphic is better. You choose the following marketing metric, where "sales" are measured in units:

$$\text{Annual \% sales change} = \frac{(2012\ \text{Sales} - 2011\ \text{Sales}) \times 100}{2011\ \text{Sales}}$$

You want to act quickly to improve sales. In your map, growth that is greater than 10 percent is green, 0 to 10 percent growth is orange, and decline is red. Notice that you (1) picked a metric and (2) made your own rules that green is good, orange is bad, and red is very bad.

Your Findings   You see that sales growth in the northeastern states is weaker than the 10 percent target, and sales are actually declining in many of the states.

Annual Percentage Change in Unit Volume, by State

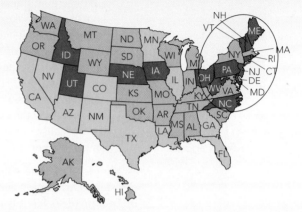

Your Action   Marketing is often about grappling with sales shortfalls. You'll need to start by trying to identify and correct the problems in the largest volume states that are underperforming—in this case in the northeastern United States.

You'll want to do marketing research to see if the problem starts with (1) an external factor involving consumer tastes or (2) an internal factor such as a breakdown in your distribution system.

How Marketing Dashboards Can Improve New-Product Performance

The Using Marketing Dashboards box shows how marketers measure actual market performance versus the goals set in new-product planning. It shows that you have set a goal of 10 percent annual growth for the new snack you developed. You have chosen a marketing metric of "annual % sales change" to measure the annual growth rate from 2011 to 2012 for each of the 50 states.

Your special concerns in the marketing dashboard are the states shown in red, where sales have actually declined. As shown in the box, having identified the northeastern United States as a problem region, you conduct in-depth marketing research to lead to corrective actions. For example, is the decline in sales in this region due to an external factor, such as consumer preference? Perhaps consumers in the northeastern United States prefer more regional snack tastes or think your snack is too sweet. Or perhaps the problem is due to your own internal marketing strategy, such as poor distribution, prices that are too high, or bad advertising.

learning review

4. What kind of innovation would an improved electric toothbrush be?

5. Why can an "insignificant point of difference" lead to new-product failure?

6. What is "groupthink," and how can it lead to new-product failures?

THE NEW-PRODUCT PROCESS

LO6

new-product process

The seven stages an organization goes through to identify business opportunities and convert them into salable products or services.

To develop new products efficiently, companies such as General Electric and 3M use a specific sequence of steps to make their products ready for market. Figure 9–5 shows the **new-product process**, the seven stages an organization goes through to identify business opportunities and convert them into salable products or services. Today many firms use a formal Stage-Gate® process to evaluate whether the results at each stage of the new-product development process are successful enough to warrant proceeding to the next stage. If problems in a stage can't be corrected, the project doesn't proceed to the next stage and product development is killed.[21]

Stage 1: New-Product Strategy Development

For companies, *new-product strategy development* is the stage of the new-product process that defines the role for a new product in terms of the firm's overall objectives. During this stage, the firm uses both a SWOT analysis (Chapter 2) and environmental scanning (Chapter 3) to assess its strengths and weaknesses relative to the trends it identifies as opportunities or threats. The outcome not only defines the vital "protocol" for each new-product idea but also identifies the strategic role it might serve in the firm's business portfolio.

New-product development in services, such as buying a stock or airline ticket or watching a National Football League game, is often difficult. Why? Because services are intangible and performance-oriented. Nevertheless, service innovations can have a huge impact on our lives. For example, the online brokerage firm E*TRADE has revolutionized the financial services industry through its online trading.

Stage 2: Idea Generation

Idea generation, the second stage of the new-product process, involves developing a pool of concepts to serve as candidates for new products, building upon the previous stage's results. Many forward-looking companies have discovered their own organizations are not generating enough useful new-product ideas. This has led to *open innovation*, in which an organization finds and executes creative new-product ideas by developing strategic relationships with outside individuals and organizations. Open innovation helps organizations overcome the not-invented-here barriers discussed earlier. Consider the following examples of open innovation relationships.[22]

Employee and Co-Worker Suggestions   Employees should be encouraged to suggest new-product ideas through suggestion boxes. The idea for Nature Valley granola bars from General Mills came when one of its marketing managers observed co-workers bringing granola to work in plastic bags.

FIGURE 9–5
Carefully using the seven stages in the new-product process increases the chances of new-product success.

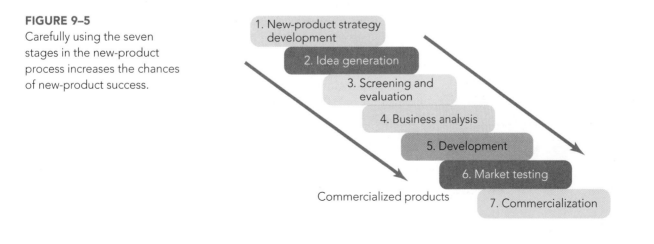

1. New-product strategy development
2. Idea generation
3. Screening and evaluation
4. Business analysis
5. Development
6. Market testing
7. Commercialization

Commercialized products

One result of Ford's chief executive officer encouraging better idea sharing among employees is its new Ford Focus shown here.

An important part of Ford's current turnaround has been chief executive officer Alan Mulally's encouraging managers and employees to speak up and volunteer ideas to improve its technology and line of new cars—an openness lacking in U.S. auto companies in the past.[23] Further, Mulally has made clear that managers and employees in different departments aren't rivals. Instead of the not-invented-here (NIH) thinking of past years, Mulally has encouraged managers and employees to see themselves as part of the "One Ford" team and share information and help one another. This emphasis on improved employee communications has helped Ford launch new models, add new technologies, and redesign its supply chain.[24]

Customer and Supplier Suggestions Firms ask their salespeople to talk to customers and ask their purchasing personnel to talk to suppliers to discover new-product ideas.[25] Whirlpool gets ideas from customers on ways to standardize components so that it can cut the number of different product platforms to reduce costs.[26] Business researchers tell firms to actively involve customers and suppliers in the new-product development process. This means the focus should be on what the new product will actually do for them rather than simply what they want.[27]

A. G. Lafley, CEO of Procter & Gamble (P&G), gave his executives a *revolutionary* thought: "Look outside the company for solutions to problems rather than insisting P&G knows best." When he ran P&G's laundry detergent business, he had to redesign the laundry boxes so they were easier to open. Why? While consumers *said* P&G's laundry boxes were "easy to open," cameras they agreed to have installed in their laundry rooms showed they opened the boxes with *screwdrivers*![28]

With a $150 million marketing budget, in 2012 P&G launched Tide Pods, a revolutionary three-chamber liquid dose that cleans, fights stains, and brightens. P&G describes Tide Pods as "its biggest laundry innovation in more than a quarter century." P&G says Tide Pods has produced the highest consumer-satisfaction scores the company has ever seen for a new laundry product. But after its successful new-product launch, P&G redesigned its packaging after discovering that some children thought the pods were candy and tried to eat them.[29]

QR 9–3
P&G's Tide Pods Ad

"Crowdsourcing" is a creative idea-generation method if an R&D-marketing team wants ideas from 10,000 or 20,000 customers or suppliers. *Crowdsourcing* involves generating insights leading to actions based on massive numbers of people's ideas. It requires a precise question to focus the idea-generation process. Dell used crowdsourcing to develop an online site to generate 13,464 ideas for new products and website and marketing improvements, of which 402 were implemented.[30]

Procter & Gamble's new Tide Pods launch shows how it has improved both planning and implementation by involving consumers earlier in its innovation activities.

Research and Development Laboratories Another source of new products is a firm's own research and development laboratories. Apple's sleek iPad, iPhone, and iMac models came out of its Apple Industrial Design Group, which continues to be driven by the obsessive concerns of its co-founder, the late Steve Jobs, for cutting-edge industrial design in all the company's products. One secret behind Apple's world-class ability to convert vague concepts into tangible products: an action-item list emerging from every meeting. This focuses on *who* does *what* by *when*![31]

Professional R&D and innovation laboratories that are outside the walls of large corporations are sources of open innovation and can provide new-product ideas.[32] IDEO is a world-class new-product development firm, having designed more than 4,000 of them. IDEO designs include the Apple mouse and the Crest Neat Squeeze toothpaste dispenser.[33]

Brainstorming sessions conducted at IDEO can generate 100 new ideas in an hour. IDEO's "shop-a-long" visits with client firms let a client's managers experience firsthand what their customers do. A sample recommendation from a shop-a-long visit with managers from

An IDEO innovation: A five-section, single-serve package for salads. Visit IDEO's website (www.ideo.com) to view its recent innovations.

Gary Schwartzberg partnered with Kraft Foods to get his cream cheese–filled bagels in stores across the United States.

a large U.S. health maintenance organization came from actually playing the part of a patient: Make examining rooms larger to enable the nervous patient to have a friend or relative in the room while waiting for the doctor.[34] Fresh Express asked IDEO to design an innovative single-serve package for salads. IDEO's solution (photo): A five-section package—one large section for the salad greens and four smaller ones for proteins, dressings, and so on—with each section sealed in plastic.

Competitive Products Analyzing the competition can lead to new-product ideas. For six months, the Marriott Corporation sent a six-person intelligence team to travel and stay at economy hotels around the country. The team assessed the competition's strengths and weaknesses on everything from the soundproof qualities of the rooms to the softness of the towels. Marriott then budgeted $500 million for a new economy hotel chain—Fairfield Inns.

Smaller Firms, Universities, and Inventors Many firms look for outside visionaries that have inventions or innovative ideas that can become products. Some sources of this open innovation strategy include:

- *Smaller, nontraditional firms.* Small technology firms and even small, nontraditional firms in adjacent industries provide creative advances. General Mills partnered with Weight Watchers to develop Progresso Light soups, the first consumer packaged product in any grocery category to carry the Weight Watchers endorsement with a 0 points value per serving.[35]
- *Universities.* Many universities have technology transfer centers that often partner with business firms to commercialize faculty inventions. The first-of-its-kind carbonated yogurt Go-Gurt Fizzix was launched in late 2007 as a result of General Mills partnering with Brigham Young University to license the university's patent to put the "fizz" into the yogurt.[36]
- *Inventors.* Many lone inventors and entrepreneurs develop brilliant new-product ideas—like Gary Schwartzberg's tube-shaped bagel filled with cream cheese. A portable breakfast for the on-the-go person, the innovative bagel couldn't get widespread distribution. So Schwartzberg sold his idea to Kraft Foods, Inc., which now markets its Bagel-Fuls filled with Kraft's best-selling Philadelphia cream cheese in supermarkets across the United States.[37]

Great ideas can come from almost anywhere—the challenge is recognizing and implementing them.

Stage 3: Screening and Evaluation

Screening and evaluation is the stage of the new-product process that internally and externally evaluates new-product ideas to eliminate those that warrant no further effort.

Internal Approach A firm's employees evaluate the technical feasibility of a proposed new-product idea to determine whether it meets the objectives defined in the new-product strategy development stage. For example, 3M scientists develop many world-class innovations in the company's labs. A recent innovation was its micro-replication technology—one that has 3,000 tiny gripping "fingers" per square inch. An internal assessment showed 3M that this technology could be used to improve the gripping of golf or work gloves.

Organizations that develop service-dominated offerings need to ensure that employees have the commitment and skills to meet customer expectations and sustain customer loyalty—an important criterion in screening a new-service idea. This is the

customer experience management (CEM)

The process of managing the entire customer experience within the company.

essence of **customer experience management (CEM)**, which is the process of managing the entire customer experience within the company. Marketers must consider employees' interactions with customers so that the new services are consistently delivered and experienced, clearly differentiated from other service offerings, and relevant and valuable to the target market.

External Approach Firms use *concept tests*, external evaluations with consumers that consist of preliminary testing of a new-product idea rather than an actual product. Generally, these tests are more useful with minor modifications of existing products than with new, innovative products with which consumers are not familiar.[38] Concept tests rely on written descriptions of the product but may be augmented with sketches, mock-ups, or promotional literature. Key questions for concept testing include: How does the customer perceive the product? Who would use it? and How would it be used?

learning review

7. What is the new-product strategy development stage in the new-product process?

8. What are the main sources of new-product ideas?

9. How do internal and external screening and evaluation approaches differ?

Stage 4: Business Analysis

Business analysis specifies the features of the product and the marketing strategy needed to bring it to market and make financial projections. This is the last checkpoint before significant resources are invested to create a *prototype*—a full-scale operating model of the product. The business analysis stage assesses the total "business fit" of the proposed new product with the company's mission and objectives—from whether the product can be economically developed and manufactured to the marketing strategy needed to have it succeed in the marketplace.

This process requires not only detailed financial projections but also assessments of the marketing and product synergies related to the company's existing operations. Will the new product require a lot of new machinery to produce it or can it be produced using the unused capacity of existing machines? Will the new product cannibalize sales of existing products or will it increase revenues by reaching new market segments? Can the new product be protected with a patent or copyright? Financial projections of expected profits require estimates of expected prices per unit and units sold, as well as detailed estimates of the costs of R&D, production, and marketing.

For services, business analysis involves using capacity management to find ways to match the availability of the service offering to when it is needed. For example, airlines and mobile phone service providers use off-peak pricing to charge different prices during different times of the day or during different days of the week to help match the supply and demand for their services.[39]

Stage 5: Development

Development is the stage of the new-product process that turns the idea on paper into a prototype. This results in a demonstrable, producible product that involves not only manufacturing the product efficiently but also performing laboratory and consumer tests to ensure it meets the standards established for it in the protocol.

As described in the text, it took a year and a half in the development stage to produce "a perfect cup" of Chobani's Greek Yogurt. New Chobani flavors in 2012: apple, cinnamon, blood orange, and passion fruit.

In 2005 Turkish immigrant Hamdi Ulukaya opened his mail in upstate New York and saw an ad that said, "Fully equipped yogurt factory for sale." He bought it, painted the walls, hired a yogurt master, and turned his attention to the task of developing a high-quality yogurt. "It took a year and a half to make a perfect cup of yogurt," says Ulukaya.

Marketing Matters > > > > > customer value

Marissa Mayer: The Talent behind Google's Familiar *White* Home Page

Unknown to you, Google Employee No. 20, Marissa Mayer, probably impacts your life at least 5 or 10 times a week.

The New York Times calls her the "gatekeeper of Google's home page," the one person who "controls the look, feel, and functionality of the Internet's most heavily trafficked search engine." Virtually every new design or feature—from the color of the Google toolbar to the exact words on a Google page—needs her stamp of approval. The very clear, very plain, very white Google home page reflects Mayer's passion about obtaining a favorable user experience.

As vice president of search products and user experience, Mayer has introduced over 100 Google products and features. Sounding like a combination English teacher and art instructor, Mayer sets the design standards based on her internal Google experiments to measure user preferences. Her precise design rules include:

- Avoid first- and second-person pronouns.
- Write "Google" instead of "we."
- Don't switch tenses.
- Avoid italics because they are hard to read on a computer screen.

Beyond the grammar lessons, there are also precise design and graphic arts guidelines: "If you want to make the design on the page simpler, take away one of these: A type of font, a color, or an image." And then there's the Saturday morning she had to find the stray slash – "/" – on Google servers that sent tens of millions of users the message in red: "THIS SITE MAY HARM YOUR COMPUTER."

Mayer has had such an impact on Google's success that she was tapped to be the new CEO of Yahoo! in mid-2012.

QR 9–4
Chobani
Video

During development, laboratory tests like this one on Barbie result in safer dolls and toys for children.

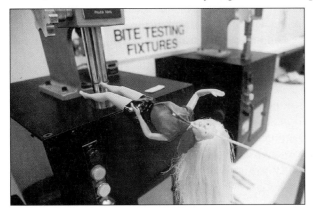

With over 40,000 new consumer packaged goods (CPG) products launched annually, who can imagine a new food category skyrocketing to success? But that's exactly what has happened with . . . Greek yogurt! The dominant brand is Ulukaya's Chobani Greek Yogurt, launched in 2007. Chobani—meaning "shepherd"—stresses (1) natural ingredients, (2) high quality, and (3) great taste!

By 2012 Chobani had a 13 percent share of the entire yogurt market and was processing 3 million pounds of milk a day to produce its Greek yogurt. Blindsided by Chobani, major competitors like Dannon—with its Oikos brand—and General Mills—with its Yoplait brand—have jumped into the Greek yogurt business. Even Kraft Foods, which had left the yogurt business and whose yogurt factory Ulukaya bought, started marketing its new Athenos brand of Greek yogurt in 2011![40]

For services, improving the delivery of customer service is critical. This involves analyzing the entire sequence of steps or "service encounters" to improve the interactions between consumers and the service provider. High-contact services such as hotels, car rental agencies, and web providers use this approach to serve customers better. That white, plain-vanilla Google home page may look like it was designed by a child. But the Marketing Matters box describes how Google's Marissa Mayer works to get exactly the right "feel" for Google's millions of users.[41]

Safety tests are also critical for when the product isn't used as planned. To make sure seven-year-olds can't bite Barbie's head off and choke, Mattel clamps her foot in steel jaws in a test stand and then pulls on her head with a wire. Similarly, car manufacturers conduct extensive safety tests by crashing their cars into concrete walls.

Consumer products companies, such as General Mills shown here, often use controlled test markets to assess the likely success of new product, promotional, or pricing strategies.

Stage 6: Market Testing

Market testing is a stage of the new-product process that involves exposing actual products to prospective consumers under realistic purchase conditions to see if they will buy. If the budget permits, consumer packaged goods firms do this by *test marketing,* which involves offering a product for sale on a limited basis in a defined area for a specific time period. The three main kinds of test markets are (1) standard, (2) controlled, and (3) simulated.[42] Because standard test markets are so time-consuming and expensive and can alert competitors to a firm's plans, some firms skip test markets entirely or use controlled or simulated test markets.

Standard Test Markets   In a *standard test market,* a company develops a product and then attempts to sell it through normal distribution channels in a number of test-market cities. Test-market cities must be demographically representative of markets targeted for the new product, have cable TV systems that can deliver different ads to different homes, and have retailers with checkout counter scanners to measure sales. A distinguishing feature of a standard test market is that the producer sells the product to distributors, wholesalers, and retailers, just as it would do for other products.

Controlled Test Markets   A *controlled test market* involves contracting the entire test program to an outside service. The service pays retailers for shelf space and can therefore guarantee a specified percentage of the test product's potential distribution volume. SymphonyIRI Group is a leader in supplying controlled test markets. Its BehaviorScan service uses five demographically representative cities to track sales made to a panel of households. In some cases the effectiveness of different TV commercials and other direct-to-consumer promotions can be measured.

Simulated Test Markets   To save time and money, companies often turn to *simulated (or laboratory) test markets (STM),* a technique that somewhat replicates a full-scale test market. STMs are often run in shopping malls, to find consumers who use the product class being tested. Next, qualified participants are shown the product or the product concept and are asked about usage, reasons for purchase, and important product attributes. They then see the company's and competitors' ads for the test product. Finally, participants are given money to decide to buy or not buy the firm's or the competitors' product from a real or simulated store environment.

When Test Markets Don't Work   Not all products can use test markets. Test marketing a service is very difficult because consumers can't see what they are buying. For example, how do you test market a new building for an art museum? Similarly, test markets for expensive consumer products such as cars or costly industrial products such as jet engines are impractical. For these products, reactions of potential buyers to mockups or one-of-a-kind prototypes are all that is feasible.

Stage 7: Commercialization

Finally, the product is brought to the point of *commercialization*—the stage of the new-product process that positions and launches a new product in full-scale production and sales. Companies proceed very carefully at the commercialization stage because this is the most expensive stage for most new products. If competitors introduce a product that leapfrogs the firm's own new product or if cannibalization of its own existing products looks significant, the firm may halt the new-product launch.

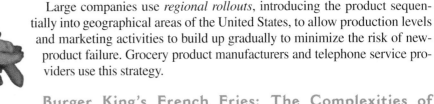

Large companies use *regional rollouts*, introducing the product sequentially into geographical areas of the United States, to allow production levels and marketing activities to build up gradually to minimize the risk of new-product failure. Grocery product manufacturers and telephone service providers use this strategy.

Burger King's French Fries: The Complexities of Commercialization

To discover the downs and ups of commercializing a new product, see the text discussion of Burger King's 15-year search for french fries that can compete with those of McDonald's.

Burger King's "improved french fries" are an example of what can go wrong at the commercialization stage. McDonald's french fries are the gold standard against which all other fries in the fast-food industry are measured. In 1997, Burger King decided to take on McDonald's fries and spent millions of R&D dollars developing a whey/starch-coated fry designed to retain heat longer and add crispiness. The launch, backed with a $70 million marketing campaign, turned into a disaster. The reason: Except under ideal conditions, the new fry proved too complicated to get right day after day in Burger King restaurants, and changes had to be made to get the "production" process correct to ensure consistent results.

Fast-forward to today. Over the past couple of years, Wendy's has introduced new fries in the fast-food war. Launched in late 2010, Wendy's Natural Cut Fries with Sea Salt have become a huge hit.

Burger King, now the number three fast-food marketer after McDonalds and Wendy's, responded with its new Thick Cut fries in late 2011. In development and testing for over two years, the new fries are "fluffier" on the inside for a more "potatoey" taste, have less sodium, and have a new "coating" on the outside. This was done to create a "crispy, golden brown deliciousness" while retaining the heat longer—for at least 10 minutes because 75 percent of customers eat their fries "on the go" in their cars, offices, or homes.

A taste test conducted by an independent market research firm stated that the new Burger King fries were preferred over McDonald's fries by a 57 to 35 percent margin. Burger King also launched the largest TV advertising campaign in its history—featuring "spokespud" Mr. Potato Head—to promote the new fries.[43]

The Special Risks in Commercializing Grocery Products

New grocery products pose special commercialization problems. Because shelf space is so limited, many supermarkets require a *slotting fee* for new products, a payment a manufacturer makes to place a new item on a retailer's shelf. This can run to several million dollars for a single product. But there's even another potential expense. If a new grocery product does not achieve a predetermined sales target, some retailers require a *failure fee*, a penalty payment a manufacturer makes to compensate a retailer for devoting valuable shelf space to a product that failed to sell. These costly slotting fees and failure fees are further examples of why large grocery product manufacturers use regional rollouts.

Speed as a Factor in New-Product Success

Companies have discovered that speed or *time to market* (TtM) is often vital in introducing a new product. Recent studies have shown that high-tech products coming to market on time are far more profitable than those arriving late. So companies like Sony, BMW, 3M, and Hewlett-Packard often overlap the sequence of stages described in this chapter.

With this approach, termed *parallel development*, cross-functional team members who conduct the simultaneous development of both the product and the production process stay with the product from conception to production. This enabled Hewlett-Packard to reduce the development time for notebook computers from 12 to 7 months. In software development, *fast prototyping* uses a "do it, try it, fix it" approach—encouraging continuing improvement even after the initial design. To speed up time to market, many firms insulate their new-product teams from routine administrative tasks to keep them from bogging down in red tape.[44]

learning review

10. How does the development stage of the new-product process involve testing the product inside and outside the firm?

11. What is a test market?

12. What is the commercialization of a new product?

LEARNING OBJECTIVES REVIEW

LO1 *Recognize the terms that pertain to products and services.*

A product is a good, service, or idea consisting of a bundle of tangible and intangible attributes that satisfies consumers and is received in exchange for money or something else of value.

A good has tangible attributes that a consumer's five senses can perceive and intangible ones such as warranties; a laptop computer is an example. Goods also can be divided into nondurable goods, which are consumed in one or a few uses, and durable goods, which usually last over many uses. Services are intangible activities or benefits that an organization provides to satisfy consumer needs in exchange for money or something else of value, such as an airline trip. An idea is a thought that leads to a product or action, such as eating healthier foods.

LO2 *Identify the ways to classify consumer and business products and services.*

By type of user, the major distinctions are consumer products, which are products purchased by the ultimate consumer, and business products, which are products that assist an organization in providing other products for resale.

Consumer products can be broken down based on the effort involved in the purchase decision process, marketing mix attributes used in the purchase, and the frequency of purchase: (*a*) convenience products are items that consumers purchase frequently and with a minimum of shopping effort; (*b*) shopping products are items for which consumers compare several alternatives on selected criteria; (*c*) specialty products are items that consumers make special efforts to seek out and buy; and (*d*) unsought products are items that consumers either do not know about or do not initially want.

Business products can be broken down into (*a*) components, which are items that become part of the final product, such as raw materials or parts, and (*b*) support products, which are items used to assist in producing other goods and services and include installations, accessory equipment, supplies, and industrial services.

Services can be classified in terms of whether they are delivered by (*a*) people or equipment, (*b*) business firms or nonprofit organizations, or (*c*) government agencies.

Firms can offer a range of products, which involve decisions regarding the product item, product line, and product mix.

LO3 *Describe four unique elements of services.*

The four unique elements of services—the four I's—are intangibility, inconsistency, inseparability, and inventory. Intangibility refers to the tendency of services to be a performance that cannot be held or touched, rather than an object. Inconsistency is a characteristic of services because they depend on people to deliver them, and people vary in their capabilities and in their day-to-day performance. Inseparability refers to the difficulty of separating the deliverer of the services (hair stylist) from the service itself (hair salon). Inventory refers to the need to have service production capability when there is service demand.

LO4 *Explain the significance of "newness" and "consumer learning" in terms of new products and services.*

From the important perspective of the consumer, "newness" is often seen as the degree of learning that a consumer must engage in to use the product. With a continuous innovation, no new behaviors must be learned. With a dynamically continuous innovation, only minor behavioral changes are needed. With a discontinuous innovation, consumers must learn entirely new consumption patterns.

LO5 *Describe the factors affecting the success or failure of a new product or service.*

A new product or service often fails for these marketing reasons: (*a*) insignificant points of difference, (*b*) incomplete market and product protocol before product development starts, (*c*) not satisfying customer needs on critical factors, (*d*) bad timing, (*e*) too little market attractiveness, (*f*) poor product quality, (*g*) poor execution of the marketing mix, and (*h*) no economical access to buyers.

LO6 *Explain the purposes of each step of the new-product process.*

The new-product process consists of seven stages a firm uses to develop salable products or services: (1) New-product strategy development involves defining the role for the new product within the firm's overall objectives. (2) Idea generation involves developing a pool of concepts from consumers, employees, basic R&D, and competitors to serve as candidates for new products. (3) Screening and evaluation involves evaluating new product ideas to eliminate those that are not feasible from a technical or consumer perspective. (4) Business analysis involves defining the features of the new product, developing the marketing strategy and marketing program to introduce it, and making a financial forecast. (5) Development involves not only producing a prototype product but also testing it in the lab and with consumers to see that it meets the standards set for it. (6) Market testing involves exposing actual products to prospective consumers under realistic purchasing conditions to see if they will buy the product. (7) Commercialization involves positioning and launching a product in full-scale production and sales with a specific marketing program.

FOCUSING ON KEY TERMS

business products p. 196
consumer products p. 196
customer experience management (CEM) p. 210

four I's of services p. 199
idle production capacity p. 199
new-product process p. 207
product p. 196

product item p. 200
product line p. 200
product mix p. 200
services p. 196

APPLYING MARKETING KNOWLEDGE

1 Products can be classified as either consumer or business products. How would you classify the following products? (*a*) Johnson's baby shampoo, (*b*) a Black & Decker two-speed drill, and (*c*) an arc welder.

2 Are Nature Valley Granola bars and Eddie Bauer hiking boots convenience, shopping, specialty, or unsought products?

3 Based on your answer to question 2, how would the marketing actions differ for each product and the classification to which you assigned it?

4 Explain how the four I's of services apply to a Marriott Hotel.

5 Idle production capacity may be related to inventory or capacity management. How would the pricing component of the marketing mix reduce idle production capacity for (*a*) a car wash, (*b*) a stage theater group, and (*c*) a university?

6 In terms of the behavioral effect on consumers, how would a PC, such as an Apple iMac, be classified? In light of this classification, what actions would you suggest to PC manufacturers to increase their sales in the market?

7 What methods would you suggest to assess the potential commercial success for the following new products? (*a*) a new, improved ketchup; (*b*) a three-dimensional television system that took the company 10 years to develop; and (*c*) a new children's toy on which the company holds a patent.

8 Concept testing is an important step in the new-product process. Outline the concept tests for (*a*) an electrically powered car and (*b*) a new loan payment system for automobiles that is based on a variable interest rate. What are the differences in developing concept tests for products as opposed to services?

building your marketing plan

In fine-tuning the product strategy for your marketing plan, do these two things:

1 Develop a simple three-column table in which (*a*) market segments of potential customers are in the first column and (*b*) the one or two key points of difference of

the product to satisfy the segment's needs are in the second column.

2 In the third column of your table, write ideas for specific new products for your business in each of the rows in your table.

video case 9 General Mills Warm Delights™: Indulgent, Delicious, and Gooey!

QR 9–5
Warm Delights
Video Case

Vivian Milroy Callaway (photo on page 216), vice president for the Center for Learning and Experimentation at General Mills, retells the story for the "indulgent, delicious, and gooey" Warm Delights™. She summarizes, "When you want something that is truly innovative, you have to look at the rules you have been assuming in your category and break them all!"

The creators of Betty Crocker Warm Delights stress that if the marketing decisions had been based on the history of the cake category, a smaller, struggling business would have resulted. The team challenged the assump-

tions of accumulated cake category business experience. Today Warm Delights is a roaring success.

PLANNING PHASE: INNOVATION, BUT A SHRINKING MARKET

"In the typical grocery store, the baking mix aisle is a quiet place," says Callaway. Shelves sigh with flavors, types, and brands. Prices are low, but there is little consumer traffic. Cake continues to be a tradition for birthdays and social occasions. But consumer demand still declines. The percentage of U.S. households that buy at least one baking mix in a year is shrinking.

Today, a promoted price of 89 cents to make a 9 × 12 inch cake is common. Many choices, but little differentiation, gradually falling sales, and low uniform prices are the hallmarks of a mature category. But it's not that consumers don't buy cake-like treats. In fact, indulgent treats are growing. The premium prices for ice cream ($3.00 a pint) and chocolate ($3.00 a bar) are not slowing consumer purchases.

The Betty Crocker marketing team challenged the food scientists at General Mills to create a great tasting, easy to prepare, single-serve cake treat. The goal: Make it indulgent, delicious, and gooey. The team focused the scientists on a product that would have:

- Consistent great taste.
- Quick preparation.
- A single portion.
- No cleanup.

The food scientists delivered the prototype! Next, the marketing team began hammering out the four Ps. They started with a descriptive name—"Betty Crocker Dessert Bowls"—and a plan to shelve it in the "quiet" cake aisle. This practical approach would meet the consumer need for a "small, fast, microwave cake" for dessert. Several marketing challenges emerged:

- *The comparison problem.* The easy shelf price comparison to 9 × 12 inch cakes selling for 89 cents would make it harder to price Dessert Bowls at $2.00.
- *The communication problem.* The product message "a small, faster-to-make cake" wasn't compelling. For example, after-school snacks should be fast and small, but "dessert" sounds too indulgent.
- *The quiet aisle problem.* The cake-aisle shopper is probably not browsing for a cake innovation.
- *The dessert problem.* Consumers' on-the-go, calorie-conscious meal plans don't generally include a planned dessert.
- *The microwave problem.* Consumers might not believe it tastes good.

In sum, the small, fast-cake product didn't resonate with a compelling consumer need. But it would be a safe bet

because the Dessert Bowl positioning fit nicely with the family-friendly Betty Crocker brand.

IMPLEMENTATION PHASE: LEAVING THE SECURITY OF FAMILY BEHIND

The consumer insights team really enjoyed the hot, gooey cake product. But they feared that it would languish in the cake aisle under the Dessert Bowl name since this didn't capture the essence of what the food delivered. They explored who the indulgent treat customers really are. The data revealed that the heaviest buyers of premium treats are women without children. This focused the team on a target consumer: "What does she want?" They asked an ad agency and consultants to come up with a name that would appeal to "her." Several independently suggested "Warm Delights," which became the brand name.

Targeting the on-the-go women who want a small, personal treat had marketing advantages:

- The $2.00 Warm Delights price compared favorably to the price of many single-serve indulgent treats.
- The product's message of "warm, convenient, delightful" is compelling.
- On-the-go women's meal plans do include the occasional delicious treat.

One major problem remained: The cake-aisle shopper is probably not browsing for an indulgent, single-serve treat.

The marketing team solved this shelving issue by using advertising and product displays outside the cake aisle. This would raise women's awareness of Warm Delights. Television advertising and in-store display programs are costly, so Warm Delights sales would have to be strong to pay back the investment.

Vivian Callaway and the team turned to market research to fine-tune the plan. The research put Warm Delights (and Dessert Bowls) on the shelf in real (different) stores to study sales. A few key findings emerged. First, the name "Warm Delights" beat "Dessert Bowls." Second, the Warm Delights with nuts simply wasn't easy to prepare, so nuts were removed. Third, the packaging with a disposable bowl beat the typical cake-mix packaging involving using your own bowl.

Another result of obtaining this consumer feedback was that many buyers said they wanted a smaller size of Warm Delights. So Callaway and her team introduced Warm Delights Minis—a smaller, 150-calorie version (photo) of the regular, 370-calorie Warm Delights.

An interesting postscript to the team's brand name research: A competitor apparently liked not only the idea of a quick, gooey, microwavable dessert but also the "Dessert Bowls" name! You may now see this competitive product on your supermarket's shelves.

EVALUATION PHASE: TURNING THE PLAN INTO ACTION

The marketing plan isn't action. Sales for "Warm Delights" required the marketing team to (1) get the retailers to stock the product, preferably somewhere other than the cake aisle, and (2) appeal to consumers enough to have them purchase, like, and repurchase the product.

The initial acceptance of a product by retailers is important. But each store manager must experience good sales of Warm Delights to be motivated to keep its shelves restocked with the product. Also, the Warm Delights team must monitor the display activity in the store. Are the displays fully stocked at all times? Do the sales increase when a display is present?

Other key questions: Did the customer buy one or two Warm Delights? Did the customer return for a second purchase a few weeks later? The syndicated services that sell household panel purchase data provide the answers. The Warm Delights team evaluates these reports to see if the number of people who try the product matches with expectations and how the repeat purchases occur.

For ongoing feedback, calls by Warm Delights consumers to the free consumer information line are monitored. This is a great source of real-time feedback. If a pattern emerges and these calls are mostly about the same problem, that is bad. However, when consumers call to say "thank you" or "it's great," that is good. This is an informal, quick way to identify if the product is on track.

GOOD MARKETING MAKES A DIFFERENCE

The team took personal and business risks by choosing a Warm Delights plan over the more conservative Dessert Bowl plan. Today, General Mills has loyal Warm Delights consumers who are open to trying new flavors, new sizes, and new forms. If you were a consultant to the Warm Delights team, what would you do to grow this brand?

Questions

1 What is the competitive set of desserts in which Warm Delights is located?

2 (*a*) Who is the target market? (*b*) What is the point of difference in regard to the positioning for Warm Delights? (*c*) What are the potential opportunities and hindrances of the target market and positioning?

3 (*a*) What marketing research did Vivian Callaway execute? (*b*) What were the critical questions for which she sought research and expert advice? (*c*) How did this affect the product's marketing mix price, promotion, packaging, and distribution decisions?

4 (*a*) What initial promotional plan directed to consumers in the target market did Callaway use? (*b*) Why did this make sense to Callaway and her team when Warm Delights was launched?

5 If you were a consultant to Vivian Callaway, what product changes would you recommend to increase sales of Warm Delights?

Managing Successful Products, Services, and Brands

10

LEARNING OBJECTIVES

After reading this chapter you should be able to:

 LO1 Explain the product life-cycle concept.

LO2 Identify ways that marketing executives manage a product's life cycle.

LO3 Recognize the importance of branding and alternative branding strategies.

LO4 Describe the role of packaging and labeling in the marketing of a product.

LO5 Recognize how the four Ps framework is expanded in the marketing of services.

GATORADE: BRINGING SCIENCE TO SWEAT

Why is the thirst for Gatorade unquenchable? Look no further than constant product improvement and masterful brand development.

Like Kleenex in the tissue market, Jell-O among gelatin desserts, and Scotch for cellophane tape, Gatorade is synonymous with sports drinks. Concocted in 1965 at the University of Florida as a rehydration beverage for the school's football team, the drink was coined "Gatorade" by an opposing team's coach after watching his team lose to the Florida Gators in the Orange Bowl. The name stuck, and a new beverage product class was born. Stokely-Van Camp Inc. bought the Gatorade formula in 1967 and commercialized the product.

The Quaker Oats Company acquired Stokely-Van Camp in 1983 and quickly increased Gatorade sales through a variety of means. More flavors were added. Multiple package sizes were offered using different containers. Distribution expanded from convenience stores and supermarkets to mass merchandisers such as Walmart. Consistent advertising and promotion effectively conveyed the product's unique performance benefits and links to athletic competition. International opportunities were vigorously pursued. Today, Gatorade is sold in more than 80 countries and is now a global brand.

Masterful brand management spurred Gatorade's success. Gatorade Frost was introduced in 1997 and aimed at expanding the brand's reach beyond organized sports to other usage occasions. Gatorade Fierce appeared in 1999. In the same year, Gatorade entered the bottled-water category with Propel Fitness Water, a lightly flavored water fortified with vitamins. The Gatorade Performance Series was introduced in 2001, featuring a Gatorade Energy Bar, Gatorade Energy Drink, and Gatorade Nutritional Shake.

Brand development accelerated after PepsiCo Inc. purchased Quaker Oats and the Gatorade brand in 2001. Gatorade Xtremo, developed with a bilingual label for Latino consumers, was launched in 2002. Gatorade X-Factor followed in 2003. In 2005, Gatorade Endurance Formula was created for serious runners, construction workers, and other people doing long, sweaty workouts. Gatorade Rain, a lighter tasting version of regular Gatorade, arrived in 2006. In 2007, Gatorade AM, with no caffeine, debuted for the morning workout consumer. A low-calorie Gatorade called G2 appeared in 2008.

In 2009, Gatorade executives unleashed a bevy of enhanced beverages in bold new packaging. "Just like any good athlete, Gatorade is taking it to the next level," said Gatorade's chief marketing officer. "Whether you're in it for the win, for the thrill or for better health, if your body is moving, Gatorade sees you as an athlete, and we're inviting you

into the brand." According to a company announcement, "The new Gatorade attitude would be most visible through a total packaging redesign." For example, Gatorade Thirst Quencher was redesigned to display the letter G front and center along with the brand's iconic bolt. "For Gatorade, G represents the heart, hustle, and soul of athleticism and will become a badge of pride for anyone who sweats, no matter where they're active."

To differentiate the range of Gatorade offerings from the traditional Gatorade Thirst Quencher, newly enhanced beverages conveyed the attitude of a tough-love coach or personal trainer through in-your-face names on the label and nutrition benefits inside. For example, Gatorade Fierce became Bring It and Gatorade X-Factor became Be Tough. Continuing product development efforts guided the creation of the G Series of products in 2010 and 2011 "that goes beyond hydration to provide fuel, fluid, and nutrients before, during, and after the game." Gatorade Prime 01 was formulated to be consumed before a game. Gatorade Perform 02 was designed for consumption during a game. Gatorade Recover 03 was created for use after a game for rehydration and to promote muscle recovery. Starting in 2012, these products were supported with the "Win From Within" advertising campaign.[1]

The marketing of Gatorade illustrates continuous product development and masterful brand management in a dynamic marketplace. Not surprisingly, Gatorade remains a vibrant multibillion-dollar brand some 45 years after its creation. This chapter shows how the actions taken by Gatorade executives exemplify those made by successful marketers.

Gatorade's marketing performance is a direct result of continuous product improvement and masterful brand management as defined by the "Gatorade bath."

QR 10–1
Gatorade Ad

CHARTING THE PRODUCT LIFE CYCLE

LO1

Products, like people, are viewed as having a life cycle. The concept of the **product life cycle** describes the stages a new product goes through in the marketplace: introduction, growth, maturity, and decline (Figure 10–1).[2] The two curves shown in this figure, total industry sales revenue and total industry profit, represent the sum of sales revenue and profit of all firms producing the product. The reasons for the changes in each curve and the marketing decisions involved are detailed next.

product life cycle
The stages a new product goes through in the marketplace: introduction, growth, maturity, and decline.

Introduction Stage

The introduction stage of the product life cycle occurs when a product is introduced to its intended target market. During this period, sales grow slowly, and profit is minimal. The lack of profit is often the result of large investment costs in product development, such as the millions of dollars spent by Gillette to develop the Gillette Fusion razor shaving system. The marketing objective for the company at this stage is to create consumer awareness and stimulate *trial*—the initial purchase of a product by a consumer.

Companies often spend heavily on advertising and other promotion tools to build awareness and stimulate product trial among consumers in the introduction stage. For example, Gillette budgeted $200 million in advertising to introduce the Fusion shaving system to male shavers. The result? Over 60 percent of male shavers became aware of the new razor within six months and 26 percent tried the product.[3]

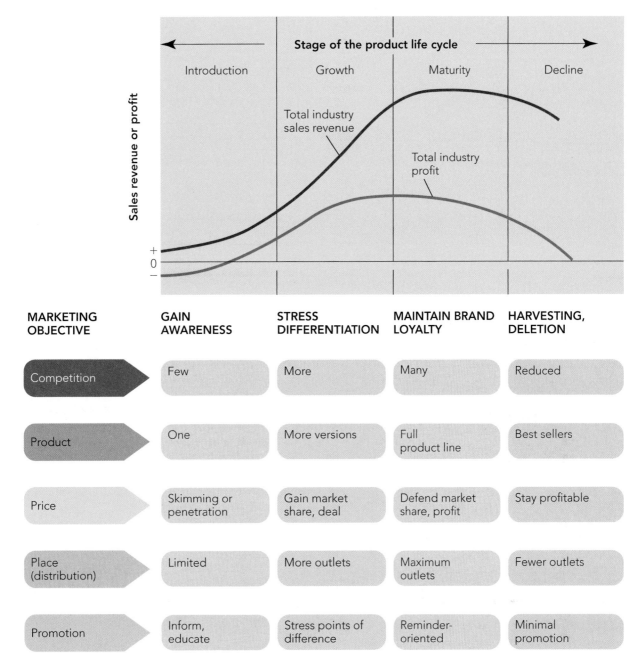

Stage of the product life cycle

	Introduction	Growth	Maturity	Decline
MARKETING OBJECTIVE	**GAIN AWARENESS**	**STRESS DIFFERENTIATION**	**MAINTAIN BRAND LOYALTY**	**HARVESTING, DELETION**
Competition	Few	More	Many	Reduced
Product	One	More versions	Full product line	Best sellers
Price	Skimming or penetration	Gain market share, deal	Defend market share, profit	Stay profitable
Place (distribution)	Limited	More outlets	Maximum outlets	Fewer outlets
Promotion	Inform, educate	Stress points of difference	Reminder-oriented	Minimal promotion

FIGURE 10–1

How stages of the product life cycle relate to a firm's marketing objectives and marketing mix actions.

Advertising and promotion spending in the introduction stage is made to stimulate *primary demand*, the desire for the product class rather than for a specific brand, since there are few competitors with the same product. As competitors launch their own products and the product progresses along its life cycle, company attention focuses on creating *selective demand*, the preference for a specific brand.

Other marketing mix variables also are important at this stage. Gaining distribution can be a challenge because channel intermediaries may be hesitant to carry a new product. Also, a company often restricts the number of variations of the product to ensure control of product quality. As an example, the original Gatorade came in only one flavor—lemon-lime.

During introduction, pricing can be either high or low. A high initial price may be used as part of a *skimming* strategy to help the company recover the costs of development as well as capitalize on the price insensitivity of early buyers. A master of this

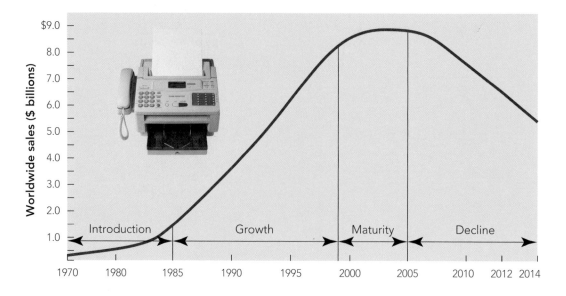

FIGURE 10–2

Product life cycle for the stand-alone fax machine for business use: 1970–2014. All four product life-cycle stages appear: introduction, growth, maturity, and decline.

strategy is 3M. According to a 3M manager, "We hit fast, price high, and get the heck out when the me-too products pour in."[4] High prices tend to attract competitors eager to enter the market because they see the opportunity for profit. To discourage competitive entry, a company can price low, referred to as *penetration pricing*. This pricing strategy helps build unit volume, but a company must closely monitor costs. These and other pricing techniques are covered in Chapter 11.

Figure 10–2 charts the stand-alone fax machine product life cycle for business use in the United States from the early 1970s to 2014.[5] As shown, sales grew slowly in the 1970s and early 1980s after Xerox pioneered the first portable fax machine. Fax machines were first sold direct to businesses by company salespeople and were premium priced. The average price for a fax machine in 1980 was a hefty $12,700. Those fax machines were primitive by today's standards. They contained mechanical parts, not electronic circuitry, and offered few features seen in today's models.

Several product classes are in the introductory stage of the product life cycle today. These include OLED 3D SmartTV and electric-powered automobiles.

Growth Stage

The growth stage of the product life cycle is characterized by rapid increases in sales. It is in this stage that competitors appear. For example, Figure 10–2 shows the dramatic increase in sales of fax machines from 1986 to 1998. The number of companies selling fax machines also increased, from one in the early 1970s to four in the late 1970s to seven manufacturers in 1983, which sold nine brands. By 1998 there were some 25 manufacturers and 60 brands from which to choose.

The result of more competitors and more aggressive pricing is that profit usually peaks during the growth stage. For instance, the average price for a fax machine plummeted from $3,300 in 1985 to $500 in 1995. At this stage, advertising shifts emphasis to stimulating selective demand; product benefits are compared with those of competitors' offerings for the purpose of gaining market share.

Product sales in the growth stage grow at an increasing rate because of new people trying or using the product and a growing proportion of *repeat purchasers*—people who tried the product, were satisfied, and bought again. For the Gillette Fusion razor, over 60 percent of men who tried the razor adopted the product permanently. For successful products, the ratio of repeat to trial purchases grows as the product moves through the life cycle. Durable fax machines meant that replacement purchases were rare. However, it became common for more than one fax machine to populate a business as the machine's use became more widespread.

Electric automobiles like the Volt made by General Motors are in the introductory stage of the product life cycle. By comparison, e-book readers such as Kindle offered by Amazon are in the growth stage of the product life cycle. Each product faces unique challenges based on its product life-cycle stage.

General Motors Company
www.gm.com

Amazon
www.amazon.com

Changes appear in the product in the growth stage. To help differentiate a company's brand from competitors, an improved version or new features are added to the original design, and product proliferation occurs. Changes in fax machines included (1) models with built-in telephones; (2) models that used plain, rather than thermal, paper for copies; and (3) models that integrated electronic mail.

In the growth stage, it is important to broaden distribution for the product. In the retail store, for example, this often means that competing companies fight for display and shelf space. Expanded distribution in the fax industry is an example. Early in the growth stage, just 11 percent of office machine dealers carried this equipment. By the mid-1990s, over 70 percent of these dealers sold fax equipment, and distribution was expanded to other stores selling electronic equipment.

Numerous product classes or industries are in the growth stage of the product life cycle today. Examples include smartphones and e-book readers.

Maturity Stage

The maturity stage is characterized by a slowing of total industry sales or product class revenue. Also, marginal competitors begin to leave the market. Most consumers who would buy the product are either repeat purchasers of the item or have tried and abandoned it. Sales increase at a decreasing rate in the maturity stage as fewer new buyers enter the market. Profit declines due to fierce price competition among many sellers, and the cost of gaining new buyers at this stage rises.

Marketing attention in the maturity stage is often directed toward holding market share through further product differentiation and finding new buyers. Fax machine manufacturers developed Internet-enabled multifunctional models with new features such as scanning, copying, and color reproduction. They also designed fax machines suitable for small and home businesses, which today represent a

Will E-mail Spell Extinction for Fax Machines?

Technological substitution that creates value for customers often causes the decline stage in the product life cycle. Will e-mail replace fax machines?

This question has been debated for years. Even though e-mail continues to grow with broadening Internet access, millions of fax machines are still sold each year. Industry analysts estimate that the number of e-mail mailboxes worldwide will be 2.5 billion in 2012 and will increase to 3.1 billion in 2014. However, the phenomenal popularity of e-mail has not brought fax machines to extinction. Why? The two technologies do not directly compete for the same messaging applications.

E-mail is used for text messages, and faxing is predominately used for communicating formatted documents by business users. Fax usage is expected to increase through 2012, even though unit sales of fax machines have declined on a worldwide basis. Internet technology and e-mail may eventually replace facsimile technology and paper and make fax machines extinct, but not in the immediate future.

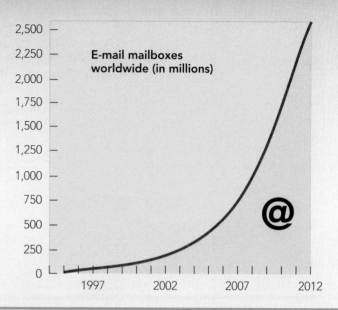

substantial portion of sales. Still, a major consideration in a company's strategy in this stage is to control overall marketing cost by improving promotional and distribution efficiency.

Fax machines entered the maturity stage in the late 1990s. At the time, about 90 percent of industry sales were captured by five producers (Hewlett-Packard, Brother, Sharp, Lexmark, and Samsung), reflecting the departure of marginal competitors. By 2004, 200 million stand-alone fax machines were installed throughout the world, sending more than 120 billion faxes annually.

Numerous product classes and industries are in the maturity stage of their product life cycle today. These include carbonated soft drinks and DVD players.

Decline Stage

The decline stage occurs when sales drop. Fax machines for business use moved to this stage in early 2005. By then, the average price for a fax machine had sunk below $100. Frequently, a product enters this stage not because of any wrong strategy on the part of companies, but because of environmental changes. For example, digital music players pushed compact discs into decline in the recorded music industry. Will Internet technology and e-mail make fax machines extinct any time soon? The Marketing Matters box offers one perspective on this question.[6]

Products in the decline stage tend to consume a disproportionate share of management and financial resources relative to their future worth. A company will follow one of two strategies to handle a declining product: deletion or harvesting.

Deletion   Product *deletion*, or dropping the product from the company's product line, is the most drastic strategy. Because a residual core of consumers still consume or use a product even in the decline stage, product elimination decisions are not taken lightly. For example, Sanford Corporation continues to sell its Liquid Paper correction fluid for use with typewriters in the era of word-processing equipment.

Harvesting   A second strategy, *harvesting*, is when a company retains the product but reduces marketing costs. The product continues to be offered, but salespeople do not allocate time in selling nor are advertising dollars spent. The purpose of harvesting is to maintain the ability to meet customer requests. Coca-Cola, for instance, still sells Tab, its first diet cola, to a small group of die-hard fans. According to Coke's CEO, "It shows you care. We want to make sure those who want Tab, get Tab."[7]

Three Aspects of the Product Life Cycle

Some important aspects of product life cycles are (1) their length, (2) the shape of their sales curves, and (3) the rate at which consumers adopt products.

Length of the Product Life Cycle   There is no set time that it takes a product to move through its life cycle. As a rule, consumer products have shorter life cycles than business products. For example, many new consumer food products such as Frito-Lay's Baked Lay's potato chips move from the introduction stage to maturity in 18 months. The availability of mass communication vehicles informs consumers quickly and shortens life cycles. Also, technological change tends to shorten product life cycles as new-product innovation replaces existing products.

Shape of the Product Life Cycle   The product life-cycle sales curve shown in Figure 10–1 is the *generalized life cycle*, but not all products have the same shape to their curve. In fact, there are several life-cycle curves, each type suggesting different marketing strategies. Figure 10–3 shows the shape of life-cycle sales curves for four different types of products: high-learning, low-learning, fashion, and fad products.

A *high-learning product* is one for which significant customer education is required and there is an extended introductory period (Figure 10–3A). It may surprise you, but personal computers had this life-cycle curve. Consumers in the 1980s had to learn the benefits of owning the product or be educated in a new way of performing familiar tasks. Convection ovens for home use required consumers to learn a new way of cooking and alter familiar recipes used with conventional ovens. As a result, these ovens spent years in the introductory period.

In contrast, sales for a *low-learning product* begin immediately because little learning is required by the consumer, and the benefits of purchase are readily understood

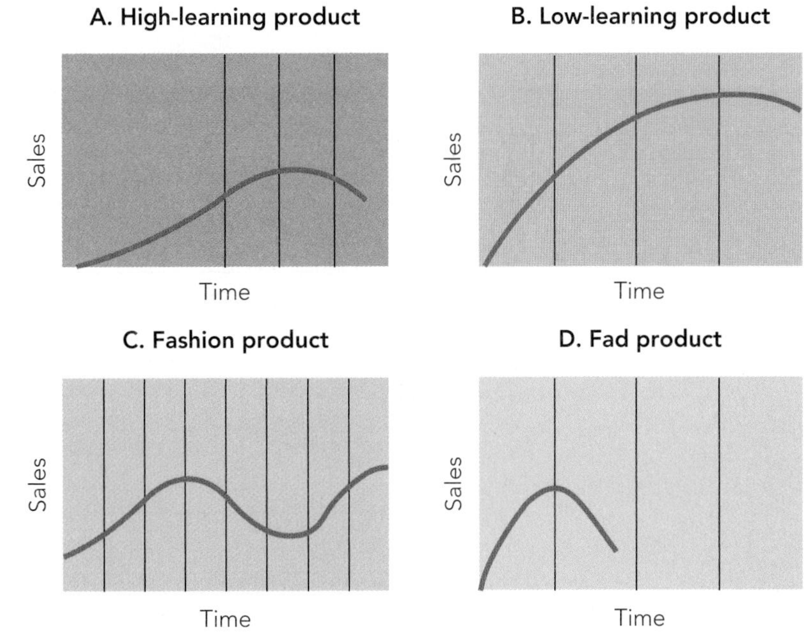

FIGURE 10–3

Alternative product life-cycle curves based on product types. Note the long introduction stage for a high-learning product compared with a low-learning product. Read the text for an explanation of different product life-cycle curves.

A. High-learning product

Sales / Time

B. Low-learning product

Sales / Time

C. Fashion product

Sales / Time

D. Fad product

Sales / Time

(Figure 10–3B). This product often can be easily imitated by competitors, so the marketing strategy is to broaden distribution quickly. In this way, as competitors rapidly enter, most retail outlets already have the innovator's product. It is also important to have the manufacturing capacity to meet demand. A successful low-learning product is Gillette's Fusion razor. This product achieved $1 billion in worldwide sales in less than three years.

A *fashion product* (Figure 10–3C) is a style of the times. Life cycles for fashion products frequently appear in women's and men's apparel. Fashion products are introduced, decline, and then seem to return. The length of the cycles may be months, years, or decades. Consider women's hosiery. Product sales have been declining for years. Women consider it more fashionable to not wear hosiery—bad news for Hanes brands, the leading marketer of women's sheer hosiery. According to an authority on fashion, "Companies might as well let the fashion cycle take its course and wait for the inevitable return of pantyhose."[8]

A *fad* experiences rapid sales on introduction and then an equally rapid decline (Figure 10–3D). These products are typically novelties and have a short life cycle. They include car tattoos, described as the first removable and reusable graphics for automobiles, and vinyl dresses and fleece bikinis.[9]

The Product Life Cycle and Consumers The life cycle of a product depends on sales to consumers. Not all consumers rush to buy a product in the introductory stage, and the shapes of the life-cycle curves indicate that most sales occur after the product has been on the market for some time. In essence, a product diffuses, or spreads, through the population, a concept called the *diffusion of innovation*.[10]

Some people are attracted to a product early. Others buy it only after they see their friends or opinion leaders with the item. Figure 10–4 shows the consumer population divided into five categories of product adopters based on when they adopt a new product. Brief profiles accompany each category. For any product to be successful, it must be purchased by innovators and early adopters. This is why manufacturers of new pharmaceuticals try to gain adoption by respected hospitals, clinics, and physicians. Once accepted by innovators and early adopters, the adoption of new products moves on to the early majority, late majority, and laggard categories.

Several factors affect whether a consumer will adopt a new product or not. Common reasons for resisting a product in the introduction stage are *usage barriers*

FIGURE 10–4

Five categories and profiles of product adopters. For a product to be successful, it must be purchased by innovators and early adopters.

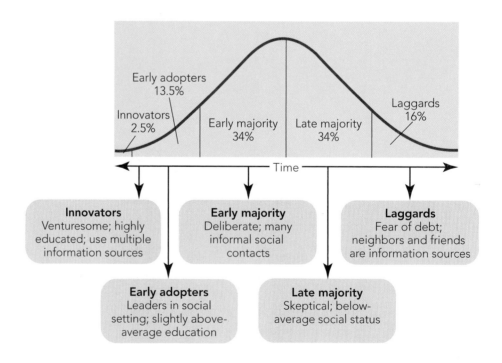

(the product is not compatible with existing habits), *value barriers* (the product provides no incentive to change), *risk barriers* (physical, economic, or social), and *psychological barriers* (cultural differences or image).[11]

Companies attempt to overcome these barriers in numerous ways. They provide warranties, money-back guarantees, extensive usage instructions, demonstrations, and free samples to stimulate initial trial of new products. For example, software developers offer demonstrations downloaded from the Internet. Cosmetics consumers can browse through the ColorMatch Custom Makeup Selector on Cover Girl's website to find out how certain makeup products will look. Free samples are one of the most popular means to gain consumer trial. In fact, 71 percent of consumers consider a sample to be the best way to evaluate a new product.[12]

---

learning review

1. Advertising plays a major role in the _____ stage of the product life cycle, and _____ plays a major role in maturity.

2. How do high-learning and low-learning products differ?

MANAGING THE PRODUCT LIFE CYCLE

LO2

An important task for a firm is to manage its products through the successive stages of their life cycles. This section describes the role of the product manager, who is usually responsible for this, and presents three ways to manage a product through its life cycle: modifying the product, modifying the market, and repositioning the product.

Role of a Product Manager

The product manager, sometimes called a *brand manager*, manages the marketing efforts for a close-knit family of products or brands. The product manager style of marketing organization is used by consumer products firms, including Procter & Gamble, General Mills, and PepsiCo, and by industrial firms such as Intel and Hewlett-Packard.

All product managers are responsible for managing existing products through the stages of the life cycle. Some are also responsible for developing new products. Product managers' marketing responsibilities include developing and executing a marketing program for the product line described in an annual marketing plan and approving ad copy, media selection, and package design.

Product managers also engage in extensive data analysis related to their products and brands. Sales, market share, and profit trends are closely monitored. Managers often supplement these data with two measures: (1) a category development index (CDI) and (2) a brand development index (BDI). These indexes help to identify strong and weak market segments (usually demographic or geographic segments) for specific consumer products and brands and provide direction for marketing efforts. The calculation, visual display, and interpretation of these two indexes for Hawaiian Punch are described in the Using Marketing Dashboards box on the next page.

Modifying the Product

Product modification involves altering one or more of a product's characteristics, such as its quality, performance, or appearance, to increase the product's value to customers and increase sales. Wrinkle-free and stain-resistant clothing made possible by nanotechnology revolutionized the men's and women's apparel business and stimulated industry sales of casual pants, shirts, and blouses.

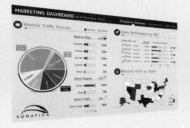

Using Marketing Dashboards
Knowing Your CDI and BDI

Where are sales for my product category and brand strongest and weakest? Data related to this question are displayed in a marketing dashboard using two indexes: (1) a category development index and (2) a brand development index.

Your Challenge You have joined the marketing team for Hawaiian Punch, the top fruit punch drink sold in the United States. The brand has been marketed to mothers with children under 13 years old. The majority of Hawaiian Punch sales are in gallon and 2-liter bottles. Your assignment is to examine the brand's performance and identify growth opportunities for the Hawaiian Punch brand among households that consume prepared fruit drinks (the product category).

Your marketing dashboard displays a category development index and a brand development index provided by a syndicated marketing research firm. Each index is based on the calculations below:

Category Development Index (CDI) =
$$\frac{\text{Percent of a product category's total U.S. sales in a market segment}}{\text{Percent of the total U.S. population in a market segment}} \times 100$$

Brand Development Index (BDI) =
$$\frac{\text{Percent of a brand's total U.S. sales in a market segment}}{\text{Percent of the total U.S. population in a market segment}} \times 100$$

A CDI over 100 indicates above-average product category purchases by a market segment. A number under 100 indicates below-average purchases. A BDI over 100 indicates a strong brand position in a segment; a number under 100 indicates a weak brand position.

You are interested in CDI and BDI displays for four household segments that consume prepared fruit drinks: (1) households without children; (2) households with children 6 years old or under; (3) households with children aged 7 to 12; and (4) households with children aged 13 to 18.

Your Findings The BDI and CDI measures displayed below show that Hawaiian Punch is consumed by households with children, and particularly households with children under age 12. The Hawaiian Punch BDI is over 100 for both segments—not surprising since the brand is marketed to these segments. Households with children 13 to 18 years old evidence high fruit drink consumption with a CDI over 100. But Hawaiian Punch is relatively weak in this segment, with a BDI under 100.

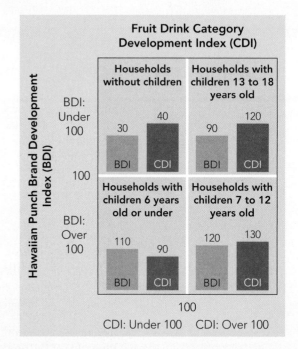

Your Action An opportunity for Hawaiian Punch exists among households with children aged 13 to 18 years old—teenagers. You might propose that Hawaiian Punch be repositioned for teens. In addition, you might recommend that Hawaiian Punch be packaged in single-serve cans or bottles to attract this segment, much like soft drinks. Teens might also be targeted for advertising and promotions.

New features, packages, or scents can be used to change a product's characteristics and give the sense of a revised product. Procter & Gamble revamped Pantene shampoo and conditioner with a new vitamin formula and relaunched the brand with a multimillion-dollar advertising and promotion campaign. The result? Pantene, a brand first introduced in the 1940s, is now the top-selling shampoo and conditioner in the United States in an industry with more than 1,000 competitors.

Harley-Davidson redesigned some of its motorcycle models to feature smaller hand grips, a lower seat, and an easier-to-pull clutch lever to create a more comfortable ride for women. According to Genevieve Schmitt, founding editor of WomenRidersNow.com, "They realize that women are an up-and-coming segment and that they need to accommodate them."

Harley-Davidson, Inc.

www.harley-davidson.com

QR 10–2
Dockers Ad

Modifying the Market

With *market modification* strategies, a company tries to find new customers, increase a product's use among existing customers, or create new use situations.

Finding New Customers   Produce companies have begun marketing and packaging prunes as dried plums to attract younger buyers. Harley-Davidson has tailored a marketing program to encourage women to take up biking, thus doubling the number of potential customers for its motorcycles.

Increasing a Product's Use   Promoting more frequent usage has been a strategy of Campbell Soup Company. Because soup consumption rises in the winter and declines during the summer, the company now advertises more heavily in warm months to encourage consumers to think of soup as more than a cold-weather food. Similarly, the Florida Orange Growers Association advocates drinking orange juice throughout the day rather than for breakfast only.

Creating a New Use Situation   Finding new uses for an existing product has been the strategy behind Dockers, the U.S. market leader in casual pants. Originally intended as a single pant for every situation, Dockers now promotes different looks for different usage situations: work, weekend, dress, and golf.

Repositioning the Product

Often a company decides to reposition its product or product line in an attempt to bolster sales. *Product repositioning* changes the place a product occupies in a consumer's mind relative to competitive products. A firm can reposition a product by changing one or more of the four marketing mix elements. Four factors that trigger the need for a repositioning action are discussed next.

Reacting to a Competitor's Position   One reason to reposition a product is because a competitor's entrenched position is adversely affecting sales and market share. New Balance, Inc., successfully repositioned its athletic shoes to focus on fit, durability, and comfort rather than competing head-on against Nike and Adidas on fashion and professional sports. The company offers an expansive range of shoes and it networks with podiatrists, not sports celebrities.

Reaching a New Market   When Unilever introduced iced tea in Britain, sales were disappointing. British consumers viewed it as leftover hot tea, not suitable for drinking. The company made its tea carbonated and repositioned it as a cold soft drink to compete as a carbonated beverage and sales improved. Johnson & Johnson effectively repositioned its St. Joseph aspirin from a product for infants to an adult low-strength aspirin to reduce the risk of heart problems or strokes.

Catching a Rising Trend   Changing consumer trends also lead to repositioning. Growing consumer interest in foods that offer health and dietary benefits is an example. Many products have been repositioned to capitalize on this trend. Quaker Oats makes the FDA-approved claim that oatmeal, as part of a low-saturated-fat, low-cholesterol diet, may reduce the risk of heart disease. Calcium-enriched products, such as Kraft American cheese and Uncle Ben's Calcium Plus rice, emphasize healthy bone structure for children and adults. Weight-conscious consumers have embraced low-fat and low-calorie diets in growing numbers. Today, most food and beverage companies offer reduced-fat and low-calorie versions of their products.

Changing the Value Offered   In repositioning a product, a company can decide to change the value it offers buyers and trade up or down. *Trading up* involves adding

Making Responsible Decisions > > > > > > > > ethics

Consumer Economics of Downsizing—Get Less, Pay More

For more than 30 years, Starkist put 6.5 ounces of tuna into its regular-sized can. Today, Starkist puts 6.125 ounces of tuna into its can but charges the same price. Frito-Lay (Doritos and Lay's snack chips), PepsiCo (Tropicana orange juice), and Nestlé (Poland Spring and Calistoga bottled waters) have whittled away at package contents 5 to 10 percent while maintaining their products' package size, dimensions, and prices. Kimberly-Clark cut its retail price on its jumbo pack of Huggies diapers from $13.50 to $12.50 but reduced the number of diapers per pack from 48 to 42. Georgia-Pacific reduced the content of its Brawny

paper towel six-roll pack by 20 percent without lowering the price.

Consumer advocates charge that downsizing the content of packages while maintaining prices is a subtle and unannounced way of taking advantage of consumer buying habits. They also say downsizing is a price increase in disguise and a deceptive, but legal, practice. Manufacturers argue that this practice is a way of keeping prices from rising beyond psychological barriers for their products.

Is downsizing an unethical practice if manufacturers do not inform consumers that the package contents are less than they were previously?

value to the product (or line) through additional features or higher-quality materials. Michelin, Bridgestone, and Goodyear have done this with a "run-flat" tire that can travel up to 50 miles at 55 miles per hour after suffering total air loss. Dog food manufacturers, such as Ralston Purina, also have traded up by offering super-premium foods based on "life-stage nutrition." Mass merchandisers, such as Target and JCPenney, can trade up by adding a designer clothes section to their stores.

Trading down involves reducing the number of features, quality, or price. For example, airlines have added more seats, thus reducing legroom, and limited snack service. Trading down also exists when companies engage in *downsizing*—reducing the package content without changing package size and maintaining or increasing the package price. Firms are criticized for this practice, as described in the Making Responsible Decisions box.[13]

The Milk Processor Education Program (MilkPEP) promotes the nutritional qualities of milk, notably vitamin D, in its advertising to capitalize on the growing consumer interest in foods that offer health and dietary benefits.

The Milk Processor Education Program
www.whymilk.com

learning review

3. What does "creating a new use situation" mean in managing a product's life cycle?

4. Explain the difference between trading up and trading down in product repositioning.

BRANDING AND BRAND MANAGEMENT

branding
An organization's use of a name, phrase, design, symbol, or combination of these to identify and distinguish its products.

brand name
Any word, device (design, shape, sound, or color), or combination of these used to distinguish a seller's goods or services.

brand personality
A set of human characteristics associated with a brand name.

QR 10–3
Dr Pepper Ad

brand equity
The added value a brand name gives to a product beyond the functional benefits provided.

A basic decision in marketing products is **branding**, in which an organization uses a name, phrase, design, symbols, or combination of these to identify its products and distinguish them from those of competitors. A **brand name** is any word, device (design, sound, shape, or color), or combination of these used to distinguish a seller's goods or services. Some brand names can be spoken, such as a Gatorade. Other brand names cannot be spoken, such as the white apple (the *logotype* or *logo*) that Apple puts on its machines and in its ads.

Consumers may benefit most from branding. Recognizing competing products by distinct trademarks allows them to be more efficient shoppers. Consumers can recognize and avoid products with which they are dissatisfied, while becoming loyal to other, more satisfying brands. As discussed in Chapter 4, brand loyalty often eases consumers' decision making by eliminating the need for an external search.

Brand Personality and Brand Equity

Product managers recognize that brands offer more than product identification and a means to distinguish their products from those of competitors.[14] Successful and established brands take on a **brand personality**, a set of human characteristics associated with a brand name. Research shows that consumers assign personality traits to products—traditional, romantic, rugged, sophisticated, rebellious—and choose brands that are consistent with their own or desired self-image. Marketers can and do imbue a brand with a personality through advertising that depicts a certain user or usage situation and conveys emotions or feelings to be associated with the brand. For example, personality traits linked with Coca-Cola are all-American and real; with Pepsi, young and exciting; and with Dr Pepper, nonconforming and unique. The traits often linked to Harley-Davidson are masculinity, defiance, and rugged individualism.

Brand name importance to a company has led to a concept called **brand equity**, the added value a brand name gives to a product beyond the functional benefits provided. This added value has two distinct advantages. First, brand equity provides a competitive advantage. The Sunkist brand implies quality fruit. The Disney name defines children's entertainment. A second advantage is that consumers are often willing to pay a higher price for a product with brand equity. Brand equity, in this instance, is represented by the premium a consumer will pay for one brand over another when the functional benefits provided are identical. Gillette razors and blades, Bose audio systems, Duracell batteries, and Louis Vuitton luggage all enjoy a price premium arising from brand equity.

Creating Brand Equity Brand equity doesn't just happen. It is carefully crafted and nurtured by marketing programs that forge strong, favorable, and unique customer associations and experiences with a brand. Brand equity resides in the minds of consumers and results from what they have learned, felt, seen, and heard about a brand over time. Marketers recognize that brand equity is not easily or

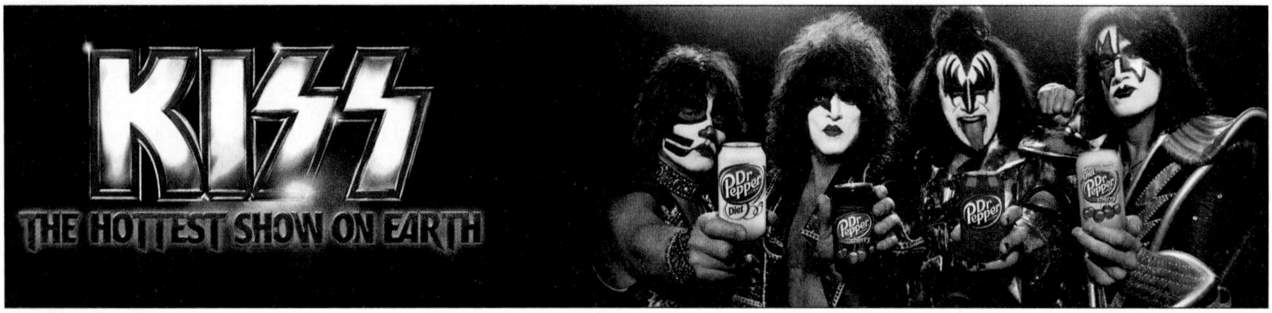

Can you describe brand personality traits for the successful Dr Pepper soft drink brand? Does the rock group KISS align with this brand personality? Read the text to learn what personality traits are often associated with the Dr Pepper brand.

Dr Pepper Snapple Group, Inc.
www.drpeppersnapplegroup.com

quickly achieved. Rather, it arises from a sequential building process consisting of four steps (see Figure 10–5).[15]

- The first step is to develop positive brand awareness and an association of the brand in consumers' minds with a product class or need to give the brand an identity. Gatorade and Kleenex have achieved this in the sports drink and facial tissue product classes, respectively.
- Next, a marketer must establish a brand's meaning in the minds of consumers. Meaning arises from what a brand stands for and has two dimensions—a functional, performance-related dimension and an abstract, imagery-related dimension. Nike has done this through continuous product development and improvement and its links to peak athletic performance in its integrated marketing communications program.
- The third step is to elicit the proper consumer responses to a brand's identity and meaning. Here attention is placed on how consumers think and feel about a brand. Thinking focuses on a brand's perceived quality, credibility, and superiority relative to other brands. Feeling relates to the consumer's emotional reaction to a brand. Michelin elicits both responses for its tires. Not only is Michelin thought of as a credible and superior-quality brand, but consumers also acknowledge a warm and secure feeling of safety, comfort, and self-assurance without worry or concern about the brand.
- The final, and most difficult, step is to create a consumer–brand connection evident in an intense, active loyalty relationship between consumers and the brand. A deep psychological bond characterizes a consumer–brand connection and the personal identification customers have with the brand. Brands that have achieved this status include Harley-Davidson, Apple, and eBay.

FIGURE 10–5
The customer-based brand equity pyramid shows the four-step building process that forges strong, favorable, and unique customer associations with a brand.

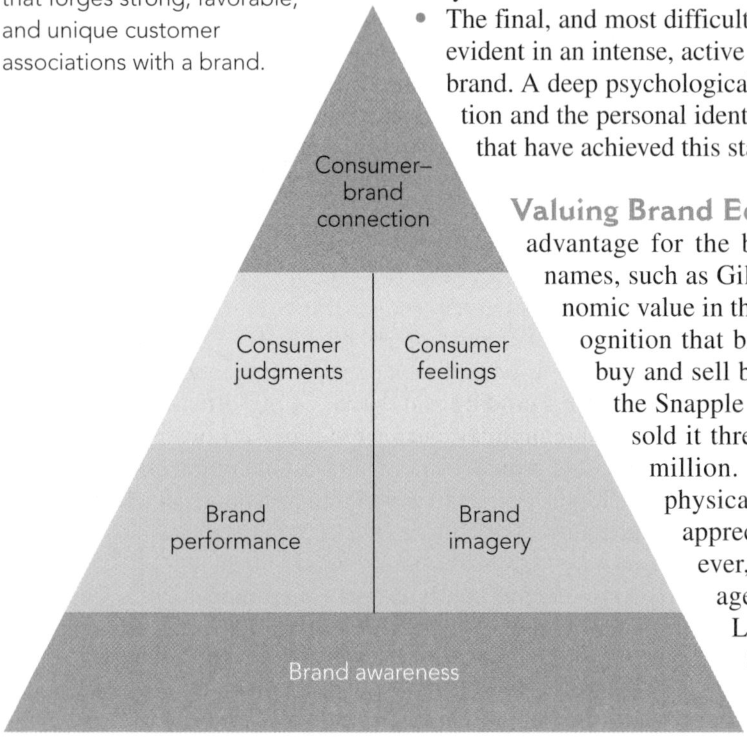

Valuing Brand Equity Brand equity also provides a financial advantage for the brand owner.[16] Successful, established brand names, such as Gillette, Nike, Gatorade, and Nokia, have an economic value in the sense that they are intangible assets. The recognition that brands are assets is apparent in the decision to buy and sell brands. For example, Triarc Companies bought the Snapple brand from Quaker Oats for $300 million and sold it three years later to Cadbury Schweppes for $900 million. This example illustrates that brands, unlike physical assets that depreciate with time and use, can appreciate in value when effectively marketed. However, brands can lose value when they are not managed properly. Consider the purchase and sale of Lender's Bagels. Kellogg bought the brand for $466 million only to sell it to Aurora Foods for $275 million three years later following deteriorating sales and profits.

Ralph Lauren has a long-term licensing agreement with Luxottica Group, S.P.A., of Milan for the design, production, and worldwide distribution of prescription frames and sunglasses under the Ralph Lauren brand. The agreement is an ideal fit for both companies. Ralph Lauren is a leader in the design, marketing, and distribution of premium lifestyle products. Luxottica is the global leader in the premium and luxury eyewear sector.

Luxottica Group, S.P.A.
www.luxottica.com

Ralph Lauren Corporation
www.ralphlauren.com

Financially lucrative brand licensing opportunities arise from brand equity.[17] *Brand licensing* is a contractual agreement whereby one company (licensor) allows its brand name(s) or trademark(s) to be used with products or services offered by another company (licensee) for a royalty or fee. Playboy earns over $37 million annually licensing its name and logo for merchandise. Disney makes billions of dollars each year licensing its characters for children's toys, apparel, and games. Winnie the Pooh fees alone exceed $3 billion annually.

Successful brand licensing requires careful marketing analysis to ensure a proper fit between the licensor's brand and the licensee's products. World-renowned designer Ralph Lauren earns over $140 million each year by licensing his Ralph Lauren, Polo, and Chaps brands for dozens of products, including paint by Glidden, furniture by Henredon, footwear by Rockport, eyewear by Luxottica, and fragrances by L'Oreal.[18] Mistakes, such as Kleenex diapers, Bic perfume, and Domino's fruit-flavored bubble gum, are a few examples of poor matches and licensing failures.

Picking a Good Brand Name

We take brand names such as Red Bull, iPad, and Axe for granted, but it is often a difficult and expensive process to pick a good name. Companies will spend between $25,000 and $100,000 to identify and test a new brand name. Five criteria are mentioned most often when selecting a good brand name.[19]

- *The name should suggest the product benefits.* For example, Accutron (watches), Easy Off (oven cleaner), Glass Plus (glass cleaner), Cling-Free (antistatic cloth for drying clothes), Chevy Volt (electric car), and Tidy Bowl (toilet bowl cleaner) all clearly describe the benefits of purchasing the product.
- *The name should be memorable, distinctive, and positive.* In the auto industry, when a competitor has a memorable name, others quickly imitate. When Ford named a car the Mustang, Pinto and Bronco soon followed. The Thunderbird name led to the Phoenix, Eagle, Sunbird, and Firebird.
- *The name should fit the company or product image.* Sharp is a name that can apply to audio and video equipment. Excedrin, Anacin, and Nuprin are scientific-sounding names, good for analgesics. Eveready, Duracell, and DieHard suggest reliability and longevity—two qualities consumers want in a battery.
- *The name should have no legal or regulatory restrictions.* Legal restrictions produce trademark infringement suits, and regulatory restrictions arise through the

improper use of words. For example, the U.S. Food and Drug Administration discourages the use of the word *heart* in food brand names. This restriction led to changing the name of Kellogg's Heartwise cereal to Fiberwise, and Clorox's Hidden Valley Ranch Take Heart Salad Dressing had to be modified to Hidden Valley Ranch Low-Fat Salad Dressing. Increasingly, brand names need a corresponding website address on the Internet. This further complicates name selection because about 140 million domain names are already registered.

- *The name should be simple* (such as Bold laundry detergent, Axe deodorant and body spray, and Bic pens) *and should be emotional* (such as Joy and Obsession perfumes). In the development of names for international use, having a nonmeaningful brand name has been considered a benefit. A name such as Exxon does not have any prior impressions or undesirable images among a diverse world population of different languages and cultures. The 7Up name is another matter. In Shanghai, China, the phrase means "death through drinking" in the local dialect. Sales have suffered as a result.

Branding Strategies

Companies can employ several different branding strategies, including multiproduct branding, multibranding, private branding, or mixed branding (see Figure 10–6).

multiproduct branding
A branding strategy in which a company uses one name for all its products in a product class.

Multiproduct Branding Strategy

With **multiproduct branding**, a company uses one name for all its products in a product class. This approach is sometimes called *family branding* or *corporate branding* when the company's trade name is used. For example, Microsoft, General Electric, Samsung, Gerber, and Sony engage in corporate branding—the company's trade name and brand name are identical. Church & Dwight uses the Arm & Hammer family brand name for all its products featuring baking soda as the primary ingredient.

There are several advantages to multiproduct branding. Capitalizing again on brand equity, consumers who have a good experience with the product will transfer this favorable attitude to other items in the product class with the same name. Therefore, this brand strategy makes possible *product line extensions*, the practice of using a current brand name to enter a new market segment in its product class.

Campbell Soup Company employs a multiproduct branding strategy with soup line extensions. It offers regular Campbell soup, home-cooking style, and chunky varieties and more than 100 soup flavors. This strategy can result in lower advertising and promotion costs because the same name is used on all products, thus raising the level of brand awareness. A risk with line extension is that sales of an extension may come at the expense of other items in the company's product line. Line extensions work best

FIGURE 10–6
Alternative branding strategies are available to marketers. Each has advantages and disadvantages described in the text.

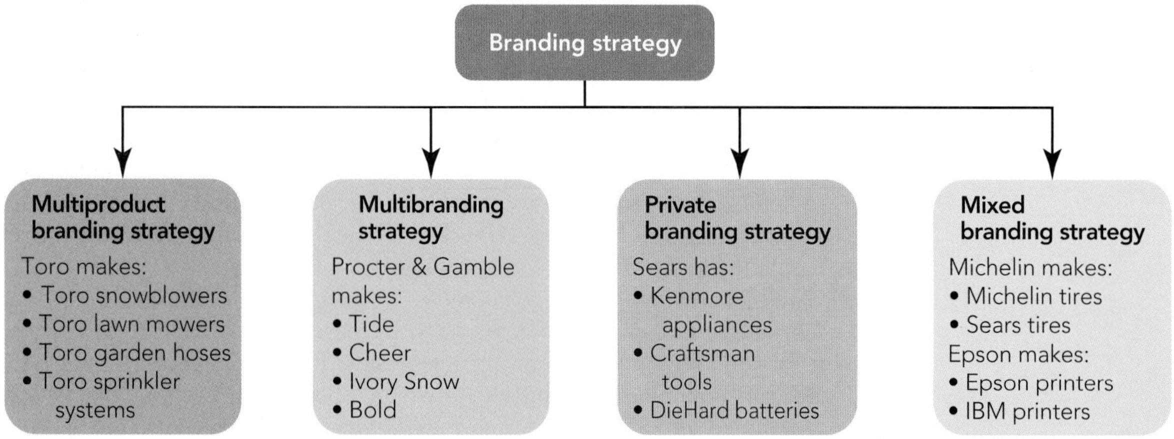

Branding strategy
Multiproduct branding strategy
Toro makes:
• Toro snowblowers
• Toro lawn mowers
• Toro garden hoses
• Toro sprinkler systems
Multibranding strategy
Procter & Gamble makes:
• Tide
• Cheer
• Ivory Snow
• Bold
Private branding strategy
Sears has:
• Kenmore appliances
• Craftsman tools
• DieHard batteries
Mixed branding strategy
Michelin makes:
• Michelin tires
• Sears tires
Epson makes:
• Epson printers
• IBM printers

Kimberly-Clark was able to leverage the strong Huggies brand equity among mothers when it introduced a full line of baby and toddler toiletries first in the United States and then globally. The success of this brand extension strategy is evident in the $500 million in annual sales generated globally.

Kimberly-Clark Corporation
www.kimberly-clark.com

---

multibranding
A branding strategy that involves giving each product a distinct name.

---

when they provide incremental company revenue by taking sales away from competing brands or attracting new buyers.

Some multiproduct branding companies employ *subbranding*, which combines a corporate or family brand with a new brand, to distinguish a part of its product line from others. Gatorade successfully used subbranding with the introduction of Gatorade G2. Similarly, Porsche successfully markets its higher-end Porsche Carrera and its lower-end Porsche Boxster.

A strong brand equity also allows for *brand extension*: the practice of using a current brand name to enter a different product class. For instance, equity in the Huggies family brand name allowed Kimberly-Clark to successfully extend its name to a full line of baby and toddler toiletries. Honda's established name for motor vehicles has extended easily to snowblowers, lawn mowers, marine engines, and snowmobiles.

However, there is a risk with brand extensions. Too many uses for one brand name can dilute the meaning of a brand for consumers. Some marketing experts claim this has happened to the Arm & Hammer brand given its use for toothpaste, laundry detergent, gum, cat litter, air freshener, carpet deodorizer, and antiperspirant.[20]

Multibranding Strategy   Alternately, a company can engage in **multibranding**, which involves giving each product a distinct name. Multibranding is a useful strategy when each brand is intended for a different market segment. P&G makes Camay soap for those concerned with soft skin and Safeguard for those who want deodorant protection. Black & Decker markets its line of tools for the household do-it-yourselfer segment with the Black & Decker name but uses the DeWalt name for its professional tool line. Disney uses the Miramax and Touchstone Pictures names for films directed at adults and its Disney name for children's films.

Multibranding is applied in a variety of ways. Some companies array their brands on the basis of price-quality segments.[21] Marriott International offers 18 hotel and resort brands, each suited for a particular traveler experience and budget. To illustrate, Marriott EDITION hotels and Vacation Clubs offer luxury amenities at a premium price. Marriott and Renaissance hotels offer medium- to high-priced accommodations. Courtyard hotels and TownePlace Suites appeal to economy-minded travelers, whereas the Fairfield Inn is for those on a very low travel budget.

Other multibrand companies introduce new product brands as defensive moves to counteract competition. Called *fighting brands*, their chief purpose is to confront competitor brands.[22] For instance, Frito-Lay introduced Santitas brand tortilla chips to go head-to-head against regional tortilla chip brands that were biting into sales of its flagship Doritos and Tostitos brand tortilla chips. Ford launched its Fusion brand to halt the defection of Ford owners who were buying competitors' midsize cars. According to Ford's car group marketing manager, "Every year we were losing around 50,000 people from our products to competitors' midsize cars. We were losing Mustang, Focus, and Taurus owners. Fusion is our interceptor."[23]

Compared with the multiproduct strategy, advertising and promotion costs tend to be higher with multibranding. The company must generate awareness among consumers and retailers for each new brand name without the benefit of any previous impressions. The advantages of this strategy are that each brand is unique to each market segment and there is no risk that a product failure will affect other products in the line. Still, some large multibrand firms have found that the complexity and expense of implementing this strategy can outweigh the benefits. For example, Unilever recently pruned its brands from some 1,600 to 400 through product deletion and sales to other companies.[24]

Creating Customer Value through Packaging—Pez Heads Dispense More than Candy

Customer value can assume numerous forms. For Pez Candy, Inc. (www.pez.com), customer value manifests itself in some 450 Pez character candy dispensers. Each refillable dispenser ejects tasty candy tablets in a variety of flavors that delight preteens and teens alike in more than 60 countries.

Pez was formulated in 1927 by Austrian food mogul Edward Haas III and successfully sold in Europe as an adult breath mint. Pez, which comes from the German word for peppermint, *pfefferminz*, was originally packaged in a hygienic, headless plastic dispenser. Pez first appeared in the United States in 1953 with a headless dispenser, marketed to adults. After conducting extensive marketing research, Pez was repositioned with fruit flavors, repackaged with licensed character heads on top of the dispenser, and remarketed as a children's product in the mid-1950s. Since then, most top-level licensed characters and hundreds of other characters have become Pez heads. Consumers buy about 80 million Pez dispensers and 4.6 billion Pez tablets a year, and company sales growth exceeds that of the candy industry as a whole.

The unique Pez package dispenses a "use experience" for its customers beyond the candy itself, namely, fun. And fun translates into a 98 percent awareness level for Pez among teenagers and an 89 percent awareness level among mothers with children. Pez has not advertised its product for years. With that kind of awareness, who needs advertising?

Private Branding Strategy A company uses *private branding*, often called *private labeling* or *reseller branding*, when it manufactures products but sells them under the brand name of a wholesaler or retailer. Rayovac, Paragon Trade Brands, and Ralcorp Holdings are major suppliers of private-label alkaline batteries, diapers, and grocery products, respectively. Radio Shack, Costco, Sears, Walmart, and Kroger are large retailers that have their own brand names. Private branding is popular because it typically produces high profits for manufacturers and resellers. Consumers also buy them. It is estimated that one of every five items purchased at U.S. supermarkets, drugstores, and mass merchandisers bears a private brand label.[25]

Mixed Branding Strategy A fourth branding strategy is *mixed branding*, where a firm markets products under its own name(s) and that of a reseller because the segment attracted to the reseller is different from its own market. Beauty and fragrance marketer Elizabeth Arden is an example. The company sells its Elizabeth Arden brand through department stores and a line of skin care products at Walmart with the "skin-simple" brand name. Companies such as Del Monte, Whirlpool, and Dial produce private brands of pet foods, home appliances, and soap, respectively.

PACKAGING AND LABELING PRODUCTS

The *packaging* component of a product refers to any container in which it is offered for sale and on which label information is conveyed. A *label* is an integral part of the package and typically identifies the product or brand, who made it, where and when it was made, how it is to be used, and package contents and ingredients. To a great extent, the customer's first exposure to a product is the package and label and both are an expensive and important part of marketing strategy. For Pez Candy, Inc., the character head-on-a-stick plastic container that dispenses a miniature tablet candy is the central element of its marketing strategy, as described in the Marketing Matters box.[26]

Creating Customer Value and Competitive Advantage through Packaging and Labeling

Packaging and labeling account for about 15 cents of every dollar spent by consumers for products.[27] Despite their cost, packaging and labeling are essential because both provide important benefits for the manufacturer, retailer, and ultimate consumer. Packaging and labeling also can provide a competitive advantage.

Communication Benefits   A major benefit of packaging is the label information on it conveyed to the consumer, such as directions on how, where, and when to use the product and the source and composition of the product, which is needed to satisfy legal requirements of product disclosure. For example, the labeling system for packaged and processed foods in the United States provides a uniform format for nutritional and dietary information. Many packaged foods contain informative recipes to promote usage of the product. Campbell Soup estimates that the green bean casserole recipe on its cream of mushroom soup can accounts for $20 million in soup sales each year![28] Other information consists of seals and symbols, either government required or commercial seals of approval (such as the Good Housekeeping seal).

Functional Benefits   Packaging often plays a functional role, such as storage, convenience, protection, or product quality. Storing food containers is one example, and beverage companies have developed lighter and easier ways to stack products on shelves and in refrigerators. Examples include Coca-Cola beverage packs designed to fit neatly onto refrigerator shelves and Ocean Spray Cranberries's rectangular juice bottles that allow 10 units per package versus 8 of its former round bottles.

The convenience dimension of packaging is increasingly important. Kraft Miracle Whip salad dressing, Heinz ketchup, and Skippy Squeez'It peanut butter are sold in squeeze bottles; microwave popcorn has been a major market success; and Chicken of the Sea tuna and Folgers coffee are packaged in single-serving portions. For the convenience of weight-conscious consumers, Nabisco offers portion-controlled, 100-calorie packs of Oreos, Cheese Nips, and other products in individual pouches.

Consumer protection is another important function of packaging, including the development of tamper-resistant containers. Today, companies commonly use safety seals or pop-tops that reveal previous opening. Consumer protection through labeling exists in "open dating," which states the expected shelf life of the product.

Functional features of packaging also can affect product quality. Pringles, with its cylindrical packaging, offers uniform chips, minimal breakage, and for some consumers, better value for the money than flex-bag packages for chips.

Cylindrical packaging for Pringles illustrates the functional role of packaging in product and brand management.

Perceptual Benefits   A third component of packaging and labeling is the perception created in the consumer's mind. Package and label shape, color, and graphics distinguish one brand from another, convey a brand's positioning, and build brand equity. According to the director of marketing for L'eggs hosiery, "Packaging is important to the positioning and equity of the L'eggs brand."[29] Why? Packaging and labeling have been shown to enhance brand recognition and facilitate the formation of strong, favorable, and unique brand associations.[30] This logic applies to Celestial Seasonings's packaging and labeling, which uses delicate illustrations, soft and warm colors, and quotations about life to reinforce the brand's positioning as a New Age, natural herbal tea.

The distinctive design of Celestial Seasonings's tea boxes reinforces the brand's positioning as a New Age, natural herbal tea.

Successful marketers recognize that changes in packages and labels can update and uphold a brand's image in the customer's mind. Pepsi-Cola embarked on a packaging change to uphold its image among teens and young adults. Beginning in 2007, Pepsi-Cola debuted new graphics on its cans and bottles to reflect the "fun, optimistic, and youthful spirit" of the brand to its customers.[31]

Because labels list a product's source, brands competing in the global marketplace can benefit from "country of origin or manufacture" perceptions as described in Chapter 6. Consumers tend to hold stereotypes about country-product pairings that they judge "best"—English tea, French perfume, Italian leather, and Japanese electronics—which can affect a brand's image. Increasingly, Chinese firms are adopting the English language and Roman letters for their brand labels. This is being done because of a common perception in many Asian countries that "things Western are good."[32]

Packaging and Labeling Challenges and Responses

Package and label designers face four challenges. They are (1) the continuing need to connect with customers; (2) environmental concerns; (3) health, safety, and security issues; and (4) cost reduction.

Connecting with Customers   Packages and labels must be continually updated to connect with customers. The challenge lies in creating aesthetic and functional design features that attract customer attention and deliver customer value in their use. If done right, the rewards can be huge.[33] For example, the marketing team responsible for Kleenex tissues converted its standard rectangular box into an oval shape with colorful seasonal graphics. Sales soared with this aesthetic change in packaging. After months of in-home research, Kraft product managers discovered that consumers often transferred Chips Ahoy! cookies to jars for easy access and to avoid staleness. The company solved both problems by creating a patented resealable opening on the top of the bag. The result? Sales of the new package doubled that of the old package with the addition of this functional feature.

Environmental Concerns   Because of widespread worldwide concern about the growth of solid waste and the shortage of viable landfill sites, the amount, composition, and disposal of packaging material continue to receive much attention. For example, PepsiCo, Coca-Cola, and Nestlé have decreased the amount of plastic in their beverage bottles to reduce solid waste. Recycling packaging material is another major thrust. Procter & Gamble now uses recycled cardboard in over 70 percent of its paper packaging. Its Spic and Span liquid cleaner is packaged in 100 percent recycled material. Other firms, such as Walmart, are emphasizing the use of less packaging material. Since 2008, Walmart has been working with its 600,000 global suppliers to reduce overall packaging and shipping material by 5 percent by 2013.[34]

Health, Safety, and Security Issues   A third challenge involves the growing health, safety, and security concerns of packaging materials. Today, most consumers believe companies should make sure products and their packages are safe and secure, regardless of the cost. Companies are responding in numerous ways. Most butane lighters sold today, like those made by Scripto, contain a child-resistant safety latch to prevent misuse and accidental fire. Child-proof caps on pharmaceutical products and household cleaners and sealed lids on food packages are now common. New packaging technology and materials that extend a product's *shelf life* (the time a product can be stored) and prevent spoilage continue to be developed.

Cost Reduction About 80 percent of packaging material used in the world consists of paper, plastics, and glass. As the cost of these materials rises, companies are constantly challenged to find innovative ways to cut packaging costs while delivering value to their customers. Many food and personal care companies have replaced bottles and cans with sealed plastic or foil pouches. Pouches cut packaging costs by 10 to 15 percent.[35]

MANAGING THE MARKETING OF SERVICES

In this section we conclude the chapter with a brief discussion of the marketing mix for services. As such, it is necessary to expand the four Ps framework to include people, physical environment, and process, which is referred to as the **seven Ps of services marketing**.[36]

Product (Service)

To a large extent, the concepts of the product component of the marketing mix apply equally well to Cheerios (a product) and to American Express (a service). Yet there are two aspects of the product/service element of the mix that warrant special attention when dealing with services: exclusivity and brand name.

Chapter 9 pointed out that one favorable dimension in a new product is its ability to be patented. However, services cannot be patented. Hence the creator of a successful quick-service restaurant chain could quickly discover the concept being copied by others. Domino's Pizza, for example, has seen competitors, such as Pizza Hut, copy the quick delivery advantage that originally propelled the company to success.

Because services are intangible and, therefore, more difficult to describe, the brand name or identifying logo of the service organization is particularly important in consumer decisions. Brand names help make the abstract nature of services more concrete. Service marketers apply branding concepts in the same way as product marketers. Consider American Express. It has applied subbranding with its American Express Green, Gold, Platinum, Optima, Blue, and Centurian credit cards, with unique service offerings for each.

McDonald's familiar Golden Arches logo is an important part of the company's branding.

Price

In the service industries, *price* is referred to in various ways. The terms used vary, depending upon whether the services are provided by hospitals (charges); consultants, lawyers, physicians, or accountants (fees); airlines (fares); or hotels (rates). Regardless of the term used, price plays two essential roles: (1) to affect consumer perceptions and (2) to be used in capacity management. Because of the intangible nature of services, price can indicate the quality of the service. Would you wonder about the quality of a $100 surgery? Studies show that when there are few cues by which to judge the quality of a product or service, consumers use price.[37]

The capacity management role of price is also important to movie theaters, airlines, restaurants, and hotels. Many service businesses use **off-peak pricing**, which consists of charging different prices during different times of the day or days of the week to reflect variations in demand for the service. Airlines offer seasonal discounts and movie theaters offer matinee prices.

Place (Distribution)

Place or distribution is a major factor in developing a service marketing strategy because of the inseparability of services from the producer. Historically, little attention has been paid to distribution in services marketing. But as competition grows, the value

The United States Postal Service uses advertising to stress the convenience of its service.

of convenient distribution is being recognized. Hairstyling chains such as Cost Cutters Family Hair Care, tax preparation offices such as H&R Block, and accounting firms such as PricewaterhouseCoopers all use multiple locations for the distribution of services. In the banking industry, customers of participating banks using the Cirrus system can access any one of thousands of automatic teller systems throughout the United States. The availability of electronic distribution through the Internet now provides global coverage for travel services, banking, entertainment, and many other information-based services.

Promotion

The purpose of promotion for services, specifically advertising, is to show the benefits of using the service. It is valuable to stress availability, location, consistent quality, and efficient, courteous service. Also, services must be concerned with their image. Promotional efforts, such as Merrill Lynch's use of the bull in its ads, contribute to image and positioning strategies. In general, promotional concerns of services are similar to those of products. Another form of promotion, *publicity,* plays a major role in the promotional strategy of nonprofit services and some professional organizations. Nonprofit organizations such as public school districts, the Chicago Symphony Orchestra, religious organizations, and hospitals use publicity to disseminate their messages. Because of the heavy reliance on publicity, many services use *public service announcements* (PSAs). PSAs are free and nonprofit groups tend to rely on them as the foundation of their media plan. However, the timing and location of a PSA are under the control of the medium, not the organization. Thus, the nonprofit service group cannot control who sees the message or when the message is delivered.

People

Many services depend on people for the creation and delivery of the customer service experience. The nature of the interaction between employees and customers strongly influences the customer's perceptions of the service experience. Customers will often judge the quality of the service experience based on the performance of the people providing the service.

This aspect of services marketing has led to a concept called *customer experience management* (CEM), which is the process of managing the entire customer experience with the firm. CEM experts suggest that the process should be intentional, planned, and consistent so that every experience is similar, differentiated from other services, relevant, and valuable to the target market. Companies such as Disney, Southwest Airlines, and Starbucks all manage the experience they offer customers. They integrate their activities to connect with customers at each contact point to move beyond customer relationships to customer loyalty. Zappos.com, an online retailer, requires that all employees complete a four-week customer loyalty training program to deliver one of the company's core concepts—"Deliver WOW through service."[38]

Physical Environment

The appearance of the environment in which the service is delivered and where the firm and customer interact can influence the customer's perception of the service. The physical evidence of the service includes all the tangibles surrounding the service: the buildings, landscaping, vehicles, furnishings, signage, brochures, and equipment. Service firms need to systematically and carefully manage physical evidence and to convey the proper impression of the service to the customer. This is sometimes referred to as impression, or evidence, management.[39] For many services, the physical environment provides an opportunity for the firm to send consistent and strong messages about the nature of the service to be delivered.

Process

Process refers to the actual procedures, mechanisms, and flow of activities by which the service is created and delivered. The actual creation and delivery steps that the customer experiences provide customers with evidence on which to judge the service. These steps involve not only "what" gets created but also "how" it is created. Grease Monkey believes that it has the right process in the vehicle oil change and fluid exchange service business. Customers do not need appointments, stores are open six days per week, the service is completed in 15–20 minutes, and a waiting room allows customers to read or work while the service is being completed.

Most services have a limited capacity due to the inseparability of the service from the service provider and the perishable nature of the service. For example, a patient must be in the hospital at the same time as the surgeon to "buy" an appendectomy, and only one patient can be helped at that time. Similarly, no additional surgery can be conducted tomorrow because of an unused operating room or an available surgeon today—the service capacity is lost if it is not used. So the service component of the marketing mix must be integrated with efforts to influence consumer demand. This is referred to as **capacity management**. Service organizations must manage the availability of the offering so that (1) demand matches capacity over the duration of the demand cycle (for example, one day, week, month, or year), and (2) the organization's assets are used in ways that will maximize the return on investment (ROI).

capacity management
Integrating the service component of the marketing mix with efforts to influence consumer demand.

---

learning review

5. What is the difference between a line extension and a brand extension?

6. Explain the role of packaging in terms of perception.

7. How do service businesses use off-peak pricing?

LEARNING OBJECTIVES REVIEW

LO1 *Explain the product life-cycle concept.*
The product life cycle describes the stages a new product goes through in the marketplace: introduction, growth, maturity, and decline. Product sales growth and profitability differ at each stage, and marketing managers have marketing objectives and marketing mix strategies unique to each stage based on consumer behavior and competitive factors. In the introductory stage, the need is to establish primary demand, whereas the growth stage requires selective demand strategies. In the maturity stage, the need is to maintain market share; the decline stage necessitates a deletion or harvesting strategy. Some important aspects of product life cycles are (*a*) their length, (*b*) the shape of the sales curves, and (*c*) the rate at which consumers adopt products.

LO2 *Identify ways that marketing executives manage a product's life cycle.*
Marketing executives manage a product's life cycle in three ways. First, they can modify the product itself by altering its

characteristics, such as product quality, performance, or appearance. Second, they can modify the market by finding new customers for the product, increasing a product's use among existing customers, or creating a new use situation for the product. Finally, they can reposition the product using any one or a combination of marketing mix elements. Four factors trigger a repositioning action. They include reacting to a competitor's position, reaching a new market, catching a rising trend, and changing the value offered to consumers.

LO3 *Recognize the importance of branding and alternative branding strategies.*
A basic decision in marketing products is branding, in which an organization uses a name, phrase, design, symbols, or a combination of these to identify its products and distinguish them from those of its competitors. Product managers recognize that brands offer more than product identification and a means to distinguish their products from competitors. Successful and

established brands take on a brand personality and acquire brand equity—the added value a given brand name gives to a product beyond the functional benefits provided—that is crafted and nurtured by marketing programs that forge strong, favorable, and unique consumer associations with a brand. A good brand name should suggest the product benefits, be memorable, fit the company or product image, be free of legal restrictions, and be simple and emotional. Companies can and do employ several different branding strategies. With multiproduct branding, a company uses one name for all its products in a product class. A multibranding strategy involves giving each product a distinct name. A company uses private branding when it manufactures products but sells them under the brand name of a wholesaler or retailer. Finally, a company can employ mixed branding, where it markets products under its own name(s) and that of a reseller.

LO4 *Describe the role of packaging and labeling in the marketing of a product.*
Packaging and labeling play numerous roles in the marketing of a product. The packaging component of a product refers to any container in which it is offered for sale and on which label information is conveyed. Manufacturers, retailers, and consumers acknowledge that packaging and labeling provide communication, functional, and perceptual benefits. Contemporary packaging and labeling challenges include (*a*) the continuing need to connect with customers, (*b*) environmental concerns, (*c*) health, safety, and security issues, and (*d*) cost reduction.

LO5 *Recognize how the four Ps framework is expanded in the marketing of services.*
The four Ps framework also applies to services with some adaptations. Because services cannot be patented, unique offerings are difficult to protect. In addition, because services are intangible, brands and logos (which can be protected) are particularly important. The inseparability of production and consumption of services means that capacity management is important to services. The intangible nature of services makes price an important indication of service quality. Distribution has become an important marketing tool for services, and electronic distribution allows some services to provide global coverage. In recent years, service organizations have increased their promotional activities. Finally, the performance of people, the appearance of the physical environment, and the process involved in delivering a service are recognized as central to the customer experience.

FOCUSING ON KEY TERMS

brand equity p. 231	**capacity management** p. 241	**off-peak pricing** p. 240
brand name p. 231	**seven Ps of services marketing** p. 239	**product life cycle** p. 220
brand personality p. 231	**multibranding** p. 235	
branding p. 231	**multiproduct branding** p. 234	

APPLYING MARKETING KNOWLEDGE

1 Listed below are three different products in various stages of the product life cycle. What marketing strategies would you suggest to these companies? (*a*) Canon digital cameras—growth stage, (*b*) Hewlett Packard tablet computers—introductory stage, and (*c*) handheld manual can openers—decline stage.

2 It has often been suggested that products are intentionally made to break down or wear out. Is this strategy a planned product modification approach?

3 The product manager of GE is reviewing the penetration of trash compactors in American homes. After more than two decades in existence, this product is in relatively few homes. What problems can account for this poor acceptance? What is the shape of the trash compactor life cycle?

4 For years, Ferrari has been known as the manufacturer of expensive luxury automobiles. The company plans to attract the major segment of the car-buying market that purchases medium-priced automobiles. As Ferrari considers this trading-down strategy, what branding strategy would you recommend? What are the trade-offs to consider with your strategy?

building your marketing plan

For the product offering in your marketing plan,

1 Identify (*a*) its stage in the product life cycle and (*b*) key marketing mix actions that might be appropriate, as shown in Figure 10–1.

2 Develop (*a*) branding and (*b*) packaging strategies, if appropriate for your offering.

QR 10–4
Mary Kay
Video Case

Sheryl Adkins-Green couldn't ask for a better assignment. As the newly appointed vice president of brand development at Mary Kay, Inc., she is responsible for development of the product portfolio around the world, including global initiatives and products specifically formulated for global markets. She is enthusiastic about her position, noting that, "There is tremendous opportunity for growth. Even in these economic times, women still want to pamper themselves, and to look good is to feel good."

Getting up to speed on her new company and her new position topped her short-term agenda. She was specifically interested in the company's efforts to date to build the Mary Kay brand in India.

THE MARY KAY WAY

Mary Kay Ash founded Mary Kay Cosmetics in 1963 with her life savings of $5,000 and the support of her 20-year-old son, Richard Rogers, who currently serves as executive chairman of Mary Kay, Inc. Mary Kay, Inc., is one of the largest direct sellers of skin care and color cosmetics in the world with more than $2.5 billion in annual sales. Mary Kay brand products are sold in more than 35 markets on five continents. The United States, China, Russia, and Mexico are the top four markets served by the company. The company's global independent sales force exceeds 2 million. About 65 percent of the company's independent sales representatives reside outside the United States.

Mary Kay Ash's founding principles were simple, time-tested, and remain a fundamental company business philosophy. She adopted the Golden Rule as her guiding principle, determining the best course of action in virtually any situation could be easily discerned by "doing unto others as you would have them do unto you." She also steadfastly believed that life's priorities should be kept in their proper order, which to her meant "God first, family second, and career third." Her work ethic, approach to business, and success have resulted in numerous awards and recognitions including, but not limited to, the Horatio Alger American Citizen Award, recognition as one of "America's 25 Most Influential Women," and induction into the National Business Hall of Fame.

Mary Kay, Inc., engages in the development, manufacture, and packaging of skin care, makeup, spa and body, and fragrance products for men and women. It offers anti-aging, cleanser, moisturizer, lip and eye care, body care, and sun care products. Overall, the company produces more than 200 premium products in its state-of-the-art manufacturing facilities in Dallas, Texas, and Hangzhou, China. The company's approach to direct selling employs the "party plan," whereby independent sales representatives host parties to demonstrate or sell products to consumers.

GROWTH OPPORTUNITIES IN ASIA-PACIFIC MARKETS

Asia-Pacific markets represent major growth opportunities for Mary Kay, Inc. These markets for Mary Kay, Inc., include Australia, China, Hong Kong, India, Korea, Malaysia, New Zealand, the Philippines, Singapore, and Taiwan.

China accounts for the largest sales revenue outside the United States, representing about 25 percent of annual Mary Kay, Inc., worldwide sales. The company entered China in 1995 and currently has some 200,000 independent sales representatives or "beauty consultants" in that country.

Part of Mary Kay's success in China has been attributed to the company's message of female empowerment and femininity, which has resonated in China, a country where young women have few opportunities to start their own businesses. Speaking about the corporate philosophy at Mary Kay, Inc., KK Chua, President, Asia-Pacific, said, "Mary Kay's corporate objective is not only to create a market, selling skin care and cosmetics; it's all about enriching women's lives by helping women reach their full potential, find their inner beauty and discover how truly great they are." This view is echoed by Sheryl Adkins-Green, who notes that the Mary Kay brand has "transformational and aspirational" associations for users and beauty consultants alike.

Mary Kay, Inc., learned that adjustments to its product line and message for women were necessary in some Asia-Pacific markets. In China, for example, the order of life's priorities—"God first, family second, and career third"—has been modified to "Faith first, family second, and career third." Also, Chinese women aren't heavy users of makeup. Therefore, the featured products include skin cream, anti-aging cream, and whitening creams. As a generalization, whitening products are popular among women in China, India, Korea, and the Philippines, where lighter skin is associated with beauty, class, and privilege.

MARY KAY, INDIA

Mary Kay, Inc., senior management believed that India represented a growth opportunity for three reasons. First, the Indian upper and consuming classes were growing and were expected to total over 500 million individuals. Second, the population was overwhelmingly young and

FIGURE 1

Social and economic statistics for India in 2007 and China in 1995.

	India 2007	China 1995
Population (million)	1,136	1,198
Population age distribution (0–24; 25-49; 50+)	52%, 33%, 15%	43%, 39%, 18%
Urban population	29.2%	29.0%
Population/square mile	990	332
Gross domestic product (U.S.$ billion)	3,113	728
Per capita income (U.S.$)	$950	$399
Direct selling sales percent of total cosmetics/skin care sales	3.3%	3.0%

optimistic. This youthful population continues to push consumerism as the line between luxury and basic items continues to blur. Third, a growing number of working women have given a boost to sales of cosmetics, skin care, and fragrances in India's urban areas, where 70 percent of the country's middle-class women reside.

Senior management also believed that India's socioeconomic characteristics in 2007 were similar in many ways to China in 1995, when the company entered that market (see Figure 1). The Mary Kay culture was viewed as a good fit with the Indian culture, which would benefit the company's venture into this market. For example, industry research has shown that continuing modernization of the country has led to changing aspirations. As a result,

the need to be good looking, well-groomed, and stylish has taken a newfound importance.

Mary Kay initiated operations in India in September 2007 with a full marketing launch in early 2008. The initial launch was in Delhi, the nation's capital and the second most populated metropolis in India, and Mumbai, the nation's most heavily populated metropolis. Delhi, with per capita income of U.S. $1,420, and Mumbai, with per capita income of $2,850, were among the wealthiest metropolitan areas in India.

According to Rhonda Shasteen, chief marketing officer at Mary Kay, Inc., "For Mary Kay to be successful in India, the company had to build a brand, build a sales force, and build an effective supply chain to service the sales force."

Building a Brand

Mary Kay, Inc., executives believed that brand building in India needed to involve media advertising; literature describing the Mary Kay culture, the Mary Kay story, and the company's image; and educational material for Mary Kay independent sales representatives. In addition, Mary Kay, Inc., became the cosmetics partner of the Miss India Worldwide Pageant 2008. At this event, Mary Kay Miss Beautiful Skin 2008 was crowned.

Brand building in India also involved product mix and pricing. Four guidelines were followed:

1. Keep the offering simple and skin care focused for the new Indian sales force and for a new operation.
2. Open with accessibly priced basic skin care products in relation to the competition in order to establish Mary Kay product quality and value.
3. Avoid opening with products that would phase out shortly after launch.
4. Address the key product categories of Skin Care, Body Care, and Color based on current market information.

Brand pricing focused on offering accessibly priced basic skin care to the average middle-class Indian consumer between the ages of 25 and 54. This strategy, called "mass-tige pricing," resulted in product price points that were above mass but below prestige competitive product prices. Following an initial emphasis on offering high-quality, high-value products, Mary Kay introduced more technologically advanced products that commanded higher price points. For example, the company introduced the Mary Kay MelaCEP Whitening System, consisting of seven products, which was specifically formulated for Asian skin in March 2009. This system was ". . . priced on the lower price end of the prestige category with a great value for money equation," said Hina Nagarajan, country manager for Mary Kay India.

Building a Sales Force

According to Adkins-Green, "Mary Kay's most powerful marketing vehicle is the direct selling organization," which is a key component of the brand's marketing strategy. Mary Kay relied on its Global Leadership Development Program directors and National Sales directors and the Mary Kay Sales Education staff from the United States and Canada for the initial recruitment and training of independent sales representatives in India. New independent sales representatives received 2 to 3 days of intensive training and a starter kit that included not only products, but also information pertaining to product demonstrations, sales presentations, professional demeanor, the company's history and culture, and team building.

"Culture training is very important to Mary Kay (independent sales representatives) because they are going to be the messengers of Mary Kay," said Hina Nagarajan. "As a direct-selling company that offers products sold person-to-person, we recognize that there's a personal relationship between consultant and client with every sale," added Rhonda Shasteen. By late 2009, there were some 4,000 independent sales representatives in India present in some 200 cities mostly in the northern, western, and northeastern regions of the country.

Creating a Supply Chain

Mary Kay, India, imported products into India from China, Korea, and the United States. Products were shipped to regional distribution centers in Delhi and Mumbai, India, where Mary Kay Beauty Centers were located. Beauty Centers served as order pick-up points for the independent sales representatives. Mary Kay beauty consultants purchased products from the company and, in turn, sold them to consumers.

LOOKING AHEAD

Mary Kay, Inc., plans to invest around $20 million in the next five years on product development, company infrastructure, and building its brand in India. "There is a tremendous opportunity for growth," says Sheryl Adkins-Green. India represents a particularly attractive opportunity. Developing the brand and brand portfolio and specifically formulating products for Indian consumers will require her attention to brand positioning and brand equity.

Questions

1 What information should be included in a written positioning statement for Mary Kay?

2 How would you draft a formal, written positioning statement for Mary Kay using the information detailed in question 1?

3 Is Mary Kay a global brand? Why or why not?

4 How has Mary Kay, India, focused on the different steps in the customer-based brand equity pyramid described in Figure 10–5?

Pricing Products and Services

11

LEARNING OBJECTIVES

After reading this chapter you should be able to:

LO1 Describe the nature and importance of pricing and the approaches used to select an approximate price level.

LO2 Explain what a demand curve is and the role of revenues in pricing decisions.

LO3 Explain the role of costs in pricing decisions and describe how combinations of price, fixed cost, and unit variable cost affect a firm's break-even point.

LO4 Recognize the objectives a firm has in setting prices and the constraints that restrict the range of prices a firm can charge.

LO5 Describe the steps taken in setting a final price.

VIZIO, INC.—WHERE VISION MEETS VALUE™ IN HDTV

Can you name North America's fastest-growing HDTV and consumer electronics company? Stumped? It's VIZIO, Inc., an entrepreneurial Irvine, California–based company with a bold agenda. "Our goal is to be the next Sony in 20 to 30 years," says William Wang, VIZIO's co-founder and chief executive officer.

In 2002, Mr. Wang was struck by an ad for a $10,000 flat-panel HDTV set and immediately saw an opportunity. Instead of marketing these sets as luxury items, Mr. Wang thought he could make and market a flat-panel HDTV that was affordable to the average customer. Like many entrepreneurs, he borrowed money from friends and family and mortgaged his home. Within a year, he formed a company that is now known as VIZIO, Inc., and delivered its first HDTV to Costco for distribution through that company's stores. VIZIO HDTVs are now sold through Costco, Walmart, BJ's Wholesale, Sears, Sam's Club, and Target stores nationwide, along with authorized online partners. The company has sold more than 30 million units since 2002.

VIZIO's ability to deliver affordable flat-panel HDTVs to the average customer is based on a novel strategy. VIZIO didn't invest in expensive manufacturing facilities but instead relied on contract manufacturers in Taiwan to build its products. Product development and marketing specialists in the United States handle product design and marketing. That's "Where Vision Meets Value," the company's motto, comes into play. "The whole goal is to ensure that we have the right product at the right time and the right price and really drive a seamless end-to-end value chain," says John Morriss, VIZIO's vice president of partner management. "VIZIO HDTVs are more popular and in greater demand than ever," added Laynie Newsome, VIZIO's co-founder and chief sales officer. "Consumers want to save money without sacrificing quality or technology, which is why we continue to be the fastest growing HDTV company in the United States." Matthew McRae, VIZIO's chief technology officer, adds that VIZIO's strategy is to make affordable products with innovative features, saying, "Everybody deserves the latest technology."

VIZIO's powerful and profitable price-value position has resonated with consumers and the company now produces annual sales of $3 billion. VIZIO is now the largest seller of flat-panel HDTVs in North America. In 2012, VIZIO entered the personal computer market, offering desktop PCs, tablet computers, and laptop computers. Not bad for a company with about 200 employees and just 10 years old![1]

Welcome to the fascinating—and intense—world of pricing, where many forces come together to determine the price buyers will be asked to pay. This chapter covers important factors used in setting prices for products and services.

QR 11–1 VIZIO Ad

NATURE AND IMPORTANCE OF PRICE

The price paid for products and services goes by many names. You pay *tuition* for your education, *rent* for an apartment, *interest* on a bank credit card, and a *premium* for car insurance. Your dentist or physician charges you a *fee*, a professional or social organization charges *dues*, and airlines charge a *fare*. And what you pay for clothes or a haircut is termed a *price*.

What Is a Price?

price

The money or other considerations (including other products and services) exchanged for the ownership or use of a product or service.

These examples highlight the many varied ways that price plays a part in our daily lives. From a marketing viewpoint, **price** is the money or other considerations (including other products and services) exchanged for the ownership or use of a product or service. Recently, Wilkinson Sword exchanged some of its knives for advertising used to promote its razor blades. This practice of exchanging products and services for other products and services rather than for money is called *barter*. These transactions account for billions of dollars annually in domestic and international trade.

For most products and services, money is exchanged. However, the amount paid is not always the same as the list, or quoted, price because of discounts, allowances, and extra fees. While discounts, allowances, and rebates make the effective price lower, other marketing tactics raise the real price. One popular pricing tactic is to use "special fees" and "surcharges." This practice is driven by consumers' zeal for low prices combined with the ease of making price comparisons on the Internet. Buyers are more willing to pay extra fees than a higher list price, so sellers use add-on charges as a way of having the consumer pay more without raising the list price.[2]

In deciding whether to buy a new Bugatti Veyron, consider incentives, allowances, and extra fees—as well as the original list price!

All the factors that increase or decrease the final price of an offering help construct a "price equation," which is shown for a few products in Figure 11–1. As an example, the following would be key considerations if you wanted to buy a Bugatti Veyron 16.4 Super Sport. The car can accelerate from 0 to 60 mph in 2.4 seconds. With its 1,200 horsepower engine, its top speed is 258 mph! The aerodynamic body is made out of carbon fiber to safely handle the speed. Fuel economy, however, is a paltry 7 mpg city and 15 mpg highway. Every 10,000 miles, you will have to replace the special 20-inch Michelin tires, which cost $42,500 for a set of four!

The Bugatti Veyron Super Sport has a list price of $2.5 million, but you want the clear-coat paint option, so it will cost an extra $430,000. An extended warranty will add an additional $70,000 to the cost. However, if you put $500,000 down and finance the balance, you will receive a rebate of $50,000 off the list or base price.

As a trade-in value for your 2005 Honda Civic DX four-door sedan that has 75,000 miles and is in good condition, the dealer gives you a trade-in allowance of $5,000. In addition, you will have to pay (1) an import duty of $60,000; (2) a gas-guzzler tax of $5,000; (3) a 7.5 percent sales tax of about $230,000; (4) an auto registration fee of $5,000 to the state; and (5) a $50,000 destination charge to ship the car. Finally, your total finance charge is $378,640 based on an annual interest rate of 5 percent over a five-year period.[3]

Applying the price equation shown in Figure 11–1 to your Bugatti Veyron purchase, your final price is:

$$\text{Final price} = [\text{List price}] - [(\text{Incentives}) + (\text{Allowances})] + [\text{Extra Fees}]$$

$$= [\$2,500,000] - [(\$500,000 + \$50,000 + 5,000)]$$

$$+ [\$430,000 + \$70,000 + \$60,000 + \$5,000 + \$230,000$$

$$+ \$5,000 + \$50,000 + \$378,640]$$

$$= \$3,173,640$$

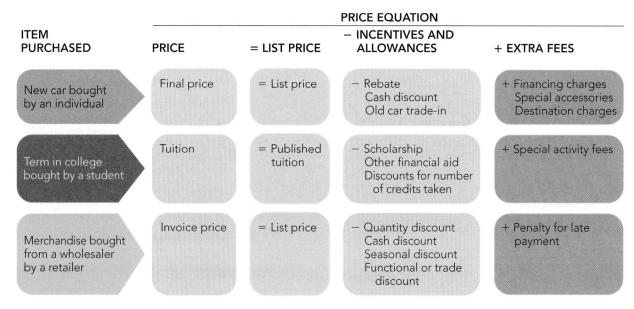

ITEM PURCHASED	PRICE	= LIST PRICE	− INCENTIVES AND ALLOWANCES	+ EXTRA FEES
New car bought by an individual	Final price	= List price	− Rebate Cash discount Old car trade-in	+ Financing charges Special accessories Destination charges
Term in college bought by a student	Tuition	= Published tuition	− Scholarship Other financial aid Discounts for number of credits taken	+ Special activity fees
Merchandise bought from a wholesaler by a retailer	Invoice price	= List price	− Quantity discount Cash discount Seasonal discount Functional or trade discount	+ Penalty for late payment

FIGURE 11–1

The "price" a buyer pays can take different names, depending on what is purchased, and can change depending on the price equation.

value
The ratio of perceived benefits to price.

profit equation
Profit equals total revenue minus total cost.

Note that your final price is $673,640 more than the list price! Are you still interested in the Bugatti Veyron 16.4 Super Sport? If so, put yourself on the waiting list!

Price as an Indicator of Value

From a consumer's standpoint, price is often used to indicate value when it is compared with the perceived benefits such as quality, durability, and so on of a product or service. Specifically, **value** is the ratio of perceived benefits to price, or

$$\text{Value} = \frac{\text{Perceived benefits}}{\text{Price}}$$

This relationship shows that for a given price, as perceived benefits increase, value increases. For example, if you're used to paying $9.99 for a medium pizza, wouldn't a large pizza at the same price be more valuable? Conversely, for a given price, value decreases when perceived benefits decrease.

For some products, price influences consumers' perception of overall quality and ultimately its value to consumers.[4] In a survey of home furnishing buyers, 84 percent agreed with the statement: "The higher the price, the higher the quality."[5] Kohler introduced a walk-in bathtub that is safer for children and the elderly. Although priced higher than conventional step-in bathtubs, it has proven very successful because buyers are willing to pay more for what they perceive as the benefit of the extra safety.

Here "value" involves the judgment by a consumer of the worth and desirability of a product or service relative to substitutes that satisfy the same need. In this instance a "reference value" emerges, which involves comparing the costs and benefits of substitute items.

Price in the Marketing Mix

Pricing is a critical decision made by a marketing executive because price has a direct effect on a firm's profits. This is apparent from a firm's **profit equation**:

Profit = Total revenue − Total cost

= (Unit price × Quantity sold) − (Fixed cost + Variable cost)

What makes this relationship even more complicated is that price affects the quantity sold, as illustrated with demand curves later in this chapter. Furthermore, since the quantity sold usually affects a firm's costs because of efficiency of production, price also indirectly affects costs. Thus, pricing decisions influence both total revenue (sales) and total cost, which makes pricing one of the most important and most difficult decisions marketing executives face.

GENERAL PRICING APPROACHES

A key for a marketing manager setting a price for a product is to find an approximate price level to use as a reasonable starting point. Four common approaches used to find this approximate price level are (1) demand-oriented, (2) cost-oriented, (3) profit-oriented, and (4) competition-oriented approaches (see Figure 11–2). Although these approaches are discussed separately below, some of them overlap, and an effective marketing manager will consider several in selecting an approximate price level.

Demand-Oriented Pricing Approaches

Demand-oriented approaches weigh factors underlying expected customer tastes and preferences more heavily than such factors as cost, profit, and competition when selecting a price level.

Skimming Pricing A firm introducing a new or innovative product can use *skimming pricing,* setting the highest initial price that customers really desiring the product are willing to pay. These customers are not very price sensitive because they weigh the new product's price, quality, and ability to satisfy their needs against the same characteristics of substitutes. As the demand of these customers is satisfied, the firm lowers the price to attract another, more price-sensitive segment. Thus, skimming pricing gets its name from skimming successive layers of "cream," or customer segments, as prices are lowered in a series of steps.

Skimming pricing is an effective strategy when (1) enough prospective customers are willing to buy the product immediately at the high initial price to make these sales profitable, (2) the high initial price will not attract competitors, (3) lowering the price has only a minor effect on increasing the sales volume and reducing the unit costs, and (4) customers interpret the high price as a signal of high quality.[6] These four conditions are most likely to exist when the new product is protected by patents or copyrights or its uniqueness is understood and valued by consumers. Gillette, for example, adopted a skimming strategy for its five-blade Fusion brand shaving system (which included no less than 70 patents!) since many of these conditions applied.

FIGURE 11–2

Four approaches for selecting an approximate price level.

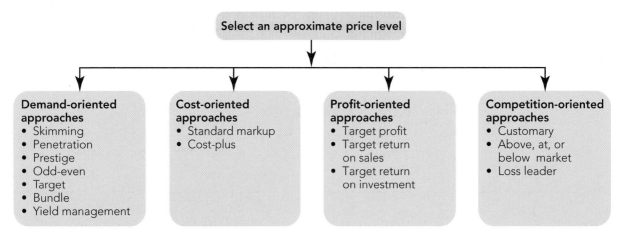

Select an approximate price level

Demand-oriented approaches	Cost-oriented approaches	Profit-oriented approaches	Competition-oriented approaches
• Skimming • Penetration • Prestige • Odd-even • Target • Bundle • Yield management	• Standard markup • Cost-plus	• Target profit • Target return on sales • Target return on investment	• Customary • Above, at, or below market • Loss leader

Marketing Matters > > > > > customer value

Energizer's Lesson in Price Perception— Value Lies in the Eye of the Beholder

Battery manufacturers are as tireless as a certain drum-thumping bunny in their efforts to create products that perform better, last longer, and, not incidentally, outsell the competition. The commercialization of new alkaline battery technology at a price that creates value for consumers is not always obvious or easy. Just ask the marketing executives at Energizer about their experience with pricing Energizer Advanced Formula and Energizer e^2 AA alkaline batteries.

When Duracell launched its high-performance Ultra brand AA alkaline battery with a 25 percent price premium over standard Duracell batteries, Energizer quickly countered with its own high-performance battery—Energizer Advanced Formula. Believing that consumers would not pay the premium price, Energizer priced its Advanced Formula brand at the same price as its standard AA alkaline battery, expecting to gain market share from Duracell. It did not happen. Why? According to industry analysts, consumers associated Energizer's low price with inferior quality in the high-performance segment. Instead of gaining market share, Energizer lost market share to Duracell and Rayovac, the No. 3 battery manufacturer.

Having learned its lesson, Energizer subsequently released its e^2 high-performance battery, this time priced 4 percent higher than Duracell Ultra and about 50 percent higher than Advanced Formula. The result? Energizer recovered lost sales and market share. The lesson learned? Value lies in the eye of the beholder.

Penetration Pricing Setting a low initial price on a new product to appeal immediately to the mass market is *penetration pricing*, the exact opposite of skimming pricing. Amazon consciously chose a penetration strategy when it introduced the Kindle Fire tablet computer at $199 when competitive models were priced at $499.

The conditions favoring penetration pricing are the reverse of those supporting skimming pricing: (1) many segments of the market are price sensitive, (2) a low initial price discourages competitors from entering the market, and (3) unit production and marketing costs fall dramatically as production volumes increase. A firm using penetration pricing may (1) maintain the initial price for a time to gain profit lost from its low introductory level or (2) lower the price further, counting on the new volume to generate the necessary profit.

QR 11–2
Rolex Ad

Prestige Pricing Although consumers tend to buy more of a product when the price is lower, sometimes the reverse is true. If consumers are using price as a measure of the quality of an item, a company runs the risk of appearing to offer a low-quality product if it sets the price below a certain point. *Prestige pricing* involves setting a high price so that quality- or status-conscious consumers will be attracted to the product and buy it. Rolex watches, Chanel perfume, and Cartier jewelry have an element of prestige pricing in them and may sell worse at lower prices than at higher ones.[7] As described in the Marketing Matters box, this is the pricing strategy Energizer used with its very successful e^2 high-performance AA batteries.[8]

Odd-Even Pricing Sears offers a Craftsman radial saw for $499.99, the suggested retail price for the Gillette Fusion shaving system is $11.99, and Kmart sells Windex glass cleaner on sale for 99 cents. Why not simply price these items at $500, $12, and $1, respectively? These firms are using *odd-even pricing*, which involves setting prices a few dollars or cents under an even number. The presumption is that consumers see the Sears radial saw as priced at "something over $400" rather than "about $500." In theory, demand increases if the price drops from $500 to $499.99. There is

McDonald's Extra Value Meal uses which pricing strategy? Read the text to find out which one and why.

some evidence to suggest this does happen. However, research suggests that overuse of odd-ending prices tends to mute their effect on demand.[9]

Target Pricing   Manufacturers will sometimes estimate the price that the ultimate consumer will pay for a product. They then work backward through markups taken by retailers and wholesalers to determine what price they can charge wholesalers for the product. This practice, called *target pricing,* results in the manufacturer deliberately adjusting the composition and features of a product to achieve the target price to consumers. Canon uses target pricing for its cameras.

Bundle Pricing   A frequently used demand-oriented pricing practice is *bundle pricing*—the marketing of two or more products in a single package price. For example, Delta Air Lines offers vacation packages that include airfare, car rental, and lodging. Bundle pricing is based on the idea that consumers value the package more than the individual items. This is due to benefits received from not having to make separate purchases and enhanced satisfaction from one item given the presence of another. This is the idea behind McDonald's Extra Value Meal. Moreover, bundle pricing often provides a lower total cost to buyers and lower marketing costs to sellers.

Yield Management Pricing   Have you ever been on an airplane and discovered the person next to you paid a lower price for her ticket than you paid? Annoying, isn't it? But what you observed is *yield management pricing*—the charging of different prices to maximize revenue for a set amount of capacity at any given time. Airlines, hotels, and car rental firms engage in capacity management (described in Chapter 11) by varying prices based on time, day, week, or season to match demand and supply. American Airlines estimates that yield management pricing produces an annual revenue that exceeds $500 million.[10]

Cost-Oriented Pricing Approaches

With cost-oriented approaches, a price setter stresses the cost side of the pricing problem, not the demand side. Price is set by looking at the production and marketing costs and then adding enough to cover direct expenses, overhead, and profit.

Standard Markup Pricing   Managers of supermarkets and other retail stores have such a large number of products that estimating the demand for each product as a means of setting price is impossible. Therefore, they use *standard markup pricing,* which entails adding a fixed percentage to the cost of all items in a specific product class. This percentage markup varies depending on the type of retail store (such as furniture, clothing, or grocery) and the product involved. High-volume products usually have smaller markups than do low-volume products. Supermarkets such as Kroger, Safeway, and Jewel have different markups for staple items and discretionary items. The markup on staple items like sugar, flour, and dairy products varies from 10 percent to 23 percent, whereas markups on discretionary items like snack foods and candy range from 27 percent to 47 percent. These markups must cover all expenses of the store, pay for overhead costs, and contribute something to profits. For supermarkets these markups, which may appear very large, result in only a 1 percent profit on sales revenue.

By comparison, consider the markups on snacks and beverages purchased at your local movie theater. The markup is 87 percent on soft drinks, 65 percent on candy bars, and 90 percent on popcorn. These markups might sound high, but consider the consequences. "If we didn't charge as much for concessions as we did, a movie ticket would cost $20," says the CEO of Regal Entertainment, the largest U.S. theater chain.[11]

How was the price of the Rock and Roll Hall of Fame and Museum determined? Read the text to find out.

Cost-Plus Pricing   Many manufacturing, professional services, and construction firms use a variation of standard markup pricing. *Cost-plus pricing* involves summing the total unit cost of providing a product or service and adding a specific amount to the cost to arrive at a price. Cost-plus pricing is the most commonly used method to set prices for business products. For example, this pricing approach was used in setting the price for the $92 million Rock and Roll Hall of Fame and Museum in Cleveland, Ohio.

Profit-Oriented Pricing Approaches

A price setter may choose to balance both revenues and costs to set price using profit-oriented approaches. These might either involve a target of a specific dollar volume of profit or express this target profit as a percentage of sales or investment.

Target Profit Pricing   When a firm sets an annual target of a specific dollar volume of profit, this is called *target profit pricing.* For example, if you owned a picture frame store and wanted to achieve a target profit of $7,000, how much would you need to charge for each frame? Because profit depends on revenues and costs, you would have to know your costs and then estimate how many frames you would sell. Based on sales in previous years, let's assume that you expect to frame 1,000 pictures next year. The cost of your time and materials to frame an average picture is $22, while your overhead expenses (rent, manager salaries, etc.) are $26,000. Finally, your goal is to achieve a profit of $7,000. How do you calculate your price per picture?

$$\text{Profit} = \text{Total revenue} - \text{Total costs}$$
$$= (\text{Pictures sold} \times \text{Price/picture}) -$$
$$[(\text{Cost/picture} \times \text{Pictures sold}) + \text{Overhead cost}]$$

Solving for price per picture, the equation becomes,

$$\text{Price/picture} = \frac{\text{Profit} + [(\text{Cost/picture} \times \text{Pictures sold}) + \text{Overhead cost}]}{\text{Pictures sold}}$$

$$= \frac{\$7,000 + [(\$22 \times 1,000) + \$26,000]}{1,000}$$

$$= \frac{\$7,000 + \$48,000}{1,000}$$

$$= \$55 \text{ per picture}$$

Clearly, this pricing method depends on an accurate estimate of demand. Because demand is often difficult to predict, this method has the potential for disaster if the estimate is too high. Generally, a target profit pricing strategy is best for firms offering new or unique products, without a lot of competition. What if other frame stores in your area were charging $40 per framed picture? As a marketing manager, you'd have to offer improved customer value with your more expensive frames, lower your costs, or settle for less profit.

Target Return-on-Sales Pricing   Firms such as supermarkets often use *target return-on-sales pricing* to set prices that will give them a profit that is a specified percentage—say, 1 percent—of the sales volume. This price method is often used because of the difficulty in establishing a benchmark of sales or investment to show how much of a firm's effort is needed to achieve the target.

Target Return-on-Investment Pricing Firms such as General Motors and many public utilities use *target return-on-investment pricing* to set prices to achieve a return-on-investment (ROI) target such as a percentage that is mandated by its board of directors or regulators. For example, an electric utility may decide to seek a 10 percent ROI. If its investment in plant and equipment is $50 billion, it would need to set the price of electricity to its customers at a level that results in $5 billion a year in profit.

Competition-Oriented Pricing Approaches

Rather than emphasize demand, cost, or profit factors, a price setter can stress what competitors or "the market" is doing.

Has Red Bull's price premium among energy-drink brands sold in convenience stores increased or decreased? The Using Marketing Dashboards box answers this question.

Customary Pricing For some products where tradition, a standardized channel of distribution, or other competitive factors dictate the price, *customary pricing* is used. Candy bars offered through standard vending machines have a customary price of 75 cents, and a significant departure from this price may result in a loss of sales for the manufacturer. Hershey typically has changed the amount of chocolate in its candy bars depending on the price of raw chocolate rather than vary its customary retail price so that it can continue selling through vending machines.

Above-, At-, or Below-Market Pricing The "market price" of a product is what customers are generally willing to pay, not necessarily the price that the firm sets. For most products it is difficult to identify a specific market price for a product or product class. Still, marketing managers often have a subjective feel for the competitors' price or the market price. Using this benchmark, they then may deliberately choose a strategy of *above-, at-,* or *below-market pricing.*

Among watch manufacturers, Rolex takes pride in emphasizing that it makes one of the most expensive watches you can buy, a clear example of above-market pricing. Manufacturers of national brands of clothing such as Hart Schaffner & Marx and retailers such as Bloomingdale's deliberately set premium prices for their products.

Large department store chains such as JCPenney generally use at-market pricing. These chains often establish the going market price in the minds of their competitors. Similarly, Revlon cosmetics and Arrow brand shirts are generally priced "at market." They also provide a reference price for competitors that use above- and below-market pricing.

In contrast, a number of firms use below-market pricing. Manufacturers of generic products and retailers that offer their own private brands of products ranging from peanut butter to shampoo deliberately set prices for these products about 8 percent to 10 percent below the prices of nationally branded competitive products such as Skippy peanut butter or Vidal Sassoon shampoo.

Companies use a "price premium" to assess whether their products and brands are above, at, or below the market. An illustration of how the price premium measure is calculated, displayed, and interpreted appears in the Using Marketing Dashboards box.[12]

Loss-Leader Pricing For a special promotion retail stores deliberately sell a product below its customary price to attract attention to it. The purpose of this *loss-leader pricing* is not to increase sales but to attract customers in hopes they will buy other products as well, particularly the discretionary items with large markups. For example, Best Buy, Target, and Walmart sell CDs at about half of music companies' suggested retail price to attract customers to their stores.[13]

Using Marketing Dashboards

Are Red Bull Prices Above, At, or Below the Market?

How would you determine whether a firm's retail prices are above, at, or below the market? You might visit retail stores and record what prices retailers are charging for products or brands. However, this laborious activity can be simplified by combining dollar market share and unit volume market share measures to create a "price premium" display on your marketing dashboard.

Your Challenge Red Bull is the leading energy-drink brand in the United States in terms of dollar market share and unit market share (see the table). Company marketing executives have research showing that Red Bull has a strong brand equity. What they want to know is whether the brand's price premium resulting from its brand equity has eroded due to heavy price discounting in the convenience store channel. This channel accounts for 60 percent of energy drink sales.

A price premium is the percentage by which the actual price charged for a specific brand exceeds (or falls short of) a benchmark established for a similar product or basket of products. As such, a price premium shows whether a brand is priced above, at, or below the market. This premium is calculated as follows:

Price premium (%)
$$= \frac{\text{Dollar sales market share for a brand}}{\text{Unit volume market share for a brand}} - 1$$

Your Findings Using 2010 energy-drink brand market share data for U.S. convenience stores, the Red Bull price premium is 1.152, or 15.2 percent, calculated as follows: (38 percent ÷ 33 percent) − 1 = .152. Red Bull's average price is 15.2 percent higher than the average price for

energy-drink brands sold in convenience stores. Red Bull's price premium based on 2009 brand market share data was 1.121, or 12.1 percent, calculated as follows: (37 percent ÷ 33 percent) −1 = 12.1. Red Bull's price premium has increased relative to its competitors, notably Monster Energy and Rockstar. The price premiums for Red Bull and these two competitive brands for 2009 and 2010 are displayed in the marketing dashboard shown below.

Your Action Red Bull has increased its price premium while retaining its unit volume share, which is not only favorable news for the brand but also evidence of price discounting by other brands. Clearly, the company's brand-building effort, reflected in sponsorships and a singular focus on brand attributes valued by consumers, should be continued.

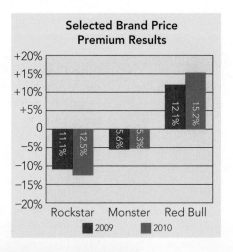

	Dollar Sales Market Share		Unit Volume Market Share	
Brand	2010	2009	2010	2009
Red Bull	38%	37%	33%	33%
Monster	18	17	19	18
Rockstar	7	8	8	9
Other brands	37	38	40	40
	100%	100%	100%	100%

---

learning review

1. Value is _____.

2. What circumstances in pricing a new product might support skimming or penetration pricing?

ESTIMATING DEMAND AND REVENUE

Basic to setting a product's price is the extent of customer demand for it. Marketing executives must also translate this estimate of customer demand into estimates of revenues the firm expects to receive.

Fundamentals of Estimating Demand

How much money would you pay for your favorite magazine? If the price kept going up, at some point you would probably quit buying it. Conversely, if the price kept going down, you might eventually decide not only to keep buying your magazine but also to get your friend a subscription, too. The lower the price, the higher the demand. The publisher wants to sell more magazines, but will it sell enough additional copies to make up for the lower price per copy? That is an important question for marketing managers. Here's how one firm decided to find out.

In a classic study, *Newsweek* conducted a pricing experiment at newsstands in 11 cities across the United States. At that time, Houston newsstand buyers paid $2.25, while in Fort Worth, New York, Los Angeles, and Atlanta they paid the regular $2.00 price. In San Diego, the price was $1.50, while in Minneapolis–St. Paul, New Orleans, and Detroit it was only $1.00. By comparison, the regular newsstand price for *Time* and *U.S. News & World Report, Newsweek's* competitors, was $1.95. Why did *Newsweek* conduct the experiment? According to a *Newsweek* executive, "We want to figure out what the demand curve for our magazine at the newsstand is."[14]

demand curve

A graph relating the quantity sold and the price, which shows how many units will be sold at a given price.

The Demand Curve A **demand curve** is a graph relating the quantity sold and the price, which shows the maximum number of units that will be sold at a given price. Demand curve D_1 in Figure 11–3A shows the newsstand demand for *Newsweek* under the existing conditions. Note that as price falls, more people decide to buy and unit sales increase. But price is not the complete story in estimating demand. Economists emphasize three other key factors:

1. *Consumer tastes.* As we saw in Chapter 3, these depend on many factors such as demographics, culture, and technology. Because consumer tastes can change quickly, up-to-date marketing research is essential.

2. *Price and availability of similar products.* The laws of demand work for one's competitors, too. If the price of *Time* magazine falls, more people will buy it. That then means fewer people will buy *Newsweek. Time* is considered by economists to be a substitute for *Newsweek.* Online magazines are also a substitute—one whose availability has increased tremendously in recent years. The point to remember is, as the price of substitutes falls or their availability increases, the demand for a product (*Newsweek,* in this case) will fall.

3. *Consumer income.* In general, as real consumer income (allowing for inflation) increases, demand for a product also increases.

The first of these two factors influences what consumers *want* to buy, and the third affects what they *can* buy. Along with price, these are often called *demand factors,* or factors that determine consumers' willingness and ability to pay for products and services. As discussed earlier in Chapters 7 and 9, it is often very difficult to estimate demand for new products, especially because consumer likes and dislikes are often so difficult to read clearly.

Movement Along versus Shift of a Demand Curve Demand curve D_1 in Figure 11–3A shows that as the price is lowered from $2.00 to $1.50, the quantity demanded increases from 3 million (Q_1) to 4.5 million (Q_2) units per year. This is an example of a *movement along a*

The text describes a creative pricing experiment undertaken by *Newsweek* magazine.

A Demand curve under initial conditions

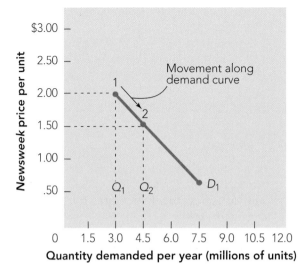

B Shift in the demand curve with more favorable conditions

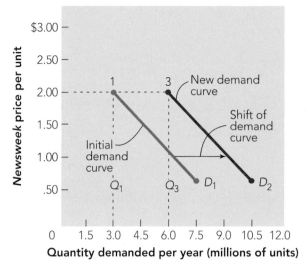

FIGURE 11–3

Demand curves for *Newsweek* showing the effect on annual sales (quantity demanded per year) by a change in price caused by (A) a movement along the demand curve and (B) a shift in the demand curve.

demand curve and assumes that other factors (consumer tastes, price and availability of substitutes, and consumer income) remain unchanged.

What if some of these factors change? For example, if advertising causes more people to want *Newsweek,* newsstand distribution is increased, or if consumer incomes rise, then the demand increases. Now the original curve, D_1 (the blue line in Figure 11–3B), no longer represents the demand; a new curve, D_2, must be drawn. D_2 (the red line in Figure 11–3B) represents the new demand curve for *Newsweek*. Economists call this a *shift in the demand curve*—in this case, a shift to the right, from D_1 to D_2. This increased demand means that more *Newsweek* magazines are wanted for a given price: At a price of $2, the demand is 6 million units per year (Q_3) on D_2 rather than 3 million units per year (Q_1) on D_1.

Price Elasticity of Demand Marketing managers are especially interested in the **price elasticity of demand**—a key consideration related to the product's demand curve. Price elasticity of demand is the percentage change in quantity demanded relative to a percentage change in price. It measures how sensitive consumer demand and the firm's revenues are to changes in the product's price.

A product with *elastic demand* is one in which a slight decrease in price results in a relatively large increase in demand, or units sold. The reverse is also true: With elastic demand, a slight increase in price results in a relatively large decrease in demand. Marketing experiments on soft drinks and snack foods show them often to have elastic demand. So marketing managers may cut price to increase the demand, the units sold, and total revenue for one of these products, depending on what competitors' prices are. Recent research studies show that price elasticity for these products is increasing, probably because consumers are more often trying to take advantage of temporary price promotions and deals.[15]

In contrast, a product with *inelastic demand* means that slight increases or decreases in price will not significantly affect the demand, or units sold, for the product. Products and services considered as necessities usually have inelastic demand. What about gasoline for your car? Will an increase of a dollar per gallon cause you to drive fewer miles and buy less gasoline? No? Then you're like millions of other Americans, which is why gasoline has inelastic demand.[16] This means that an increase of a dollar per gallon may have a relatively minor impact on the number of gallons sold and will actually increase the total revenue of a gasoline producer, such as ExxonMobil.

price elasticity of demand
The percentage change in the quantity demanded relative to a percentage change in price.

Price elasticity of demand =

$$E = \frac{\text{Percentage change in quantity demanded}}{\text{Percentage change in price}}$$

Price elasticity of demand is determined by a number of factors. First, the more substitutes a product or service has, the more likely it is to be price elastic. For example, a new sweater, shirt, or blouse has many possible substitutes and is price elastic, but gasoline has almost no substitutes and is price inelastic. Second, products and services considered to be nondiscretionary are price inelastic, so open-heart surgery is price inelastic, whereas airline tickets for a vacation are price elastic. Third, items that require a large cash outlay compared with a person's disposable income are price elastic. Accordingly, cars and yachts are price elastic; pulp fiction books tend to be price inelastic.

Fundamentals of Estimating Revenue

total revenue
The total money received from the sale of a product; the unit price of a product multiplied by the quantity sold.

While economists may talk about "demand curves," marketing executives are more likely to speak in terms of "revenue generated." Demand curves lead directly to an essential revenue concept critical to pricing decisions: **total revenue**. Total revenue (TR) equals the unit price (P) times the quantity sold (Q). Using this equation, let's recall our picture frame shop and assume our annual demand has improved so we can set a price of $100 per picture framed and sell 400 pictures per year. So,

$$TR = P \times Q$$
$$= \$100 \times 400$$
$$= \$40,000$$

This combination of price and quantity sold annually will give us a total revenue of $40,000 per year. Is that good? Are you making money, making a profit? Alas, total revenue is only part of the profit equation that we saw earlier:

Total profit = Total revenue − Total cost

The next section covers the other part of the profit equation: cost.

learning review

3. What three key factors are necessary when estimating consumer demand?

4. Price elasticity of demand is _____.

DETERMINING COST, VOLUME, AND PROFIT RELATIONSHIPS

While revenues are the moneys received by the firm from selling its products or services to customers, costs or expenses are the monies the firm pays out to its employees and suppliers. Marketing managers often use break-even analysis to relate revenues and costs, topics covered in this section.

The Importance of Controlling Costs

total cost
The total expenses incurred by a firm in producing and marketing a product; total cost is the sum of fixed costs and variable costs.

Understanding the role and behavior of costs is critical for all marketing decisions, particularly pricing decisions. Four cost concepts are important in pricing decisions: **total cost**, *fixed cost, variable cost,* and *unit variable cost* (see Figure 11–4).

Many firms go bankrupt because their costs get out of control, causing their total costs—the sum of their fixed costs and variable costs—to exceed their total revenues over an extended period of time. So firms constantly try to control their fixed costs, like insurance and executive salaries, and reduce the variable costs in their manufactured items by having production done outside the United States. This is why sophisticated marketing managers make pricing decisions that balance both revenues and costs.

Total cost (TC) is the total expense incurred by a firm in producing and marketing a product. Total cost is the sum of fixed cost and variable cost.

Fixed cost (FC) is the sum of the expenses of the firm that are stable and do not change with the quantity of a product that is produced and sold. Examples of fixed costs are rent on the building, executive salaries, and insurance.

Variable cost (VC) is the sum of the expenses of the firm that vary directly with the quantity of a product that is produced and sold. For example, as the quantity sold doubles, the variable cost doubles. Examples are the direct labor and direct materials used in producing the product and the sales commissions that are tied directly to the quantity sold. As mentioned above,

$$TC = FC + VC$$

Unit variable cost (UVC) is expressed on a per unit basis, or

$$UVC = \frac{VC}{Q}$$

Break-Even Analysis

break-even analysis

A technique that examines the relationship between total revenue and total cost to determine profitability at different levels of output.

Marketing managers often employ an approach that considers cost, volume, and profit relationships based on the profit equation. **Break-even analysis** is a technique that analyzes the relationship between total revenue and total cost to determine profitability at various levels of output. The *break-even point (BEP)* is the quantity at which total revenue and total cost are equal. Profit then comes from all units sold beyond the BEP. In terms of the definitions in Figure 11–4,

$$BEP_{Quantity} = \frac{\text{Fixed cost}}{\text{Unit price} - \text{Unit variable cost}} = \frac{FC}{P - UVC}$$

Calculating a Break-Even Point Consider a picture frame store. Suppose you wish to identify how many pictures you must sell to cover your fixed cost at a given price. Let's assume demand for your framed pictures is strong so the average price customers are willing to pay for each picture is $120. Also, suppose your fixed cost (FC) is $32,000 (for real estate taxes, interest on a bank loan, and other fixed expenses) and unit variable cost (UVC) for a picture is $40 (for labor, glass, frame, and matting). Your break-even quantity (BEP$_{Quantity}$) is 400 pictures, as follows:

$$BEP_{Quantity} = \frac{\text{Fixed cost}}{\text{Unit price} - \text{Unit variable cost}} = \frac{FC}{P - UVC}$$

$$= \frac{\$32,000}{\$120 - \$40}$$

$$= 400 \text{ pictures}$$

The row shaded in orange in Figure 11–5 on the next page shows that your break-even quantity at a price of $120 per picture is 400 pictures. At less than 400 pictures, your picture frame store incurs a loss. At more than 400 pictures, it makes a profit. Figure 11–5 also shows that if you could increase your annual picture sales to 1,000— the row shaded in green—your store would make a profit of $48,000.

Figure 11–6 on the next page shows a graphic presentation of the break-even analysis, called a *break-even analysis chart*. It shows that total revenue and total cost intersect and are equal at a quantity of 400 pictures sold, which is the break-even point at which profit is exactly $0. You want to do better? If your frame store could increase the quantity

Quantity of Pictures Sold (Q)	Price per Picture (P)	Total Revenue (TR) = (P × Q)	Unit Variable Cost (UVC)	Total Variable Cost (VC) = (UVC × Q)	Fixed Cost (FC)	Total Cost (TC) = (FC + VC)	Profit = (TR − TC)
0	$120	$ 0	$40	$ 0	$32,000	$32,000	$–32,000
200	120	24,000	40	8,000	32,000	40,000	–16,000
400	120	48,000	40	16,000	32,000	48,000	0
600	120	72,000	40	24,000	32,000	56,000	16,000
800	120	96,000	40	32,000	32,000	64,000	32,000
1,000	120	120,000	40	40,000	32,000	72,000	48,000
1,200	120	144,000	40	48,000	32,000	80,000	64,000

FIGURE 11–5
Calculating a break-even point for the picture frame store in the text example shows its profit starts at 400 framed pictures per year.

sold annually to 1,000 pictures, the graph in Figure 11–6 shows you can earn an annual profit of $48,000, just as shown by the row shaded in green in Figure 11–5.

Applications of Break-Even Analysis Because of its simplicity, break-even analysis is used extensively in marketing, most frequently to study the impact on profit of changes in price, fixed cost, and variable cost. The mechanics of break-even analysis are the basis of the widely used electronic spreadsheets. Spreadsheets permit managers to answer hypothetical "what if" questions about the effect of changes in price and cost on their profit.

FIGURE 11–6
A break-even analysis chart for the picture frame store example shows the break-even point at 400 pictures and $48,000 in revenue.

learning review

5. What is the difference between fixed costs and variable costs?
6. What is a break-even point?

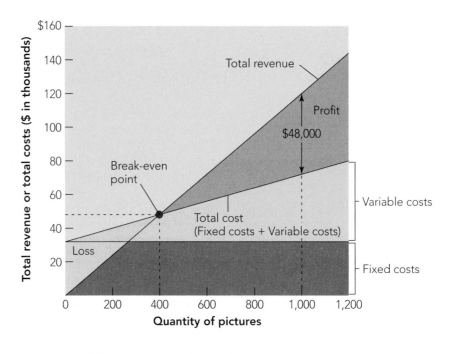

PRICING OBJECTIVES AND CONSTRAINTS

With such a variety of alternative pricing strategies available, a marketing manager must consider the pricing objectives and constraints that will narrow the range of choices. While pricing objectives frequently reflect corporate goals, pricing constraints often relate to conditions existing in the marketplace.

Identifying Pricing Objectives

pricing objectives
Expectations that specify the role of price in an organization's marketing and strategic plans.

Pricing objectives specify the role of price in an organization's marketing and strategic plans. To the extent possible, these pricing objectives are carried to lower levels in the organization, such as in setting objectives for marketing managers responsible for an individual brand. These objectives may change depending on the financial position of the company as a whole, the success of its products, or the segments in which it is doing business. Apple, for example, has specific pricing objectives for its iPhone brand that vary by country.

Profit   Three different objectives relate to a firm's profit, which is often measured in terms of return on investment. These objectives have different implications for pricing strategy. One objective is *managing for long-run profits,* in which a company—such as many Japanese car or HDTV set manufacturers—gives up immediate profit by developing quality products to penetrate competitive markets over the long term. Products are priced relatively low compared to their cost to develop, but the firm expects to make greater profits later because of its high market share.

A *maximizing current profit* objective, such as for a quarter or year, is common in many firms because the targets can be set and performance measured quickly. American firms are sometimes criticized for this short-run orientation. As noted earlier, a *target return* objective occurs when a firm sets a profit goal (such as 20 percent for return on investment), usually determined by its board of directors. These three profit objectives have different implications for a firm's pricing objectives.

Another profit consideration for marketers is to ensure that firms in their channels of distribution make an adequate profit. Without profits for channel members, a marketer is cut off from its customers. Figure 11–7 shows where each customer dollar spent for designer denim jeans goes. For brand name companies that market designer denim jeans, 50 cents of each dollar spent by a customer goes to a specialty retailer to cover its costs and profit.[17] So, the next time you spend $200 for a pair of designer denim jeans, remember that $100 goes to the retailer that stocked, displayed, and sold the jeans to you.

Sales   Given that a firm's profit is high enough for it to remain in business, an objective may be to increase sales revenue, which can lead to increases in market share and profit. Objectives related to sales revenue or unit sales have the advantage of being translated easily into meaningful targets for marketing managers responsible for a product line or brand. However, while cutting the price on one product in a firm's line may increase its sales revenue, it may also reduce the sales revenue of related products.

Market Share   Market share is the ratio of the firm's sales revenues or unit sales to those of the industry (competitors plus the firm itself). Companies often pursue a market share objective when industry

FIGURE 11–7

Where each dollar goes when you buy a pair of designer denim jeans

Material = 9¢ (fabric)

Trim = 1¢ (zipper, rivets)

Labor = 3¢ (sewing, cutting)

Manufacturing Contractor = 3¢

Brand Name Company = 34¢

Specialty Retailer = 50¢

sales are relatively flat or declining. In the late 1990s, Boeing cut prices drastically to try to maintain its 60 percent market share and encountered huge losses. Although increased market share is a primary goal of some firms, others see it as a means to other ends: increasing sales and profits.

Unit Volume   Many firms use unit volume, the quantity produced or sold, as a pricing objective. These firms often sell multiple products at very different prices and need to match the unit volume demanded by customers with price and production capacity. Using unit volume as an objective can be counterproductive if a volume objective is achieved, say, by drastic price cutting that drives down profit.

Survival   In some instances, profits, sales, and market share are less important objectives of the firm than mere survival. Frontier Airlines attracted passengers with low fares and aggressive promotions to improve the firm's cash flow. This pricing objective helped Frontier stay alive in the competitive airline industry following its bankruptcy in 2008.

Social Responsibility   A firm may forgo higher profit on sales and follow a pricing objective that recognizes its obligations to customers and society in general. For example, Gerber supplies a specially formulated product free of charge to children who cannot tolerate foods based on cow's milk.

Identifying Pricing Constraints

pricing constraints

Factors that limit the range of prices a firm may set.

Factors that limit the range of prices a firm may set are **pricing constraints**. Consumer demand for the product clearly affects the price that can be charged. Other constraints on price vary from factors within the organization to competitive factors outside the organization.

Demand for the Product Class, Product, and Brand   The number of potential buyers for a product class (cars), product (sports cars), and brand (Bugatti Veyron) clearly affects the price a seller can charge. Generally, the greater the demand for a product, or brand, the higher the price that can be set. For example, the New York Mets set different ticket prices for their games based on the appeal of their opponent—prices are higher when they play the New York Yankees and lower when they play the Pittsburgh Pirates.[18]

Newness of the Product: Stage in the Product Life Cycle   The newer a product and the earlier it is in its life cycle, the higher is the price that can usually be charged. Willing to spend $5,399 for a Samsung Smart TV 65-inch 3D LED HDTV? The high initial price is possible because of patents and limited competition early in its product life cycle. By the time you read this, the price probably will be much lower.

Cost of Producing and Marketing the Product   In the long run, a firm's price must cover all the costs of producing and marketing a product. If the price doesn't cover these costs, the firm will fail; so in the long run, a firm's costs set a floor under its price. The cost to produce HDTVs and flat-panel displays is decreasing by 15 percent per year. However, manufacturers have adopted aggressive pricing tactics, thus decreasing profit margins.[19]

Competitors' Prices   When Apple introduced its iPad in 2010, it was not only unique and in the introductory stage of its product life cycle but also the first commercially successful tablet device sold. As a result, Apple had great latitude in setting a price. Now, with a wide range of competition in tablets from Samsung's Galaxy Tab, Motorola's Xoom, and others, Apple's pricing latitude is less broad.[20]

What pricing constraints do high-definition television manufacturers face? Read the text to appreciate the pricing challenges in this market.

Legal and Ethical Considerations   Setting a final price is clearly a complex process. The task is further complicated by legal and ethical issues. Four pricing practices that have received special scrutiny are described below:

- *Price fixing.* A conspiracy among firms to set prices for a product is termed price fixing. Price fixing is illegal under the Sherman Act. When two or more competitors collude to explicitly or implicitly set prices, this practice is called *horizontal price fixing.* For example, six foreign vitamin companies recently pled guilty to price fixing in the human and animal vitamin industry and paid the largest fine in U.S. history: $335 million.[21] *Vertical price fixing* involves controlling agreements between independent buyers and sellers (a manufacturer and a retailer) whereby sellers are required to not sell products below a minimum retail price.

- *Price discrimination.* The Clayton Act as amended by the Robinson-Patman Act prohibits price discrimination—the practice of charging different prices to different buyers for goods of like grade and quality. However, not all price differences are illegal; only those that substantially lessen competition or create a monopoly are deemed unlawful.

- *Deceptive pricing.* Price deals that mislead consumers fall into the category of deceptive pricing. Deceptive pricing is outlawed by the Federal Trade Commission. *Bait and switch* is an example of deceptive pricing. This occurs when a firm offers a very low price on a product (the bait) to attract customers to a store. Once in the store, the customer is persuaded to purchase a higher-priced item (the switch) using a variety of tricks, including (1) degrading the promoted item and (2) not having the promised item in stock or refusing to take orders for it.

- *Predatory pricing.* Predatory pricing is the practice of charging a very low price for a product with the intent of driving competitors out of business. Once competitors have been driven out, the firm raises its prices. Proving the presence of this practice has been difficult and expensive because it must be shown that the predator explicitly attempted to destroy a competitor and the predatory price was below the defendant's average cost.

learning review

7. What is the difference between pricing objectives and pricing constraints?

8. Explain what bait and switch is and why it is an example of deceptive pricing.

SETTING A FINAL PRICE

LO5

The final price set by the marketing manager serves many functions. It must be high enough to cover the cost of providing the product or service *and* meet the objectives of the company. Yet it must be low enough that customers are willing to pay it. But not too low, or customers may think they're purchasing an inferior product. Dizzy yet? Setting price is one of the most difficult tasks the marketing manager faces, but three generalized steps are useful to follow.

Step 1: Select an Approximate Price Level

Before setting a final price, the marketing manager must understand the market environment, the features and customer benefits of the particular product, and the goals of the firm. A balance must be struck between factors that might drive a price higher (such as a profit-oriented approach) and other forces (such as increased competition from substitutes) that may drive a price down.

Marketing managers consider pricing objectives and constraints first, then choose among the general pricing approaches—demand-, cost-, profit-, or competition-oriented—to arrive at an approximate price level. This price is then analyzed in terms of cost, volume, and profit relationships. Break-even analyses may be run at this point, and finally, if this approximate price level "works," it is time to take the next step: setting a specific list or quoted price.

Step 2: Set the List or Quoted Price

QR 11–3
CarMax Ad

A seller must decide whether to follow a one-price or flexible-price policy.

One-Price Policy A *one-price policy*, also called *fixed pricing,* is setting one price for all buyers of a product or service. CarMax uses this approach in its stores and features a "no haggle, one price" price for cars. Some retailers have married this policy with a below-market approach. Dollar Value Stores and 99¢ Only Stores sell everything in their stores for $1 or less. Family Dollar Stores sell everything for $2.

Flexible-Price Policy In contrast, a *flexible-price policy* involves setting different prices for products and services depending on individual buyers and purchase situations in light of demand, cost, and competitive factors. Dell Inc. uses flexible pricing as it continually adjusts prices in response to changes in its own costs, competitive pressures, and demand from its various personal computer segments (home, small business, corporate, etc.). "Our flexibility allows us to be [priced] different even within a day," says a Dell spokesperson.[22]

Flexible pricing is not without its critics because of its discriminatory potential. For example, car dealers have traditionally used flexible pricing on the basis of buyer–seller negotiations to agree on a final sales price. However, flexible pricing may result in discriminatory practices in car buying, as detailed in the Making Responsible Decisions box.[23]

Step 3: Make Special Adjustments to the List or Quoted Price

When you pay 75 cents for a bag of M&Ms in a vending machine or receive a quoted price of $10,000 from a contractor to renovate a kitchen, the pricing sequence ends with the last step just described: setting the list or quoted price. But when you are a

Making Responsible Decisions > > > > > > > ethics

Flexible Pricing—Is There Discrimination in Bargaining for a New Car?

What do 60 percent of prospective buyers dread when looking for a new car? That's right! They dread negotiating the price. Price bargaining demonstrates shortcomings of flexible pricing when purchasing a new car: the potential for race and gender price discrimination.

A National Bureau of Economic Research study of 750,000 car purchases indicated that African Americans, Hispanics, and women, on average, paid roughly $423, $483, and $105 more, respectively, for a new car in the $21,000 range than the typical purchaser. Smaller price premiums remained after adjusting for income, education, and other factors that may affect price negotiations.

Research shows that searching automotive and car dealer websites before buying a new car reduces price premiums paid by African Americans, Hispanics, and women.

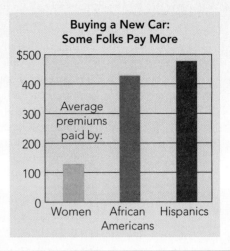

Buying a New Car: Some Folks Pay More

Average premiums paid by: Women, African Americans, Hispanics

---

manufacturer of M&M candies and sell your product to dozens or hundreds of wholesalers and retailers in your channel of distribution, you may need to make a variety of special adjustments to the list or quoted price. Wholesalers also must adjust the list or quoted prices they set for retailers. Two adjustments to the list or quoted price are (1) discounts and (2) allowances.

Discounts *Discounts* are reductions from list price that a seller gives a buyer as a reward for some activity of the buyer that is favorable to the seller. Four kinds of discounts are especially important in marketing strategy: (1) quantity, (2) seasonal, (3) trade (functional), and (4) cash.

- *Quantity discounts.* To encourage customers to buy larger quantities of a product, firms at all levels in the channel of distribution offer quantity discounts, which are reductions in unit costs for a larger order. For example, an instant photocopying service might set a price of 10 cents a copy for 1 to 24 copies, 9 cents a copy for 25 to 99 copies, and 8 cents a copy for 100 copies or more.
- *Seasonal discounts.* To encourage buyers to stock inventory earlier than their normal demand would require, manufacturers often use seasonal discounts. A firm such as Toro that manufactures lawn mowers and snow throwers offers seasonal discounts to encourage wholesalers and retailers to stock up on lawn mowers in January and February and snow throwers in July and August—five or six months before the seasonal demand by ultimate consumers.
- *Trade (functional) discounts.* To reward wholesalers and retailers for marketing functions they will perform in the future, a manufacturer often gives trade, or functional, discounts. These reductions off the list or base price are offered to resellers in the channel of distribution on the basis of (1) where they are in the channel and (2) the marketing activities they are expected to perform in the future.
- *Cash discounts.* To encourage retailers to pay their bills quickly, manufacturers offer them cash discounts. Cash discounts are typically expressed as a percentage off the list price.

Manufacturers provide a variety of discounts to assist channel members such as Payless ShoeSource, a shoe retailer promoting an early fall sale.

A retailer like Payless ShoeSource that plans an early fall sale often tries to take advantage of several of these discounts to increase its revenues and profits.

Allowances Allowances—like discounts—are reductions from list or quoted prices to buyers for performing some activity.

- *Trade-in allowances.* A new-car dealer can offer a substantial reduction in the list price of that new Toyota Camry by offering you a trade-in allowance of $2,500 for your Chevrolet. A trade-in allowance is a price reduction given when a used product is part of the payment on a new product. Trade-ins are an effective way to lower the price a buyer has to pay without formally reducing the list price.
- *Promotional allowances.* Sellers in the channel of distribution can qualify for promotional allowances for undertaking certain advertising or selling activities to promote a product. Various types of allowances include an actual cash payment or an extra amount of "free goods" (as with a free case of pizzas to a retailer for every dozen cases purchased). Frequently, a portion of these savings is passed on to the consumer by retailers.

Some companies, such as Procter & Gamble, have chosen to reduce promotional allowances for retailers by using everyday low pricing. *Everyday low pricing* (EDLP) is the practice of replacing promotional allowances with lower manufacturer list prices. EDLP promises to reduce the average price to consumers while minimizing promotional allowances that cost manufacturers billions of dollars every year.

---

learning review

9. What are the three steps in setting a final price?

10. What is the purpose of (*a*) quantity discounts and (*b*) promotional allowances?

LEARNING OBJECTIVES REVIEW

LO1 *Describe the nature and importance of pricing and the approaches used to select an approximate price level.*
Price is the money or other considerations (such as barter) exchanged for the ownership or use of a product or service. Although price typically involves money, the amount exchanged is often different from the list or quoted price because of incentives (rebates, discounts, etc.), allowances (trade), and extra fees (finance charges, surcharges, etc.).

Demand, cost, profit, and competition influence the initial consideration of the approximate price level for a product or service. Demand-oriented pricing approaches stress consumer demand and revenue implications of pricing and include seven types: skimming, penetration, prestige, odd-even, target, bundle, and yield management. Cost-oriented pricing approaches emphasize the cost aspects of pricing and include two types: standard markup and cost-plus pricing. Profit-oriented pricing approaches focus on a balance between revenues and costs to set a price and include three types: target profit, target return-on-sales, and target return-on-investment pricing. And finally, competition-oriented pricing approaches stress what competitors or the marketplace are doing and include three types: customary; above-, at-, or below-market; and loss-leader pricing.

LO2 *Explain what a demand curve is and the role of revenues in pricing decisions.*
A demand curve is a graph relating the quantity sold and price, which shows the maximum number of units that will be sold at a given price. Three demand factors affect price: (*a*) consumer tastes, (*b*) price and availability of substitute products, and (*c*) consumer income. These demand factors determine consumers' willingness and ability to pay for products and services. Assuming these demand factors remain unchanged, if the price of a product is lowered or raised, then the quantity demanded for it will increase or decrease, respectively. The demand curve relates to a firm's total revenue, which is the total money received from the sale of a product, or the price of one unit times the quantity of units sold.

LO3 *Explain the role of costs in pricing decisions and describe how combinations of price, fixed cost, and unit variable cost affect a firm's break-even point.*
Four important costs impact a firm's pricing decisions: (*a*) total cost, or total expenses, the sum of the fixed costs and variable costs incurred by a firm in producing and marketing a product; (*b*) fixed cost, the sum of the expenses of the firm that are stable and do not change with the quantity of a product that is produced and sold; (*c*) variable cost, the sum of the expenses of the firm that vary directly with the quantity of a product that is produced and sold; and (*d*) unit variable cost, the variable cost expressed on a per unit basis.

Break-even analysis is a technique that analyzes the relationship between total revenue and total cost to determine profitability at various levels of output. The break-even point is the quantity at which total revenue and total cost are equal.

Assuming no change in price, if the costs of a firm's product increase due to higher fixed costs (manufacturing or advertising) or variable costs (direct labor or materials), then its break-even point will be higher. And if total cost is unchanged, an increase in price will reduce the break-even point.

LO4 *Recognize the objectives a firm has in setting prices and the constraints that restrict the range of prices a firm can charge.*
Pricing objectives specify the role of price in a firm's marketing strategy and may include profit, sales revenue, market share, unit volume, survival, or some socially responsible price level. Pricing

constraints that restrict a firm's pricing flexibility include demand, product newness, production and marketing costs, prices of competitive substitutes, and legal and ethical considerations.

LO5 *Describe the steps taken in setting a final price.*
Three common steps marketing managers often use in setting a final price are (1) select an approximate price level as a starting point; (2) set the list or quoted price, choosing between a one-price policy or a flexible-price policy; and (3) modify the list or quoted price by considering discounts and allowances.

FOCUSING ON KEY TERMS

break-even analysis p. 259
demand curve p. 256
price p. 248
price elasticity of demand p. 257

pricing constraints p. 262
pricing objectives p. 261
profit equation p. 249
total cost p. 258

total revenue p. 258
value p. 249

APPLYING MARKETING KNOWLEDGE

1 How would the price equation apply to the purchase price of (*a*) gasoline, (*b*) an airline ticket, and (*c*) a checking account?

2 Under what conditions would a camera manufacturer adopt a skimming price approach for a new product? A penetration approach?

3 What are some similarities and differences between skimming pricing, prestige pricing, and above-market pricing?

4 Touché Toiletries Inc. has developed an addition to its Lizardman Cologne line tentatively branded Ode

d'Toade Cologne. Unit variable costs are 45 cents for a 3-ounce bottle, and heavy advertising expenditures in the first year would result in total fixed costs of $900,000. Ode d'Toade Cologne is priced at $7.50 for a 3-ounce bottle. How many bottles of Ode d'Toade must be sold to break even?

5 What would be your response to the statement, "Profit maximization is the only legitimate pricing objective for the firm"?

building your marketing plan

In starting to set a final price:

1 List two pricing objectives and three pricing constraints.
2 Think about your customers and competitors and set three possible prices.

3 Assume a fixed cost and unit variable cost and (*a*) calculate the break-even points and (*b*) plot a break-even chart for the three prices specified in step 2.

video case 11 Washburn Guitars: Using Break-Even Points to Make Pricing Decisions

QR 11–4
Washburn
Guitars
Video Case

"We offer a guitar at every price point for every skill level," explains Kevin Lello, vice president of marketing at Washburn Guitars. Washburn is one of the most prestigious guitar manufacturers in the world, offering instruments that range from one-of-a-kind, custom-made acoustic and electric guitars and basses to less-expensive, mass-produced guitars. Lello has responsibility for marketing Washburn's products and ensuring that the price of

each product matches the company's objectives related to sales, profit, and market share. "We do pay attention to break-even points," adds Lello. "We need to know exactly how much a guitar costs us, and how much the overhead is for each guitar."

THE COMPANY

The modern Washburn Guitars company started in 1977 when a small Chicago firm bought the century-old Washburn brand name and a small inventory of guitars, parts, and promotional supplies. At that time, annual company sales of about 2,500 guitars generated revenues of $300,000. Washburn's first catalog, appearing in 1978, told a frightening truth:

> Our designs are translated by Japan's most experienced craftsmen, assuring the consistent quality and craftsmanship for which they are known.

At that time, the American guitar-making craft was at an all-time low. Guitars made by Japanese firms, such as Ibane and Yamaha, were in use by an increasing number of professionals.

Times have changed for Washburn. Today, the company sells about 50,000 guitars each year and annual revenues exceed $40 million. All this resulted from Washburn's aggressive marketing strategies to develop product lines with different price points targeted at musicians in distinctly different market segments.

THE PRODUCTS AND MARKET SEGMENTS

One of Washburn's early successes was the trendsetting Festival Series of cutaway, thin-bodied flattops, with built-in bridge pickups and controls. This guitar became the standard for live performances as its popularity with rock and country stars increased. Over the years several generations of musicians have used Washburn guitars. Early artists included Bob Dylan, Dolly Parton, Greg Allman, and the late George Harrison of the Beatles. In recent years, Mike Kennerty of the All American Rejects, Rick Savage of Def Leppard, and Hugh McDonald of Bon Jovi have been among the many musicians who use Washburn products.

Until 1991, all Washburn guitars were manufactured in Asia. That year Washburn started building its high-end guitars in the United States. Today, Washburn marketing executives divide its product line into four categories to appeal to different market segments. From high end to low end these are:

- One-of-a-kind, custom instruments.
- Batch-custom instruments.
- Mass-customized instruments.
- Mass-produced instruments.

The one-of-a-kind custom products appeal to the many stars who use Washburn instruments as well as collectors. The batch-custom products appeal to professional musicians. The mass-customized products appeal to musicians with intermediate skill levels who may not yet be professionals. Finally, the mass-produced units are targeted at first-time buyers and are still manufactured in Asian factories.

PRICING ISSUES

Setting prices for its various lines presents a continuing challenge for Washburn. Not only do the prices have to reflect the changing tastes of its various segments of musicians, but the prices must also be competitive with the prices of other guitars manufactured and marketed globally. The price elasticity of demand, or price sensitivity, for Washburn's products varies between its segments. To reduce the price sensitivity for some of its products, Washburn uses endorsements by internationally known musicians who play its instruments and lend their names to lines of Washburn signature guitars. Stars playing Washburn guitars, such as Nuno Bettencourt of Extreme, Paul Stanley of KISS, Scott Ian of Anthrax, and Dan Donegan of Disturbed, have their own lines of signature guitars—the "batch-custom" units mentioned earlier. These guitars receive excellent reviews. *Total Guitar* magazine, for example, recently said, "If you want a truly original axe that has been built with great attention to detail . . . then the Washburn Maya Pro DD75 could be the one."

Bill Abel, Washburn's vice president of sales, is responsible for reviewing and approving prices for the company's lines of guitars. Setting a sales target of 2,000 units for a new line of guitars, he is considering a suggested retail price of $349 per unit for customers at one of the hundreds of retail outlets carrying the Washburn line. For planning purposes, Abel estimates half of the final retail price will be the price Washburn nets when it sells its guitar to the wholesalers and dealers in its channel of distribution.

Looking at Washburn's financial data for its present plant, Abel estimates that this line of guitars must bear these fixed costs:

Rent and taxes	= $14,000
Depreciation of equipment	= $ 4,000
Management and quality control program	= $20,000

In addition, he estimates the variable costs for each unit to be:

Direct materials	= $25/unit
Direct labor	= 15 hours/unit @ $8/hour

Carefully kept production records at Washburn's plant make Abel believe that these are reasonable estimates. He explains, "Before we begin a production run, we have a good feel for what our costs will be. The U.S.–built N-4, for example, simply costs more than one of our foreign-produced electrics."

Caught in the global competition for guitar sales, Washburn continually searches for ways to reduce and control costs. For example, Washburn recently purchased Parker Guitar, another guitar manufacturer that designed products for professionals and collectors, and will combine the two production facilities in a new location. Washburn expects the acquisition to lower its fixed and variable costs. Specifically, Washburn projects that its new factory location will reduce its rent and taxes expense by 40 percent, and the new skilled employees will reduce the hours of work needed for each unit by 15 percent.

By managing the prices of its products, Washburn also helps its dealers and retailers. In fact, Abel believes it is another reason for Washburn's success: "We have excellent relationships with the independent retailers. They're our lifeblood, and our outlet to sell our product. We sell through chains and online dealers, but it's the independent dealer that sells the guitars. So we take a smaller margin from them because they have to do more work. They appreciate it, and they go the extra mile for us."

Questions

1 What factors are most likely to affect the demand for the lines of Washburn guitars (*a*) bought by a first-time guitar buyer and (*b*) bought by a sophisticated musician who wants a signature model?

2 For Washburn, what are examples of (*a*) shifting the demand curve to the right to get a higher price for a guitar line (movement of the demand curve) and (*b*) pricing decisions involving moving along a demand curve?

3 In Washburn's factory, what is the break-even point for the new line of guitars if the retail price is (*a*) $349, (*b*) $389, and (*c*) $309? Also, (*d*) if Washburn achieves the sales target of 2,000 units at the $349 retail price, what will its profit be?

4 Assume that the merger with Parker leads to the cost reductions projected in the case. What will be the (*a*) new break-even point at a $349 retail price for this line of guitars and (*b*) new profit if it sells 2,000 units?

5 If for competitive reasons, Washburn eventually has to move all its production back to Asia, (*a*) which specific fixed and variable costs might be lowered and (*b*) what additional fixed and variable costs might it expect to incur?

PLAY WITH AN
EDGE.
FOUR-PIECE FUSED TITANIUM
Callaway
DIABLO EDGE
The Diablo Edge™ Technology Alvaro Quiros plays on TOUR is also available in the new Callaway Diablo Edge Driver, the most precisely engineered titanium Driver we've ever developed. Four optimized parts are fused together to give you more power, more fire and the edge you need to hit it longer than ever before. Learn more at callawaygolf.com
Engineering Performance For You.
Callaway®

Managing Marketing Channels and Supply Chains

12

LEARNING OBJECTIVES

After reading this chapter you should be able to:

 LO1 Explain what is meant by a marketing channel of distribution and why intermediaries are needed.

LO2 Distinguish among traditional marketing channels, electronic marketing channels, and different types of vertical marketing systems.

LO3 Describe factors that marketing executives consider when selecting and managing a marketing channel.

LO4 Explain what supply chain and logistics management are and how they relate to marketing strategy.

CALLAWAY GOLF: DESIGNING AND DELIVERING THE GOODS FOR GREAT GOLF

What do Morgan Pressel and Ernie Els, two world-class golf professionals, and Justin Timberlake, a pop icon and avid amateur golfer, have in common? All three use Callaway Golf equipment, accessories, and apparel when playing their favorite sport.

With annual sales approaching $900 million, Callaway Golf is one of the most recognized and highly regarded companies in the golf industry. With its commitment to continuous product innovation and broad distribution in the United States and more than 110 countries worldwide, Callaway Golf has built a strong reputation for designing and delivering the goods for great golf for golfers of all skill levels, both amateur and professional.

Callaway Golf primarily markets its products through more than 15,000 on- and off-course golf retailers and sporting goods retailers, such as Golf Galaxy, Inc., Dick's Sporting Goods, Inc., and PGA Tour Superstores, which sell quality golf products and provide a level of customer service appropriate for the sale of such products.

The company also has its own online store (Shop.Callawaygolf.com), which makes it a full-fledged multichannel marketer, and a successful one as well. Soon after the online store was launched, the chief executive of PGA America called the store "innovative in that it combines that old legacy relationship with the retail channel with the new innovation of the Web." Callaway's president and chief executive officer says Callaway's online store is useful for consumers who are looking for accessories or apparel and for those who know their preferred golf club specifications: "There are always going to be certain people that will not feel comfortable buying online. But for those that do feel comfortable, we really represent the most seamless process."

Callaway Golf considers its marketing channel partners a valued marketing asset. For example, when the company opened its online store, careful attention was given to how Callaway Golf "could satisfy the consumer but do so in a way that didn't violate our relationships with our loyal trade partners," according to a company spokesperson. The solution? Callaway Golf has one of its retailers get credit for the sale. This retailer then fulfills a buyer's order within 24 hours. Consumers, retailers, and Callaway Golf all benefit from this arrangement.[1]

This chapter focuses on managing marketing channels of distribution and supply chains. Each is an important element in the marketing mix.

NATURE AND IMPORTANCE OF MARKETING CHANNELS

LO1

Reaching prospective buyers, either directly or indirectly, is a prerequisite for successful marketing. At the same time, buyers benefit from distribution systems used by companies.

What Is a Marketing Channel of Distribution?

You see the results of distribution every day. You may have purchased Lay's Potato Chips at a 7-Eleven convenience store, a book online through Amazon.com, and Levi's jeans at a Kohl's department store. Each of these items was brought to you by a marketing channel of distribution, or simply a **marketing channel**, which consists of individuals and firms involved in the process of making a product or service available for use or consumption by consumers or industrial users.

Marketing channels can be compared with a pipeline through which water flows from a source to a terminus. Marketing channels make possible the flow of products and services from a producer, through intermediaries, to a buyer. Intermediaries go by various names (see Figure 12–1) and perform various functions. Some intermediaries purchase items from the seller, store them, and resell them to buyers. For example, Celestial Seasonings produces specialty teas and sells them to food wholesalers. The wholesalers then sell these teas to supermarkets and grocery stores, which, in turn, sell them to consumers. Other intermediaries such as brokers and agents represent sellers but do not actually take title to products—their role is to bring a seller and buyer together. Century 21 real estate agents are examples of this type of intermediary.

marketing channel
Individuals and firms involved in the process of making a product or service available for use or consumption by consumers or industrial users.

Value Is Created by Intermediaries

The importance of intermediaries is made even clearer when we consider the functions they perform and the value they create for buyers.

Important Functions Performed by Intermediaries Intermediaries make possible the flow of products from producers to ultimate consumers by performing three basic functions (see Figure 12–2). Intermediaries perform a

FIGURE 12–1
Terms used for marketing intermediaries vary in specificity and use in consumer and business markets.

TERM	DESCRIPTION
Middleman	Any intermediary between the manufacturer and end-user markets
Agent or broker	Any intermediary with legal authority to act on behalf of the manufacturer
Wholesaler	An intermediary who sells to other intermediaries, usually to retailers; term usually applies to consumer markets
Retailer	An intermediary who sells to consumers
Distributor	An imprecise term, usually used to describe intermediaries who perform a variety of distribution functions, including selling, maintaining inventories, extending credit, and so on; a more common term in business markets but may also be used to refer to wholesalers
Dealer	A more imprecise term than *distributor* that can mean the same as distributor, retailer, wholesaler, and so forth

TYPE OF FUNCTION	ACTIVITIES RELATED TO FUNCTION
Transactional function	• *Buying*: Purchasing products for resale or as an agent for supply of a product • *Selling*: Contacting potential customers, promoting products, and seeking orders • *Risk taking*: Assuming business risks in the ownership of inventory that can become obsolete or deteriorate
Logistical function	• *Assorting*: Creating product assortments from several sources to serve customers • *Storing*: Assembling and protecting products at a convenient location to offer better customer service • *Sorting*: Purchasing in large quantities and breaking into smaller amounts desired by customers • *Transporting*: Physically moving a product to customers
Facilitating function	• *Financing*: Extending credit to customers • *Grading*: Inspecting, testing, or judging products and assigning them quality grades • *Marketing information and research*: Providing information to customers and suppliers, including competitive conditions and trends

FIGURE 12–2

Marketing channel intermediaries perform these fundamental functions, each of which consists of different activities.

transactional function when they buy and sell products or services. But an intermediary such as a wholesaler also performs the function of sharing risk with the producer when it stocks merchandise in anticipation of sales. If the stock is unsold for any reason, the intermediary—not the producer—suffers the loss.

The logistics of a transaction (described at length later in this chapter) involve the details of preparing and getting a product to buyers. Gathering, sorting, and dispersing products are some of the *logistical functions* of the intermediary—imagine the several books required for a literature course sitting together on one shelf at your college bookstore! Finally, intermediaries perform *facilitating functions* that, by definition, make a transaction easier for buyers. For example, JCPenney issues credit cards to consumers so they can buy now and pay later.

All three functions must be performed in a marketing channel, even though each channel member may not participate in all three. Channel members often negotiate about which specific functions they will perform and for what price.

Consumers Also Benefit from Intermediaries Consumers also benefit from intermediaries. Having the products and services you want, when you want them, where you want them, and in the form you want them is the ideal result of marketing channels.

In more specific terms, marketing channels help create value for consumers through the four utilities described in Chapter 1: time, place, form, and possession. *Time utility* refers to having a product or service when you want it. For example, FedEx provides next-morning delivery. *Place utility* means having a product or service available where consumers want it, such as having a Chevron gas station located on a long stretch of lonely highway. *Form utility* involves enhancing a product or service to make it more appealing to buyers. Consider the importance of bottlers in the soft-drink industry. Coca-Cola and Pepsi-Cola manufacture the flavor concentrate (cola, lemon-lime) and sell it to bottlers—intermediaries—which then add sweetener and the concentrate to carbonated water and package the beverage in bottles and cans, which are then sold to retailers. *Possession utility* entails efforts by intermediaries to help buyers take possession of a product or service, such as having airline tickets delivered by a travel agency.

learning review	1. What is meant by a marketing channel? 2. What are the three basic functions performed by intermediaries?

CHANNEL STRUCTURE AND ORGANIZATION

LO2

A product can take many routes on its journey from a producer to buyers. Marketers continually search for the most efficient route from the many alternatives available. As you'll see, there are some important differences between the marketing channels used for consumer products and business products.

Marketing Channels for Consumer Products and Services

Figure 12–3 shows the four most common marketing channels for consumer products and services. It also shows the number of levels in each marketing channel, as evidenced by the number of intermediaries between a producer and ultimate buyers. As the number of intermediaries between a producer and buyer increases, the channel is viewed as increasing in length. Thus, the producer → wholesaler → retailer → consumer channel is longer than the producer → consumer channel.

Direct Channel   Channel A represents a *direct channel* because the producer and the ultimate consumers deal directly with each other. Many products and services are distributed this way. Many insurance companies sell their services using a direct channel and branch sales offices. The Schwan Food Company of Marshall, Minnesota, the largest direct-to-home provider of frozen foods in the United States, uses route salespeople who sell from refrigerated trucks. Because there are no intermediaries with a direct channel, the producer performs all three channel functions.

Indirect Channel   The remaining three channel forms in Figure 12–3 are *indirect channels* because intermediaries are inserted between the producer and consumers and perform numerous channel functions. Channel B, with a retailer added, is most common when a retailer is large and can buy in large quantities from a producer or when the cost of inventory makes it too expensive to use a wholesaler. Automobile manufacturers such as Toyota use this channel, and a local car dealer acts as a retailer. Why is there no wholesaler? So many variations exist in the product that it would be impossible for a wholesaler to stock all the models required to satisfy buyers; in addition, the cost of maintaining an inventory would be too high. However, large retailers such as Target, 7-Eleven, Staples, Safeway, and Home Depot buy in sufficient quantities to make it cost effective for a producer to deal with only a retail intermediary.

FIGURE 12–3

Common marketing channels for consumer products and services differ by the kind and number of intermediaries involved.

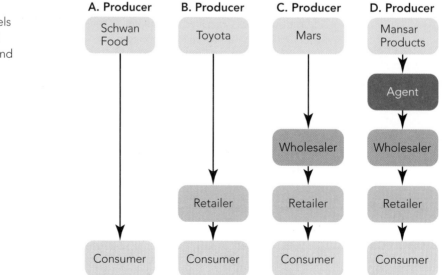

Adding a wholesaler in Channel C is most common for low-cost, low-unit value items that are frequently purchased by consumers, such as candy, confectionary items, and magazines. For example, Mars sells case quantities of its line of candies to wholesalers, who then break down (sort) the cases so that individual retailers can order in boxes or much smaller quantities.

Channel D, the most indirect channel, is employed when there are many small manufacturers and many small retailers; in this type of channel, an agent is used to help coordinate a large supply of the product. Mansar Products, Ltd., is a Belgian producer of specialty jewelry that uses agents to sell to wholesalers in the United States, who then sell to many small independent jewelry retailers.

Marketing Channels for Business Products and Services

The four most common channels for business products and services are shown in Figure 12–4. In contrast with channels used for consumer products, business channels typically are shorter and rely on one intermediary or none at all because business users are fewer in number, tend to be more concentrated geographically, and buy in larger quantities.

Direct Channel Channel A in Figure 12–4, represented by IBM's large, mainframe computer business, is a direct channel. Firms using this channel maintain their own salesforce and perform all channel functions. This channel is employed when buyers are large and well defined, the sales effort requires extensive negotiations, and the products are of high unit value and require hands-on expertise in terms of installation or use.

Indirect Channel Channels B, C, and D in Figure 12–4 are indirect channels with one or more intermediaries between the producer and the industrial user. In Channel B, an industrial distributor performs a variety of marketing channel functions, including selling, stocking, delivering a full product assortment, and financing. In many ways, industrial distributors are like wholesalers in consumer channels. Caterpillar uses industrial distributors to sell its construction and mining equipment in over 200 countries. In addition to selling, Caterpillar distributors stock 40,000 to 50,000 parts and service equipment using highly trained technicians.

Channel C introduces a second intermediary, an agent, who serves primarily as the independent selling arm of producers and represents a producer to industrial users. For example, Stake Fastener Company, a producer of industrial fasteners, has an agent call on industrial users rather than employing its own salesforce.

FIGURE 12–4

Common marketing channels for business products and services differ by the kind and number of intermediaries involved.

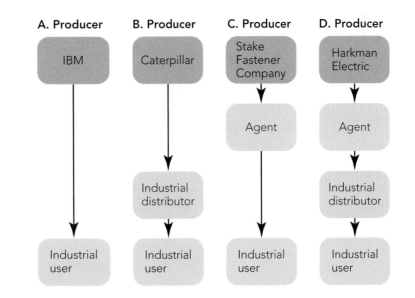

Channel D is the longest channel and includes both agents and industrial distributors. For instance, Harkman Electric, a producer of electric products, uses agents to call on electrical distributors who sell to industrial users.

Electronic Marketing Channels

These common marketing channels for consumer and business products and services are not the only routes to the marketplace. Advances in electronic commerce have opened new avenues for reaching buyers and creating customer value.

Interactive electronic technology has made possible *electronic marketing channels*, which employ the Internet to make products and services available for consumption or use by consumers or organizational buyers. A unique feature of these channels is that they combine electronic and traditional intermediaries to create time, place, form, and possession utility for buyers.

Figure 12–5 shows the electronic marketing channels for books (Amazon.com), automobiles (Autobytel.com), reservation services (Orbitz.com), and personal computers (Dell.com). Are you surprised that they look a lot like common consumer product marketing channels? An important reason for the similarity resides in the channel functions detailed in Figure 12–2. Electronic intermediaries can and do perform transactional and facilitating functions effectively and at a relatively lower cost than traditional intermediaries because of efficiencies made possible by information technology. But electronic intermediaries are incapable of performing elements of the logistical function, particularly for products such as books and automobiles. This function remains with traditional intermediaries or with the producer, as evident with Dell, Inc., and its direct channel.

Many services can be distributed through electronic marketing channels, such as car rental reservations marketed by Alamo.com, financial securities by Schwab.com, and insurance by MetLife.com. However, many other services, such as health care and auto repair, still involve traditional intermediaries.

Direct and Multichannel Marketing

Many firms also use direct and multichannel marketing to reach buyers. *Direct marketing channels* allow consumers to buy products by interacting with various advertising media without a face-to-face meeting with a salesperson. Direct marketing channels include mail-order selling, direct-mail sales, catalog sales, telemarketing, interactive media, and televised home shopping (the Home Shopping Network). Some firms sell products almost entirely through direct marketing. These firms include L.L. Bean

FIGURE 12–5

Consumer electronic marketing channels look much like those for consumer products and services. Read the text to learn why.

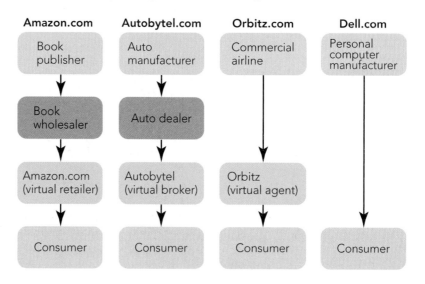

Eddie Bauer successfully engages in multichannel marketing through its 425 retail and outlet stores in North America, Japan, and Germany, its website, and its catalog.

Eddie Bauer
www.eddiebauer.com

multichannel marketing
The blending of different communication and delivery channels that are mutually reinforcing in attracting, retaining, and building relationships with consumers.

(apparel) and Newegg.com (consumer electronics). Marketers such as Nestlé, in addition to using traditional channels composed of wholesalers and retailers, also employ direct marketing through catalogs and telemarketing to reach more buyers.

Multichannel marketing is the *blending* of different communication and delivery channels that are *mutually reinforcing* in attracting, retaining, and building relationships with consumers who shop and buy in traditional intermediaries and online. Multichannel marketing seeks to integrate a firm's electronic marketing and delivery channels. At Eddie Bauer, for example, every effort is made to make the apparel shopping and purchase experience for its customers the same across its retail store, catalog, and website channels. According to an Eddie Bauer marketing manager, "We don't distinguish between channels because it's all Eddie Bauer to our customers."[2]

Multichannel marketing also can leverage the value-adding capabilities of different channels. For example, retail stores leverage their physical presence by allowing customers to pick up their online orders at a nearby store or return or exchange nonstore purchases if they wish. Catalogs can serve as shopping tools for online purchasing, as they do for store purchasing. Websites can help consumers do their homework before visiting a store. Staples has leveraged its store, catalog, and website channels with impressive results. It is the second largest Internet retailer in the United States.[3]

Dual Distribution and Strategic Channel Alliances

dual distribution
An arrangement whereby a firm reaches different buyers by using two or more different types of channels for the same basic product.

In some situations, producers use **dual distribution**, an arrangement whereby a firm reaches different buyers by employing two or more different types of channels for the same basic product. For example, GE sells its large appliances directly to home and apartment builders but uses retail stores, including Lowe's home centers, to sell to consumers. In some instances, firms pair multiple channels with a multibrand strategy (see Chapter 10). This is done to minimize cannibalization of the firm's family brand and differentiate the channels. For example, Hallmark sells its Hallmark greeting cards through Hallmark stores and select department stores and its Ambassador brand of cards through discount and drugstore chains.

A recent innovation in marketing channels is the use of *strategic channel alliances*, whereby one firm's marketing channel is used to sell another firm's products. Strategic alliances are popular in global marketing, where the creation of marketing channel relationships is expensive and time-consuming. For example, General Mills and Nestlé

Can you say Nestlé Cheerios *miel amandes*? Millions of French start their day with this European equivalent of General Mills's Honey Nut Cheerios, made possible by Cereal Partners Worldwide (CPW). CPW is a strategic alliance designed from the start to be a global business. It joined the cereal manufacturing and marketing capability of U.S.–based General Mills with the worldwide distribution clout of Swiss-based Nestlé.

From its headquarters in Switzerland, CPW first launched General Mills cereals under the Nestlé label in France, the United Kingdom, Spain, and Portugal in 1991. Today, CPW competes in more than 130 international markets.

The General Mills–Nestlé strategic channel alliance also increased the ready-to-eat cereal worldwide market share of these companies, which are already rated as the two best-managed firms in the world. CPW currently accounts for more than 8 percent of global breakfast cereal sales, with more than $2 billion in annual revenue.

QR 12–1
Honey Nut
Cheerios Ad

vertical marketing systems
Professionally managed and centrally coordinated marketing channels designed to achieve channel economies and maximum marketing impact.

have an extensive alliance that spans about 130 international markets from Mexico to China. Read the Marketing Matters box so you won't be surprised when you are served Nestlé (not General Mills) Cheerios when traveling outside North America.[4]

Vertical Marketing Systems

The traditional marketing channels described so far represent a loosely knit network of independent producers and intermediaries brought together to distribute products and services. However, other channel arrangements exist for the purpose of improving efficiency in performing channel functions and achieving greater marketing effectiveness. These arrangements are called vertical marketing systems. **Vertical marketing systems** are professionally managed and centrally coordinated marketing channels designed to achieve channel economies and maximum marketing impact.[5] Figure 12–6 depicts the three major types of vertical marketing systems: corporate, contractual, and administered.

Corporate Systems The combination of successive stages of production and distribution under a single ownership is a *corporate vertical marketing system*. For example, a producer might own the intermediary at the next level down in the channel. This practice, called *forward integration*, is exemplified by Ralph Lauren, which manufactures clothing and also owns apparel shops. Other examples of forward integration include Goodyear, Apple, and Sherwin-Williams. Alternatively, a retailer might own a manufacturing operation, a practice called *backward integration*. For example, Kroger supermarkets operate manufacturing facilities that produce everything from aspirin to cottage cheese for sale under the Kroger label. Tiffany & Co., the exclusive jewelry retailer, manufactures about half of the fine jewelry items for sale through its over 230 stores and boutiques worldwide.

Companies seeking to reduce distribution costs and gain greater control over supply sources or resale of their products pursue forward and backward integration. However,

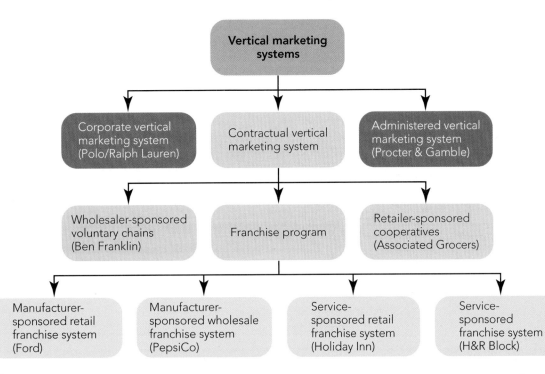

FIGURE 12–6

There are three major types of vertical marketing systems—corporate, contractual, and administered. Contractual systems are the most popular for reasons described in the text.

both types of integration increase a company's capital investment and fixed costs. For this reason, many companies favor contractual vertical marketing systems to achieve channel efficiencies and marketing effectiveness.

Contractual Systems Under a *contractual vertical marketing system*, independent production and distribution firms integrate their efforts on a contractual basis to obtain greater functional economies and marketing impact than they could achieve alone. Contractual systems are the most popular among the three types of vertical marketing systems.

Three variations of contractual systems exist. *Wholesaler-sponsored voluntary chains* involve a wholesaler that develops a contractual relationship with small, independent retailers to standardize and coordinate buying practices, merchandising programs, and inventory management efforts. With the organization of a large number of independent retailers, economies of scale and volume discounts can be achieved to compete with chain stores. IGA and Ben Franklin variety and craft stores represent wholesaler-sponsored voluntary chains. *Retailer-sponsored cooperatives* exist when small, independent retailers form an organization that operates a wholesale facility cooperatively. Member retailers then concentrate their buying power through the wholesaler and plan collaborative promotional and pricing activities. Examples of retailer-sponsored cooperatives include Associated Grocers and Ace Hardware.

The most visible variation of contractual systems is franchising. *Franchising* is a contractual arrangement between a parent company (a franchisor) and an individual or firm (a franchisee) that allows the franchisee to operate a certain type of business under an established name and according to specific rules.

Four types of franchise arrangements are most popular. *Manufacturer-sponsored retail franchise systems* are prominent in the automobile industry, where a manufacturer such as Ford licenses dealers to sell its cars subject to various sales and service conditions. *Manufacturer-sponsored wholesale franchise systems* exist in the soft-drink industry, where PepsiCo licenses wholesalers (bottlers) that purchase concentrate from PepsiCo and then carbonate, bottle, promote, and distribute its products to retailers, vending machines, and restaurants. *Service-sponsored retail franchise systems* are used by firms that have designed a unique approach for performing a service and wish to profit by selling the franchise to others. Holiday Inn, Avis, and McDonald's represent this type of franchising approach. *Service-sponsored franchise systems* exist when franchisors license individuals or firms to dispense a service under a trade name and specific guidelines. Examples include Snelling and Snelling, Inc., employment services and H&R Block tax services.

Administered Systems   In comparison, *administered vertical marketing systems* achieve coordination at successive stages of production and distribution by the size and influence of one channel member rather than through ownership. Procter & Gamble, given its broad product assortment ranging from disposable diapers to detergents, is able to obtain cooperation from supermarkets in displaying, promoting, and pricing its products. Walmart can obtain cooperation from manufacturers in terms of product specifications, price levels, and promotional support, given its position as the world's largest retailer.

---

learning review

3. What is the difference between a direct and an indirect channel?

4. Why are channels for business products typically shorter than channels for consumer products?

5. What is the principal distinction between a corporate vertical marketing system and an administered vertical marketing system?

MARKETING CHANNEL CHOICE AND MANAGEMENT

Marketing channels not only link a producer to its buyers but also provide the means through which a firm implements various elements of its marketing strategy. Therefore, choosing a marketing channel is a critical decision.

Factors Affecting Channel Choice and Management

Marketing executives consider three questions when choosing a marketing channel and intermediaries:

1. Which channel and intermediaries will provide the best coverage of the target market?
2. Which channel and intermediaries will best satisfy the buying requirements of the target market?
3. Which channel and intermediaries will be the most profitable?

Target Market Coverage   Achieving the best coverage of the target market requires attention to the *density*—that is, the number of stores in a geographical area—and type of intermediaries to be used at the retail level of distribution. Three degrees of distribution density exist: intensive, exclusive, and selective.

Intensive distribution means that a firm tries to place its products and services in as many outlets as possible. Intensive distribution is usually chosen for convenience products or services such as candy, fast food, newspapers, and soft drinks. For example, Coca-Cola's retail distribution objective is to place its products "within an arm's reach of desire." Cash, yes cash, is distributed intensively by Visa. It operates over 1.8 million automatic teller machines in more than 200 countries.

Exclusive distribution is the extreme opposite of intensive distribution because only one retailer in a specified geographical area carries the firm's products. Exclusive distribution is typically chosen for specialty products or services, such as some women's fragrances and men's and women's apparel and accessories. Gucci, one of the world's leading luxury products companies, uses exclusive distribution in the marketing of its Yves Saint Laurent, Sergio Rossi, Boucheron, Opium, and Gucci brands.

intensive distribution
When a firm tries to place its products or services in as many outlets as possible.

exclusive distribution
When only one retail outlet in a specific geographical area carries the firm's products.

Retailers and industrial distributors prefer exclusive distribution for two reasons. First, it limits head-to-head competition for an identical product. Second, it provides a point of difference for a retailer or distributor. For instance, luxury retailer Saks Inc. seeks exclusive product lines for its stores. According to the company CEO, "It's incumbent on us not to be just a place where you can buy the big brands. Those brands are still critical—the Chanels, the Pradas, the Guccis—but even with those brands, we need to find things unique to us."[6]

selective distribution

When a firm selects a few retail outlets in a specific geographical area to carry its products.

Selective distribution lies between these two extremes and means that a firm selects a few retailers in a specific geographical area to carry its products. Selective distribution weds some of the market coverage benefits of intensive distribution to the control over resale evident with exclusive distribution. For example, Dell, Inc., chose selective distribution when it decided to sell its products through U.S. retailers along with its direct channel.[7] According to Michael Dell, the company CEO, "There were plenty of retailers who said, 'sell through us,' but we didn't want to show up everywhere." The company now sells a limited range of its products through Walmart, Sam's Club, Best Buy, and Staples. Dell's decision was consistent with current trends. Today, selective distribution is the most common form of distribution intensity.

Buyer Requirements   A second consideration in channel choice is gaining access to channels and intermediaries that satisfy at least some of the interests buyers might want fulfilled when they purchase a firm's products or services. These interests fall into four broad categories: (1) information, (2) convenience, (3) variety, and (4) pre- or postsale services. Each relates to customer experience.

Information is an important requirement when buyers have limited knowledge or desire specific data about a product or service. Properly chosen intermediaries communicate with buyers through in-store displays, demonstrations, and personal selling. Consumer electronics manufacturers such as Apple have opened their own retail outlets staffed with highly trained personnel to communicate how their products can better satisfy each customer's needs.

Convenience has multiple meanings for buyers, such as proximity or driving time to a retail outlet. For example, 7-Eleven stores, with more than 36,000 outlets worldwide, many of which are open 24 hours a day, satisfy this interest for buyers. Candy and snack-food firms benefit by gaining display space in these stores. For other consumers, convenience means a minimum of time and hassle. Jiffy Lube, which promises to change engine oil and filters quickly, appeals to this aspect of convenience. For those who shop on the Internet, convenience means that websites must be easy to locate and navigate, and image downloads must be fast. A commonly held view among website

Which buying requirements are satisfied by Jiffy Lube and PETCO? Read the text to find out.

Using Marketing Dashboards

Channel Sales and Profit at Charlesburg Furniture

Charlesburg Furniture is one of 1,000 wood furniture manufacturers in the United States. The company sells its furniture through furniture store chains, independent furniture stores, and department store chains, mostly in the southern United States. The company has traditionally allocated its marketing funds for cooperative advertising, in-store displays, and retail sales support on the basis of dollar sales by channel.

Your Challenge As the vice president of sales & marketing at Charlesburg Furniture, you have been asked to review the company's sales and profit in its three channels and recommend a course of action. The question: Should Charlesburg Furniture continue to allocate its marketing funds on the basis of channel dollar sales or profit?

Your Findings Charlesburg Furniture tracks the sales and profit from each channel (and individual customer) and the three-year trend of sales by channel on its marketing dashboard. This information is displayed in the marketing dashboard below.

Several findings stand out. Furniture store chains and independent furniture stores account for 85.2 percent of Charlesburg Furniture sales and 93 percent of company profit. These two channels also evidence growth as measured by annual percentage change in sales. By comparison, department store chains annual percentage sales growth has declined and recorded negative growth in 2011. This channel accounts for 14.8 percent of company sales and 7 percent of company profit.

Your Action Charlesburg Furniture should consider abandoning the practice of allocating marketing funds solely on the basis of channel sales volume. The importance of independent furniture stores to Charlesburg's profitability warrants further spending, particularly given this channel's favorable sales trend. Doubling the percentage allocation for marketing funds for this channel may be too extreme, however. Charlesburg Furniture might also reconsider the role of department store chains as a marketing channel.

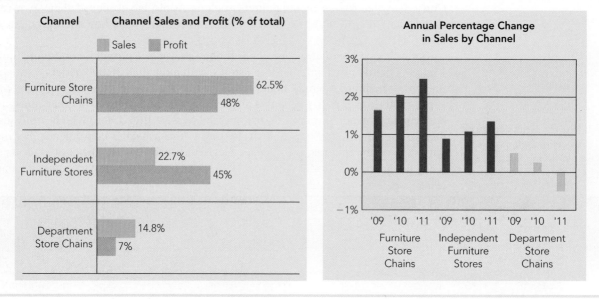

developers is the "eight second rule": Consumers will abandon their efforts to enter or navigate a website if download time exceeds eight seconds.[8]

Variety reflects buyers' interest in having numerous competing and complementary items from which to choose. Variety is evident in the breadth and depth of products and brands carried by intermediaries, which enhances their attraction to buyers. Thus, manufacturers of pet food and supplies seek distribution through pet superstores such as PETCO and PetSmart, which offer a wide array of pet products.

Pre- or postsale services provided by intermediaries are an important buying requirement for products such as large household appliances that require delivery, installation, and credit. Therefore, Whirlpool seeks dealers that provide such services.

Profitability The third consideration in choosing a channel is profitability, which is determined by the margins earned (revenue minus cost) for each channel member and for the channel as a whole. Channel cost is the critical dimension of profitability. These costs include distribution, advertising, and selling expenses associated with different types of marketing channels. The extent to which channel members share these costs determines the margins received by each member and by the channel as a whole.

Companies routinely monitor the performance of their marketing channels. Read the Using Marketing Dashboards box to see how Charlesburg Furniture views the sales and profit performance of its marketing channels.

Managing Channel Relationships: Conflict and Cooperation

Unfortunately, because channels consist of independent individuals and firms, there is always the potential for disagreements concerning who performs which channel functions, how profits are allocated, which products and services will be provided by whom, and who makes critical channel-related decisions. These channel conflicts necessitate measures for dealing with them.

Sources of Conflict in Marketing Channels
Channel conflict arises when one channel member believes another channel member is engaged in behavior that prevents it from achieving its goals. Two types of conflict occur in marketing channels: vertical conflict and horizontal conflict.

Vertical conflict occurs between different levels in a marketing channel—for example, between a manufacturer and a wholesaler or retailer or between a wholesaler and a retailer. Three sources of vertical conflict are most common.[9] First, conflict arises when a channel member bypasses another member and sells or buys products direct, a practice called **disintermediation**. This conflict emerged when American Airlines decided to terminate its relationship with Orbitz and Expedia, two online ticketing and travel sites, and sell directly through AA Direct Connect. Second, conflict occurs due to disagreements over how profit margins are distributed among channel members. This happened when the world's biggest music company, Universal Music Group, adopted a pricing policy for CDs that squeezed the profit margins for specialty music retailers. A third conflict situation arises when manufacturers believe wholesalers or retailers are not giving their products adequate attention. For example, Nike stopped shipping popular sneakers such as Nike Shox NZ to Foot Locker in retaliation for the retailer's decision to give more shelf space to shoes costing under $120.

Horizontal conflict occurs between intermediaries at the same level in a marketing channel, such as between two or more retailers (Target and Kmart) or two or more wholesalers that handle the same manufacturer's brands. Two sources of horizontal conflict are common.[10] First, horizontal conflict arises when a manufacturer increases its distribution coverage in a geographical area. For example, a franchised Buick dealer in Chicago might complain to General Motors that another franchised Buick dealer has located too close to its dealership. Second, dual distribution causes conflict when different types of retailers carry the same brands. For instance, independent Goodyear tire dealers became irate when Goodyear Tire Company decided to sell its brands through Sears, Walmart, and Sam's Club. Many switched to competing tire makers.

Securing Cooperation in Marketing Channels
Conflict can have destructive effects on the workings of a marketing channel so it is necessary to secure cooperation among channel members. One means

Channel conflict is sometimes visible to consumers. Read the text to learn what antagonized independent Goodyear tire dealers.

is through a *channel captain,* a channel member that coordinates, directs, and supports other channel members. Channel captains can be producers, wholesalers, or retailers. P&G assumes this role because it has a strong consumer following in brands such as Crest, Tide, and Pampers. Therefore, it can set policies or terms that supermarkets will follow. McKesson, a pharmaceutical drug wholesaler, is a channel captain because it coordinates and supports the product flow from numerous small drug manufacturers to drugstores and hospitals nationwide. Walmart is a retail channel captain because of its strong consumer image, number of outlets, and purchasing volume.

A firm becomes a channel captain because it is the channel member with the ability to influence the behavior of other members. Influence can take four forms. First, economic influence arises from the ability of a firm to reward other members given its strong financial position or customer franchise. Microsoft Corporation and Walmart have such influence. Expertise is a second source of influence. For example, American Hospital Supply helps its customers (hospitals) manage inventory and streamline order processing for hundreds of medical supplies. Third, identification with a particular channel member can create influence for that channel member. For instance, retailers may compete to carry the Ralph Lauren line, or clothing manufacturers may compete to be carried by Neiman Marcus, Nordstrom, or Bloomingdale's. In both instances, the desire to be identified with a channel member gives that firm influence over others. Finally, influence can arise from the legitimate right of one channel member to direct the behavior of other members. This situation is likely to occur in contractual vertical marketing systems where a franchisor can legitimately direct how a franchisee behaves.

learning review

6. What are the three questions marketing executives consider when choosing a marketing channel and intermediaries?

7. What are the three degrees of distribution density?

LOGISTICS AND SUPPLY CHAIN MANAGEMENT

LO4

logistics
Those activities that focus on getting the right amount of the right products to the right place at the right time at the lowest possible cost.

A marketing channel relies on logistics to make products available to consumers and industrial users. **Logistics** involves those activities that focus on getting the right amount of the right products to the right place at the right time at the lowest possible cost. The performance of these activities is *logistics management,* the practice of organizing the cost-effective flow of raw materials, in-process inventory, finished goods, and related information from point of origin to point of consumption to satisfy customer requirements.

Three elements of this definition deserve emphasis. First, logistics deals with decisions needed to move a product from the source of raw materials to consumption—that is, the *flow* of the product. Second, those decisions have to be *cost effective.* Third, while it is important to drive down logistics costs, there is a limit: A firm needs to drive down logistics costs as long as it can deliver expected customer service, which means satisfying *customer requirements.* The role of management is to see that customer needs are satisfied in the most cost-effective manner. When properly done, the results can be spectacular. Consider Procter & Gamble. The company set out to meet consumer needs more effectively by collaborating and partnering with its suppliers and retailers to ensure that the right products reached store shelves at the right time and at a lower cost. The effort was judged a success when, during an 18-month period, P&G's retail customers posted a $65 million savings in logistics costs and customer service increased.[11]

The Procter & Gamble experience is not an isolated incident. Companies now recognize that getting the right items needed for consumption or production to the right place at the right time in the right condition at the right cost is often beyond their individual capabilities and control. Instead, collaboration, coordination, and information

FIGURE 12–7

Relating logistics management and supply chain management to supplier networks and marketing channels.

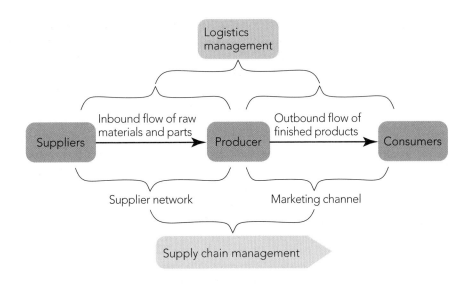

sharing among manufacturers, suppliers, and distributors are necessary to create a seamless flow of products and services to customers. This perspective is represented in the concept of a supply chain and the practice of supply chain management.

Supply Chains versus Marketing Channels

A **supply chain** refers to the various firms involved in performing the activities required to create and deliver a product or service to consumers or industrial users. It differs from a marketing channel in terms of the firms involved. A supply chain includes suppliers that provide raw material inputs to a manufacturer as well as the wholesalers and retailers that deliver finished products to consumers. The management process is also different. *Supply chain management* is the integration and organization of information and logistics activities *across firms* in a supply chain for the purpose of creating and delivering products and services that provide value to consumers. The relation among marketing channels, logistics management, and supply chain management is shown in Figure 12–7. An important feature of supply chain management is its application of sophisticated information technology that allows companies to share and operate systems for order processing, transportation scheduling, and inventory and facility management.

Sourcing, Assembling, and Delivering a New Car: The Automotive Supply Chain

FIGURE 12–8

The automotive supply chain includes thousands of firms that provide the functional components, software codes, and parts in a typical car.

All companies are members of one or more supply chains. A supply chain is essentially a series of linked suppliers and customers in which every customer is, in turn, a supplier to another customer until a finished product reaches the ultimate consumer. Even the simplified supply chain diagram for carmakers shown in Figure 12–8 illustrates how

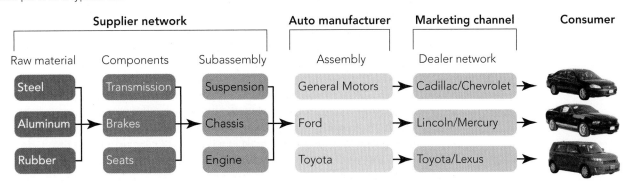

complex a supply chain can be.[12] A carmaker's supplier network includes thousands of firms that provide the 2,000 functional components, 30,000 parts, and 10 million lines of software code in a typical automobile. They provide items ranging from raw materials, such as steel and rubber, to components, including transmissions, tires, brakes, and seats, to complex subassemblies and assemblies such as in chassis and suspension systems that make for a smooth, stable ride.

The process of coordinating and scheduling material and component flows for their assembly into actual automobiles by carmakers is heavily dependent on logistical activities, including transportation, order processing, inventory control, materials handling, and information technology. A central link is the carmaker supply chain manager, who is responsible for translating customer requirements into actual orders and arranging delivery dates and financing for automobile dealers.

Logistical aspects of the automobile marketing channel are also an important part of the supply chain. Major responsibilities include transportation (which involves the selection and oversight of external carriers—trucking, airline, railroad, and shipping companies—for cars and parts to dealers), the operation of distribution centers, the management of finished goods inventories, and order processing for sales. Supply chain managers also play an important role in the marketing channel. They work with car dealer networks to ensure that the right mix of automobiles is delivered to each location. In addition, they make sure that spare and service parts are available so that dealers can meet the car maintenance and repair needs of consumers. All of this is done with the help of information technology that links the entire automotive supply chain. What does all of this cost? It is estimated that logistics costs represent 25 to 30 percent of the retail price of a typical new car.

QR 12–2
IBM Video

Supply Chain Management and Marketing Strategy

The automotive supply chain illustration shows how information and logistics activities are integrated and organized across firms to create and deliver a car to you, the consumer. What's missing from this illustration is the linkage between a specific company's supply chain and its marketing strategy. Just as companies have different marketing strategies, they also design and manage supply chains differently. The goals to be achieved by a firm's marketing strategy determine whether its supply chain needs to be more responsive or efficient in meeting customer requirements.

Aligning a Supply Chain with Marketing Strategy There are a variety of supply chain configurations, each of which is designed to perform different tasks well. Marketers today recognize that the choice of a supply chain follows from a clearly defined marketing strategy and involves three steps:[13]

1. *Understand the customer.* To understand the customer, a company must identify the needs of the customer segment being served. These needs, such as a desire for a low price or convenience of purchase, help a company define the relative importance of efficiency and responsiveness in meeting customer requirements.

2. *Understand the supply chain.* Second, a company must understand what a supply chain is designed to do well. Supply chains range from those that emphasize being responsive to customer requirements and demand to those that emphasize efficiency with a goal of supplying products at the lowest possible delivered cost.

3. *Harmonize the supply chain with the marketing strategy.* Finally, a company needs to ensure that what the supply chain is capable of doing well is consistent with the targeted customer's needs and its marketing strategy. If a mismatch exists between what the supply chain does particularly well and a company's marketing strategy, the company will need to either redesign the supply chain to support the marketing strategy or change the marketing strategy. Read the Marketing Matters box to learn how IBM overhauled its complete supply chain to support its marketing strategy.[14]

Marketing Matters > > > > > customer value

IBM's Integrated Supply Chain—Delivering a Total Solution for Its Customers

IBM is one of the world's great business success stories because of its ability to reinvent itself to satisfy shifting customer needs in a dynamic global marketplace. The company's transformation of its supply chain is a case in point.

IBM set about to build a single integrated supply chain that would handle raw material procurement, manufacturing, logistics, customer support, order entry, and customer fulfillment across all of IBM—something that had never been done before. Why would IBM do this? According to IBM's CEO, "You cannot hope to thrive in the IT industry if you are a high-cost, slow-moving company. Supply chain is one of the new competitive battlegrounds. We are committed to being the most efficient and productive player in our industry."

The task was not easy. With factories in 10 countries, IBM buys 2 billion parts a year from 33,000 suppliers, offers 78,000 products available in 3 million possible variations, moves over 2 billion pounds of machines and parts annually, processes 1.7 million customer orders annually in North America alone, and operates in 150 countries. Yet with surprising efficiency, IBM overhauled its supply chain from raw material sourcing to postsales support.

Today, IBM is uniquely poised to configure and deliver a tailored mix of hardware, software, and service to provide a total solution for its customers. Not surprisingly, IBM's integrated supply chain is now heralded as one of the best in the world!

How are these steps applied and how are efficiency and responsive considerations built into a supply chain? Let's look at how two well-known companies—Dell and Walmart—have harmonized their supply chain and marketing strategy.[15]

Dell: A Responsive Supply Chain   The Dell marketing strategy primarily targets customers who desire having the most up-to-date computer systems customized to their needs. These customers are also willing to (1) wait to have their customized computer system delivered in a few days, rather than picking out a model at a retail store, and (2) pay a reasonable, though not the lowest, price in the marketplace. Given Dell's customer segment, the company has the option of adopting an efficient or responsive supply chain.

An efficient supply chain may use inexpensive, but slower, modes of transportation, emphasize economies of scale in its production process by reducing the variety of system configurations offered, and limit its assembly and inventory storage facilities to a single location. If Dell opted only for efficiency in its supply chain, it would be difficult to satisfy its target customers' desire for rapid delivery and a wide variety of customizable products with its assembly and storage facilities confined to its headquarters in Austin, Texas.

Dell instead has opted for a responsive supply chain. It relies on more expensive express transportation for receipt of components from suppliers and delivery of finished products to customers. The company achieves product variety and manufacturing efficiency by designing common platforms across several products and using common components. Also, Dell has invested heavily in information technology to link itself with suppliers and customers.

Walmart: An Efficient Supply Chain   Now let's consider Walmart. Walmart's marketing strategy is to be a reliable, lower-price retailer for a wide variety of mass consumption consumer goods. This strategy favors an efficient supply chain designed to deliver products to 200 million consumers each week at the lowest possible cost. Efficiency is achieved in a variety of ways. For instance, Walmart keeps relatively low inventory levels, and most of it is stocked in stores available for sale, not in warehouses gathering dust. The low inventory arises from Walmart's use of *cross-docking*—a practice that involves unloading products from suppliers, sorting products for individual stores, and

quickly reloading products onto its trucks for a particular store. No warehousing or storing of products occurs, except for a few hours or, at most, a day. Cross-docking allows Walmart to operate only a small number of distribution centers to service its vast network of Walmart stores, Supercenters, Neighborhood Markets, Marketside stores, and Sam's Clubs, which contributes to efficiency. On the other hand, the company runs its own fleet of trucks to service its stores. This does increase cost and investment, but the benefits in terms of responsiveness justify the cost in Walmart's case.

Walmart has invested much more than its competitors in information technology to operate its supply chain. The company feeds information about customer requirements and demand from its stores back to its suppliers, which manufacture only what is being demanded. This large investment has improved the efficiency of Walmart's supply chain and made it responsive to customer needs.

Three lessons can be learned from these two examples. First, there is no one best supply chain for every company. Second, the best supply chain is the one that is consistent with the needs of the customer segment being served and complements a company's marketing strategy. And finally, supply chain managers are often called upon to make trade-offs between efficiency and responsiveness on various elements of a company's supply chain.

TWO CONCEPTS OF LOGISTICS MANAGEMENT IN A SUPPLY CHAIN

The objective of logistics management in a supply chain is to minimize total logistics costs while delivering the appropriate level of customer service.

Total Logistics Cost Concept

total logistics cost
Expenses associated with transportation, materials handling and warehousing, inventory, stockouts, order processing, and return products handling.

For our purposes, **total logistics cost** includes expenses associated with transportation, materials handling and warehousing, inventory, stockouts (being out of inventory), order processing, and return products handling. Note that many of these costs are interrelated so that changes in one will impact the others. For example, if a firm attempts to reduce its transportation costs by shipping in larger quantities, it will increase its inventory levels. While larger inventory levels will increase inventory costs, they should also reduce stockouts. It is important, therefore, to study the impact on all of the logistics decision areas when considering a change.

Customer Service Concept

customer service
The ability of logistics management to satisfy users in terms of time, dependability, communication, and convenience.

Because a supply chain is a *flow,* the end of it—or *output*—is the service delivered to customers. Within the context of a supply chain, **customer service** is the ability of logistics management to satisfy users in terms of time, dependability, communication, and convenience. As suggested by Figure 12–9, a supply chain manager's key task is to balance these four customer service factors against total logistics cost factors.

Time   In a supply chain setting, time refers to *order cycle* or *replenishment* time for an item, which means the time between the ordering of an item and when it is received and ready for use or sale. The various elements that make up the typical order cycle include recognition of the need to order, order transmittal, order processing, documentation, and transportation. A current emphasis in supply chain management is to reduce order cycle time so that the inventory levels of customers may be minimized. Another emphasis is to make the process of reordering and receiving products as simple as possible, often through inventory systems called *quick response* and *efficient consumer response* delivery systems. For example, at Saks Fifth Avenue, point-of-sale scanner technology records each day's sales. When stock falls below a minimum level, a replenishment order is automatically produced. Vendors such as Donna Karan (DKNY) receive the order, which is processed and delivered within 48 hours.[16]

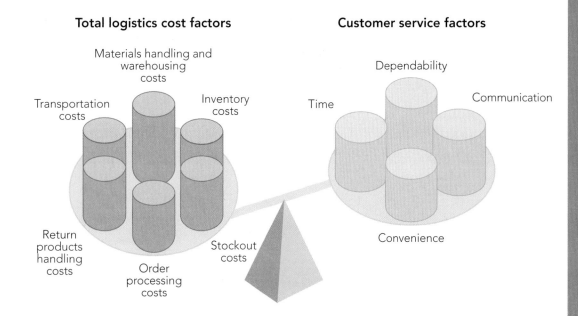

Total logistics cost factors

Materials handling and warehousing costs

Transportation costs

Inventory costs

Return products handling costs

Order processing costs

Stockout costs

Customer service factors

Dependability

Time

Communication

Convenience

FIGURE 12–9
Supply chain managers balance total logistics cost factors against customer service factors.

Dependability Dependability is the consistency of replenishment. This is important to all firms in a supply chain—and to consumers. How often do you return to a store if it fails to have in stock the item you want to purchase? Dependability can be broken into three elements: consistent lead time, safe delivery, and complete delivery. Consistent service allows planning (such as appropriate inventory levels), whereas inconsistencies create surprises. Intermediaries may be willing to accept longer lead times if they know about them in advance and can thus make plans.

Communication Communication is a two-way link between the buyer and seller that helps in monitoring service and anticipating future needs. Status reports on orders are a typical example of communication between the buyer and seller.

Convenience The concept of convenience for a supply chain manager means that there should be a minimum of effort on the part of the buyer in doing business with the seller. Is it easy for the customer to order? Are the products available from many outlets? Will the seller arrange all necessary details, such as transportation? This customer service factor has promoted the use of **vendor-managed inventory** (VMI), whereby the *supplier* determines the product amount and assortment a customer (such as a retailer) needs and automatically delivers the appropriate items.

Campbell Soup's system illustrates how VMI works.[17] Every morning, retailers electronically inform the company of their demand for all Campbell products and the inventory levels in their distribution centers. Campbell uses that information to forecast future demand and determine which products need replenishment based on upper and lower inventory limits established with each retailer. Trucks leave the Campbell shipping plant that afternoon and arrive at the retailer's distribution centers with the required replenishments the same day.

vendor-managed inventory

An inventory management system whereby the supplier determines the product amount and assortment a customer (such as a retailer) needs and automatically delivers the appropriate items.

reverse logistics

A process of reclaiming recyclable and reusable materials, returns, and reworks from the point of consumption or use for repair, remanufacturing, redistribution, or disposal.

CLOSING THE LOOP: REVERSE LOGISTICS

The flow of products in a supply chain does not end with the ultimate consumer or industrial user. Companies today recognize that a supply chain can work in reverse. **Reverse logistics** is a process of reclaiming recyclable and reusable materials, returns, and reworks from the point of consumption or use for repair, remanufacturing, redistribution, or disposal. The effect of reverse logistics can be seen in the reduced waste in landfills

Reverse Logistics and Green Marketing Go Together at Hewlett-Packard: Recycling e-Waste

About 53 million tons of electronic and electronic equipment find their way to landfills around the world annually. Americans alone discarded 400 million analog TV sets and computer monitors and Japanese consumers trashed 610 million cell phones in 2010. The result? Landfills are seeping lead, chromium, mercury, and other toxins, prevalent in digital debris, into the environment.

Fortunately, Hewlett-Packard has taken it upon itself to act responsibly and address this issue through its highly regarded reverse logistics program. Hewlett-Packard has recycled computer and printer hardware since 1987 and is an industry leader in this practice. The company's recycling service is available today in more than 40 countries, regions, and territories. By 2010, Hewlett-Packard will have recycled over 1 billion pounds of used products to be refurbished for resale or donation or for recovery of materials.

Recycling at Hewlett-Packard is part of the company's Design for Supply Chain program. Among other initiatives in this program, emphasis is placed on product and packaging changes to reduce reverse supply chain and environmental costs. For example, design changes have increased the recycling of its popular ink-jet supplies by 25 percent.

and lowered operating costs for companies. The Making Responsible Decisions box on the next page describes the successful reverse logistics initiative at Hewlett-Packard.[18]

Companies such as Motorola and Nokia (return and reuse of mobile phones) and Caterpillar, Xerox, and IBM (remanufacturing and recycling) have implemented acclaimed reverse logistics programs.[19] Other firms have enlisted third-party logistics providers such as UPS, FedEx, and Penske Logistics to handle this process along with other supply chain functions. GNB Technologies, Inc., a manufacturer of lead-acid batteries for automobiles and boats, has outsourced much of its supply chain activity to UPS Supply Chain Services.[20] The company contracts with UPS to manage its shipments between plants, distribution centers, recycling centers, and retailers. This includes movement of both new batteries and used products destined for recycling and covers both truck and railroad shipments. This partnership, along with the initiatives of other battery makers, has paid economic and ecological dividends. By recycling 90 percent of the lead from used batteries, manufacturers have kept the demand for new lead in check, thereby holding down costs to consumers. Also, solid waste management costs and the environmental impact of lead in landfills are reduced.

QR 12–3
UPS Video

learning review

8. What is the principal difference between a marketing channel and a supply chain?

9. The choice of a supply chain involves what three steps?

10. A manager's key task is to balance which four customer service factors against which six logistics cost factors?

LEARNING OBJECTIVES REVIEW

LO1 *Explain what is meant by a marketing channel of distribution and why intermediaries are needed.*

A marketing channel of distribution, or simply a marketing channel, consists of individuals and firms involved in the process of making a product or service available for use or consumption by consumers or industrial users. Intermediaries make possible the flow of products from producers to buyers by performing three basic functions. The transactional function involves buying, selling, and risk taking because intermediaries stock merchandise in anticipation of sales. The logistical function involves the gathering, storing, and dispensing of products. The facilitating function assists producers in making products and services more attractive to buyers. The performance of these functions by intermediaries creates time, place, form, and possession utility for consumers.

LO2 *Distinguish among traditional marketing channels, electronic marketing channels, and different types of vertical marketing systems.*

Traditional marketing channels describe the route taken by products and services from producers to buyers. This route can range from a direct channel with no intermediaries, because a producer and the ultimate consumer deal directly with each other, to indirect channels where intermediaries (agents, wholesalers, distributors, or retailers) are inserted between a producer and consumer and perform numerous channel functions. Electronic marketing channels employ the Internet to make products and services available for consumption or use by consumer or business buyers. Vertical marketing systems are professionally managed and centrally coordinated marketing channels designed to achieve channel economies and maximum marketing impact. There are three major types of vertical marketing systems (VMSs). A corporate VMS combines successive stages of production and distribution under a single ownership. A contractual VMS exists when independent production and distribution firms integrate their efforts on a contractual basis to obtain greater functional economies and marketing impact than they could achieve alone. An administered VMS achieves coordination at successive stages of production and distribution by the size and influence of one channel member rather than through ownership.

LO3 *Describe factors that marketing executives consider when selecting and managing a marketing channel.*

Marketing executives consider three questions when selecting and managing a marketing channel and intermediaries. (1) Which channel and intermediaries will provide the best coverage of the target market? Marketers typically choose one of three levels of market coverage: intensive, selective, or exclusive distribution. (2) Which channel and intermediaries will best satisfy the buying requirements of the target market? These buying requirements fall into four categories: information, convenience, variety, and pre- or postsale services. (3) Which channel and intermediaries will be the most profitable? Here marketers look at the margins earned (revenues minus cost) for each channel member and for the channel as a whole.

LO4 *Explain what supply chain and logistics management are and how they relate to marketing strategy.*

A supply chain refers to the various firms involved in performing the various activities required to create and deliver a product or service to consumers or industrial users. Supply chain management is the integration and organization of information and logistics across firms for the purpose of creating value for consumers. Logistics involves those activities that focus on getting the right amount of the right products to the right place at the right time at the lowest possible cost. Logistics management includes the coordination of the flows of both inbound and outbound products, an emphasis on making these flows cost effective, and customer service. A company's supply chain follows from a clearly defined marketing strategy. The alignment of a company's supply chain with its marketing strategy involves three steps. First, a supply chain must reflect the needs of the customer segment being served. Second, a company must understand what a supply chain is designed to do well. Supply chains range from those that emphasize being responsive to customer requirements and demands to those that emphasize efficiency with the goal of supplying products at the lowest possible delivered cost. Finally, a supply chain must be consistent with the targeted customer's needs and the company's marketing strategy. The Dell and Walmart examples in the chapter illustrate how this alignment is achieved by two market leaders.

FOCUSING ON KEY TERMS

channel conflict p. 283
customer service p. 288
disintermediation p. 283
dual distribution p. 277
exclusive distribution p. 280

intensive distribution p. 280
logistics p. 284
marketing channel p. 272
multichannel marketing p. 277
reverse logistics p. 289

selective distribution p. 281
supply chain p. 285
total logistics cost p. 288
vendor-managed inventory p. 289
vertical marketing systems p. 278

APPLYING MARKETING KNOWLEDGE

1 A distributor for Celanese Chemical Company stores large quantities of chemicals, blends these chemicals to satisfy the requests of customers, and delivers the blends to a customer's warehouse within 24 hours of receiving an order. What utilities does this distributor provide?

2 Suppose the president of a carpet manufacturing firm has asked you to look into the possibility of bypassing the firm's wholesalers (who sell to carpet, department, and furniture stores) and selling direct to these stores. What caution would you voice on this matter, and what type of information would you gather before making this decision?

3 What type of channel conflict is likely to be caused by dual distribution, and what type of conflict can be reduced by direct distribution? Why?

4 How does the channel captain idea differ among corporate, administered, and contractual vertical marketing systems with particular reference to the use of the different forms of influence available to firms?

5 List the customer service factors that would be vital to buyers in the following types of companies: (*a*) manufacturing, (*b*) retailing, (*c*) hospitals, and (*d*) construction.

building your marketing plan

Does your marketing plan involve selecting channels and intermediaries? If the answer is "no," read no further and do not include this element in your plan. If the answer is "yes,"

1 Identify which channel and intermediaries will provide the best coverage of the target market for your product or service.

2 Specify which channel and intermediaries will best satisfy the important buying requirements of the target market.

3 Determine which channel and intermediaries will be the most profitable.

4 Select your channel(s) and intermediary(ies).

5 If inventory is involved, (*a*) identify the three or four major kinds of inventory needed for your organization (retail stock, finished products, raw materials, supplies, and so on), and (*b*) suggest ways to reduce their costs.

6 (*a*) Rank the four customer service factors (time, dependability, communication, and convenience) from most important to least important from your customers' point of view, and (*b*) identify actions for the one or two most important factors that will help you better serve your customers.

video case 12 Amazon: Delivering the Goods . . . Millions of Times a Day

QR 12–4
Amazon
Video Case

"The new economy means that the balance of power has shifted toward the consumer," explains Jeff Bezos, CEO of Amazon.com, Inc. The global online retailer is a pioneer of fast, convenient, low-cost virtual shopping that has attracted millions of consumers. Of course, while Amazon has changed the way many people shop, the company still faces the traditional and daunting task of creating a seamless flow of deliveries to its customers—often millions of times each day.

THE COMPANY

Bezos started Amazon.com with a simple idea: to use the Internet to transform book buying into the fastest, easiest, and most enjoyable shopping experience possible. The company was incorporated in 1994 and opened its virtual doors in July 1995. At the forefront of a huge growth of dot-com businesses, Amazon pursued a get-big-fast business strategy. Sales grew rapidly and Amazon began adding products and services other than books. In fact, Amazon soon set its goal on being the world's most customer-centric company, where customers can find and discover anything they might want to buy online.

Today Amazon claims to have the "Earth's Biggest Selection™" of products and services in the following categories: Books; Movies, Music & Games; Digital Downloads; Kindle; Computers & Office; Electronics; Home & Garden; Grocery, Health & Beauty; Toys, Kids & Baby; Clothing, Shoes & Jewelry; Sports & Outdoors; and Tools, Auto & Industrial. Other services allow customers to:

- Search for a product or brand using all or part of its name.
- Place orders with one click using the "Buy Now with 1-Click" button.
- Receive personalized recommendations based on past purchases through opt-in e-mails.

These products and services have attracted millions of people around the globe. This has made Amazon.com, along with its international sites in Austria, Canada, the United Kingdom, Germany, Japan, France, and China, the leading online retailer.

SUPPLY CHAIN AND LOGISTICS MANAGEMENT AT AMAZON.COM

What happens after an order is submitted on Amazon's website but before it arrives at the customer's door? A lot. Amazon.com maintains huge distribution, or "fulfillment," centers where it keeps inventory of millions of products. This is one of the key differences between Amazon.com and some of its competitors—it actually stocks products. So Amazon must manage the flow of products from its 15 million suppliers to its distribution and customer service centers with the flow of customer orders from the distribution centers to individuals' homes or offices.

The process begins with the suppliers. "Amazon's goal is to collaborate with our suppliers to increase efficiencies and improve inventory turnover," explains Amazon's vice president of supply chain. "We want to bring to suppliers the kind of interactive relationship that has inspired customers to shop with us." For example, Amazon is using software to more accurately forecast purchasing patterns by region, which allows it to give its suppliers better information about delivery dates and volumes. Before the development of this software, 12 percent of incoming inventory was sent to the wrong location, leading to lost time and delayed orders. Now only 4 percent of the incoming inventory is mishandled.

At the same time, Amazon has been improving the part of the process that sorts the products into the individual orders. Amazon's senior vice president of operations says, "We spent the whole year really focused on increasing productivity." Again, technology has been essential. According to the senior vice president of operations, "The speed at which telecommunications networks allow us to pass information back and forth has enabled us to do the real-time work that we keep talking about. In the past, it

would have taken too long to get this many items through a system." Once the order is in the system, computers ensure that all items are included in the box before it is taped and labeled. A network of trucks and regional postal hubs then concludes the process with delivery of the order.

The success of Amazon's logistics and supply chain management activities may be most evident during the year-end holiday shopping season. Amazon received orders for 37.9 million items between November 9 and December 21 one year, including orders for 450,000 Harry Potter books and products, and orders for 36,000 items placed just before the holiday delivery deadline. Well over 99 percent of the orders were shipped and delivered on time.

AMAZON'S CHALLENGES

Several sales growth options are possible for Amazon. First, it can continue to pursue growth through sales of hundreds of thousands of electronic books, magazines, and newspapers through its new Kindle devices and store. Second, Amazon can continue its expansion into new product and service categories. Recently, it launched its Outdoor Recreation store—the latest in over a dozen such categories. This approach would prevent Amazon from becoming a niche merchant and position it as a true online retail department store. Third, Amazon can increase the availability of products from other retailers through its Amazon WebStore. These retailers can create a customized, branded website that uses Amazon eCommerce technology. Finally, Amazon can pursue a strategy of providing access to its existing operations for other retailers through its Fulfillment by Amazon (FBA) service. Online retailers store their products at Amazon's distribution centers and when they sell a product—Amazon ships it!

Amazon.com has come a long way toward proving that online retailing can work. Its logistics and supply chain management activities have provided Amazon with a cost-effective and efficient distribution system that combines automation and communication technology with superior customer service. To continue its drive to increase future sales, profits, and customer service, Amazon acquired Zappos.com in mid-2009. According to Bezos, "We see great opportunities for both companies to learn from each other and create even better experiences for our customers."

Questions

1 How do Amazon.com's logistics and supply chain management activities help the company create value for its customers?

2 What systems did Amazon develop to improve the flow of products from suppliers to Amazon distribution centers? What systems improved the flow of orders from the distribution centers to customers?

3 Why will logistics and supply chain management play an important role in the future success of Amazon.com?

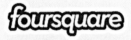

Already a member? **Log In**

Search places, people and tips 🔍

CHECK IN
FIND YOUR FRIENDS
UNLOCK YOUR CITY

Foursquare gives you & your friends new ways to explore your city.
Earn points & unlock badges for discovering new things. LEARN MORE

JOIN NOW

RECENT ACTIVITY

 A.Muzzill in Petaling Jaya, Selangor:
wrote a tip @ **Subway**

 Huseyin C. in Fakıbeyli, Yozgat:
unlocked the **'Adventurer'** badge.

 Reva Vidmala S. in New York, NY:
unlocked the **'Fitbit 1k lifetime miles'** badge.

GET IT NOW

iPhone →

BlackBerry →

ANDROID →

palm →

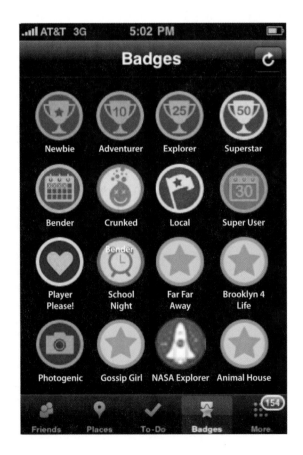

Retailing and Wholesaling

13

LEARNING OBJECTIVES

After reading this chapter you should be able to:

LO1 Identify retailers in terms of the utilities they provide.

LO2 Explain the alternative ways to classify retail outlets.

LO3 Describe the many methods of nonstore retailing.

LO4 Specify the retailing mix actions used to implement a retailing strategy.

LO5 Explain changes in retailing with the wheel of retailing and the retail life cycle concepts.

LO6 Describe the types of firms that perform wholesaling activities and their functions.

RETAILERS LOVE IT WHEN THE MAYOR VISITS!

Dennis Crowley is certain that he knows how you want to plan your evening. First, your smartphone checks your schedule to determine when classes are over or when you are off work. Next, it sees that some of your friends are nearby, and then it helps make a reservation at a restaurant. Best of all, you get a discount because you are the virtual "mayor" of the restaurant!

Is this really possible? According to Crowley, co-founder of foursquare, it's very close to reality, and retailers are thrilled. Foursquare is a location-based social networking app for smartphones that gives consumers points and "badges" for reporting their location and allows businesses to reward customers for visiting their stores. For example, you might "check-in" with your phone's GPS locator each time you visit your favorite restaurant and, if you become its most frequent visitor, foursquare will designate you as the mayor of that establishment. The restaurant may offer a discount or special promotion to encourage the current mayor—who is likely to bring friends—to visit. Many Starbucks locations, for example, offer $1 discounts to foursquare mayors.

There are other location services also. Gowalla, Booyah, Brightkite, and Loopt are similar to foursquare. In addition, Facebook offers its own location service. When shoppers check into Facebook Places, nearby stores send personal offers. Retailers see location services such as these as an opportunity to personalize their offerings to potential customers. In the past, it was difficult to attract nearby shoppers or to know who they were when they visited the store. Location services provide a unique opportunity to reach people on the way to a mall, in a store, or with their friends out on the town. Because phones are typically used by only one person, marketers can personalize their communication to each individual shopper based on their past shopping activities.

In addition, location services can complement the many geographical information systems and mapping services available to marketers today. Crowley believes that location services like foursquare will grow in popularity and observes that "users seem to love it." Currently his company boasts 100 employees, 750,000 participating stores, restaurants, and bars, and more than 20 million users![1]

Location-based social networking services are just a few examples of the many exciting changes occurring in retailing today. This chapter examines the critical role of retailing in the marketplace and the challenging decisions retailers face as they strive to create value for customers.

What types of products will consumers buy through catalogs, television, the Internet, or by telephone? In what type of store will

retailing

All activities involved in selling, renting, and providing products and services to ultimate consumers for personal, family, or household use.

consumers look for products they don't buy directly? How important is the location of the store? Will customers expect services such as alterations, delivery, installation, or repair? What price should be charged for each product? These are difficult and important questions that are an integral part of retailing. In the channel of distribution, retailing is where the customer meets the product. It is through retailing that exchange (a central aspect of marketing) occurs. **Retailing** includes all activities involved in selling, renting, and providing products and services to ultimate consumers for personal, family, or household use.

THE VALUE OF RETAILING

LO1

Retailing is an important marketing activity. Not only do producers and consumers meet through retailing actions, but retailing also creates customer value and has a significant impact on the economy. To consumers, the value of retailing is in the form of utilities provided (see Figure 13–1). Retailing's economic value is represented by the people employed in retailing as well as by the total amount of money exchanged in retail sales.

Consumer Utilities Offered by Retailing

The utilities provided by retailers create value for consumers. Time, place, form, and possession utilities are offered by most retailers in varying degrees, but one utility is often emphasized more than others. Look at Figure 13–1 to see how well you can match the retailer with the utility being emphasized in the description.

FIGURE 13–1

Which retailer best provides which utilities?

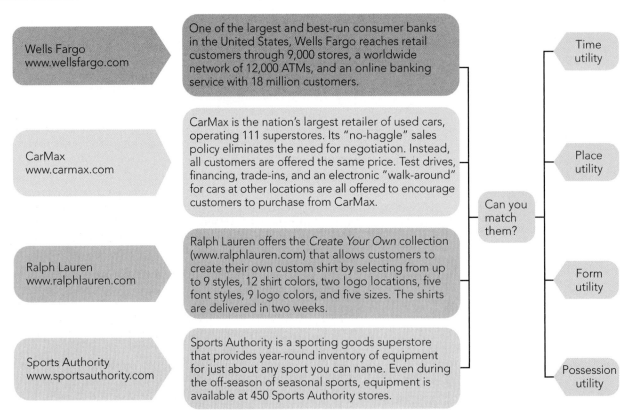

Tesco is one of the largest retailers outside the United States.

QR 13–1
CarMax Video

Providing mini banks in supermarkets, as Wells Fargo does, puts the bank's products and services close to the consumer, providing place utility. By providing financing or leasing and taking used cars as trade-ins, CarMax makes the purchase easier and provides possession utility. Form utility—production or alteration of a product—is offered by Ralph Lauren through its online *Create Your Own* program, which offers shirts that meet each customer's specifications. Finding the right sporting equipment during the off-season is the time utility provided by Sports Authority. Many retailers offer a combination of the four basic utilities. Some supermarkets, for example, offer convenient locations (place utility); are open 24 hours a day (time utility); customize purchases in the bakery, deli, and florist (form utility); and allow several payment and credit options (possession utility).

The Global Economic Impact of Retailing

Retailing is important to the U.S. and global economies. Four of the 30 largest businesses in the United States are retailers (Walmart, Costco, Home Depot, and Target). Walmart's $447 billion in annual sales in 2011 surpassed the gross domestic product of all but 26 countries for that same year. Walmart, Costco, Home Depot, and Target together have more than 2.9 million employees—more than the combined populations of Jacksonville, Florida; El Paso, Texas; and Stockton, California.[2] Many retailers, including food stores, automobile dealers, and general merchandise outlets, are also significant contributors to the U.S. economy.[3]

Outside the United States large retailers include Aeon in Japan, Carrefour in France, Metro Group in Germany, and Tesco in Britain.[4] In emerging economies such as China and Mexico, a combination of local and global retailers is evolving. Walmart, for example, has more than 5,700 stores outside the United States, including stores in Argentina, Brazil, China, India, Japan, Mexico, and the United Kingdom.[5]

learning review

1. When Ralph Lauren makes shirts to a customer's exact preferences, what utility is being provided?

2. Two measures of the impact of retailing in the global economy are _____ and _____.

CLASSIFYING RETAIL OUTLETS

LO2

For manufacturers, consumers, and the economy, retailing is an important component of marketing that has several variations. Because of the large number of alternative forms of retailing, it is easier to understand the differences among retail institutions by recognizing that outlets can be classified in several ways. First, *form of ownership* distinguishes retail outlets based on whether independent retailers, corporate chains, or contractual systems own the outlet. Second, *level of service* is used to describe the degree of service provided to the customer. Three levels of service are provided by self-, limited-, and full-service retailers. Finally, the type of *merchandise line* describes how many different types of products a store carries and in what assortment. The alternative types of outlets are discussed in greater detail in the following pages. For many consumers today, each of the types of outlets discussed is viewed in terms of its environmentally friendly, or green, activities. The Making Responsible Decisions box on the next page gives examples of the green activities of several retailers.[6]

Green Isn't Just a Color to Retailers. It's a Value!

You might remember when "going green" was an expression used to describe consumers and the products they purchased. Initially, retailers responded by offering products that met consumers' new environmental interests. Over time, however, retailers have come to realize that consumers want products that are consistent with their personal values and they want to purchase them from retailers with similar values. Today, many retailers are developing comprehensive and sophisticated business practices that reflect a new focus on social and environmental responsibility.

The U.S. Green Retail Association offers guidance for retailers implementing new "green" practices and also provides a third-party certification that recognizes a commitment to green values. Some practices are intuitive and simple, such as encouraging the use of reusable shopping bags, installing LED lighting, and using nontoxic cleaning products. Other practices, such as reducing CO_2 emissions with economical delivery vehicles, using rainwater for landscape maintenance, or finding alternative uses for landfill waste require a larger effort. Very often, however, these environmental initiatives also have financial benefits. When Home Depot switched its in-store light fixture displays to compact fluorescent light bulbs, for example, it saved $16 million per year.

Many retailers are also requiring that their suppliers make similar efforts and meet the same standards. When Walmart noticed that some packaging led to waste, it required its toy suppliers to trim one square-inch of packaging from its lines and thus reduced packaging by 3,500 tons.

Target has even taken the green concept to its advertising agency and requires that waste from shooting new commercials be recycled or composted. Are your favorite retailers green? Do sustainability practices such as these influence your purchase decisions?

Form of Ownership

There are three general forms of retail ownership—independent retailer, corporate chain, and contractual systems.

Independent Retailer   One of the most common forms of retail ownership is the independent business owned by an individual. Independent retailers account for most of the 1.1 million retail establishments in the United States and include hardware stores, convenience stores, clothing stores, and computer and software stores. In addition, there are 26,700 jewelry stores, 18,500 florists, and 31,300 sporting goods and hobby stores. The advantage of this form of ownership for the owner is that he gets to be his own boss. For customers, the independent store can offer convenience, personal service, and lifestyle compatibility.[7]

Corporate Chain   A second form of ownership, the corporate chain, involves multiple outlets under common ownership. Macy's Inc., for example, operates 800 Macy's department stores in 45 states. Macy's also owns 37 Bloomingdale's, which compete with other chain stores such as Saks Fifth Avenue and Neiman Marcus. In a chain operation, centralization in decision making and purchasing is common. Chain stores have advantages in dealing with manufacturers, particularly as the size of the chain grows. A large chain can bargain with a manufacturer to obtain good service or volume discounts on orders. Target's large volume makes it a strong negotiator with manufacturers of most products. The buying power of chains is seen when consumers compare chain store prices with other types of stores. Consumers also benefit in dealing with chains because there are multiple outlets with similar merchandise and consistent management policies.

Retailing has become a high-tech business for many large chains. Walmart, for example, has developed a sophisticated inventory management and cost control system that allows rapid price changes for each product in every store. In addition, stores such as Walmart and Target are implementing pioneering new technologies such as radio

Subway is a popular business-format franchisor.

frequency identification (RFID) tags to improve the quality of information available about products.

Contractual Systems Contractual systems involve independently owned stores that band together to act like a chain. The three kinds described in Chapter 12 are retailer-sponsored cooperatives, wholesaler-sponsored voluntary chains, and franchises. One retailer-sponsored cooperative is the Associated Grocers, which consists of neighborhood grocers that all agree with several other independent grocers to buy their goods directly from food manufacturers. In this way, members can take advantage of volume discounts commonly available to chains and also give the impression of being a large chain, which may be viewed more favorably by some consumers. Wholesaler-sponsored voluntary chains such as Independent Grocers' Alliance (IGA) try to achieve similar benefits.

In a franchise system an individual or firm (the franchisee) contracts with a parent company (the franchisor) to set up a business or retail outlet. The franchisor usually assists in selecting the location, setting up the store or facility, advertising, and training personnel. The franchisee usually pays a onetime franchise fee and an annual royalty, usually tied to the franchise's sales. There are two general types of franchises: *business-format franchises*, such as McDonald's, Radio Shack, and Subway, and *product-distribution franchises*, such as a Ford dealership or a Coca-Cola distributor. In business-format franchising, the franchisor provides step-by-step procedures for most aspects of the business and guidelines for the most likely decisions a franchisee will face. In product-distribution franchising, the franchisor provides a few general guidelines and the franchisee is much more independent.

Franchise fees paid to the franchisor can range from $15,000 for a Subway franchise to $45,000 for a McDonald's restaurant franchise. When the fees are combined with other costs such as real estate and equipment, however, the total investment can be much higher. Franchisees also pay an ongoing royalty fee that ranges from 2 percent for a Sonic Drive-In to 30 percent for an H&R Block. By selling franchises, an organization reduces the cost of expansion but loses some control. A good franchisor, however, will maintain strong control of the outlets in terms of delivery and presentation of merchandise and try to enhance recognition of the franchise name.[8]

Level of Service

Even though most customers perceive little variation in retail outlets by form of ownership, differences among retailers are more obvious in terms of level of service. In some department stores, such as Loehmann's, very few services are provided. Some grocery stores, such as the Cub Foods chain, encourage customers to bag the food themselves. Other outlets, such as Neiman Marcus, provide a wide range of customer services from gift wrapping to wardrobe consultation.

Self-Service Self-service requires that customers perform many functions during the purchase process. Warehouse clubs such as Costco, for example, are usually self-service, with all nonessential customer services eliminated. Similarly, many gas stations, supermarkets, and airlines today have self-service lanes and terminals. Video retailer Redbox has more than 30,000 kiosks throughout the United States, without a single clerk. New forms of self-service are being developed at convenience stores, fast-food restaurants, and even libraries! In California, fully automated convenience stores that dispense gasoline, snacks, and hot coffee are being developed. At Pizza Hut you can place an order through an iPhone app or on the website. Similarly, the Palm Beach County library system has added self-service checkout machines at each of its branches. In general, the trend is toward retailing experiences that make customers co-creators of the value they receive.[9]

Limited Service Limited-service outlets provide some services, such as credit and merchandise return, but not others, such as clothing alterations. General merchandise stores such as Walmart, Kmart, and Target are usually considered limited service outlets. Customers are responsible for most shopping activities, although salespeople are available in departments such as consumer electronics, jewelry, and lawn and garden.

Full Service Full-service retailers, which include most specialty stores and department stores, provide many services to their customers. Neiman Marcus, Nordstrom, and Saks Fifth Avenue, for example, all rely on better service to sell more distinctive, higher-margin goods and to retain their customers. Nordstrom offers a wide variety of services, including free exchanges, easy returns, gift cards, credit cards through Nordstrom bank, a 7-days-a-week customer service line, a live chat line with beauty, design, and wedding specialists, online shopping with in-store pick-up, catalogs, and a four-level loyalty program called Nordstrom Fashion Rewards. Some Nordstrom stores also offer a "Personal Stylist" department, which provides shopping assistants for consumers who need help with style, color, and size selection, and a concierge service for assistance with anything else. Nordstrom stores typically have 50 percent more salespeople on the floor than similarly sized stores, and the salespeople are renowned for their professional and personalized attention to customers. Nordstrom also offers e-mail and RSS (Really Simple Syndication) feeds to notify customers when new merchandise is available, and it recently purchased an online retailer to offer its customers "flash sales."[10]

Type of Merchandise Line

Retail outlets also vary by their merchandise lines, the key distinction being the breadth and depth of the items offered to customers (see Figure 13–2). *Depth of product line* means the store carries a large assortment of each item, such as a shoe store that offers running shoes, dress shoes, and children's shoes. *Breadth of product line* refers to the variety of different items a store carries, such as appliances and books.

Depth of Line Stores that carry a considerable assortment (depth) of a related line of items are limited-line stores. Sports Authority sporting goods stores carry considerable depth in sports equipment ranging from weight-lifting accessories to running shoes. Stores that carry tremendous depth in one primary line of merchandise are single-line stores. Victoria's Secret, a nationwide chain, carries great depth in women's lingerie. Both limited- and single-line stores are often referred to as *specialty outlets*.

Specialty discount outlets focus on one type of product, such as electronics (Best Buy), office supplies (Staples), or books (Barnes and Noble), at very competitive prices. These outlets are referred to in the trade as *category killers* because they often dominate the market. Best Buy, for example, is the largest consumer electronics retailer with more than 1,000 stores.

Staples is the category killer in office supplies because it dominates the market in that category.

FIGURE 13–2

Stores vary in terms of the breadth and depth of their merchandise lines.

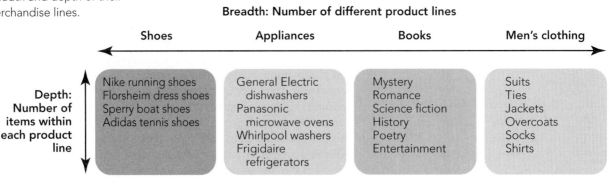

Breadth: Number of different product lines

Shoes	Appliances	Books	Men's clothing

Nike running shoes
Florsheim dress shoes
Sperry boat shoes
Adidas tennis shoes
	General Electric
	  dishwashers
	Panasonic
	  microwave ovens
	Whirlpool washers
	Frigidaire
	  refrigerators
		Mystery
		Romance
		Science fiction
		History
		Poetry
		Entertainment
			Suits
			Ties
			Jackets
			Overcoats
			Socks
			Shirts

Depth: Number of items within each product line

scrambled merchandising

Offering several unrelated product lines in a single retail store.

Breadth of Line Stores that carry a broad product line, with limited depth, are referred to as *general merchandise stores*. For example, large department stores such as Dillard's, Macy's, and Neiman Marcus carry a wide range of different types of products but not unusual sizes. The breadth and depth of merchandise lines are important decisions for a retailer. Traditionally, outlets carried related lines of goods. Today, however, **scrambled merchandising**, offering several unrelated product lines in a single store, is common. The modern drugstore carries food, camera equipment, magazines, paper products, toys, small hardware items, and pharmaceuticals. Supermarkets sell videos and flowers and print photos.

---

learning review

3. Centralized decision making and purchasing are an advantage of _____ ownership.

4. What are some examples of new forms of self-service retailers?

5. Would a shop for big men's clothes carrying pants in sizes 40 to 60 have a broad or deep product line?

NONSTORE RETAILING

LO3

Most of the retailing examples discussed thus far in the chapter, such as corporate chains, department stores, and limited- and single-line specialty stores, involve store retailing. Many retailing activities today, however, are not limited to sales in a store. Nonstore retailing occurs outside a retail outlet through activities that involve varying levels of customer and retailer involvement. The six forms of nonstore retailing are automatic vending, direct mail and catalogs, television home shopping, online retailing, telemarketing, and direct selling.

Vending machines offer a variety of products. Which types of products are most common in a vending machine? For the answer, see the text.

Automatic Vending

Nonstore retailing includes vending machines, or *v-commerce,* which make it possible to serve customers when and where stores cannot. Machine maintenance, operating costs, and location leases can add to the cost of the products, so prices in vending machines are often higher than those in stores. About 29 percent of the products sold from vending machines are cold beverages, another 19 percent are candy and snacks, and 6 percent are food. Many new types of products are quickly becoming available in vending machines. Best Buy now uses vending machines to sell mobile phone and computer accessories, digital cameras, flash drives, and other consumer electronics products in airports, hospitals, and businesses. Similarly, Healthy You Vending manufactures machines designed to distribute healthy drinks, snacks, and entrees in offices, health clubs, hospitals, schools, and colleges. The 5.4 million vending machines currently in use in the United States generate about $19 billion in annual sales.[11]

Improved technology is making v-commerce easier to use. Many vending machines now have touch screens and credit card readers. In addition, some vending machine companies are testing wireless technology to allow consumers to make vending machine purchases using their mobile phones. Wireless technology is also being used by companies to monitor sales; this information is used to schedule trips to restock machines when items are sold out. Another improvement in vending machines is the trend toward "green" machines, which consume less energy by using more efficient compressors, more efficient lighting, and better insulation. For today's consumers, vending machines represent an extension of brands that are already available in stores, through catalogs, and online.[12]

Specialty catalogs appeal to market niches. They create value by providing a fast and convenient way to shop.

QR 13–2
IKEA Video

Direct Mail and Catalogs

Direct-mail and catalog retailing has been called "the store that comes to the door." It is attractive for several reasons. First, it can eliminate the cost of a store and clerks. Dell, for example, is one of the largest computer and information technology retailers, and it does not have any stores. Second, direct mail and catalogs improve marketing efficiency through segmentation and targeting, and they create customer value by providing a fast and convenient means of making a purchase. Finally, many catalogs now serve as a tool to encourage consumers to visit a website, a social media page, or even a store. Online retailers such as Zappos, Amazon, and eBay, for example, now offer catalogs. The average U.S. household today receives 24 direct-mail items or catalogs each week. The Direct Marketing Association estimates that direct-mail and catalog retailing creates $669 billion in sales. Direct-mail and catalog retailing is popular outside the United States, also. Furniture retailer IKEA delivered 190 million copies of its catalog in 25 languages to 35 countries last year.[13]

Several factors have had an impact on direct-mail and catalog retailing in recent years. The influence of large retailers such as IKEA, Crate and Barrel, L.L. Bean, and others has been positive as their marketing activities have increased the number and variety of products consumers purchase through direct mail and catalogs. Higher paper costs and increases in postage rates, the growing interest in do-not-mail legislation, the concern for "green" mailings and catalogs, and the possibility of the U.S. Postal Service reducing delivery to five days, however, have caused direct-mail and catalog retailers to search for ways to provide additional customer value. One approach has been to send specialty catalogs to market niches identified in their databases. L.L. Bean, for example, has developed an individual catalog for fly-fishing enthusiasts.[14]

Television Home Shopping

Television home shopping is possible when consumers watch a shopping channel on which products are displayed; orders are then placed over the telephone or the Internet. Currently, the three largest programs are QVC, HSN, and ShopNBC. QVC ("quality, value, convenience") broadcasts live 24 hours each day, 364 days a year, and reaches 200 million cable and satellite homes in the United States, United Kingdom, Germany, Japan, and Italy. The company generates sales of $8.3 billion from its 70 million customers by offering more than 1,150 products each week.[15]

Television home shopping programs serve millions of customers each year. See the text to learn how they are attracting new customers.

In the past, television home shopping programs have attracted mostly 40- to 60-year-old women. To begin to attract a younger audience, QVC has invited celebrities onto the show. For example, Kim, Khloe, and Kourtney Kardashian have been hosts selling their apparel line. Broadcasting live acts such as LeAnn Rimes also help attract new customers. The shopping programs are also using other forms of retailing. In addition to its television program, QVC has two types of retail stores: a studio store at its headquarters and six outlet stores. Similarly, the Home Shopping Network now offers retail experiences on TV, online, in catalogs, and in stores. Finally, several television shopping programs are developing online platforms, which may attract as many as 50 percent of all new customers, and interactive technology that allows viewers to place orders using their remote control rather than the telephone.[16]

Online Retailing

Online retailing allows consumers to search for, evaluate, and order products through the Internet. For many consumers the advantages of this form of retailing are the 24-hour access, the ability to comparison shop, in-home privacy, and variety. Traditional and online retailers—"bricks and clicks"—are melding, using experiences from both approaches to create better value and experiences for customers. For example, Walmart (www.walmart.com) recently introduced its "Pick Up Today" service that allows customers to order online and receive free same-day pickup at a local store. In addition, Walmart offers its Site-to-Store service for online items not available in stores as well as free shipping for pick up at a FedEx office. The Walmart Mobile app allows shoppers to browse and order products using their smartphones. Two of the biggest days for online retailing are the Friday after Thanksgiving—Black Friday—and the Monday after Thanksgiving—Cyber Monday—which recently generated $816 million and $1.25 billion, respectively. Online sales account for approximately 9 percent of all retail sales and are expected to reach $327 billion in 2016.[17]

Online retail purchases can be the result of several very different approaches. First, consumers can pay dues to become a member of an online discount service such as www.netMarket.com. The service offers thousands of products and hundreds of brand names at very low prices to its 25 million subscribers. Another approach to online retailing is to use a shopping "bot" such as www.mysimon.com. This site searches the Internet for a product specified by the consumer and provides a report on the locations of the best prices available. Consumers can also use the Internet to go directly to online malls (www.fashionmall.com), apparel retailers (www.gap.com), bookstores (www.amazon.com), computer manufacturers (www.dell.com), grocery stores (www.peapod.com), music and video stores (www.tower.com), and travel agencies (www.travelocity.com). A final approach to online retailing is the online auction, such as www.ebay.com, where consumers bid on more than 50,000 categories of products.[18]

Shopping "bots" like mysimon.com find the best prices for products specified by consumers.

One of the biggest problems online retailers face is that nearly two-thirds of online shoppers make it to "checkout" and then leave the website to compare shipping costs and prices on other sites. Of the shoppers who leave, 70 percent do not return. One way online retailers are addressing this issue is to offer consumers a comparison of competitors' offerings. At allbookstores.com, for example, consumers can use a "comparison engine" to compare prices with amazon.com, barnesandnoble.com, and as many as 25 other bookstores. Experts suggest that online retailers should think of their websites as dynamic billboards and be visible to search engines if they are

to attract and retain customers.[19] Online retailers are also trying to improve the online retailing experience by adding experiential or interactive activities to their websites. Similarly, car manufacturers such as BMW, Mercedes, and Jaguar encourage website visitors to "build" a vehicle by selecting interior and exterior colors, packages, and options and then view the customized virtual car.

Telemarketing

Another form of nonstore retailing, called **telemarketing**, involves using the telephone to interact with and sell directly to consumers. Compared with direct mail, telemarketing is often viewed as a more efficient means of targeting consumers. Insurance companies, brokerage firms, and newspapers have often used this form of retailing as a way to cut costs but still maintain access to their customers. According to the Direct Marketing Association, annual telemarketing sales exceed $305 billion.[20]

The telemarketing industry has recently gone through dramatic changes as a result of new legislation related to telephone solicitations. Issues such as consumer privacy, industry standards, and ethical guidelines have encouraged discussion among consumers, Congress, the Federal Trade Commission, and businesses. The result was legislation that created the National Do-Not-Call registry (www.donotcall.gov) for consumers who do not want to receive telephone calls related to company sales efforts. Currently, there are more than 209 million phone numbers on the registry. Companies that use telemarketing have already adapted by adding compliance software to ensure that numbers on the list are not called.[21]

Direct Selling

QR 13–3
Mary Kay
Video

Direct selling, sometimes called door-to-door retailing, involves direct sales of goods and services to consumers through personal interactions and demonstrations in their home or office. A variety of companies, including familiar names such as Avon, Fuller Brush, Mary Kay Cosmetics, and World Book, have created an industry with more than $30 billion in U.S. sales by providing consumers with personalized service and convenience. In the United States, there are more than 16 million direct salespeople working full-time and part-time in 70 product categories.[22]

Growth in the direct-selling industry is the result of two trends. First, many direct-selling retailers are expanding into markets outside of the United States. Avon, for example, has 6.4 million sales representatives in 100 countries. Approximately one-third of Amway's $11 billion in sales now comes from China.[23] The second trend is the growing number of companies that are using direct selling to reach consumers who prefer one-on-one customer service and a social shopping experience rather than online shopping or big discount stores. The Direct Selling Association reports that the number of companies using direct selling has increased by 30 percent in the past five years. Pampered Chef, for example, has 60,000 independent sales reps who sell the company's products at in-home kitchen parties. Interest among potential sales representatives has grown during the recent economic downturn as people seek independence and control of their work activities.[24]

---

learning review

6. Successful catalog retailers often send _____ catalogs to _____ markets identified in their databases.

7. How are retailers increasing consumer interest and involvement in online retailing?

8. Where are direct selling retail sales growing? Why?

RETAILING STRATEGY

LO4

This section describes how a retailer develops and implements a retailing strategy. In developing a retailing strategy, managers work with the **retailing mix**, which includes activities related to managing the store and the merchandise in the store. The retailing mix is shown in Figure 13–3. It is similar to the marketing mix and includes retail pricing, store location, retail communication, and merchandise.

retailing mix
The activities related to managing the store and the merchandise in the store, which includes retail pricing, store location, retail communication, and merchandise.

Retail Pricing

In setting prices for merchandise, retailers must decide on the markup, markdown, and timing for markdowns. The *markup* refers to how much should be added to the cost the retailer paid for a product to reach the final selling price. Retailers decide on the *original markup*, but by the time the product is sold, they end up with a *maintained markup*. The original markup is the difference between retailer cost and initial selling price. When products do not sell as quickly as anticipated, their price is reduced. The difference between the final selling price and retailer cost is the maintained markup, which is also called the *gross margin*.

Discounting a product, or taking a *markdown*, occurs when the product does not sell at the original price and an adjustment is necessary. Often new models or styles force the price of existing models to be marked down. Discounts may also be used to increase demand for complementary products.[25] For example, retailers might take a markdown on the price of cake mix to generate frosting purchases. The *timing* of a markdown can be important. Many retailers take a markdown as soon as sales fall off to free up valuable selling space and cash. However, other stores delay markdowns to discourage bargain hunters and maintain an image of quality. There is no clear answer, but retailers must consider how the timing might affect future sales. Research indicates that frequent promotions increase consumers' ability to remember regular prices.[26]

Although most retailers plan markdowns, many retailers use price discounts as a part of their regular merchandising policy. Walmart and Home Depot, for example, emphasize consistently low prices and eliminate most markdowns with a strategy often called *everyday low pricing* (EDLP).[27] Because consumers often use price as an indicator of product quality, however, the brand name of the product and the image of the store become important decision factors in these situations.[28] Another strategy, *everyday fair pricing*, is advocated by retailers that may not offer the lowest price but try to create value for customers through service and the total buying experience.[29] Consumers often use the prices of *benchmark* or *signpost* items, such as a can of Coke, to form an

Walmart uses an Everyday Low Pricing strategy to attract shoppers to its stores.

FIGURE 13–3
Retailing strategy is related to store positioning and the retailing mix. Note the similarity between the retailing mix and the marketing mix.

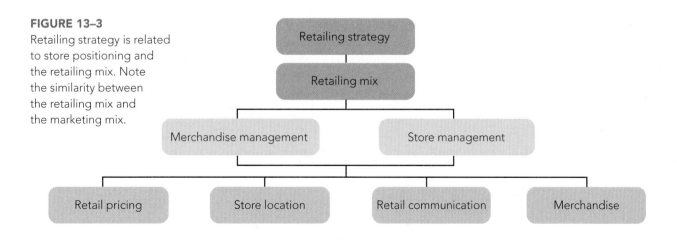

T.J. Maxx is a popular off-price retailer where prices are low but selection may be unpredictable.

overall impression of the store's prices.[30] In addition, price is the most likely factor to influence consumers' assessment of merchandise value.[31] When store prices are based on rebates, retailers must be careful to avoid negative consumer perceptions if the rebate processing time is long (e.g., six weeks).[32]

Off-price retailing is a retail pricing practice that is used by retailers such as T.J. Maxx, Burlington Coat Factory, and Ross Stores. *Off-price retailing* involves selling brand-name merchandise at lower than regular prices. The difference between the off-price retailer and a discount store is that off-price merchandise is bought by the retailer from manufacturers with excess inventory at prices below wholesale prices. The discounter, however, buys at full wholesale prices but takes less of a markup than traditional department stores. Because of this difference in the way merchandise is purchased by the retailer, selection at an off-price retailer is unpredictable, and searching for bargains has become a popular activity for many consumers. "It's more like a sport than it is like ordinary shopping," says Christopher Boring of Columbus, Ohio's Retail Planning Associates.[33] Savings to the consumer at off-price retailers are reportedly as high as 70 percent off the prices of a traditional department store. A variation of off-price retailing includes outlet stores such as Nordstrom Rack and Off 5th (Saks Fifth Avenue outlet) which allow retailers to sell excess merchandise and still maintain an image of offering merchandise at full price in their primary store.

Off 5th provides an outlet for excess merchandise from Saks Fifth Avenue.

Store Location

A second aspect of the retailing mix involves deciding where to locate the store and how many stores to have. Department stores, which started downtown in most cities, have followed customers to the suburbs, and in recent years more stores have been opened in large regional malls. Most stores today are near several others in one of four settings: the central business district, the regional shopping center, the strip mall, or the power center.

The *central business district* is the oldest retail setting, the community's downtown area. Until the regional outflow to suburbs, it was the major shopping area, but the suburban population has grown at the expense of the downtown shopping area. Consumers often view central business district shopping as less convenient because of lack of parking, higher crime rates, and exposure to the weather. Many cities such as Louisville, Denver, and San Antonio have implemented plans to revitalize shopping in central business districts by attracting new offices, entertainment, and residents to downtown locations.

Regional shopping centers consist of 50 to 150 stores that typically attract customers who live or work within a 5- to 10-mile range. These large shopping areas often contain two or three *anchor stores*, which are well-known national or regional stores such as Sears, Saks Fifth Avenue, and Bloomingdale's. The largest variation of a regional center in North America is the West Edmonton Mall in Alberta, Canada. This shopping center is a conglomerate of more than 800 stores, the world's largest indoor amusement park, more than 100 restaurants, a movie complex, and two hotels, all of which attract 30 million visitors each year.[34]

Not every suburban store is located in a shopping mall. Many neighborhoods have clusters of stores, referred to as a *strip mall,* to serve people who are within a 5- to 10-minute drive. Gas station, hardware, laundry, grocery, and pharmacy outlets are commonly found in a strip mall. Unlike the larger shopping centers, the composition of these stores is usually unplanned. A variation of the strip mall is called the *power center,* which is a huge shopping strip with multiple anchor (or national) stores such as Home Depot, Best Buy, or JCPenney. Power centers are seen as having the convenient location found in many strip malls and the additional power of national stores. These large strip malls often have two to five anchor stores and often contain a supermarket, which brings the shopper to the power center on a weekly basis.[35]

The many retailing formats described in this chapter represent an exciting menu of choices for creating customer value in the marketplace. Each format allows retailers to offer unique benefits and meet the particular needs of various customer groups. While each format has many successful applications, retailers in the future are likely to combine many of the formats to offer a broader spectrum of benefits and experiences and to appeal to different segments of consumers.[36] These **multichannel retailers** will utilize and integrate a combination of traditional store formats and nonstore formats such as catalogs, television, home shopping, and online retailing.[37] Barnes & Noble, for example, has created barnesandnoble.com to compete with amazon.com. Similarly, Office Depot has integrated its store, catalog, and Internet operations.

multichannel retailers
Retailers that use a combination of traditional store formats and nonstore formats, such as catalogs, television, and online retailing.

Retail Communication

A retailer's communication activities can play an important role in positioning a store and creating its image. While the typical elements of communication and promotion are discussed in Chapter 15 on advertising, sales promotion, and public relations, Chapter 16 on social media, and Chapter 17 on personal selling, the message communicated by the many other elements of the retailing mix is also important.

Deciding on the image of a retail outlet is an important retailing mix factor that has been widely recognized and studied since the late 1950s. Pierre Martineau described image as "the way in which the store is defined in the shopper's mind," partly by its functional qualities and partly by an aura of psychological attributes.[38] In this definition, *functional* refers to mix elements such as price ranges, store layouts, and breadth and depth of merchandise lines. The psychological attributes are the intangibles such as a sense of belonging, excitement, style, or warmth. Image has been found to include impressions of the corporation that operates the store, the category or type of store, the product categories in the store, the brands in each category, merchandise and service quality, and the marketing activities of the store.[39]

Closely related to the concept of image is the store's atmosphere or ambience. Many retailers believe that sales are affected by layout, color, lighting, music, and other elements of the retail environment. This concept leads many retailers to use **shopper marketing**—the use of displays, coupons, product samples, and other brand communications to influence shopping behavior in a store. Shopper marketing can also influence behavior in an online shopping environment and when shoppers use smartphone apps to identify shopping needs or make purchase decisions.[40] In creating the right image and atmosphere, a retail store tries to attract a target audience and fortify beliefs about the store, its products, and the shopping experience in the store. While store image perceptions can exist independently of shopping experiences, consumers' shopping experiences also influence their perceptions of a store.[41] In addition, the physical surroundings also influence a store's employees.[42]

shopper marketing
The use of displays, coupons, product samples, and other brand communications to influence shopping behavior in a store.

Merchandise

A final element of the retailing mix is the merchandise offering. Managing the breadth and depth of the product line requires retail buyers who are familiar with the needs of the target market and the alternative products available from the many manufacturers that might be interested in having a product available in the store. A popular approach to managing the assortment of merchandise today is called **category management**. This approach assigns a manager the responsibility for selecting all products that consumers in a market segment might view as substitutes for each other, with the objective of maximizing sales and profits in the category. For example, a category manager might be responsible for shoes in a department store or paper products in a grocery store, and would consider trade deals, order costs, and the between-brand effects of price range changes to determine brand assortment, order quantities, and prices.[43]

category management
An approach to managing the assortment of merchandise that maximizes sales and profits.

Retailers have a variety of marketing metrics that can be used to assess the effectiveness of a store or retail format. First, there are measures related to customers such as the number of transactions per customer, the average transaction size per customer, the number of customers per day or per hour, and the average length of a store visit. Second, there are measures related to products such as number of returns, inventory

Using Marketing Dashboards

Why Apple Stores May Be the Best in the United States!

How effective is my retail format compared to other stores? How are my stores performing this year compared to last year? Information related to this question is often displayed in a marketing dashboard using two measures: (1) sales per square foot, and (2) same-store sales growth.

Your Challenge You have been assigned to evaluate the Apple Store retail format. The store's simple, inviting, and open atmosphere has been the topic of discussion among many retailers. Apple, however, is relatively new to the retailing business and many experts have been skeptical of the format. To allow an assessment of Apple Stores, use *sales per square foot* as an indicator of how effectively retail space is used to generate revenue and *same-store sales growth* to compare the increase in sales of stores that have been open for the same period of time. The calculations for these two indicators are:

$$\text{Sales per square foot} = \frac{\text{Total sales}}{\text{Selling area in square feet}}$$

Same-store sales growth

$$= \frac{\text{Store sales in year 2} - \text{Store sales in year 1}}{\text{Store sales in year 1}}$$

Your Findings You decide to collect sales information for Target, Neiman Marcus, Best Buy, Tiffany, and Apple stores to allow comparisons with other successful retailers. The information you collect allows the calculation of *sales per square foot* and *same-store growth* for each store. The results are then easy to compare in the graphs below.

Your Action The results of your investigation indicate that in terms of sales per square foot, Apple Stores are higher than any of the comparison stores at $5,348. In addition, Apple's same-store growth rate of 44.2 percent is higher than all of the other retailers. You conclude that the elements of Apple's format are very effective and even indicate that Apple may currently be the best retailer in the United States.

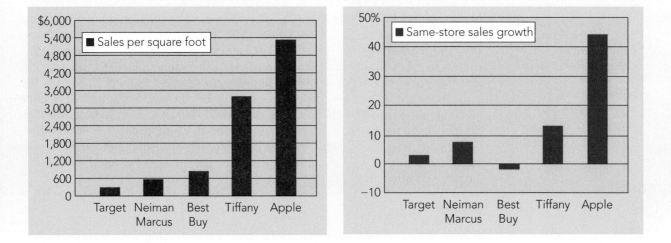

turnover, inventory carrying cost, and average number of items per transaction. Finally, there are financial measures, such as gross margin, sales per employee, return on sales, and markdown percentage.[44] The two most popular measures for retailers are *sales per square foot* and *same-store sales growth*. The Using Marketing Dashboards box describes the calculation of these measures for Apple Stores.[45]

learning review	**9.** How does original markup differ from maintained markup?
	10. A huge shopping strip mall with multiple anchor stores is a _____ center.
	11. What is a popular approach to managing the assortment of merchandise in a store?

THE CHANGING NATURE OF RETAILING

Retailing is the most dynamic aspect of a channel of distribution. New types of retailers are always entering the market, searching for a new position that will attract customers. The reason for this continual change is explained by two concepts: the wheel of retailing and the retail life cycle.

The Wheel of Retailing

The **wheel of retailing** describes how new forms of retail outlets enter the market.[46] Usually they enter as low-status, low-margin stores such as a drive-in hamburger stand with no indoor seating and a limited menu (Figure 13–4, box 1). Gradually these outlets add fixtures and more embellishments to their stores (in-store seating, plants, and chicken sandwiches as well as hamburgers) to increase the attractiveness for customers. With these additions, prices and status rise (box 2). As time passes, these outlets add still more services and their prices and status increase even further (box 3). These retail outlets now face some new form of retail outlet that again appears as a low-status, low-margin operator (box 4), and the wheel of retailing turns as the cycle starts to repeat itself.

When Ray Kroc bought McDonald's in 1955, it opened shortly before lunch and closed just after dinner, offering a limited menu for the two meals without any inside seating for customers. Over time, the wheel of retailing has led to new products and services. In 1975, McDonald's introduced the Egg McMuffin and turned breakfast into a fast-food meal. Today, McDonald's offers an extensive menu, including oatmeal and premium coffee, and it provides seating and services such as wireless Internet connections. For the future, McDonald's is testing new products, such as oven-baked Texas chicken skewers, a chicken parmesan burger, and blueberry McGriddles, and new formats, such as touchscreen ordering and table service![47]

These changes are leaving room for new forms of outlets such as Checkers Drive-In Restaurants. The chain opened fast-food stores that offered only basics—burgers, fries, and cola, a drive-through window, and no inside seating—and now has more than 800 stores. The wheel is turning for other outlets, too—Boston Market has added pick-up, delivery, and full-service catering to its original restaurant format, and it also provides Boston Market meal solutions through supermarket delis and Boston Market frozen meals in the frozen food

Outlets such as Checkers enter the wheel of retailing as low-status, low-margin stores.

FIGURE 13–4
The wheel of retailing describes how retail outlets change. Read the text to learn how retailers like McDonald's follow the cycle.

FIGURE 13–5
The retail life cycle describes
stages of growth and decline
for retail outlets.

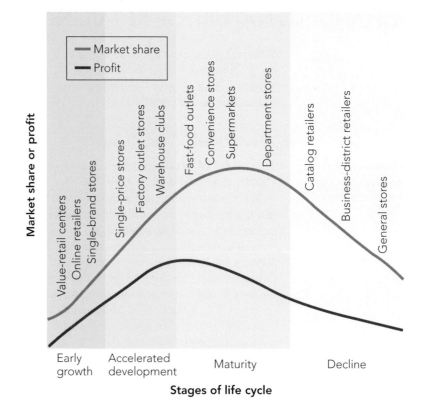

Stages of life cycle

QR 13–4
Checkers Video

sections of groceries. For still others, the wheel has come full circle. Taco Bell is now opening small, limited-offering outlets in gas stations, discount stores, or "wherever a burrito and a mouth might possibly intersect."[48]

The Retail Life Cycle

The process of growth and decline that retail outlets, like products, experience is described by the **retail life cycle**.[49] Figure 13–5 shows the retail life cycle and the position of various current forms of retail outlets on it. Early growth is the stage of emergence of a retail outlet, with a sharp departure from existing competition. Market share rises gradually, although profits may be low because of start-up costs. In the next stage, accelerated development, both market share and profit achieve their greatest growth rates. Usually multiple outlets are established as companies focus on the distribution element of the retailing mix. In this stage, some later competitors may enter. Wendy's, for example, appeared on the hamburger chain scene almost 20 years after McDonald's had begun operation. The key goal for the retailer in this stage is to establish a dominant position in the fight for market share.

The battle for market share is usually fought before the maturity stage, and some competitors drop out of the market. In the war among hamburger chains, Jack in the Box, Gino's Hamburgers, and Burger Chef used to be more dominant outlets. New retail forms, such as Fatburger and In-N-Out Burger in the hamburger chain market, enter in the maturity stage, stores try to maintain their market share, and price discounting occurs.

retail life cycle

The process of growth and decline that retail outlets experience over time.

---

learning review

12. According to the wheel of retailing, when a new retail form appears, how would you characterize its image?

13. Market share is usually fought out before the _____ stage of the retail life cycle.

WHOLESALING

Many retailers depend on intermediaries that engage in wholesaling activities—selling products and services for the purposes of resale or business use. There are several types of intermediaries, including wholesalers and agents (described briefly in Chapter 12), as well as manufacturers' sales offices, which are important to understand as part of the retailing process.

Merchant Wholesalers

merchant wholesalers
Independently owned firms that take title to the merchandise they handle.

Merchant wholesalers are independently owned firms that take title to the merchandise they handle. They go by various names, including industrial distributor. Most firms engaged in wholesaling activities are merchant wholesalers.

Merchant wholesalers are classified as either full-service or limited-service wholesalers, depending on the number of functions performed. Two major types of full-service wholesalers exist. *General merchandise* (or *full-line*) *wholesalers* carry a broad assortment of merchandise and perform all channel functions. This type of wholesaler is most prevalent in the hardware, drug, and clothing industries. However, these wholesalers do not maintain much depth of assortment within specific product lines. *Specialty merchandise* (or *limited-line*) *wholesalers* offer a relatively narrow range of products but have an extensive assortment within the product lines carried. They perform all channel functions and are found in the health foods, automotive parts, and seafood industries.

Four major types of limited-service wholesalers exist. *Rack jobbers* furnish the racks or shelves that display merchandise in retail stores, perform all channel functions, and sell on consignment to retailers, which means they retain the title to the products displayed and bill retailers only for the merchandise sold. Familiar products such as hosiery, toys, housewares, and health and beauty items are sold by rack jobbers. *Cash and carry wholesalers* take title to merchandise but sell only to buyers who call on them, pay cash for merchandise, and furnish their own transportation for merchandise. They carry a limited product assortment and do not make deliveries, extend credit, or supply market information. This wholesaler is common in electric supplies, office supplies, hardware products, and groceries.

Drop shippers, or *desk jobbers*, are wholesalers that own the merchandise they sell but do not physically handle, stock, or deliver it. They simply solicit orders from retailers and other wholesalers and have the merchandise shipped directly from a producer to a buyer. Drop shippers are used for bulky products such as coal, lumber, and chemicals, which are sold in extremely large quantities. *Truck jobbers* are small wholesalers that have a small warehouse from which they stock their trucks for distribution to retailers. They usually handle limited assortments of fast-moving or perishable items that are sold for cash directly from trucks in their original packages. Truck jobbers handle products such as bakery items, dairy products, and meat.

Agents and Brokers

Unlike merchant wholesalers, agents and brokers do not take title to merchandise and typically perform fewer channel functions. They make their profit from commissions or fees paid for their services, whereas merchant wholesalers make their profit from the sale of the merchandise they own.

manufacturer's agents
Agents who work for several producers and carry noncompetitive, complementary merchandise in an exclusive territory.

Manufacturer's agents and selling agents are the two major types of agents used by producers. **Manufacturer's agents**, or *manufacturer's representatives*, work for several producers and carry noncompetitive, complementary merchandise in an exclusive territory. Manufacturer's agents act as a producer's sales arm in a territory and are principally responsible for the transactional channel functions, primarily selling. They are used extensively in the automotive supply, footwear, and fabricated steel industries.

By comparison, *selling agents* represent a single producer and are responsible for the entire marketing function of that producer. They design promotional plans, set prices, determine distribution policies, and make recommendations on product strategy. Selling agents are used by small producers in the textile, apparel, food, and home furnishing industries.

brokers

Independent firms or individuals whose main function is to bring buyers and sellers together to make sales.

Brokers are independent firms or individuals whose principal function is to bring buyers and sellers together to make sales. Brokers, unlike agents, usually have no continuous relationship with the buyer or seller but negotiate a contract between two parties and then move on to another task. Brokers are used extensively by producers of seasonal products (such as fruits and vegetables) and in the real estate industry.

A unique broker that acts in many ways like a manufacturer's agent is a food broker, representing buyers and sellers in the grocery industry. Food brokers differ from conventional brokers because they act on behalf of producers on a permanent basis and receive a commission for their services. For example, Nabisco uses food brokers to sell its candies, margarine, and Planters peanuts, but it sells its line of cookies and crackers directly to retail stores.

Manufacturer's Branches and Offices

Unlike merchant wholesalers, agents, and brokers, manufacturer's branches and sales offices are wholly owned extensions of the producer that perform wholesaling activities. Producers assume wholesaling functions when there are no intermediaries to perform these activities, customers are few in number and geographically concentrated, or orders are large or require significant attention. A *manufacturer's branch office* carries a producer's inventory and performs the functions of a full-service wholesaler. A *manufacturer's sales office* does not carry inventory, typically performs only a sales function, and serves as an alternative to agents and brokers.

---

learning review

14. What is the difference between merchant wholesalers and agents?

15. Under what circumstances do producers assume wholesaling functions?

LEARNING OBJECTIVES REVIEW

LO1 *Identify retailers in terms of the utilities they provide.*
Retailers provide time, place, form, and possession utilities. Time utility is provided by stores with convenient time-of-day (e.g., open 24 hours) or time-of-year (e.g., seasonal sports equipment available all year) availability. Place utility is provided by the number and location of the stores. Possession utility is provided by making a purchase possible (e.g., financing) or easier (e.g., delivery). Form utility is provided by producing or altering a product to meet the customer's specifications (e.g., custom-made shirts).

LO2 *Explain the alternative ways to classify retail outlets.*
Retail outlets can be classified by their form of ownership, level of service, and type of merchandise line. The forms of ownership include independent retailers, corporate chains, and contractual systems that include retailer-sponsored cooperatives, wholesaler-sponsored voluntary chains, and franchises. The levels of service include self-service, limited-service, and full-service outlets. Stores classified by their merchandise line include stores with depth, such as sporting goods specialty stores, and stores with breadth, such as large department stores.

LO3 *Describe the many methods of nonstore retailing.*
Nonstore retailing includes automatic vending, direct mail and catalogs, television home shopping, online retailing, telemarketing, and direct selling. The methods of nonstore retailing vary by the level of involvement of the retailer and the level of involvement of the customer. Vending, for example, has low involvement, whereas both the consumer and the retailer have high involvement in direct selling.

LO4 *Specify the retailing mix actions used to implement a retailing strategy.*
Retailing mix actions are used to manage a retail store and the merchandise in a store. The mix variables include pricing, store location, communication activities, and merchandise. Two common forms of assessment for retailers are "sales per square foot" and "same-store growth."

LO5 *Explain changes in retailing with the wheel of retailing and the retail life cycle concepts.*
The wheel of retailing concept explains how retail outlets typically enter the market as low-status, low-margin stores. Over time,

stores gradually add new products and services, increasing their prices, status, and margins, and leaving an opening for new low-status, low-margin stores. The retail life cycle describes the process of growth and decline for retail outlets through four stages: early growth, accelerated development, maturity, and decline.

LO6 *Describe the types of firms that perform wholesaling activities and their functions.*
There are three types of firms that perform wholesaling functions. First, merchant wholesalers are independently owned and take title to merchandise. They include general merchandise wholesalers, specialty merchandise wholesalers, rack jobbers, cash and carry wholesalers, drop shippers, and truck jobbers and can perform a variety of channel functions. Second, agents and brokers do not take title to merchandise and primarily perform marketing functions. Finally, manufacturer's branches, which may carry inventory, and sales offices, which perform sales functions, are wholly owned by the producer.

FOCUSING ON KEY TERMS

APPLYING MARKETING KNOWLEDGE

1 Discuss the impact of changes in household income on (*a*) nonstore retailing and (*b*) the retail mix.

2 In retail pricing, retailers often have a maintained markup. Explain how this maintained markup differs from original markup and why it is so important.

3 What are the similarities and differences between the product and retail life cycles?

4 How would you classify Walmart in terms of its position on the wheel of retailing versus that of an off-price retailer?

5 Develop a chart to highlight the role of each of the four main elements of the retailing mix across the four stages of the retail life cycle.

6 Breadth and depth are two important components in distinguishing among types of retailers. Discuss the breadth and depth implications of the following retailers discussed in this chapter: (*a*) Nordstrom, (*b*) Walmart, (*c*) IKEA, and (*d*) Best Buy.

7 According to the wheel of retailing and the retail life cycle, what will happen to factory outlet stores?

8 The text discusses the development of online retailing in the United States. How does the development of this retailing form agree with the implications of the retail life cycle?

9 Comment on this statement: The only distinction among merchant wholesalers and agents and brokers is that merchant wholesalers take title to the products they sell.

building your marketing plan

Does your marketing plan involve using retailers? If the answer is "no," read no further and do not include a retailing element in your plan. If the answer is "yes":

1 Use Figure 13–3 to develop your retailing strategy by specifying the details of the retailing mix.

2 Describe an appropriate combination of retail pricing, store location, retail communication, and merchandise assortment.

3 Confirm that the wholesalers needed to support your retailing strategy are consistent with the channels and intermediaries you selected in Chapter 12.

video case 13 Mall of America®: Shopping and a Whole Lot More

QR 13–5
Mall of America
Video Case

"If you build it, they will come" not only worked in the movie *Field of Dreams* but also applies—big time—to Mall of America®.

Located in a suburb of Minneapolis, Mall of America (www.mallofamerica.com) is the largest completely enclosed retail and family-entertainment complex in the United States. "We're more than a mall, we're a destination," explains Maureen Cahill, executive vice president at Mall of America. More than 100,000 people each day—40 million visitors each year—visit the one-stop complex offering retail shopping, guest services, convenience, a huge variety of entertainment, and fun for all. "Guest services" include everything from high school classrooms to a wedding chapel.

THE CONCEPT AND CHALLENGE

The idea for Mall of America came from the West Edmonton Mall in Alberta, Canada. The Ghermezian Brothers, who developed that mall, sought to create a unique mall that would attract not only local families but also tourists from the Upper Midwest, the nation, and even from abroad.

The two challenges for Mall of America: How can it (1) attract and keep the large number of retail establishments needed to (2) continue to attract even more millions of visitors than today? A big part of the answer is in Mall of America's positioning—"A place for fun!"

THE STAGGERING SIZE AND OFFERINGS

Opened August 1992 amid tremendous worldwide publicity, Mall of America faced skeptics who had their doubts because of its size, its unique retail-entertainment mix, and the nationwide recession. Despite these concerns, it opened with more than 80 percent of its space leased and attracted more than 1 million visitors its first week.

Mall of America is 4.2 million square feet, the equivalent of 88 football fields. This makes it three to four times the size of most other regional malls. It includes four anchor department stores: Nordstrom, Macy's, Bloomingdale's, and Sears. It also includes more than 520 specialty stores, from Armani Exchange to DSW Shoe Warehouse. Approximately 36 percent of Mall of America's space is devoted to anchors and 64 percent to specialty stores. This makes the space allocation the reverse of most regional malls.

The retail-entertainment mix of Mall of America is incredibly diverse. For example, there are more than 165 apparel and accessory stores, 14 jewelry stores, and 26 shoe stores. Two food courts with 27 restaurants plus more than 20 other restaurants scattered throughout the building meet most food preferences of visitors. Another surprise: Mall of America is home to many "concept stores," where retailers introduce a new type of store or design. In addition, it has an entrepreneurial program for people with an innovative retail idea and limited resources. They can open a kiosk, wall unit, or small store for a specified time period or as a temporary seasonal tenant.

Unique features of Mall of America include:

- Nickelodeon Universe®, a seven-acre theme park with more than 30 attractions and rides, including a roller coaster, Ferris wheel, and games in a glass-enclosed, skylighted area with more than 400 trees.
- Sea Life® Minnesota aquarium, where visitors are surrounded by sharks, stingrays, and sea turtles; can adventure among fish native to the north woods; and can discover what lurks at the bottom of the Mississippi River.
- Entertainment choices that include a 14-screen theater, A.C.E.S. Flight Simulation, the Amazing Mirror Maze, and Moose Mountain Adventure Golf.
- The House of Comedy, featuring comedians from Last Comic Standing, Saturday Night Live, and Just for Laughs.

As a host to corporate events and private parties, Mall of America has a rotunda that opens to all four floors facilitating presentations, demonstrations, and exhibits. Organizations such as PepsiCo, Visa-USA, and Ford have used the facilities to gain shopper awareness. Mall of America is a rectangle with the anchor department stores at the corners and amusement park in the skylighted central area, making it easy for shoppers to understand and navigate. It has 12,550 free parking ramp spaces on site and another 7,000 spaces nearby during peak times.

THE MARKET

The Minneapolis–St. Paul metropolitan area is a market with more than 3 million people. A total of 30 million people live within a day's drive of Mall of America. A survey of its shoppers showed that 32 percent of the shoppers travel 150 miles or more and account for more than 50 percent of the sales revenues. Located three miles

from the Minneapolis/St. Paul International Airport, Mall of America has a light-rail service from the airport and downtown Minneapolis available.

Tourism accounts for 4 out of 10 visits to Mall of America. About 6 percent of visitors come from outside the United States. Some come just to see and experience Mall of America, while others take advantage of the cost savings available on goods (Japan) or taxes (Canada and states with sales taxes on clothing).

THE FUTURE: FACING THE CHALLENGES

Where is Mall of America headed in the future? "Mall of America is one of the most recognized brands in the world," Cahill says. "They might not know where we are sometimes, but they've heard of Mall of America and they know they want to come.

"What we've learned since 1992 is to keep Mall of America fresh and exciting," she explains. "We're constantly looking at what attracts people and adding to that. We're adding new stores, new attractions, and new events." For example, the mall holds more than 400 events each year including book signings, an inventors fair, fashion shows, and live Cirque du Soleil performances.

Mall of America announced a plan for a 5.6 million-square-foot expansion, the area of another 117 football fields, connected by pedestrian skyway to the present building. "The second phase will not be a duplicate of what we have," Cahill says. "We have plans for boutique, family, and business hotels, 20,000 square feet of event space, an ice rink, a spa and wellness center, museum-quality exhibit space, and new restaurants and retail offerings."

The expansion is expected to attract an additional 20 million visitors annually. In addition, the development is designed to exceed environmental certification standards. All of these new additions and the many offerings of the current mall reinforce that Mall of America is a shopping destination and a whole lot more!

Questions

1 Why has Mall of America been such a marketing success so far?

2 What (*a*) retail and (*b*) consumer trends have occurred since Mall of America was opened in 1992 that it should consider when making future plans?

3 (*a*) What criteria should Mall of America use in adding new facilities to its complex? (*b*) Evaluate (*1*) retail stores, (*2*) entertainment offerings, and (*3*) hotels on these criteria.

4 What specific marketing actions would you propose that Mall of America managers take to ensure its continuing success in attracting visitors (*a*) from the local metropolitan area and (*b*) from outside of it?

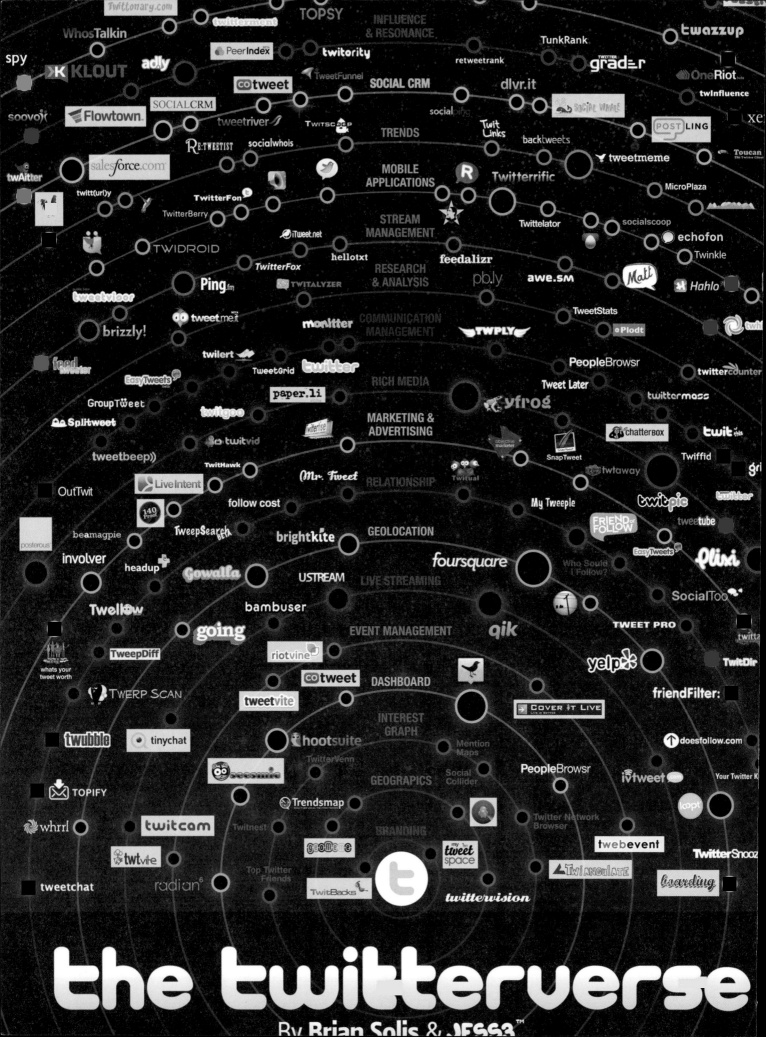

the twitterverse

By Brian Solis & JESS3

Integrated Marketing Communications and Direct Marketing

14

LEARNING OBJECTIVES

After reading this chapter you should be able to:

LO1 Discuss integrated marketing communications and the communication process.

LO2 Describe the promotional mix and the uniqueness of each component.

LO3 Select the promotional approach appropriate to a product's target audience, life-cycle stage, and channel strategy.

LO4 Describe the elements of the promotion decision process.

LO5 Explain the value of direct marketing for consumers and sellers.

GET ENGAGED. . . IN THE TWITTERVERSE!

How do companies such as VW, Google, Old Spice, Ford, Papa John's, and Hollywood Records engage today's consumers? They build integrated marketing communications programs with many media, including Twitter!

Many experts have observed that our marketplace is in the midst of an "age of engagement." Many consumers are no longer responsive to one-way communication from advertisers. They want interaction with companies and brands. Twitter accommodates this new perspective by charging advertisers for promoted tweets based on "engagement." At Twitter, *engagement* means the recipient takes some action—a re-tweet, a response, a click on a link, or designating a tweet as a "favorite." Advertisers don't pay if their tweet is ignored. As Twitter executive Adam Bain explains, "Marketers are rewarded if they are good, not just if they're loud."

Twitter offers several suggestions to ensure the success of a Twitter-based component of an integrated campaign. First, the message should be about something new and important such as a product launch. Second, the campaign should take place in real time as events actually happen. Finally, the tweet should include a link that allows consumers to be involved with and participate in the announcement. VW, for example, sent the following tweet: "The 21st Century VW Beetle was just revealed. Check out the revolutionary new take on the iconic design at http://vwoa.us/hZdaLm." The engagement rate was an extraordinary 52 percent!

Traditional media are also finding ways to engage customers. Television networks provide online video streams for many series, encourage audience participation and voting on reality shows such as *Dancing With the Stars*, and even offer iPhone and iPad apps for fans. The popular Fox network program *Glee*, for example, had 200,000 users of its app just two weeks after its launch. Brands such as Pepsi and Mountain Dew have also created partnerships with networks by announcing contests to encourage consumers to create videos that can be viewed on the programs or their websites.

E-mail, blogs, gift cards, magazines, and sweepstakes are also potential forms of media that can engage today's consumers. What is the newest way to engage consumers? QR codes, or quick-response codes. A QR code is a bar code arranged in a square pattern. Consumers scan the codes with their smartphones to receive detailed information about a product. Best Buy added QR codes to all of its in-store product-information tags to link shoppers to the product detail page on the Best Buy website. In the future, QR codes will also link to videos and product ratings and will allow the customer to add the product to a gift registry.[1]

The many types of promotion illustrated in these examples demonstrate the opportunity for engaging potential customers and the importance of integrating the various elements of a marketing communications program. Promotion represents the fourth element in the marketing mix. The promotional element consists of communication tools, including advertising, personal selling, sales promotion, public relations, and direct marketing. The combination of one or more of these communication tools is called the **promotional mix**. All of these tools can be used to (1) inform prospective buyers about the benefits of the product, (2) persuade them to try it, and (3) remind them later about the benefits they enjoyed by using the product. In the past, marketers often viewed these communication tools as separate and independent. The advertising department, for example, often designed and managed its activities without consulting departments or agencies that had responsibility for sales promotion or public relations. The result was often an overall communication effort that was uncoordinated and, in some cases, inconsistent. Today, the concept of designing marketing communications programs that coordinate all promotional activities—advertising, personal selling, sales promotion, public relations, and direct marketing—to provide a consistent message across all audiences is referred to as **integrated marketing communications (IMC)**. In addition, by taking consumer expectations into consideration, IMC is a key element in a company's customer experience management strategy.[2]

This chapter provides an overview of the communication process, a description of the promotional mix elements, several tools for integrating the promotional mix, and a process for developing a comprehensive promotion program. One of the promotional mix elements, direct marketing, is also discussed in this chapter. Chapter 15 covers advertising, sales promotion, and public relations, Chapter 16 covers social media, and Chapter 17 discusses personal selling.

promotional mix
The combination of one or more of the communication tools used to inform, persuade, or remind prospective buyers.

integrated marketing communications
The concept of designing marketing communications programs that coordinate all promotional activities to provide a consistent message across all audiences.

THE COMMUNICATION PROCESS

communication
The process of conveying a message to others; it requires six elements: a source, a message, a channel of communication, a receiver, and the processes of encoding and decoding.

Communication is the process of conveying a message to others and it requires six elements: a source, a message, a channel of communication, a receiver, and the processes of encoding and decoding[3] (see Figure 14–1). The *source* may be a company or person who has information to convey. The information sent by a source, such as a description of a new cellular telephone, forms the *message*. The message is conveyed by means of a *channel of communication* such as a salesperson, advertising media, or public relations tools. Consumers who read, hear, or see the message are the *receivers*.

FIGURE 14–1
The communication process consists of six key elements. See the text to learn about factors that influence the effectiveness of the process.

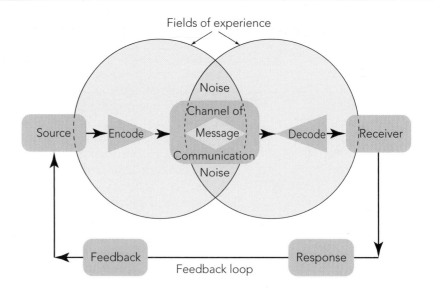

NEVER STOP EXPLORING

MATT SEGAL SENDING PASSPORT TO INSANITY, GRAMPIANS, AUSTRALIA. THENORTHFACE.COM

How would you decode this ad? What message is The North Face trying to send?

The North Face

www.thenorthface.com

QR 14–1
The North
Face Ad

Encoding and Decoding

Encoding and decoding are essential to communication. *Encoding* is the process of having the sender transform an idea into a set of symbols. *Decoding* is the reverse, or the process of having the receiver take a set of symbols, the message, and transform the symbols back to an idea. Look at the accompanying outdoor products advertisement: Who is the source, and what is the message?

Decoding is performed by the receivers according to their own frame of reference: their attitudes, values, and beliefs.[4] The North Face is the source and the advertisement is the message, which appeared in *Outside* magazine (the channel). How would you interpret (decode) this advertisement? The picture and text in the advertisement show that the source's intention is to generate interest in its product with the headline "Never stop exploring"—a statement the source believes will appeal to the readers of the magazine.

The process of communication is not always a successful one. Errors in communication can happen in several ways. The source may not adequately transform the abstract idea into an effective set of symbols, a properly encoded message may be sent through the wrong channel and never make it to the receiver, the receiver may not properly transform the set of symbols into the correct abstract idea, or finally, feedback may be so delayed or distorted that it is of no use to the sender. Although communication appears easy to perform, truly effective communication can be very difficult.

For the message to be communicated effectively, the sender and receiver must have a mutually shared *field of experience*—a similar understanding and knowledge they apply to the message. Figure 14–1 shows two circles representing the fields of experience of the sender and receiver, which overlap in the message. Some of the better-known message problems have occurred when U.S. companies have taken their messages to cultures with different fields of experience. Many misinterpretations are merely the result of bad translations. For example, KFC made a mistake when its "finger-lickin' good" slogan was translated into Mandarin Chinese as "eat your fingers off"![5]

Feedback

Figure 14–1 shows a line labeled *feedback loop*, which consists of a response and feedback. A *response* is the impact the message had on the receiver's knowledge, attitudes, or behaviors. *Feedback* is the sender's interpretation of the response and indicates whether the message was decoded and understood as intended. Chapter 15 reviews approaches called *pretesting*, which ensure that messages are decoded properly.

Noise

Noise includes extraneous factors that can work against effective communication by distorting a message or the feedback received (see Figure 14–1). Noise can be a simple error, such as a printing mistake that affects the meaning of a newspaper advertisement or using words or pictures that fail to communicate the message clearly. Noise can also occur when a salesperson's message is misunderstood by a prospective buyer, such as when a salesperson's accent, use of slang terms, or communication style make hearing and understanding the message difficult.

learning review	1. What are the six elements required for communication to occur?
	2. A difficulty for U.S. companies advertising in international markets is that the audience does not share the same _____.
	3. A misprint in a newspaper ad is an example of _____.

THE PROMOTIONAL ELEMENTS

To communicate with consumers, a company can use one or more of five promotional alternatives: advertising, personal selling, public relations, sales promotion, and direct marketing. Figure 14–2 summarizes the distinctions among these five elements. Three of these elements—advertising, sales promotion, and public relations—are often said to use *mass selling* because they are used with groups of prospective buyers. In contrast, personal selling uses *customized interaction* between a seller and a prospective buyer. Personal selling activities include face-to-face, telephone, and interactive electronic communication. Direct marketing also uses messages customized for specific customers.

Advertising

advertising

Any paid form of nonpersonal communication about an organization, product, service, or idea by an identified sponsor.

Advertising is any paid form of nonpersonal communication about an organization, product, service, or idea by an identified sponsor. The *paid* aspect of this definition is important because the space for the advertising message normally must be bought. An occasional exception is the public service announcement, where the advertising time or space is donated. A full-page, four-color ad in *Time* magazine, for example, costs $320,100. The *nonpersonal* component of advertising is also important. Advertising involves mass media (such as TV, radio, and magazines), which are nonpersonal and do not have an immediate feedback loop as does personal selling. So before the message is sent, marketing research plays a valuable role; for example, it determines that the target market will actually see the medium chosen and that the message will be understood.

PROMOTIONAL ELEMENT	MASS OR CUSTOMIZED	PAYMENT	STRENGTHS	WEAKNESSES
Advertising	Mass	Fees paid for space or time	• Efficient means for reaching large numbers of people	• High absolute costs • Difficult to receive good feedback
Personal selling	Customized	Fees paid to salespeople as either salaries or commissions	• Immediate feedback • Very persuasive • Can select audience • Can give complex information	• Extremely expensive per exposure • Messages may differ between salespeople
Public relations	Mass	No direct payment to media	• Often most credible source in the consumer's mind	• Difficult to get media cooperation
Sales promotion	Mass	Wide range of fees paid, depending on promotion selected	• Effective at changing behavior in short run • Very flexible	• Easily abused • Can lead to promotion wars • Easily duplicated
Direct marketing	Customized	Cost of communication through mail, telephone, or computer	• Messages can be prepared quickly • Facilitates relationship with customer	• Declining customer response • Database management is expensive

FIGURE 14–2

Each of the five elements of the promotional mix has strengths and weaknesses.

There are several advantages to a firm using advertising in its promotional mix. It can be attention-getting—as with the Havaianas ad shown on the next page—and also can communicate specific product benefits to prospective buyers. By paying for the advertising space, a company can control *what* it wants to say and, to some extent, to *whom* the message is sent. Advertising also allows the company to decide *when* to send its message (which includes how often). The nonpersonal aspect of advertising also has its advantages. Once the message is created, the same message is sent to all receivers in a market segment. If the pictorial, text, and brand elements of an advertisement are properly pretested, an advertiser can ensure the ad's ability to capture consumers' attention and trust that the same message will be decoded by all receivers in the market segment.[6]

Advertising has some disadvantages. As shown in Figure 14–2 and discussed in depth in Chapter 15, the costs to produce and place a message are significant, and the lack of direct feedback makes it difficult to know how well the message has been received.

Personal Selling

The second major promotional alternative is **personal selling**, which is the two-way flow of communication between a buyer and seller designed to influence a person's or group's purchase decision. Unlike advertising, personal selling is usually face-to-face communication between the sender and receiver. Why do companies use personal selling?

There are important advantages to personal selling, as summarized in Figure 14–2. A salesperson can control to *whom* the presentation is made, reducing the amount of *wasted coverage*, or communication with consumers who are not in the target audience.

personal selling

The two-way flow of communication between a buyer and seller, often in a face-to-face encounter, designed to influence a person's or group's purchase decision.

The personal component of selling has another advantage in that the seller can see or hear the potential buyer's reaction to the message. If the feedback is unfavorable, the salesperson can modify the message.

The flexibility of personal selling can also be a disadvantage. Different salespeople can change the message so that no consistent communication is given to all customers. The high cost of personal selling is probably its major disadvantage. On a cost-per-contact basis, it is generally the most expensive of the five promotional elements.

Public Relations

Public relations is a form of communication management that seeks to influence the feelings, opinions, or beliefs held by customers, prospective customers, stockholders, suppliers, employees, and other publics about a company and its products or services.[7] Many tools such as special events, lobbying efforts, annual reports, press conferences, social media (including Facebook and Twitter), and image management may be used by a public relations department, although publicity often plays the most important role.[8] **Publicity** is a nonpersonal, indirectly paid presentation of an organization, product, or service. It can take the form of a news story, editorial, or product announcement. A difference between publicity and both advertising and personal selling is the "indirectly paid" dimension. With publicity a company does not pay for space in a mass medium (such as television or radio) but attempts to get the medium to run a favorable story on the company. In this sense, there is an indirect payment for publicity in that a company must support a public relations staff.

An advantage of publicity is credibility. When you read a favorable story about a company's product (such as a glowing restaurant review), there is a tendency to believe it. Travelers throughout the world have relied on Frommer's guides such as *Italy from $90 a Day*. These books describe out-of-the-way, inexpensive restaurants and hotels, giving invaluable publicity to these establishments. Such businesses do not (nor can they) buy a mention in the guide.

The disadvantage of publicity relates to the lack of the user's control over it. A company can invite media to cover an interesting event such as a store opening or a new product release, but there is no guarantee that a story will result, if it will be positive, or who will be in the audience. Social media, such as blogs, have grown dramatically and allow uncontrollable public discussions of almost any company activity. Many public relations departments now focus on facilitating and responding to online discussions.

The Havianas ad, Frommer's travel guide, and Ford Focus Sweepstakes are examples of three elements of the promotional mix—advertising, public relations, and sales promotion.

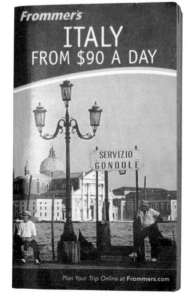

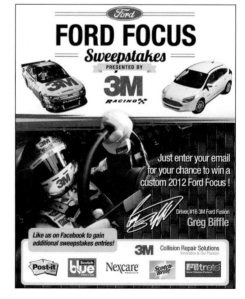

McDonald's, for example, responds to comments about McDonald's products and promotions on its corporate social responsibility blog, *Open for Discussion*.[9] Generally, publicity is an important element of most promotional campaigns, although the lack of control means that it is rarely the primary element. Research related to the sequence of IMC elements, however, indicates that publicity followed by advertising with the same message increases the positive response to the message.[10]

Sales Promotion

sales promotion
A short-term offer designed to arouse interest in buying a product or service.

A fourth promotional element is **sales promotion**, a short-term inducement of value offered to arouse interest in buying a product or service. Used in conjunction with advertising or personal selling, sales promotions are offered to intermediaries as well as to ultimate consumers. Coupons, rebates, samples, contests, and sweepstakes such as the Ford Focus promotion are just a few examples of sales promotions discussed later in this chapter.

The advantage of sales promotion is that the short-term nature of these programs (such as a coupon or sweepstakes with an expiration date) often stimulates sales for their duration. Offering value to the consumer in terms of a cents-off coupon or rebate may increase store traffic from consumers who are not store-loyal.[11]

Sales promotions cannot be the sole basis for a campaign because gains are often temporary and sales drop off when the deal ends. Advertising support is needed to convert the customer who tried the product because of a sales promotion into a long-term buyer. If sales promotions are conducted continuously, they lose their effectiveness. Customers begin to delay purchase until a coupon is offered, or they question the product's value. Some aspects of sales promotions also are regulated by the federal government.[12] These issues are reviewed in detail in Chapter 15.

Direct Marketing

direct marketing
Promotional element that uses direct communication with consumers to generate a response in the form of an order, a request for further information, or a visit to a retail outlet.

Another promotional alternative, **direct marketing**, uses direct communication with consumers to generate a response in the form of an order, a request for further information, or a visit to a retail outlet. The communication can take many forms, including face-to-face selling, direct mail, catalogs, telephone solicitations, direct response advertising (on television and radio and in print), and online marketing.[13] Like personal selling, direct marketing often consists of interactive communication. It also has the advantage of being customized to match the needs of specific target markets. Messages can be developed and adapted quickly to facilitate one-to-one relationships with customers.

While direct marketing has been one of the fastest-growing forms of promotion, it has several disadvantages. First, most forms of direct marketing require a comprehensive and up-to-date database with information about the target market. Developing and maintaining the database can be expensive and time-consuming. In addition, growing concern about privacy has led to a decline in response rates among some customer groups. Companies with successful direct marketing programs are sensitive to these issues and often use a combination of direct marketing alternatives together, or direct marketing combined with other promotional tools, to increase value for customers.

learning review

4. Explain the difference between advertising and publicity when both appear on television.

5. Cost per contact is high with the _____ element of the promotional mix.

6. Which promotional element should be offered only on a short-term basis?

INTEGRATED MARKETING COMMUNICATIONS—DEVELOPING THE PROMOTIONAL MIX

LO3

A firm's promotional mix is the combination of one or more of the promotional tools it chooses to use. In putting together the promotional mix, a marketer must consider two issues. First, the balance of the elements must be determined. Should advertising be emphasized more than personal selling? Should a promotional rebate be offered? Would public relations activities be effective? Several factors affect such decisions: the target audience for the promotion, the stage of the product's life cycle, the characteristics of the product, the decision stage of the buyer, and even the channel of distribution. Second, because the various promotional elements are often the responsibility of different departments, coordinating a consistent promotional effort is necessary. A promotional planning process designed to ensure integrated marketing communications can facilitate this goal.

Publications such as *Restaurant Business* reach business buyers.

The Target Audience

Promotional programs are directed to the ultimate consumer, to an intermediary (retailer, wholesaler, or industrial distributor), or to both. Promotional programs directed to buyers of consumer products often use mass media because the number of potential buyers is large. Personal selling is used at the place of purchase, generally the retail store. Direct marketing may be used to encourage first-time or repeat purchases. Combinations of many media alternatives are a necessity for some target audiences today. The Marketing Matters box describes how Generation Y consumers can be reached through mobile marketing programs.[14]

Advertising directed to business buyers is used selectively in trade publications, such as *Restaurant Business* magazine for buyers of restaurant equipment and supplies. Because business buyers often have specialized needs or technical questions, personal selling is particularly important. The salesperson can provide information and the necessary support after the sale.

Intermediaries are often the focus of promotional efforts. As with business buyers, personal selling is the major promotional ingredient. The salespeople assist intermediaries in making a profit by coordinating promotional campaigns sponsored by the manufacturer and by providing marketing advice and expertise. Intermediaries' questions often pertain to the allowed markup, merchandising support, and return policies.

Purina sponsors the Incredible Dog Challenge to maintain existing buyers.

The Product Life Cycle

All products have a life cycle (see Chapter 10), and the composition of the promotional mix changes over the four life-cycle stages (as shown for Purina Dog Chow in Figure 14-3):

- *Introduction stage.* Informing consumers in an effort to increase their level of awareness is the primary promotional objective in the introduction stage of the product life cycle. In general, all the promotional mix elements are used at this time.
- *Growth stage.* The primary promotional objective of the growth stage is to persuade the consumer to buy the product. Advertising is used to communicate brand differences, and personal selling is used to solidify the channel of distribution.

How Can You Reach Generation Y? With Mobile Marketing!

The American Marketing Association recently commissioned research to better understand marketing targeted at cell phones, or mobile marketing. The findings were eye-opening! While approximately 25 percent of the world's population has access to and uses the Internet, more than 65 percent use mobile phones. Of the 331 million mobile phone users in the United States, approximately 45 percent use smartphones. And who is most likely to access the Internet or respond to ads on their phone? By a huge margin, the answer is Generation Y.

Generation Y consists of "digital natives" who have grown up with technology. They have and use laptop computers, high definition televisions, game consoles, tablet PCs, and smartphones; they access Facebook, Netflix, Twitter, and foursquare; and they have downloaded apps, used mobile coupons, scanned QR codes, posted comments on blogs, connected with Bluetooth, and used SMS and MMS messaging. To cope with the variety of technology options, millennials use media multitasking—the practice of using more than one medium at the same time.

One-third of all Internet activity, for example, takes place while watching television. In fact, this time-compression behavior is so common that researchers estimate that a typical media day for these consumers is 31 hours!

To communicate with Generation Y consumers, marketers have added mobile marketing to their integrated marketing communications campaigns. Several guidelines help ensure the success of mobile campaigns. First, the messages must be short and fast. MTV, for example, recently hired a "Twitter Jockey" to provide 140 character messages to its millennial viewers. Second, messages must be honest, authentic, and transparent about the purpose and value of the brand. Finally, campaigns should encourage multitasking. *American Idol* and other television programs, for example, ask viewers to use their televisions, computers, and phones to watch, review, and vote for favorite performers.

Watch for other brands that use these guidelines as mobile marketing becomes an essential element of IMC programs targeted at Generation Y.

- *Maturity stage.* In the maturity stage the need is to maintain existing buyers. Advertising's role is to remind buyers of the product's existence. Sales promotion, in the form of discounts, coupons, and events, is important in maintaining loyal buyers.
- *Decline stage.* The decline stage of the product life cycle is usually a period of phase-out for the product, and little money is spent in the promotional mix.

FIGURE 14–3

Promotional objectives and activities change over the four stages of the product life cycle of Purina Dog Chow.

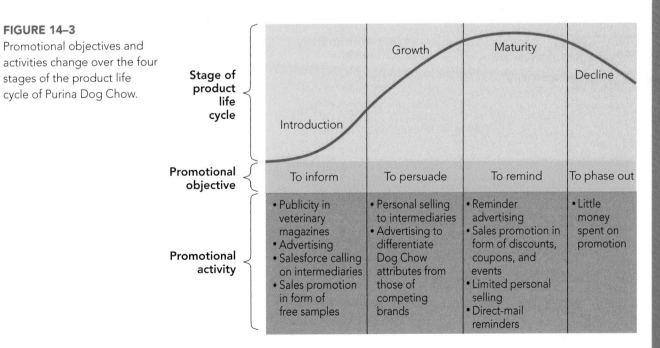

Why does this ad for a drug that helps lower cholesterol suggest readers should "Ask your doctor if Zetia is right for you"? For the answer, see the text.

FIGURE 14–4

Push and pull strategies direct the promotional mix to different points in the channel of distribution.

Channel Strategies

Chapter 12 discussed the channel flow from a producer to intermediaries to consumers. Achieving control of the channel is often difficult for the manufacturer, and promotional strategies can assist in moving a product through the channel of distribution. This is where a manufacturer has to make an important decision about whether to use a push strategy, pull strategy, or both in its channel of distribution.[15]

Push Strategy Figure 14–4A shows how a manufacturer uses a **push strategy**, directing the promotional mix to channel members to gain their cooperation in ordering and stocking the product. In this approach, personal selling and sales promotions play major roles. Salespeople call on wholesalers to encourage orders and provide sales assistance. Sales promotions, such as case discount allowances (20 percent off the regular case price), are offered to stimulate demand. By pushing the product through the channel, the goal is to get channel members to push it to their customers.

Ford Motor Company, for example, provides support and incentives for its 3,430 Ford dealers. Through a multilevel program, Ford provides incentives to reward dealers for meeting sales goals. Dealers receive an incentive when they are near a goal, another when they reach a goal, and an even larger one if they exceed sales projections. Ford also offers some dealers special incentives for maintaining superior facilities or improving customer service. All of these actions are intended to encourage Ford dealers to "push" the Ford products through the channel to consumers.[16]

Pull Strategy In some instances, manufacturers face resistance from channel members who do not want to order a new product or increase inventory levels of an existing brand. As shown in Figure 14–4B, a manufacturer may then elect to implement a **pull strategy** by directing its promotional mix at ultimate consumers to encourage them to ask the retailer for a product. Seeing demand from ultimate consumers, retailers order the product from wholesalers and thus the item is pulled

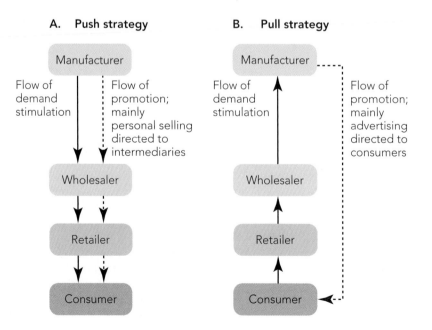

through the intermediaries. Pharmaceutical companies, for example, now spend more than $4.2 billion annually on *direct-to-consumer* prescription drug advertising, to complement traditional personal selling and free samples directed only at doctors.[17] The strategy is designed to encourage consumers to ask their doctor for a specific drug by name—pulling it through the channel. Successful campaigns such as the print ad which says, "Ask your doctor if Zetia is right for you," can have dramatic effects on the sales of a product.

learning review

7. Promotional programs can be directed to _____, _____, or both.

8. Describe the promotional objective for each stage of the product life cycle.

9. Explain the differences between a push strategy and a pull strategy.

DEVELOPING AN IMC PROGRAM

LO4

Because media costs are high, promotion decisions must be made carefully, using a systematic approach. Paralleling the planning, implementation, and evaluation steps described in the strategic marketing process (Chapter 2), the promotion decision process is divided into (1) developing, (2) executing, and (3) assessing the promotion program (see Figure 14–5).

Identifying the Target Audience

The first step in developing the promotion program involves identifying the *target audience,* the group of prospective buyers toward which a promotion program will be directed. To the extent that time and money permit, the target audience for the promotion program is the target market for the firm's product, which is identified from primary and secondary sources of marketing information. The more a firm knows about its target audiences—including demographics, interests, preferences, and behaviors—the easier it is to develop a promotional program. A firm might use a profile based on gender, age, and income, for example, to place ads on specific TV programs or in particular magazines. Similarly, a firm might use *behavioral targeting*—collecting information about your web-browsing behavior to determine the banner and display ads that you will see as you surf the Web. Behavioral targeting is discussed in more detail in Chapter 18.[18]

FIGURE 14–5
The promotion decision process includes planning, implementation, and evaluation.

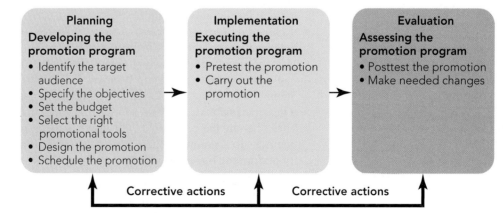

Specifying Promotion Objectives

hierarchy of effects

The sequence of stages a prospective buyer goes through: awareness, interest, evaluation, trial, and adoption.

After the target audience is identified, a decision must be reached on what the promotion should accomplish. Consumers can be said to respond in terms of a **hierarchy of effects**, which is the sequence of stages a prospective buyer goes through from initial awareness of a product to eventual action (either trial or adoption of the product).[19] The five stages are:

- *Awareness*—the consumer's ability to recognize and remember the product or brand name.
- *Interest*—an increase in the consumer's desire to learn about some of the features of the product or brand.
- *Evaluation*—the consumer's appraisal of the product or brand on important attributes.
- *Trial*—the consumer's actual first purchase and use of the product or brand.
- *Adoption*—through a favorable experience on the first trial, the consumer's repeated purchase and use of the product or brand.

For a totally new product, the sequence applies to the entire product category, but for a new brand competing in an established product category, it applies to the brand itself. These steps can serve as guidelines for developing promotion objectives.

Although sometimes an objective for a promotion program involves several steps in the hierarchy of effects, it often focuses on a single stage. Regardless of what the specific objective might be, from building awareness to increasing repeat purchases, promotion objectives should possess three important qualities. They should (1) be designed for a well-defined target audience, (2) be measurable, and (3) cover a specified time period.

Setting the Promotion Budget

After setting the promotion objectives, a company must decide how much to spend. The promotion expenditures needed to reach U.S. households are enormous. Nine companies—including P&G, AT&T, General Motors, and Verizon—each spend a total of more than $2 billion annually on promotion.[20] Determining the ideal amount for the budget is difficult because there is no precise way to measure the exact results of spending promotion dollars. However, several methods can be used to set the promotion budget.[21]

- *Percentage of sales.* In the percentage of sales budgeting approach, the amount of money spent on promotion is a percentage of past or anticipated sales. A common budgeting method,[22] this approach is often stated in terms such as "our promotion budget for this year is 3 percent of last year's gross sales." See the Using Marketing Dashboards box for an application of the promotion-to-sales ratio to the automotive industry.[23]
- *Competitive parity.* Competitive parity budgeting matches the competitor's absolute level of spending or the proportion per point of market share.[24]
- *All you can afford.* Common to many businesses, the all-you-can-afford budgeting method allows money to be spent on promotion only after all other budget items—such as manufacturing costs—are covered.[25]
- *Objective and task.* The best approach to budgeting is objective and task budgeting, whereby the company (1) determines its promotion objectives, (2) outlines the tasks to accomplish those objectives, and (3) determines the promotion cost of performing those tasks.[26]

Of the various methods, only the objective and task method takes into account what the company wants to accomplish and requires that the objectives be specified.[27]

Using Marketing Dashboards

How Much Should You Spend on IMC?

Integrated marketing communications programs coordinate a variety of promotion alternatives to provide a consistent message across audiences. The amount spent on the various promotional elements, or on the total campaign, may vary depending on the target audience, the type of product, where the product is in the product life cycle, and the channel strategy selected. Managers often use the promotion-to-sales ratio on their marketing dashboard to assess how effective the IMC program expenditures are at generating sales.

Your Challenge As a manager at General Motors you've been asked to assess the effectiveness of all promotion expenditures during the past year. The promotion-to-sales ratio can be used by managers to make year-to-year comparisons of their programs, to compare the effectiveness of their program with competitors' programs, or to make comparisons with industry averages. You decide to calculate the promotion-to-sales ratio for General Motors. In addition, to allow a comparison, you decide to make the same calculation for one of your competitors, Ford, and for the entire automobile industry. The ratio is calculated as follows:

Promotion-to-sales ratio =
Total promotion expenditures/Total sales

Your Findings The information needed for these calculations is readily available from trade publications and annual reports. The following graph shows the promotion-to-sales ratio for General Motors and Ford and the automotive industry. General Motors spent $2.21 billion on its IMC program to generate $49 billion in U.S. sales for a ratio of 4.5 (percent). Ford's ratio was 2.8, and the industry average was 3.2.

Your Action General Motors's promotion-to-sales ratio is higher than Ford's and higher than the industry average. This suggests that the current mix of promotional activities and the level of expenditures may not be creating an effective IMC program. In the future you will want to monitor the factors that may influence the ratio. The average ratio for the beverage industry has fallen to 5.7 while the average for grocery stores is less than 1.

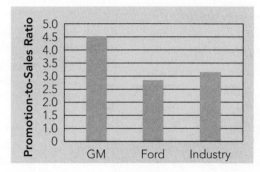

QR 14–2
Olympics Video

The 2014 Winter Olympics in Sochi, Russia, created a comprehensive IMC program.

Selecting the Right Promotional Tools

Once a budget has been determined, the combination of the five basic IMC tools—advertising, personal selling, sales promotion, public relations, and direct marketing—can be specified. While many factors provide direction for selection of the appropriate mix, the large number of possible combinations of the promotional tools means that many combinations can achieve the same objective. Therefore, an analytical approach and experience are particularly important in this step of the promotion decision process. The specific mix can vary from a simple program using a single tool to a comprehensive program using all forms of promotion. The Olympics have become a very visible example of a comprehensive integrated communications program. Because the Games are repeated every two years, the promotion is continuous during "on" and "off" years. Included in the program are advertising campaigns, personal selling efforts by the Olympic committee and organizers, sales promotion activities such as product tie-ins and sponsorships, public relations programs managed by the host cities, online and digital communication, and direct marketing efforts targeted at a variety of audiences, including governments, organizations, firms, athletes, and individuals.[28] At this stage, it is also important to assess the relative importance of the various tools. While it may be desirable to utilize and integrate several forms of promotion, one may deserve emphasis. The Olympics, for example, place primary importance on public relations and publicity.

Designing the Promotion

The central element of a promotion program is the promotion itself. Advertising consists of advertising copy and the artwork that the target audience is intended to see or hear. Personal selling efforts depend on the characteristics and skills of the salesperson. Sales promotion activities consist of the specific details of inducements such as coupons, samples, and sweepstakes. Public relations efforts are readily seen in tangible elements such as news releases, and direct marketing actions depend on written, verbal, and electronic forms of delivery. The design of the promotion will play a primary role in determining the message that is communicated to the audience. This design activity is frequently viewed as the step requiring the most creativity. In addition, successful designs are often the result of insight regarding consumers' interests and purchasing behavior. All of the promotion tools have many design alternatives. Advertising, for example, can utilize fear, humor, attractiveness, or other themes in its appeal. Similarly, direct marketing can be designed for varying levels of personal or customized appeals. One of the challenges of IMC is to design each promotional activity to communicate the same message.[29]

Scheduling the Promotion

What promotional tools did Disney use to support the release of *Pirates of the Caribbean: On Stranger Tides?*

Once the design of each of the promotional program elements is complete, it is important to determine the most effective timing of their use. The promotion schedule describes the order in which each promotional tool is introduced and the frequency of its use during the campaign. Walt Disney Pictures studio, for example, uses a schedule of several promotional tools for its movies. To generate interest in the movie *Pirates of the Caribbean: On Stranger Tides,* the studio first released footage from the film on the television program *Entertainment Tonight.* The trailer for the movie was then released (about six months prior to the movie's release) in both regular and 3D formats. A television commercial for the movie also debuted during the Super Bowl, and a *Pirates of the Caribbean* video game in Xbox, PlayStation, and Wii formats was released before the movie. In addition, Disney created a partnership with retailer Hot Topic which promoted "Pirates Day" to the 4.5 million members of its loyalty program and the 2.5 million visitors to its website. In-store re-creations of the ships in the movie generated thousands of photos that fans posted on Facebook and Twitter. Free toys created by Lego were given away at selected toy stores and at Tesco stores in Europe. After the movie was released, Disney used online promotions to encourage fans to purchase the DVD.[30]

Overall, the scheduling of the various promotions was designed to generate interest, bring consumers into theaters, and then encourage additional purchases after seeing the movie. Several factors such as seasonality and competitive promotion activity can also influence the promotion schedule. Businesses such as ski resorts, airlines, and professional sports teams are likely to reduce their promotional activity during the "off" season. Similarly, restaurants, retail stores, and health clubs are likely to increase their promotional activity when new competitors enter the market.

EXECUTING AND ASSESSING THE PROMOTION PROGRAM

As shown earlier in Figure 14–5, the ideal execution of a promotion program involves pretesting each design before it is actually used to allow for changes and modifications that improve its effectiveness. Similarly, posttests are recommended to evaluate the impact of each promotion and the contribution of the promotion toward achieving the program objectives. The most sophisticated pretest and posttest procedures have been developed for advertising and are discussed in Chapter 15. Testing procedures for sales promotion and direct marketing efforts currently focus on comparisons of different designs or responses of different segments. To fully benefit from IMC programs, companies must create and maintain a test-result database that allows comparisons of the relative impact of the promotional tools and their execution options in varying situations. Information from the database will allow informed design and execution decisions and provide support for IMC activities during internal reviews by financial or administrative personnel. The San Diego Padres baseball team, for example, developed a database of information relating attendance to its integrated campaign using a new logo, special events, merchandise sales, and a loyalty program.

Carrying out the promotion program can be expensive and time-consuming. One researcher estimates that "an organization with sales less than $10 million can successfully implement an IMC program in one year, one with sales between $200 million and $500 million will need about three years, and one with sales between $2 billion and $5 billion will need five years." In addition, firms with a market orientation are more likely to implement an IMC program.[31] To facilitate the transition, approximately 200 integrated marketing communications agencies are in operation. In addition, some of the largest agencies are adopting approaches that embrace "total communications solutions."

QR 14–3
Geico Ad

Media agency Horizon, which recently won *Advertising Age* magazine's Media Agency of the Year award, for example, is part of a multinational partnership of media agencies servicing 40 markets across Europe, North America, Latin America, the Middle East, and Asia. The agency's services include communication planning, brand strategy development, and television, digital, and out-of-home media buying, research, and direct response marketing. One of its integrated campaigns for Geico included TV advertising, YouTube videos that generated more than 5 million impressions, and postings on Hulu. Horizon has also used its holistic approach with other clients including Google, Kraft, NBC Universal, Weight Watchers, and Quiznos. CEO and founder Bill Koenigsberg explains that one of the keys to the agency's success is its focus on increasing brand sales, awareness, and purchase intent. Brand strategy teams accomplish this by including account managers, channel experts, media specialists, and a planning supervisor. While many agencies may still be specialists, the trend today is clearly toward an integrated perspective that includes all forms of promotion.[32]

An important factor in developing successful IMC programs is to create a process that facilitates their design and use. A tool used to evaluate a company's current process is the IMC audit. The audit analyzes the internal communication network of the company; identifies key audiences; evaluates customer databases; assesses messages in recent advertising, public relations releases, packaging, websites, e-mail communication, signage, sales promotions, and direct mail; and determines the IMC expertise of company and agency personnel.[33] This process is becoming increasingly important as consumer-generated media such as blogs, RSS, podcasts, and social networks become more popular and as the use of search engines increases. According to Professor Judy Franks, marketers should also be cognizant of consumers she calls "accelerators" who easily move content from medium to medium—from TV to YouTube to a mobile phone text message, for example—without any influence or control from the message source.[34]

learning review

10. What are the stages of the hierarchy of effects?

11. What are the four approaches to setting the promotion budget?

12. How have advertising agencies changed to facilitate the use of IMC programs?

DIRECT MARKETING

Direct marketing has many forms and utilizes a variety of media. Several forms of direct marketing—direct mail and catalogs, television home shopping, telemarketing, and direct selling—were discussed as methods of nonstore retailing in Chapter 13. In addition, although advertising is discussed in Chapter 15, a form of advertising—direct response advertising—is an important form of direct marketing. Finally, interactive marketing is discussed in detail in Chapter 18. In this section, the growth of direct marketing, its value for consumers and sellers, and key global, technological, and ethical issues are discussed.

The Growth of Direct Marketing

The increasing interest in customer relationship management is reflected in the dramatic growth of direct marketing. The ability to customize communication efforts and create one-to-one interactions is appealing to most marketers, particularly those with IMC programs. While many direct marketing methods are not new, the ability to design and use them has increased with the availability of customer information databases and new printing technologies. In recent years, direct marketing growth has outpaced total economic growth. Direct marketing expenditures exceed $160 billion and are growing at a rate of 3.8 percent. Similarly, revenues are expected to grow to $2.5 trillion by 2016. Direct marketing currently accounts for 8.3 percent of the total U.S. gross domestic product. E-mail, the most popular form of direct marketing, is used by 93 percent of marketers and generates a 1.7 percent response rate.[35] While e-mail is the most common form of direct marketing, most campaigns use several methods. Many companies also integrate their direct marketing with other forms of promotion. Porsche, for example, recently launched television ads to change consumer perceptions of its cars and supported the campaign with direct-mail brochures, a mobile application, and an online video contest. Mobile direct marketing sales and social network direct marketing sales are growing at 31 percent and 17 percent, respectively, the fastest of all direct marketing tools.[36]

E-mail has become the most popular form of direct marketing.

The Value of Direct Marketing

One of the most visible indicators of the value of direct marketing for consumers is its level of use. For example, 53 percent of the U.S. population have ordered merchandise or services by mail; 64 percent of households with Internet access shop online; consumers spent more than $144 billion on products available through offers; and 24 percent of social media users are more likely to purchase a product after seeing a positive post. Consumers report many benefits, including the following: They don't have to go to a store; they can usually shop 24 hours a day; buying direct saves time; they avoid hassles with salespeople; they can save money; it's fun and entertaining; and direct marketing offers more privacy than in-store shopping. Many consumers also believe that direct marketing provides excellent customer service. Toll-free telephone numbers, customer service representatives with access to information regarding purchasing preferences, overnight delivery services, and unconditional guarantees all help create value for direct marketing customers. At Landsend.com, when customers need assistance they can click the Live Help icon to receive help from a sales representative on the phone or through online chat or online video until the correct product is found. "It's like we were walking down the aisle in a store!" says one Lands' End customer.[37]

The value of direct marketing for sellers can be described in terms of the responses it generates. **Direct orders** are the result of offers that contain all the information necessary for a prospective buyer to make a decision to purchase and complete the

QR 14–4
Priceline Ad

direct orders
The result of direct marketing offers that contain all the information necessary for a potential buyer to make a decision to purchase and complete the transaction.

Target uses direct mail to motivate people to visit its stores.

transaction. Priceline.com, for example, will send *PriceBreaker* RSS alerts to people in its database. The messages offer discounted fares and rates to customers who can travel on very short notice. **Lead generation** is the result of an offer designed to generate interest in a product or service and a request for additional information. Four Seasons Hotels now sell private residences in several of their properties and send direct mail to prospective residents asking them to request additional information on the telephone or through a website. Finally, **traffic generation** is the outcome of an offer designed to motivate people to visit a business. Home Depot, for example, uses an opt-in e-mail alert to announce special sales that attract consumers to the store. Similarly, Target uses direct mail to generate traffic in new and remodeled stores.[38]

Technological, Global, and Ethical Issues in Direct Marketing

The information technology and databases described in Chapter 7 are key elements in any direct marketing program. Databases are the result of organizations' efforts to create profiles of customers so that direct marketing tools, such as e-mail and catalogs, can be directed at specific customers. While most companies try to keep records of their customers' past purchases, many other types of data are needed to use direct marketing to develop one-to-one relationships with customers. Some data, such as lifestyles, media use, and demographics, are best collected from the consumer. Other types of data, such as price, quantity, and brand, are best collected from the businesses where purchases are made. Increases in postage rates and the decline in the economy have also increased the importance of information related to the cost of direct marketing activities. Brookstone, for example, uses its database to mail more than 70 million catalogs to a specific profile of target customer each year. In addition, when the number of catalogs being sent to individual carrier routes is small, the database can add names to qualify for U.S. Postal Service discounts. This approach saves Brookstone $5,000 to $15,000 in postage each time it mails a catalog.[39]

Direct marketing faces several challenges and opportunities in global markets today. Several countries such as Italy and Denmark, for example, have requirements for mandatory "opt-in"—that is, potential customers must give permission to include their name on a list for direct marketing solicitations. In addition, the mail, telephone, and Internet systems in many countries are not as well developed as they are in the United States. The need for improved reliability and security in these countries has slowed the growth of direct mail, while the dramatic growth of mobile phone penetration has created an opportunity for direct mobile marketing campaigns. Another issue for global direct marketers is payment. The availability of credit and credit cards varies throughout the world, creating the need for alternatives such as C.O.D. (cash on delivery), bank deposits, and online payment accounts.[40]

Global and domestic direct marketers both face challenging ethical issues today. Concerns about privacy, for example, have led to various attempts to provide guidelines that balance consumer and business interests. The European Union passed a consumer privacy law, called the *Data Protection Directive*, after several years of discussion with the Federation of European Direct Marketing and the U.K.'s Direct Marketing Association. In the United States, the Federal Trade Commission and many state legislatures have also been concerned about privacy. Several bills that call for a do-not-mail registry similar to the Do-Not-Call Registry are being discussed. Similarly, there are growing concerns about the web "tracking" tools used by direct marketers to segment consumers and match them with advertising. The Making Responsible Decisions box on the next page describes some of the issues under consideration.[41]

Making Responsible Decisions > > > > > > ethics

What Information Should Be Private?

In 2003 the Federal Trade Commission opened the National Do-Not-Call Registry to give Americans a tool for maintaining their privacy on home telephone lines. More than two-thirds of all households registered. Since then several state legislatures have passed laws to create do-not-call lists for mobile phone numbers. In addition, new discussions about privacy related to mail and computer use have begun.

Generally, the question being discussed is, What information is private? Are telephone numbers, addresses of residences, and online activities private or public information? Proponents of a Do-Not-Mail registry argue that, like telephone calls, citizens should be able to stop unsolicited mail. Proponents of Do-Not-Track regulations suggest that website owners who use cookies to collect information about consumers' shopping habits should only do so with consumers' consent. Marketers suggest that consumers who share this information are more likely to receive messages and advertising that better match their interests.

The Direct Marketing Association currently advocates several solutions. First, it created DMAchoice, an online tool to help consumers manage the types of mail and e-mail they receive. Second, the organization designed a Self-Regulatory Program for Online Behavioral Advertising which encourages advertisers to include an Advertising Option icon in the corner of online ads to allow consumers to opt out of having data collected about their online activities. The European Union, however, recently passed the *E-Privacy Directive* to provide explicit laws for website owners. In the United States, the Senate is evaluating the *Do-Not-Track Online Act*. State legislatures are also considering a variety of laws related to mail and online tracking.

What is your opinion? What types of information should be private? Can we find a balance between self-regulation and legislation?

---

learning review

13. The ability to design and use direct marketing programs has increased with the availability of _____ and _____.

14. What are the three types of responses generated by direct marketing activities?

LEARNING OBJECTIVES REVIEW

LO1 *Discuss integrated marketing communications and the communication process.*

Integrated marketing communications is the concept of designing marketing communications programs that coordinate all promotional activities—advertising, personal selling, sales promotion, public relations, and direct marketing—to provide a consistent message across all audiences. The communication process conveys messages with six elements: a source, a message, a channel of communication, a receiver, and encoding and decoding. The communication process also includes a feedback loop and can be distorted by noise.

LO2 *Describe the promotional mix and the uniqueness of each component.*

There are five promotional alternatives. Advertising, sales promotion, and public relations are mass selling approaches, whereas personal selling and direct marketing use customized messages. Advertising can have high absolute costs but reaches large numbers of people. Personal selling has a high cost per contact but provides immediate feedback. Public relations is often difficult to obtain but is very credible. Sales promotion influences short-term consumer behavior. Direct marketing can help develop customer relationships, although maintaining a database can be very expensive.

LO3 *Select the promotional approach appropriate to a product's target audience, life-cycle stage, and channel strategy.*

The promotional mix depends on the target audience. Programs for consumers, business buyers, and intermediaries might emphasize advertising, personal selling, and sales promotion, respectively. The promotional mix also changes over the product life-cycle stages. During the introduction stage, all promotional mix elements are used. During the growth stage advertising is emphasized, while the maturity stage utilizes sales promotion and direct marketing. Little promotion is used during the decline stage. Finally, the promotional mix can depend on the channel strategy. Push strategies require personal selling and sales promotions directed at channel members, while pull strategies depend on advertising and sales promotions directed at consumers.

LO4 *Describe the elements of the promotion decision process.*
The promotion decision process consists of three steps: planning, implementation, and evaluation. The planning step consists of six elements: identify the target audience, specify the objectives, set the budget, select the right promotional elements, design the promotion, and schedule the promotion. The implementation step includes pretesting. The evaluation step includes posttesting.

LO5 *Explain the value of direct marketing for consumers and sellers.*
The value of direct marketing for consumers is indicated by its level of use. For example, 49 percent of the U.S. population have made a purchase by mail and 64 percent have shopped online. The value of direct marketing for sellers can be measured in terms of three types of responses: direct orders, lead generation, and traffic generation.

FOCUSING ON KEY TERMS

advertising p. 320
communication p. 318
direct marketing p. 323
direct orders p. 332
hierarchy of effects p. 328
integrated marketing
   communications (IMC) p. 318

lead generation p. 333
personal selling p. 321
promotional mix p. 318
public relations p. 322
publicity p. 322

pull strategy p. 326
push strategy p. 326
sales promotion p. 323
traffic generation p. 333

APPLYING MARKETING KNOWLEDGE

1   After listening to a recent sales presentation, Mary Smith signed up for membership at the local health club. On arriving at the facility, she learned there was an additional fee for racquetball court rentals. "I don't remember that in the sales talk; I thought they said all facilities were included with the membership fee," complained Mary. Describe the problem in terms of the communication process.

2   Develop a matrix to compare the five elements of the promotional mix on three criteria—to *whom* you deliver the message, *what* you say, and *when* you say it.

3   Explain how the promotional tools used by an airline would differ if the target audience were (*a*) consumers who travel for pleasure and (*b*) corporate travel departments that select the airlines to be used by company employees.

4   Suppose you introduced a new consumer food product and invested heavily both in national advertising (pull strategy) and in training and motivating your field salesforce to sell the product to food stores (push strategy). What kinds of feedback would you receive from both the advertising and your salesforce? How could you increase both the quality and quantity of each?

5   Fisher-Price Company, long known as a manufacturer of children's toys, has introduced a line of clothing for children. Outline a promotional plan to get this product introduced in the marketplace.

6   Many insurance companies sell health insurance plans to companies. In these companies the employees pick the plan, but the set of offered plans is determined by the company. Recently Blue Cross–Blue Shield, a health insurance company, ran a television ad stating, "If your employer doesn't offer you Blue Cross–Blue Shield coverage, ask why." Explain the promotional strategy behind the advertisement.

7   Identify the sales promotion tools that might be useful for (*a*) Tastee Yogurt, a new brand introduction, (*b*) 3M self-sticking Post-it® Notes, and (*c*) Wrigley's Spearmint Gum.

8   Design an integrated marketing communications program—using each of the five promotional elements—for Rhapsody, the online music service.

9   BMW introduced its first sport activity vehicle, the X6, to compete with other popular crossover vehicles such as the Acura ZDX. Design a direct marketing program to generate (*a*) leads, (*b*) traffic in dealerships, and (*c*) direct orders.

10   Develop a privacy policy for database managers that provides a balance of consumer and seller perspectives. How would you encourage voluntary compliance with your policy? What methods of enforcement would you recommend?

building your marketing plan

To develop the promotion strategy for your marketing plan, follow the steps suggested in the planning phase of the promotion decision process described in Figure 14–5.

1   You should (*a*) identify the target audience, (*b*) specify the promotion objectives, (*c*) set the promotion budget, (*d*) select the right promotional tools, (*e*) design the promotion, and (*f*) schedule the promotion.

2   Also specify the pretesting and posttesting procedures needed in the implementation and evaluation phases.

3   Finally, describe how each of your promotional tools is integrated to provide a consistent message.

"When you look at a brand like Mountain Dew, and actually many of our brands, we absolutely used to have a focus on creating iconic TV advertising. That was how the marketing model worked. Right now when you look at what the brand needs going forward, that's just not going to do it. That's not going to be able to break through. So we are completely changing our approach," observes Lauren Hobart, chief marketing officer for Sparkling Beverages at PepsiCo, Inc. Pepsi's new model is to apply an integrated marketing communications (IMC) approach that utilizes traditional promotion tools and new social media to engage consumers. Mountain Dew has based its extraordinarily successful "Dewmocracy" campaigns on this new model. "No longer is it OK to just stand and talk to your consumers one way," observes Hobart.

THE BRAND

Mountain Dew is a citrus-flavored carbonated soft drink invented by Barney and Ally Hartman in Tennessee during the 1940s. The name was derived from a slang term for moonshine whiskey and matched the unique energizing effect created by carbonated water, extra sugar, caffeine, concentrated orange juice, and citric acid. The beverage became very popular in local markets and attracted the attention of PepsiCo, Inc., in the early 1960s, when it acquired Mountain Dew as its first flavored soft drink.

During the past 50 years terms used to describe the brand image have changed from "hillbilly," to "country cool," to "young and irreverent," but all have conveyed a common underlying theme. As Frank Cooper, senior vice president and chief consumer engagement officer, explains, "There is a thread that went throughout the Mountain Dew experience throughout the years." The thread had three dimensions:

- A "Do-It-Yourself" Ethic
- An "Operating Outside of the Mainstream" Perspective
- A "Remain True to Yourself" Attitude

These elements were part of all of Mountain Dew's advertising campaigns as it moved from popularity in rural areas to distribution in suburbs and metropolitan areas. The expansion really took off when the "Do the Dew" campaign began. This campaign positioned Mountain Dew as a product for "edgy" young consumers involved in activities such as skateboarding, snowboarding, skydiving, windsurfing, extreme sports, and video gaming.

Today Mountain Dew is a megabrand in the soft drink category, with about 6 percent of all carbonated soft drink sales in the United States and about 80 percent of the citrus soft drink market. Mountain Dew has more than 30 flavors and variations including caffeine-free, diet, Code Red, LiveWire, Pitch Black, Baja Blast, Voltage, Throwback, Cherry Fusion, and White Out. Its main competition includes Fault, Mello Yello, and Sun Drop. It is one of 19 brands at PepsiCo with sales greater than $1 billion, and it is the company's second largest beverage, behind only Pepsi-Cola. PepsiCo, Inc., has annual revenues of approximately $60 billion from several businesses, which also include the Frito-Lay, Quaker, Tropicana, and Gatorade brands.

THE DEWMOCRACY CAMPAIGNS

The general concept of the Dewmocracy campaigns is to harness the passion of Mountain Dew's loyal customers. The need for the concept resulted from several changes in the marketplace. First, the carbonated beverage market became very competitive. Hobart describes the situation: "There has been a proliferation of new products. With the rise of energy drinks, with the rise of enhanced water, there has been growth coming from all places, and the model of how we compete has dramatically had to change over the last few years." Second, consumers became more interested in authentic, high-involvement brand experiences. These types of experiences were difficult to offer through a single media outlet. "We had noticed that traditional ways of connecting with consumers weren't working as well," observes Mark Hanson, brand manager for Mountain Dew.

The first Dewmocracy campaign began in late 2007 by asking consumers to choose the next Dew's flavor, color, name, and graphics. More than 1 million people participated in the process, which utilized a website, DEWmocracy.com, and featured gaming elements and a discussion board. The results led to three final concepts—Supernova, Revolution, and Voltage—being introduced to the market. Three months later, Voltage, which featured a citrus-charged flavor and a deep blue color, was announced as the winner. Voltage has gone on to exceed its sales volume projections, selling more than 17 million cases after its introduction as the winner.

The success of the first Dewmocracy campaign led to another Dewmocracy campaign and the integration of more communication tools. In addition to the website, the second campaign utilized many social media such as Facebook, Twitter, 12seconds.tv, and YouTube. Dewmocracy 2 involved a seven-stage process (described in Table 1). Stage One was a truck stop tour that allowed consumers to try seven new flavors of Mountain Dew. During this stage Mountain Dew also gave away home testing kits to winners of a video testimonial contest. The second stage organized loyal fans into "Flavor Nations" based on their preference for one of the top

TABLE 1
The seven stages of the Dewmocracy 2 campaign

Stage	Name	Description
1	Truck Stop: Taste the Flavors	In the first stage, trucks traveled to 17 markets in 12 states, giving consumers a chance to sample seven possible new flavors.
2	Make Your Voice Heard: Flavor Nations	The top three flavors from Stage One were sent to 4,000 loyal Dew consumers. Each participant selected their favorite flavor and joined the corresponding Flavor Nation.
3	Shoot Your Shade: Color Selection	The members of each Flavor Nation selected three colors from an 18-color palette, and then all consumers voted on Facebook to select the best of the nine final colors.
4	Name Game: Name the Product	Flavor Nation members submitted name suggestions and then selected the top three. Dew fans could become followers of their favorite name on Twitter. The winners of the Twitter race were Typhoon, Distortion, and White Out.
5	Dew Art: Design Your Can	Mountain Dew asked designers, art schools, and Dew fans to submit labels for each flavor. Fan votes were used to select the top 10 labels, and each Flavor Nation selected the best of the top 10. Dew brand teams then adjusted them to look good on the shelf.
6	Creative Juices: Advertising	Advertising agencies, film students, and individuals were asked to submit 12-second commercials on 12seconds.tv, where fans voted to select the top ads. The winners then prepared 15-second versions to air on television.
7	Vote in the Flavor Battle	The three products were introduced in stores and consumers voted for their favorite. The winner was added to the Dew product line!

three flavors from Stage One. In the third stage, fans chose product colors. Stage Four used a Twitter race to determine the names of each flavor. Stage Five determined the design of the cans and Stage Six selected television advertising for each flavor. The seventh and final stage introduced each of the three flavors to the market for voting.

Each Flavor Nation used Facebook and Twitter to generate votes for their flavor. After two months of competition and voting, Mountain Dew White Out was declared the winner with 44 percent of the votes. Consumers had played an active role in the design and selection of a new Mountain Dew flavor. In addition, for the first time, consumers also had played a role in the selection of paid media, which ran on television.

THE RESULTS

The effectiveness of the Dewmocracy 2 campaign can be measured in many ways. Each stage of the process can be evaluated in terms of a variety of statistics. For example:

- The Truck Stop Tour generated a total attendance of 1.5 million people.
- The Color Selection stage generated 538 total viewer hours.
- The Twitter Race attracted more than 1,900 followers.
- The Advertising Challenge videos received 202,000 views.
- The final stage, the Flavor Battle, generated almost 3 million votes.

In addition, there was dramatic growth in the general interest in Mountain Dew. Prior to the campaign Mountain Dew had about 125,000 Facebook members. By the end of the campaign, Mountain Dew had 1 million Facebook members. This is critically important because, as Frank Cooper

explains, "You have to move cases, so volume is important," however, "the second piece of it is . . . deepening the connection with the people who love the brand."

Dewmocracy 2 represents an excellent example of an integrated marketing communications campaign utilizing many media alternatives to reinforce a central message. The process included sales promotion activities such as the truck events, video contests, and retail displays; advertising such as the online messages during the seven-stage process and traditional (television) advertising following the selection of the winner; and public relations activities such as the press releases and news coverage generated by the interest in the Dewmocracy campaign. Mountain Dew also used new forms of communication such as prompting Xbox users to vote for one of the new flavors.

Mark Hanson offers a good summary of the Dewmocracy approach: "I think what Dewmocracy 1 and ultimately Dewmocracy 2 have done, is solidify Mountain Dew's position as a brand that acknowledges and embraces the desires of its fans. There is tangible proof that we are listening to the voice of the consumer throughout. It uniquely situates Mountain Dew in the consumer landscape as a brand for the people, by the people." Since the first two Dewmocracy campaigns have been so successful, watch for the announcement of a third one soon!

Questions

1 What changes in the environment provided the opportunity for the Dewmocracy approach?

2 Which of the promotional elements described in Figure 14–2 were used by Mountain Dew in its Dewmocracy 2 campaign?

3 What are some of the different ways Mountain Dew can assess the success of its campaign?

Advertising, Sales Promotion, and Public Relations

15

LEARNING OBJECTIVES

After reading this chapter you should be able to:

LO1 Explain the differences between product advertising and institutional advertising and the variations within each type.

LO2 Describe the steps used to develop, execute, and evaluate an advertising program.

LO3 Explain the advantages and disadvantages of alternative advertising media.

LO4 Discuss the strengths and weaknesses of consumer-oriented and trade-oriented sales promotions.

LO5 Recognize public relations as an important form of communication.

WHERE CAN YOU WATCH TV? WHERE CAN'T YOU?

It started with broadcast TV. Then came cable TV. Now, the world of television is about to change again. Get ready, because it's coming quickly. The new TV looks like the old TV, except, it's not on TV!

Television has been a key element of the advertising landscape for decades. Over the years there have been many changes and experiments to try to improve its advertising. For example, traditional 60-second ads were reduced to 30-, 15-, 5-, and even 1-second ads. Some advertisers tried two-minute ads or bought all of the advertising during an entire program. As viewers began to use digital video recorders (DVRs) to "time-shift" their viewing and skip the ads, advertisers placed subliminal messages in the ads that could only be seen by playing the ad slowly on the DVR. As technology improved, programming and advertising experimented with 3D formats. All of these changes were attempts to adjust to the behaviors and preferences of consumers. None of them, however, are likely to compare to the changes coming during the next few years.

The next big thing in TV is that, in addition to traditional broadcast and cable, programming will also be available through the Internet. OTV, or online TV, is the growing capability to view streaming video that is available online. You may already be familiar with some of the early versions of this new capability. Hulu, for example, is an ad-supported subscription service offering streaming video of TV shows, movies, and other content from NBC, Fox, ABC, and other networks. Similarly, Machinima is a YouTube channel that offers how-to clips, user-generated video, and original series such as "Mortal Kombat: Legacy" and "Bite Me." The channel currently has an audience of 67 million unique viewers each month. Netflix, Apple, and Amazon also offer video-on-demand services.

Advertisers are excited because OTV will offer targeted audiences who are engaged in the programming. According to Allen DeBevoise, CEO of Machinima, "People are not only watching these videos; they're also embedding, ranking, and replying to them." One aspect of these new offerings may change TV viewing dramatically: They are available on any device with connectivity. Televisions, computers, tablets, and smartphones will all provide access to OTV. Early evidence suggests that OTV will provide many challenges and opportunities for advertisers. Watch closely, from wherever you are![1]

The growth of OTV is just one of the many exciting changes occurring in the field of advertising today. They illustrate the importance of advertising as one of the five promotional mix elements in marketing communications programs. This chapter describes three of the promotional mix elements—advertising, sales promotion, and public relations. Direct marketing was covered in Chapter 14, and personal selling is covered in Chapter 17.

TYPES OF ADVERTISEMENTS

Chapter 14 described **advertising** as any paid form of nonpersonal communication about an organization, a product, a service, or an idea by an identified sponsor. As you look through any magazine, watch television, listen to the radio, or browse the Internet, the variety of advertisements you see or hear may give you the impression that they have few similarities. Advertisements are prepared for different purposes, but they basically consist of two types: product advertisements and institutional advertisements.

Product Advertisements

Focused on selling a good or service, **product advertisements** take three forms: (1) pioneering (or informational), (2) competitive (or persuasive), and (3) reminder. Look at the ads for Campbell's, 1&1, and Red Bull to determine the type and objective of each ad.

Used in the introductory stage of the product life cycle, *pioneering* advertisements tell people what a product is, what it can do, and where it can be found. The key objective of a pioneering advertisement (such as the ad for Campbell's new Slow Kettle® Style soups) is to inform the target market. Informational ads, particularly those with specific information, have been found to be interesting, convincing, and effective.[2]

Advertising that promotes a specific brand's features and benefits is *competitive*. The objective of these messages is to persuade the target market to select the firm's brand rather than that of a competitor. An increasingly common form of competitive advertising is *comparative* advertising, which shows one brand's strengths relative to those of competitors.[3] The 1&1 ad, for example, highlights the competitive advantages of 1&1's domain registration service compared to GoDaddy and Network Solutions. Studies indicate that comparative ads attract more attention and increase the perceived quality of the advertiser's brand although their impact may vary by product type, message content, and audience gender.[4] Firms that use comparative advertising need market research to provide legal support for their claims.[5]

Reminder advertising is used to reinforce previous knowledge of a product. The Red Bull ad shown reminds consumers about a special event, in this case, Valentine's Day. Reminder advertising is good for products that have achieved a well-recognized

Product advertisements serve varying purposes. Which ad would be considered a (1) pioneering, (2) competitive, and (3) reminder ad?

position and are in the mature phase of their product life cycle. Another type of reminder ad, *reinforcement*, is used to assure current users they made the right choice. One example is used in Dial soap advertisements: "Aren't you glad you use Dial. Don't you wish everybody did?"

Institutional Advertisements

The objective of **institutional advertisements** is to build goodwill or an image for an organization rather than promote a specific good or service. Institutional advertising has been used by companies such as Texaco, Pfizer, and IBM to build confidence in the company name.[6] Often this form of advertising is used to support the public relations plan or counter adverse publicity. Four alternative forms of institutional advertisements are often used:

QR 15–1
Chevron Video

1. *Advocacy* advertisements state the position of a company on an issue. Chevron's "We Agree" campaign places ads stating its position on issues such as renewable energy, growth and jobs, and community development. Another form of advocacy advertisement is used when organizations make a request related to a particular action or behavior, such as a request by the American Red Cross for blood donations.

2. *Pioneering institutional* advertisements, like the pioneering ads for products discussed earlier, are used for announcements about what a company is, what it can do, or where it is located. Recent Bayer ads stating, "We cure more headaches than you think," are intended to inform consumers that the company produces many products in addition to aspirin. Bridgestone uses pioneering institutional ads in its "One Team. One Planet" campaign to inform people about its rubber tree farms, tire recycling, and environmentally friendly factories.

3. *Competitive institutional* advertisements promote the advantages of one product class over another and are used in markets where different product classes compete for the same buyers. America's milk processors and dairy farmers use their "Got Milk?" campaign to increase demand for milk as it competes against other beverages.

4. *Reminder institutional* advertisements, like the product form, simply bring the company's name to the attention of the target market again. The Army branch of the U.S. military sponsors a campaign to remind potential recruits of the opportunities in the Army.

A reminder institutional ad by the U.S. Army tries to keep the attention of the target market.

learning review

1. What is the difference between pioneering and competitive ads?
2. What is the purpose of an institutional advertisement?

DEVELOPING THE ADVERTISING PROGRAM

LO2

The promotion decision process described in Chapter 14 can be applied to each of the promotional elements. Advertising, for example, can be managed by following the three steps (developing, executing, and evaluating) of the process.

Identifying the Target Audience

To develop an effective advertising program, advertisers must identify the target audience. All aspects of an advertising program are likely to be influenced by the characteristics of the prospective consumer. Understanding the lifestyles, attitudes, and demographics of the target market is essential. Dr Pepper, for example, promoted its reduced-calorie soda, Dr Pepper Ten, to 25- to 34-year-old men, while Kraft targeted 20- to 30-year-old women for its Greek yogurt, Athenos. Both campaigns emphasized advertising techniques that matched the audience—a mobile "man cave" parked at baseball fields and car shows for men, and a Facebook Page with nutritional information for women. Similarly, the placement of the advertising depends on the audience. When Gatorade introduced G Series Fit it placed ads on E! and MapMyFitness.com to reach "fitness" athletes who exercise regularly. Even scheduling can depend on the audience. Nike schedules advertising, sponsorships, deals, and endorsements to correspond with the Olympics to appeal to "hard-core" athletes.[7] To eliminate possible bias that might result from subjective judgments about some population segments, the Federal Communications Commission suggests that advertising program decisions be based on market research about the target audience.[8]

Specifying Advertising Objectives

The guidelines for setting promotion objectives described in Chapter 14 also apply to setting advertising objectives. This step helps advertisers with other choices in the promotion decision process, such as selecting media and evaluating a campaign. Advertising with an objective of creating awareness, for example, would be better matched with a magazine than a directory such as the Yellow Pages. The Association of Magazine Media believes objectives are so important that it offers an award each year to the campaign that demonstrates "both creative excellence and effectiveness in meeting campaign objectives." Similarly, the Advertising Research Foundation sponsors an Advertising Effectiveness Forum to "advance the practice of measuring and evaluating the effectiveness of advertising and marketing communication."[9]

QR 15–2
E*TRADE Video

Setting the Advertising Budget

During the 1990 Super Bowl, it cost companies $700,000 to place a 30-second ad. By 2012, the cost of placing a 30-second ad during Super Bowl XLVI was $3.5 million. The reason for the escalating cost is the growing number of viewers: 111 million people, or about 50 percent of the viewing public, watch the game. In addition, the audience is attractive to advertisers because research indicates it is equally split between men and women and many viewers look forward to watching the ads and then using social media to share comments with friends. More than 50 percent of the Super Bowl XLVI ads mentioned a website, about 15 percent included prompts for Facebook or Twitter, and 10 percent included QR codes or text messages. The ads are effective too: The most recent commercials generated 985,000 social media comments, including 10,000 tweets per second during the last three minutes of the game. As a result, the Super Bowl attracts many advertisers such Anheuser-Busch, Chrysler, M&Ms, Coca-Cola, E*TRADE, CareerBuilder.com, and GoDaddy. The consumer-generated Doritos ad of a grandmother who used a sling-wearing baby to snatch a bag of Doritos was rated the highest and won $1 million![10]

Do you remember this Doritos ad from the Super Bowl?

Designing the Advertisement

An advertising message usually focuses on the key benefits of the product that are important to a prospective buyer in making trial and adoption decisions. The message depends on the general form or appeal used in the ad and the actual words included in the ad.

Message Content   Most advertising messages are made up of both informational and persuasional elements. Information and persuasive content can be combined in the form of an appeal to provide a basic reason for the consumer to act. Although the marketer can use many different types of appeals, common advertising appeals include fear, sex, and humor.

Fear appeals suggest to the consumer that he or she can avoid some negative experience through the purchase and use of a product or service, a change in behavior, or a reduction in the use of a product. Examples with which you may be familiar include

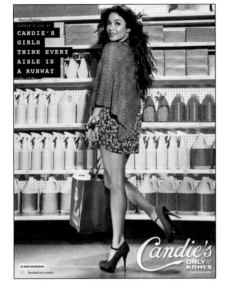

automobile safety ads that depict an accident or injury; political candidate endorsements that warn against the rise of other, unpopular ideologies; or social cause ads warning of the serious consequences of drug and alcohol use. When using fear appeals, the advertiser must be sure that the appeal is strong enough to get the audience's attention and concern but not so strong that it will lead them to tune out the message. In fact, research on antismoking ads indicates that stressing the severity of long-term health risks may actually enhance smoking's allure among youth.[11]

In contrast, *sex appeals* suggest to the audience that the product will increase the attractiveness of the user. Sex appeals can be found in almost any product category, from automobiles to toothpaste. The contemporary women's clothing store Bebe, for example, designs its advertising to "attract customers who are intrigued by the playfully sensual and evocative imagery of the Bebe lifestyle." Studies indicate that sex appeals increase attention by helping advertising stand out in today's cluttered media environment. Unfortunately, sexual content does not always lead to changes in recall, recognition, or purchase intent. Experts suggest that sexual content is most effective when there is a strong fit between the use of a sex appeal in the ad and the image and positioning of the brand, as seen in the Candie's ad.[12]

Read the text to learn why Candie's uses a sex appeal in its advertising.

Humorous appeals imply either directly or subtly that the product is more fun or exciting than competitors' offerings. As with fear and sex appeals, the use of humor is widespread in advertising and can be found in many product categories. You may have smiled at the popular Geico ads that use cavemen, a gecko, a stack of money with eyes named Kash, and a Rod Serling look-alike actor. These ads use humor to differentiate the company from its competitors. The ads have been so popular that Geico has created viral videos and posted them on video-sharing websites such as YouTube, where millions of viewers watch them within days.[13] You may have a favorite humorous ad character, such as the Energizer battery bunny, the AFLAC duck, or Travelocity's gnome. Advertisers believe that humor improves the effectiveness of their ads, although some studies suggest that humor wears out quickly, losing the interest of consumers. Another problem with humorous appeals is that their effectiveness may vary across cultures if used in a global campaign.[14]

QR 15–3
Chrysler Ad

Creating the Actual Message   Copywriters are responsible for creating the text portion of the messages in advertisements. Translating the copywriter's ideas into an actual advertisement is a complex process.

Designing quality artwork, layout, and production for advertisements is costly and time-consuming. The American Association of Advertising Agencies reports that high-quality TV commercials typically cost about $324,000 to produce a 30-second ad. One reason for the high costs is that as companies have developed global campaigns, the need to shoot commercials in several locations has increased. Audi recently filmed commercials in Germany, Australia, and Morocco. Actors are also expensive: Compensation for a typical TV ad is $16,000.[15]

Advertising agency Wieden + Kennedy was recently designated *Advertising Age* magazine's U.S. Agency of the Year for its creative approach to bringing "brands closer to consumers." Examples of the agency's approach include the "Imported from Detroit" campaign for Chrysler, "The Man Your Man Could Smell Like" campaign for Old Spice, and the "Curve ID" campaign for Levi's. W+K was also recognized for its use of digital and social media. The Old Spice television campaign, for example, was followed by an online "Response" campaign that generated 40 million views in one week, a 2,700 percent increase in Twitter followers, an 800 percent increase in Facebook fan interaction, a 300 percent increase in traffic to www.oldspice.com, and a 107 percent increase in sales.[16]

QR 15–4
Levi's Ad

---

learning review

3. The Federal Communications Commission suggests that advertising program decisions be based on _____.

4. Describe three common forms of advertising appeals.

Selecting the Right Media

Every advertiser must decide where to place its advertisements. The alternatives are the *advertising media*, the means by which the message is communicated to the target audience. Newspapers, magazines, radio, and TV are examples of advertising media. This decision on media selection is related to the target audience, type of product, nature of the message, campaign objectives, available budget, and the costs of the alternative media. Figure 15–1 shows the distribution of the $209 billion spent on advertising among the many media alternatives.[17]

In deciding where to place advertisements, a company has several media to choose from and a number of alternatives, or vehicles, within each medium. Often advertisers use a mix of media forms and vehicles to maximize the exposure of the message to the target audience while at the same time minimizing costs. These two conflicting goals are of central importance to media planning.

Because advertisers try to maximize the number of individuals in the target market exposed to the message, they must be concerned with reach. *Reach* is the number of

FIGURE 15–1

Television and direct mail account for more than 50 percent of all advertising expenditures (in millions).

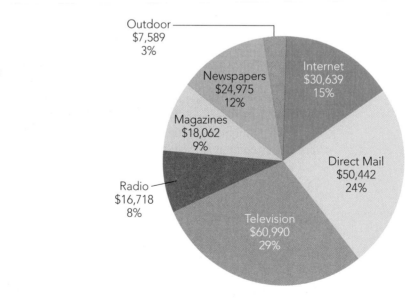

Using Marketing Dashboards
What Is the Best Way to Reach 1,000 Customers?

Marketing managers must choose from many advertising options as they design a campaign to reach potential customers. Because there are so many media alternatives (television, radio, magazines, etc.) and multiple options within each of the media, it is important to monitor the efficiency of advertising expenditures on your marketing dashboard.

Your Challenge As the marketing manager for a company about to introduce a new soft drink into the U.S. market, you are preparing a presentation in which you must make recommendations for the advertising campaign. You have observed that competitors use magazine ads, newspaper ads, and even Super Bowl ads! To compare the cost of some of the alternatives you decide to use one of the most common measures in advertising: cost per thousand impressions (CPM). The CPM is calculated as follows:

Cost per thousand impressions =
 Advertising cost ($)/Impressions generated (in 1,000s)

Your challenge is to determine the most efficient use of your advertising budget.

Your Findings Your research department helps you collect cost and audience size information for three options: full-page color ads in *Bloomberg Businessweek* magazine and *USA Today* newspaper, and a 30-second television ad during

Media Alternative	Cost of Ad	Audience Size	Cost per Thousand Impressions
Bloomberg Businessweek (magazine)	$156,800	980,000	$160
USA Today (newspaper)	$242,600	1,981,016	$122
Super Bowl (television)	$3,500,000	111,300,000	$31

the Super Bowl. With this information you are able to calculate the cost per thousand impressions for each alternative.

Your Action Based on the calculations for these options, you see that there is a large variation in the cost of reaching 1,000 potential customers (CPM) and also in the absolute cost of the advertising. Although advertising during the Super Bowl has the lowest CPM, $31 for each 1,000 impressions, it also has the largest absolute cost! Your next step will be to consider other factors such as your total available budget, the profiles of the audiences each alternative reaches, and whether the type of message you want to deliver is better communicated in print or on television.

different people or households exposed to an advertisement. The exact definition of reach sometimes varies among alternative media. Newspapers often use reach to describe their total circulation or the number of different households that buy the paper. Television and radio stations, in contrast, describe their reach using the term *rating*—the percentage of households in a market that are tuned to a particular TV show or radio station. In general, advertisers try to maximize reach in their target market at the lowest cost.

Although reach is important, advertisers are also interested in exposing their target audience to a message more than once. This is because consumers often do not pay close attention to advertising messages, some of which contain large amounts of relatively complex information. When advertisers want to reach the same audience more than once, they are concerned with *frequency*, the average number of times a person in the target audience is exposed to a message or advertisement. Like reach, greater frequency is generally viewed as desirable. Studies indicate that with repeated exposure to advertisements consumers respond more favorably to brand extensions.[18]

When reach (expressed as a percentage of the total market) is multiplied by frequency, an advertiser will obtain a commonly used reference number called *gross rating points* (GRPs). To obtain the appropriate number of GRPs to achieve an advertising campaign's objectives, the media planner must balance reach and frequency. The balance will also be influenced by cost. *Cost per thousand* (CPM) refers to the cost of reaching 1,000 individuals or households with the advertising message in a given medium (*M* is the Roman numeral for 1,000). See the Using Marketing Dashboards box for an example of the use of CPM in media selection.

Different Media Alternatives

LO3

Figure 15–2 summarizes the advantages and disadvantages of the major advertising media, which are described in more detail below. Direct mail was discussed in Chapter 14.

Television Television is a valuable medium because it communicates with sight, sound, and motion. Print advertisements alone could never give you the sense of a sports car accelerating from a stop or cornering at a high speed. In addition, network television reaches 96.7 percent of all households—114.7 million—more than any other advertising option. There are also many opportunities for out-of-home TV viewing as televisions can be seen in many bars, hotels, offices, airports, and on college campuses.

Television's major disadvantage is cost: The price of a prime-time, 30-second ad can range from $502,900 to run on *American Idol,* to $203,078 to run on *Grey's Anatomy,* to $55,358 to run on *Grimm.* Because of these high charges, many advertisers choose less expensive "spot" ads, which run between programs, or 15-second ads, rather than the traditional 30- or 60-second lengths. Approximately 25 percent of all TV ads are now 15 seconds long. In addition, there is some indication that advertisers are shifting their interest to live events rather than programs that might be watched on a DVR days later.[19]

FIGURE 15–2

Advertisers must consider the advantages and disadvantages of the many media alternatives.

MEDIUM	ADVANTAGES	DISADVANTAGES
Television	Reaches extremely large audience; uses picture, print, sound, and motion for effect; can target specific audiences	High cost to prepare and run ads; short exposure time and perishable message; difficult to convey complex information
Radio	Low cost; can target specific local audiences; ads can be placed quickly; can use sound, humor, and intimacy effectively	No visual element; short exposure time and perishable message; difficult to convey complex information
Magazines	Can target specific audiences; high-quality color; long life of ad; ads can be clipped and saved; can convey complex information	Long time needed to place ad; relatively high cost; competes for attention with other magazine features
Newspapers	Excellent coverage of local markets; ads can be placed and changed quickly; ads can be saved; quick consumer response; low cost	Ads compete for attention with other newspaper features; short life span; poor color
Yellow Pages	Excellent coverage of geographic segments; long use period; available 24 hours/365 days	Proliferation of competitive directories in many markets; difficult to keep up-to-date
Internet	Video and audio capabilities; animation can capture attention; ads can be interactive and link to advertiser	Animation and interactivity require large files and more time to load; effectiveness is still uncertain
Outdoor	Low cost; local market focus; high visibility; opportunity for repeat exposures	Message must be short and simple; low selectivity of audience; criticized as a traffic hazard
Direct mail	High selectivity of audience; can contain complex information and personalized messages; high-quality graphics	High cost per contact; poor image (junk mail)

Oxygen is one of many specialized channels available to advertisers on cable networks.

Magazines such as *Sports Illustrated for Kids* appeal to narrowly defined segments such as children and teenagers.

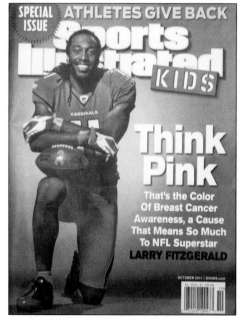

Another problem with television advertising is the likelihood of *wasted coverage*—having people outside the market for the product see the advertisement. The cost and wasted coverage problems of TV advertising can be reduced through the specialized cable and satellite channels. Advertising time is often less expensive on cable and satellite channels than on the broadcast networks. According to the National Cable and Telecommunications Association, there are 565 cable networks, such as ESPN, MTV, Lifetime, Oxygen, the Speed Channel, the History Channel, the Science Channel, and the Food Network, that reach very narrowly defined audiences. Cable networks are also "tagging" their programs to allow advertisers to place ads in scenes with particular themes. Advertisements for golf equipment, for example, might be placed after a program scene that shows characters playing golf.[20]

Another popular form of television advertising is the infomercial. **Infomercials** are program-length (30-minute) advertisements that take an educational approach to communication with potential customers. You may remember seeing products such as the Magic Bullet, ThighMaster, and OxiClean on infomercials with Ron Popeil, Suzanne Somers, and Billy Mays as their respective spokespersons. Infomercials are increasingly popular because the slow economy has reduced the average cost of a 30-minute block of television time to an average of $425.

Radio The United States has more than 24,700 radio stations. These stations consist of approximately 4,800 AM, 9,800 FM, and 10,100 HD and Internet stations. The major advantage of radio is that it is a segmented medium. For example, the Farm Radio Network, the Family Life Network, Business Talk Radio, and the Performance Racing Network are all listened to by different market segments. The large number of media options today has reduced the amount of time spent listening to radio, also. The average 18- to 24-year-old, however, still listens to radio an average of 12.5 hours each week, making radio an important medium for businesses with college students as a target market.[21]

A disadvantage of radio is that it has limited use for products that must be seen. Another problem is the ease with which consumers can tune out a commercial by switching stations. Satellite radio service SiriusXM offers more than 135 commercial-free, digital, coast-to-coast channels to consumers for a monthly fee. Radio is also a medium that competes for people's attention as they do other activities such as driving, working, or relaxing. Radio listening time reaches its peak during the morning drive time (7 to 8 A.M.), remains high during the day, and then begins to decline in the afternoon (after 4 P.M.) as people return home and start evening activities.[22]

Magazines Magazines have become a very specialized medium, primarily because there are currently more than 16,500 magazines. Some 180 new magazines were introduced last year, including *Athlon Sports,* a monthly magazine distributed through newspapers; *Bound by Ink,* a quarterly about tattoos and tattoo artists; *Chop Chop,* a food magazine for families whose kids want to be in the kitchen; and *Emerge,* a business magazine that focuses on the people involved in the stories. Many publishers are also adding new digital versions of existing magazines. The *New Yorker,* for example, can now be read in its entirety on an iPad. Some magazines, such as *Accountancy Age* and *Computer Weekly,* are dropping their print format to offer only an online version.[23]

The marketing advantage of this medium is the great number of special-interest publications that appeal to narrowly defined segments. Runners read *Runner's World,* sailors buy *Yachting,* gardeners subscribe to *Garden Design,* and children peruse *Sports Illustrated for Kids.* More than 829 publications focus on travel, 128 are dedicated to interior design and decoration, and 140 are related to golf. Each magazine's

Print advertising can help attract readers to newspapers such as *USA Today*.

USA Today
www.usatoday.com

Yellow pages are used more than 11 billion times each year. See the text for advantages and disadvantages of this media alternative.

readers often represent a unique profile. Take the *Rolling Stone* reader, who tends to listen to music more than most people; Sirius XM satellite radio knows an ad in *Rolling Stone* is reaching the desired target audience. In addition, recent studies comparing advertising in different media suggest that magazine advertising is perceived to be more "trustworthy," "inspirational," and engaging than other media.[24]

The cost of advertising in national magazines is a disadvantage, but many national publications publish regional and even metro editions, which reduces the absolute cost and wasted coverage. *Time* publishes many editions, including Latin American, Canadian, Asian, South Pacific, European, and U.S. editions.

Newspapers Newspapers are an important local medium with excellent reach potential. Daily publication allows advertisements to focus on specific current events, such as a 24-hour sale. Local retailers often use newspapers as their sole advertising medium. Newspapers are rarely saved by the purchaser, however, so companies are generally limited to ads that call for an immediate customer response (although customers can clip and save ads they select). Companies also cannot depend on newspapers for color reproduction as good as that in most magazines.

National advertising campaigns rarely include this medium except in conjunction with local distributors of their products. In these instances, both parties often share the advertising costs using a cooperative advertising program, which is described later in this chapter. Another exception is the use of newspapers such as *The Wall Street Journal* and *USA Today*, which have national distribution of more than 1.5 and 2.0 million readers, respectively. One newspaper, *Metro*, offers a global audience of 20 million daily readers in Boston, New York, Philadelphia, and 100 cities in Europe, North and South America, and Asia.[25]

Yellow Pages Yellow pages represent an advertising media alternative comparable to radio and magazines in terms of expenditures—about $10 billion in the United States and $23 billion globally. According to the Local Search Association, consumers turn to print yellow pages more than 11 billion times annually and online yellow pages an additional 5.6 billion times per year. One reason for this high level of use is that the 6,500 yellow pages directories reach almost all households with telephones. Yellow pages are a directional medium because they help consumers know where purchases can be made after other media have created awareness and demand. A disadvantage faced by yellow pages today is the proliferation of directories. AT&T (Real Yellow Pages), SuperMedia (Verizon Superpages), and R.H. Donnelley (DEX) now produce competing directories for many cities, neighborhoods, and ethnic groups.[26]

Internet The Internet represents a relatively new medium for many advertisers although it has already attracted a wide variety of industries. Online advertising is similar to print advertising in that it offers a visual message. It has additional advantages, however, because it can also use the audio and video capabilities of the Internet. Sound and movement may simply attract more attention from viewers, or they may provide an element of entertainment to the message. Online advertising also has the unique feature of being interactive. Called *rich media*, these interactive ads have drop-down menus, built-in games, or search engines to engage viewers. Although online advertising is relatively small compared to other traditional media, it offers an opportunity to reach younger consumers who have developed a preference for online communication.

A disadvantage of online advertising is the difficulty of measuring impact. Several companies are testing methods of tracking where viewers go on their computer in the days and weeks after seeing an ad. Nielsen's online rating service, for example, measures actual Internet use through meters installed on the computers of 500,000 individuals in 20 countries. Measuring the relationship between online and offline behavior is

Who Is Responsible for Click Fraud?

Spending on Internet advertising is expected to exceed $20 billion in 2014 as many advertisers shift their budgets from print and TV to the Internet. For most advertisers one advantage of online advertising is that they pay only when someone clicks on their ad. Unfortunately, the growth of the medium has led to "click fraud," which is the deceptive clicking of ads solely to increase the amount advertisers must pay. There are several forms of click fraud. One method is the result of Paid-to-Read (PTR) websites that recruit and pay members to simply click on ads. Another method is the result of "click-bots," which are software programs that produce automatic clicks on ads, sometimes through mobile devices. While the activity is difficult to detect and stop, experts estimate that up to 19 percent of clicks may be the result of fraud and may be costing advertisers as much as $800 million each year!

Two of the largest portals for Internet advertising are Google and Yahoo! Both firms try to filter out illegitimate clicks, although some advertisers claim that they are still

being charged for PTR and clickbot traffic. Although the laws that govern click fraud are not very clear, Google and Yahoo! have each settled class action lawsuits and agreed to provide rebates or credits to advertisers who were charged for fraudulent clicks.

Investigations of the online advertising industry have discovered a related form of click fraud that occurs when legitimate website visitors click on ads without any intention of looking at the site. As one consumer explains, "I always try and remember to click on the ad banners once in a while to try and keep the sites free." Stephen Dubner calls this "webtipping"!

As the Internet advertising industry grows it will become increasingly important to resolve the issue of click fraud. Consumers, advertisers, websites that carry paid advertising, and the large web portals are all involved in a complicated technical, legal, and social situation. Who do you think is responsible for click fraud? Who should lead the way in the effort to find a solution?

Every dog can be identified by its unique nose print.
We can help you sniff out your customers. →

The Science of Digital Marketing

24/7 REAL MEDIA

24/7 Real Media's service can provide an assessment of the effectiveness of a website by monitoring "click-through" rates.

also important. Recent research by comScore, which studied 139 online ad campaigns, revealed that online ads didn't always result in a "click," but they increased the likelihood of a purchase by 17 percent and they increased visits to the advertiser's website by 40 percent.[27] The Making Responsible Decisions box describes how click fraud is increasing the necessity of assessing online advertising effectiveness.[28]

Outdoor   A very effective medium for reminding consumers about your product is outdoor advertising, such as the scoreboard at San Diego's Qualcomm Stadium. The most common form of outdoor advertising, called *billboards*, often results in good reach and frequency and has been shown to increase purchase rates.[29] The visibility of this medium is good supplemental reinforcement for well-known products, and it is a relatively low-cost, flexible alternative. A company can buy space just in the desired geographical market. A disadvantage to billboards, however, is that no opportunity exists for lengthy advertising copy. Also, a good billboard site depends on traffic patterns and sight lines.

If you have ever lived in a metropolitan area, chances are you might have seen another form of outdoor advertising, *transit advertising*. This medium includes messages on the interior and exterior of buses, subway and light-rail cars, and taxis. As the use of mass transit grows, transit advertising may become increasingly important. Selectivity is available to advertisers, who can buy space by neighborhood or bus route. One disadvantage to this medium is that the heavy travel times, when the audiences are the largest, are not conducive to reading advertising copy. People are standing shoulder to shoulder on the subway, hoping not to miss their stop, and little attention is paid to the advertising.

Other Media   As traditional media have become more expensive and cluttered, advertisers have been attracted to a variety of nontraditional advertising

options called out-of-home advertising, or *place-based media*. Messages are placed in locations that attract a specific target audience such as airports, doctors' offices, health clubs, theaters (where ads are played on the screen before the movies are shown), grocery stores, storefronts, and even the bathrooms of bars, restaurants, and nightclubs. Soon there will be advertising on video screens on gas pumps, ATMs, and in elevators, and increasingly it will be interactive. The $2.5 billion industry has attracted advertisers such as AT&T and JCPenney, which use in-store campaigns, and Geico, Sprint, and FedEx, which use out-of-home advertising to reach mobile professionals in health clubs, airports, and hotels. Research suggests that creative use of out-of-home advertising, such as preshow theater ads, enhances consumer recall of the ads.[30]

Outdoor advertising can be an effective medium for reminding consumers about a product.

Scheduling the Advertising

There is no correct schedule to advertise a product, but three factors must be considered. First is the issue of *buyer turnover*, which is how often new buyers enter the market to buy the product. The higher the buyer turnover, the greater the amount of advertising required. A second issue in scheduling is the *purchase frequency*; the more frequently the product is purchased, the less repetition is required. Finally, companies must consider the *forgetting rate*, the speed at which buyers forget the brand if advertising is not seen.

Setting schedules requires an understanding of how the market behaves. Most companies tend to follow one of three basic approaches:

1. *Continuous (steady) schedule.* When seasonal factors are unimportant, advertising is run at a continuous or steady schedule throughout the year.
2. *Flighting (intermittent) schedule.* Periods of advertising are scheduled between periods of no advertising to reflect seasonal demand.
3. *Pulse (burst) schedule.* A flighting schedule is combined with a continuous schedule because of increases in demand, heavy periods of promotion, or the introduction of a new product.

For example, products such as breakfast cereals have a stable demand throughout the year and would typically use a continuous schedule of advertising. In contrast, products such as snow skis and suntan lotions have seasonal demands and receive flighting-schedule advertising during the seasonal demand period. Some products such as toys or automobiles require pulse-schedule advertising to facilitate sales throughout the year and during special periods of increased demand (such as holidays or new car introductions). Some evidence suggests that pulsing schedules are superior to other advertising strategies.[31] In addition, research indicates the effectiveness of a particular ad wears out quickly and, therefore, many alternative forms of a commercial may be more effective.[32]

Out-of-home advertising such as this storefront display is becoming interactive to engage consumers.

learning review

5. You see the same ad in *Time* and *Fortune* magazines and on billboards and TV. Is this an example of reach or frequency?

6. Why has the Internet become a popular advertising medium?

7. Describe three approaches to scheduling advertising.

EXECUTING THE ADVERTISING PROGRAM

Executing the advertising program involves pretesting the advertising copy and actually carrying out the advertising program. John Wanamaker, the founder of Wanamaker's Department Store in Philadelphia, remarked, "I know half my advertising is wasted, but I don't know what half." By evaluating advertising efforts, marketers can try to ensure that their advertising expenditures are not wasted.[33] Evaluation is done usually at two separate times: before and after the advertisements are run in the actual campaign. Several methods used in the evaluation process at the stages of idea formulation and copy development are discussed below.

Pretesting the Advertising

To determine whether the advertisement communicates the intended message or to select among alternative versions of the advertisement, **pretests** are conducted before the advertisements are placed in any medium.

pretests

Tests conducted before an advertisement is placed in any medium to determine whether it communicates the intended message or to select among alternative versions of the advertisement.

Portfolio Tests   Portfolio tests are used to test copy alternatives. The test ad is placed in a portfolio with several other ads and stories, and consumers are asked to read through the portfolio. Afterward, subjects are asked for their impressions of the ads on several evaluative scales, such as from "very informative" to "not very informative."

Jury Tests   Jury tests involve showing the ad copy to a panel of consumers and having them rate how they liked it, how much it drew their attention, and how attractive they thought it was. This approach is similar to the portfolio test in that consumer reactions are obtained. However, unlike the portfolio test, a test advertisement is not hidden within other ads.

Theater Tests   Theater testing is the most sophisticated form of pretesting. Consumers are invited to view new television shows or movies in which test commercials are also shown. Viewers register their feelings about the advertisements either on handheld electronic recording devices used during the viewing or on questionnaires afterward.

Carrying Out the Advertising Program

The responsibility for actually carrying out the advertising program can be handled by one of three types of agencies. The *full-service agency* provides the most complete range of services, including market research, media selection, copy development, artwork, and production. In the past, agencies that assisted a client by both developing and placing advertisements often charged a commission of 15 percent of the media costs. As corporations introduced integrated marketing approaches, however, many advertisers switched from paying commissions to incentive plans based on performance. These plans typically pay for agency costs and a 5 to 10 percent profit, plus bonuses if specific performance goals related to brand preference, lead generation, sales, and market share are met. In the future, clients may move to a value-based approach where compensation is dependent on sales of the advertised product or brand.[34]

Limited-service agencies specialize in one aspect of the advertising process, such as providing creative services to develop the advertising copy, buying previously unpurchased media (media agencies), or providing Internet services (Internet agencies). Limited-service agencies that deal in creative work are compensated by a contractual agreement for the services performed. Finally, *in-house agencies* made up of the company's own advertising staff may provide full services or a limited range of services.

ASSESSING THE ADVERTISING PROGRAM

The advertising decision process does not stop with executing the advertising program. The advertisements must be evaluated to determine whether they are achieving their intended objectives, and results may indicate that changes must be made in the advertising program.

Posttesting the Advertising

An advertisement may go through **posttests** after it has been shown to the target audience to determine whether it accomplished its intended purpose. Five approaches common in posttesting are discussed here.[35]

Aided Recall   After being shown an ad, respondents are asked whether their previous exposure to it was through reading, viewing, or listening. The Starch test uses aided recall to determine the percentage of those (1) who remember seeing a specific magazine ad (*noted*), (2) who saw or read any part of the ad identifying the product or brand (*seen-associated*), (3) who read any part of the ad's copy (read some), and (4) who read at least half of the ad (*read most*). Elements of the ad are then tagged with the results.[36]

Unaided Recall   A question such as, "What ads do you remember seeing yesterday?" is asked of respondents without any prompting to determine whether they saw or heard advertising messages.

Attitude Tests   Respondents are asked questions to measure changes in their attitudes after an advertising campaign, such as whether they have a more favorable attitude toward the product advertised.[37]

The Starch test uses aided recall to evaluate an ad on four dimensions. See the text to learn more.

Inquiry Tests   Additional product information, product samples, or premiums are offered to an ad's readers or viewers. Ads generating the most inquiries are presumed to be the most effective.

Sales Tests   Sales tests involve studies such as controlled experiments (e.g., using radio ads in one market and newspaper ads in another and comparing the results) and consumer purchase tests (measuring retail sales that result from a given advertising campaign). The most sophisticated experimental methods today allow a manufacturer, a distributor, or an advertising agency to manipulate an advertising variable (such as schedule or copy) through cable systems and observe subsequent sales effects by monitoring data collected from checkout scanners in supermarkets.[38]

---

learning review

8. Explain the difference between pretesting and posttesting advertising copy.

9. What is the difference between aided and unaided recall posttests?

SALES PROMOTION

LO4

Sales promotion has become a key element of the promotional mix, which now accounts for more than $71.9 billion in annual expenditures. In a recent survey by *Promo* magazine, marketing professionals reported that approximately 32 percent of their budgets were allocated to advertising, 37 percent to consumer promotion, 24 percent to trade promotion, and 7 percent to other marketing activities.[39] The allocation of marketing expenditures reflects the trend toward integrated promotion programs, which include a variety of promotion elements. Selection and integration of the many promotion techniques require a good understanding of the advantages and disadvantages of each kind of promotion.[40]

Consumer-Oriented Sales Promotions

consumer-oriented sales promotions

Sales tools, such as coupons, sweepstakes, and samples, used to support a company's advertising and personal selling efforts directed to ultimate consumers.

Directed to ultimate consumers, **consumer-oriented sales promotions**, or simply *consumer promotions*, are sales tools used to support a company's advertising and personal selling. The alternative consumer-oriented sales promotion tools include coupons, deals, premiums, contests, sweepstakes, samples, loyalty programs, point-of-purchase displays, rebates, and product placements.

Coupons   Coupons are sales promotions that usually offer a discounted price to the consumer, which encourages trial. Approximately 332 billion coupons worth $470 billion are distributed in the United States each year. Most coupons are distributed as freestanding inserts in newspapers and reach 60 million households each week. Research indicates that 81 percent of consumers use coupons. Coupon redemption rates have been increasing in recent years as the weak economy has increased the attractiveness of coupons. Consumers redeemed $2.8 billion of the coupons, which was approximately $8.57 per person. Companies that have increased their use of coupons include Procter & Gamble, Nestlé, and Kraft, while the top retailers for coupon redemption were Walmart and Kroger. The number of coupons generated at Internet sites (e.g., www.valpak.com and www.coupon.com) and on mobile phones has been increasing although they account for less than 2 percent of all coupons. The redemption rate for online coupons, however, is substantially higher than other forms of coupons. Groupon and other daily coupon services generated $873 million in sales last year and expect the market to reach $3.9 billion by 2015. The extraordinary growth has attracted competitors such as LivingSocial and Facebook![41]

Coupons are often far more expensive than the face value of the coupon; a 25-cent coupon can cost three times that after paying for the advertisement to deliver it, dealer handling, clearinghouse costs, and redemption. In addition, misredemption, or attempting to redeem a counterfeit coupon or a valid coupon when the product was not purchased, should be added to the cost of the coupon. The Coupon Information Corporation estimates that companies pay out refunds worth hundreds of millions of dollars each year as a result of coupon fraud. Recent growth in coupon fraud has marketers considering adding holograms and visual aids to coupons to help cashiers identify valid coupons.[42]

Coupons encourage trial by offering a discounted price. See the text to learn if coupons increase sales.

There's something in it for you®

Deals   Deals are short-term price reductions, commonly used to increase trial among potential customers or to retaliate against a competitor's actions. For example, if a rival manufacturer introduces a new cake mix, the company responds with a "two packages for the price of one" deal. This short-term price reduction builds up the stock on the kitchen shelves of cake mix buyers and makes the competitor's introduction more difficult.

Premiums   A promotional tool often used with consumers is the premium, which consists of merchandise offered free or at a significant savings over its retail price. This latter type of premium is called self-

McDonald's Monopoly sweepstakes offers a grand prize of $1 million.

liquidating because the cost charged to the consumer covers the cost of the item. McDonald's, for example, used a free premium in a promotional partnership with 20th Century Fox during the release of the movie *Rio*. Collectible toys that portrayed movie characters were given away free with the purchase of a Happy Meal. What are the most popular premiums? According to the Promotional Products Association International, the top premiums are apparel, writing instruments, shopping bags, cups and mugs, and desk accessories. By offering a premium, companies encourage customers to return frequently or to use more of the product. Research suggests that deal-prone consumers and value seekers are attracted to premiums.[43]

Contests   Contests represent a fourth sales promotion tool in which consumers apply their skill or analytical or creative thinking to try to win a prize. This form of promotion has been growing as requests for videos, photos, and essays are a good match with the trend toward consumer-generated content. For example, PepsiCo sponsored the "Crash the Super Bowl" contest, asking people to create their own 30-second ad about Doritos and Pepsi MAX. A panel of judges selected 10 finalists from the 5,600 entries, and the public voted online for its favorite. The winner aired on the Super Bowl, and when one of the ads hit No. 1 on *USA Today*'s Super Bowl Ad Meter, it was awarded a $1 million bonus! If you like contests, you can enter online now at websites such as www.contests.about.com.[44]

Sweepstakes   Sweepstakes are sales promotions that require participants to submit some kind of entry but are purely games of chance requiring no analytical or creative effort by the consumer. Popular sweepstakes include the HGTV "Dream Home Giveaway," which receives more than 76 million entries each year, and McDonald's Monopoly, which offers a grand prize of $1 million.[45]

Two variations of sweepstakes are popular now. First are the sweepstakes that offer products that consumers value as prizes. Mars Chocolate, for example, created a sweepstakes where consumers enter a UPC code from M&M's products for a chance to win one of five Toyota automobiles. Coca-Cola has a similar sweepstakes called "My Coke Rewards" that allows consumers to use codes from bottle caps to enter to win prizes or to collect points to be redeemed for rewards. The second are the sweepstakes that offer an "experience" as the prize. For example, one of television's most popular series, *American Idol*, and AT&T sponsor a sweepstakes for a chance to win a trip for two to the season finale of *American Idol* in Los Angeles. Similarly, Coca-Cola and Celebrity Cruises created a sweepstakes where consumers enter for a chance to win a trip to the Olympics. Federal laws, the Federal Trade Commission, and state legislatures have issued rules covering sweepstakes, contests, and games to regulate fairness, ensure that the chance for winning is represented honestly, and guarantee that the prizes are actually awarded. Several well-known sweepstakes created by Publishers Clearing House and *Reader's Digest* have paid fines and agreed to new sweepstakes guidelines in response to regulatory scrutiny.[46]

Samples   Another common consumer sales promotion is sampling, which is offering the product free or at a greatly reduced price. Often used for new products, sampling puts the product in the consumer's hands. A trial size is generally offered that is smaller than the regular package size. If consumers like the sample, it is hoped they will remember and buy the product. When Mars changed its Milky Way Dark to Milky Way Midnight, it gave away more than 1 million samples to college students at nightclubs, several hundred campuses, and popular spring break locations. Awareness of the candy bar rose to 60 percent, trial rose 166 percent, and sales rose 25 percent. Recent research indicates that 63 percent of college students who receive a sample will also purchase the product. Overall, companies invest more than $2.3 billion in sampling programs each year.[47]

Point-of-purchase displays help increase consumers' attention in a store.

Loyalty Programs   Loyalty programs are a sales promotion tool used to encourage and reward repeat purchases by acknowledging each purchase made by a consumer and offering a premium as purchases accumulate. The most popular loyalty programs today are credit card reward programs. More than 75 percent of all cards offer incentives for use of their card. Citibank, for example, offers "Thank You" points for using Citi credit or debit cards. The points can be redeemed for books, music, gift cards, cash, travel, and special limited time rewards. Airlines, retailers, hotels, and grocery stores also offer popular loyalty programs. Specialty retailers such as Toys 'Я' Us and Best Buy have enhanced their reward programs to add value to their offerings as they compete with low-cost merchandise. There are now more than 2.1 billion loyalty program memberships, for an average of 18 for each household in the United States, which accumulate $48 billion worth of points each year.[48]

Point-of-Purchase Displays   In a store aisle, you often encounter a sales promotion called a point-of-purchase display. These product displays take the form of advertising signs, which sometimes actually hold or display the product, and are often located in high-traffic areas near the cash register or the end of an aisle. The point-of-purchase display for Nabisco's annual back-to-school program is designed to maximize the consumer's attention to lunch box and after-school snacks and to provide storage for the products. Annual expenditures on point-of-purchase promotions now exceed $20.3 billion and are expected to grow as point-of-purchase becomes integrated with all forms of promotion.

Rebates   Another consumer sales promotion tool, the cash rebate, offers the return of money based on proof of purchase. For example, Apple recently offered a $100 rebate to consumers who purchased an Apple computer and a printer during a three-month promotion period. When a rebate is offered on lower-priced items, the time and trouble of mailing in a proof of purchase to get the rebate check often means that many buyers never take advantage of it. However, this "slippage" is less likely to occur with frequent users of rebate promotions. In addition, online consumers are more likely to take advantage of rebates.[49]

Product Placements   A final consumer promotion tool, **product placement**, involves the use of a brand-name product in a movie, television show, video game, or commercial for another product. It was Steven Spielberg's placement of Hershey's Reese's Pieces in *E.T.* that first brought a lot of interest to the candy. Similarly, when Tom Cruise wore Bausch and Lomb's Ray-Ban sunglasses in *Risky Business* and its Aviator glasses in *Top Gun*, sales skyrocketed from 100,000 pairs to 7,000,000 pairs in five years. After *Toy Story*, Etch-A-Sketch sales increased 4,500 percent and Mr. Potato Head sales increased 800 percent. Product placement has also grown in television programs. *American Idol* ranks No. 1 with Coca-Cola, Ford, and AT&T

product placement

A consumer sales promotion that uses a brand-name product in a movie, television show, video, or commercial for another product.

Product placement can take many forms today. Are you familiar with these examples?

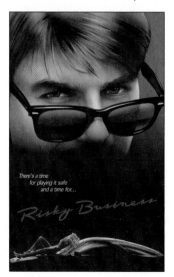

product appearances, followed by *Celebrity Apprentice* and *The Biggest Loser.* Companies are usually eager to gain exposure for their products, and studios believe that product placements can add authenticity to the film or program. The producers usually receive fees in exchange for the exposure. The latest James Bond film, for example, recently earned $45 million in product placement revenue. Complaints that product placement has become excessive have led the Federal Communications Commission to begin development of guidelines for TV product placement, while the British government recently passed a law allowing product placement if a bold "P" logo is shown before and after the program.[50]

Trade-Oriented Sales Promotions

Trade-oriented sales promotions, or simply *trade promotions*, are sales tools used to support a company's advertising and personal selling directed to wholesalers, retailers, or distributors. Some of the sales promotions just reviewed are used for this purpose, but three other common approaches are targeted uniquely to these intermediaries: (1) allowances and discounts, (2) cooperative advertising, and (3) training of distributors' salesforces.

Allowances and Discounts   Trade promotions often focus on maintaining or increasing inventory levels in the channel of distribution. An effective method for encouraging such increased purchases by intermediaries is the use of allowances and discounts. However, overuse of these price reductions can lead to retailers changing their ordering patterns in the expectation of such offerings. Although there are many variations that manufacturers can use with discounts and allowances, three common approaches are the merchandise allowance, the case allowance, and the finance allowance.[51]

Reimbursing a retailer for extra in-store support or special featuring of the brand is a *merchandise allowance*. Performance contracts between the manufacturer and trade member usually specify the activity to be performed, such as a picture of the product in a newspaper with a coupon good at only one store. The merchandise allowance then consists of a percentage deduction from the list case price ordered during the promotional period. Allowances are not paid by the manufacturer until it sees proof of performance (such as a copy of the ad placed by the retailer in the local newspaper).

A second common trade promotion, a *case allowance*, is a discount on each case ordered during a specific time period. These allowances are usually deducted from the invoice. A variation of the case allowance is the "free goods" approach, whereby retailers receive some amount of the product free based on the amount ordered, such as 1 case free for every 10 cases ordered.[52]

A final trade promotion, the *finance allowance*, involves paying retailers for financing costs or financial losses associated with consumer sales promotions. This trade promotion is regularly used and has several variations. One type is the floor stock protection program—manufacturers give retailers a case allowance price for products in their warehouse, which prevents shelf stock from running down during the promotional period. Also common are freight allowances, which compensate retailers that transport orders from the manufacturer's warehouse.

Cooperative Advertising   Resellers often perform the important function of promoting the manufacturer's products at the local level. One common sales promotional activity is to encourage both better quality and greater quantity in the local advertising efforts of resellers through **cooperative advertising**. These are programs by which a manufacturer pays a percentage of the retailer's local advertising expense for advertising the manufacturer's products.

Usually, the manufacturer pays a percentage, often 50 percent, of the cost of advertising up to a certain dollar limit, which is based on the amount of the purchases the retailer makes of the manufacturer's products. In addition to paying for the advertising, the manufacturer often furnishes the retailer with a selection of different ad executions, sometimes suited for several different media. A manufacturer may provide, for example, several different print layouts as well as a few broadcast ads for the retailer to adapt and use.[53]

Training of Distributors' Salesforces One of the many functions the intermediaries perform is customer contact and selling for the producers they represent. Both retailers and wholesalers employ and manage their own sales personnel. A manufacturer's success often rests on the ability of the reseller's salesforce to represent its products.

Thus, it is in the best interest of the manufacturer to help train the reseller's salesforce. Because the reseller's salesforce is often less sophisticated and knowledgeable about the products than the manufacturer might like, training can increase their sales performance. Training activities include producing manuals and brochures to educate the reseller's salesforce. The salesforce then uses these aids in selling situations. Other activities include national sales meetings sponsored by the manufacturer and field visits to the reseller's location to inform and motivate the salesforce to sell the products. Manufacturers also develop incentive and recognition programs to motivate a reseller's salespeople to sell their products.

---

learning review

10. Which sales promotional tool is most common for new products?

11. Which trade promotion is used to encourage the local advertising efforts of resellers?

PUBLIC RELATIONS

LO5

publicity tools
Methods of obtaining nonpersonal presentation of an organization, product, or service without direct cost.

As noted in Chapter 14, public relations is a form of communication management that seeks to influence the image of an organization and its products and services. In developing a public relations campaign, several methods of obtaining nonpersonal presentation of an organization, product, or service without direct cost—**publicity tools**—are available to the public relations director. Many companies frequently use the *news release*, consisting of an announcement regarding changes in the company or the product line. The objective of a news release is to inform a newspaper, radio station, or other medium of an idea for a story.

A second common publicity tool is the *news conference*. Representatives of the media are all invited to an informational meeting, and advance materials regarding the content are sent. This tool is often used when new products are introduced or significant changes in corporate structure and leadership are being made.

Nonprofit organizations rely heavily on *public service announcements* (PSAs), which are free space or time donated by the media. For example, the charter of the American Red Cross prohibits any local chapter from advertising, so to solicit blood donations local chapters often depend on PSAs on radio or television to announce their needs.

---

learning review

12. What is a news release?

13. What type of publicity tool is used most often by nonprofit organizations?

LEARNING OBJECTIVES REVIEW

LO1 *Explain the differences between product advertising and institutional advertising and the variations within each type.*

Product advertisements focus on selling a good or service and take three forms: Pioneering advertisements tell people what a product is, what it can do, and where it can be found; competitive advertisements persuade the target market to select the firm's brand rather than a competitor's; and reminder advertisements reinforce previous knowledge of a product. Institutional advertisements are used to build goodwill or an image for an organization. They include advocacy advertisements, which state the position of a company on an issue, and pioneering, competitive, and reminder advertisements, which are similar to the product ads but focused on the institution.

LO2 *Describe the steps used to develop, execute, and evaluate an advertising program.*

The promotion decision process can be applied to each of the promotional elements. The steps to develop an advertising program include the following: identify the target audience, specify the advertising objectives, set the advertising budget, design the advertisement, create the message, select the media, and schedule the advertising. Executing the program requires pretesting, and evaluating the program requires posttesting.

LO3 *Explain the advantages and disadvantages of alternative advertising media.*

Television advertising reaches large audiences and uses pictures, print, sound, and motion; its disadvantages, however, are that it is expensive and perishable. Radio advertising is inexpensive and can be placed quickly, but it has no visual element and is perishable. Magazine advertising can target specific audiences and can convey complex information, but it takes a long time to place the ad and is relatively expensive. Newspapers provide excellent coverage of local markets and can be changed quickly, but they have a short life span and poor color. Yellow pages advertising has a long use period and is available 24 hours per day; its disadvantages, however, are that there is a proliferation of directories and they cannot be updated frequently. Internet advertising can be interactive, but its effectiveness is difficult to measure. Outdoor advertising provides repeat exposures, but its message must be very short and simple. Direct mail can be targeted at very selective audiences, but its cost per contact is high.

LO4 *Discuss the strengths and weaknesses of consumer-oriented and trade-oriented sales promotions.*

Coupons encourage retailer support but may delay consumer purchases. Deals reduce consumer risk but reduce perceived value. Premiums offer consumers additional merchandise they want, but they may be purchasing only for the premium. Contests create involvement but require creative thinking. Sweepstakes encourage repeat purchases, but sales drop after the sweepstakes. Samples encourage product trial but are expensive. Loyalty programs help create loyalty but are expensive to run. Displays provide visibility but are difficult to place in retail space. Rebates stimulate demand but are easily copied. Product placements provide a positive message in a noncommercial setting that is difficult to control. Trade-oriented sales promotions include (*a*) allowances and discounts, which increase purchases but may change retailer ordering patterns, (*b*) cooperative advertising, which encourages local advertising, and (*c*) salesforce training, which helps increase sales by providing the salespeople with product information and selling skills.

LO5 *Recognize public relations as an important form of communication.*

Public relations activities usually focus on communicating positive aspects of the business. A frequently used public relations tool is publicity. Publicity tools include news releases and news conferences. Nonprofit organizations often use public service announcements.

FOCUSING ON KEY TERMS

APPLYING MARKETING KNOWLEDGE

1 How does competitive product advertising differ from competitive institutional advertising?

2 Suppose you are the advertising manager for a new line of children's fragrances. Which form of media would you use for this new product?

3 You have recently been promoted to be director of advertising for the Timkin Tool Company. In your first meeting with Mr. Timkin, he says, "Advertising is a waste! We've been advertising for six months now and sales haven't increased. Tell me why we should continue." Give your answer to Mr. Timkin.

4 A large life insurance company has decided to switch from using a strong fear appeal to a humorous approach. What are the strengths and weaknesses of such a change in message strategy?

5 Some national advertisers have found that they can have more impact with their advertising by running a large number of ads for a period and then running no ads at all for a period. Why might such a flighting schedule be more effective than a continuous schedule?

6 Which medium has the lowest cost per thousand?

Medium	Cost	Audience
TV show	$5,000	25,000
Magazine	2,200	6,000
Newspaper	4,800	7,200
FM radio	420	1,600

7 Each year managers at Bausch and Lomb evaluate the many advertising media alternatives available to them as they develop their advertising program for contact lenses. What advantages and disadvantages of each alternative should they consider? Which media would you recommend to them?

8 What are two advantages and two disadvantages of the advertising posttests described in the chapter?

9 Federated Banks is interested in consumer-oriented sales promotions that would encourage senior citizens to direct deposit their Social Security checks with the bank. Evaluate the sales promotion options, and recommend two of them to the bank.

10 How can public relations be used by Firestone and Ford following investigations into complaints about tire failures?

building your marketing plan

To augment your promotion strategy from Chapter 14:

1 Use Figure 15–2 to select the advertising media you will include in your plan by analyzing how combinations of media (e.g., television and Internet advertising, radio and yellow pages advertising) can complement each other.

2 Select your consumer-oriented sales promotion activities (coupons, deals, premiums, contests, sweepstakes, samples, loyalty programs, point-of-purchase displays, rebates, and/or product placements).

3 Specify which trade-oriented sales promotions and public relations tools you will use.

video case 15 Google, Inc.: The Right Ads at the Right Time

QR 15–5
Google Video
Case

"So what we did, in essence, is we said advertising should be useful to a consumer just as much as the organic search results, and we don't want people just to buy advertising and be able to show an ad if it's irrelevant to the consumer's need," says Richard Holden, director of product management at Google. To accomplish this, Google developed a "Quality Score" model to predict how effective an ad will be. The model uses many factors, such as click-through rates, advertiser history, and keyword performance, to develop a score for each advertisement. "Essentially, what we're trying to do is predict ahead, before we actually show an ad, how a consumer will react to that ad, and our interest is in showing fewer ads, not more ads; just the right ads at the right time," Holden continues. The Google advertising model has revolutionized the advertising industry, and it continues to improve every day!

THE COMPANY

Google began in 1996 as a research project for Stanford computer science students Larry Page and Sergey Brin.

They started with a simple idea—that a search engine based on the relationships between websites would provide a better ranking than a search engine based only on the number of times a key term appeared on a website. The success of their model led to rapid growth and the founders moved the company from their dorm room, to a friend's garage, to offices in Palo Alto, California, and eventually to its current location, known as the Googleplex, in Mountain View, California. In 2000, Google began selling advertising as a means of generating revenue. Its advertising model allowed advertisers to bid on search words and pay for each "click" by a search-engine user. The ads were required to be simple and text-based so that the search result pages remained uncluttered and the search time was as fast as possible.

Page and Brin's first search engine was called "Back-Rub" because their technique was based on relationships, or backlinks, between websites. The name quickly changed, however. The name "Google" is a misspelling of the word "googol," which is a mathematical term for a 1 followed by 100 zeros. Page and Brin used the name in the original domain, www.google.stanford.edu, to reflect their interest in organizing the immense amount of information available on the Web. The domain name, of course, became www.google.com and eventually Webster's dictionary added the verb "google" with the definition "to use the Google search engine to obtain information on the Internet." The name has become so familiar that *Advertising Age* recently reported that Google is "the world's most powerful brand"!

Today Google receives several hundred million inquiries each day as it pursues its mission: to organize the world's information and make it universally accessible and useful. The company generates more than $21 billion in annual revenue and has more than 20,000 employees. As Google has grown it has developed 10 guidelines that represent the corporate philosophy. They are:

1. Focus on the user and all else will follow.
2. It's best to do one thing really, really well.
3. Fast is better than slow.
4. Democracy on the Web works.
5. You don't need to be at your desk to need an answer.
6. You can make money without doing evil.
7. There's always more information out there.
8. The need for information crosses all borders.
9. You can be serious without a suit.
10. Great just isn't good enough.

Using these guidelines Google strives to continually improve its search engine. "The perfect search engine," explains Google co-founder Larry Page, "would understand exactly what you mean and give back exactly what you want."

ONLINE ADVERTISING

Google generates revenue by offering online advertising opportunities—next to search results or on specific web pages. The company always distinguishes ads from the search results or the content of a web page and it never sells placement in the search results. This approach ensures that Google website visitors always know when someone has paid to put a message in front of them. The advantage of online advertising is that it is measurable and allows immediate assessment of its effectiveness. As Gopi Kallayil, product marketing manager, explains: "There is a very high degree of measurability and trackability that you get through online advertising." In addition, he says, "With online advertising you can actually track the value of every single dollar that you spend, understand which particular customers the ad reached, and what they did after they received the advertising message."

The online advertising market has grown from its initial focus on simple text ads to a much larger set of options. There are five key categories of online advertising. They are:

- Search: 47%
- Display: 35%
- Classified: 10%
- Referral: 7%
- E-mail: 1%

Google is the dominant provider of online search requests and receives more than 60 percent of the search advertising revenue. The fastest-growing advertising category, however, is display advertising where Yahoo! and Microsoft are established providers. Google believes that there is an opportunity to grow its display advertising sales by making the ads useful information instead of visual clutter. According to Google co-founder Sergey Brin, "It's like search—matching people with information they want. It just happens to be promotional."

Several improvements in technology and business practice tools contributed to Google's success. First, Google developed its patented PageRank™ algorithm, which evaluates the entire link structure of the Web and uses the link structure to determine which pages are most important. Then the process uses hypertext-matching analysis to determine which pages are relevant to a specific search. A combination of the importance and the relevance of web pages provides the search results—in just a fraction of a second. Second, Google developed two business practice tools—AdWords and AdSense—to help (1) advertisers create ads, and (2) content providers generate advertising revenue. Both tools have become essential elements of Google's advertising model.

AdWords

To help advertisers place ads on their search-engine results, Google developed an online tool called AdWords. Advertisers can use AdWords to create ad text, select target keywords, and manage their account. The process allows advertisers to reach targeted audiences. Frederick Vallaeys, Adwords evangelist, explains: "One of my favorite things about AdWords is the fact that it really helps you find the right customer at the right time and show them the right message. With AdWords you can very specifically target your market because you're targeting them at a time when they do a search on Google. At that time they've told you a keyword, you know exactly what they're looking for, and here is your opportunity as a marketer to give them the exact answer to what they've just told you they wanted to find." Google has found that text ads that are relevant to the person reading them have much higher response ("click-through") rates than ads that are not targeted.

AdWords is also easy for any advertiser to use. Large or small businesses can simply open an account with a credit card and have ads appear within minutes. "When AdWords rolled out their self-service product, it really was one of the first times when it was very easy for a small business to put their ad up on the Internet on a search engine and compete on a level playing field alongside Fortune 1000 companies," says Vallaeys. Google has an experienced sales and service team available to help any advertiser select appropriate keywords, generate ad copy, and monitor campaign performance. The team is dedicated to helping its advertisers improve click-through rates because high click-through rates are an indication that ads are relevant to a user's interests. Methods of improving advertising performance include changing the keywords and rewriting copy. Because there is no limit to the number of keywords that an advertiser can select and each keyword can be matched with different ad copy, the potential for many very customer-specific options is high.

Another advantage of Google's AdWords program is that it allows advertisers to easily control costs. The ads appear as a "Sponsored Link" next to search results each time the Google search engine matches the search request with the ad's keywords and Quality Score, although the advertiser is not charged unless someone "clicks" on the link. In a traditional advertising model, advertisers were charged using a CPM (cost-per-thousand) approach, which charged for the impressions made by an ad. According to Holden, the Google model "transformed that to what we call a CPC, or a cost-per-click model, and this is a model that an advertiser, instead of paying for an impression, only pays when somebody actually clicks on that ad and is delivered to their website. So, in effect, they may be getting the benefit from impressions being shown, but we're not actually charging them anything unless there's a definite lead being delivered to their website." Google also offers advertisers real-time analytical services to allow assessment of and changes to any component of an advertising campaign.

AdSense

The AdSense program was designed for website owners as a tool for placing ads next to their web page content rather than next to search results. Currently, thousands of website managers use AdSense to place ads on their sites and generate revenue. Google applies the same general philosophy to matching ads with websites as it does to matching ads to search requests. By delivering ads that precisely target the content on the site's pages, Google believes the advertising enhances the experience for visitors to the website. In this way advertisers, website publishers, and information seekers all benefit.

AdSense is one of the tools Google is using to pursue its goal of increasing its display advertising business. Yahoo! and Microsoft's Bing are leaders in display advertising because they can put ads on their own websites such as Yahoo! Finance and MSN Money. To provide additional outlets for display ads, Google recently purchased YouTube.

In addition, Google purchased DoubleClick, an advertising exchange where websites put space up for auction and ad agencies bid to place ads for their clients. Google is also trying to make it easy for anyone to create a display ad by introducing a new tool called Display Ad Builder. Some experts observe that because Google is so dominant at search advertising, its future growth will depend on success in display advertising.

GOOGLE'S FUTURE STRATEGY

How will Google continue its success? One possibility is that it will begin to try to win advertising away from the U.S. TV industry. While this is a new type of advertising requiring creative capabilities and relationships with large advertising agencies, Google has dedicated many of its resources to becoming competitive for television advertising expenditures. For example, Google recently helped Volvo develop a campaign that included a YouTube ad and Twitter updates. Google is also likely to develop new websites, establish blogs, and build relationships with existing sites.

Another opportunity for Google will be mobile telephone advertising. There are currently more than 5.4 billion mobile phones in use, and 1 billion of those are Internet-capable. Just as Google's search engine provides a means to match relevant information with consumers, phones offer a chance to provide real-time and location-specific information. Some of the challenges in mobile advertising will be that the networks are not fast and that the ad formats are not standardized. Google believes its new phone and its Android operating system will also help.

Finally, as Google pursues its mission it will continue to expand throughout the world. Search results are already available in 35 languages and volunteers are helping with many others. It is obvious that Google is determined to "organize the world's information" and make it "accessible and useful."

Questions

1   Describe several unique characteristics about Google and its business practices.
2   What is Google's philosophy about advertising? How can less advertising be preferred to more advertising?
3   Describe the types of online advertising available today. Which type of advertising does Google currently dominate? Why?
4   How can Google be successful in the display advertising business? What other areas of growth are likely to be pursued by Google in the future?

Using Social Media to Connect with Consumers

 16

LEARNING OBJECTIVES

After reading this chapter you should be able to:

LO1 Define social media and describe how they differ from traditional advertising media.

LO2 Identify the four major social networks and how brand managers integrate them into their organizations' marketing actions.

LO3 Describe the differing roles of those receiving messages through traditional media versus social media and the factors brand managers use to select a social network.

LO4 Explain how social media can produce sales revenues for a brand and compare the performance measures linked to inputs or costs versus outputs or revenues.

LO5 Describe how the convergence of the real and digital worlds affects the future of social media.

CONNECTING WITH TODAY'S COLLEGE STUDENTS USING FACEBOOK AND TWITTER

Like Kimmy Summers at the University of North Carolina (wearing cap in photo), thousands of "brand ambassadors" at colleges and universities across the United States face a special challenge right before freshman week.[1]

Getting Help for Freshman Move-In Day

The challenge: How can she recruit student volunteers to help incoming freshmen during campus move-in day? Use the campus newspaper?

The answer is a no-brainer for most upperclassmen working as brand ambassadors for firms like American Eagle Outfitters (AE), Target, and Apple: Use Facebook and Twitter! Here's a somewhat generic marketing plan they use for freshman week, with AE as an example:

- Use the college Facebook Page and Twitter messages to recruit about 40 volunteers to assist freshmen on move-in day.

- Tell incoming freshmen about the volunteers on the college Facebook Page with teasers like: "Need help moving in? No worries. AE will be there."

- Have these volunteers help freshmen move into their college dorms.

- Give each freshman who was helped a coupon for a free pair of AE flip-flops.

The volunteers often get a free American Eagle T-shirt (photo).

The New Age of Social Media

"College students are wary of old-school marketing," says Paul Himmelfarb, managing director of Youth Marketing Connection, which links marketers with college students. "You have to take a brand and incorporate it into the college lifestyle by peer-to-peer marketing."[2]

In the past decade, college students have more than doubled their use of the Internet and social media to collect information and buy products and services. College marketers increasingly use social media to reach students because they work better than traditional print and TV ads.[3] More than 10,000 student brand ambassadors on the 4,000 U.S. college campuses use social media to connect with other students. Sample websites for Facebook, Twitter, LinkedIn, and YouTube are shown on the opposite page.

This chapter defines social media, describes four widely used social networks, explains how organizations use social networks in developing marketing strategies, and considers where social media are headed in the future.

UNDERSTANDING SOCIAL MEDIA

LO1

Defining *social media* is challenging, but it's necessary to help a brand or marketing manager select the right one. This section defines social media, positions a number of social networks, and compares social and traditional media. As you read this, consider how you might choose a social network if *you*—like college students around the globe—were using one to launch a start-up business.

The text describes how Web 2.0 and user generated content are the foundations of today's social media.

blog

A contraction of "web log," a web page that serves as a publicly accessible personal journal and online forum for an individual organization.

user generated content (UGC)

The various forms of online media content that are publicly available and created by end users.

social media

Online media where users submit comments, photos, and videos—often accompanied by a feedback process to identify "popular" topics.

What Are Social Media?

This section describes how social media came about (remember that the word "media" is plural—"medium" being singular), defines social media, and provides a means of classifying the countless social media networks available to assist marketing managers in choosing among them.

How Social Media Came About Researchers Andreas M. Kaplan and Michael Haenlein note that the term "social media" is sometimes used interchangeably with the terms "Web 2.0" and "user generated content"—two concepts that are the foundations of today's social media.[4]

The term "Web 2.0" first appeared in 2004 to describe a new way to utilize the World Wide Web. Web 2.0 does not refer to any technical update of the World Wide Web, but refers to functionalities that make possible today's high degree of interactivity among users. So with Web 2.0, content is no longer seen as being created and published in final form exclusively by one author. Instead, the content can be modified continuously by all users in a participatory fashion, such as with blogs and wikis.

A **blog**—a contraction of "web log"—is a web page that serves as a publicly accessible personal journal and online forum for an individual or organization. Companies like Hewlett-Packard and Frito-Lay routinely monitor blogs to gain insight into customer complaints and suggestions. A *wiki* is a website whose content is created and edited by the ongoing collaboration of end users, for example, to generate and improve new product ideas. They differ in that a blog is a diary that shows a sequential journey while a wiki shows the end result as a single entry.[5]

User generated content (UGC) refers to the various forms of online media content that are publicly available and created by end users. The term "user generated content" was in common use by 2005 and covers all the ways people can use social media. UGC satisfies three basic criteria:[6]

1. It is published either on a publicly accessible website or on a social networking site, so it is not simply an e-mail.
2. It shows a significant degree of creative effort, so it is more than simply posting a newspaper article on a personal blog without editing or comments.
3. It is consumer-generated by an individual outside of a professional organization, without a commercial market in mind.

Defining Social Media Social media represent a unique blending of technology and social interaction to create personal value for users. **Social media** are online media where users submit comments, photos, and videos—often accompanied by a feedback process to identify "popular" topics.[7] Most social media involve a genuine online conversation among people about a subject of mutual interest, one built on their personal thoughts and experiences. However, other social media sites involve games and virtual worlds, in which the online interaction includes playing a game, completing a quest, controlling an avatar, and so on. Business firms also refer to social media as "consumer-generated media." A single social media site like Facebook or YouTube is referred to as a *social network.*

Classifying Social Media Most of us would probably say that Flickr, YouTube, Facebook, and Twitter are well-known social networks. But marketing managers trying to reach potential customers need a system to classify the more than 400 specialized and diverse social networks to select the best among them. Kaplan and Haenlein have proposed a classification system for marketers based on two factors:[8]

1. *Media richness.* This involves the degree of acoustic, visual, and personal contact between two communication partners—face-to-face communications, say, being higher in media richness than telephone or e-mail communications. The higher the media richness and quality of presentation, the greater the social influence that communication partners have on each other's behavior.

2. *Self-disclosure.* In any type of social interaction, individuals want to make a positive impression to achieve a favorable image with others. This favorable image is affected by the degree of self-disclosure about a person's thoughts, feelings, likes, and dislikes—where greater self-disclosure is likely to increase one's influence on those reached.

Figure 16–1 uses these two factors of media richness and self-disclosure to position a number of social media sites in two-dimensional space. For example, blogs like Flickr and Tumblr are in the upper left because they are high in self-disclosure but relatively low in media richness, while Wikipedia is low on both factors.[9] LinkedIn contains detailed career and résumé information for business networking and is high in self-disclosure, while YouTube's videos are strong on the media richness scale but are moderate in terms of self-disclosure. Second Life, high in both self-disclosure and media richness, is a 3D virtual social world where users create a personal avatar to explore and interact with others in that world to "live a life without boundaries." World of Warcraft is high in media richness but low in self-disclosure.

Marketing managers look carefully at the positioning of the social networks shown in Figure 16–1 in selecting those to use in their plans. For example, World of Warcraft (WoW),

With the countless social networks available on smartphones and computer screens, how do marketing managers choose the best ones to reach their target markets? As a first step, the text describes how social media can be classified and how they differ from traditional media.

FIGURE 16–1

A sample of social media, classified by media richness and self-disclosure. Note that in moving from words to photos, videos, and animation, media richness increases. Also, in moving from very impersonal messages to highly personal ones, self-disclosure increases.

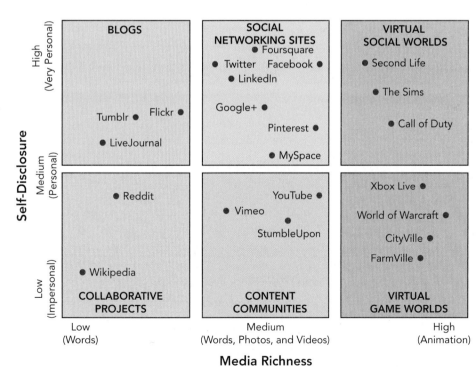

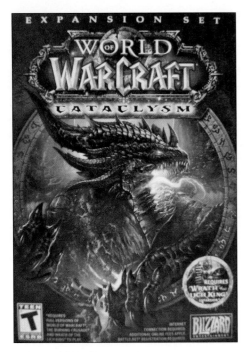

World of Warcraft is a multiplayer, online role-playing game where players control a character avatar within a fantasy world. It is one of the social media positioned in Figure 16–1.

positioned in the Virtual Game Worlds segment in Figure 16–1, is a multi-player, online role-playing game in the fantasy Warcraft universe. Toyota recently used mechanics and pictures from the World of Warcraft in a commercial to reach the millions of people who play the game in the United States.

Comparing Social and Traditional Media

Consumers receive information, news, and education from print (newspapers, magazines) and electronic media (radio, television). But marketing managers know that social media are very different from traditional media like newspapers or even radio or television. Social media and traditional media have both similarities and differences that impact marketing strategies, as described below:[10]

- *Ability to reach both large and niche audiences.* Both kinds of media can be designed to reach either a mass market or specialized segments; however, good execution is critical, and audience size is not guaranteed.
- *Expense and access.* Messages and ads in traditional media like newspapers or television generally are expensive to produce and have restricted access by individuals. Also, traditional media are typically owned privately or by the government. In contrast, messages on social media networks are generally accessible everywhere to those with smartphones, computers, and tablet devices and can be produced cheaply.
- *Training and number of people involved.* Producing traditional media typically requires specialized skills and training and often involves teams of people. In contrast, sending messages on social media requires only limited skills, so practically anyone can post a message that includes words and images.
- *Time to delivery.* Traditional media can involve days or even months of continuing effort to deliver the communication, and time lags can be extensive. In contrast, individuals using social media can post virtually instantaneous content.
- *Permanence.* Traditional media, once created, cannot be altered. For example, once a magazine article is printed and distributed, it cannot be changed. But social media can be altered almost instantaneously by comments or editing.
- *Credibility and social authority.* Individuals and organizations can establish themselves as an "expert" in their given field, thereby becoming an "influencer" in that field. For example, *The New York Times* has immense credibility among newspaper media. But with social media, a sender often simply begins to participate in the "conversation," hoping that the quality of the message will establish credibility with the receivers, thereby enhancing the sender's influence.

In terms of privacy, with minor exceptions, recipients of traditional media like TV or radio ads are completely anonymous. Subscribers to newspapers or magazines are somewhat less so because publishers can sell subscription lists to advertisers. Social media have much less privacy and anonymity. When they breach expectations for privacy, unethical outsiders can access users' names.[11]

learning review

1. What do we mean by social media?

2. In classifying social media, what do we mean by (a) media richness and (b) self-disclosure?

3. Compare traditional media and social media in terms of time to delivery of the communication.

A LOOK AT FOUR IMPORTANT SOCIAL NETWORKS

Facebook, Twitter, LinkedIn, and YouTube are four widely used networks in the world of social media. So marketing managers need a special understanding of these four website platforms as they integrate social media into their marketing strategies to supplement the traditional media they already use. This section briefly defines and describes each of these four major social media and outlines some guidelines for a brand manager using each of them. Because of its importance, Facebook merits more detailed coverage.

Facebook

Facebook is the first choice among people seeking to create and maintain online connections with others by using photos, videos, and short text entries.[12] Facebook enhanced its photo-sharing capability with its acquisition of Instagram in early 2012.[13] With a billion active users expected by late 2012—1 in every 7 people on the planet—Facebook is truly the 900-pound gorilla among all social media. Also, Facebook has a global presence, now accessible in more than 70 languages.[14]

Facebook

A website where users may create a personal profile, add other users as friends, and exchange comments, photos, videos, and "likes" with them.

Facebook: An Overview   **Facebook** is a website where users create a personal profile, add other users as friends, and exchange comments, photos, videos, and "likes" with them. Facebook users today can keep friends and family updated on what a user is thinking, doing, and feeling. Additionally, users may chat with friends and create and join common-interest groups, organized by workplace, high school, college, and Pages—some of the latter maintained by organizations as a means of advertising. While Facebook is currently open to anyone age 13 and over, the social network is exploring the possibility of adding users under 13 years of age.

Time magazine's selection of Mark Zuckerberg as its "Person of the Year" reflects the staggering impact of Facebook today.[15] Consider that Facebook users:

- Have over 15 billion photos on the site and are adding over 300 million more every day.
- Include more than over 500 million people who tap into Facebook on mobile phones.
- Spend one out of every seven minutes logged onto the Internet.[16]

The average American Facebook user has 245 friends on the site.[17]

Mark Zuckerberg, a *Time* magazine "Person of the Year," may connect a billion Facebook users by late 2012.

Facebook in a Brand Manager's Strategy
Facebook Pages were created as a method for brand managers to generate awareness for their product, service, or brand within Facebook. They allow brand managers to promote their business on Facebook, separate from their private and personal profiles. Done well, these are magnets for feedback. Additionally, Facebook Page information is generally public and cataloged by search engines so brand managers can identify influencers within their customer base.

Figure 16–2 on the next page shows the Facebook Page for Bitter Girls, which is featured in the video case at the end of this chapter. This start-up business targets 13- to 17-year-old girls with a dark but empowering theme. The notes in the margin in Figure 16–2 show how elements on the Bitter Girls Facebook Page seek to connect with fans and generate conversations. Several also help measure the successfulness of the Facebook Page. The brand manager for Bitter Girls works with the website designer to present an attention-getting Facebook Page.

FIGURE 16–2

This Facebook Page for Bitter Girls shows elements that are of interest to its brand manager.

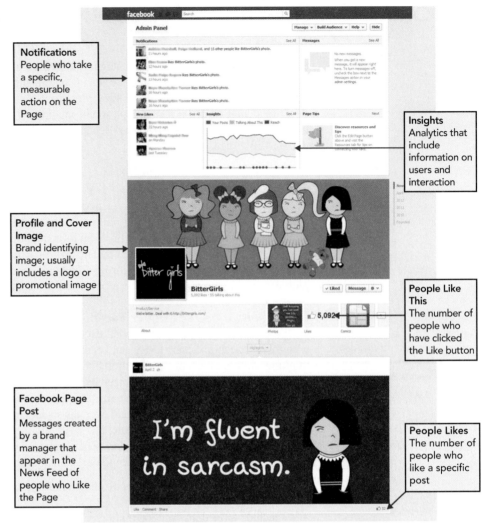

Notifications
People who take a specific, measurable action on the Page

Insights
Analytics that include information on users and interaction

Profile and Cover Image
Brand identifying image; usually includes a logo or promotional image

People Like This
The number of people who have clicked the Like button

Facebook Page Post
Messages created by a brand manager that appear in the News Feed of people who Like the Page

People Likes
The number of people who like a specific post

To generate new customers and increase traffic to their Facebook Pages, brand managers can use paid ads and sponsored stories within the Facebook advertising platform.[18] Most ads within Facebook appear on the right-hand side of the website. An advantage of these Facebook ads is that the content can migrate into Facebook conversations among friends—to the delight of advertisers.

The marketing challenge for an organization's Facebook Page is to post and create the content that will generate the best response. Brand managers using Facebook seek to maintain a continuing, positive conversation with their fans. Buddy Media, an online consulting group, has suggested the following guidelines to engage fans on Facebook:[19]

- *Make it familiar, but with a twist.* Focus content strategy on imagery and messaging that is familiar to fans—punctuated with something unique. For example, Aflac uses its Aflac Duck—the well-known "spokes-duck"—to treat fans to Aflac Duck commercials and virtual Duck gifts. These, in turn, link to a point-of-purchase site for supplemental insurance.
- *Keep it fresh.* Redbox uses frequent posts to keep fans informed about its latest film releases.
- *Let users get engaged and guide content.* Taco Bell polls users to see which menu item they'd like featured in the following week's menu profile photo.

BASIS OF COMPARISON	SOCIAL NETWORKS			
	facebook	**twitter**	**Linked in**	**You Tube**
User Characteristics	40% male, 60% female; 78% have some college; 35% are under 35 years old	40% male, 60% female; 79% have some college; 44% are under 35 years old	47% male, 53% female; 56% have some college; 22% are under 35 years old	45% male, 55% female; 79% have some college; 36% are under 35 years old
Brand Exposure	Great for brand exposure; jump start it through the Facebook ad platform; connect with other brand pages.	Offers unique opportunities for website integration and to engage with customers.	Effective to demonstrate an organization's professionalism; have employees maintain complete profiles to do this.	Can be powerful tool to build your channel, to explain a complex product, and to brand your videos.
Customer Communication	Great for engaging people who like your brand, want to share their opinions, and have customer service questions.	Use Twitter monitoring programs such as CoTweet or HootSuite to track what people are saying about your brand.	Not the primary focus, but engagement opportunities exist through industry-related groups and company profiles.	Whether you seek to entertain, inform, or both, video is a powerful tool for quickly engaging your customers.
Traffic to Website	Traffic is decent and on the rise; use links and customized tabs to direct visitors back to your website.	Potential can be large, but focus on sending out info relevant to your brand and audience interested in your tweets.	Traffic may be small but can be valuable from a B2B and business development perspective.	Traffic goes to the videos; if the goal is to get traffic back to your site, then add a hyperlink in the video description.

GOOD! OK! BAD!

FIGURE 16–3

How brand managers can use four social networks in developing their marketing strategies.

Figure 16–3 compares four major social networks (Facebook, Twitter, LinkedIn, and YouTube) from the point of view of a brand manager.[20] The figure suggests that using Facebook can increase brand exposure by engaging brand-loyal customers to share their opinions with their Facebook friends and involving them in brand contests.

Twitter

Now that "tweets" have become part of our everyday language, it's apparent that Twitter has entered the mainstream of American life. In mid-2012, Twitter globally had over 170 million registered users but only 140 million active users who send 340 million tweets a day.[21]

Twitter

A website that enables users to send and receive "tweets," messages up to 140 characters long.

Twitter: An Overview **Twitter** is a website that enables users to send and receive *tweets*, messages up to 140 characters long. Twitter is based on the principle of "followers." So when you choose to follow another Twitter user, that user's tweets appear in reverse chronological order on your Twitter page.

Because of its short message length, the ease of posting and receiving tweets, and its convenience on a smartphone, Twitter can be a good source of information about a brand or product. Carma Laboratories, the maker of Carmex lip balm and skin care products, uses Twitter as an important tool in its social media program to communicate brand messages to its followers. As part of Carmex's social media outreach, the brand is active on Twitter with daily messages, retweets, and replies.

The immediacy of Twitter messaging allows brands like Carmex to operate promotions in real time. For example, Carmex partnered with @LeBronJamescom to conduct a scavenger hunt on Twitter where members of TeamLeBron tweeted clues to their location. The first person to arrive at the destination won a jar of Carmex with a 14 karat gold cap.

Beyond sending out messages, Carmex relies on Twitter as a listening device. Carmex's social media team monitors mentions of Carmex on Twitter to see what people are saying. If there are product concerns, Carmex can reach out to consumers to make sure their concerns are addressed.

Carmex (@Carmex) used Twitter to partner with members of TeamLeBron to win a jar of Carmex lip balm.

Twitter in a Brand Manager's Strategy With the 140-character limit on tweets, brand managers cannot expect extensive comments on their brands. But they can use social media management tools like CoTweet to see what Twitter users are saying—good and bad—about both their own brands and competitive ones. They then respond to the negative comments and re-tweet the positive ones.

Brand managers have various other strategies for listening to and interacting with present and potential consumers using Twitter. For example, they can:[22]

- Generate brand buzz by developing an official Twitter profile, recruiting followers, and showing photos of their products.
- Follow the Twitter profiles that mention their product and monitor what is being said, responding to user criticisms to develop happier customers.
- Tweet on topics that provide information of value to their consumers. Starbucks successfully used Twitter to supplement its "Free Pastry Day" on Facebook—a promotion that awarded a free pastry to those buying a Starbucks beverage.

As with Facebook, Twitter can actively engage customers if done well and creatively. In promoting its new Ford Fiesta subcompact car, Ford received 4 million mentions on Twitter about its "Fiesta movement."

LinkedIn

LinkedIn

A business-oriented website that lets users post their professional profiles to connect to a network of businesspeople.

Unlike Facebook and Twitter, the LinkedIn site's main purpose is professional networking and job searching.

LinkedIn: An Overview **LinkedIn** is a business-oriented website that lets users post their professional profiles to connect to a network of businesspeople, who are also called *connections*. This social network has more than 160 million registered users in over 200 countries. By 2013, users will conduct over 5.3 billion professionally-oriented searches. Because of its popularity, over 2 million companies have LinkedIn Company Pages to post news and job openings.[23]

Experts give the following tips to LinkedIn users:

- Focus your profile to make sure it is both complete and current and includes who you are professionally, who you can help, and how you can help them.
- Brand yourself as an expert with "answers" by searching through relevant questions to let your answers showcase your abilities.

Also, make a point of growing your network to connect with new people.[24]

Professor Steven Hartley, a coauthor of this textbook, uses LinkedIn to connect with a network of educators and businesspeople.

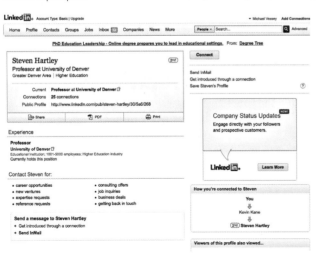

LinkedIn in a Brand Manager's Strategy Marketing managers can use LinkedIn to promote their brand in subtle ways. This is done mainly for business-to-business (B2B) image building and networking with industry-related groups. A company can also use LinkedIn for business development to find sales leads and vendors and to organize focus groups. Using LinkedIn, brand managers can demonstrate the organization's expertise and create and moderate discussion groups.

Rebecca Black uses YouTube to promote her music, which allows her fans to "like," "share," and "comment" on her video.

YouTube

A video-sharing website in which users can upload, distribute view, and comment on videos.

For how OK Go has used "Here It Goes Again" (14.0 million views) and "This Too Shall Pass" (36.5 million views) on YouTube to gain fans, licensees, live shows, and sponsors, see the text.

YouTube

The ability of YouTube to reach its audience stretches the imagination. Think about this: In mid-2012, its 800 million users (1) watched 3 billion hours of video a month, (2) uploaded 72 hours of video each minute, and (3) got 1 trillion page views a day."[25]

YouTube: An Overview **YouTube** is a video-sharing website in which users can upload, view, and comment on videos. YouTube uses streaming video technology to display user generated video content that includes movie and TV clips, music videos, and original videos developed by amateurs. While most of the content is uploaded by amateurs, many companies offer material on the site through a YouTube partnership program.

In December 2011, YouTube redesigned its home page—to the dismay of many of its loyal users. Its goal in doing so was to provide a more organized structure to steer users to "channels," rather than simply encourage them to browse like in the past.[26] An interesting issue is whether the greater structure might hurt single YouTube videos like Rebecca Black's "Friday" (35+ million views), which went viral."[27] Also in 2012, YouTube announced that to attract big advertisers, it would begin producing its own video programs.

YouTube in a Brand Manager's Strategy YouTube offers great opportunity for a brand manager to produce and show a video that explains the benefits of a complex product (Figure 16–3). Since YouTube is owned by Google, it incorporates a search engine so users interested in a specific topic can find it easily. In terms of cost advantages, while a brand manager must pay the cost of creating a video, launching a new channel on YouTube is free.

In 2012, YouTube announced a new program to help small businesses create video ads on its social medium. Small businesses will now be able to buy and manage key words for their video ads on YouTube. So, a baker who runs a YouTube video ad for her bakery can buy words like "baking," "cookies," and "cake," and her video will appear when someone searches for those terms on YouTube.[28]

OK Go, a music group, watched downloaded songs from the Internet cause a meltdown in its CD sales and experienced difficulty in getting its own record label. So it used YouTube to win fans, licensees, and sponsors for its *very* offbeat music creations. OK Go's YouTube music videos—what it calls "treadmill videos"—are the foundation

Marketing Matters >>>>>>> technology

What Are Some of Your Other Favorite Social Networks?

Other social networks that are popular among college students with diverse interests include the following:

 Vimeo—A community of creative people who are passionate about sharing the videos they make

 Google+—A social sharing network from Google that allows you to organize friends in "circles" for easy sharing, host "hangouts," and more

 Foursquare—A location-based mobile platform that helps you explore cities through "check-ins" and rewards

GROUPON Groupon—A way to get daily discounts of 50% to 90% on "the best stuff to do, see, eat, and buy." The catch: A time limit for which a minimum number of people must take the deal to receive the discount

 StumbleUpon—A discovery engine for finding and sharing the best content on the web

 Flickr—An online photo management and sharing network that allows you to show off and organize your favorite photos and videos

 LivingSocial—Helps more than 60 million members find, share, and enjoy the best of their neighborhoods in over 650 markets globally by connecting them with hand-picked local businesses

 Pinterest—A content sharing network where members "pin" images, videos, and more to "pinboards" they create, which are categorized into different themes

 Tumblr—A feature-rich, micro-blogging platform that allows users to share text, photos, music, links, videos, and more

MeetUp—A network that helps people with shared interests plan meetings and events in their communities

---

QR 16–1
OK Go Music Video

for its success. Examples include:[29] an animation with 2,300 pieces of toast, a dance with a dozen trained dogs, and the first-ever Rube Goldberg machine that operates in time to music.

The following guidelines on marketing and promoting a brand using YouTube videos include:[30]

- Create a branded channel rich in key words to improve the odds of the video showing up in user searches.
- Target viewers by using YouTube's insights and analytics research to reveal the number of views, the number of visits to your website, and what key words are driving user visits.

For the hundreds of social networks in the secondary tier, the ones discussed in the Marketing Matters box are among the most widely used.

---

learning review

4. How is "user generated content" presented by someone using Facebook?

5. What are some ways brand managers use Facebook to converse with a brand's fans?

6. What are the major differences between Facebook and YouTube that are of interest to brand managers?

INTEGRATING SOCIAL MEDIA INTO TODAY'S MARKETING STRATEGIES

LO3

Thousands of marketing managers around the globe understand how to use traditional media to generate sales for their brand. Some are successful, and others are not. But many of these same managers will admit that social networks are so new and complex they are not sure how best to use them.

This section looks at (1) how social media tie to the strategic marketing process, (2) how to select a social network, (3) how social media can be used to generate sales, and (4) how to measure the results of social media programs. The section closes by describing Nestlé's Kit Kat meltdown on Facebook.

Social Media and the Strategic Marketing Process

The strategic marketing process described in Chapter 2 and the communications process running from sender to receiver discussed in Chapter 14 apply to both traditional and social media. But note these important differences in the communication process:

- Traditional media like magazine or TV ads generally use one-way communication from sender to receiver, who the marketer hopes will buy the product advertised. A little word-of-mouth chatting may occur among the "passive receivers" but communications generally end with the receiver.
- Social media deliberately seek to ensure that the message *does not end* with an individual receiver. Instead, the goal is to reach "active receivers," those who will become "influentials" and be "delighted" with the brand advertised. These will then become "evangelists," who will send messages to their online friends and then back to the advertiser about the joys of using the brand.

So success in social media marketing relies heavily on the ability of a marketing program to convert passive "receivers" of the message to active "evangelists" who will spread favorable messages about the brand.

Selecting the Social Network

In using social media, a brand manager tries to select and use one or more social networks from the hundreds that exist. This often entails assessing (1) the number of daily visitors to the website and (2) the characteristics of these visitors.

Recent Growth of the Four Social Networks   Figure 16–4 on the next page shows the recent growth of Facebook, Twitter, LinkedIn, and YouTube. In terms of millions of unique U.S. visitors to the website per month, it shows the dramatic growth of Facebook, which reached 210 million visitors per month in May 2012. At that time Figure 16–4 shows that YouTube had 170 million daily unique visitors, while Twitter had 42 million and LinkedIn had 34 million.[31]

Audience Data Available for Social Networks   Google and other services provide user profile data for the social networks to help brand managers choose among them. The top row of Figure 16–3 shows a recent profile of audience demographics for four major social networks. As shown in the figure, Facebook users are 60 percent female and 40 percent male; 78 percent have at least some college education; and 35 percent are under 35 years old.[32]

FIGURE 16–4

The monthly unique U.S. visitors to four social network sites: Facebook, YouTube, Twitter, and LinkedIn.

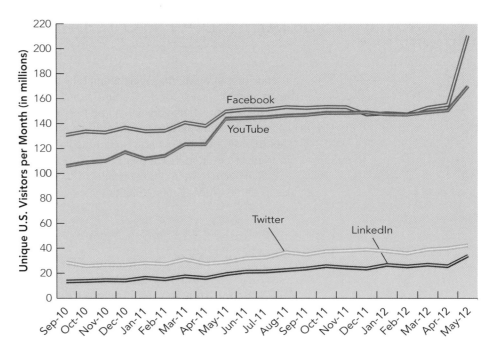

How Social Media Produce Sales

An example shows how a Pepsi brand manager can use social media to produce sales and profits for her product or brand. Consider the roles of both the Pepsi brand manager and social media in the following example.[33]

Role of the Pepsi Brand Manager   The Pepsi brand manager composes title, copy, and images or photos for the ad. She also specifies the web address to which its ad should link based on the brand's social media marketing goals. To increase awareness and build up a fan base, she might link the ad to the Pepsi website or its Facebook, Twitter, or Pinterest sites. To encourage and produce new sales that can be tracked, she must link the ad to a coupon code, a specific product on the Pepsi website, or other promotional offer.

The brand manager then defines the characteristics of the one or more market segments she wants to reach on the social media she has selected. This starts with demographic characteristics like geographic region, sex, age range, and education. She then adds factors like relationship status and user interests.

In choosing to run a social media ad campaign, brand managers like those at Pepsi must assess the potential sales likely to result, as compared to a campaign using traditional media.

Role of Social Media   As an example, Facebook generates its sales revenue by selling ads that appear along the right-hand section throughout the website. Facebook sells ads directly to its advertisers in both cost-per-click and cost-per-thousand metrics (see Figure 16–5). In mid-2012, Facebook charged Pepsi and other advertisers $8 every 1,000 times their sponsored story ads were viewed or loaded in the main news feed. So $1 million bought 125 million views or impressions for Facebook advertisers, Advertisers who are increasingly asking how many of these impression lead to a sale and whether other traditional media are better. For example, $1 million gets an advertiser two 30-second TV commercials on "American Idol" or 6.5 full-page color ads in *People* magazine.[34]

Performance Measure	Costs to Advertisers	Who Provides It	Who Uses It	An Assessment	
				Advantages	Disadvantages
Cost per thousand (CPM)	"I will pay $0.50 for every 1,000 times this ad loads, up to $100 per month."	Small websites that sell ads directly (may be using a third party service)	Advertisers who simply want to build "awareness"	Simple to use	Impressions don't always lead to sales
Cost per click (CPC)	"I will pay $1.00 for every visitor who clicks on this ad and goes from your website to mine."	Most websites use this method—executed by a third-party like Google/AdWords	Advertisers who want to pay for success, but may not be able to track sales from advertisement to purchase	Only pay for a visitor who has expressed an interest in my ad	Ads may not display if they are a poor fit for the viewing audience
Cost per action (CPA)	"I will pay $5 for every purchase that originated from an ad on your site."	Usually executed through third parties; Google AdSense recently added this feature	Sophisticated advertisers who want to pay for success	Only pay for what works	Similar to CPC but harder to track and more expensive per action

FIGURE 16–5

Performance measures for social networks linked mainly to inputs or costs, as seen by a brand manager.

QR 16–2
Pepsi Pulse
Video

In using social media ads, unlike traditional print media, the Pepsi brand manager is not buying placement on a specific section on a Facebook site. For example, Facebook determines the most effective placement for the ads based on the demographic and other user criteria the brand manager sets to reach the target market.

As an example, in early 2012, Pepsi announced its "Live for Now" pop-culture campaign to reinvigorate its brand. Its new social-media driven, interactive Pepsi Pulse website (www.pepsi.com) gives the Top 10 pop-culture entertainment and sports events, news, photos, videos, and so on. Pepsi Pulse allows fans "to easily share content on Facebook, Twitter, and Pinterest." Pepsi Pulse also offers geo-targeting and special deals with its selected partners to enhance the value of the site.[35]

Measuring the Results of Social Media Programs

Performance measures for social media divide into (1) those linked to inputs or costs (Figure 16–5) and (2) those tied to the outputs or revenues resulting from social media. Clearly, the ideal performance measure for both conventional and social media is one that ties actual sales revenues to the cost of the ad or other promotion. With the explosion in the growth of social media, marketing and brand managers are being challenged to connect the cost of these new social network promotions to the sales they generate. The result has been an emergence of many new performance measures, often requiring a whole new language.

Performance Measures Linked to Inputs or Costs Figure 16–5 shows three performance measures for social networks linked mainly to inputs or costs. Moving down the list of measures shown in Figure 16–5, one starts with a measure tied only to costs (the cost per thousand measure) and then moves to a measure linked more closely to the sales revenues generated from the social media ad or action (cost per action, or CPA).

The cost per thousand (CPM) measure ties to the number of times the ad loads and a user might see it—but not whether the user has actually reacted to it. This measure is roughly equivalent to the CPM for traditional media discussed in Chapter 15. The cost per click (CPC) measure gives the rate the advertiser pays, say to Facebook, every time a visitor clicks on the ad and jumps from that page to the advertiser's website. Finally, the CPA measure ties loosely to actual sales—for example, paying $5 for every purchase that originates from an ad, say, on the Facebook site. By summing up the revenues from all these purchases, a difficult task, this CPA measure most closely ties the cost of the social media ad to the sales revenues the ad generates.

Performance Measures Linked to Outputs or Revenues Many of the measures for evaluating how a brand manager's social network promotion is doing reflect the two-way communications present in social media. These measures often tie to output results in terms of "fans," "friends," "followers," or "visitors" to a social network site, which can be a first step to estimating the sales revenue generated. From a brand manager's viewpoint, here are some of the frequently used Facebook measures, moving from the more general to the more specific:

- *Fans.* The number of people who have opted in to a brand's messages through a social media platform at a given time.
- *Share of voice.* The brand's share or percentage of all the online social media chatter related to, say, its product category or a topic.
- *Page views.* The number of times a Facebook Page is loaded in a given time period.
- *Visitors.* The total number of visitors to a Facebook Page in a given time period; if someone visits three times in one day, she is counted three times.
- *Unique visitors.* The total number of unique visitors to a Facebook Page in a given time period; if someone visits three times in one day, he is counted only once.
- *Average Page views per visitor.* Page views divided by visitors in a given time period.
- *Interaction rate.* The number of people who interact with a Post ("like," make a comment, and so on) divided by the total number of people seeing the Post.
- *Click-through rate (CTR).* Percentage of recipients who have clicked on a link on the Page to visit a specific site.
- *Fan source.* Where a social network following comes from—with fans coming from a friend being more valuable than those coming from an ad.

Note that while sales revenues resulting from social media do not appear in these measures, as we move down the list above, the measures are often more specific than comparable ones used in traditional media. This is because it is far simpler to electronically track the social network users who click on a website or ad than it is to track consumers who receive traditional media.

Specialized Focus for Other Social Networks One of the advantages of social media is that communities can form around ideas and commonalities, regardless of the physical location of their members. While major social networks such as Facebook or YouTube may garner the majority of the traffic, smaller networks like Pinterest may be more successful for some products and services.

Pinterest, a virtual pinboard and content-sharing social network, allows people to "pin" or share images of their favorite things such as clothing, craft ideas, home décor, and recipes. Pinterest members create customized, themed "pinboards" to categorize their images such as "Odds & Ends," "Food," and "Knitting" shown on the Pinterest screen on the opposite page. These images are shared with other members of the Pinterest community. Members can also share their pinned images on Facebook and Twitter.[36]

Many of the items that members pin include products that are available for purchase online. As Pinterest recently surpassed LinkedIn to become the third largest social network, it has become a major sales driver for retailers and manufacturers. In using Pinterest, brand managers can post images of their company's products on their

Pinterest allows users to "pin" or share images of favorite interests on its site, which is useful for brand managers promoting their company's products.

Pinterest board and link them back to their websites. This can be done effectively by ensuring that all website links are associated with unique images and adding share features like the "pin it" button to the brand's online content.

Greenpeace vs. Nestlé's Kit Kat: A Nightmarish Meltdown

For the way Nestlé's Kit Kat Facebook Page was "brand-jacked" with Greenpeace activists dressed as orangutans, see the text.

While an intense level of social media communications on Facebook or Twitter can be a brand manager's dream, it can also be his worst nightmare. The Greenpeace campaign against Nestlé and its Kit Kat candy bar brand is an example.[37]

The Background Currently, palm oil is an ingredient in several of Nestlé's products, including the Kit Kat chocolate bar. In March 2010, Nestlé reported that 18 percent of its palm oil was "nonsustainable," meaning its suppliers were cutting down rainforests in places like Indonesia without enough concern for the environmental harm or equivalent remediation. These Indonesian rainforests are home to orangutans. Nestlé announced that its goal was to be using "100 percent sustainable palm oil" by 2015. Nestlé's plan seemed to demonstrate a sense of social responsibility and to support the goal of global sustainability.

Greenpeace's Actions and Results Greenpeace, a social and environmental advocacy organization, decided that Nestlé's effort to find sustainable palm oil suppliers was moving too slowly. So it launched an all-out "shock campaign" against Nestlé with the proclamation: "Caught Red-Handed: How Nestlé's Use of Palm Oil Is Having a Devastating Impact on Rainforests, the Climate, and Orangutans." Then Greenpeace posted a very graphic and provocative video on YouTube, including activists

dressed as orangutans. The Greenpeace campaign triggered customer complaints on the Kit Kat Facebook Page, some with a "Killer Kat" logo (at left), a play on Nestlé's "Kit Kat" logo. Also, Nestlé management received 200,000 e-mails, and its 1-800 customer service numbers were jammed by protest calls.

Nestlé's Overreaction and Its Effects Nestlé's response unwittingly led to increased online attention and animosity. At Nestlé's request, YouTube removed the video that Nestlé believed infringed on its Kit Kat brand. The result: Views of the video on other sites like Flickr and Vimeo skyrocketed in the next 24 hours.

QR 16–3
Greenpeace
Kit Kat Video

Nestlé's Kit Kat Facebook users who were violently opposed to its deforestation actions swelled. One commentator noted that Greenpeace had "brand-jacked" the Nestlé Kit Kat Facebook Page. Within 60 days, Nestlé's management capitulated. It took steps to drop palm oil suppliers linked to deforestation—in effect recognizing the power of social media.

Social Media Lessons for Brand Managers Rather than being aggressive, brand managers should respond to a crisis situation with transparency and an approachable tone. Also, a brand manager facing a crisis situation should communicate directly with "key influencers," emphasizing the company's concern about the issue, and communicate often, using Twitter, Facebook, blogs, YouTube, and other relevant social media. Above all, it is critical to have an emergency social media plan for the brand in place—*before* an actual crisis erupts.

---

learning review

7. What is the difference between (and marketing significance of) a "passive receiver" for conventional media and an "active receiver" for social media?

8. Stated simply, how can an advertiser on Facebook expect to generate sales?

9. How did Nestlé's initial overreaction to the Greenpeace campaign heighten its problems?

THE FUTURE: SOCIAL MEDIA + SMARTPHONES + EXOTIC APPS

LO5

Trends in marketing's use of social media reflect what scientists call "mirror worlds" or "smart systems" that are really the convergence of the real and digital worlds. A *smart system* is a computer-based network that triggers actions by sensing changes in the real or digital world. This section discusses (1) the convergence of real and digital worlds, (2) how this convergence links social media to marketing actions, and (3) where all this *may* be headed in *your* future. The section closes by describing the impact of social media on global marketing.

The Convergence of Real and Digital Worlds

apps
Small, downloadable software programs that can run on smartphones and tablet devices.

Saying that our physical and virtual worlds are converging sounds like science fiction. But placing your online order for jeans or providing your demographic characteristics and personal interests when joining Facebook involves converting real-world decisions or personal characteristics into a digital format that starts to approximate your own personal world.[38] This convergence of real and digital worlds is the result of an unlimited proliferation of interlinked smartphones, tablet devices, sensors, special identification tags, databases, algorithms, apps, and other elements (Figure 16–6).

Smartphones and their apps are speeding up this convergence. **Apps** (or *mobile apps* or *applications*) are small, downloadable software programs that run on smartphones and tablet devices. When Apple launched its iPhone in 2007, it didn't expect smartphone apps to be very important. Wrong! By mid-2012, its App Store was selling and offering over 650,000 apps. And Google's Android has over 500,000 apps available through the Google Content Play Store.[39]

The Marketing Matters box describes six popular apps for use on digital devices. Many apps are video games. Some, like Angry Birds, achieve astounding success. Launched by a tiny Finnish firm in 2009, by early 2012 Angry Birds had been downloaded 700 million times.

Marketing Matters >>>>>>>> technology

The Coolest, Wildest, Weirdest, and . . . Best . . . Apps???

Here are six apps that were popular among college students in mid-2012.

 Draw Something—The fastest growing social drawing game where two players cooperate and take turns drawing a picture for the other to guess.

 Words With Friends—A multiplayer word game where players take turns building words using a crossword puzzle style similar to Scrabble.

 Tiny Wings—In this game, a player helps a bird with tiny wings fly as long as possible by using hills to gain speed and momentum.

 Pandora—An app offering free, personalized radio that helps listeners discover new music based on the artists and songs the listener likes.

 Temple Run—An action video game where wandering explorers attempting to steal an idol from a temple navigate through a maze of booby traps and try to outrun demonic monkeys.

 Hanging With Friends—A multiplayer word game where players take turns guessing words within a limited amount of guesses, similar to hangman.

But how popular are these apps as you read this? Your answer relates to the product life cycle for today's apps, which is discussed in the text.

FIGURE 16–6

An array of diverse elements leads to a convergence of the real world and the digital world. This, in turn, triggers marketing actions whose results are often more easily measurable.

But due to intense competition, the product life cycle of video game apps is often two or three years or less. Even Angry Birds appeared to be in its decline stage in mid-2012. An example of this competition: Draw Something was downloaded 35 million times in the first six weeks of its existence—and in early 2012 it supplanted Words With Friends as the No. 1 free app for Apple and paid app for Android.[40]

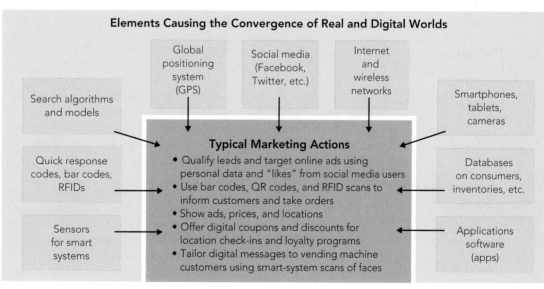

Elements Causing the Convergence of Real and Digital Worlds

Search algorithms and models · Global positioning system (GPS) · Social media (Facebook, Twitter, etc.) · Internet and wireless networks · Smartphones, tablets, cameras

Quick response codes, bar codes, RFIDs · Databases on consumers, inventories, etc.

Sensors for smart systems · Applications software (apps)

Typical Marketing Actions
- Qualify leads and target online ads using personal data and "likes" from social media users
- Use bar codes, QR codes, and RFID scans to inform customers and take orders
- Show ads, prices, and locations
- Offer digital coupons and discounts for location check-ins and loyalty programs
- Tailor digital messages to vending machine customers using smart-system scans of faces

Mobile Marketing: Tightening Links to Marketing Actions

This convergence of the real and digital worlds has resulted in increasing use of *mobile marketing*, any marketing activity conducted through several Internet networks to which consumers are continuously connected using a personal mobile device[41] This continuous connection present in mobile marketing has led to three recent smartphone apps:[42]

- *Price-comparison searches*: Scan product bar codes and research 500,000 stores, synchronizing searches between your computer and smartphone.
- *Location-based promotions*: Use your GPS-enabled smartphone for location check-ins to receive discounts at stores such as JCPenney.
- *Loyalty programs*: Win loyalty points for walking into stores like Target or Macy's and receive discounts from them.

The number of smartphone shopping searches and purchases has exploded in recent years, causing huge problems for conventional brick-and-mortar retailers.

Where to Now?

The clear point of difference in mobile marketing is its unique ability to empower users by connecting with them individually and continuously—learning about their likes and personal characteristics and sharing this information with online friends and (often) marketers selling products.[43] This shifting mind-set to a socially networked world will lead to connected users having more influence in the marketplace.[44] In the future, it seems we will see:

- New, creative ways to personalize social media connections.
- An increasing number of purchases made with a fob (a small device with embedded software) or a smartphone linked to a credit card.
- An enhanced focus on socially networked "communities" like neighborhoods, loyal users of a brand, and alumni associations—groups with common interests.
- An increased emphasis on measuring the marketing return on investment for social media initiatives.

Too busy to visit your supermarket this week? If you are in South Korea, do it on the wall of your subway station with your smartphone—and have your purchases delivered to your door.

Tesco Home Plus, a South Korean supermarket chain, provides a quick spur-of-the-moment opportunity for grocery shopping. Shoppers use their smartphones to scan images on the wall of a subway station to buy Tesco's grocery products while waiting for their train. They use the smartphone app to pay for the groceries, which are delivered to their door right after they get home.[45]

The convergence of social media, tablet devices, smartphones, and new apps will lead to companies having a more dynamic interaction with their customers.[46] Another futuristic example: A vending machine scans your face to identify your age and sex and changes its display (this already exists in Japan) and—in the future—gives you a quantity discount for buying two of your favorite candy bars (it knows about your Facebook "likes") while showing an electronic dinner coupon for a nearby restaurant if you appear between 7:00 and 9:00 P.M. this evening. The results of the candy and dinner offer are directly measurable for marketers. Note how many of the "convergence elements" in Figure 16–6 are present in this scenario.

This "smart systems" convergence is also having a dynamic impact on entrepreneurship and small business. This is because, unlike the huge cash investment needed to start a bricks-and-mortar business, today's social media enable new businesses to begin life on a financial shoestring. The launch of Bitter Girls in the video case at the end of the chapter is an example of a low-cost start-up.

What? American action-hero Chuck Norris is afraid to take a mallet to the live, flapping carp that is planned for a Czech holiday dinner? The text example shows how social media are now part of marketing strategies around the globe.

The Global Marketing Reach of Social Media

Computers, television, the Internet, smartphones, tablet devices, and social media have changed forever the way businesses around the world market products and services.

A T-Mobile promotion illustrates the impact of social media on global marketing strategies. T-Mobile and its global satellite-TV service were trying to reach consumers in the Czech Republic. So they decided to feature Chuck Norris, the U.S. action-movie hero in 1980s films like *The Delta Force* and the 1990s TV show *Walker, Texas Ranger*. These were huge hits among Czechs, from children to adults.[47]

A recent holiday T-Mobile TV spot there showed a Czech woman in her kitchen preparing a traditional Christmas Eve dinner of fresh carp. She hands Chuck Norris, her guest, a mallet to kill the still flapping fish. Norris shakes his head, "No." The woman then raises the mallet herself to smash the carp's head, and our action-hero Chuck Norris . . . faints! In trying to revive him, the woman hears her husband gleefully say, "On TV, anybody can be tough!"

This Czech TV ad campaign surpassed T-Mobile's expectations, and it had to add extra people to answer customer phone and Facebook questions. The reasons: More than 40,000 people became fans of T-Mobile's Czech unit on Facebook, and 4.5 million people viewed the ads on YouTube—in a country whose population is 10 million. Neighboring Poles and Slovaks—whose languages are similar to Czech—loved the ads as well.

So marketing strategies linked to social media are moving around the world. They often cross country boundaries, like the T-Mobile promotion accidentally did by also reaching consumers in Poland and Slovakia.

learning review

10. What is an example of how the real (physical) and digital (virtual) worlds are converging?

11. What are apps and why are they important?

12. How does T-Mobile's Czech ad campaign featuring Chuck Norris show the global marketing reach of social media?

LEARNING OBJECTIVES REVIEW

L01 *Define social media and describe how they differ from traditional advertising media.*

Social media are online media where active users submit news, photos, videos, and opinions, often accompanied by a feedback process to identify "popular" topics. Social media can be classified based on two factors: (1) media richness, which involves the degree of acoustic, visual, and physical contact between the social network and the user, and (2) self-disclosure, which is the degree to which individuals can control the impressions they want to make to others. Social media differ from traditional advertising media (newspapers, magazines, radio, and television) in that user generated content (1) is relatively inexpensive to create, publish, and access, (2) requires little training to develop, (3) can deliver virtually instantaneous responses, (4) can quickly alter and repost, and (5) may not be as private or anonymous as users expect.

L02 *Identify the four major social networks and how brand managers integrate them in their organizations' marketing actions.*

The four major social networks are Facebook, Twitter, LinkedIn, and YouTube. Facebook is a social network where users create a personal profile, add other users as "friends," and exchange messages, photos, videos, and opinions with them. To increase traffic to a Facebook Page, brand managers can use paid ads and sponsored stories. Twitter enables users to send and receive "tweets," messages up to 140 characters long. For Twitter, brand managers can use monitoring programs to track what people are saying about their organization's brand. LinkedIn lets users post their personal profiles to a network of businesspeople. LinkedIn can be used to create a company profile to share brand information and career opportunities with LinkedIn users and to demonstrate the company's expertise and professionalism. YouTube is a video-sharing social network where users can upload, distribute, view, and comment on videos. YouTube also allows marketers to create a brand channel to promote a product, show ads for it, and have viewers comment on it. YouTube also allows a company to inform consumers about itself and direct traffic by featuring a link back to its website.

L03 *Describe the differing roles of those receiving messages through traditional media versus social media and the factors brand managers use to select a social network.*

With promotional messages received through traditional media, recipients are generally "passive receivers" and the communication ends with them. In contrast, recipients of social media messages are "active receivers," and the company sending them messages hopes they will become "evangelists" and send positive messages back to the company and to online friends. The factors a marketer uses to select a specific social network involve assessing (1) the number of daily visitors to the company's website, (2) the characteristics (or profile) of those visitors, and (3) the focus of the social network. Of the four major social networks, Facebook has the largest number of daily visitors, followed by YouTube, Twitter, and LinkedIn. Each of these has a unique user profile that allows marketers to develop marketing programs to reach specific target segments. Also, because each social network has a unique focus (videos, short messaging, and so on), marketers can modify their marketing programs to take advantage of these differences.

L04 *Explain how social media can produce sales revenues for a brand and compare the performance measures linked to inputs or costs versus outputs or revenues.*

Measuring the sales generated from social media is more difficult than with traditional media because in many cases there is no direct link between a social network user and a sale. Brand managers can use social media platforms to send messages or paid advertisements to the brand's audience that include links to the special promotions, to coupon codes, or to specific products in an online store. By tracking the performance of these links, the brand manager can identify the ones that produce sales revenues. Performance measures linked to inputs and costs include (1) cost per thousand (similar to the CPM for a print ad), which is the number of times an ad is displayed to a user, (2) cost per click, which gives the rate the advertiser pays each time a visitor clicks on the ad and then jumps to the web page of the advertiser's choice, and (3) cost per action, which is the amount paid for every purchase that originates from an ad on a social media network site. Examples of performance measures linked to outputs or revenues include (1) the number of unique monthly users viewing the website at a given time; (2) page views, or the number of times a specific web page is loaded; and (3) visitors, or the total number of users viewing a particular web page during a specified time period.

L05 *Describe how the convergence of the real and digital worlds affects the future of social media.*

The convergence of the real and digital worlds in social networking is made possible by means of a "smart system," which is a computer-based network that triggers actions by sensing changes in the real or digital world. An example is how Japanese vending machines are able to recognize a customer's sex and age and respond with a new digital display on the vending machine. Other components of a smart system include sensors; radio frequency identification (RFID) tags; and apps, which are small, downloadable software programs that can run on smartphones and tablet devices to add functionality to these devices. In the future, there will be: (1) new ways to personalize social media connections; (2) an explosion of bar codes, RFIDs, and quick response (QR) codes linked to new apps available with social media; (3) an increased focus on socially networked "communities;" (4) social networks beginning to charge for user actions that generate more sales for advertisers; and (5) an increased emphasis on measuring the marketing return on investment for social media initiatives. The convergence of social media, smartphones, tablet devices, and new apps will lead to companies having a more dynamic interaction with their customers.

FOCUSING ON KEY TERMS

apps p. 378
blog p. 364
Facebook p. 367

LinkedIn p. 370
social media p. 364
Twitter p. 369

user generated content (UGC) p. 364
YouTube p. 371

APPLYING MARKETING KNOWLEDGE

1 Why was Kimmy Summers more successful using Facebook and Twitter to get volunteers and promote freshman move-in day at her university than she might have been using more conventional print media?

2 You and three college friends have decided to launch an online business selling clothes college students wear—T-shirts, shorts, sweats, and so on. You plan to use Facebook ads. What "likes" or interests do (*a*) college men and (*b*) college women have that might help you in planning your Facebook strategy?

3 You graduated from college four years ago and now have an information technology (IT) job. Your company just announced it will move all the IT work overseas in three months. Go to the LinkedIn site and determine what information you would put on your LinkedIn site to help you find a new job.

4 What is the significance of "user generated content" when contrasted with social media and traditional media?

5 You are a brand manager for a sneaker manufacturer like Nike or Under Armour and are trying to use Facebook to reach (*a*) college-age women and (*b*) men over 55 years of age. What three or four "likes" or interests would you expect each segment to have when you try to reach it with Facebook?

6 In measuring the results of a social network, what are the (*a*) advantages and (*b*) disadvantages of performance measures linked directly to revenues versus costs?

7 Looking back with perfect hindsight, what should the brand manager for Nestlé's Kit Kat have done when the Greenpeace e-mails first appeared?

building your marketing plan

Remembering the target market segments you identified in Chapter 8 for your marketing plan:

1 (*a*) Identify which one of the four social networks described in the chapter would be most useful and (*b*) give your reasons.

2 Briefly describe (*a*) how you would use this social network to try to increase sales of your products and (*b*) why you expect target market customers to respond to it.

video case 16 AOI Marketing: Using Facebook to Launch Bitter Girls®

QR 16–4
Bitter Girls
Video Case

"Today's successful women often march to their own unique drums, are highly motivated, and are very concerned about the greater good for society," says Jennifer Katz, president of AOI Marketing, Inc., a new media marketing firm.

THE CONCEPT: EMPOWERING TEENAGE GIRLS

A start-up team at AOI Marketing was charged with developing a concept that can be used to license and to market a variety of products to the "tween and teen" female market. The team observed that many of today's successful women don't fit into the most-popular-girl-in-their-high-school-class model. "So we developed the concept of communicating a message that is uplifting and empowering for girls," says Katz.

POSITIONING THE BITTER GIRLS CONCEPT FOR ITS TARGET MARKET

The team's initial idea was to cast Bitter Girls® in a happy, upbeat position. Through trial-and-error promotions and research, the marketing positioning changed 180 degrees from the original to today's concept:

- *Original concept.* The product started as "My Better Self"—a blog to give ideas to teenage girls to improve their self-confidence and ability to take on the world they will be facing soon. The problem: The goodie-goodie tone to the blog couldn't attract the attention and interest of these girls.
- *Today's concept.* The original concept was turned on its head to use irony and sometimes dark humor to help provide the same positive self-image for the girls.

    "This same dark-humor positioning partly underlies the success

of the TV classic *The Simpsons,*" says Amanda Axvig, the firm's vice president of marketing. She goes on, "This revised positioning strategy is reflected in how AOI Marketing ultimately defined Bitter Girls in its marketing plan," which is:

> Bitter Girls are smart, motivated, creative, authentic girls making a difference in the world. Based on real-life people, the Bitter Girls represent girls who grew up to become doctors, architects, human rights activists, writers, and more.

Note the deliberate disconnect between the Bitter Girls name and the positive nature of the girls in the description of them. However, feedback from females in the target market who like the brand on Facebook indicate there is more interest in keeping Bitter Girls dark, sullen, and "edgy."

PRODUCT INTEGRITY AND COMPETITION

With brand awareness growing, the team wrote precise development guidelines to ensure the product's integrity, look, and feel in order to meet the needs of the licensee. The AOI team worked with graphic artists Alexandra Amrami and Clay Williams to develop the logo and initial characters. Note the level of detail in the examples below:

- *Logo and font.* The official logo of the Bitter Girls® (above) should always appear as a specific font with the bow on the letter B and the heart on the letter I, followed by the Registered Trademark symbol, ®, after the brand name or logo. The only allowable typefaces on the main product are the handwritten logotype or the Harrowprint font by Stephen Doonan.
- *Identifying names.* Each girl in the collection has a name, such as Jenny, Ariel, Kari, and so on. The identifying name and career aspirations of Bitter Girls must also be written in Harrowprint font, as shown above.
- *Quotes and phrases.* On the Facebook Page, people who like Bitter Girls can suggest new "quotes and phrases" or rate existing ones. Some examples:

1. If I want your opinion, I'll give it to you.
2. Bitter is the new black.
3. Just put on your big girl pants and get it done.
4. If you were just a little smarter, I could teach you to fetch.
5. It's not me, it's definitely you.

A number of competitors in the "tween and teen" female market promote individualism, girl power, and self-esteem. For example, in 1993, artist Rob Reger created "Emily the Strange" for a black cat–loving 13-year-old girl who tells the world to "Get Lost." In 1994, Lela Lee created her first "Angry Little Girls" that now appear in a variety of products and books.

USING SOCIAL MEDIA TO CREATE BRAND AWARENESS

The goal in launching the business is to popularize the logo and cartoon drawings of Bitter Girls. "That makes it possible to license the concept to manufacturers and retailers selling products like apparel or mobile phone cases bought by tween and teen girls," says Brian Stuckey, vice president of operations for AOI Marketing.

Studying competitors that use social media is of great value to Bitter Girls because actions such as "people like this," "comments," and "likes" are transparent on Facebook Pages. This gives Bitter Girls real-time insight as to what is grabbing the attention of the market segments it is targeting.

The AOI team first had to create awareness in the target market that the Bitter Girls brand exists. Looking at strategies of competitors and with a limited marketing budget, the AOI team has decided that its own website and Facebook are the best low-cost ways to acquire a "seed" following. This process involves "creating an official Facebook Page, developing a story line, and running highly targeted Facebook ads," says Stuckey. The ads appear on the right-hand side of Facebook Pages targeting fans of complementary brands such as *Seventeen Magazine* and Justin Bieber.

Innovation never stops at AOI Marketing. As the Bitter Girls brand continues moving forward, the AOI Marketing team is developing a new brand targeting the same tween and teen female audience. Following a business model similar to Bitter Girls, the new Brighter Girls® brand empowers young girls to be confident and inspiring. The goal is to help them successfully address issues that impact them most, such as body image and relationships.

Review Figure 16–2 and use your knowledge of websites, social media, and Facebook in answering the questions below.

Questions

1 (*a*) What is the image you first have when you hear the brand name "Bitter Girls"? What are both (*b*) the strengths and (*c*) the weaknesses in linking this brand name to the concept of empowering tweens and teens?

2 How can social media be used to drive traffic to the Bitter Girls website?

3 How can Bitter Girls (*a*) bring people from its website to its Facebook Page and (*b*) increase their involvement and participation on its Facebook Page? (*c*) Why are these important goals?

4 (*a*) How can Bitter Girls find new likes? (*b*) On what other Facebook Pages should Bitter Girls advertise?

5 (*a*) What products besides apparel and mobile phone cases might Bitter Girls license? (*b*) How can Bitter Girls promote its products through Facebook?

Personal Selling and Sales Management

17

LEARNING OBJECTIVES

After reading this chapter you should be able to:

 LO1 Discuss the nature and scope of personal selling and sales management in marketing.

LO2 Identify the different types of personal selling.

LO3 Explain the stages in the personal selling process.

LO4 Describe the major functions of sales management.

MEET TODAY'S SALES PROFESSIONAL

Have you been considering sales as a career opportunity? If so, then consider Lindsey Smith as a role model (see opposite page).

Ms. Smith represents Molecular Imaging Products within the Medical Diagnostics Division of GE Healthcare, having joined the company ten years ago right out of college with a BBA degree. The epitome of today's sales professional, she lists integrity, motivation, trust and relationship building, and a team orientation as just a few of the ingredients necessary for a successful sales career.

As a sales professional, she recognizes the importance of constantly updating and refining her product knowledge, analytical and communication skills, and strategic thinking about opportunities to more fully satisfy each customer's clinical, economic, and technical requirements. And for good reason. Her customer contacts include physicians (radiologists, neurologists, and cardiologists), medical technologists, nurses, and health care provider CEOs, CFOs, and other administrators.

Lindsey Smith's selling orientation and customer relationship philosophy rest on four pillars. First, she is committed to creating value for her clients: "I believe every sales call and client interaction should create value for both the customer and the company." Second, she seeks to serve her clients as a trusted consultant: "I emphasize being a resource for my customers by providing novel solutions for them." Third, she continually reinforces GE Healthcare's competitive advantage: "I emphasize my company's value proposition and showcase the company's product innovation, solutions, and service." Finally, she regards challenges as opportunities: "I consider challenges as opportunities to provide solutions and resources to customers and to build client trust and long-term relationships."

Lindsey Smith's approach to selling and customer relationships has served her well. She is among the company's top revenue-producers and has a long list of loyal customers.[1]

This chapter describes the scope and significance of personal selling and sales management in marketing and creating value for customers. It first highlights the many forms of personal selling. Next, the major steps in the selling process are outlined with an emphasis on building buyer–seller relationships. Attention is then focused on salesforce management and its critical role in achieving a company's broader marketing objectives. Three major salesforce management functions are then detailed. They are sales plan formulation, sales plan implementation, and salesforce evaluation. Finally, technology's persuasive influence on how selling is done and how salespeople are managed is described.

SCOPE AND SIGNIFICANCE OF PERSONAL SELLING AND SALES MANAGEMENT

Chapter 14 described personal selling and management of the sales effort as being part of the firm's promotional mix. Although it is important to recognize that personal selling is a useful vehicle for communicating with present and potential buyers, it is much more.

Nature of Personal Selling and Sales Management

Personal selling involves the two-way flow of communication between a buyer and seller, often in a face-to-face encounter, designed to influence a person's or group's purchase decision. However, with advances in telecommunications, personal selling also takes place over the telephone and through video teleconferencing and Internet-enabled links between buyers and sellers.

Personal selling remains a highly human-intensive activity despite the use of technology. Accordingly, the people involved must be managed. **Sales management** involves planning the selling program and implementing and evaluating the personal selling effort of the firm. The tasks involved in managing personal selling include setting objectives; organizing the salesforce; recruiting, selecting, training, and compensating salespeople; and evaluating the performance of individual salespeople.

personal selling
The two-way flow of communication between a buyer and seller, often in a face-to-face encounter, designed to influence a person's or group's purchase decision.

sales management
Planning the selling program and implementing and evaluating the personal selling effort of the firm.

QR 17–1
Cambridge
Sales Video

Selling Happens Almost Everywhere

"Everyone lives by selling something," wrote author Robert Louis Stevenson a century ago. His observation still holds true today. The U.S. Bureau of Labor Statistics reports that about 14 million people are employed in sales positions in the United States. Included in this number are manufacturing sales personnel, real estate brokers, stockbrokers, and salesclerks who work in retail stores. In reality, however, virtually every occupation that involves customer contact has an element of personal selling. For example, attorneys, accountants, bankers, and company personnel recruiters perform sales-related activities, whether or not they acknowledge it.

Personal Selling in Marketing

Personal selling serves three major roles in a firm's overall marketing effort. First, salespeople are the critical link between the firm and its customers. This role requires that salespeople match company interests with customer needs to satisfy both parties in the exchange process. Second, salespeople *are* the company in a consumer's eyes. They represent what a company is or attempts to be and are often the only personal contact a customer has with the company. IBM's chief executive officer calls the company's 40,000-strong salesforce "our face to the client."[2] Third, personal selling may play a dominant role in a firm's marketing program. This situation typically arises when a firm uses a push marketing strategy, described in Chapter 14. Avon, for example, pays almost 40 percent of its total sales dollars for selling expenses. Pharmaceutical firms and office and educational equipment manufacturers also rely heavily on personal selling in the marketing of their products.

Creating Customer Solutions and Value through Salespeople: Relationship Selling

As the critical link between the firm and its customers, salespeople can create customer value in many ways. For instance, by being close to the customer, salespeople can identify creative solutions to customer problems. Salespeople at Medtronic, Inc.,

Could this be a salesperson in the operating room? Read the text to find out why Medtronic salespeople visit hospital operating rooms.

Medtronic
www.medtronic.com

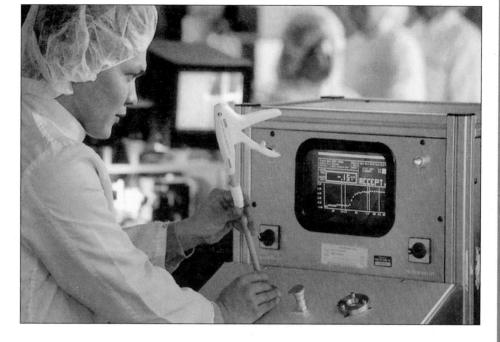

the world leader in the heart pacemaker market, are in the operating room for more than 90 percent of the procedures performed with their product and are on call, wearing pagers, 24 hours a day. "It reflects the willingness to be there in every situation, just in case a problem arises—even though nine times out of ten the procedure goes just fine," notes a satisfied customer.[3]

Salespeople can create value by easing the customer buying process. This happened at TE Connectivity, a producer of electrical products. Salespeople and customers had a difficult time getting product specifications and performance data on the company's 70,000 products quickly and accurately. The company now has all of its information on its website, which can be downloaded instantly by salespeople and customers.

Customer value is also created by salespeople who follow through after the sale. At Jefferson Smurfit Corporation, a multibillion-dollar supplier of packaging products, one of its salespeople juggled production from three of the company's plants to satisfy an unexpected demand for boxes from General Electric. This person's action led to the company being given GE's Distinguished Supplier Award.

relationship selling
The practice of building ties to customers based on a salesperson's attention and commitment to customer needs over time.

Relationship Selling Customer value creation is made possible by **relationship selling**, the practice of building ties to customers based on a salesperson's attention and commitment to customer needs over time. Relationship selling involves mutual respect and trust among buyers and sellers. It focuses on creating long-term customers, not a one-time sale. A survey of 300 senior sales executives revealed that 96 percent consider "building long-term relationships with customers" to be the most important activity affecting sales performance. Companies such as Xerox, American Express, Motorola, and Owens-Corning have made relationship building a core focus of their sales effort.[4]

Relationship selling represents another dimension of customer relationship management. It emphasizes the importance of learning about customer needs and wants and tailoring solutions to customer problems as a means to customer value creation.

learning review

1. What is personal selling?

2. What is involved in sales management?

THE MANY FORMS OF PERSONAL SELLING

Personal selling assumes many forms based on the amount of selling done and the amount of creativity required to perform the sales task. Broadly speaking, two types of personal selling exist: order taking and order getting. While some firms use only one of these types of personal selling, others use a combination of the two.

Order-Taking Salespeople

order taker
A salesperson who processes routine orders or reorders for products that were already sold by the company.

Typically, an **order taker** processes routine orders or reorders for products that were already sold by the company. The primary responsibility of order takers is to preserve an ongoing relationship with existing customers and maintain sales.

Two types of order takers exist. *Outside order takers* visit customers and replenish inventory stocks of resellers, such as retailers or wholesalers. For example, Frito-Lay salespeople call on supermarkets, convenience stores, and other establishments to ensure that the company's line of snack products (such as Doritos and Tostitos tortilla chips) is in adequate supply. In addition, outside order takers often provide assistance in arranging displays.

Inside order takers, also called *order clerks* or *salesclerks*, answer simple questions, take orders, and complete transactions with customers. Many retail clerks are inside order takers. Inside order takers are employed by companies that use *inbound telemarketing*, the use of toll-free telephone numbers that customers can call to obtain information about products or services and make purchases. In business-to-business settings, order taking arises in straight rebuy situations, as described in Chapter 5.

Order takers generally do little selling in a conventional sense. They engage in modest problem solving with customers. They often represent products that have few options, such as magazine subscriptions and highly standardized industrial products. Inbound telemarketing is also an essential selling activity for more "customer-service" driven firms, such as Dell. At these companies, order takers undergo extensive training so that they can better assist callers with their purchase decisions.

Order-Getting Salespeople

order getter
A salesperson who sells in a conventional sense and identifies prospective customers, provides customers with information, persuades customers to buy, closes sales, and follows up on customers' use of a product or service.

An **order getter** sells in a conventional sense and identifies prospective customers, provides customers with information, persuades customers to buy, closes sales, and

A Frito-Lay salesperson takes inventory of snacks for the store manager to sign. In this situation, the manager will make a straight rebuy decision.

Frito-Lay, Inc.
www.fritolay.com

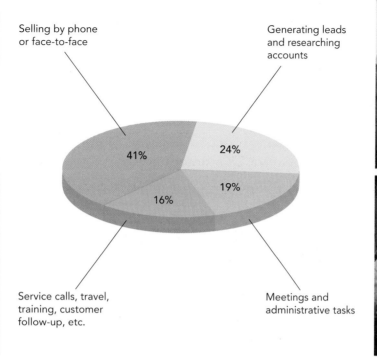

Selling by phone or face-to-face — 41%

Generating leads and researching accounts — 24%

19% — Meetings and administrative tasks

16% — Service calls, travel, training, customer follow-up, etc.

FIGURE 17–1

How do outside order-getting salespeople spend their time each week? You might be surprised after reading the text.

follows up on customers' use of a product or service. Like order takers, order getters can be inside (an automobile salesperson) or outside (a Xerox salesperson).

Order getting involves a high degree of creativity and customer empathy and is typically required for selling complex or technical products with many options, so considerable product knowledge and sales training are necessary. In modified rebuy or new-buy purchase situations in business-to-business selling, an order getter acts as a problem solver who identifies how a particular product may satisfy a customer's need. Similarly, in the purchase of a service, such as insurance, a Metropolitan Life insurance agent can provide a mix of plans to satisfy a buyer's needs depending on income, stage of the family's life cycle, and investment objectives.

Order getting is not a 40-hour-per-week job. Industry research shows that outside order getters, or field service representatives, often work over 50 hours per week. As shown in Figure 17–1, 41 percent of an average field sales representative's time is actually spent selling by phone or face-to-face. Another 24 percent is devoted to generating leads and researching customer accounts. The remainder of a sales representative's workweek is occupied by administrative tasks, meetings, service calls, travel, and training.[5]

Order getting by outside salespeople is also expensive. It is estimated that the average cost of a single field sales call on a business customer is about $350, factoring in the salesperson's compensation, benefits, and travel-and-entertainment expenses. This cost illustrates why outbound telemarketing is popular. *Outbound telemarketing* is the practice of using the telephone rather than personal visits to contact current and prospective customers. A much lower cost per sales call (from $20 to $25) and little or no field expenses account for its widespread appeal.

learning review

3. What is the principal difference between an order taker and an order getter?

4. What percentage of an order-getting salesperson's time is spent selling?

THE PERSONAL SELLING PROCESS: BUILDING RELATIONSHIPS

Selling, and particularly order getting, is a complicated activity that involves building buyer–seller relationships. Although the salesperson–customer interaction is essential to personal selling, much of a salesperson's work occurs before this meeting and continues after the sale itself. The **personal selling process** consists of six stages: (1) prospecting, (2) preapproach, (3) approach, (4) presentation, (5) close, and (6) follow-up (see Figure 17–2).

personal selling process
Sales activities occurring before and after the sale itself, consisting of six stages: (1) prospecting, (2) preapproach, (3) approach, (4) presentation, (5) close, and (6) follow-up.

Prospecting: Identifying and Qualifying Prospective Customers

Personal selling begins with the *prospecting stage*—the search for and qualification of potential customers. There are three types of prospects. A *lead* is the name of a person who may be a possible customer. A *prospect* is a customer who wants or needs the product. If an individual wants the product, can afford to buy it, and is the decision maker, this individual is a *qualified prospect*.

FIGURE 17–2
Stages and objectives of the personal selling process. Each stage is critical for successful selling and building a customer relationship.

STAGE	OBJECTIVE	COMMENTS
1. Prospecting	Search for and qualify prospects	Start of the selling process; prospects produced through advertising, referrals, and cold canvassing
2. Preapproach	Gather information and decide how to approach the prospect	Information sources include personal observation, other customers, and own salespeople
3. Approach	Gain a prospect's attention, stimulate interest, and make transition to the presentation	First impression is critical; gain attention and interest through reference to common acquaintances, a referral, or product demonstration
4. Presentation	Begin converting a prospect into a customer by creating a desire for the product or service	Different presentation formats are possible; however, involving the customer in the product or service through attention to particular needs is critical; important to deal professionally and ethically with prospect skepticism, indifference, or objections
5. Close	Obtain a purchase commitment from the prospect and create a customer	Salesperson asks for the purchase; different approaches include the trial close and assumptive close
6. Follow-up	Ensure that the customer is satisfied with the product or service	Resolve any problems faced by the customer to ensure customer satisfaction and future sales possibilities

Trade shows are a popular source for leads and prospects. Companies like TSCentral provide comprehensive trade show information.

TSCentral

www.tscentral.com

Leads and prospects are generated using several sources. For example, advertising may contain a coupon or a toll-free number to generate leads. Some companies use exhibits at trade shows, professional meetings, and conferences to generate leads or prospects. Staffed by salespeople, these exhibits are used to attract the attention of prospective buyers and disseminate information. Others utilize the Internet for generating leads and prospects. Today, salespeople are using websites, e-mail, and social networks, suched as LinkedIn, to connect to individuals and companies that may be interested in their products or services.

Another approach for generating leads is through *cold canvassing* or *cold calling*, either in person or by telephone. This approach simply means that a salesperson may open a directory, pick a name, and contact that individual or business. Despite its high refusal rate, cold canvassing can be successful.[6]

Cold canvassing is often criticized by U.S. consumers and is now regulated. Research shows that 75 percent of U.S. consumers consider this practice an intrusion on their privacy, and 72 percent find it distasteful.[7] *The Telephone Consumer Protection Act* (1991) contains provisions to curb abuses such as early morning or late night calling. Additional federal regulations require more complete disclosure regarding solicitations, include provisions that allow consumers to avoid being called at any time through the Do-Not-Call Registry, and impose fines for violations. For example, satellite television provider DirecTV was fined $5.3 million for making thousands of calls to consumers who had put their telephone numbers on the Do-Not-Call Registry.[8]

Preapproach: Preparing for the Sales Call

Once a salesperson has identified a qualified prospect, preparation for the sale begins with the preapproach. The *preapproach* stage involves obtaining further information on the prospect and deciding on the best method of approach. Knowing how the prospect prefers to be approached and what the prospect is looking for in a product or service is essential.

For instance, a Merrill Lynch stockbroker will need information on a prospect's discretionary income, investment objectives, and preference for discussing brokerage services over the telephone or in person. For business product companies such as

Texas Instruments, the preapproach involves identifying the buying role of a prospect (for example, influencer or decision maker), important buying criteria, and the prospect's receptivity to a formal or informal presentation. Identifying the best time to contact a prospect is also important. Northwestern Mutual Life Insurance Company suggests the best times to call on people in different occupations: dentists before 9:30 A.M., lawyers between 11:00 A.M. and 2:00 P.M., and college professors between 7:00 and 8:00 P.M.

Successful salespeople recognize that the preapproach stage should never be short-changed. Their experience coupled with research on customer complaints indicates that failure to learn as much as possible about the prospect is unprofessional and the ruin of a sales call.

Approach: Making the First Impression

The *approach* stage involves the initial meeting between the salesperson and the prospect, where the objectives are to gain the prospect's attention, stimulate interest, and build the foundation for the sales presentation itself and the basis for a working relationship. The first impression is critical at this stage, and it is common for salespeople to begin the conversation with a reference to common acquaintances, a referral, or even the product or service itself. Which tactic is taken will depend on the information obtained in the prospecting and preapproach stages.

How business cards are exchanged with Asian customers is very important. Read the text to learn the appropriate protocol in the approach stage of the personal selling process.

The approach stage is very important in international settings.[9] In many societies outside the United States, considerable time is devoted to nonbusiness talk designed to establish a rapport between buyers and sellers. For instance, it is common for two or three meetings to occur before business matters are discussed in the Middle East and Asia. Gestures are also very important. The initial meeting between a salesperson and a prospect in the United States customarily begins with a firm handshake. Handshakes also apply in France, but they are gentle, not firm. Forget the handshake in Japan. An appropriate bow is expected. What about business cards? Business cards should be printed in English on one side and the language of the prospective customer on the other. Knowledgeable U.S. salespeople know that their business cards should be handed to Asian customers using both hands, with the name facing the receiver. In Asia, anything involving a person's name demands respect.

Presentation: Tailoring a Solution for a Customer's Needs

The *presentation* stage is at the core of the order-getting selling process, and its objective is to convert a prospect into a customer by creating a desire for the product or service. Three major presentation formats exist: (1) stimulus-response format, (2) formula selling format, and (3) need-satisfaction format.

Stimulus-Response Format The *stimulus-response presentation* format assumes that given the appropriate stimulus by a salesperson, the prospect will buy. With this format the salesperson tries one appeal after another, hoping to hit the right button. A counter clerk at McDonald's is using this approach when he or she asks whether you'd like an order of french fries or a dessert with your meal. The counter clerk is engaging in what is called *suggestive selling*. Although useful in this setting, the stimulus-response format is not always appropriate, and for many products a more formalized format is necessary.

Formula Selling Format   The *formula selling presentation* format is based on the view that a presentation consists of information that must be provided in an accurate, thorough, and step-by-step manner to inform the prospect. A popular version of this format is the *canned sales presentation*, which is a memorized, standardized message conveyed to every prospect. Used frequently by firms in telephone and door-to-door selling of consumer products (for example, Kirby vacuum cleaners), this approach treats every prospect the same, regardless of differences in needs or preferences for certain kinds of information.

Canned sales presentations can be advantageous when the differences between prospects are unknown or with novice salespeople who are less knowledgeable about the product and selling process than experienced salespeople. Although it guarantees a thorough presentation, it often lacks flexibility and spontaneity and, more important, does not provide for feedback from the prospective buyer—a critical component in the communication process and the start of a relationship.

Rockport sales representatives are adept at adaptive selling to retail buyers.

The Rockport Company
www.rockport.com

adaptive selling
A need-satisfaction sales presentation style that involves adjusting the presentation to fit the selling situation.

consultative selling
A need-satisfaction sales presentation style that focuses on problem identification, where the salesperson serves as an expert on problem recognition and resolution.

Need-Satisfaction Format   The stimulus-response and formula selling formats share a common characteristic: The salesperson dominates the conversation. By comparison, the *need-satisfaction presentation* format emphasizes probing and listening by the salesperson to identify the needs and interests of prospective buyers. Once these are identified, the salesperson tailors the presentation to the prospect and highlights product benefits that may be valued by the prospect. The need-satisfaction format, which emphasizes problem solving and customer solutions, is the most consistent with the marketing concept and relationship building.

Two selling styles are common with this format.[10] **Adaptive selling** involves adjusting the presentation to fit the selling situation, such as knowing when to offer solutions and when to ask for more information. Sales research and practice show that knowledge of the customer and sales situation are key ingredients for adaptive selling. Many consumer service firms such as brokerage and insurance firms and consumer product firms like Rockport, AT&T, and Gillette effectively apply this selling style.

Consultative selling focuses on problem identification, where the salesperson serves as an expert on problem recognition and resolution. With consultative selling, problem solution options are not simply a matter of choosing from an array of existing products or services. Rather, novel solutions often arise, thereby creating unique value for the customer.

Consultative selling is prominent in business-to-business marketing. Johnson Controls's Automotive Systems Group, IBM's Global Services, DHL Worldwide Express, GE Healthcare, and Xerox offer customer solutions through their consultative selling style. According to a senior Xerox sales executive, "Our business is no longer about selling boxes. It's about selling digital, networked-based information management solutions, and this requires a highly customized and consultative selling process." But what does a customer solution really mean? The Marketing Matters box on the next page offers a unique answer.[11]

Handling Objections   A critical concern in the presentation stage is handling objections. *Objections* are excuses for not making a purchase commitment or decision. Some objections are valid and are based on the characteristics of the product or service or price. However, many objections reflect prospect skepticism or indifference. Whether valid or not, experienced salespeople know that objections do not put an end to the presentation. Rather, techniques can be used to deal with

Imagine This . . . Putting the Customer into Customer Solutions!

Solutions for problems are what companies are looking for from suppliers. At the same time, suppliers focus on customer solutions to differentiate themselves from competitors. So what is a customer solution and what does it have to do with selling?

Sellers view a solution as a customized and integrated combination of products and services for meeting a customer's business needs. But what do buyers think? From a buyer's perspective, a solution is one that (1) meets their requirements, (2) is designed to uniquely solve their problem, (3) can be implemented, and (4) ensures follow-up. This insight arose from a field study conducted by three researchers at Emory University. Their in-depth study also yielded insight into what an effective customer solution offers. According to one buyer interviewed in their study:

They (the supplier) make sure that their sales and marketing guys know what's going on. The sales and technical folks know what's going on, and the technical and support guys know what's going on with me. All these guys are in the loop, and it's not a puzzle for them.

So what does putting the customer into customer solutions have to do with selling? Three things stand out. First, considerable time and effort is necessary to fully understand a specific customer's requirements. Second, effective customer solutions are based on relationships among sellers and buyers. And finally, consultative selling is central to providing novel solutions for customers, thereby creating value for them.

---

objections in a courteous, ethical, and professional manner. Six techniques are most common:[12]

1. *Acknowledge and convert the objection.* This technique involves using the objection as a reason for buying. For example, a prospect might say, "The price is too high." The reply: "Yes, the price is high because we use the finest materials. Let me show you. . . ."
2. *Postpone.* The postpone technique is used when the objection will be dealt with later in the presentation: "I'm going to address that point shortly. I think my answer would make better sense then."
3. *Agree and neutralize.* Here a salesperson agrees with the objection, then shows that it is unimportant. A salesperson would say, "That's true. Others have said the same. But, they thought that issue was outweighed by other benefits."
4. *Accept the objection.* Sometimes the objection is valid. Let the prospect express such views, probe for the reason behind it, and attempt to stimulate further discussion on the objection.
5. *Denial.* When a prospect's objection is based on misinformation and clearly untrue, it is wise to meet the objection head on with a firm denial.
6. *Ignore the objection.* This technique is used when it appears that the objection is a stalling mechanism or is clearly not important to the prospect.

Each of these techniques requires a calm, professional interaction with the prospect and is most effective when objections are anticipated in the preapproach stage. Handling objections is a skill requiring a sense of timing, appreciation for the prospect's state of mind, and adeptness in communication. Objections also should be handled ethically. Lying or misrepresenting product or service features are grossly unethical practices.

Close: Asking for the Customer's Order or Business

The *closing* stage in the selling process involves obtaining a purchase commitment from the prospect. This stage is the most important and the most difficult because the salesperson must determine when the prospect is ready to buy. Telltale signals indicating

The closing stage involves obtaining a purchase commitment from the prospect. Read the text to learn how the close itself can take several forms.

a readiness to buy include body language (prospect reexamines the product or contract closely), statements ("This equipment should reduce our maintenance costs"), and questions ("When could we expect delivery?").

The close itself can take several forms. Three closing techniques are used when a salesperson believes a buyer is about ready to make a purchase: (1) trial close, (2) assumptive close, and (3) urgency close. A *trial close* involves asking the prospect to make a decision on some aspect of the purchase: "Would you prefer the blue or gray model?" An *assumptive close* entails asking the prospect to consider choices concerning delivery, warranty, or financing terms under the assumption that a sale has been finalized. An *urgency close* is used to commit the prospect quickly by making reference to the timeliness of the purchase: "The low interest financing ends next week," or "That is the last model we have in stock." Of course, these statements should be used only if they accurately reflect the situation; otherwise, such claims would be unethical. When a prospect is clearly ready to buy, the final close is used, and a salesperson asks for the order.

Follow-Up: Solidifying the Relationship

The selling process does not end with the closing of a sale; rather, professional selling requires customer follow-up. One marketing authority equated the follow-up with courtship and marriage, by observing, "The sale merely consummates the courtship. Then the marriage begins. How good the marriage is depends on how well the relationship is managed."[13] The *follow-up* stage includes making certain the customer's purchase has been properly delivered and installed and difficulties experienced with the use of the item are addressed. Attention to this stage of the selling process solidifies the buyer–seller relationship. Research shows that the cost and effort to obtain repeat sales from a satisfied customer is roughly half of that necessary to gain a sale from a new customer.[14] In short, today's satisfied customers become tomorrow's qualified prospects or referrals.

learning review

5. What are the six stages in the personal selling process?

6. Which presentation format is most consistent with the marketing concept? Why?

THE SALES MANAGEMENT PROCESS

LO4

Selling must be managed if it is going to contribute to a firm's marketing objectives. Although firms differ in the specifics of how salespeople and the selling effort are managed, the sales management process is similar across firms. Sales management consists of three interrelated functions: (1) sales plan formulation, (2) sales plan implementation, and (3) salesforce evaluation (see Figure 17–3 on the next page).

Sales Plan Formulation: Setting Direction

Formulating the sales plan is the most basic of the three sales management functions. According to the vice president of the Harris Corporation, a global communications company, "If a company hopes to implement its marketing strategy, it really needs a

FIGURE 17–3
The sales management
process involves sales plan
formulation, sales plan
implementation, and
salesforce evaluation.

Sales plan formulation
- Setting objectives
- Organizing the salesforce
- Developing account management policies

Sales plan implementation
- Salesforce recruitment and selection
- Salesforce training
- Salesforce motivation and compensation

Salesforce evaluation
- Quantitative assessments
- Behavioral evaluation

sales plan
A statement describing what is to be achieved and where and how the selling effort of salespeople is to be deployed.

detailed sales planning process."[15] The **sales plan** is a statement describing what is to be achieved and where and how the selling effort of salespeople is to be deployed. Sales plan formulation involves three tasks: (1) setting objectives, (2) organizing the salesforce, and (3) developing account management policies.

Setting Objectives   Setting objectives is central to sales management because this task specifies what is to be achieved. In practice, objectives are set for the total salesforce and for each salesperson.

Selling objectives can be output related and focus on dollar or unit sales volume, number of new customers added, and profit. Alternatively, they can be input related and emphasize the number of sales calls and selling expenses. Output- and input-related objectives are used for the salesforce as a whole and for each salesperson. A third type of objective that is behaviorally related is typically specific for each salesperson and includes his or her product knowledge, customer service satisfaction ratings, and selling and communication skills.

Whatever objectives are set, they should be precise and measurable and specify the time period over which they are to be achieved. Once established, these objectives serve as performance standards for the evaluation of the salesforce, the third function of sales management.

Organizing the Salesforce   Establishing a selling organization is the second task in formulating the sales plan. Companies organize their salesforce on the basis of (1) geography, (2) customer, or (3) product or service.

A geographical structure is the simplest organization, where the United States, or indeed the globe, is first divided into regions and each region is divided into districts or territories. Salespeople are assigned to each district with defined geographical boundaries and call on all customers and represent all products sold by the company. The main advantage of this structure is that it can minimize travel time, expenses, and duplication of selling effort. However, if a firm's products or customers require specialized knowledge, then a geographical structure is not suitable.

A customer sales organizational structure is used when different types of buyers have different needs. In practice this means that a different salesforce calls on each separate type of buyer or marketing channel. For example, Kodak recently switched from a geographical to a marketing channel structure with different sales teams serving specific retail channels: mass merchandisers, photo specialty outlets, and food and drug stores. The rationale for this approach is that more effective, specialized customer support and knowledge are provided to buyers. However, this structure often leads to higher administrative costs and some duplication of selling effort, because two separate salesforces are used to represent the same products.

major account management
The practice of using team selling to focus on important customers so as to build mutually beneficial, long-term, cooperative relationships; also called key account management.

A variation of the customer organizational structure is **major account management**, or *key account management,* the practice of using team selling to focus on important customers so as to build mutually beneficial, long-term, cooperative relationships. Major account management involves teams of sales, service, and often technical personnel who work with purchasing, manufacturing, engineering, logistics, and financial executives in customer organizations. This approach, which often assigns company

Marketing Matters > > > > > > customer value

Creating and Sustaining Customer Value through Cross-Functional Team Selling

The day of the lone salesperson calling on a customer is rapidly becoming history. Today, 75 percent of companies employ cross-functional teams of professionals to work with customers to improve relationships, find better ways of doing things, and, of course, create and sustain value for their customers.

Xerox and IBM pioneered cross-functional team selling, but other firms were quick to follow as they spotted the potential to create and sustain value for their customers. Recognizing that corn growers needed a herbicide they could apply less often, a DuPont team of chemists, sales and marketing executives, and regulatory specialists created just the right product that recorded sales of $57 million in its first year. Procter & Gamble uses teams of marketing, sales, advertising, computer systems, and supply chain personnel to work with its major retailers, such as Walmart, to identify ways to develop, promote, and deliver products. Pitney Bowes, Inc., which produces sophisticated computer systems that weigh, rate, and track packages for firms such as UPS and FedEx, also uses sales teams to meet customer needs. These teams consist of sales personnel, "carrier management specialists," and engineering and administrative executives who continually

find ways to improve the technology of shipping goods across town and around the world.

Efforts to create and sustain customer value through cross-functional team selling have become a necessity as customers seek greater value for their money. According to the vice president for procurement of a *Fortune* 500 company, "Today, it's not just getting the best price but getting the best value—and there are a lot of pieces to value."

personnel to a customer account, results in "customer specialists" who can provide exceptional service. Procter & Gamble uses this approach with Walmart as does Black & Decker with Home Depot. Other companies also have embraced this practice, as described in the Marketing Matters box.[16]

A product sales organizational structure is used when specific knowledge is required to sell a product. For example, Maxim Steel has a salesforce that sells drilling pipe to oil companies and another that sells specialty steel products to manufacturers. The primary advantage of this structure is that salespeople can develop expertise with technical characteristics, applications, and selling methods associated with a particular product or family of products. However, this structure also produces high administrative costs and duplication of selling effort because two company salespeople may call on the same customer.

In short, there is no one best sales organization for all companies in all situations.[17] The organization of the salesforce should reflect the marketing strategy of the firm.

Developing Account Management Policies   The third task in formulating a sales plan involves developing **account management policies** specifying who salespeople should contact, what kinds of selling and customer service activities should be engaged in, and how these activities should be carried out. These policies might state which individuals in a buying organization should be contacted, the amount of sales and service effort that different customers should receive, and the kinds of information salespeople should collect before or during a sales call.

An example of an account management policy in Figure 17–4 on the next page shows how different accounts or customers can be grouped according to level of opportunity and the firm's competitive sales position.[18] When specific account names

account management policies
Policies that specify who salespeople should contact, what kinds of selling and customer service activities should be engaged in, and how these activities should be carried out.

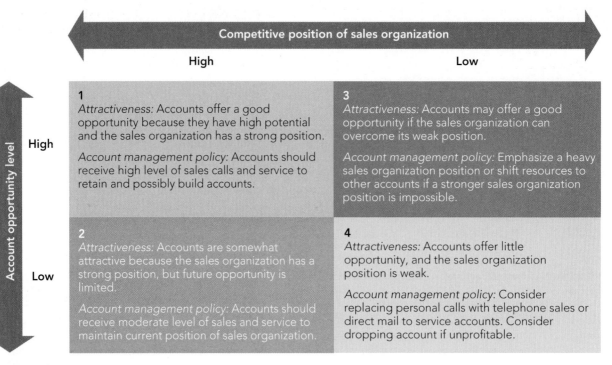

Competitive position of sales organization

High | Low

Account opportunity level — High | Low

1
Attractiveness: Accounts offer a good opportunity because they have high potential and the sales organization has a strong position.

Account management policy: Accounts should receive high level of sales calls and service to retain and possibly build accounts.

3
Attractiveness: Accounts may offer a good opportunity if the sales organization can overcome its weak position.

Account management policy: Emphasize a heavy sales organization position or shift resources to other accounts if a stronger sales organization position is impossible.

2
Attractiveness: Accounts are somewhat attractive because the sales organization has a strong position, but future opportunity is limited.

Account management policy: Accounts should receive moderate level of sales and service to maintain current position of sales organization.

4
Attractiveness: Accounts offer little opportunity, and the sales organization position is weak.

Account management policy: Consider replacing personal calls with telephone sales or direct mail to service accounts. Consider dropping account if unprofitable.

FIGURE 17–4

An account management policy grid grouping customers according to level of opportunity and the firm's competitive sales position.

are placed in each cell, salespeople clearly see which accounts should be contacted, with what level of selling and service activity, and how to deal with them. Accounts in cells 1 and 2 might have high frequencies of personal sales calls and increased time spent on a call. Cell 3 accounts will have lower call frequencies, and cell 4 accounts might be contacted through telemarketing or direct mail rather than in person. For example, Union Pacific Railroad put its 20,000 smallest accounts on a telemarketing program. A subsequent survey of these accounts indicated that 84 percent rated Union Pacific's sales effort "very effective" compared with 67 percent before the switch.

Sales Plan Implementation: Putting the Plan into Action

The sales plan is put into practice through the tasks associated with sales plan implementation. Whereas sales plan formulation focuses on "doing the right things," implementation emphasizes "doing things right." The three major tasks involved in implementing a sales plan are (1) salesforce recruitment and selection, (2) salesforce training, and (3) salesforce motivation and compensation.

Salesforce Recruitment and Selection   Effective recruitment and selection of salespeople is one of the most crucial tasks of sales management. It entails finding people who match the type of sales position required by a firm. Recruitment and selection practices will differ greatly between order-taking and order-getting sales positions, given the differences in the demands of these two jobs. Therefore, recruitment and selection begin with a carefully crafted job analysis and job description followed by a statement of job qualifications.

A *job analysis* is a study of a particular sales position, including how the job is to be performed and the tasks that make up the job. Information from a job analysis is used to write a *job description*, a written document that describes job relationships and requirements that characterize each sales position. It explains (1) to whom a salesperson reports, (2) how a salesperson interacts with other company personnel, (3) the customers to be called on, (4) the specific activities to be carried out, (5) the physical and mental demands of the job, and (6) the types of products and services to be sold.

Salesforce training is an ongoing process. Read the text to learn how training is conducted.

The job description is then translated into a statement of job qualifications, including the aptitudes, knowledge, skills, and a variety of behavioral characteristics considered necessary to perform the job successfully. Qualifications for order-getting sales positions often mirror the expectations of buyers: (1) imagination and problem-solving ability, (2) strong work ethic, (3) honesty, (4) intimate product knowledge, (5) effective communication and listening skills, and (6) attentiveness reflected in responsiveness to buyer needs and customer loyalty and follow-up. Firms use a variety of methods for evaluating prospective salespeople. Personal interviews, reference checks, and background information provided on application forms are the most frequently used methods.

Salesforce Training

Whereas the recruitment and selection of salespeople is a one-time event, salesforce training is an ongoing process that affects both new and seasoned salespeople.[19] Sales training covers much more than selling practices. For example, IBM Global Services salespeople, who sell consulting and various information technology services, take at least two weeks of in-class and Internet-based training on both consultative selling and the technical aspects of business.

On-the-job training is the most popular type of training, followed by individual instruction taught by experienced salespeople. Formal classes, seminars taught by sales trainers, and computer-based training are also popular.

Salesforce Motivation and Compensation

A sales plan cannot be successfully implemented without motivated salespeople. Research on salesperson motivation suggests that (1) a clear job description, (2) effective sales management practices, (3) a personal need for achievement, and (4) proper compensation, incentives, or rewards will produce a motivated salesperson.[20]

The importance of compensation as a motivating factor means that close attention must be given to how salespeople are financially rewarded for their efforts. Salespeople are paid using one of three plans: (1) straight salary, (2) straight commission, or (3) a combination of salary and commission. Under a *straight salary compensation plan*, a salesperson is paid a fixed fee per week, month, or year. With a *straight commission compensation plan*, a salesperson's earnings are directly tied to the sales or profit generated. For example, an insurance agent might receive a 2 percent commission of $2,000 for selling a $100,000 life insurance policy. A *combination compensation plan* contains a specified salary plus a commission on sales or profit generated.

Why is Jamie Cruse Vrinios, a successful Mary Kay Cosmetics Independent National Sales Director, posing with a Cadillac Escalade Hybrid? Read the text to learn how Mary Kay rewards its top sales performers.

Mary Kay Cosmetics, Inc.
www.marykay.com

Each compensation plan has its advantages and disadvantages.[21] A straight salary plan is easy to administer and gives management a large measure of control over how salespeople allocate their efforts. However, it provides little incentive to expand sales volume. This plan is used when salespeople engage in many nonselling activities, such as account or customer servicing. A straight commission plan provides the maximum amount of selling incentive but can discourage salespeople from providing customer service. This plan is common when nonselling activities are minimal. Combination plans are most preferred by salespeople and attempt to build on the advantages of salary and commission plans while reducing the potential shortcomings of each. A majority of companies use combination plans today.

Nonmonetary rewards are also given to salespeople for meeting or exceeding objectives. These rewards include trips, honor societies, distinguished salesperson awards, and letters of commendation. Some unconventional rewards include the new pink Cadillacs and Buicks and jewelry given by Mary Kay Cosmetics to outstanding salespeople. Mary Kay, with 12,000 cars, has the largest fleet of General Motors cars in the world.[22]

Salesforce Evaluation: Measuring Results

The final function in the sales management process involves evaluating the salesforce. It is at this point that salespeople are assessed as to whether sales objectives were met and account management policies were followed. Both quantitative and behavioral measures are used to tap different selling dimensions.

Quantitative Assessments Quantitative assessments are based on input- and output-related objectives set forth in the sales plan. Input-related measures focus on the actual activities performed by salespeople such as those involving sales calls, selling expenses, and account management policies. The number of sales calls made, selling expense related to sales made, and the number of reports submitted to superiors are frequently used input measures.

sales quota

Specific goals assigned to a salesperson, sales team, branch sales office, or sales district for a stated time period.

Output measures often appear in a sales quota. A **sales quota** contains specific goals assigned to a salesperson, sales team, branch sales office, or sales district for a stated time period. Dollar or unit sales volume, last year/current sales ratio, sales of specific products, new accounts generated, and profit achieved are typical goals. The time period can range from one month to one year.

Behavioral Evaluation Behavioral measures are also used to evaluate salespeople. These include assessments of a salesperson's attitude, attention to customers, product knowledge, selling and communication skills, appearance, and professional demeanor. Even though these assessments are sometimes subjective, they are frequently considered and, in fact, inevitable, in salesperson evaluation. Why? These factors are often important determinants of quantitative outcomes.

About 60 percent of U.S. companies now include customer satisfaction as a behavioral measure of salesperson performance. For example, at Microsoft, half of a salesperson's commission is dependent on customer satisfaction ratings.[23]

Increasingly, companies are using marketing dashboards to track salesperson performance for evaluation purposes. An illustration appears in the Using Marketing Dashboards box.

Salesforce Automation and Customer Relationship Management

Personal selling and sales management have undergone a technological revolution with the integration of salesforce automation and customer relationship management processes. In fact, the convergence of computer, information, communication, and Internet technologies has transformed the sales function in many companies and made the promise of customer relationship management a reality. **Salesforce automation** (SFA) is the use of these technologies to make the sales function more effective and efficient. SFA applies to a wide range of activities, including each stage in the personal selling process and management of the salesforce itself.[24]

salesforce automation (SFA)

The use of technology to make the sales function more effective and efficient.

Salesforce automation exists in many forms. Examples of SFA applications include computer hardware and software for account analysis, time management, order processing and follow-up, sales presentations, proposal generation, and product and sales training. Each application is designed to ease administrative tasks and free time for salespeople to be with customers building relationships, designing solutions, and providing service.

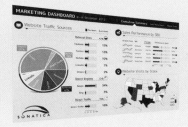

Using Marketing Dashboards

Tracking Salesperson Performance at Moore Chemical & Sanitation Supply, Inc.

Moore Chemical & Sanitation Supply, Inc. (MooreChem) is a large midwestern supplier of cleaning chemicals and sanitary products. MooreChem sells to janitorial companies that clean corporate and professional office buildings.

MooreChem recently installed a sales and account management planning software package that included a dashboard for each of its sales representatives. Salespeople had access to their dashboards as well. These dashboards included seven metrics—sales revenue, gross margin, selling expense, profit, average order size, new customers, and customer satisfaction. Each metric was gauged to show actual salesperson performance relative to target goals.

Your Challenge   As a newly promoted district sales manager at MooreChem, your responsibilities include tracking each salesperson's performance in your district. You are also responsible for directing the sales activities and practices of district salespeople.

In anticipation of a performance review with one of your salespeople, Brady Boyle, you review his dashboard for the previous quarter. This information can be used to provide a constructive review of his performance.

Your Findings   Brady Boyle's quarterly performance is displayed below. Boyle has exceeded targeted goals for sales revenue, selling expense, and customer satisfaction. All of these metrics show an upward trend. He has met his target for gaining new customers and average order size. But, Boyle's gross margin and profit are below targeted goals. These metrics evidence a downward trend as well. Brady Boyle's mixed performance requires a constructive and positive correction.

Your Action   Brady Boyle should already know how his performance compares with targeted goals. Remember, Boyle has access to his dashboard. Recall that he has exceeded his sales target, but is considerably under his profit target. Boyle's sales trend is up, but his profit trend is down.

You will need to focus attention on Boyle's gross margin and selling expense results and trend. Boyle, it seems, is spending time and money selling lower margin products that produce a targeted average order size. It may very well be that Boyle is actually expending effort selling more products to his customers. Unfortunately, the product mix yields lower gross margins, resulting in a lower profit.

Metric	Actual as % of Target	Trend	Actual
Sales Revenue		↗	$913,394
Gross Margin		↘	$356,212
Selling Expense		↗	$162,356
Profit		↘	$193,856
Average Order Size		→	$5,766
New Customers		→	10
Customer Satisfaction		↗	4.73 / 5

0%   50%   100%   150%

Salesforce Technology   Technology has become an integral part of field selling.[25] Today, most companies supply their field salespeople with laptop computers. For example, salespeople for Godiva Chocolates use their laptop computers to process orders, plan time allocations, forecast sales, and communicate with Godiva personnel and customers. While in a department store candy buyer's office, such as Neiman Marcus, a salesperson can calculate the order cost (and discount), transmit the order, and obtain a delivery date within minutes from Godiva's order processing department.

Toshiba America Medical Systems salespeople use laptop computers with built-in DVD capabilities to provide interactive presentations for their computerized tomography (CT) and magnetic resonance imaging (MRI) scanners. The computer technology allows the customer to see elaborate three-dimensional animations, high-resolution scans, and

Toshiba America Medical Systems salespeople have found computer technology to be an effective sales presentation tool and training device.

Toshiba America Medical Systems
www.toshiba.com

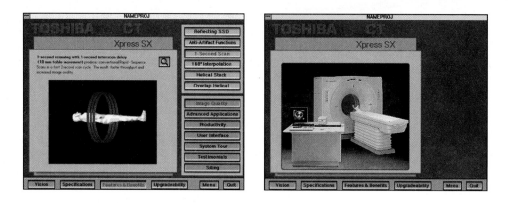

video clips of the company's products in operation as well as narrated testimonials from satisfied customers. Toshiba has found this application to be effective both for sales presentations and for training its salespeople.

Salesforce Communication Technology has changed the way salespeople communicate with customers, other salespeople and sales support personnel, and management. Facsimile, electronic mail, and voice mail are common communication technologies used by salespeople today. Mobile phone and tablet device technologies now allow salespeople to exchange data, text, and voice transmissions. Whether traveling or in a customer's office, these technologies provide information at the salesperson's fingertips to answer customer questions and solve problems.

Perhaps the greatest impact on salesforce communication is the application of Internet technology. Today, salespeople are using their company's intranet for a variety of purposes. At HP Enterprise Services, a professional services firm, salespeople access its intranet to download client material, marketing content, account information, technical papers, and competitive profiles. In addition, HP Enterprise Services offers training classes that salespeople can take anytime and anywhere.

Salesforce automation is clearly changing how selling is done and how salespeople are managed. Its numerous applications promise to boost selling productivity, improve customer relationships, and decrease selling cost.

---

learning review

7. What are the three types of selling objectives?

8. What three factors are used to structure sales organizations?

LEARNING OBJECTIVES REVIEW

LO1 *Discuss the nature and scope of personal selling and sales management in marketing.*
Personal selling involves the two-way flow of communication between a buyer and seller, often in a face-to-face encounter, designed to influence a person's or group's purchase decision. Sales management involves planning the selling program and implementing and controlling the personal selling effort of the firm. The scope of selling and sales management is apparent in three ways. First, virtually every occupation that involves customer contact has an element of personal selling. Second, selling plays a significant role in a company's overall marketing effort. Salespeople occupy a boundary position between buyers and sellers; they *are* the company to many buyers and

account for a major cost of marketing in a variety of industries; and they can create value for customers. Finally, through relationship selling, salespeople play a central role in tailoring solutions to customer problems as a means to customer value creation.

LO2 *Identify the different types of personal selling.*
Two types of personal selling exist: (*a*) order taking and (*b*) order getting. Each type differs from the others in terms of actual selling done and the amount of creativity required to perform the sales task. Order takers process routine orders or reorders for products that were already sold by the company. They generally do little selling in a conventional sense and engage in

only modest problem solving with customers. Order getters sell in a conventional sense and identify prospective customers, provide customers with information, persuade customers to buy, close sales, and follow up on customers' use of a product or service. Order getting involves a high degree of creativity and customer empathy and is typically required for selling complex or technical products with many options.

LO3 *Explain the stages in the personal selling process.*
The personal selling process consists of six stages: (*a*) prospecting, (*b*) preapproach, (*c*) approach, (*d*) presentation, (*e*) close, and (*f*) follow-up. Prospecting involves the search for and qualification of potential customers. The preapproach stage involves obtaining further information on the prospect and deciding on the best method of approach. The approach stage involves the initial meeting between the salesperson and prospect. The presentation stage involves converting a prospect into a customer by creating a desire for the product or service.

The close involves obtaining a purchase commitment from the prospect. The follow-up stage involves making certain that the customer's purchase has been properly delivered and installed and difficulties experienced with the use of the item are addressed.

LO4 *Describe the major functions of sales management.*
Sales management consists of three interrelated functions: (*a*) sales plan formulation, (*b*) sales plan implementation, and (*c*) evaluation of the salesforce. Sales plan formulation involves setting objectives, organizing the salesforce, and developing account management policies. Sales plan implementation involves salesforce recruitment, selection, training, motivation, and compensation. Finally, salesforce evaluation focuses on quantitative assessments of sales performance and behavioral measures such as customer satisfaction that are linked to selling objectives and account management policies.

FOCUSING ON KEY TERMS

account management policies p. 399	**order taker** p. 390	**sales plan** p. 398
adaptive selling p. 395	**personal selling** p. 388	**sales quota** p. 402
consultative selling p. 395	**personal selling process** p. 392	**salesforce automation (SFA)** p. 402
major account management p. 398	**relationship selling** p. 389	
order getter p. 390	**sales management** p. 388	

APPLYING MARKETING KNOWLEDGE

1 Jane Dawson is a new sales representative for the Charles Schwab brokerage firm. In searching for clients, Jane purchased a mailing list of subscribers to *The Wall Street Journal* and called them all regarding their interest in discount brokerage services. She asked if they have any stocks and if they have a regular broker. Those people without a regular broker were asked their investment needs. Two days later Jane called back with investment advice and asked if they would like to open an account. Identify each of Jane Dawson's actions in terms of the steps of selling.

2 Using a continuum with "Order taker" at one end and "Order getter" at the other, where would you place each of the following sales jobs? (*a*) Burger King counter clerk, (*b*) automobile insurance salesperson, (*c*) IBM computer salesperson, (*d*) life insurance salesperson, and (*e*) shoe salesperson.

3 Of the two firms described below, which compensation plan would you recommend for each firm and what reasons would you give for your recommendations? (*a*) A newly formed company that sells lawn care equipment on a door-to-door basis directly to consumers; and (*b*) the Nabisco Company, which sells heavily advertised products in supermarkets by having the salesforce call on these stores and arrange shelves, set up displays, and make presentations to store buying committees.

4 Suppose someone said to you, "The only real measure of a salesperson is the amount of sales produced." How might you respond?

building your marketing plan

Does your marketing plan involve a personal selling activity? If the answer is no, read no further and do not include a personal selling element in your plan. If the answer is yes:

1 Identify the likely prospects for your product or service.
2 Determine what information you should obtain about the prospect.

3 Describe how you would approach the prospect.
4 Outline the presentation you would make to the prospect for your product or service.
5 Develop a sales plan, focusing on the organizational structure you would use for your salesforce (geography, product, or customer).

"I'm like the quarterback of the team. I manage 250 accounts, and anything from billing issues, to service issues, to selling the products. I'm really the face to the customer," says Alison Capossela, a Washington, DC–based Xerox sales representative.

As the primary company contact for Xerox customers, Alison is responsible for developing and maintaining customer relationships. To accomplish this she uses a sophisticated selling process which requires many activities from making presentations, to attending training sessions, to managing a team of Xerox personnel, to monitoring competitors' activities. The face-to-face interactions with customers, however, are the most rewarding for Capossela. "It's an amazing feeling; the more they challenge me the more I fight back. It's fun!" she explains.

THE COMPANY

Xerox Corporation's mission is to "help people find better ways to do great work by constantly leading in document technologies, products, and services that improve customers' work processes and business results." To accomplish this mission Xerox employs 136,500 people in 160 countries. Xerox is the world's leading document management enterprise and a *Fortune* 500 company. Xerox offers a wide range of products and services. These include printers, copiers and fax machines, multifunction and network devices, high-speed color presses, digital imaging and archiving products and services, and supplies such as toner, paper, and ink. The entire company is guided by customer-focused and employee-centered core values (e.g., "We succeed through satisfied customers") and a passion for innovation, speed, and adaptability.

Xerox was founded in 1906 as a manufacturer of photographic paper called The Haloid Company. In 1947, the company purchased the license to basic xerographic patents. The following year it received a trademark for the word "Xerox." By 1973, Xerox had introduced the automatic, plain-paper copier, opened offices in Japan, and its Palo Alto Research Center (PARC) had invented the world's first personal computer (the Alto), the "mouse," and graphical user interface software. In 1994, Xerox adopted "The Document Company" as its signature and the partially digitized red "X" as its corporate symbol.

In 2001, Anne M. Mulcahy was named CEO of Xerox Corporation and became chairperson of the board in 2002. Mulcahy began her career as a sales representative at Xerox. She brought her experience as a sales rep to her position in senior management. In particular, she focused on reenergizing the Xerox sales organization with a focus on customer relationships. "We started winning when we listened to customers," Mulcahy says. "We did that by providing greater value than our competitors—and that meant selling the way customers want to buy." She adds, "Doing what's right for the customer—that's our guiding principle." As Kevin Warren, vice president of sales, explains: "One of the reasons she was so successful is that she absolutely resonated with all the people. I think [because of] the fact that she started out as a sales rep, people felt like she was one of them."

THE SELLING PROCESS AT XEROX

When Mulcahy became CEO, Xerox began a shift to a consultative selling model that focused on helping customers solve their business problems rather than just placing more equipment in their office. The shift meant that sales reps needed to be less product-oriented and more relationship- and value-oriented. Xerox wanted to be a provider of total solutions. Today, Xerox has more than 8,000 sales professionals throughout the world who spend a large amount of their day developing customer relationships. Capossela explains: "Fifty percent of my day is spent with my customers, 25 percent is following up with phone calls or e-mails, and another 25 percent involves preparing proposals." The approach has helped Xerox attract new customers and keep existing customers.

The sales process at Xerox typically follows the six stages of the personal selling process identified in Figure 17–2: (1) Xerox identifies potential clients through responses to advertising, referrals, and telephone calls; (2) the salesforce prepares for a presentation by familiarizing themselves with the potential client and its document needs; (3) a Xerox sales representative approaches the prospect and suggests a meeting and presentation; (4) as the presentation begins, the salesperson summarizes relevant information about potential solutions Xerox can offer, states what he or she hopes to get out of the meeting, explains how the products and services work, and reinforces the benefits of working with Xerox; (5) the salesperson engages in an action close (gets a signed document or a firm confirmation of the sale); and then (6) continues to meet and communicate with the client to provide assistance and monitor the effectiveness of the installed solution.

Xerox sales representatives also use the selling process to maintain relationships with existing customers. In today's competitive environment it is not unusual to have customers who have been approached by competitors or who are required to obtain more than one bid before renewing a contract. Xerox has teams of people who collect and analyze information about competitors and their products. The information is sent out to sales reps or offered to them through workshops and seminars. The most difficult competitors are the ones that have also invested in customer relationships. The selling process allows Xerox to continually react and respond to new information and take advantage of opportunities in the marketplace.

THE SALES MANAGEMENT PROCESS AT XEROX

The Xerox salesforce is divided into four geographic organizations: North America, which includes the United States and Canada; Europe, which includes 17 countries; Global Accounts, which manages large accounts that operate in multiple locations; and Developing Markets, which includes all other geographic territories that may require Xerox products and services. Within each geographic area, the majority of Xerox products and services are typically sold through its direct salesforce. Xerox also utilizes a variety of other channels, including value-added resellers, independent agents, dealers, systems integrators, telephone, and Internet sales channels.

Motivation and compensation is an important aspect of any salesforce. At Xerox there is a passion for winning that provides a key incentive for sales reps. In addition, the compensation plan plays an important role. As Warren explains, "Our compensation plans are a combination of salary as well as an opportunity to leverage earnings through sales commissions and bonuses." Xerox also has a recognition program called the President's Club where the top performers are awarded a five-day trip to one of the top resorts in the world. The program has been a huge success and has now been offered for more than 30 years.

Perhaps the most well-known component of Xerox's sales management process is its sales representative training program. For example, Xerox developed the "Create and Win" program to help sales reps learn the new consultative selling approach. The components of the program consisted of interactive training sessions and distance-learning webinars. Every new sales representative at Xerox receives eight weeks of training development in the field and at the Xerox Corporate University in Virginia. "The training program is phenomenal!" according to Capossela. The training and its focus on the customer is part of the Xerox culture outside of the sales organization also. Every senior executive at Xerox is responsible for working with at least one customer. They also spend a full day every month responding to incoming customer calls and inquiries.

WHAT IS IN THE FUTURE FOR THE XEROX SALESFORCE?

The recent growth and success at Xerox is creating many opportunities for the company and for its sales representatives. For example, Xerox is accelerating the development of its top salespeople. Mentors are used to provide advice for day-to-day issues and long-term career planning. In addition, globalization has become such an important initiative at Xerox that experienced and successful sales representatives are quickly given opportunities to manage large global accounts. Xerox is also moving toward an approach that empowers sales representatives to make decisions about how to handle accounts. The large number of Xerox customers means there are a variety of different corporate styles, and the sales reps are increasingly the best qualified to manage the relationship. This approach is just one more example of Xerox's commitment to customers and creating customer value.

Questions

1 Why was Anne Mulcahy's experience as a sales representative an important part of Xerox's growth in recent years?

2 How did the sales approach change after Mulcahy became the CEO of Xerox?

3 *(a)* How does Xerox create customer value through its personal selling process? *(b)* How does Alison Capossela provide solutions for Xerox customers?

4 Why is the Xerox training program so important to the company's success?

Implementing Interactive and Multichannel Marketing

18

LEARNING OBJECTIVES

After reading this chapter you should be able to:

 LO1 Describe what interactive marketing is and how it creates customer value, customer relationships, and customer experiences.

LO2 Explain why certain types of products and services are particularly suited for interactive marketing.

 LO3 Describe why consumers shop and buy online and how marketers influence online purchasing behavior.

 LO4 Define cross-channel shoppers and the role of transactional and promotional websites in reaching these shoppers.

SEVEN CYCLES. ONE BIKE. YOURS.

"One Bike. Yours." is the company tagline for Seven Cycles, Inc., located in Watertown, Massachusetts. And for good reason.

Seven Cycles is the world's largest custom bicycle frame builder in the world. The company produces a broad range of road, mountain, cyclocross, tandem, touring, single-speed, and commuter bikes annually, and no two bikes are exactly alike. At Seven Cycles, attention is focused on each customer's unique cycling experience through the optimum fit, function, performance, and comfort of his or her very own bike. According to one satisfied customer, "Getting a Seven is more of a creation than a purchase."

The marketing success of Seven Cycles is due to its state-of-the-art bicycle frames. But as Rob Vandermark, company founder and president, says, "Part of our success is that we are tied to a business model that includes the Internet."

Seven uses its multilanguage (English, German, Chinese, Japanese, Korean, and Flemish) website (www.sevencycles.com) to let customers get deeply involved in the frame-building process and the selection of components to outfit their complete bike. It enables customers to collaborate on the design of their own bike using the company's Custom Kit fitting system, which considers the rider's size, aspirations, and riding habits. Then customers can monitor their bike's progress through the development and production process by clicking "Where's My Frame?" on the Seven Cycles website.

This customization process and continuous feedback make for a collaborative relationship between Seven Cycles, its 233 authorized retailers and distributors, and customers in 40 countries. "Each bike we build is unique, so each customer's experience deserves to be unique as well," explains Mattison Crowe, marketing manager at Seven Cycles.

In addition to the order process, website visitors can peruse weekly news stories and learn about new product introductions to get a unique perspective on the business. They can read employee biographies online to learn more about the people who build the bikes. The website also offers a retailer-specific section as a 24/7 repository of updated information for the company's channel partners.

Beyond the website, current Seven owners can interact with the company on the Seven Cycles blog to learn about its activities and products. Seven Cycles also uses its company Facebook Page and Twitter account to post brief and timely updates and build a stronger sense of community around the brand.[1]

This chapter describes how companies design and implement interactive marketing programs. It begins by explaining how Internet technology can create customer value, build customer relationships, and produce customer experiences in novel ways. Next, it describes how Internet technology affects and is affected by consumer behavior and marketing practice. Finally, the chapter shows how marketers integrate and leverage their communication and delivery channels using Internet technology to implement multichannel marketing programs.

CREATING CUSTOMER VALUE, RELATIONSHIPS, AND EXPERIENCES IN MARKETSPACE

LO1

Consumers and companies populate two market environments today. One is the traditional *marketplace*. Here buyers and sellers engage in face-to-face exchange relationships in a material environment characterized by physical facilities (stores and offices) and mostly tangible objects. The other is the *marketspace*, an Internet-enabled digital environment characterized by face-to-screen exchange relationships and electronic images and offerings.

The existence of two market environments has been a boon for consumers. Today, consumers can shop for and purchase a wide variety of products and services in either market environment. Actually, many consumers now browse and buy in both market environments, and more are expected to do so in the future. Figure 18–1 shows the growth in online shoppers and estimated retail sales in the United States since 2007. About 90 percent of Internet users ages 15 and older shop online in the United States. They are expected to buy $304 billion worth of products and services in 2015 (excluding travel, automobile, and prescription drugs).[2]

Creating Customer Value in Marketspace

Why has the marketspace captured the eye and imagination of marketers worldwide? Recall from Chapter 1 that marketing creates time, place, form, and possession utilities, thereby providing value. Marketers believe that the possibilities for customer value creation are greater in the digital marketspace than in the physical marketplace.

Consider place and time utility. In marketspace, the provision of direct, on-demand information is possible from marketers *anywhere* to customers *anywhere, at any time.*

FIGURE 18–1

Trends in online shoppers and online retail sales revenue in the United States.

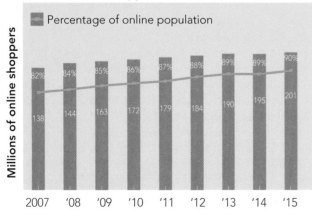

Why? Operating hours and geographical constraints do not exist in marketspace. For example, Recreational Equipment (www.rei.com), an outdoor gear marketer, reports that 35 percent of its orders are placed between 10:00 P.M. and 7:00 A.M., long after and before retail stores are open for business. Similarly, a U.S. consumer from Chicago can access Marks & Spencer (www.marks-and-spencer.co.uk), the well-known British department store, to shop for clothing as easily as a person living near London's Piccadilly Square.

Possession utility—getting a product or service to consumers so they can own or use it—is accelerated. Airline, car rental, and lodging electronic reservation systems such as Orbitz (www.orbitz.com) allow comparison shopping for the lowest fares, rents, and rates and almost immediate access to and confirmation of travel arrangements and accommodations.

The greatest marketspace opportunity for marketers, however, lies in its potential for creating form utility. Interactive two-way Internet-enabled communication capabilities in marketspace invite consumers to tell marketers specifically what their requirements are, making customization of a product or service to fit their exact needs possible. For instance, customers can arrange for a custom-made mountain bike from Seven Cycles as described in the chapter-opening example.

Seven Cycles creates form utility in the creation of customized bikes for its customers in 40 countries.

Seven Cycles, Inc.
www.sevencycles.com

Creating Interactivity, Individuality, and Customer Relationships in Marketspace

Marketers also benefit from two unique capabilities of Internet technology that promote and sustain customer relationships. One is *interactivity*; the other is *individuality*.[3] Both capabilities are important building blocks for buyer–seller relationships.

Mars, Inc., uses choiceboard technology to decorate M&Ms with personal photos and messages. Other applications for choiceboards are described in the text.

Mars, Inc.

www.mymms.com

For these relationships to occur, companies need to interact with their customers by listening and responding to their needs. Marketers must also treat customers as individuals and empower them to (1) influence the timing and extent of the buyer–seller interaction and (2) have a say in the kind of products and services they buy, the information they receive, and in some cases, the prices they pay.

Internet technology allows for interaction, individualization, and customer relationship building to be carried out on a scale never before available and makes interactive marketing possible. **Interactive marketing** involves two-way buyer–seller electronic communication in a computer-mediated environment in which the buyer controls the kind and amount of information received from the seller. Interactive marketing is characterized by sophisticated choiceboard and personalization systems that transform information supplied by customers into customized responses to their individual needs.

Choiceboards A **choiceboard** is an interactive, Internet-enabled system that allows individual customers to design their own products and services by answering a few questions and choosing from a menu of product or service attributes (or components), prices, and delivery options.[4] Customers today can design their own computers with Dell's online configurator, style their own athletic shoe at www.reebok.com, assemble their own investment portfolios with Schwab's mutual fund evaluator, build their own bicycle at www.sevencycles.com, create a diet and fitness program to fit their lifestyle at www.ediet.com, and decorate M&Ms with photos of themselves and unique messages at www.mymms.com. Because choiceboards collect precise information about the preferences and behavior of individual buyers, a company becomes more knowledgeable about a customer and better able to anticipate and fulfill that customer's needs.

QR 18–1
My M&Ms
Video

Most choiceboards are essentially transaction devices. However, companies such as Dell have expanded the functionality of choiceboards using collaborative filtering technology. **Collaborative filtering** is a process that automatically groups people with similar buying intentions, preferences, and behaviors and predicts future purchases.[5] For example, say two people who have never met buy a few of the same DVDs over time. Collaborative filtering software is programmed to reason that these two buyers might have similar musical tastes: If one buyer likes a particular DVD, then the other will like it as well. The outcome? Collaborative filtering gives marketers the ability to make a dead-on sales recommendation to a buyer in *real time*. You see collaborative filtering applied each time you view a selection at Amazon.com and see "Customers who bought this (item) also bought. . . ."

Personalization Choiceboards and collaborative filtering are marketer-initiated efforts to provide customized responses to the needs of individual buyers. Personalization systems are typically buyer-initiated efforts. **Personalization** is the consumer-initiated practice of generating content on a marketer's website that is custom tailored to an individual's specific needs and preferences. For example, Yahoo! (www.yahoo.com) allows users to create personalized MyYahoo! pages. Users can add or delete a variety of types of information from their personal pages, including specific stock quotes, weather conditions in any city in the world, and local television schedules. In turn, Yahoo! can use the buyer profile data entered when users register at the site to tailor e-mail messages, advertising, and content to the individual—and post a happy birthday greeting on the user's special day.

Reebok has effectively used choiceboard technology for customizing athletic shoes as described in the text.

Reebok
www.reebok.com

permission marketing
Asking for a consumer's consent (called opt-in*) to receive e-mail and advertising based on personal data supplied by the consumer.*

An aspect of personalization is a buyer's willingness to have tailored communications brought to his or her attention. Obtaining this approval is called **permission marketing**—the solicitation of a consumer's consent (called *opt-in*) to receive e-mail and advertising based on personal data supplied by the consumer. Permission marketing is a proven vehicle for building and maintaining customer relationships, provided it is properly used.

Companies that successfully employ permission marketing adhere to three rules.[6] First, they make sure opt-in customers receive only information that is relevant and meaningful to them. Second, their customers are given the option to *opt-out*, or change the kind, amount, or timing of information sent to them. Finally, their customers are assured that their name or buyer profile data will not be sold or shared with others. This assurance is important because a majority of adult Internet users express concern about the privacy of their personal information.[7]

Creating an Online Customer Experience

A continuing challenge for companies is the design and execution of marketing programs that capitalize on the unique customer value-creation capabilities of Internet technology. Companies realize that applying Internet technology to create time, place, form, and possession utility is just a starting point for creating a meaningful marketspace presence. Today, the quality of the customer experience produced by a company is the standard by which a meaningful marketspace presence is measured.

From an interactive marketing perspective, *customer experience* is defined as the sum total of the interactions that a customer has with a company's website, from the initial look at a home page through the entire purchase decision process. Companies produce a customer experience through seven website design elements.[8] These elements are context, content, community, customization, communication, connection, and commerce. Each is summarized in Figure 18–2 on the next page. A closer look at these elements illustrates how each contributes to customer experience.

Context *Context* refers to a website's aesthetic appeal and functional look and feel reflected in site layout and visual design. A functionally oriented website focuses largely on the company's offering, be it products, services, or information. Deal-oriented travel websites, such as Priceline.com, tend to be functionally oriented with an emphasis on destinations, scheduling, and prices. In contrast, beauty websites, such as Revlon.com, are more aesthetically oriented. As these examples suggest, context attempts to convey the core consumer benefit provided by the company's offerings.

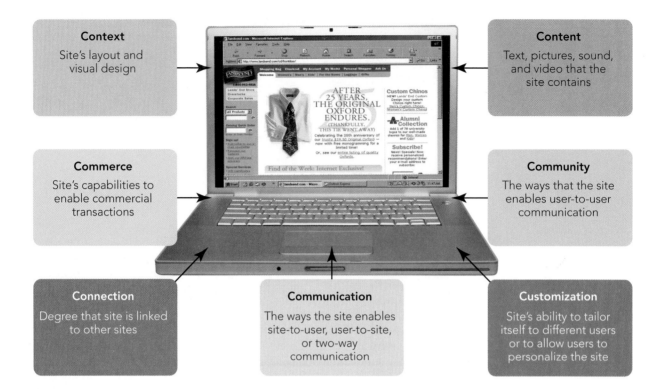

Context
Site's layout and visual design

Content
Text, pictures, sound, and video that the site contains

Commerce
Site's capabilities to enable commercial transactions

Community
The ways that the site enables user-to-user communication

Connection
Degree that site is linked to other sites

Communication
The ways the site enables site-to-user, user-to-site, or two-way communication

Customization
Site's ability to tailor itself to different users or to allow users to personalize the site

FIGURE 18–2
Seven website design elements that drive customer experience.

Content *Content* applies to all digital information on a website, including the presentation form—text, video, audio, and graphics. Content quality and presentation along with context dimensions combine to engage a website visitor and provide a platform for the five remaining design elements.

Customization Website *customization* is the ability of a site to modify itself to, or be modified by, each individual user. This design element is prominent in websites that offer personalized content, such as My eBay and MyYahoo!

Connection The *connection* element is the network of linkages between a company's site and other sites. These links are embedded in the website; appear as highlighted words, a picture, or graphic; and allow a user to effortlessly visit other sites with a mouse click. Connection is a major design element for informational websites such as *The New York Times*. Users of NYTimes.com can access the book review section and link to Barnes & Noble to order a book or browse related titles without ever visiting a store.

Communication *Communication* refers to the dialogue that unfolds between the website and its users. Consumers—particularly those who have registered at a website—expect that communication to be interactive and individualized in real time much like a personal conversation. In fact, some websites now enable a user to talk directly with a customer representative while shopping the site. For example, two-thirds of the sales through Dell.com involve human sales representatives.

Community In addition, an increasing number of company websites encourage user-to-user communications hosted by the company to create virtual communities, or simply, *community*. This design element is popular because it has been shown to enhance customer experience and build favorable buyer–seller relationships. Examples of communities range from the Pampers Village hosted by Procter & Gamble (www.pampers.com) to the Harley Owners Group (HOG) sponsored by Harley-Davidson (www.harley-davidson.com).

Travelocity pays close attention to creating a favorable customer experience by employing all seven website design elements.

Travelocity
www.travelocity.com

Commerce The seventh design element is *commerce*—the website's ability to conduct sales transactions for products and services with a mouse click. Online transactions are quick and simple in well-designed websites.

Most websites do not include every design element. Although every website has context and content, they differ in the use of the remaining five elements. Why? Websites have different purposes. Only websites that emphasize the actual sale of products and services include the commerce element. Websites that are used primarily for advertising and promotion purposes emphasize the communication element. The difference between these two types of websites is discussed later in the chapter in the description of cross-channel shoppers and multichannel marketing.

Companies use a broad array of measures to assess website performance. For example, the amount of time per month visitors spend on their website, or "stickiness," is used to gauge customer experience.[9] Read the Using Marketing Dashboards box on the next page to learn how stickiness is measured and interpreted at Sewell Automotive Companies.

---

learning review

1. The consumer-initiated practice of generating content on a marketer's website that is custom tailored to an individual's specific needs and preferences is called _____.

2. Companies produce a customer experience through what seven website design elements?

ONLINE CONSUMER BEHAVIOR AND MARKETING PRACTICE IN MARKETSPACE

Who are online consumers, and what do they buy? Why do they choose to shop and purchase products and services in the digital marketspace rather than (or in addition to) the traditional marketplace? Answers to these questions have a direct bearing on marketspace marketing practices.

Who Is the Online Consumer?

Online consumers are the subsegment of all Internet users who employ this technology to research products and services and make purchases. As a group, online consumers are equally likely to be women and men and tend to be better educated, younger, and more affluent than the general U.S. population.[10] This makes them an attractive market. Even though online shopping and buying is popular, a small percentage of online consumers still account for a disproportionate share of online retail sales in the United States. It is estimated that 20 percent of online consumers who spend $1,000-plus per year online account for 87 percent of total consumer online sales. Also, women tend to purchase more products and services online than men.[11]

Using Marketing Dashboards

Sizing Up Site Stickiness at Sewell Automotive Companies

Automobile dealerships have invested significant time, effort, and money in their websites. Why? Car browsing and shopping on the Internet is now commonplace.

Dealerships commonly measure website performance by tracking visits, visitor traffic, and "stickiness"—the amount of time per month visitors spend on their website. Website design, easy navigation, involving content, and visual appeal combine to enhance the interactive customer experience and website stickiness.

To gauge stickiness, companies monitor the average time spent per unique monthly visitor (in minutes) on their websites. This is done by tracking and displaying the average visits per unique monthly visitor and the average time spent per visit, in minutes, in their marketing dashboards. The relationship is as follows:

Average Time Spent per Unique Monthly Visitor (minutes) =

$$\left(\begin{array}{c} \text{Average Visits per} \\ \text{Unique Monthly Visitor} \end{array} \right) \times \left(\begin{array}{c} \text{Average Time Spent} \\ \text{per Visit (minutes)} \end{array} \right)$$

Your Challenge As the manager responsible for Sewell .com, the Sewell Automotive Companies's website, you have been asked to report on the effect of recent improvements in the company's website on the amount of time per month visitors spend on the website. Sewell ranks among the largest

U.S. automotive dealerships and is a recognized customer service leader in the automotive industry. Its website reflects the company's commitment to an unparalleled customer experience at its family of dealerships.

Your Findings Examples of monthly marketing dashboard traffic and time measures are displayed below for June 2008, three months before the website improvements (green arrow), and June 2009, three months after the improvements were made (red arrow).

The average time spent per unique monthly visitor increased from 8.5 minutes in June 2008 to 11.9 minutes in June 2009—a sizable jump. The increase is due primarily to the upturn in the average time spent per visit from 7.1 minutes to 8.5 minutes. The average number of visits also increased, but the percentage change was much less.

Your Action Improvements in the website have noticeably "moved the needle" on average time spent per unique monthly visitor. Still, additional action may be required to increase average visits per unique monthly visitor. These actions might include an analysis of Sewell's web advertising program, search engine initiatives with Google, links to automobile manufacturer corporate websites, and broader print and electronic media advertising.

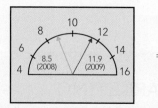

Average Time Spent per
Unique Monthly Visitor (minutes)

=

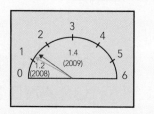

Average Visits per
Unique Monthly Visitor

×

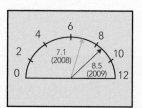

Average Time Spent
per Visit (minutes)

Numerous marketing research firms have studied the lifestyles and shopping habits of online consumers. A recurrent insight is that online consumers are diverse and represent different kinds of people seeking different kinds of online experiences. As an illustration, the Marketing Matters box provides an in-depth look at the lifestyle and shopping habits of today's "Internet mom."[12]

What Online Consumers Buy

LO3

Much still needs to be learned about online consumer purchase behavior. Although research has documented the most frequently purchased products and services bought online, marketers also need to know why these items are popular in the digital marketspace.

Marketing Matters > > > >> > > technology

Meet Today's Internet Mom on a Mission

Do you have fond childhood memories of surfing the Internet with your mother?

Research indicates that 95 percent of mothers with children under 18 years old will be online regularly by 2015. Internet moms are typically 38 years old. They tend to be married, college educated, and work outside the home.

Results from a recent Disney Online M.O.M.—Mom on a Mission—study show how today's mother uses the Internet. Consider that:

1. Internet moms spend the most time online between the hours of 5 A.M. and noon.
2. Seventy-five percent of moms go online with a specific task or goal in mind. They are not surfers.
3. Moms spend an average of 6.9 hours per week online connecting with family and friends: 84 percent stay connected through e-mail and 69 percent through social networks.
4. For subjects other than their child's health, moms turn to the Internet as their primary source of information about: (a) shopping deals or discounts; (b) cooking/baking recipes and nutrition/dieting; (c) family activities, entertainment, and travel; (d) holiday planning and activities; (e) beauty/style suggestions; and (f) financial planning.

According to a Disney Online spokesperson, "Moms juggle so many roles, from being the caregiver and household CEO, to coordinating the family's activities. Our study results showed that the Internet is helping to make moms' lives more manageable, so they can spend more quality time with their families."

Six general product and service categories account for over 80 percent of online consumer buying today and for the foreseeable future.[13] One category consists of items for which product information is an important part of the purchase decision, but prepurchase trial is not necessarily critical. Items such as computers, computer accessories, and consumer electronics sold by Dell.com fall into this category. So do books, which accounts for the sales growth of Amazon.com and Barnes & Noble (www.barnesandnoble.com). Both booksellers publish short reviews of new books that visitors to their websites can read before making a purchase decision.

A second category includes items for which audio or video demonstration is important. This category consists of DVDs sold by Columbia House.com. The third category contains items that can be delivered digitally, including computer software, music, video, and electronic ticketing. Popular websites for these items include apple.com/iTunes, Netflix.com, and Ticketmaster.com.

Unique items, such as specialty products, foods, beverages, and gifts, represent a fourth category. Food and gift merchants such as HarryandDavid.com sell these products. A fifth category includes items that are regularly purchased and where convenience is very important. Many consumer-packaged goods, such as grocery products, personal care items, and office products, fall into this category. A final category of items consists of highly standardized products and services for which information about price is important. Certain kinds of home improvement products, small appliances, casual apparel, and toys make up this category.

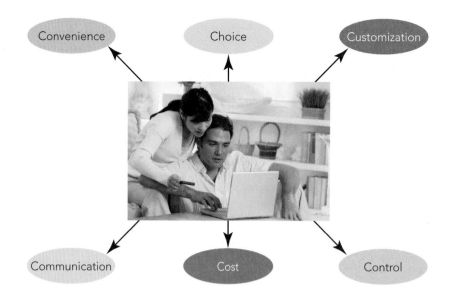

Why Consumers Shop and Buy Online

Marketers emphasize the customer value-creation possibilities, the importance of interactivity, individuality and relationship building, and producing customer experience in the new marketspace. However, consumers typically refer to six reasons they shop and buy online: convenience, choice, customization, communication, cost, and control (Figure 18–3).

Convenience   Online shopping and buying is *convenient*. Consumers can visit Walmart at www.walmart.com to scan and order from among thousands of displayed products without fighting traffic, finding a parking space, walking through long aisles, and standing in store checkout lines. Alternatively, online consumers can use **bots**, electronic shopping agents or robots that comb websites to compare prices and product or service features. In either instance, an online consumer has never ventured into a store. However, for convenience to remain a source of customer value creation, websites must be easy to locate and navigate, and image downloads must be fast.

A commonly held view among online marketers is the **eight-second rule**: Customers will abandon their efforts to enter and navigate a website if download time exceeds eight seconds. Furthermore, the more clicks and pauses between clicks required to access information or make a purchase, the more likely it is a customer will exit a website.

Choice   *Choice*, the second reason consumers shop and buy online, has two dimensions. First, choice exists in the product or service selection offered to consumers. Buyers desiring selection can avail themselves of numerous websites for almost anything they want. For instance, online buyers of consumer electronics can shop individual manufacturers such as Bose (www.bose.com) and QVC.com, a general merchant that showcases more than 1,000 products each week.

Choice assistance is the second dimension. Here, the interactive capabilities of Internet-enabled technologies invite customers to engage in an electronic dialogue with marketers for the purpose of making informed choices. Choice assistance is one of the reasons for the continued success of Zappos.com. The company offers an online chat room that enables prospective buyers to ask questions and receive answers in real time. In addition, carefully designed search capabilities permit consumers to review products by brand and particular items.

bots
Electronic shopping agents or robots that comb websites to compare prices and product or service features.

eight-second rule
A view that customers will abandon their efforts to enter and navigate a website if download time exceeds eight seconds.

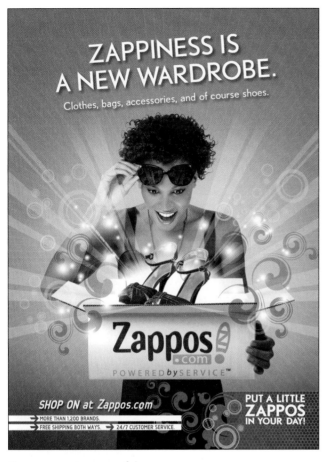

Zappos.com is successful because it meets all the requirements necessary for consumers to shop and buy online. The company has posted significant annual sales of shoes, apparel, bags, accessories, housewares, and jewelry.

Zappos.com

www.zappos.com

Customization Even with a broad selection and choice assistance, some customers prefer one-of-a-kind items that fit their specific needs. *Customization* arises from Internet-enabled capabilities that make possible a highly interactive and individualized information and exchange environment for shoppers and buyers. Remember the earlier Reebok, Schwab, Dell, and Seven Cycles examples? To varying degrees, online consumers also benefit from *customerization*—the growing practice of not only customizing a product or service but also personalizing the marketing and overall shopping and buying interaction for each customer.[14] Customerization seeks to do more than offer consumers the right product, at the right time, and at the right price. It combines choiceboard and personalization systems to expand the exchange environment beyond a transaction and makes shopping and buying an enjoyable, personal experience.

Communication Online consumers particularly welcome the *communication* capabilities of Internet-enabled technologies. This communication can take three forms: (1) marketer-to-consumer e-mail notification, (2) consumer-to-marketer buying and service requests, and (3) consumer-to-consumer chat rooms and instant messaging, plus social networking websites such as Twitter and Facebook.

Communication has proven to be a double-edged sword for online consumers. On the one hand, the interactive communication capabilities of Internet-enabled technologies increase consumer convenience, reduce information search costs, and make choice assistance and customization possible. Communication also promotes the development of company-hosted and independent **web communities**—websites that allow people to congregate online and exchange views on topics of common interest. For instance, Coca-Cola hosts MyCoke.com, and iVillage.com is an independent web community for women and includes topics such as career management, personal finances, parenting, relationships, beauty, and health.

Web logs, or *blogs,* are another form of communication. Blogs are popular because they provide online forums on a wide variety of subjects ranging from politics to car repair. Companies such as Hewlett-Packard, PepsiCo, and Harley-Davidson routinely monitor blogs and social media posts to gather customer insights.[15]

On the other hand, communications can take the form of electronic junk mail or unsolicited e-mail, called **spam**. The prevalence of spam has prompted many online services to institute policies and procedures to prevent spammers from spamming their subscribers, and several states have antispamming laws. In 2004, the *CAN-SPAM (Controlling the Assault of Non-Solicited Pornography and Marketing) Act* became effective and restricts information collection and unsolicited e-mail promotions on the Internet.

Internet-enabled communication capabilities also make possible *buzz,* a popular term for word-of-mouth behavior in marketspace. Chapter 4 described the importance of word of mouth in consumer behavior. Internet technology has magnified its significance. According to Jeff Bezos, president of Amazon.com, "If you have an unhappy customer on the Internet, he doesn't tell his six friends, he tells his 6,000 friends!"[16] Buzz is particularly influential for toys, cars, sporting goods, motion pictures, apparel, consumer electronics, pharmaceuticals, health and beauty products, and health care services. Some marketers have capitalized on this phenomenon by creating buzz through viral marketing.

Staffers sit in Gatorade's "Mission Control" room in Chicago, Illinois, to monitor the Internet and social media outlets, such as Facebook and Twitter, 24 hours a day. Whenever someone uses Twitter to say they are drinking a Gatorade or mentions the brand on Facebook or in a blog, it pops up on screen at Mission Control. In this way, conversations featuring Gatorade can provide useful consumer insights into how the brand is viewed and used.

Gatorade
www.gatorade.com

viral marketing
An Internet-enabled promotional strategy that encourages users to forward marketer-initiated messages to others via e-mail.

dynamic pricing
The practice of changing prices for products and services in real time in response to supply and demand conditions.

Viral marketing is an Internet-enabled promotional strategy that encourages individuals to forward marketer-initiated messages to others via e-mail, social networking websites, and blogs. There are three approaches to viral marketing. Marketers can embed a message in the product or service so that customers hardly realize they are passing it along. The classic example is Hotmail, which was one of the first companies to provide free, Internet-based e-mail. Each outgoing e-mail message has the tagline: "Get Your Private, Free Email from MSN Hotmail." Today, Windows Live Hotmail has more than 350 million users.

QR 18–2
Frito-Lay Video

Second, marketers can make the website content so compelling that viewers want to share it with others. Careerbuilders.com has done this with its Monk-e-mail site, which allows users to send personalized, private-themed e-cards for all occasions. More than 100 million Monk-e-mails have been sent since 2006. Finally, marketers can offer incentives (discounts, sweepstakes, or free merchandise). For example, Burger King asked, "What do you love more, your friend or the Whopper?" in its Whopper Sacrifice campaign. Facebook users were asked to "unfriend" 10 people from their Facebook friends list in exchange for a free burger.[17]

Cost Consumer *cost* is a fifth reason for online shopping and buying. Many popular items bought online can be purchased at the same price or cheaper than in retail stores. Lower prices also result from Internet-enabled software that permits **dynamic pricing**, the practice of changing prices for products and services in real time in response to supply and demand conditions. As described in Chapter 11, dynamic pricing is a form of flexible pricing and can often result in lower prices. It is typically used for pricing time-sensitive items such as airline seats, scarce items found at art or collectible auctions, and out-of-date items such as last year's models of computer equipment and accessories. Ticketmaster has recently experimented with dynamic pricing to adjust the price of sports and concert tickets in response to demand.[18]

Careerbuilder.com, an online career placement company, has had great viral marketing success with its Monk-e-mail featuring talking monkeys. People can stylize their monkeys by choosing headgear, clothes, glasses, backgrounds, and other features. They can also record a message using one of four monkey voices or their own voice. Monk-e-mail can be sent to friends or posted on Twitter.

CareerBuilder

www.careerbuilder.com

A consumer's cost of external information search, including time spent and often the hassle of shopping, is also reduced. Greater shopping convenience and lower external search costs are two major reasons for the popularity of online shopping and buying among women—particularly those who work outside the home.

Control The sixth reason consumers prefer to buy online is the *control* it gives them over their shopping and purchase decision process. Online shoppers and buyers are empowered consumers. They deftly use Internet technology to seek information, evaluate alternatives, and make purchase decisions on their own time, terms, and conditions. For example, studies show that shoppers spend an average of five hours researching cars online before setting foot in a showroom.[19] The result of these activities is a more informed and discerning shopper.

Even though consumers have many reasons for shopping and buying online, a segment of Internet users refrains from making purchases for privacy and security reasons. These consumers are concerned about a rarely mentioned seventh C—cookies.

Cookies are computer files that a marketer can download onto the computer and mobile phone of an online shopper who visits the marketer's website. Cookies allow the marketer's website to record a user's visit, track visits to other websites, and store and retrieve this information in the future. Cookies also contain visitor information such as expressed product preferences, personal data, passwords, and credit card numbers.

Cookies make possible customized and personal content for online shoppers. They also make possible the practice of behavioral targeting for marketers. **Behavioral targeting** uses information provided by cookies for directing online advertising from marketers to those online shoppers whose behavioral profiles suggest they would be interested in such advertising. A controversy surrounding cookies is summed up by an authority on the technology: "At best cookies make for a user-friendly web world: like a salesclerk who knows who you are. At worst, cookies represent a potential loss of privacy."[20] Read the Making Responsible Decisions box on the next page to learn more about privacy and security issues in the digital marketspace.[21]

When and Where Online Consumers Shop and Buy

Shopping and buying also happen at different times in marketspace than in the traditional marketplace.[22] About 80 percent of online retail sales occur Monday through Friday. The busiest shopping day is Wednesday. By comparison, 35 percent of retail store sales are registered on the weekend. Saturday is the most popular shopping day. Monday through Friday online shopping and buying often occur during normal work hours—some 30 percent of online consumers say they visit websites from their place

cookies
Computer files that a marketer can download onto the computer of an online shopper who visits the marketer's website.

behavioral targeting
Uses information provided by cookies for directing online advertising from marketers to those online shoppers whose behavioral profiles suggest they would be interested in such advertising.

Who Is Responsible for Internet Privacy and Security?

Privacy and security are two key reasons consumers are leery of online shopping and buying. A recent Pew Internet & American Life Project poll reported that 76 percent of online consumers have privacy and security concerns about the Internet. Even more telling, many have stopped shopping a website or forgone an online purchase because of these concerns. Industry analysts estimate that over $30 million in e-commerce sales are lost annually because of privacy and security concerns among online shoppers.

Consumer concerns are not without merit. According to the Federal Trade Commission, 46 percent of fraud complaints are Internet related, costing consumers $560 million. In addition, consumers lose millions of dollars each year due to identity theft resulting from breaches in company security systems.

A percolating issue is whether the U.S. government should pass more stringent Internet privacy and security laws. About 70 percent of online consumers favor such action. Companies, however, favor self-regulation. For example, TRUSTe (www.truste.com) awards its trademark to company websites that comply with standards of privacy protection and disclosure. Still, consumers are ultimately responsible for using care and caution when engaging in online behavior, including e-commerce. Consumers have a choice of whether or not to divulge personal information and monitor how their information is being used.

What role should the U.S. government, company self-regulation, and consumer vigilance play in dealing with privacy and security issues in the digital marketspace?

of work, which partially accounts for the sales level during the workweek. Favorite websites for workday shopping and buying include those featuring event tickets, auctions, online periodical subscriptions, flowers and gifts, consumer electronics, and travel. Websites offering health and beauty items, apparel and accessories, and music and video tend to be browsed and bought from a consumer's home.

---

learning review

3. What is viral marketing?

4. What are the six reasons consumers prefer to shop and buy online?

CROSS-CHANNEL SHOPPERS AND MULTICHANNEL MARKETING

Consumers are more likely to browse than buy online. Consumer marketspace browsing and buying in the traditional marketplace has given rise to the cross-channel shopper and the importance of multichannel marketing.

Who Is the Cross-Channel Shopper?

cross-channel shopper
An online consumer who researches products online and then purchases them at a retail store.

A **cross-channel shopper** is an online consumer who researches products online and then purchases them at a retail store.[23] Recent research shows that 51 percent of U.S. online consumers are cross-channel shoppers. These shoppers represent both genders equally and are only slightly younger than online consumers. They tend to have a higher education, earn significantly more money, and are more likely to embrace technology in their lives than online consumers who don't cross-channel shop.

Cross-channel shoppers want the right product at the best price, and they don't want to wait several days for delivery. The top reasons these shoppers research items online before buying in stores include (1) the desire to compare products among different retailers; (2) the need for more information than is available in stores; and (3) the ease of comparing their options without having to trek to multiple retail locations.

Research shows that sales arising from cross-channel shoppers dwarf exclusive online retail sales. Retail sales revenue from cross-channel shoppers is estimated to be about five times greater than online retail sales.

Implementing Multichannel Marketing

The prominence of cross-channel shoppers has focused increased attention on multichannel marketing. Recall from Chapter 12 that *multichannel marketing* is the blending of different communication and delivery channels that are mutually reinforcing in attracting, retaining, and building relationships with consumers who shop and buy in the traditional marketplace and online—the cross-channel shopper.

The most common cross-channel shopping and buying path is to browse one or more websites and then purchase an item at a retail store. This shopping path might suggest that company websites for cross-channel shoppers should be similar. But they are not. Websites play a multifaceted role in multichannel marketing because they can serve as either a communication or delivery channel. Two general applications of websites exist based on their intended purpose: (1) transactional websites and (2) promotional websites.

Victoria's Secret, a specialty retailer of intimate apparel for women, reports that a sizeable percentage of its website customers are men. Read the text to find out the exact percentage.

Multichannel Marketing with Transactional Websites *Transactional websites* are essentially electronic storefronts. They focus principally on converting an online browser into an online, catalog, or in-store buyer using the website design elements described earlier. Transactional websites are most common among store and catalog retailers and direct selling companies, such as Tupperware. Retailers and direct selling firms have found that their websites, while cannibalizing sales volume from stores, catalogs, and sales representatives, attract new customers and influence sales. Consider Victoria's Secret, the well-known specialty retailer of intimate apparel for women ages 18 to 45. It reports that almost 60 percent of its website customers are men, most of whom generate new sales volume for the company.[24]

Transactional websites are used less frequently by manufacturers of consumer products. A recurring issue for manufacturers is the threat of *channel conflict*, described in Chapter 12, and the potential harm to trade relationships with their retailing intermediaries. Still, manufacturers do use transactional websites, often cooperating with retailers. For example, Callaway Golf Company markets its golf merchandise at www.callawaygolf.com but relies on a retailer close to the buyer to fill the order. The retailer ships the order to the buyer within 24 hours and is credited with the sale. The majority of retailers that sell Callaway merchandise participate in this relationship, including retail chains Golf Galaxy and Dick's Sporting Goods. According to Callaway's chief executive officer, "This arrangement allows us to satisfy the consumer but to do so in a way that didn't violate our relationship with our loyal trade partners—those 15,000 outlets that sell Callaway products."[25]

In addition, Callaway, like other manufacturers, lists stores on its website where its merchandise can be shopped and bought. More often than not, however, manufacturers using multichannel marketing channels employ websites for advertising and promotion purposes.

Multichannel Marketing with Promotional Websites *Promotional websites* have a very different purpose than transactional websites. They advertise and promote a company's products and services and provide information on how items can

FIGURE 18–4
Implementing multichannel
marketing with promotional
websites is common today.
Two successes are found at
Hyundai Motor America and
the Clinique Division of Estée
Lauder, Inc.

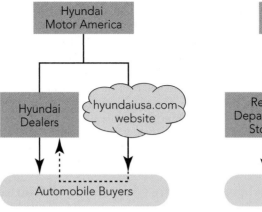
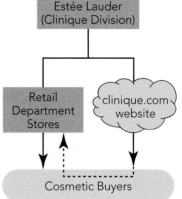

• 70% of Hyundai leads come from its
website.

• 80% of people visiting a Hyundai
dealer first visited its website.

• 80% of current Clinique buyers who visit
its website later purchase a Clinique
product at a store.

• 37% of non-Clinique buyers make a
Clinique purchase after visiting its website.

be used and where they can be purchased. They often engage the visitor in an interactive experience involving games, contests, and quizzes with electronic coupons and other gifts as prizes. Procter & Gamble maintains separate websites for many of its leading brands, including Scope mouthwash (www.getclose.com) and Pampers diapers (www.pampers.com). Promotional websites are effective in generating interest in and trial of a company's products (see Figure 18–4).[26] Hyundai Motor America reports that 80 percent of the people visiting a Hyundai store first visited the brand's website (www.hyundaiusa.com) and 70 percent of Hyundai leads come from its website.

QR 18–3
Pampers Video

Promotional websites also can be used to support a company's traditional marketing channel and build customer relationships. This is the objective of the Clinique Division of Estée Lauder, Inc., which markets cosmetics through department stores. Clinique reports that 80 percent of current customers who visit its website (www.clinique.com) later purchase a Clinique product at a department store, while 37 percent of non-Clinique buyers make a Clinique purchase after visiting the company's website.

The popularity of multichannel marketing is apparent in its impact on online retail sales.[27] Fully 70 percent of U.S. online retail sales are made by companies that practice multichannel marketing. Multichannel marketers are expected to register over 90 percent of U.S. online retail sales in 2015.

learning review

5. A cross-channel shopper is _____.

6. Channel conflict between manufacturers and retailers is likely to arise when manufacturers use _____ websites.

LEARNING OBJECTIVES REVIEW

LO1 *Describe what interactive marketing is and how it creates customer value, customer relationships, and customer experiences.* Interactive marketing involves two-way buyer–seller electronic communication in a computer-mediated environment in which the buyer controls the kind and amount of information received from the seller. It creates customer value by providing time, place, form, and possession utility for consumers. Customer relationships are created and sustained through two unique capabilities of Internet technology: interactivity and individuality. From an interactive marketing perspective, customer experience represents the sum total of the interactions that a customer has with a company's website, from the initial look at a home page through the entire purchase decision process. Companies produce a customer experience through seven website design elements. These elements are context, content, community, customization, communication, connection, and commerce.

LO2 *Explain why certain types of products and services are particularly suited for interactive marketing.*

Certain types of products and services seem to be particularly suited for interactive marketing. One category consists of items for which product information is an important part of the purchase decision, but prepurchase trial is not necessarily critical. A second category involves items for which audio or video demonstration is important. A third category contains items that can be digitally delivered. Unique items represent a fourth category. A fifth category includes items that are regularly purchased and where convenience is very important. A final category consists of highly standardized items for which information about price is important.

LO3 *Describe why consumers shop and buy online and how marketers influence online purchasing behavior.*

There are six reasons consumers shop and buy online. They are convenience, choice, customization, communication, cost, and control. Marketers have capitalized on these reasons through a variety of means. For example, they provide choice assistance using choiceboard and collaborative filtering technology, which also provides opportunities for customization. Company-hosted web communities and viral marketing practices capitalize on the communications dimensions of Internet-enabled technologies. Dynamic pricing provides real-time responses to supply and demand conditions, often resulting in lower prices to consumers. Permission marketing is popular given consumer interest in control.

LO4 *Define cross-channel shoppers and the role of transactional and promotional websites in reaching these shoppers.*

A cross-channel shopper is an online consumer who researches products online and then purchases them at a retail store. These shoppers are reached through multichannel marketing. Websites play a multifaceted role in multichannel marketing because they can serve as either a delivery or communication channel. In this regard, transactional websites are essentially electronic storefronts. They focus principally on converting an online browser into an online, catalog, or in-store buyer using the website design elements described earlier. On the other hand, promotional websites serve to advertise and promote a company's products and services and provide information on how items can be used and where they can be purchased.

FOCUSING ON KEY TERMS

behavioral targeting p. 421
bots p. 418
choiceboard p. 412
collaborative filtering p. 412
cookies p. 421
cross-channel shopper p. 422
dynamic pricing p. 420
eight-second rule p. 418
interactive marketing p. 412
permission marketing p. 413
personalization p. 412
spam p. 419
viral marketing p. 420
web communities p. 419

APPLYING MARKETING KNOWLEDGE

1 About 70 percent of Internet users have actually purchased something online. Have you made an online purchase? If so, why do you think so many people who have access to the Internet are not also online buyers? If not, why are you reluctant to do so? Do you think that electronic commerce benefits consumers even if they don't make a purchase?

2 Like the traditional marketplace, marketspace offers marketers opportunities to create greater time, place, form, and possession utility. How do you think Internet-enabled technology rates in terms of creating these values? Take a shopping trip at a virtual retailer of your choice (don't buy anything unless you really want to). Then compare the time, place, form, and possession utility provided by this virtual retailer with the time, place, form, and possession utility provided by a nonelectronic retailer that offers the same product category.

3 Visit Amazon.com (www.amazon.com) or Barnes & Noble (www.barnesandnoble.com). As you tour the company's website, think about how shopping for books online compares with a trip to your university bookstore to buy books. Specifically, compare and contrast your shopping experiences with respect to convenience, choice, customization, communication, cost, and control.

4 Visit the website for your university or college. Based on your visit, would you conclude that the website is a transactional website or a promotional website? Why? How would you rate the website in terms of the seven website design elements that affect customer experience?

building your marketing plan

Does your marketing plan involve a marketspace presence for your product or service? If the answer is "no," read no further and do not include this element in your plan. If the answer is "yes," then attention must be given to developing a website in your marketing plan. A useful starting point is to:

1 Describe how each website element—context, content, community, customization, communication, connection, and commerce—will be used to create a customer experience.

2 Identify a company's website that best reflects your website conceptualization.

QR 18–4
Pizza Hut
Video Case

It's no surprise that Pizza Hut is the world's largest pizza chain with more than 10,000 restaurants in 100 countries. But did you know that Pizza Hut became one of the top 35 U.S. Internet retailers in 2009?

According to Brian Niccol, Pizza Hut's chief marketing officer (CMO), "We've done what many would say is impossible. We successfully built an online business in three years that produces hundreds of millions of dollars in annual revenue. Today, Pizza Hut is a category leader in the interactive and emerging marketplace." So how did they do it? Pizza Hut simply revolutionized the quick serve restaurant (QSR) world through a multichannel marketing approach that created a customer experience and a customer engagement platform that was second to none.

THE RETAIL PIZZA BUSINESS

With three national competitors dominating the marketplace, the pizza business is very competitive. Even customers who could be considered heavy users of a particular brand regularly purchase from competitors on the basis of timing, pricing, and convenience.

In general, Pizza Hut's most frequent customers (and likely those of the other two major competitors) divide into two categories: (1) families, primarily time-starved mothers, looking for a quick and simple mealtime solution; and (2) young adult males who fuel their active lifestyle with one of the world's most versatile and convenient foods (no cooking, no utensils, no cleanup, and leftovers are perfect for breakfast). While these two groups could not be more dissimilar on the surface, value and convenience are important for both groups. Cost-conscious mothers look for a good quality product and a hassle-free eating experience. Deal-seeking young adult males seek more of the food they love with less time and cash invested in the process.

The importance of the take-home and delivery segment of the U.S. pizza market is illustrated by the fact that Pizza Hut's principal national competitors focus exclusively on this aspect of the business. Most take-home and delivery sales are ordered before a customer enters the restaurant. By 2006, a growing number of retail pizza customers had become comfortable ordering pizza online. Pizza ordering, as it turned out, was an ideal product for the digital world. People understood the basic menu, generally knew

that they could customize their order in a variety of ways, and were accustomed to not being in the store when ordering. Brand retail presence and established customer delivery networks also made the shift to online ordering easier for national pizza chains than other national quick serve restaurants. But as Pizza Hut understood, there is still an incredible level of complexity in making something truly sophisticated, simple, and easy for the customer.

CREATING A PLAN OF ACTION

For the most part, the intent of online ordering for the pizza business was to make transactions with the customer easier and cheaper for the brand. Pizza Hut recognized the opportunity to engage people with its brand and with other people directly and do something special; namely, build sustainable relationships with its customers and enable Pizza Hut to engage people in a more meaningful and profitable way. In short, Pizza Hut set about to reinvent the retail pizza business by breaking away from a transactional platform to an efficient and powerful customer engagement platform by reaching out to customers' kitchens and couches to offer a better mealtime ordering, delivery, and dining experience.

Pizza Hut selected imc² (www.imc2.com) as one of its lead agencies to plan a comprehensive interactive strategy that focused first on the redesign of the Pizza Hut corporate website (including redefining the customer experience online and across all of the brand's touchpoints) and then on a series of progressively sophisticated and industry-leading customer engagement strategies. imc² brought 15 years of experience in interactive marketing and brand engagement to the assignment. Its clients have included Coca-Cola, Johnson & Johnson, Pfizer, Omni Hotels, Hasbro, Procter & Gamble, and Samsung, among a host of other companies, large and small.

PIZZAHUT.COM, CUSTOMER EXPERIENCE, AND BRAND ENGAGEMENT

Pizza Hut and imc² executives agreed that the strategy for reinventing the retail pizza business would involve developing opportunities for customers to engage with the brand by using the right technologies to enable and encourage interaction. A new website was necessary to better address all major design elements. How Pizza Hut and imc² executed these design elements not only created

value for its customers, but also served as a basis for differentiation in the retail pizza business. Let's look at these design elements and PizzaHut.com's performance.

The Pizza Hut website was completely redesigned to support nationwide online ordering in 2007 (including all franchise locations for the first time) and is updated frequently to keep up with the company's fast-paced marketing strategy and ambitious product innovation rollout schedule. Since promotions are an important expectation in pizza purchasing and speak to the brand's consumers in a language that clearly connects with their desire for value, the website *context* and *content* balance the ability to shop for a deal with quick and easy ordering access for people who arrive at PizzaHut.com ready to purchase. The website presents a number of Pizza Hut's current offers in the central viewing window as well as through the rolling navigation directly underneath the main content. Primary navigation for information, such as the menu, locations, and nutrition facts, are displayed horizontally across the top of the rotating content.

Website *customization* is achieved in several ways, but the primary utility is to simplify ordering. For customers who have already registered, there are several personalization options, including rapid ordering called *Express Checkout*—a feature that's based on saved preferences similar to a "playlist." For example, if you have a group of friends that likes to watch movies together, you might create an order named *Movie Night* that has your group's favorite pizzas. Using the *Express Checkout* option accessible directly on the home page, you can select *Movie Night*, quickly review the order, click the "submit" button, and the pizzas are on their way, relying on saved delivery and payment options through a stored *cookie* (a piece of digital code that is used to identify previous visitors) to speed the transaction. With this type of functionality, you can think of convenience as an investment that creates loyalty and somewhat insulates the brand against switching down the line when customers would have to register with and learn a competitor's system, and where access to their favorite features might not be available.

Website *content* and *communications* are integrated with the company's overall communications programs—including traditional media—with product innovations, promotions, and special events shared across platforms. True to the brand, communications are fun and energetic, matching bold images and vibrant color with a smart, clever, and lighthearted voice. One noteworthy example includes the 2008 April Fools' Day rebranding of the company as "Pasta Hut" to coincide with the launch of the brand's innovative line of Tuscani Pastas. This campaign included online support in the form of display media (banner ads) and the temporary rebranding of PizzaHut.com as PastaHut.com with special imagery and copy supporting the name change. Not only did the brand get plenty of coverage in the press, but it deepened the connection with customers by showing their willingness to be spontaneous and fun, inviting people to play along with the joke.

Pizza Hut's integrated marketing communications approach enables the company to easily test and incorporate other items and brands under the larger corporate umbrella, such as the WingStreet operation and the pasta extension. This demonstrates the brand's ability to stretch the QSR concept way beyond its pizza roots and suggests the kind of direction the company may pursue in the future.

PizzaHut.com and the brand's other online assets are all about getting the world's favorite pizza and signature products into the hands and stomachs of customers. Since *commerce* is a huge consideration on the site, there are multiple pathways for ordering, including several onsite methods, a

Facebook app (the first national pizza chain to produce an ordering application for the world's leading social networking site), a branded desktop widget, mobile ordering (also known as Total Mobile Access, added in 2008, that includes both a WAP [wireless application protocol] site and text ordering), and a sophisticated and simple iPhone app released in 2009 that lets customers build and submit their order visually. Additional revenue streams can also be quickly built online, as demonstrated by the eGift Card program conceived and implemented by imc^2 over a weekend during the 2008 holiday season.

Realizing that it did not make sense for the company or its customers to create a *community* on the site, Pizza Hut tapped into Facebook to achieve results in a very cost-effective manner. With approximately 1 million fans and the first of its kind Facebook ordering application, the brand can efficiently engage a huge group of people in a very natural way without disrupting their daily routine. Again, the brand understands that if you make something convenient, you can increase trust while securing greater transactional loyalty. Pizza Hut's 2009 program to identify a summer intern, or *Twintern*, responsible for monitoring and encouraging dialogue on Twitter and other social media networks is another example of how the brand is building on existing platforms and making effective use of the massive social marketing infrastructure.

PizzaHut.com connects mobile, desktop, social networks, and other digital gateways to complement traditional media and its retail presence. So when Pizza Hut thinks about the *connection* design element, it includes more than just linking to other websites online. Rather, it provides a comprehensive approach to creating a seamless customer experience wherever and whenever people want to engage the brand.

PERFORMANCE MEASUREMENT AND OUTCOMES

Pizza Hut diligently measures the performance of Pizza Hut. com. The company created a customized marketing dashboard that allows the Pizza Hut management team to monitor various aspects of the brand's marketing program and provides an almost constant stream of fresh information that it can use to optimize engagement with people or tweak various aspects of performance.

The results have been remarkable, but understand that due to the highly competitive nature of the industry, they are fluid and only represent a moment in time. Consider, for example:

1. PizzaHut.com dominates the pizza category with number one rankings in website traffic and search volume. According to comScore, a global leader in digital analytics and measurement, the Pizza Hut site achieves the most traffic per online dollars spent in the pizza category.
2. PizzaHut.com became one of the top 35 Internet retailers in the United States in 2009, up from 45th in 2008.
3. Pizza Hut's iPhone app had more than 100,000 downloads in the first two weeks after release.

WHAT'S NEXT

So what's next for PizzaHut.com? While the brand has made huge gains in a very short time period, staying on top in the rapidly evolving digital marketplace requires constant attention. Pizza Hut envisions that its online business will surpass the $1 billion mark within the next five years and that digital transactions will lead all revenue within a decade.

While understandably protective of the company's future strategy, Pizza Hut CMO Niccol has ambitious goals and he's not joking when he deadpans, "I want Pizza Hut to become the Amazon of food service and be pioneers for the digital space. I do not want us to be a brick-and-mortar company that just dabbles in the space." The transition to something along the lines of the Amazon model suggests that the brand might further evolve its identity as a pizza business and stretch or completely redefine the QSR model.

Most brands that want to grow in the evolving economy will have to think and plan long-term and be able to act swiftly as marketplace conditions change. imc² Chief Marketing Officer Ian Wolfman, when assessing the future of the marketing, sums up the opportunity neatly. "Our agency believes that marketing's current transformation will result in a complete reorientation of how brands and companies engage with their consumers and other stakeholders. Brands that thrive will be those, like Pizza Hut, that can efficiently build sustainable relationships with people—relationships that have both high trust and high transactions" (see Figure 1). He goes on to explain that "brands taking a longer view have an unexpected advantage over traditional models that often focus too tightly on hitting near-term quarterly targets." Referring to research his agency has done on the subject, Wolfman points out that the most successful brands in the future will likely be those that resonate with people on a deeply emotional level and operate with a clearly defined sense of purpose.

Pizza Hut, with its focus on digitally enabled customer convenience and category innovation, is ideally positioned to connect with people on a level that builds trust and increases transactions. Referring to the initial time investment, however modest, that customers have to make in registering with the system and enabling various devices, Niccol sees the landscape as very promising for brands that put their customers' interests and preferences first. "If we do our job right—creating authentic engagement and making it convenient and valuable for people to interact with the brand—the numbers follow."

Questions

1 What kind of website is PizzaHut.com?

2 How does PizzaHut.com incorporate the seven website design elements?

3 How are choiceboard and personalization systems used in the PizzaHut.com website?

FIGURE 1

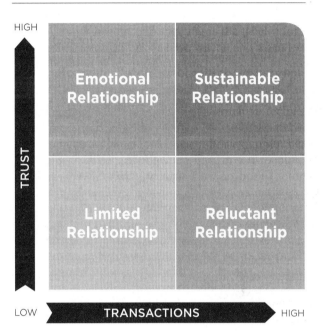

imc² Brand Sustainability Map

APPENDIX B

Planning a Career in Marketing

GETTING A JOB: THE PROCESS OF MARKETING YOURSELF

Getting a job is usually a lengthy process, and it is exactly that—a *process* that involves careful planning, implementation, and evaluation. You may have everything going for you: a respectable grade point average (GPA), relevant work experience, several extracurricular activities, superior communication skills, and demonstrated leadership qualities. Despite these, you still need to market yourself systematically and aggressively; after all, even the best products lie dormant on a retailer's shelves unless marketed effectively.

The process of getting a job involves the same activities marketing managers use to develop and introduce products and brands into the marketplace.[1] The only difference is that you are marketing yourself, not a product. You need to conduct marketing research by analyzing your personal qualities (performing a self-audit) and by identifying job opportunities. Based on your research results, select a target market—those job opportunities that are compatible with your interests, goals, skills, and abilities—and design a marketing mix around that target market. *You* are the "product;" you must decide how to "position" and "brand" yourself in the job market.[2] The price component of the marketing mix is the salary range and job benefits (such as health and life insurance, vacation time, and retirement benefits) that you hope to receive. Promotion involves communicating with prospective employers through written and electronic correspondence (advertising) and job interviews (personal selling). The place element focuses on how to reach prospective employers—at the career services office, job fairs, or online, for example.

This appendix will assist you in career planning by (1) providing information about careers in marketing and (2) outlining a job search process.

CAREERS IN MARKETING

The diversity of marketing opportunities is reflected in the many types of marketing jobs, including product management, marketing research, and public relations. While many of these jobs are found at traditional employers such as manufacturers, retailers, and advertising agencies, there are also many opportunities in a variety of other types of organizations. The diversity of marketing jobs is also changing because of changes in the marketing discipline. The growth of interactive marketing and social media has created a variety of new jobs such as data miners and social media managers. The growth of multichannel marketing has led to the need for communication channel managers and integration specialists. Specialties in demand now include digital marketing, multicultural marketing, social media, and viral marketing.[3]

Recent studies of career paths and salaries suggest that marketing careers can also provide excellent opportunities for advancement and substantial pay. For example, one of every eight chief executive officers (CEOs) of the nation's 500 most valuable publicly held companies held positions in marketing before becoming CEO.[4] Similarly, reports of average starting salaries of college graduates indicate that salaries in marketing compare favorably with those in many other fields. The median starting salary of new marketing undergraduates in 2012 was $49,600, compared with $44,700 for advertising majors and $37,500 for journalism majors.[5] The future is likely to be even better. The U.S. Department of Labor reports that employment of advertising, marketing, promotions, public relations, and sales managers is expected to grow at a rate of 13 percent through 2018, spurred by competition for a growing number of products and services, both foreign and domestic.[6]

Figure B–1 describes marketing occupations in seven major categories: product management and physical distribution, sales, nonprofit marketing, global marketing, advertising and promotion, retailing, and marketing research. One of these may be right for you. Additional sources of marketing career information are provided at the end of this appendix.

FIGURE B–1

Seven major categories of marketing occupations

Product Management and Physical Distribution

Product development manager creates a road map for new products by working with customers to determine their needs and with designers to create the product.

Product or brand manager is responsible for integrating all aspects of a product's marketing program including research, sales, sales promotion, advertising, and pricing.

Supply chain manager oversees the part of a company that transports products to consumers and handles customer service.

Operations manager supervises warehousing and other physical distribution functions and often is directly involved in moving goods on the warehouse floor.

Inventory control manager forecasts demand for goods, coordinates production with plant managers, and tracks shipments to keep customers supplied.

Physical distribution specialist is an expert in the transportation and distribution of goods and also evaluates the costs and benefits of different types of transportation.

Sales

Direct or retail salesperson sells directly to consumers in the salesperson's office, the consumer's home, or a retailer's store.

Trade salesperson calls on retailers or wholesalers to sell products for manufacturers.

Industrial or semi-technical salesperson sells supplies and services to businesses.

Complex or professional salesperson sells complicated or custom-designed products to businesses. This requires understanding of the product technology.

Customer service manager maintains good relations with customers by coordinating the sales staff, marketing management, and physical distribution management.

Nonprofit Marketing

Marketing manager develops and directs marketing campaigns, fund-raising, and public relations.

Global Marketing

Global marketing manager is an expert in world-trade agreements, international competition, cross-cultural analysis, and global market-entry strategies.

Advertising and Promotion

Account executive maintains contact with clients while coordinating the creative work among artists and copywriters. Account executives work as partners with the client to develop marketing strategy.

Media buyer deals with media sales representatives in selecting advertising media and analyzes the value of media being purchased.

Copywriter works with art director in conceptualizing advertisements and writes the text of print or radio ads or the storyboards of television ads.

Art director handles the visual component of advertisements.

Sales promotion manager designs promotions for consumer products and works at an ad agency or a sales promotion agency.

Public relations manager develops written or video messages for the public and handles contacts with the press.

Online marketing manager develops and executes the e-business marketing plan and manages all aspects of the advertising, promotion, and content for the online business.

Social media marketing manager plans and manages the delivery of marketing messages through all social media and monitors and responds to the feedback received.

Retailing

Buyer selects products a store sells, surveys consumer trends, and evaluates the past performance of products, services, and suppliers.

Store manager oversees the staff and services at a store.

Marketing Research

Project manager for the supplier coordinates and oversees the market studies for a client.

Account executive for the supplier serves as a liaison between the client and the market research firm, like an advertising agency account executive.

In-house project director acts as project manager (see above) for the market studies conducted by the firm for which he or she works.

Competitive intelligence researcher uses new information technologies to monitor the competitive environment.

Marketing database manager compiles and analyzes consumer data to identify behavior patterns, preferences, and user profiles for personalized marketing programs.

Source: Adapted from Lila B. Stair and Leslie Stair, *Careers in Marketing* (New York: McGraw-Hill, 2008); and David W. Rosenthal and Michael A. Powell, *Careers in Marketing,* ©1984, pp. 352–54.

Product Management and Physical Distribution

Product or brand managers are involved in all aspects of a product's marketing program.

Many organizations assign one manager the responsibility for a particular product. For example, Procter & Gamble (P&G) has separate brand managers for Tide, Cheer, Gain, and Bold. Product or brand managers are involved in all aspects of a product's marketing program, such as marketing research, sales, sales promotion, advertising, and pricing, as well as manufacturing. Managers of similar products typically report to a category manager, or marketing director, and may be part of a *product management team* to encourage interbrand cooperation.[7]

Several other jobs related to product management (Figure B–1) deal with physical distribution issues such as storing the manufactured product (inventory), moving the product from the firm to the customers (transportation), and engaging in many other aspects of the manufacture and sale of goods. Prospects for these jobs are likely to increase as wholesalers try to differentiate themselves from competitors by increasing their involvement with selling activities and by offering more services such as installation, maintenance, assembly, and even repair.[8]

Advertising and Promotion

Advertising positions are available in three kinds of organizations: advertisers, media companies, and agencies. Advertisers include manufacturers, retail stores, service firms, and many other types of companies. Often they have an advertising department responsible for preparing and placing their own ads. Advertising careers are also possible with the media: television, radio stations, magazines, newspapers, and the Internet. Finally, advertising agencies offer job opportunities through their use of account management, research, media, and creative services.

Starting positions with advertisers and advertising agencies are often as assistants to employees with several years of experience. An assistant copywriter facilitates the development of the message, or copy, in an advertisement. An assistant art director participates in the design of visual components of advertisements. Entry-level media positions involve buying the media that will carry the ad or selling airtime on radio or television or page space in print media. Advancement to supervisory positions requires planning skills, a broad vision, and an affinity for spotting an effective advertising idea. Students interested in advertising should develop good communication skills and try to gain advertising experience through summer employment opportunities or internships.[9]

Retailers such as Macy's and Bloomingdale's offer careers in merchandise management and store management.

Retailing

There are two separate career paths in retailing: merchandise management and store management. The key position in merchandising is that of a buyer, who is responsible for selecting merchandise, guiding the promotion of the merchandise, setting prices, bargaining with wholesalers, training the salesforce, and monitoring the competitive environment. The buyer must also be able to organize and coordinate many critical activities under severe time constraints. In contrast, store management involves the supervision of personnel in all departments and the general management of all facilities, equipment, and merchandise displays. In addition, store managers are responsible for the financial performance of each department and for the store as a whole. Typical positions beyond the store manager level include district manager, regional manager, and divisional vice president.[10]

Most starting jobs in retailing are trainee positions. A trainee is usually placed in a management training program and then given a position as an assistant buyer or assistant department manager. Advancement and responsibility can be achieved quickly because there is a shortage of qualified personnel in

Xerox is well-known for its sales career opportunities.

retailing and because superior performance of an individual is quickly reflected in sales and profits—two visible measures of success. In addition, the growth of multichannel retailing has created new opportunities such as website management and online merchandise procurement.[11]

Sales

College graduates from many disciplines are attracted to sales positions because of the increasingly professional nature of selling jobs and the many opportunities they can provide. A selling career offers benefits that are hard to match in any other field: (1) the opportunity for rapid advancement (into management or to new territories and accounts); (2) the potential for extremely attractive compensation; (3) the development of personal satisfaction, feelings of accomplishment, and increased self-confidence; and (4) independence—salespeople often have almost complete control over their time and activities.

Employment opportunities in sales occupations are found in a wide variety of organizations, including insurance agencies, retailers, and financial service firms. In addition, many salespeople work as manufacturers' representatives for organizations that have selling responsibilities for several manufacturers.[12] Activities in sales jobs include *selling duties*, such as prospecting for customers, demonstrating the product, or quoting prices; *sales-support duties*, such as handling complaints and helping solve technical problems; and *nonselling duties*, such as preparing reports, attending sales meetings, and monitoring competitive activities. Salespeople who can deal with these varying activities and have empathy for customers are critical to a company's success. According to *Bloomberg Businessweek*, "Great salespeople feel for their customers. They understand their needs and pressures; they get the challenges of their business. They see every deal through the customer's eyes."[13]

Marketing Research

Marketing researchers play important roles in many organizations today. They are responsible for obtaining, analyzing, interpreting, and presenting data to facilitate making marketing decisions. This means marketing researchers are basically problem solvers. Success in the area requires not only an understanding of statistical analysis, research methods, and programming, but also a broad base of marketing knowledge, writing and verbal presentation skills, and an ability to communicate with colleagues and clients. According to Stan Sthanunathan, vice president of marketing strategy and insights at Coca-Cola, a researcher's job "is to bring out opportunities."[14] Individuals who are inquisitive, methodical, analytical, and solution-oriented find the field particularly rewarding.

Buckle is an example of a company that encourages students to think about a job and a career.

The responsibilities of the men and women currently working in the market research industry include defining the marketing problem, selecting the research methods, designing the questions, selecting the sample, collecting and analyzing the data, and, finally, reporting the results of the research. These jobs are available in three kinds of organizations. *Marketing research consulting firms* contract with large companies to provide research about their products or services.[15] *Advertising agencies* may provide research services to help clients with questions related to advertising and promotional problems. Finally, some companies have an *in-house research staff* to design and execute their research projects. Online marketing research, which is likely to become the most common form of marketing research in the near future, requires an understanding of new tools such as dynamic scripting, response validation, intercept sampling, instant messaging surveys, and online consumer panels.[16]

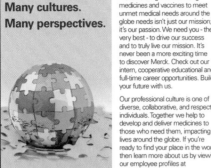
Merck seeks diverse and collaborative employees and offers them challenging career opportunities throughout the world.

International Careers

Many of the careers just described can be found in international settings—in large transnational or multinational corporations, small- to medium-size firms with export business, and franchises. The international consulting firm Accenture, for example, has thousands of consultants around the world. Similarly, many franchises such as 7-Eleven, which has 32,880 foreign locations, are rapidly expanding outside of the United States.[17] The changes in the European Union, Brazil, Russia, India, China, and other growing markets are likely to provide many opportunities for international careers. Several methods of gaining international experience are possible. For example, some companies may alternate periods of work at domestic locations with assignments outside of the United States. In addition, working for a firm with headquarters outside of the United States at one of its local offices may be appealing. In many organizations, international experience has become a necessity for promotion and career advancement. "If you are going to succeed, an expatriate assignment is essential," says Eric Kraus of Gillette Co. in Boston.[18]

THE JOB SEARCH PROCESS

Activities you should consider during your job search process include assessing yourself, identifying job opportunities, preparing your résumé and related correspondence, and going on job interviews.

Assessing Yourself

You must know your product—you—so that you can market yourself effectively to prospective employers. Consequently, a critical first step in your job search is conducting a self-inquiry or self-assessment. This activity involves understanding your interests, abilities, personality, preferences, and individual style. You must be confident that you know what work environment is best for you, what makes you happy, the balance you seek between personal and professional activities, and how you can be most effective at reaching your goals. This process helps ensure that you are matching your profile to the right job, or as business consultant and author Jim Collins explains, "Finding the right seat on the bus."[19]

A self-analysis, in part, entails identifying your strengths and weaknesses. To do so, draw a vertical line down the middle of a sheet of paper and label one side of the paper "strengths" and the other side "weaknesses." Record your strong and weak points in their respective columns. Ideally, this cataloging should be done over a few days to give you adequate time to reflect on your attributes. In addition, you might seek input from others who know you well (such as parents, close relatives, friends, professors, or employers) and can offer more objective views. A hypothetical list of strengths and weaknesses is shown in Figure B–2.

FIGURE B–2
Hypothetical list of a job candidate's strengths and weaknesses

Strengths	Weaknesses
I have good communication skills.	I have minimal work experience.
I work well independently.	I have a mediocre GPA.
I am honest and dependable.	I will not relocate.
I am willing to travel in the job.	I lack a customer orientation.
I am a good problem solver.	I have poor technical skills.

Personality and vocational interest tests, provided by many colleges and universities, can give you other ideas about yourself. After tests have been administered and scored, test takers meet with testing service counselors to discuss the results. Test results generally suggest jobs for which students have an inclination. The most common tests at the college level are the Strong Interest Inventory and the Campbell Interest and Skill Survey. Some counseling centers and career coaches also use the Myers-Briggs® Type Indicator personality inventory and the Peoplemap™ assessment to help identify professions you may enjoy.[20] If you have not already done so, you may wish to see whether your school offers such testing services.

Identifying Job Opportunities

To identify and analyze the job market, you must conduct some marketing research to determine what industries *and* companies offer promising job opportunities that relate to the results of your self-analysis. Several sources that can help in your search are discussed next.

Career Services Office   Your campus career services office is an excellent source of job information. Personnel in that office can: (1) inform you about which companies will be recruiting on campus; (2) alert you to unexpected job openings; (3) advise you about short-term and long-term career prospects; (4) offer advice on résumé construction; (5) assess your interviewing strengths and weaknesses; and (6) help you evaluate a job offer. In addition, the office usually contains a variety of written materials focusing on different industries and companies and tips on job hunting.

Campus career centers and online databases such as Monster.com are excellent sources for job information.

Online Career and Employment Services   Many companies no longer make frequent on-campus visits. Instead, they may use the many online services available to advertise an employment opportunity or to search for candidate information. The National Association of Colleges and Employers, for example, maintains a site on the Internet called JobWeb (www.jobweb.org). Similarly, Monster.com and Careerbuilder.com are online databases of employment ads, candidate résumés, and other career-related information. Some of the information resources include career guidance, a cover letter library, occupational profiles, résumé templates, and networking services.[21] Employers may contact students directly when the candidate's qualifications meet their specific job requirements.

Library   The public or college library can provide you with reference material that, among other things, describes successful firms and their operations, defines the content of various jobs, and forecasts job opportunities. For example, *Fortune* publishes a list of the 1,000 largest U.S. and global companies and their respective sales and profits, and Dun & Bradstreet publishes directories of more than 26 million companies in the United States. The *Occupational Outlook Handbook* is an annual publication of the U.S. Department of Labor that provides projections for specific job prospects, as well as information pertaining to those jobs. A librarian can indicate reference materials that will be most pertinent to *your* job search.

Advertisements   Help-wanted advertisements provide an overview of what is happening in the job market. Local (particularly Sunday editions) and college newspapers, trade press (such as *Marketing News* or *Advertising Age*), and business magazines (such as *Sales & Marketing Management*) contain classified advertisement sections that generally have job opening announcements, often for entry-level positions. Reviewing the want ads can help you identify what kinds of positions are available and their requirements and job titles, which firms offer certain kinds of jobs, and levels of compensation.

Employment Agencies   An employment agency can make you aware of several job opportunities very quickly because of its large number of job listings available through computer databases. Many agencies specialize in a particular field (such as sales and marketing). The advantages of using an agency include that it (1) reduces the cost of a job search by bringing applicants and employers together, (2) often has exclusive job listings available only by working through the agency, (3) performs much of the job search for you, and (4) tries to find a job that is compatible with your qualifications and interests.[22]

Personal Contacts and Networking   An important source of job information that students often overlook is their personal contacts. People you know often may know of job opportunities, so you should advise them that you're looking for a job. Relatives and friends might aid your job search. Instructors you know well and business contacts can provide a wealth of information about potential jobs and even help arrange an interview with a prospective employer. They may also help arrange *informational interviews* with employers that do not have immediate openings. These interviews allow you to collect information about an industry or an employer and give you an advantage if a position does become available. Creating and maintaining a network of professional contacts is one of the most important career-building activities you can undertake.[23] There are many popular social networking sites available to job seekers. LinkedIn, for example, has 160 million users, including recruiters. Other sites include Plaxo, Twitter, Jobster, Facebook, Craigslist, MyWorkster, VisualCV, JobFox, and Ecademy.[24]

State Employment Office   State employment offices have listings of job opportunities in their state and counselors to help arrange a job interview for you. Although state employment offices perform functions similar to employment agencies, they differ in listing only job opportunities in their state and providing their services free.

Direct Contact   Another means of obtaining job information is direct contact—personally communicating with prospective employers (either by mail, e-mail, telephone, or in person) that you would be interested in pursuing job opportunities with them. Often you may not even know whether jobs are available in these firms. If you correspond with the companies in writing, a letter of introduction and an attached résumé should serve as your initial form of communication. Your goals in direct contact are to create a positive impression and, ultimately, to arrange a job interview.

Preparing Your Résumé

A résumé is a document that communicates to prospective employers who you are. An employer reading a résumé is looking for a snapshot of your qualifications to decide if you should be invited to a job interview. It is imperative that you design a résumé that presents you in a favorable light and allows you to get to that next important step.[25] Personnel in your career services office can provide assistance in designing résumés.

The Résumé Itself   A well-constructed résumé generally contains up to nine major sections: (1) identification (name, address, telephone number, and e-mail address); (2) job or career objective; (3) educational background; (4) honors and awards; (5) work experience or history; (6) skills or capabilities (that pertain to a particular kind of job for which you may be interviewing); (7) extracurricular activities; (8) personal interests; and (9) personal references.[26] If possible, you should include quantitative information about your accomplishments and experience, such as "increased sales revenue by 20 percent" for the year you managed a retail clothing store.[27]

Technology has created a need for a new type of résumé—the digital résumé. Although traditional versions of résumés may be visually appealing, today most career experts suggest that résumés accommodate delivery through mail, e-mail, and fax machines. In addition, résumés must accommodate employers who use scanning technology to enter résumés into their own databases or who search commercial online databases.

Some prospective employers may require that you complete an online form that asks for much of the data included in your résumé. To fully utilize online opportunities, an electronic résumé with a popular font (e.g., New Times Roman) and relatively large font size (e.g., 10–14 pt.)—and without italic text, graphics, shading, underlining, or vertical lines—must be available. In addition, because online recruiting starts with a keyword search, it is important to include keywords, focus on nouns rather than verbs, and avoid abbreviations. Related to this use of technology, don't forget that many employers may visit social networking sites, such as Facebook, or simply "Google" your name to see what comes up. Review your online profiles before you start your job search to provide a positive and accurate image![28]

The Cover Letter   The letter accompanying a résumé, or cover letter, serves as the job candidate's introduction. As a result, it must gain the attention and interest of the reader or it will fail to give the incentive to examine the résumé carefully. In designing a letter to accompany your résumé, address the following issues:

- Address the letter to a specific person.
- Identify the position for which you are applying and how you heard of it.
- Indicate why you are applying for the position.
- Summarize your most significant credentials and qualifications.
- Refer the reader to the enclosed résumé.
- Request a personal interview, and advise the reader when and where you can be reached.

As a general rule, nothing works better than an impressive cover letter and good academic credentials.[29]

Interviewing for Your Job

The job interview is a conversation between a prospective employer and a job candidate that focuses on determining whether the employer's needs can be satisfied by the candidate's qualifications. The interview is a "make or break" situation: If the interview goes well, you have increased your chances of receiving a job offer; if it goes poorly, you probably will be eliminated from further consideration.

Preparing for a Job Interview   To be successful in a job interview, you must prepare for it so you can exhibit professionalism and indicate to a prospective employer that you are serious about the job. When preparing for the interview, several critical activities need to be performed.

Before the interview, gather facts about the industry, the prospective employer, and the job. Relevant information might include the general description for the occupation; the firm's products or services; the firm's size, number of employees, and financial and competitive position; the requirements of the position; and the name and personality of the interviewer. Obtaining this information will provide you with additional insight into the firm and help you formulate questions to ask the interviewer. This information might be gleaned, for example, from corporate annual reports, *The Wall Street Journal*, Moody's manuals, Standard & Poor's *Register of Corporations, Directors, and Executives, The Directory of Corporate Affiliations*, selected issues of *Bloomberg Businessweek*, or trade publications. You should also study the LinkedIn profiles, Twitter feeds, and blogs of the people you'll be meeting. If information is not readily available, you could call the company and indicate that you wish to obtain some information about the firm before your interview.[30]

FIGURE B–3

Anticipate questions
frequently asked by
interviewers to practice how
you might respond.

Interviewer Questions

1. What do you consider to be your greatest strengths and weaknesses?
2. What do you see yourself doing in 5 years? In 10 years?
3. What are three important leadership qualities that you have demonstrated?
4. What jobs have you enjoyed the most? The least? Why?
5. Why do you want to work for our company?

Preparation for the job interview should also involve role playing, or pretending that you are in the "hot seat" being interviewed. Before role playing, anticipate questions interviewers may pose and how you might address them (see Figure B–3). Do not memorize your answers, though, because you want to appear spontaneous, yet logical and intelligent. Nonetheless, it is helpful to practice how you might respond to the questions. In addition, develop questions you might ask the interviewer that are important and of concern to you (see Figure B–4). "It's an opportunity to show the recruiter how smart you are," comments one recruiter.[31]

Before the job interview you should attend to several details. Know the exact time and place of the interview; write them down—do not rely on your memory. Get the full company name straight. Find out what the interviewer's name is and how to pronounce it. Bring a notepad and pen along to the interview, in case you need to record anything. Make certain that your appearance is clean, neat, professional, and conservative. And be punctual; arriving tardy to a job interview gives you an appearance of being unreliable.

View the interview as a
conversation between the
prospective employer and you.

Succeeding in Your Job Interview   You have done your homework, and at last the moment arrives and it is time for the interview. Although you may experience some apprehension, view the interview as a conversation between the prospective employer and you. Both of you are in the interview to look over the other party, to see whether there might be a good match. When you meet the interviewer, greet him or her by name, be cheerful, smile, and maintain good eye contact. Take your lead from the interviewer at the outset. Sit down after the interviewer has offered you a seat. Sit up straight in your chair, and look alert and interested at all times. Appear relaxed, not tense. Be enthusiastic.

During the interview, be yourself. If you try to behave in a manner that is different from the real you, your attempt may be transparent to the interviewer or you may ultimately get the job but discover that you aren't suited for it. In addition to assessing how well your skills match those of the job, the interviewer will probably try to assess your long-term interest in the firm.

As the interview comes to a close, leave it on a positive note. Thank the interviewer for his or her time and the opportunity to discuss employment possibilities. If you are still interested in the job, express this to the interviewer. The interviewer will normally tell you what the employer's next step is—probably a visit to the company.[32] Rarely will a job offer be made at the end of the initial interview. If it is and you want the job, accept the offer; if there is any doubt in your mind about the job, however, ask for time to consider the offer.

FIGURE B–4

Interviewees should develop
questions about topics that
are important to them.

Interviewee Questions

1. What is the company's promotion policy?
2. Describe the typical first-year assignment for this job.
3. How is an employee evaluated?
4. Why do you enjoy working for this firm?
5. How much responsibility would I have in this job?

Following Up on Your Job Interview   After your interview, send a thank-you note to the interviewer and indicate whether you are still interested in the job. If you want to continue pursuing the job, polite persistence may help you get it. While e-mail is a common form of communication today, it is often viewed as less personal than a letter or telephone call, so be confident that e-mail is preferred before using it to correspond with the interviewer.[33]

As you conduct your follow-up, be persistent but polite. If you are too eager, one of two things could happen to prevent you from getting the job: The employer might feel that you are a nuisance and would exhibit such behavior on the job, or the employer may perceive that you are desperate for the job and thus are not a viable candidate.

Handling Rejection   You have put your best efforts into your job search. You developed a well-designed résumé and prepared carefully for the job interview. Even the interview appears to have gone well. Nevertheless, a prospective employer may send you a rejection letter. ("We are sorry that our needs and your superb qualification don't match.") Although you will probably be disappointed, not all interviews lead to a job offer because there normally are more candidates than there are positions available.

If you receive a rejection letter, you should think back through the interview. What appeared to go right? What went wrong? Perhaps personnel from your career services office can shed light on the problem, particularly if they are in the custom of having interviewers rate each interviewee. Try to learn lessons to apply in future interviews. Keep interviewing and gaining interview experience; your persistence will eventually pay off.

SELECTED SOURCES OF MARKETING CAREER INFORMATION

The following is a selected list of marketing information sources that you should find useful during your academic studies and professional career.

Business and Marketing Publications

Scott Dacko, *The Advanced Dictionary of Marketing: Putting Theory to Use* (Oxford University Press, 2008). This dictionary focuses on leading edge terminology for individuals who are serious about the theory and practice of marketing. Each term includes six elements: description, key insights, key words, implications, applications, and a bibliography.

Hoover's Handbook of World Business (Austin, TX: Hoover's Business Press, 2011). A detailed source of information about companies outside of the United States, including firms from Canada, Europe, Japan, China, India, and Taiwan.

Jadish Sheth and Naresh Malhotra, eds., *International Encyclopedia of Marketing* (West Sussex: John Wiley & Sons Ltd., 2011). This six-volume reference contains 360 entries from over 500 global experts. Entries are arranged alphabetically within each subject volume, and each volume carries an index.

Ray Poynter, *The Handbook of Online and Social Media Research: Tools and Techniques for Market Researchers* (West Sussex: John Wiley & Sons, Ltd., 2010). This reference book covers new innovations in the fields of online and social media research, including community panels, blog mining, social networks, mobile research, and ethnography.

Career Planning Publications

Richard N. Bolles, *What Color Is Your Parachute? 2012: A Practical Manual for Job-Hunters and Career-Changers* (Berkeley, CA: Ten Speed Press, 2011). A companion workbook is also available. See www.jobhuntersbible.com.

Dennis V. Damp, *The Book of U.S. Government Jobs: Where They Are, What's Available & How to Complete a Federal Resume,* 11th Edition (McKees Rocks, PA: Bookhaven Press, 2011).

Margaret Riley Dikel and Frances E. Roehm, *Guide to Internet Job Searching* (New York: McGraw-Hill, 2008).

The National Job Bank, 2011(CD): The Complete Employment Guide to Over 20,000 American Companies (Avon, MA: Adams Media Corporation, 2010). See www.adamsmedia.com.

Miriam Salpeter, *Social Networking for Career Success: Using Online Tools to Create a Personal Brand* (New York, NY: Learning Express, 2011).

Selected Periodicals

Advertising Age, Crain Communications, Inc. (weekly). See www.adage.com. (Subscription rate: $99 per year)

Bloomberg Businessweek, McGraw-Hill Companies (weekly). See www.businessweek.com. (Subscription rate: $39.97)

Journal of Marketing, American Marketing Association (quarterly). See www.marketingpower.com. (Subscription rates: $135 print; $162 print and online)

Marketing Management, American Marketing Association (six times per year). See www.marketingpower .com. (Subscription rate: $105)

Marketing News, American Marketing Association (biweekly). See www.marketingpower.com. (Subscription rates: $85 nonmembers; $53 members)

Marketing Research, American Marketing Association (quarterly). See www.marketingpower.com. (Subscription rate: $100)

The Wall Street Journal Interactive, Dow Jones & Company, Inc. (weekly). See www.wsj.com. (Subscription rates: $103 online; $119 print; $140 online and print)

Professional and Trade Associations

American Advertising Federation
1101 Vermont Ave. N.W., Suite 500
Washington, DC 20005-6306
(202) 898-0089
www.aaf.org

American e-Commerce Association
2346 Camp St.
New Orleans, LA 70130
(504) 495-1748
www.aeaus.com

American Marketing Association
311 S. Wacker Dr., Suite 5800
Chicago, IL 60606
(800) AMA-1150
www.marketingpower.com

Direct Marketing Association
1120 Avenue of the Americas
New York, NY 10036-6700
(212) 768-7277
www.the-dma.org

Marketing Science Institute
1000 Massachusetts Ave.
Cambridge, MA 02138-5396
(617) 491-2060
www.msi.org

Sales and Marketing Executive International
P.O. Box 1390
Suma, WA 98295-1390
(312) 893-0751
www.smei.org

GLOSSARY

80/20 rule A concept that suggests 80 percent of a firm's sales are obtained from 20 percent of its customers. p. 180

account management policies Specifies who salespeople should contact, what kinds of selling and customer service activities should be engaged in, and how these activities should be carried out. p. 399

adaptive selling A need-satisfaction presentation format that involves adjusting the presentation to fit the selling situation, such as knowing when to offer solutions and when to ask for more information. p. 395

advertising Any paid form of nonpersonal communication about an organization, product, service, or idea by an identified sponsor. pp. 320, 340

apps Small, downloadable software programs that can run on smartphones and tablet devices. Also called *mobile apps* or *applications*. p. 378

attitude A learned predisposition to respond to an object or class of objects in a consistently favorable or unfavorable way. p. 91

baby boomers Includes the generation of 76 million among the U.S. population born between 1946 and 1964. p. 61

back translation The practice where a translated word or phrase is retranslated into the original language by a different interpreter to catch errors. p. 133

behavioral targeting Uses information provided by cookies for directing online advertising from marketers to those online shoppers whose behavioral profiles suggest they would be interested in such advertising. p. 421

beliefs A consumer's subjective perception of how a product or brand performs on different attributes based on personal experience, advertising, and discussions with other people. p. 91

blog A contraction of "web log," is a web page that serves as a publicly accessible personal journal and online forum for an individual or organization. p. 364

bots Electronic shopping agents or robots that comb websites to compare prices and product or service features. p. 418

brand equity The added value a brand name gives to a product beyond the functional benefits provided. p. 231

brand loyalty A favorable attitude toward and consistent purchase of a single brand over time. p. 90

brand name Any word, device (design, sound, shape, or color), or combination of these used to distinguish a seller's goods or services. p. 231

brand personality A set of human characteristics associated with a brand name. p. 231

branding A marketing decision in which an organization uses a name, phrase, design, symbols, or combination of these to identify its products and distinguish them from those of competitors. p. 231

break-even analysis A technique that analyzes the relationship between total revenue and total cost to determine profitability at various levels of output. p. 259

brokers Independent firms or individuals whose principal function is to bring buyers and sellers together to make sales. p. 312

business The clear, broad, underlying industry or market sector of an organization's offering. p. 26

business marketing The marketing of products and services to companies, governments, or not-for-profit organizations for use in the creation of products and services that they can produce and market to others. p. 106

business plan A road map for the entire organization for a specified future period of time, such as one year or five years. p. 44

business portfolio analysis A technique that managers use to quantify performance measures and growth targets to analyze their firms' strategic business units (SBUs) as though they were a collection of separate investments. p. 31

business products Products organizations buy that assist in providing other products for resale. Also called *B2B products* or *industrial products*. p. 196

buy classes Consist of three types of organizational buying situations: straight rebuy, new buy, and modified rebuy. p. 114

buying center The group of people in an organization who participate in the buying process and share common goals, risks, and knowledge important to a purchase decision. p. 113

capacity management Integrating the service component of the marketing mix with efforts to influence consumer demand. p. 241

category management An approach to managing the assortment of merchandise in which a manager is assigned the responsibility for selecting all products that consumers in a market segment might view as substitutes for each other, with the objective of maximizing sales and profits in the category. p. 307

cause marketing Occurs when the charitable contributions of a firm are tied directly to the customer revenues produced through the promotion of one of its products. p. 73

channel conflict Arises when one channel member believes another channel member is engaged in behavior that prevents it from achieving its goals. p. 283

choiceboard An interactive, Internet-enabled system that allows individual customers to design their own products and services by answering a few questions and choosing from a menu of product or service attributes (or components), prices, and delivery options. p. 412

code of ethics A formal statement of ethical principles and rules of conduct. p. 71

collaborative filtering A process that automatically groups people with similar buying intentions, preferences, and behaviors and predicts future purchases. p. 412

communication The process of conveying a message to others that requires six elements: a source, a message, a channel of communication, a receiver, and the processes of encoding and decoding. p. 318

competition The alternative firms that could provide a product to satisfy a specific market's needs. p. 66

constraints In a decision, the restrictions placed on potential solutions to a problem. p. 150

consultative selling A need-satisfaction presentation format that focuses on problem identification, where the salesperson serves as an expert on problem recognition and resolution. p. 395

consumer behavior The actions a person takes in purchasing and using products and services, including the mental and social processes that come before and after these actions. p. 80

Consumer Bill of Rights (1962) A law that codified the ethics of exchange between buyers and sellers, including the rights to safety, to be informed, to choose, and to be heard. p. 70

consumer products Products purchased by the ultimate consumer. p. 196

consumerism A grassroots movement started in the 1960s to increase the influence, power, and rights of consumers in dealing with institutions. p. 68

consumer-oriented sales promotion Sales tools used to support a company's advertising and personal selling directed to ultimate consumers. Also called *consumer promotions.* p. 353

cookies Computer files that a marketer can download onto the computer and mobile phone of an online shopper who visits the marketer's website. p. 421

cooperative advertising Advertising programs by which a manufacturer pays a percentage of the retailer's local advertising expense for advertising the manufacturer's products. p. 356

core values The fundamental, passionate, and enduring principles of an organization that guide its conduct over time. p. 25

cross-channel shopper An online consumer who researches products online and then purchases them at a retail store. p. 422

cross-cultural analysis The study of similarities and differences among consumers in two or more nations or societies. p. 130

cultural symbols Things that represent ideas and concepts. p. 131

culture The set of values, ideas, and attitudes that are learned and shared among the members of a group. p. 62

currency exchange rate The price of one country's currency expressed in terms of another country's currency. p. 135

customer experience management (CEM) The process of managing the entire customer experience within the company. p. 210

customer service The ability of logistics management to satisfy users in terms of time, dependability, communication, and convenience. p. 288

customer value The unique combination of benefits received by targeted buyers that include quality, convenience, on-time delivery, and both before-sale and after-sale service at a specific price. p. 10

customer value proposition A cluster of benefits that an organization promises customers to satisfy their needs. p. 9

customs The normal and expected ways of doing things in a specific country. p. 131

data The facts and figures related to the problem that are divided into two main parts: secondary data and primary data. p. 151

demand curve A graph relating the quantity sold and price, which shows the maximum number of units that will be sold at a given price. p. 256

demographics Describing a population according to selected characteristics such as age, gender, ethnicity, income, and occupation. p. 60

derived demand The demand for industrial products and services that is driven by, or derived from, demand for consumer products and services. p. 108

direct marketing A promotion alternative that uses direct communication with consumers to generate a response in the form of an order, a request for further information, or a visit to a retail outlet. p. 323

direct orders The result of direct marketing offers that contain all the information necessary for a prospective buyer to make a decision to purchase and complete the transaction. p. 332

disintermediation Channel conflict that arises when a channel member bypasses another member and sells or buys products direct. p. 283

diversification analysis A technique that helps a firm search for growth opportunities from among current and new markets as well as current and new products. p. 33

dual distribution An arrangement whereby a firm reaches different buyers by employing two or more different types of channels for the same basic product. p. 277

dynamic pricing The practice of changing prices for products and services in real time in response to supply and demand conditions. p. 420

economy Pertains to the income, expenditures, and resources that affect the cost of running a business and household. p. 63

eight-second rule A view that customers will abandon their efforts to enter and navigate a website if download time exceeds eight seconds. p. 418

e-marketplaces Online trading communities that bring together buyers and supplier organizations to make possible the real time exchange of information, money, products, and services. Also called *B2B exchanges* or *e-hubs.* p. 116

environmental forces The uncontrollable forces in a marketing decision involving social, economic, technological, competitive, and regulatory forces. p. 9

environmental scanning The process of continually acquiring information on events occurring outside the organization to identify and interpret potential trends. p. 60

ethics The moral principles and values that govern the actions and decisions of an individual or group. p. 69

exchange The trade of things of value between a buyer and seller so that each is better off after the trade. p. 5

exclusive distribution A level of distribution density whereby only one retailer in a specific geographical area carries the firm's products. p. 280

exporting A global market-entry strategy in which a company produces goods in one country and sells them in another country. p. 136

Facebook A website where users may create a personal profile, add other users as friends, and exchange comments, photos, videos, and "likes" with them. p. 367

family life cycle The distinct phases that a family progresses through from formation to retirement, each phase bringing with it identifiable purchasing behaviors. p. 96

Foreign Corrupt Practices Act (1977) A law, amended by the *International Anti-Dumping and Fair Competition Act* (1998), that makes it a crime for U.S. corporations to bribe an official of a foreign government or political party to obtain or retain business in a foreign country. p. 131

four I's of services he four unique elements to services: intangibility, inconsistency, inseparability, and inventory. p. 199

Generation X Includes the 15 percent of the population born between 1965 and 1976. Also called *baby bust.* p. 61

Generation Y Includes the 72 million Americans born between 1977 and 1994. Also called *millennials, echo-boom,* or *baby boomlet.* p. 61

global brand A brand marketed under the same name in multiple countries with similar and centrally coordinated marketing programs. p. 128

global competition Exists when firms originate, produce, and market their products and services worldwide. p. 127

global consumers Consumer groups living in many countries or regions of the world who have similar needs or seek similar features and benefits from products or services. p. 128

global marketing strategy A strategy that a transnational firm uses that employs the practice of standardizing marketing activities when there are cultural similarities and adapting them when cultures differ. p. 128

goals Statements of an accomplishment of a task to be achieved, often by a specific time. Also called *objectives*. p. 26

green marketing Marketing efforts to produce, promote, and reclaim environmentally sensitive products. p. 73

hierarchy of effects The sequence of stages a prospective buyer goes through from initial awareness of a product to eventual action (either trial or adoption of the product). The stages include awareness, interest, evaluation, trial, and adoption. p. 328

idle production capacity Occurs when the service provider is available but there is no demand for the service. p. 199

infomercials Program-length (30-minute) advertisements that take an educational approach to communication with potential customers. p. 347

information technology Involves operating computer networks that can store and process data. p. 162

institutional advertisements Advertisements designed to build goodwill or an image for an organization rather than promote a specific product or service. p. 341

integrated marketing communications (IMC) The concept of designing marketing communications programs that coordinate all promotional activities—advertising, personal selling, sales promotion, public relations, and direct marketing—to provide a consistent message across all audiences. p. 318

intensive distribution A level of distribution density whereby a firm tries to place its products and services in as many outlets as possible. p. 280

interactive marketing Two-way buyer-seller electronic communication in a computer-mediated environment in which the buyer controls the kind and amount of information received from the seller. p. 412

involvement The personal, social, and economic significance of the purchase to the consumer. p. 83

joint venture A global market-entry strategy in which a foreign company and a local firm invest together to create a local business in order to share ownership, control, and profits of the new company. p. 138

lead generation The result of a direct marketing offer designed to generate interest in a product or service and a request for additional information. p. 333

learning Those behaviors that result from (1) repeated experience and (2) reasoning. p. 90

LinkedIn A business-oriented website that lets users post their professional profiles to connect to a network of businesspeople, who are also called *connections*. p. 370

logistics Those activities that focus on getting the right amount of the right products to the right place at the right time at the lowest possible cost. p. 284

major account management The practice of using team selling to focus on important customers so as to build mutually beneficial, long-term, cooperative relationships. Also called *key account management*. p. 398

manufacturer's agents Agents who work for several producers and carry noncompetitive, complementary merchandise in an exclusive territory. Also called *manufacturer's representatives*. p. 311

market People with both the desire and the ability to buy a specific offering. p. 8

market orientation An organization that focuses its efforts on (1) continuously collecting information about customers' needs, (2) sharing this information across departments, and (3) using it to create customer value. p. 14

market segmentation Involves aggregating prospective buyers into groups, or segments, that (1) have common needs and (2) will respond similarly to a marketing action. pp. 35, 174

market segments The relatively homogeneous groups of prospective buyers that result from the market segmentation process. p. 174

market share The ratio of sales revenue of the firm to the total sales revenue of all firms in the industry, including the firm itself. p. 26

marketing The activity for creating, communicating, delivering, and exchanging offerings that benefit its customers, the organization, its stakeholders, and society at large. p. 5

marketing channel Consists of individuals and firms involved in the process of making a product or service available for use or consumption by consumers or industrial users. p. 272

marketing concept The idea that an organization should (1) strive to satisfy the needs of consumers (2) while also trying to achieve the organization's goals. p. 13

marketing dashboard The visual computer display of the essential information related to achieving a marketing objective. p. 28

marketing metric A measure of the quantitative value or trend of a marketing activity or result. p. 28

marketing mix The marketing manager's controllable factors—product, price, promotion, and place—that can be used to solve a marketing problem. p. 9

marketing plan A road map for the marketing activities of an organization for a specified future time period, such as one year or five years. p. 30

marketing program A plan that integrates the marketing mix to provide a good, service, or idea to prospective buyers. p. 11

marketing research The process of defining a marketing problem and opportunity, systematically collecting and analyzing information, and recommending actions. p. 148

marketing strategy The means by which a marketing goal is to be achieved, usually characterized by a specified target market and a marketing program to reach it. p. 39

marketing tactics Detailed day-to-day operational decisions essential to the overall success of marketing strategies. p. 39

market-product grid A framework to relate the market segments of potential buyers to products offered or potential marketing actions by an organization. p. 175

marketspace Information- and communication-based electronic exchange environment mostly occupied by sophisticated computer and telecommunication technologies and digitized offerings. p. 66

measures of success Criteria or standards used in evaluating proposed solutions to the problem. p. 149

merchant wholesalers Independently owned firms that take title to the merchandise they handle. p. 311

microfinance The practice of offering small, collateral-free loans to individuals who otherwise would not have access to the capital necessary to begin small businesses or other income-generating activities. p. 134

mission A statement of the organization's function in society that often identifies its customers, markets, products, and technologies. Often used interchangeably with *vision*. p. 25

moral idealism A personal moral philosophy that considers certain individual rights or duties as universal, regardless of the outcome. p. 72

motivation The energizing force that stimulates behavior to satisfy a need. p. 86

multibranding A branding strategy that involves giving each product a distinct name when each brand is intended for a different market segment. p. 235

multichannel marketing The blending of different communication and delivery channels that are mutually reinforcing in attracting, retaining, and building relationships with consumers who shop and buy in traditional intermediaries and online. p. 277

multichannel retailers Retailers that utilize and integrate a combination of traditional store formats and nonstore formats such as catalogs, television home shopping, and online retailing. p. 307

multicultural marketing Combinations of the marketing mix that reflect the unique attitudes, ancestry, communication preferences, and lifestyles of different races and ethic groups. p. 62

multidomestic marketing strategy A strategy that a multinational firms uses that have as many different product variations, brand names, and advertising programs as countries in which they do business. p. 128

multiproduct branding A branding strategy in which a company uses one name for all its products in a product class. p. 234

new-product process The seven stages an organization goes through to identify business opportunities and convert them into salable products or services. p. 207

North American Industry Classification System (NAICS) Provides common industry definitions for Canada, Mexico, and the United States, which makes it easier to measure economic activity in the three member countries of the *North American Free Trade Agreement* (NAFTA). p. 107

objectives Statements of an accomplishment of a task to be achieved, often by a specific time. Also called *goals*. p. 26

observational data Facts and figures obtained by watching, either mechanically or in person, how people actually behave. p. 154

off-peak pricing Charging different prices during different times of the day or days of the week to reflect variations in demand for the service. p. 239

opinion leaders Individuals who are considered to be knowledgeable about or users of particular products or services and therefore can exert direct or indirect social influence over others. p. 93

order getter Sells in a conventional sense and identifies prospective customers, provides customers with information, persuades customers to buy, closes sales, and follows up on customers' use of a product or service. p. 390

order taker Processes routine orders or reorders for products that were already sold by the company. p. 390

organizational buyers Those manufacturers, wholesalers, retailers, and government agencies that buy products and services for their own use or for resale. pp. 15, 106

organizational buying behavior The decision-making process that organizations use to establish the need for products and services and identify, evaluate, and choose among alternative brands and suppliers. p. 112

organizational culture The set of values, ideas, attitudes, and norms of behavior that is learned and shared among the members of an organization. p. 26

perceived risk The anxiety felt because the consumer cannot anticipate the outcomes of a purchase but believes there may be negative consequences. p. 89

perception The process by which an individual selects, organizes, and interprets information to create a meaningful picture of the world. p. 88

perceptual map A means of displaying in two dimensions the location of products or brands in the minds of consumers to enable a manager to see how consumers perceive competing products or brands, as well as the firm's own product or brand. p. 189

permission marketing The solicitation of a consumer's consent (called "*opt-in*") to receive e-mail and advertising based on personal data supplied by the consumer. p. 413

personal selling The two-way flow of communication between a buyer and seller, often in a face-to-face encounter, designed to influence a person's or group's purchase decision. pp. 321, 388

personal selling process Sales activities occurring before, during, and after the sale itself, consisting of six stages: (1) prospecting, (2) preapproach, (3) approach, (4) presentation, (5) close, and (6) follow-up. p. 392

personality A person's consistent behaviors or responses to recurring situations. p. 87

personalization The consumer-initiated practice of generating content on a marketer's website that is custom tailored to an individual's specific needs and preferences. p. 412

points of difference Those characteristics of a product that make it superior to competitive substitutes. p. 36

posttests Tests conducted after an advertisement has been shown to the target audience to determine whether it accomplished its intended purpose. p. 352

pretests Tests conducted before an advertisement is placed in any medium to determine whether it communicates the intended message or to select among alternative versions of the advertisement. p. 351

price (P) The money or other considerations (including other products and services) exchanged for the ownership or use of a product or service. p. 248

price elasticity of demand The percentage change in quantity demanded relative to a percentage change in price. p. 257

pricing constraints Factors that limit the range of prices a firm may set. p. 262

pricing objectives Specifying the role of price in an organization's marketing and strategic plans. p. 261

primary data Facts and figures that are newly collected for the project. p. 151

product A good, service, or idea consisting of a bundle of tangible and intangible attributes that satisfies consumers' needs and is received in exchange for money or something else of value. pp. 15, 196

product advertisements Advertisements that focus on selling a product or service and which take three forms: (1) pioneering (or informational), (2) competitive (or persuasive), and (3) reminder. p. 340

product differentiation A marketing strategy that involves a firm using different marketing mix activities to help consumers perceive the product as being different and better than competing products. p. 174

product item A specific product that has a unique brand, size, or price. p. 200

product life cycle Describes the stages a new product goes through in the marketplace: introduction, growth, maturity, and decline. p. 220

product line A group of product or service items that are closely related because they satisfy a class of needs, are used together, are sold to the same customer group, are distributed through the same outlets, or fall within a given price range. p. 200

product mix Consists of all of the product lines offered by an organization. p. 200

product placement A consumer sales promotion tool that uses a brand-name product in a movie, television show, video game, or a commercial for another product. p. 355

product positioning The place a product occupies in consumers' minds on important attributes relative to competitive products. p. 188

product repositioning Changing the place a product occupies in a consumer's mind relative to competitive products. p. 188

profit The money left after a business firm's total expenses are subtracted from its total revenues and is the reward for the risk it undertakes in marketing its offerings. p. 22

profit equation Profit = Total revenue − Total cost; or Profit = (Unit price × Quantity sold) − (Fixed cost + Variable cost). p. 249

promotional mix The combination of one or more communication tools used to: (1) inform prospective buyers about the benefits of the product, (2) persuade them to try it, and (3) remind them later about the benefits they enjoyed by using the product. p. 318

protectionism The practice of shielding one or more industries within a country's economy from foreign competition through the use of tariffs or quotas. p. 124

public relations A form of communication management that seeks to influence the feelings, opinions, or beliefs held by customers, prospective customers, stockholders, suppliers, employees, and other publics about a company and its products or services. p. 322

publicity A nonpersonal, indirectly paid presentation of an organization, product, or service. p. 322

publicity tools Methods of obtaining nonpersonal presentation of an organization, product, or service without direct cost, such as news releases, news conferences, and public service announcements. p. 357

pull strategy Directing the promotional mix at ultimate consumers to encourage them to ask the retailer for a product. p. 326

purchase decision process The five stages a buyer passes through in making choices about which products and services to buy: (1) problem recognition, (2) information search, (3) alternative evaluation, (4) purchase decision, and (5) postpurchase behavior. p. 80

push strategy Directing the promotional mix to channel members to gain their cooperation in ordering and stocking the product. p. 326

questionnaire data Facts and figures obtained by asking people about their attitudes, awareness, intentions, and behaviors. p. 156

quota A restriction placed on the amount of a product allowed to enter or leave a country. p. 124

reference groups People to whom an individual looks as a basis for self-appraisal or as a source of personal standards. p. 95

regulation Restrictions state and federal laws place on business with regard to the conduct of its activities. p. 67

relationship marketing Links the organization to its individual customers, employees, suppliers, and other partners for their mutual long-term benefit. p. 11

relationship selling The practice of building ties to customers based on a salesperson's attention and commitment to customer needs over time. p. 389

retail life cycle The process of growth and decline that retail outlets, like products, experience. Consists of the early growth, accelerated development, maturity, and decline stages. p. 310

retailing All activities involved in selling, renting, and providing products and services to ultimate consumers for personal, family, or household use. p. 296

retailing mix The activities related to managing the store and the merchandise in the store, which includes retail pricing, store location, retail communication, and merchandise. p. 305

reverse auction In an e-marketplace, it is an online auction in which a buyer communicates a need for a product or service and would-be suppliers are invited to bid in competition with each other. p. 117

reverse logistics A process of reclaiming recyclable and reusable materials, returns, and reworks from the point of consumption or use for repair, remanufacturing, redistribution, or disposal. p. 289

sales forecast The total sales of a product that a firm expects to sell during a specified time period under specified environmental conditions and its own marketing efforts. p. 166

sales management Planning the selling program and implementing and evaluating the personal selling effort of the firm. p. 388

sales plan A statement describing what is to be achieved and where and how the selling effort of salespeople is to be deployed. p. 398

sales promotion A short-term inducement of value offered to arouse interest in buying a product or service. p. 323

sales quota Specific goals assigned to a salesperson, sales team, branch sales office, or sales district for a stated time period. p. 402

salesforce automation (SFA) The use of computer, information, communication, and Internet technologies to make the sales function more effective and efficient. p. 402

scrambled merchandising Offering several unrelated product lines in a single store. p. 301

secondary data Facts and figures that have already been recorded prior to the project at hand. p. 151

selective distribution A level of distribution density whereby a firm selects a few retailers in a specific geographical area to carry its products. p. 281

self-regulation An alternative to government regulation where an industry attempts to police itself. p. 69

services Intangible activities or benefits that an organization provides to satisfy consumers' needs in exchange for money or something else of value. p. 196

seven Ps of services marketing An expanded marketing mix for services that includes the four Ps (product, price, promotion, and place or distribution) as well as people, physical environment, and process. p. 239

shopper marketing The use of displays, coupons, product samples, and other brand communications to influence shopping behavior in a store. p. 307

situation analysis Taking stock of where the firm or product has been recently, where it is now, and where it is headed in terms of the organization's marketing plans and the external forces and trends affecting it. p. 34

social forces The demographic characteristics and the culture of the population. p. 60

social media Online media where users submit comments, photos, and videos—often accompanied by a feedback process to identify "popular" topics. p. 364

social responsibility The idea that organizations are part of a larger society and are accountable to that society for their actions. p. 72

societal marketing concept The view that organizations should discover and satisfy the needs of consumers in a way that provides for society's well-being. p. 15

spam Communications that take the form of electronic junk mail or unsolicited e-mail. p. 419

strategic marketing process The approach whereby an organization allocates its marketing mix resources to reach its target markets. p. 34

strategy An organization's long-term course of action designed to deliver a unique customer experience while achieving its goals. p. 22

subcultures Subgroups within the larger, or national, culture with unique values, ideas, and attitudes. p. 98

supply chain The various firms involved in performing the activities required to create and deliver a product or service to consumers or industrial users. p. 285

SWOT analysis An acronym describing an organization's appraisal of its internal **S**trengths and **W**eaknesses and its external **O**pportunities and **T**hreats. p. 34

target market One or more specific groups of potential consumers toward which an organization directs its marketing program. p. 9

tariff A government tax on goods or services entering a country that primarily serves to raise prices on imports. p. 124

technology Inventions or innovations from applied science or engineering research. p. 65

telemarketing Using the telephone to interact with and sell directly to consumers. p. 304

total cost (TC) The total expense incurred by a firm in producing and marketing a product. Total cost is the sum of fixed cost and variable cost. TC = FC + VC. p. 258

total logistics cost Expenses associated with transportation, materials handling and warehousing, inventory, stockouts (being out of inventory), order processing, and return products handling. p. 288

total revenue (TR) The total money received from the sale of a product; or the unit price (P) times the quantity (Q) sold. TR = P × Q. p. 258

trade-oriented sales promotions Sales tools used to support a company's advertising and personal selling directed to wholesalers, distributors, or retailers. Also called *trade promotions*. p. 356

traditional auction In an e-marketplace, it is an online auction in which a seller puts an item up for sale and would-be buyers are invited to bid in competition with each other. p. 117

traffic generation The outcome of a direct marketing offer designed to motivate people to visit a business. p. 333

Twitter A website that enables users to send and receive "tweets," messages up to 140 characters long. p. 369

ultimate consumers The people who use the products and services purchased for a household. Also called consumers, buyers, or customers. p. 15

usage rate The quantity consumed or patronage (store visits) during a specific period. Also called *frequency marketing*. p. 180

user generated content (UGC) The various forms of online media content that are publicly available and created by end users. p. 364

utilitarianism A personal moral philosophy that focuses on "the greatest good for the greatest number" by assessing the costs and benefits of the consequences of ethical behavior. p. 72

utility The benefits or customer value received by users of the product. p. 16

value The ratio of perceived benefits to price; or Value = (Perceived benefits ÷ Price). p. 249

values A society's personally or socially preferable modes of conduct or states of existence that tend to persist over time. p. 130

vendor-managed inventory (VMI) An inventory-management system whereby the supplier determines the product amount and assortment a customer (such as a retailer) needs and automatically delivers the appropriate items. p. 289

vertical marketing systems Professionally managed and centrally coordinated marketing channels designed to achieve channel economies and maximum marketing impact. p. 278

viral marketing An Internet-enabled promotional strategy that encourages individuals to forward marketer-initiated messages to others via e-mail, social networking websites, and blogs. p. 420

web communities Websites that allow people to congregate online and exchange views on topics of common interest. p. 419

wheel of retailing A concept that describes how new forms of retail outlets enter the market. p. 309

word of mouth The influencing of people during conversations. p. 94

World Trade Organization (WTO) An institution that sets rules governing trade between its members through panels of trade experts who decide on trade disputes between members and issue binding decisions. p. 124

YouTube A video-sharing website in which users can upload, view, and comment on videos. p. 371

LEARNING REVIEW ANSWERS

CHAPTER 1

1. What is marketing?

Answer: Marketing is the activity for creating, communicating, delivering, and exchanging offerings that benefit its customers, the organization, its stakeholders, and society at large.

2. Marketing focuses on _____ and _____ consumer needs.

Answer: discovering; satisfying

3. What four factors are needed for marketing to occur?

Answer: The four factors are: (1) two or more parties (individuals or organizations) with unsatisfied needs; (2) a desire and ability to have their needs satisfied; (3) a way for the parties to communicate; and (4) something to exchange.

4. An organization can't satisfy the needs of all consumers, so it must focus on one or more subgroups, which are its _____.

Answer: target market

5. What are the four marketing mix elements that make up the organization's marketing program?

Answer: product, price, promotion, place

6. What are environmental forces?

Answer: Environmental forces are those that the organization's marketing department can't control. These include social, economic, technological, competitive, and regulatory forces.

7. What are the two key characteristics of the marketing concept?

Answer: An organization should (1) strive to satisfy the needs of consumers (2) while also trying to achieve the organization's goals.

8. What is the difference between ultimate consumers and organizational buyers?

Answer: Ultimate consumers are the people who use the products and services purchased for a household. Organizational buyers are those manufacturers, wholesalers, retailers, and government agencies that buy products and services for their own use or for resale.

CHAPTER 2

1. What is the difference between a business firm and a nonprofit organization?

Answer: A business firm is a privately owned organization that serves its customers to earn a profit so that it can survive. A nonprofit organization is a nongovernmental organization that serves its customers but does not have profit as an organizational goal. Instead, its goals may be operational efficiency or client satisfaction.

2. What are examples of a functional level in an organization?

Answer: The functional level in an organization is where groups of specialists from the marketing, finance, manufacturing/operations, accounting, information systems, research & development, and/or human resources departments focus on a specific strategic direction to create value for the organization.

3. What is the meaning of an organization's mission?

Answer: A mission is a statement of the organization's function in society, often identifying its customers, markets, products, and technologies. It is often used interchangeably with *vision*.

4. What is the difference between an organization's business and its goals?

Answer: An organization's business describes the clear, broad, underlying industry or market sector of an organization's offering. An organization's goals (or objectives) are statements of an accomplishment of a task to be achieved, often by a specific time. Goals convert an organization's mission and business into long- and short-term performance targets to measure how well it is doing.

5. What is the difference between a marketing dashboard and a marketing metric?

Answer: A marketing dashboard is the visual computer display of the essential information related to achieving a marketing objective. Each variable in a marketing dashboard is a marketing metric, which is a measure of the quantitative value or trend of a marketing activity or result.

6. What is business portfolio analysis?

Answer: Business portfolio analysis is a technique that managers use to quantify performance measures and growth targets to analyze their firms' strategic business units (SBUs) as though they were a collection of separate investments.

7. Explain the four market-product strategies in diversification analysis.

Answer: The four market-product strategies in diversification analysis are: (1) Market penetration, which is a marketing strategy to increase sales of current products in current markets. There is no change in either the basic product line or the markets served. Rather, selling more of the product or selling the product at a higher price generates increased sales. (2) Market development, which is a marketing strategy to sell current products to new markets. (3) Product development, which is a marketing strategy of selling new products to current markets. (4) Diversification, which is a potentially high-risk marketing strategy of developing new products and selling them in new markets.

8. What are the three steps of the planning phase of the strategic marketing process?

Answer: The three steps of the planning phase of the strategic marketing process are: (1) Situation (SWOT) analysis, which involves taking stock of where the firm or product has been recently, where it is now, and where it is headed in terms of the organization's marketing plans and the external forces and trends affecting it. To do this, an organization uses a SWOT analysis, an acronym that describes an organization's appraisal of its internal **S**trengths and **W**eaknesses and its external **O**pportunities and **T**hreats. (2) Market-product focus and goal setting, which determines what products an organization will offer to which customers. This is often based on market segmentation—aggregating prospective buyers into groups or segments that have common needs and will respond similarly to a marketing action. (3) Marketing program, which is where an organization develops the marketing mix elements and budget for each offering.

9. What are points of difference and why are they important?

Answer: Points of difference are those characteristics of a product that make it superior to competitive substitutes—offerings it faces in the marketplace. They are the single most important factor in the success or failure of a new product.

10. What is the implementation phase of the strategic marketing process?

Answer: The implementation phase carries out the marketing plan that emerges from the planning phase and consists of: (1) obtaining resources; (2) designing the marketing organization; (3) developing planning schedules; and (4) executing the marketing program designed in the planning phase.

11. How do the goals set for a marketing program in the planning phase relate to the evaluation phase of the strategic marketing process?

Answer: The planning phase objectives are used as the benchmarks with which the actual performance results are compared in the evaluation phase to identify deviations from the written marketing plans and then correct negative ones or exploit positive ones.

CHAPTER 3

1. Describe three generational cohorts.

Answer: (1) Baby boomers are the generation of 76 million among the U.S. population born between 1946 and 1964. These Americans are growing older and will all be 65 or older by 2030. (2) Generation X are those among the 15 percent of the U.S. population born between 1965 and 1976. These well-educated Americans, also known as the baby bust cohort because of declining birth rates, are supportive of racial and ethic diversity. (3) Generation Y are the 72 million Americans among the U.S. population born between 1977 and 1994. The rising birth rate of this "baby boomlet" cohort is the result of baby boomers having children. A subset of this generational cohort are millennials, who are younger Americans born since 1994. Because each generational cohort has its distinct attitudes and behaviors, marketers have developed generational marketing programs for each of them.

2. Why are many companies developing multicultural marketing programs?

Answer: Multicultural marketing programs consist of combinations of the marketing mix that reflect the unique attitudes, ancestry, communication preferences, and lifestyles of different races and ethnic groups. The reasons for developing these programs are: (1) The racial and ethnic diversity of the U.S. is changing rapidly due to the increases in the African American, Asian, and Hispanic populations, which increases their economic impact. (2) An accurate understanding of the culture of each group is essential if marketing efforts are to be successful. (3) Based on an analysis of population demographic data, racial and ethnic groups tend to be concentrated in specific geographic regions.

3. How are important values such as sustainability reflected in the marketplace today?

Answer: Many Americans desire and practice sustainability to preserve the environment. Specifically, these consumers buy hybrid gas-electric cars and energy-efficient light bulbs. Consumers also prefer brands that have a strong link to social action (like Ben & Jerry's—see Chapter 2). Companies are responding to this consumer trend by producing products that use renewable energy and less packaging.

4. What is the difference between a consumer's disposable and discretionary income?

Answer: Disposable income is the money a consumer has left after paying taxes to use for necessities such as food, housing, clothing, and transportation. Discretionary income is the money that remains after paying for taxes and necessities and is usually spent on luxury items.

5. How does technology impact customer value?

Answer: (1) Consumers can now assess value on the basis of other dimensions, such as quality, service, and relationships, due to the decline in the cost of technology. (2) Technology provides value through the development of new products.

6. In pure competition there are a _____ number of sellers.

Answer: large

7. The _____ Act was punitive toward monopolies, whereas the _____ Act was preventive.

Answer: Sherman Antitrust; Clayton

8. The Federal Trade Commission (FTC) monitors _____.

Answer: unfair business practices

9. How does the Better Business Bureau encourage companies to follow its standards for commerce?

Answer: The Better Business Bureau (BBB) uses moral suasion to get members to comply with its standards.

10. What rights are included in the Consumer Bill of Rights?

Answer: The rights to safety, to be informed, to choose, and to be heard.

11. Economic espionage includes what kinds of activities?

Answer: Economic espionage is the clandestine collection of trade secrets or proprietary information about a company's competitors. This practice includes trespassing, theft, fraud, misrepresentation, wiretapping, searching competitors' trash, and violations of written and implicit employment agreements with noncompete clauses.

12. What is meant by moral idealism?

Answer: Moral idealism is a personal moral philosophy that considers certain individual rights or duties as universal, regardless of the outcome.

13. What is meant by social responsibility?

Answer: Social responsibility means that organizations are part of a larger society and are accountable to that society for their actions. It comprises three concepts: (1) profit responsibility—maximizing profits for the organization's shareholders; (2) stakeholder responsibility—the obligations an organization has to those who can affect the achievement of its objectives; and (3) societal responsibility—the obligations an organization has to preserve the ecological environment and to the general public.

14. Marketing efforts to produce, promote, and reclaim environmentally sensitive products are called _____.

Answer: green marketing

15. What is sustainable development?

Answer: Sustainable development involves conducting business in such a way that protects the natural environment while making economic progress. Green marketing is an ecological example of such an initiative.

CHAPTER 4

1. What is the first stage in the consumer purchase decision process?

Answer: problem recognition

2. The brands a consumer considers buying out of the set of brands in a product class of which the consumer is aware are collectively called the _____.

Answer: consideration set

3. What is the term for postpurchase anxiety?

Answer: cognitive dissonance

4. The problem with the Toro Snow Pup was an example of selective _____.

Answer: comprehension

5. What three attitude-change approaches are most common?

Answer: (1) Change beliefs about the extent to which a brand has certain attributes. (2) Change the perceived importance of the attributes. (3) Add new attributes to the product.

6. What does *lifestyle* mean?

Answer: Lifestyle is a mode of living that is identified by how people spend their time and resources, what they consider important in their environment, and what they think of themselves and the world around them.

7. What are the two primary forms of personal influence?

Answer: opinion leadership; word of mouth activity

8. Marketers are concerned with which types of reference groups?

Answer: membership groups; aspiration groups; dissociative groups

9. What two challenges must marketers overcome when marketing to Hispanics?

Answer: (1) The diversity of nationalities among this subculture. (2) The language barrier that can lead to misinterpretation or mistranslation of commercial messages.

CHAPTER 5

1. What are the three main types of organizational buyers?

Answer: industrial firms; resellers; government units

2. What is the North American Industry Classification System (NAICS)?

Answer: The NAICS provides common industry definitions for Canada, Mexico, and the United States, which makes it easier to measure economic activity in the three member countries of NAFTA.

3. **What one department is almost always represented by a person in the buying center?**

Answer: purchasing department

4. **What are the three types of buying situations or buy classes?**

Answer: new buy; straight rebuy; modified rebuy

5. **What are e-marketplaces?**

Answer: E-marketplaces are online trading communities that bring together buyers and supplier organizations to make possible the real-time exchange of information, money, products, and services.

6. **In general, which type of online auction creates upward pressure on bid prices and which type creates downward pressure on bid prices?**

Answer: traditional auction; reverse auction

CHAPTER 6

1. **What is protectionism?**

Answer: Protectionism is the practice of shielding one or more industries within a country's economy from foreign competition through the use of tariffs or quotas.

2. **The North American Free Trade Agreement was designed to promote free trade among which countries?**

Answer: The United States, Canada, and Mexico

3. **What is the difference between a multidomestic marketing strategy and a global marketing strategy?**

Answer: Multinational firms view the world as consisting of unique markets. As a result, they use a multidomestic marketing strategy because they have as many different product variations, brand names, and advertising programs as countries in which they do business. Transnational firms view the world as one market. As a result, they use a global marketing strategy to standardize marketing activities when there are cultural similarities and adapt it when cultures differ.

4. **Cross-cultural analysis involves the study of _____.**

Answer: similarities and differences among consumers in two or more nations or societies

5. **When foreign currencies can buy more U.S. dollars, are U.S. products more or less expensive for a foreign consumer?**

Answer: less expensive

6. **What mode of entry could a company follow if it has no previous experience in global marketing?**

Answer: indirect exporting through intermediaries

7. **How does licensing differ from a joint venture?**

Answer: Under licensing, a company offers the right to a trademark, patent, trade secret, or other similarly valued items of intellectual property in return for a fee or royalty. In a joint venture, a foreign company and a local firm invest together to create a local business to produce some product or service. The two companies share ownership, control, and profits of the new entity.

8. **Products may be sold globally in three ways. What are they?**

Answer: Products can be sold: (1) in the same form as in their home market (product extension); (2) with some adaptations (product adaptation); and (3) as a totally new product (product invention).

9. **What is dumping?**

Answer: Dumping is when a firm sells a product in a foreign country below its domestic price or below its actual cost to produce.

CHAPTER 7

1. **What is marketing research?**

Answer: Marketing research is the process of defining a marketing problem and opportunity, systematically collecting and analyzing information, and recommending actions.

2. **What is the five-step marketing research approach?**

Answer: The five-step marketing research approach provides a systematic checklist for making marketing decisions and actions. The five

steps are: (1) define the problem; (2) develop the research plan; (3) collect relevant information (data); (4) develop findings; and (5) take marketing actions.

3. **What are constraints, as they apply to developing a research plan?**

Answer: Constraints in a decision are the restrictions placed on potential solutions to a problem, such as time and money. These set the parameters for the research plan—due dates, budget, etc.

4. **What is the difference between secondary and primary data?**

Answer: Secondary data are facts and figures that have already been recorded prior to the project at hand, whereas primary data are facts and figures that are newly collected for the project.

5. **What are some advantages and disadvantages of secondary data?**

Answer: Advantages of secondary data are the time-savings, the low cost, and the greater level of detail that may be available. Disadvantages of secondary data are that the data may be out of date, unspecific, or have definitions, categories, or age groupings that are wrong for the project at hand.

6. **What is the difference between observational and questionnaire data?**

Answer: Observational data are facts and figures obtained by watching, either mechanically or in person, how people actually behave. Questionnaire data are facts and figures obtained by asking people about their attitudes, awareness, intentions, and behaviors.

7. **Which type of survey provides the greatest flexibility for asking probing questions: mail, telephone, or personal interview?**

Answer: personal interview (or individual/depth interview)

8. **What is the difference between a panel and an experiment?**

Answer: A panel is a sample of consumers or stores from which researchers take a series of measurements. An experiment involves obtaining data by manipulating factors under tightly controlled conditions to test cause and effect, such as changing a variable in a customer purchase decision (marketing drivers) and seeing what happens (increase/decrease in unit or dollar sales).

9. **How does data mining differ from traditional marketing research?**

Answer: Data mining is the extraction of hidden predictive information from large databases to find statistical links between consumer purchasing patterns and marketing actions. Marketing research identifies possible drivers and then collects data.

10. **In the marketing research for Tony's Pizza, what is an example of (*a*) a finding and (*b*) a marketing action?**

Answer: (*a*) Figure 7-6A depicts annual sales from 2009 to 2012; the finding is that annual sales are relatively flat, rising only about 5 million units over the 4-year period. (*b*) Figure 7-6D shows a finding (the decline in pizza consumption) that leads to a recommendation to develop an ad targeting children 6 to 12 years old (the marketing action).

11. **What are the three kinds of sales forecasting techniques?**

Answer: They are: (1) judgments of the decision maker; (2) surveys of knowledgeable groups; and (3) statistical methods.

12. **How do you make a lost-horse forecast?**

Answer: To make a lost-horse forecast, begin with the last known value of the item being forecast, list the factors that could affect the forecast, assess whether they have a positive or negative impact, and then make the final forecast.

CHAPTER 8

1. **Market segmentation involves aggregating prospective buyers into groups that have two key characteristics. What are they?**

Answer: The groups (1) should have common needs and (2) will respond similarly to a marketing action.

2. **In terms of market segments and products, what are the three market segmentation strategies?**

Answer: The three market segmentation strategies are: (1) one product and multiple market segments; (2) multiple products and multiple market segments; and (3) "segments of one," or mass customization.

3. **The process of segmenting and targeting markets is a bridge between which two marketing activities?**

Answer: identifying market needs and executing the marketing program

4. **What is the difference between the demographic and behavioral bases of market segmentation?**

Answer: Demographic segmentation is based on some objective physical (gender, race), measurable (age, income), or other classification attribute (birth era, occupation) of prospective customers. Behavioral segmentation is based on some observable actions or attitudes by prospective customers—such as where they buy, what benefits they seek, how frequently they buy, and why they buy.

5. **What factor is estimated or measured for each of the cells in a market-product grid?**

Answer: Each cell in the grid can show the estimated market size of a given product sold to a specific market segment.

6. **What are some criteria used to decide which segments to choose for targets?**

Answer: Possible criteria include market size, expected growth, competitive position, cost of reaching the segment, and compatibility with the organization's objectives and resources.

7. **How are marketing and product synergies different in a market-product grid?**

Answer: Marketing synergies run horizontally across a market-product grid. Each row represents an opportunity for efficiency in the marketing efforts to a market segment. Product synergies run vertically down the market-product grid. Each column represents an opportunity for efficiency in research and development (R&D) and production.

8. **What is the difference between product positioning and product repositioning?**

Answer: Product positioning refers to the place a product occupies in consumers' minds based on important attributes relative to competitive products. Product repositioning involves changing the place a product occupies in a consumer's mind relative to competitive products.

9. **Why do marketers use perceptual maps in product positioning decisions?**

Answer: Perceptual maps are a means of displaying or graphing in two dimensions the location of products or brands in the minds of consumers. Marketers use perceptual maps to see how consumers perceive competing products or brands as well as their own product or brand. Then, they can develop marketing actions to move their product or brand to an ideal position.

CHAPTER 9

1. **What are the four main types of consumer products?**

Answer: They are convenience products, shopping products, specialty products, and unsought products.

2. **What are the four I's of services?**

Answer: intangibility, inconsistency, inseparability, and inventory

3. **What is the difference between a product line and a product mix?**

Answer: A product line is a group of product or service items that are closely related because they satisfy a class of needs, are used together, are sold to the same customer group, are distributed through the same outlets, or fall within a given price range. The product mix consists of all the product lines offered by an organization.

4. **What kind of innovation would an improved electric toothbrush be?**

Answer: continuous innovation—no new learning is required

5. **Why can an "insignificant point of difference" lead to new-product failure?**

Answer: The product must have superior characteristics that deliver unique benefits to the user compared to those of competitors. Without these, the product will probably fail.

6. **What is "groupthink," and how can it lead to new-product failures?**

Answer: "Groupthink" occurs when someone in a new-product planning meeting knows or suspects the product concept is a dumb idea but is afraid to speak up for fear of being cast as a "negative thinker" and "not a

team player," with the result of being ostracized from real participation in the group. This can lead to new-product failure because a strong public commitment to a new product by its key advocate may make it difficult to kill the product even when new negative information comes to light.

7. **What is the new-product strategy development stage in the new-product process?**

Answer: New-product strategy development is the stage of the new-product process that defines the role for a new product in terms of the firm's overall objectives.

8. **What are the main sources of new-product ideas?**

Answer: Employee and co-worker suggestions, customer and supplier suggestions, R&D laboratories, competitive products, and smaller, non-traditional firms, universities, and inventors.

9. **How do internal and external screening and evaluation approaches differ?**

Answer: In internal screening, company employees evaluate the technical feasibility of new-product ideas to determine whether they meet the objectives defined in the new-product strategy development step. For services, employees are assessed to determine that they have the commitment and skills to meet customer expectations and sustain customer loyalty. In external screening, evaluation consists of preliminary testing of the new-product idea (not the actual product) with consumers.

10. **How does the development stage of the new-product process involve testing the product inside and outside the firm?**

Answer: Internally, laboratory tests are done to see if the product achieves the physical, quality, and safety standards; externally, market testing is done to expose actual products to prospective consumers under realistic purchase conditions to see if they will buy.

11. **What is a test market?**

Answer: A test market is a city that is viewed as being demographically representative of markets targeted for the new product, having cable TV systems that can deliver different ads to different homes, and having retailers with checkout counter scanners to measure sales results.

12. **What is the commercialization of a new product?**

Answer: Commercialization, the last stage of the new-product process, involves positioning and launching a new product in full-scale production and sales and is the most expensive stage for most new products.

CHAPTER 10

1. **Advertising plays a major role in the _____ stage of the product life cycle, and _____ plays a major role in maturity.**

Answer: introductory; product differentiation

2. **How do high-learning and low-learning products differ?**

Answer: A high-learning product requires significant customer education and there is an extended introductory period. A low-learning product requires little customer education because the benefits of purchase are readily understood, resulting in immediate sales.

3. **What does "creating a new use situation" mean in managing a product's life cycle?**

Answer: Creating a new use situation means finding new uses or applications for an existing product.

4. **Explain the difference between trading up and trading down in product repositioning.**

Answer: Trading up involves adding value to the product (or line) through additional features or higher-quality materials. Trading down involves reducing the number of features, quality, or price or downsizing—reducing the content of packages without changing package size and maintaining or increasing the package price.

5. **What is the difference between a line extension and a brand extension?**

Answer: A line extension uses a current brand name to enter a new market segment in its product class, whereas a brand extension uses a current brand name to enter a completely different product class.

6. **Explain the role of packaging in terms of perception.**

Answer: A package's shape, color, and graphics distinguish one brand from another, convey a brand's positioning, and build brand equity.

7. How do service businesses use off-peak pricing?

Answer: Service businesses charge different prices during different times of the day or days of the week to reflect variations in demand for the service.

CHAPTER 11

1. Value is _____.

Answer: the ratio of perceived benefits to price; or Value 5 (Perceived benefits 4 Price)

2. What circumstances in pricing a new product might support skimming or penetration pricing?

Answer: Skimming pricing is an effective strategy when: (1) enough prospective customers are willing to buy the product immediately at the high initial price to make these sales profitable; (2) the high initial price will not attract competitors; (3) lowering the price has only a minor effect on increasing the sales volume and reducing the unit costs; and (4) customers interpret the high price as signifying high quality. These four conditions are most likely to exist when the new product is protected by patents or copyrights or its uniqueness is understood and valued by consumers. The conditions favoring penetration pricing are the reverse of those supporting skimming pricing: (1) many segments of the market are price sensitive; (2) a low initial price discourages competitors from entering the market; and (3) unit production and marketing costs fall dramatically as production volumes increase. A firm using penetration pricing may (1) maintain the initial price for a time to gain profit lost from its low introductory level or (2) lower the price further, counting on the new volume to generate the necessary profit.

3. What three key factors are necessary when estimating consumer demand?

Answer: consumer tastes, price and availability of similar products, and consumer income

4. Price elasticity of demand is _____.

Answer: the percentage change in the quantity demanded relative to a percentage change in price

5. What is the difference between fixed costs and variable costs?

Answer: Fixed cost is the sum of the expenses of the firm that are stable and do not change with the quantity of a product that is produced and sold. Variable cost is the sum of the expenses of the firm that vary directly with the quantity of a product that is produced and sold.

6. What is a break-even point?

Answer: A break-even point (BEP) is the quantity at which total revenue and total cost are equal.

7. What is the difference between pricing objectives and pricing constraints?

Answer: Pricing objectives specify the role of price in an organization's marketing and strategic plans. Pricing constraints are factors that limit the range of prices a firm may set.

8. Explain what bait and switch is and why it is an example of deceptive pricing.

Answer: Bait and switch is the practice of offering a very low price on a product (the bait) to attract customers to a store. Once in the store, the customer is persuaded to purchase a higher-priced item (the switch) using a variety of tricks, including (1) degrading the promoted item and (2) not having the promised item in stock or refusing to take orders for it.

9. What are the three steps in setting a final price?

Answer: They are: (1) select an appropriate price level; (2) set the list or quoted price; and (3) make special adjustments to the list or quoted price.

10. What is the purpose of (*a*) quantity discounts and (*b*) promotional allowances?

Answer: Quantity discounts are used to encourage customers to buy larger quantities of a product. Promotional allowances are used to encourage sellers in the channel of distribution to undertake certain advertising or selling activities to promote a product.

CHAPTER 12

1. What is meant by a marketing channel?

Answer: A marketing channel consists of individuals and firms involved in the process of making a product or service available for use or consumption by consumers or industrial users.

2. What are the three basic functions performed by intermediaries?

Answer: Intermediaries perform transactional, logistical, and facilitating functions.

3. What is the difference between a direct and an indirect channel?

Answer: A direct channel is one in which a producer of consumer or business products and services and ultimate consumers or industrial users deal directly with each other. An indirect channel has intermediaries that are inserted between the producer and ultimate consumers or industrial users and perform numerous channel functions.

4. Why are channels for business products typically shorter than channels for consumer products?

Answer: Business channels are typically shorter than consumer channels because business users are fewer in number, tend to be more concentrated geographically, and buy in larger quantities.

5. What is the principal distinction between a corporate vertical marketing system and an administered vertical marketing system?

Answer: A corporate vertical marketing system combines successive stages of production and distribution under a single ownership. An administered vertical marketing system achieves coordination by the size and influence of one channel member rather than through ownership.

6. What are the three questions marketing executives consider when choosing a marketing channel and intermediaries?

Answer: The three questions to consider when choosing a marketing channel and intermediaries are: (1) Which will provide the best coverage of the target market? (2) Which will best satisfy the buying requirements of the target market? (3) Which will be the most profitable?

7. What are the three degrees of distribution density?

Answer: intensive; exclusive; selective

8. What is the principal difference between a marketing channel and a supply chain?

Answer: A marketing channel consists of individuals and firms involved in the process of making a product or service available for use or consumption by consumers or industrial users. A supply chain differs from a marketing channel in terms of membership. It includes suppliers who provide raw materials to a manufacturer as well as the wholesalers and retailers—the marketing channel—that deliver the finished goods to ultimate consumers.

9. The choice of a supply chain involves what three steps?

Answer: (1) Understand the customer. (2) Understand the supply chain. (3) Harmonize the supply chain with the marketing strategy.

10. A manager's key task is to balance which four customer service factors against which six logistics cost factors?

Answer: The four customer service factors are time, dependability, communication, and convenience. The logistics cost factors are transportation costs, materials handling and warehousing costs, inventory costs, stockout costs (being out of inventory), and order processing costs. Another cost identified in Figure 12-9 and in the text is return products handling costs.

CHAPTER 13

1. When Ralph Lauren makes shirts to a customer's exact preferences, what utility is being provided?

Answer: form utility

2. Two measures of the impact of retailing in the global economy are _____ and _____.

Answer: the total annual sales; the number of employees working at large retailers

3. Centralized decision making and purchasing are an advantage of _____ ownership.

Answer: corporate chain

4. **What are some examples of new forms of self-service retailers?**
Answer: New forms of self-service are being developed at convenience stores, fast-food restaurants, and even libraries.

5. **Would a shop for big men's clothes carrying pants in sizes 40 to 60 have a broad or deep product line?**
Answer: deep product line; the range of sizes relates to the assortment of a product item (pants) rather than the variety of product lines (pants, shirts, shoes, etc.).

6. **Successful catalog retailers often send _____ catalogs to _____ markets identified in their databases.**
Answer: specialty; niche

7. **How are retailers increasing consumer interest and involvement in online retailing?**
Answer: Retailers have improved the online retailing experience by adding experiential or interactive activities to their websites, allowing customers to "build" virtual products by customizing their purchases.

8. **Where are direct selling retail sales growing? Why?**
Answer: Direct-selling retailers are (1) expanding into other global markets outside the United States and (2) reaching consumers who prefer one-on-one customer service and a social shopping experience rather than shopping online or at big discount stores.

9. **How does original markup differ from maintained markup?**
Answer: The original markup is the difference between retailer cost and initial selling price, whereas maintained markup is the difference between the final selling price and retailer cost, which is also called the gross margin.

10. **A huge shopping strip mall with multiple anchor stores is a _____ center.**
Answer: power

11. **What is a popular approach to managing the assortment of merchandise in a store?**
Answer: category management

12. **According to the wheel of retailing, when a new retail form appears, how would you characterize its image?**
Answer: a low-status, low-margin, low-price outlet

13. **Market share is usually fought out before the _____ stage of the retail life cycle.**
Answer: maturity

14. **What is the difference between merchant wholesalers and agents?**
Answer: Merchant wholesalers are independently owned firms that take title to the merchandise they handle. Agents do not take title to merchandise and typically perform fewer channel functions.

15. **Under what circumstances do producers assume wholesaling functions?**
Answer: Producers assume wholesaling functions when there are no intermediaries to perform these activities, customers are few in number and geographically concentrated, or orders are large or require significant attention.

CHAPTER 14

1. **What are the six elements required for communication to occur?**
Answer: The six elements required for communication to occur are: a source, a message, a channel of communication, a receiver, and the processes of encoding and decoding.

2. **A difficulty for U.S. companies advertising in international markets is that the audience does not share the same _____.**
Answer: field of experience

3. **A misprint in a newspaper ad is an example of _____.**
Answer: noise

4. **Explain the difference between advertising and publicity when both appear on television.**
Answer: Since advertising space on TV is paid for, a firm can control what it wants to say and to whom and how often the message is sent over a broadcast, cable, satellite, or local TV network. Since publicity is an indirectly paid presentation of a message about a firm or its products or services, the firm has little control over what is said to whom or

when. Instead, it can only suggest to the TV medium that it run a favorable story on the firm or its offerings.

5. **Cost per contact is high with the _____ element of the promotional mix.**
Answer: personal selling

6. **Which promotional element should be offered only on a short-term basis?**
Answer: sales promotion

7. **Promotional programs can be directed to _____, _____, or both.**
Answer: the ultimate consumer; an intermediary (retailer, wholesaler, or industrial distributor)

8. **Describe the promotional objective for each stage of the product life cycle.**
Answer: Introduction—to inform; Growth—to persuade; Maturity—to remind; and Decline—to phase out.

9. **Explain the differences between a push strategy and a pull strategy.**
Answer: In a push strategy, a firm directs the promotional mix to channel members to gain their cooperation in ordering and stocking the product. In a pull strategy, a firm directs the promotional mix at ultimate consumers to encourage them to ask retailers for the product, who then order it from wholesalers or the firm itself.

10. **What are the stages of the hierarchy of effects?**
Answer: The five stages of the hierarchy of effects are awareness, interest, evaluation, trial, and adoption.

11. **What are the four approaches to setting the promotion budget?**
Answer: The four approaches to setting the promotion budget are percentage of sales, competitive parity, all you can afford, and objective and task.

12. **How have advertising agencies changed to facilitate the use of IMC programs?**
Answer: Some agencies have adopted: (1) a total communications solutions approach that includes all forms of promotion; (2) an IMC audit to analyze the internal communication network of their clients; and (3) the use of both pretesting and posttesting to improve the effectiveness of IMC programs.

13. **The ability to design and use direct marketing programs has increased with the availability of _____ and _____.**
Answer: customer information databases; new printing technologies

14. **What are the three types of responses generated by direct marketing activities?**
Answer: They are direct orders, lead generation, and traffic generation.

CHAPTER 15

1. **What is the difference between pioneering and competitive ads?**
Answer: Pioneering ads, used in the introductory stage of the product life cycle, tell people what a product is, what it can do, and where it can be found. Competitive ads promote a specific brand's features and benefits to persuade the target market to select the firm's brand rather than that of a competitor.

2. **What is the purpose of an institutional advertisement?**
Answer: The purpose of an institutional advertisement is to build goodwill or an image for an organization.

3. **The Federal Communications Commission suggests that advertising program decisions be based on _____.**
Answer: market research about the target audience

4. **Describe three common forms of advertising appeals.**
Answer: The three common forms of advertising appeals are: (1) fear appeals, which suggest to the consumer that he or she can avoid some negative experience through the purchase and use of a product or service, a change in behavior, or a reduction in the use of a product; (2) sex appeals, which suggest to the audience that the product will increase the attractiveness of the user; and (3) humorous appeals, which imply either directly or subtly that the product is more fun or exciting than competitors' offerings.

5. **You see the same ad in *Time* and *Fortune* magazines and on billboards and TV. Is this an example of reach or frequency?**

Answer: Reach—using more of the same media type (magazines) as well as using more of different types of media (magazines, billboards, and TV)—is an attempt to maximize the number of individuals in a target market that are exposed to the advertisement. Frequency uses the same medium/media more than once to present the advertising message.

6. **Why has the Internet become a popular advertising medium?**

Answer: The Internet offers a visual message, can use both audio and video, is interactive through rich media, and tends to reach younger consumers.

7. **Describe three approaches to scheduling advertising.**

Answer: The three approaches to scheduling advertising are: (1) a continuous (steady) schedule, which is when advertising is run at a continuous or steady schedule throughout the year because seasonal factors are unimportant; (2) a flighting (intermittent) schedule, which is when periods of advertising are scheduled between periods of no advertising to reflect seasonal demand; and (3) a pulse (burst) schedule, which is when a flighting schedule is combined with a continuous schedule because of increases in demand, heavy periods of promotion, or introduction of a new product.

8. **Explain the difference between pretesting and posttesting advertising copy.**

Answer: Pretests are conducted before ads are placed in any medium to determine whether they communicate the intended message or to select among alternative versions of the ad. Posttests are shown to the target audience to determine whether it accomplished its intended purpose.

9. **What is the difference between aided and unaided recall posttests?**

Answer: Aided recall involves showing an ad to respondents who then are asked if their previous exposure to it was through reading, viewing, or listening. Unaided recall involves specifically asking respondents if they remember an ad without any prompting to determine if they saw or heard its message.

10. **Which sales promotional tool is most common for new products?**
Answer: samples

11. **Which trade promotion is used to encourage the local advertising efforts of resellers?**
Answer: cooperative advertising

12. **What is a news release?**
Answer: A news release is an announcement regarding changes in the company or the product line.

13. **What type of publicity tool is used most often by nonprofit organizations?**
Answer: public service announcements (PSAs)

CHAPTER 16

1. **What do we mean by social media?**
Answer: Social media are online media where users submit comments, photos, and videos—often accompanied by a feedback process to identify "popular" topics. Business firms also refer to social media as "consumer-generated media."

2. **In classifying social media, what do we mean by (a) media richness and (b) self-disclosure?**
Answer: Social media can be classified based on two factors: (a) Media richness involves the degree of acoustic, visual, and personal contact between two communication partners. For example, face-to-face communication is higher in media richness than telephone or e-mail communication. The higher the media richness and quality of presentation, the greater the social influence that these communication partners have on each other's behavior. (b) Self-disclosure involves the degree to which an individual shares his or her thoughts, feelings, likes, and dislikes when engaged in a social interaction. Typically, this person wants to make a positive impression to achieve a favorable image with others. The greater the self-disclosure, the greater the likelihood that the person will increase his or her influence on those reached.

3. **Compare traditional media and social media in terms of time to delivery of the communication.**
Answer: Traditional media can involve days or even months of continuing effort to deliver the communication, and time lags can be extensive. In contrast, individuals using social media can post virtually instantaneous content.

4. **How is "user generated content" presented by someone using Facebook?**
Answer: User generated content (UGC) refers to the various forms of online media content that are publicly available and created by end users. Facebook is a website where users create a personal profile, add other users as friends, and exchange comments, photos, videos, and "likes" with them. Facebook users today can keep friends and family updated on what a user is thinking, doing, and feeling. Additionally, users may chat with friends and create and join common-interest groups.

5. **What are some ways brand managers use Facebook to converse with a brand's fans?**
Answer: A brand manager can create awareness for a product, service, or brand by creating a Facebook Page for it. Done well, this is a magnet for feedback. Facebook allows brand managers to request a range of user data like addresses and phone numbers—with the users' permission (an "opt-in" approach). Brand managers can also use Facebook's "sponsored stories" to buy and republish Facebook messages about their brands. The marketing challenge for a Facebook Page is to post and create the content that will generate the best response. Most ads for a brand on a Facebook site appear on the right-hand side of the page. An advantage of a Facebook ad for a brand is that it can migrate into Facebook conversations among friends—to the delight of advertisers. If a brand manager uses Facebook's News Feed, which appears on every user's home page, it can be used to highlight profile changes, identify upcoming events regarding the brand, and provide links so users can participate in the activity.

6. **What are the major differences between Facebook and YouTube that are of interest to brand managers?**
Answer: According to Figure 16-3, Facebook has slightly more female users than YouTube. So, if a brand manager wants to reach males with an ad for a brand, he/she more likely would use YouTube. Both Facebook and YouTube enable a brand manager to promote the brand but in different ways: Facebook has a platform that connects with the firm's brand website. YouTube allows brand managers to create an actual brand channel to host its advertisements and other video clips that can explain complex information and/or provide product demonstrations that may be of interest to users. It too can link to a brand's website. Both Facebook and YouTube allow users to share their opinions with other users through the "Like" and the "Comment" features. However, YouTube, because it's a more visual medium, allows a brand manager to entertain as well as inform users about the brand. YouTube traffic goes directly to the video; a hyperlink is needed to get users back to the brand's website. Facebook, on the other hand, uses customized tabs and buttons to direct users to the brand's website.

7. **What is the difference between (and marketing significance of) a "passive receiver" for conventional media and an "active receiver" for social media?**
Answer: Traditional media, like magazine or TV ads, generally use one-way communication from sender to receiver, who the marketer hopes will buy the product advertised. A little word-of-mouth chatting may occur among the consumer "passive receivers" but communications generally end with the receiver. Social media deliberately seek to ensure that the message does not end with an individual receiver. Instead, the goal is to reach "active receivers," those who will become "influentials" and be "delighted" with the brand advertised. These will then become "evangelists," who will send messages—user generated content—to their online friends and then back to the advertiser about the joys of using the brand. So success in social media marketing relies heavily on the ability of a marketing program to convert passive "receivers" of the message to active "evangelists" who will spread favorable messages about the brand.

8. Stated simply, how can an advertiser on Facebook expect to generate sales?

Answer: The brand manager composes title, copy, and images or photos in an ad that would be placed on Facebook through its Facebook Ad Platform. A website address would link the ad to the brand's website or its Facebook Page. To encourage and produce new sales that can be tracked, the brand manager could also link the ad to a coupon code or some other promotional offer.

9. How did Nestlé's initial overreaction to the Greenpeace campaign heighten its problems?

Answer: Greenpeace created its "Killer" campaign against Nestlé's Kit Kat candy bar because it used palm oil from palm trees in Indonesia—ones that were not only cut down but also were home to orangutans. Nestlé's response to Greepeace's campaign unwittingly led to increased online attention and animosity. At Nestlé's request, YouTube removed the video that Nestlé believed infringed on its Kit Kat brand. The result: Views of the video on other sites like Vimeo skyrocketed in the next 24 hours. Also, Nestlé's Kit Kat Facebook users who were violently opposed to its deforestation actions had "brand-jacked" the Nestlé Kit-Kat Facebook Page. Within 60 days, Nestlé's management took steps to drop palm oil suppliers linked to deforestation. Greenpeace thus effectively orchestrated the crowd power of social media to pressure Nestlé into a strategic policy change.

10. What is an example of how the real (physical) and digital (virtual) worlds are converging?

Answer: Social media will increasingly migrate into smart systems, consisting of interlinked smartphones, tablet devices, sensors, special identification tags, databases, algorithms, apps, and other elements (see Figure 16–6).

11. What are apps and why are they important?

Answer: Apps are small, downloadable software programs that run on smartphones and tablet devices. They are speeding up the convergence of the real (physical) and digital (virtual) worlds. Many apps are related to social media, such as programs for (1) price-comparison searches, (2) loyalty programs, and (3) location-based promotions.

12. How does T-Mobile's Czech ad campaign featuring Chuck Norris show the global marketing reach of social media?

Answer: In terms of global marketing, an ad using social media can go "viral," meaning that thousands or millions of people can view, like, and comment on it—if effective, entertaining, or informative. An example is the Czech Republic T-Mobile TV ad that caused thousands of people to become fans of T-Mobile on its Facebook Page while millions watched it on YouTube. In addition, consumers in Poland and Slovakia loved the ads as well.

CHAPTER 17

1. What is personal selling?

Answer: Personal selling involves the two-way flow of communication between a buyer and seller, often in a face-to-face encounter, designed to influence a person's or group's purchase decision.

2. What is involved in sales management?

Answer: Sales management involves planning the selling program and implementing and evaluating the personal selling effort of the firm.

3. What is the principal difference between an order taker and an order getter?

Answer: An order taker processes routine orders or reorders for products that were already sold by the company. An order getter sells in a conventional sense and identifies prospective customers, provides customers with information, persuades customers to buy, closes sales, and follows up on customers' use of a product or service.

4. What percentage of an order-getting salesperson's time is spent selling?

Answer: 41 percent

5. What are the six stages in the personal selling process?

Answer: The six stages in the personal selling process are: (1) prospecting, (2) preapproach, (3) approach, (4) presentation, (5) close, and (6) follow-up.

6. Which presentation format is most consistent with the marketing concept? Why?

Answer: The need-satisfaction presentation format emphasizes probing and listening by the salesperson to identify the needs and interests of prospective buyers and then tailors the presentation to the prospect and highlights product benefits, which is consistent with the marketing concept and its focus on relationship building.

7. What are the three types of selling objectives?

Answer: The three types of selling objectives are: (1) output-related (dollars or unit sales, new customers, profit); (2) input-related (sales calls, selling expenses); and (3) behavioral-related (product knowledge, customer service, selling and communication skills).

8. What three factors are used to structure sales organizations?

Answer: geography; customer; product/service

CHAPTER 18

1. The consumer-initiated practice of generating content on a marketer's website that is custom tailored to an individual's specific needs and preferences is called _____.

Answer: personalization

2. Companies produce a customer experience through what seven website design elements?

Answer: The seven website design elements are: context, content, community, customization, communication, connection, and commerce.

3. What is viral marketing?

Answer: Viral marketing is an Internet-enabled promotional strategy that encourages individuals to forward marketer-initiated messages to others via e-mail.

4. What are the six reasons consumers prefer to shop and buy online?

Answer: The six reasons why consumers prefer to shop and buy online are: convenience, choice, customization, communication, cost, and control.

5. A cross-channel shopper is _____.

Answer: an online consumer who researches products online and then purchases them at a retail store

6. Channel conflict between manufacturers and retailers is likely to arise when manufacturers use _____ websites.

Answer: transactional

CHAPTER NOTES

Chapter 1

1. The 3M Post-it® Flag Highlighter and Post-it® Flag Pen examples are based on a series of interviews and meetings with David Windorski, 3M, from 2004 to 2011.
2. The *Oprah Winfrey Show,* January 15, 2008.
3. Lev Grossman, "2010 Person of the Year: Mark Zuckerberg," *Time,* December 27, 2010–January 3, 2011, pp. 44–75; and Ben Mezrich, *The Accidental Billionaire* (New York: Anchor Books, 2009), pp. 92–150.
4. To compare the 2004 and 2007 American Marketing Association definitions of "marketing," see Lisa M. Keefe, "Marketing Defined," *Marketing News,* January 15, 2008, pp. 28–29.
5. Richard P. Bagozzi, "Marketing as Exchange," *Journal of Marketing,* October 1975, pp. 32–39; and Gregory T. Gundlach and Patrick E. Murphy, "Ethical and Legal Foundations of Relational Marketing Exchanges," *Journal of Marketing,* October 1993, pp. 35–46.
6. "The Rise of the Creative Consumer," *The Economist,* March 12, 2005, pp. 54–60.
7. Productscan® Online database of new products, from *Marketing Intelligence Service,* December 17, 2003, www.productscan.com.
8. Robert M. McMath and Thom Forbes, "What *Were* They Thinking?" (New York: Times Business, 1998), pp. 3–22; also see http://www .gfkamerica.com/practice_areas/gfk_innovation/ newproductworks/index.en.html.
9. Ibid.
10. W. J. Hennigan, "Wheels Up," *Star Tribune,* April 27, 2012, p. M1; and from the Terrafugia website, http://www.terrafugia.com.
11. Martinne Geller, "Pepsi Counts on 'Next' to Lure Back Lost Drinkers," *Reuters,* March 13, 2012. See http://www.reuters.com/ article/2012/03/13/pepsico-idUSL2E8E9HSP20120313.
12. Kara McGuire, "New Credit Rules Are No Reason to Let Guard Down," *Star Tribune,* January 31, 2010, pp. D1, D2; and Sandra Block, "How the Credit Card Reforms Will Affect You," *USA Today,* February 22, 2010, p. 38.
13. Jerome McCarthy, *Basic Marketing: A Managerial Approach* (Homewood, IL: Richard D. Irwin, 1960); and Walter van Waterschool and Christophe Van den Bulte, "The 4P Classification of the Marketing Mix Revisited," *Journal of Marketing,* October 1992, pp. 83–93.
14. David J. Collis and Michael G. Rukstad, "Can You Say What Your Strategy Is?" *Harvard Business Review,* April 2008, pp. 82–90; and Roger A. Kerin and Robert A. Peterson, *Strategic Marketing Problems: Cases and Comments,* 12th ed. (Upper Saddle River, NJ: Prentice-Hall, 2010), p. 12.
15. Ashish Kothari and Joseph Lackner, "A Value Based Approach to Management," *Journal of Business and Industrial Marketing,* 21, no. 4, pp. 243–49; and James C. Anderson, James A. Narius, and Wouter van Rossum, "Customer Value Propositions in Business Markets," *Harvard Business Review,* March 2006, pp. 91–99.
16. For an examination of both the drivers and outcomes of consumer satisfaction programs, see Leslie M. Fine, "Spotlight on Marketing," *Business Horizons,* 49 (2006), pp. 179–83.
17. V. Kumar, *Managing Customers for Profit* (Upper Saddle River, NJ: Pearson Education, 2008); and "What's a Loyal Customer Worth?" *Fortune,* December 11, 1995, p. 182.
18. Michael Treacy and Fred D. Wiersema, *The Discipline of Market Leaders* (Reading, MA: Addison-Wesley, 1995); Michael Treacy and Fred Wiersema, "How Market Leaders Keep Their Edge," *Fortune* (February 6, 1995), pp. 88–89; and Michael Treacy, "You Need a Value Discipline—But Which One?" *Fortune* (April 17, 1995), p. 195.
19. Robert W. Palmatier, Rajiv P. Dant, Dhruv Grewal, and Kenneth R. Evans, "Factors Influencing the Effectiveness of Relationship Marketing: A Meta-Analysis," *Journal of Relationship Marketing,* October 2006, pp. 136–53; and William Boulding, Richard Staelin, Michael Ehret, and Wesley J. Johnson, "A Customer Relationship Management Roadmap: What Is Known, Potential Pitfalls, and Where to Go," *Journal of Marketing,* October 2005, pp. 155–66.
20. Susan Foumier, Susan Dobscha, and David Glen Mick, "Preventing the Premature Death of Relationship Marketing," *Harvard Business Review,* January–February 1998, pp. 42–51.
21. See www.oprah.com for January 15, 2008; and "Post-it® Flags Co-Sponsors Oprah's Live Web Event," *3M Stemwinder,* March 4–17, 2008, p. 3.
22. Reservations about and elaborations of these simplified stages appear in D. G. Brian Jones and Eric H. Shaw, "A History of Marketing Thought," Chapter 2 in *Handbook of Marketing,* edited by Barton Weitz and Robin Wensley (London: Sage Publications, 2006), pp. 39–65; Frederic E. Webster, Jr., "The Role of Marketing and the Firm," Chapter 3 in *Handbook of Marketing,* ed. Barton Weitz and Robin Wensley (London: Sage Publications, 2006), pp. 66–82; and Frederick E. Webster, Jr., "Back to the Future: Integrating Marketing as Tactics, Strategy and Organizational Culture," *Journal of Marketing,* October 2005, pp. 4–8.
23. Robert F. Keith, "The Marketing Revolution," *Journal of Marketing,* January 1960, pp. 35–38.
24. *Annual Report* (New York: General Electric Company, 1952), p. 21.
25. John C. Narver, Stanley F. Slater, and Brian Tietje, "Creating a Market Orientation," *Journal of Market Focused Management,* no. 2 (1998), pp. 241–55; Stanley F. Slater and John C. Narver, "Market Orientation and the Learning Organization," *Journal of Marketing,* July 1995, pp. 63–74; and George S. Day, "The Capabilities of Market-Driven Organizations," *Journal of Marketing,* October 1994, pp. 37–52.
26. The definition of customer relationship management is adapted from Rajendra K. Srivastava, Tasadduq A. Shervani, and Liam Fahey, "Marketing, Business Processes, and Shareholder Value: An Embedded View of Marketing Activities and the Discipline of Marketing," *Journal of Marketing,* special issue (1999), pp. 168–79; Gary F. Gebhardt, Gregory S. Carpenter, and John F. Sherry Jr., "Creating a Market Orientation: A Longitudinal, Multifirm, Grounded Analysis of Cultural Transformation," *Journal of Marketing,* October 2006, pp. 37–55; and Christopher Meyer and Andre Schwager, "Understanding Customer Experience," *Harvard Business Review,* February 2007, pp. 117–26.
27. Gary F. Gebhardt, Gregory S. Carpenter, and John F. Sherry Jr., "Creating a Market Orientation: A Longitudinal, Multifirm, Grounded Analysis of Cultural Transformation," *Journal of Marketing,* October 2006, pp. 37–55.
28. Beth Kowitt, "Inside Trader Joe's," *Fortune,* September 6, 2010, p. 87.
29. Christopher Meyer and Andre Schwager, "Understanding Customer Experience," *Harvard Business Review,* February 2007, pp. 117–26.
30. Michael E. Porter and Claas van der Linde, "Green and Competitive Ending the Stalemate," *Harvard Business Review,* September–October 1995, pp. 120–34; Jacquelyn Ottman, "Edison Winners Show Smart Environmental Marketing," *Marketing News,* July 17, 1995, pp. 16, 19; and Jacquelyn Ottman, "Mandate for the '90s: Green Corporate Image," *Marketing News,* September 11, 1995, p.8.
31. Philip Kotler and Sidney J. Levy, "Broadening the Concept of Marketing," *Journal of Marketing,* January 1969, pp. 10–15; and Jim Rendon, "When Nations Need a Little Marketing," *The New York Times,* November 23, 2003, p. BU6.

32. Peter Gumbel, "Louvre, Inc." *Time,* August 11, 2008, pp. 51–52; and Stella Wai-Art Law, *A Branding Context: The Guggenheim and the Louvre* (Columbus, OH: The Ohio State University, M.A. Thesis, 2008).

33. William L. Wilkie and Elizabeth S. Moore, "Marketing's Relationship to Society," Chapter 1 in *Handbook of Marketing,* ed. Barton Weitz and Robin Wensley (London: Sage Publications, 2006), pp. 9–38.

3M's Post-it® Flag Highlighters: This case was written by Michael J. Vessey and William Rudelius and is based on a series of personal interviews with David Windorski and 3M from 2004 to 2011.

Chapter 2

1. Information obtained from selected web pages and press releases from the Ben & Jerry's website. See www.benjerry.com.

2. "Ice Cream: Global Industry Guide," *Datamonitor,* April 27, 2010, press release posted at MarketResearch.com.

3. Roger Kerin and Robert Peterson, *Strategic Marketing Problems: Cases and Comments,* 12th ed. (Upper Saddle River, NJ: Prentice Hall, 2010), p. 140.

4. See http://www.teachforamerica.org; and Wendy Kaufman, "Ex-Starbucks Exec Helps Develop Global Eye Banks," *National Public Radio,* March 8, 2011.

5. For a discussion on how industries are defined and offerings are classified, see the following resources: the American Marketing Association website, which provides one definition of an industry (www.marketingpower.com/mg-dictionary-view1509.php); and the Census Bureau's Economic Classification Policy Committee Issues Paper #1 (www.census.gov/epcd/naics/issues1), which aggregates industries in the NAICS (www.census.gov/epcd/www/naicsdev.htm) from a "production-oriented" view (see Chapter 6).

6. W. Chan Kim and Reneé Mauborgne, "Blue Ocean Strategy: From Theory to Practice," *California Management Review* 47, no. 3 (Spring 2005), p. 105; Michael E. Porter, "What Is Strategy?" *Harvard Business Review* OnPoint Article, November–December 1996, p. 2.

7. The definition of *strategy* reflects thoughts appearing in Porter, "What Is Strategy?" pp. 4, 8; a condensed definition of strategy is found on the American Marketing Association website www.marketingpower.com; Gerry Johnson, Kevan Scholes, and Richard Wittington, *Exploring Corporate Strategy* (Upper Saddle River, NJ: Prentice Hall, 2005), p. 10; and Costas Markides, "What Is Strategy and How Do You Know If You Have One?" *Business Strategy Review* 15, no. 2 (Summer 2004), p. 5.

8. John Kador, "The View from Marketing: How to Get the Most from Your CMO," *Chief Executive,* July/August 2011, pp. 60–61; Jessica Shambora, "Wanted: Fearless Marketing Execs," *Fortune,* April 15, 2011, p. 27; Roger A. Kerin, "Strategic Marketing and the CMO," *Journal of Marketing,* October 2005, pp. 12–13; and The CMO Council: Biographies of Selected Advisory Board Members. See www.cmocouncil.org/advisoryboard.html.

9. Taken in part from Jim Collins and Jerry I. Porras, *Built to Last: Successful Habits of Visionary Companies* (New York: HarperCollins Publishers, 2002), p. 54.

10. Ibid., p. 73; Patrick M. Lencioni, "Make Your Values Mean Something," *Harvard Business Review,* July 2002, p. 6; and Aubrey Malphurs, *Values-Driven Leadership: Discovering and Developing Your Core Values for Ministry,* 2nd ed. (Grand Rapids, MI: Baker-Books, 2004), p. 31.

11. Collins and Porras, *Built to Last,* p. 73; and Lencioni, "Make Your Values Mean Something," p. 6.

12. Catherine M. Dalton, "When Organizational Values Are Mere Rhetoric," *Business Horizons* 49 (September–October 2006), p. 345.

13. Collins and Porras, *Built to Last,* pp. 94–95; and Tom Krattenmaker, "Write a Mission Statement That Your Company Is Willing to Live," *Harvard Management Communication Letter,* March 2002, pp. 3–4.

14. Janet Moore, "Change of Pace," *Star Tribune,* May 23, 2010, pp. D1, D8.

15. Tom Holloran, "Remarks to Medtronic Employees at the Celebration of the 50th Anniversary of Earl Bakken's Invention of the Wearable Pacemaker," December 6, 2007; and Janet Moore, "An Enduring Mission," *Star Tribune,* December 27, 2010, pp. D1, D2.

16. Kenneth E. Goodpaster and Thomas E. Holloran, "Anatomy of Spiritual and Social Awareness: The Case of Medtronic, Inc.," *Third International Symposium on Catholic Social Thought and Management Education,* Goa, India, 1999, pp. 9–11.

17. Theodore Levitt, "Marketing Myopia," *Harvard Business Review,* July–August 1960, pp. 45–56.

18. David Phelps, "Debt Threat," *Star Tribune,* January 26, 2009, pp. D1, D6.

19. Jeffrey A. Trachtenberg, "E-Books Rewrite Bookselling," *The Wall Street Journal,* May 20, 2010, pp. A1, A12.

20. Nick Wingfied, "Netflix Warns Price Rise Will Clip Growth," *The Wall Street Journal,* July 26, 2011, p. B9; Ronald Grover, "Netflix: Premium Cable's Worst Nightmare," *Bloomberg Businessweek,* September 20–September 26, 2010, pp. A1, A2; Stephen Gandel, "How Blockbuster Failed at Failing," *Time,* October 11, 2010, pp. 38–40; Damon Darlin, "Always Pushing beyond the Envelope," *The New York Times,* August 8, 2010, p. BU5; Alyssa Abkowitz, "The Movie Man," *Fortune,* February 2, 2009, p. 24; David Pogue, "Any Movie, Any Time," *Star Tribune,* February 4, 2009, p. D6; and Nick Wingfield, "Netflix Boss Plots Life after the DVD," *The Wall Street Journal,* June 23, 2009, pp. A1, A12.

21. The definition is adapted from Stephen Few, *Information Dashboard Design: The Effective Visual Communication of Data* (Sebastopol, CA: O'Reilly Media, Inc., 2006), pp. 2–46.

22. Koen Pauwels et al., *Dashboards & Marketing: Why, What, How and What Research Is Needed?* (Hanover, NH: Tuck School, Dartmouth, May 2008).

23. Few, *Information Dashboard Design;* Bruce H. Clark, Andrew V. Abela, and Tim Ambler, "Behind the Wheel," *Marketing Management,* May–June 2006, pp. 19–23; Spencer E. Ante, "Giving the Boss the Big Picture," *BusinessWeek,* February 13, 2006, pp. 48–49; *Dashboard Tutorial* (Cupertino, CA: Apple Computer, Inc., 2006).

24. Few, *Information Dashboard Design,* p. 13.

25. Mark Jeffrey, *Data-Driven Marketing: The 15 Metrics Everyone in Marketing Should Know* (Hoboken, NJ: John Wiley & Sons, Inc., 2010), Chapter 1; Michael Krauss, "Balance Attention to Metrics with Intuition," *Marketing News,* June 1, 2007, pp. 6–8; John Davis, *Measuring Marketing: 103 Key Metrics Every Marketer Needs* (Singapore: John Wiley & Sons [Asia] Pte Ltd., 2007); and Paul W. Farris, Neil T. Bendle, Phillip E. Pfeifer, and David J. Reibstein, *Marketing Metrics,* 2nd ed. (Upper Saddle River, NJ: Wharton School Publishing, 2010).

26. Alexander Chiang, "Special Interview with Stephen Few, Dashboard and Data Visualization Expert," *Dundas Dashboard,* July 14, 2011; Stephen Few, *Now You See It* (Oakland, CA: Analytics Press, 2009), Chapters 1–3; Jacques Bughin, Amy Guggenheim Shenkan, and Mark Singer, "How Poor Metrics Undermine Digital Marketing," *The McKinsey Quarterly,* October 2008.

27. The now-classic reference on effective graphic presentation is Edward R. Tufte, *The Visual Display of Quantitative Information,* 2nd Edition (Cheshire, CN: Graphic Press, 2001); also see Few, *Information Dashboard Design,* chaps. 3–5.

28. George Stalk, Phillip Evans, and Lawrence E. Shulman, "Competing on Capabilities: The New Rules of Corporate Strategy," *Harvard Business Review,* March–April 1992, pp. 57–69; and Darrell K. Rigby, *Management Tools 2007: An Executive's Guide* (Boston: Bain & Company, 2007), p. 22.

29. Michael Arndt, "High-Tech and Handcrafted," *BusinessWeek,* July 5, 2004, pp. 86–87.

30. Kerin and Peterson, *Strategic Marketing Problems,* pp. 2–3; and Derek F. Abell, *Defining the Business* (Englewood Cliffs, NJ: Prentice Hall, 1980), p. 18.

31. Robert D. Hof, "How to Hit a Moving Target," *BusinessWeek,* August 21, 2006, p. 3; and Peter Kim, *Reinventing the Marketing Organization* (Cambridge, MA: Forrester, July 13, 2006), pp. 7, 9, and 17.

32. Adapted from *The Experience Curve Reviewed, IV. The Growth Share Matrix of the Product Portfolio* (Boston: The Boston Consulting Group, 1973).

33. Roger A. Kerin, Vijay Mahajan, and P. Rajan Varadarajan, *Contemporary Perspectives on Strategic Marketing Planning* (Boston: Allyn & Bacon, 1990), p. 52.

34. "The Last Kodak Moment?" *The Economist,* January 14, 2012, pp. 63–64; and "Turn Around?" *The Economist,* January 21, 2012, p. 8.

35. Mike Spector and Dana Mattioli, "Kodak Teeters on the Brink," *The Wall Street Journal,"* January 5, 2012, pp. A1, A2; John Bussey, "Kodak's Long, Slow Slide," *The Wall Street Journal,* January 5, 2012, p. A2; "Kodak Focuses Consumer Business on More Profitable Growth Opportunities: Plans to Phase Out Dedicated Capture Device Business," press release, February 9, 2012, see http://www.kodak.com/ek/US/en/Kodak_Focuses_Consumer_Business_On_More_Profitable_Growth_Opportunities.htm; "Camera Industry Trends," *6Sight Magazine,* February–March 2012, p. 5, see http://6sightreport.com/wp-content/uploads/2012/03/March-2012-6Sight-Report.pdf; and Yukihiko Matsumoto, "Fine-Tuning the Niche Markets," *PMA Magazine,* November–December 2011, p. 16.

36. "Internet Imaging: Facebook Filing Shows Photo Focus," *6Sight Magazine,* February–March 2012, p. 41; and Yukihiko Matsumoto, "Fine-Tuning the Niche Markets," pp. 16–17, see http://www.nxtbook.com/nxtbooks/pmamag/20111112/index.php.

37. Paul Worthington, "Lessons from the Eastman Kodak Bankruptcy Filing," *PMA Magazine,* Winter 2012, pp. 4, 6–8, see http://www.nxtbook.com/nxtbooks/pmamag/2012winter/index.php; "1 million Facebookers Printing from Kodak Kiosks," Kiosk marketplace.com, January 8, 2012, see http://www.kioskmarketplace.com/article/188799/1-million-Facebookers-printing-from-Kodak-kiosks; "New Picture Printing Products from Fujifilm," *6Sight Magazine,* February–March 2012, p. 45; and Dan Balaban, "Photo Kiosks to Get Instant Bluetooth Pairing with NFC Tags" *NFC Times,* March 26, 2012, see http://www.nfctimes.com/news/photo-kiosks-get-instant-bluetooth-pairing-nfc-tags.

38. H. Igor Ansoff, "Strategies for Diversification," *Harvard Business Review,* September–October 1957, pp. 113–24.

39. Linda Swenson and Kenneth E. Goodpaster, *Medtronic in China (A)* (Minneapolis, MN: University of St. Thomas, 1999), pp. 4–5.

IBM: This case was written by Steven Hartley. Sources: Jessi Hempel, "IBM's Super Second Act," *Fortune,* March 21, 2011, pp. 114–124; Bruce Upbin, "IBM Plays Jeopardy!" *Forbes,* January 17, 2011, pp. 36–37; Kurt Badenhausen, "The World's Most Valuable Brands," *Forbes,* August 30, 2010, p. 34; Jeffrey M. O'Brien, "IBM's Grand Plan to Save the Planet," *Fortune,* May 4, 2009, pp. 84–91; *IBM 2009 Annual Report; IBM 2010 Annual Report;* Samuel J. Palmisano, "Our Values at Work on Being an IBMer," IBM website, http://www.ibm.com/ibm/values/us/, accessed July 5, 2011; "Welcome to the Decade of Smart," IBM website, http://www.ibm.com/smarterplanet/global/files/us_en_us_overview_decade_of_smart_011310.pdf, accessed July 7, 2011.

Appendix A

1. Personal interview with Arthur R. Kydd, St. Croix Management Group.

2. Examples of guides to writing marketing plans include William A. Cohen, *The Marketing Plan,* 5th ed. (New York: Wiley and Sons, 2006); and Roman G. Hiebing, Jr., and Scott W. Cooper, *The Successful Business Plan: A Disciplined and Comprehensive Approach* (New York: McGraw-Hill, 2008).

3. Examples of guides to writing business plans include Steven D. Peterson, Peter Jaret, and Barbara Findlay Schenck, *Business Plans Kit for Dummies,* 3rd. ed. (Hoboken, NJ: Wiley Publishing, Inc., 2010); Rhonda Abrams, *Business Plan in a Day,* 2nd ed. (Palo Alto, CA: The Planning Shop, a Division of Rhonda, Inc., 2009); Rhonda Abrams, *The Successful Business Plan,* 5th ed. (Palo Alto, CA: The Planning Shop, a Division of Rhonda, Inc., 2010); Joseph A. Covello and Brian J. Hazelgren, *The Complete Book of Business Plans,* 2nd ed. (Naperville, IL: Sourcebooks, 2006); Joseph A. Covello and Brian J. Hazelgren, *Your First Business Plan,* 5th ed. (Naperville, IL: Sourcebooks, 2005); and Mike McKeever, *How to Write a Business Plan,* 8th ed. (Berkeley, CA: Nolo, 2007).

4. Abrams, *The Successful Business Plan,* p. 41.

5. Some of these points are adapted from Abrams, *The Successful Business Plan,* pp. 41–49; others were adapted from William Rudelius, *Guidelines for Technical Report Writing* (Minneapolis: University of Minnesota, undated). See also William Strunk, Jr., and E. B. White, *The Elements of Style,* 4th ed. (Needham Heights, MA: Allyn & Bacon, 2000).

6. Rebecca Zimoch, "The Dawn of the Frozen Age," *Grocery Headquarters,* December 2002; see www.groceryheadquarters.com.

7. ACNielsen Strategic Planner as reported to the National Frozen & Refrigerated Foods Association for the week ending February 24, 2007; see www.nfraweb.org.

8. Chuck Van Hyning, *NPD's National Eating Trends;* see www.npdfoodworld.com.

9. Jeffrey M. Humphreys, "The Multicultural Economy 2009," *Georgia Business and Economic Conditions* 69, no. 3 (Third Quarter, 2009), pp. 1–13.

Chapter 3

1. David Kirkpatrick, *The Facebook Effect* (New York: Simon and Schuster, 2010); Barry Libert, *Social Nation* (Hoboken, New Jersey: John Wiley & Sons, Inc.); Lev Grossman, "2010 Person of the Year: Mark Zuckerberg," *Time,* December 27, 2010–January 3, 2011, pp. 44–75; and http://gold.insidenetwork.com/facebook/facebook_stats.

2. "The HBR Agenda," *Harvard Business Review,* January–February 2011, pp. 47–59; Ann Marie Kerwin, "10 Trends That Are Shaping Global Media Consumption," *Advertising Age,* December 6, 2010, p. 3; Christine Birkner and Piet Levy, "Marketing in 2011," *Marketing News,* January 30, 2011, pp. 14–36; Thomas Miner, "FTC Releases Revised Green Guides for Public Input," www.sustainablelifemedia.com, October 7, 2010; and Ann M. Mack, "100 Things to Watch in 2011," www.jwintelligence.com, December 2010.

3. *2011 World Population Data Sheet* (Washington, D.C.: Population Reference Bureau, 2011), pp. 2, 6.

4. "2010 Census Count," United States Census, April 1, 2010, www.2010.census.gov, February 14, 2011; Ellen Byron, "How to Market to an Aging Boomer: Flattery, Subterfuge and Euphemism," *The Wall Street Journal,* February 5, 2011, p. A1; "Projections of the Population and Components of Change for the United States," U.S. Census Bureau, Table 1, August 14, 2008; and "Projections of the Population by Selected Age Groups and Sex for the United States," U.S. Census Bureau, Table 2, August 14, 2008.

5. Ellen Byron, "How to Market to an Aging Boomer,": p. A1; Emily Bryson York and Natalie Zmuda, "Baby Boomers Help PepsiCo's Frito-Lay See a Boom in Business," *Advertising Age,* March 29, 2010, p. 4; and Emily Brandon, "10 Things You Didn't Know about Baby Boomers," *USNews.com,* January 15, 2009.

6. Anne Fisher, "When Gen X Runs the Show," *Time,* May 25, 2009, pp. 48–49; "New Hyatt Place Will Have No Front Desk," *Grand Rapids Press,* June 25, 2008, p. C1; Kimberly Palmer, "Gen X-ers: Stingy or Strapped?" *USNews.com,* February 14, 2007; Paul J. Lim, "Baby Boomers Outpace Gen X-ers," *USNews.com,* March 12, 2007; and Megan Rowe, "Marketing to Gen X," Financial & Insurance Meetings, July 1, 2006, p. 19.

7. Elizabeth Olson, "For Millennials, It's More about Personal Style Than Luxury," *The New York Times,* November 3, 2010, p. 3; Laura Vanderkam, "Graduates, You Can Have It All," *USA Today,* May 27, 2010, p. 11A; Carla Seaquist, "Hope for Reversing America's Decline: the Millennial Generation," *The Christian Science Monitor,* September 24, 2010; Geoff Gloeckler, "Here Come the Millennials," *BusinessWeek,* November 24, 2008, p. 47; Sarah Littman, "Welcome to the New Millennials," *Response,* May 1, 2008, p. 74; "The Echo Boom Gets Louder," *Multi-Housing News,* December 4, 2008; Eileen P. Gunn, "Is Your Company Really Eco-Conscious?" *USNews.com,* October 9, 2008; "Welcome Generation Y," *Management Today,* July 10, 2008; and Eileen P. Gunn, "10 Hot Green Careers for You," *USNews.com,* February 15, 2009.

8. "An Older and More Diverse Nation by Midcentury," Public Information Office, U.S. Census Bureau, Last Revised: February 2, 2011, Table 4: Projections of the Population by Sex, Race, and Hispanic Origin for the United States: 2010 to 2050 (NP2008-T4), Population Division, U.S. Census Bureau, August 14, 2008; "Mapping Census 2000: The Geography of U.S. Diversity," Population Division, U.S. Census Bureau; "The New Now: Defining the Future Together," *PR Newswire,* February 18, 2011; "African-American Consumer Buying Power Nearing $1 Trillion in 2010," *Progressive Grocer,* January 21, 2010; Jeffrey M. Humphreys, *The Multicultural Economy 2009,* volume 69, no. 3, Selig Center for Economic Growth, The University of Georgia; and Sam Fahmy, "Despite Recession, Hispanic and Asian Buying Power Expected to Surge in U.S.," *Multicultural Economy Study,* UGA Selig Center, http://www.terry.uga.edu/news/releases/2010/minority-buying-power-report.html.

9. Robin M. Williams Jr., *American Society: A Sociological Interpretation,* Third Edition (New York: Knoph, 1970); L. Robert Kohls, Why Do Americans Act Like That? International Programs, San Francisco State University; Eric Pooley, David Welch, and Alan Ohnsman, "Charged for Battle," *Bloomberg Businessweek,* January 3, 2011, pp. 48–56; Christopher Martin, Jim Efsathiou, Jr., and Esme E. Deprez, "How to Go on a Carbon Diet," *Bloomberg Businessweek,* June 7, 2010, pp. 50–52, p. 2; Monica Ginsburg, "Goodwill Hunting Gets Harder," *Crain's Chicago Business,* January 24, 2011, p. 19; and "Despite Economic Crisis, Consumers Value Brands' Commitment to Social Purpose," *PR Newswire,* November 17, 2008.

10. Patrick M. Callan, "The 2008 National Report Card: Modest Improvements, Persistent Disparities, Eroding Global Competitiveness," The National Center for Public Policy and Higher Education, Figure 5; and "College Cost in U.S. Hitting a High Note," *UPI,* December 3, 2008.

11. Azhar Iqbal and Mark Vitner, "The Deeper the Recession, the Stronger the Recovery: Is It Really That Simple?" *Business Economics* (2011), pp. 22–31.

12. Carmen Donavan-Walt, Bernadette D. Proctor, and Jessica C. Smith, "Income, Poverty and Health Insurance Coverage in the United States: 2010," *Current Population Reports* (Washington, D.C.: U.S. Census Bureau, September, 2011), pp. 6, 34.

13. Betsy Bohlen, Steve Carlotti, and Liz Mihas, "How the Recession Has Changed U.S. Consumer Behavior," *McKinsey Quarterly,* Issue 1 (2010), pp. 17–20; and Mark Trumbull, "In Tough Times, U.S. Consumers Forging New Behaviors," *Christian Science Monitor,* February 3, 2009, p. 25.

14. "Consumer Expenditure Survey: 2009," U.S. Department of Labor, Bureau of Labor Statistics, October 2010, Table 3; Mark Trumbull, "Consumers Holding Back on Spending," *Christian Science Monitor,* August 4, 2010; and Kara McGuire, "Saving Back in Vogue," *Chattanooga Times Free Press,* February 4, 2009, p. C3.

15. "Accenture Identifies Eight Trends Driving the Future of Information Technology," *Business Wire,* February 7, 2011; Matt Warman, "When Your Computer Knows You," *The Daily Telegraph,* February 24, 2011, p. 29; "CEA's Five Technology Trends to Watch," *Business Wire,* October 18, 2010; and Stephen Doyle and Zack Zavala, "The Future of Food," *Wired,* March 2007, p. 188.

16. Eric Griffith, "The Best Free Software of 2010," *PC Magazine,* March 30, 2010; and Koen Pauwels and Allen Weiss, "Moving from Free to Fee: How Online Firms Market to Change Their Business Model Successfully," *Journal of Marketing,* May 2008, pp. 14–31.

17. David Sarno and Jessica Guynn, "Apple Is Expected to Unveil New iPad," *Los Angeles Times,* February 23, 2011; and Steven Levy, "The A.I. Revolution," *Wired,* January 2011, p. 88.

18. "United States Telecommunications Report: Q4, 2010," Business Monitor International, Ltd.; "Economic Consequences of Armaments Production: Institutional Perspectives of J.K. Galbraith and T.B. Veblen," *Journal of Economic Issues,* March 1, 2008, p. 37.

19. "Google Asks EU Guidelines for Anti-Monopoly Compliance," *Tendersinfo News,* February 7, 2011; "Microsoft Anti-Trust Ruling: April 3, 2000, No Monopoly," *Dataquest,* December 30, 2010; Tim Hughes, "Way Out of This Crisis—Solution Lies in Deregulation, Not Renewed Regulation," *The Courier Mail,* February 7, 2009, p. 69; Adam Aston, "Sempra Energy: All Charge Up in California," *BusinessWeek,* June 11, 2007, p. 62; Aaron Pressman, "New Spark in Utility Stocks," *BusinessWeek,* June 4, 2007, p. 102; and Harry Maurer and Cristina Linblad, "Tackling Microsoft Again," *BusinessWeek,* January 28, 2008, p. 8.

20. "Frequently Asked Questions," Small Business Administration, Office of Advocacy, www.sba.gov/advo, September 2008.

21. "Legal Roundup," *Billboard,* January 31, 2009; and "A New Copyright Law?" *BusinessWeek,* August 3, 1998, p. 45.

22. "The Internet Browsing Cops," *The Wall Street Journal,* January 21, 2011, p. A12; Edmund Lee, "Government Says Self-Regulation of Online Privacy Is Coming Up Short," *Advertising Age,* December 6, 2010, p. 1; Julia Angwin and Jennifer Valentino-Devries, "Web Privacy 'Inadequate,'" *The Wall Street Journal,* December 2, 2010, p. B1; "FTC Refines CAN-SPAM Act," *Marketing News,* August 15, 2008, p. 4; "Time's Up," *Marketing News,* December 15, 2007, p. 14; D'Arcy Doran, "Internet Marketer Sues over Unwanted Spam," *Marketing News,* April 1, 2007, p. 20; Allison Enright, "Cingular Moves to Protect Its Turf," *Marketing News,* November 15, 2006, p. 4; Maxine L. Retsky, "Stakes Are High for Direct Mail Sweepstakes Promotions," *Marketing News,* July 3, 2000, p. 8; Catherine Arnold, "Picky, Picky, Picky," *Marketing News,* February 15, 2004, p. 17; and Catherine Arnold, "No Can Spam," *Marketing News,* January 15, 2004, p. 3.

23. Dorothy Cohen, "Trademark Strategy Revisited," *Journal of Marketing,* July 1991, pp. 46–59; and Maxine L. Retsky, "Review Int'l Filing Process for Marks," *Marketing News,* September 29, 2003, p. 8.

24. For a discussion of the definition of ethics, see Patrick E. Murphy, Gene R. Laezniak, Norman E. Bowie, and Thomas A. Klein, *Ethical Marketing: Basic Ethics in Action* (Upper Saddle River, NJ: Prentice Hall 2005).

25. See, for example, Linda K. Trevino and Katherine A. Nelson, *Managing Business Ethics: Straight Talk about How to Get It Right,* 5th ed. (New York: John Wiley & Sons, 2011).

26. Thomas Donaldson, "Values in Tension: Ethics Away from Home," *Harvard Business Review,* September–October 1996, pp. 48–62.

27. Ethisphere Institute, "2010 World's Most Ethical Companies," ethisphere.com, March 2010.

28. Vern Terpstra and Kenneth David, *The Cultural Environment of International Business,* 3rd ed. (Cincinnati: South-Western Publishing, 1991), p. 12.

29. Hedich Nasheri, *Economic Espionage and Industrial Spying* (Cambridge: Cambridge University Press, 2005).

30. "Coke Employee Faces Charges in Plot to Sell Secrets," *The Wall Street Journal,* July 6, 2006, p. B6; "Do the Right Thing? Not with a Rival's Inside Info," *Advertising Age,* July 17, 2006, p. 4; and "You Can't Beat the Real Thing," *Time,* July 17, 2006, pp. 10–11.

31. www.transparency.org, downloaded March 10, 2011.

32. *The 2009 National Business Ethics Survey.*

33. "Critics Blow Whistle on Law," *The Wall Street Journal,* November 1, 2010, pp. B1, B11; "Whistleblowers: Tales from the Back Office," *The Economist,* March 25, 2006, p. 67.

34. "Scotchgard Working Out Recent Stain on Its Business," Mercurynews.com, downloaded June 22, 2003.

35. James Q. Wilson, "Adam Smith on Business Ethics," *California Management Review,* Fall 1989, pp. 57–72.

36. Harvey S. James and Farhad Rassekh, "Smith, Friedman, and Self-Interest in Ethical Society," *Business Ethics Quarterly,* July 2000, pp. 659–74.

37. "Perrier—Overresponding to a Crisis," in Robert F. Hartley, *Marketing Mistakes and Successes,* 10th ed. (New York: John Wiley & Sons, 2006), pp. 119–130.

38. Andrew W. Savitz and Karl Weber, *The Triple Bottom Line: How Today's Best Run Companies Are Achieving Economic, Social and Environmental Success* (San Francisco, CA: Josey Bass, 2006).

39. "3M Marks 35 Years of Pollution Prevention Pays," 3M.com, April 22, 2010; "Xerox 2010 Report on Global Citizenship," Xerox.com, downloaded January 30, 2011; and "Walmart 2010 Global Sustainability Report," walmart.com, downloaded January 30, 2011.

40. For seminal discussion on this topic, see P. Rajan Varadarajan and Anil Menon, "Cause-Related Marketing: A Coalignment of Marketing Strategy and Corporate Philanthropy," *Journal of Marketing,* July 1988, pp. 58–74.

41. "Even as Cause Marketing Grows, 83 Percent of Consumers Still Want to See More," Press Release, Cone LLC, September 15, 2010; and Larry Chiagouris and Ipshita Ray, "Saving the World with Cause-Related Marketing," *Marketing Management,* July–August 2007, pp. 48–51.

42. Unmesh Kher, "Getting Smart at Being Good. . . Are Companies Better Off for It?" *Time,* January 2006, pp. A1–A37; and Pete Engardio, "Beyond the Green Corporation," *Bloomberg Businessweek,* January 29, 2007, pp. 50–64.

43. "Economics—Creating Environmental Capital," *The Wall Street Journal,* March 24, 2008, Section R; Remi Trudel and June Cotte, "Does Being Ethical Pay?" *The Wall Street Journal,* May 12, 2008, p. R4; and Pete Engardio, "Beyond the Green Corporation," *Bloomberg Businessweek,* January 29, 2007, pp. 50–64.

Toyota Inc.: This case was written by Steven Hartley. Sources: "Global 500: The World's Largest Corporations," *Fortune,* July 25, 2011, p. F-1; *2010 North America Environmental Report,* Toyota Motor North America, Inc., p. 1; "Toyota's Mobile Hybrid Tour and the Power of Partnership," Presentation by Mary Nickerson, National Marketing Manager, Toyota Motor sales, U.S.A., Inc.; Toyota website, http://www.toyota.com/sitemap.html, accessed, August 23, 2011; Tim Higgins, "Luxury Cars Are Neck and Neck in the U.S.," Bloomberg *Businessweek,* October 18, 2010, p. 26; and Mark Rechtin, "Toyota Reputation Starts to Recover," *Advertising Age,* January 24, 2011, p. 34.

Chapter 4

1. Jerry Hirsch, "Car Buying: How Men and Women Compare," latimes.com, April 7, 2011; "What Matters the Most When People Buy Cars," *BrandWeek,* October 11, 2010, p. 23; "Gender Wars and Car Shopping: Men Want Power, Women Want Cloth Seats," autos.aol.com, July 16, 2010; and Mark Dolliver, "What Matters to Women as Car Buyers," brandweek.com, November 6, 2009.

2. Roger D. Blackwell, Paul W. Miniard, and James F. Engel, *Consumer Behavior,* 10th ed. (Mason, OH: South-Western Publishing, 2006).

3. For thorough descriptions of consumer expertise, see Joseph W. Alba and J. Wesley Hutchinson, "Knowledge Calibration: What Consumers Know and What They Think They Know," *Journal of Consumer Research,* September 2000, pp. 123–57.

4. For in-depth studies on external information search patterns, see Brian T. Ratchford, Debabrata Talukdar, and Myung-Soo Lee, "The Impact of the Internet on Consumers' Use of Information Sources for Automobiles: A Re-Inquiry," *Journal of Consumer Research,* June 2007, pp. 111–119; Joel E. Urbany, Peter R. Dickson, and William L. Wilkie, "Buyer Uncertainty and Information Search," *Journal of Consumer Research,* March 1992, pp. 452–63; and Sharon E. Beatty and Scott M. Smith, "External Search Effort: An Investigation across Several Product Categories," *Journal of Consumer Research,* June 1987, pp. 83–95.

5. "Best Phones & Plans," *Consumer Reports,* August 2011, pp. 26–38.

6. For an extended discussion on evaluative criteria, see Del. J. Hawkins and David L. Mothersbaugh, *Consumer Behavior,* 11th ed. (Burr Ridge, IL: McGraw-Hill/Irwin, 2010).

7. John A. Howard, *Buyer Behavior in Marketing Strategy,* 2nd ed. (Englewood Cliffs, NJ: Prentice Hall, 1994). For an extended discussion on consumer choice sets, see Allan D. Shocker, Moshe Ben-Akiva, Brun Boccara, and Prakesh Nedungadi, "Consideration Set Influences on Consumer Decision Making and Choice: Issues, Models, and Suggestions," *Marketing Letters,* August 1991, pp. 181–98.

8. Robert J. Donovan, John R. Rossiter, Gillian Marcoolyn, and Andrew Nesdale, "Store Atmosphere and Purchasing Behavior," *Journal of Retailing,* Fall 1994, pp. 283–94; and Eric A. Greenleaf and Donald R. Lehman, "Reasons for Substantial Delay in Consumer Decision Making," *Journal of Consumer Research,* September 1995, pp. 186–99.

9. "Phone-Wielding Shoppers Strike Fear into Retailers," *The Wall Street Journal,* December 16, 2010, pp. A1, A9.

10. Sunil Gupta and Valarie Zeithaml, "Customer Metrics and Their Impact on Financial Performance," *Marketing Science,* November–December 2006, pp. 718–39.

11. These estimates given in Jagdish N. Sheth and Banwari Mitral, *Consumer Behavior,* 2nd ed. (Mason, OH: South-Western Publishing, 2003), p. 32.

12. For an in-depth examination of this topic, see Sunil Gupta and Donald R. Lehmann, *Managing Customers as Investments* (Upper Saddle River, NJ: Pearson Education, Inc., 2005).

13. For an overview of research on involvement, see John C. Mowen and Michael Minor, *Consumer Behavior: A Framework,* 5th ed. (Upper Saddle River, NJ: Prentice Hall, 2001); and Wayne D. Hoyer and Deborah J. MacInnis, *Consumer Behavior,* 5th ed. (Florence, KY: South-Western Education Publishing, 2009).

14. Russell Belk, "Situational Variables and Consumer Behavior," *Journal of Consumer Research,* December 1975, pp. 157–63. The examples are found in Martin Lindstrom, *buy.ology: Truth and Lies about Why We Buy* (New York: Doubleday Publishing, 2008).

15. A. H. Maslow, *Motivation and Personality* (New York: Harper & Row, 1970). Also see Richard Yalch and Frederic Brunel, "Need Hierarchies in Consumer Judgments of Product Design: Is It Time to Reconsider Maslow's Hierarchy?" in Kim Corfman and John Lynch, eds., *Advances in Consumer Research* (Provo, UT: Association for Consumer Research, 1996), pp. 405–10.

16. Bernardo J. Carducci, *The Psychology of Personality,* 2nd ed. (Oxford, UK: John Wiley & Sons, 2009), pp. 182–84.

17. Jane Spencer, "Lenovo Puts Style in New Laptop," *The Wall Street Journal,* January 3, 2008, p. B5.

18. This example is provided in Michael R. Solomon, *Consumer Behavior*, 4th ed. (Upper Saddle River, NJ: Prentice Hall, 1999), p. 59.

19. For further reading on subliminal perception, see Lindstrom, *buy.ology;* B. Bahrami, N. Lavie, and G. Rees, "Attentional Load Modulates Responses of Human Primary Visual Cortex to Invisible Stimuli," *Current Biology,* March 2007, pp. 39–47; and J. Karremans, W. Stroebe, and J. Claus, "Beyond Vicary's Fantasies: The Impact of Subliminal Priming and Brand Choice," *Journal of Experimental Social Psychology* 42 (2006), pp. 792–98.

20. August Bullock, *The Secret Sales Pitch* (San Jose, CA: Norwich Publishers, 2004); and Dave Lakhani, *Subliminal Persuasion* (Hoboken, NJ: John Wiley & Sons, 2008).

21. Sholnn Freeman, "Brand Breakdown," *The Washington Post,* March 26, 2006, p. F1ff.

22. Martin Fishbein and I. Aizen, *Belief, Attitude, Intention and Behavior: An Introduction to Theory and Research* (Reading, MA: Addison-Wesley, 1975), p. 6.

23. Richard J. Lutz, "Changing Brand Attitudes through Modification of Cognitive Structure," *Journal of Consumer Research,* March 1975, pp. 49–59.

24. "The VALS™ Types," www.strategicbusinessinsights.com, downloaded March 10, 2012.

25. This discussion is based on Ed Keller and Jon Berry, *The Influentials* (New York: Simon and Schuster, 2003).

26. Emanuel Rosen, *The Anatomy of Buzz Revisited* (New York: Crown Business, 2009).

27. BzzAgent.com, downloaded March 6, 2012; and Matthew Creamer, "BzzAgent Seeks to Turn Word of Mouth into a Saleable Medium," *Advertising Age,* February 13, 2006, p. 12.

28. Emanuel Rosen, "Conversation Starter," *BrandWeek,* April 12, 2010, p. 16.

29. For an extensive review on consumer socialization of children, see Deborah Roedder John, "Consumer Socialization of Children: A Retrospective Look at Twenty-Five Years of Research," *Journal of Consumer Research,* December 1999, pp. 183–213. Also see, Gwen Bachmann Achenreinver and Deborah Roedder John, "The Meaning of Brand Names to Children: A Developmental Investigation," *Journal of Consumer Psychology* 13, no. 3 (2003), pp. 205–19; and Elizabeth S. Moore, William L. Wilkie, and Richard J. Lutz, "Passing the Torch: Intergenerational Influences as a Source of Brand Equity," *Journal of Marketing,* April 2002, pp. 17–37.

30. J. Paul Peter and Jerry C. Olson, *Consumer Behavior and Marketing Strategy,* 9th ed. (Burr Ridge, IL: McGraw-Hill/Irwin, 2010); and Rich Morin and d'Vera Cohn, "Women Call the Shots at Home: Public Mixed on Gender Roles in Jobs," www.pewresearch.org, downloaded February 4, 2011. Also see, Rex Y. Du and Wagner A. Kamakura, "Household Life Cycles and Lifestyles in the United States," *Journal of Marketing Research,* February 2006, pp. 121–32.

31. This discussion is based on Lisa Mundy, "Women, Power, and Money," *Time,* March 26, 2012, pp. 26–34; Carl Bialik, "Who Makes the Call at the Mall, Men or Women?" *The Wall Street Journal*, April 23–24, 2011, p. A2; Jack Neff, "Time to Rethink Your Message: Now the Cart Belongs to Daddy," *Advertising Age,* January 17, 2011, pp. 1, 20; *The Kids and Tweens Market in the U.S., 9th Edition* (Rockville, MD: Packaged Facts, August 1, 2008); and *How Teens Use Media* (New York: Neilsen Company, June 2009).

32. Jeffrey M. Humphreys, "The Multicultural Economy in 2010," Selig Center for Economic Growth, Terry College of Business, The University of Georgia, downloaded February 14, 2011; and "The American Consumer," *Marketing News,* Special Edition, May 15, 2011.

33. The remainder of this discussion is based on Hoyer and MacInnis, *Consumer Behavior*; and *Hispanic Fact Pack: 2012 Edition* (New York: Crain Communications, January 25, 2012).

34. The remainder of this discussion is based on Peter and Olson, *Consumer Behavior and Marketing Strategy*; and Marissa Miley,

"Don't Bypass African-Americans," *Advertising Age,* February 2, 2009, pp. 3, 26.

35. The remainder of this discussion is based on Hawkins and Mothersbaugh, *Consumer Behavior: Building Marketing Strategy*; and "Marketing to Asian-Americans," *BrandWeek,* May 20, 2012, Special Section.

Groupon: This case was written by Steven Hartley. Sources: Bari Weiss, "The Journal Interview with Andrew Mason: Groupon's $6 Billion Gambler," *The Wall Street Journal,* December 20, 2010, p. 12; Brad Stone and Douglas MacMillan, "Are Four Words Worth $25 Billion?" *Bloomberg Businessweek* March 21, 2011, pp. 70–75; Brendan Coffey, "What's The Deal?" *Forbes,* April 25, 2011, pp. 20–22; Brad Stone and Douglas MacMillan, "Groupon's $6 Billion Snub," *Bloomberg Businessweek,* December 13, 2010, pp. 6–7; Christopher Steiner, "Meet the Fastest Growing Company Ever," *Forbes,* August 30, 2010; Rupal Parekh, "Groupon," *Advertising Age,* November 15, 2010, p. 20; "10 Big Stories for the Week," *Advertising Age,* December 13, 2010, pp. 12–13; Jessi Hempel, "Social Media Meets Retailing," *Fortune,* March 22, 2010, p. 30; Kunur Patel, "Suddenly, Everyone Wants to Be Groupon," *Advertising Age,* November 1, 2010, p. 1; and Brad Stone, "Coupon Deathmatch, Party of Two?" *Bloomberg Businessweek,* October 4, 2010, pp. 37–38.

Chapter 5

1. Interview with Gary Pats and Kim Nagele, JCPMedia, March 15, 2011.

2. Jason Busch, "Digging in to IBM's Procurement Outsourcing Strategy and Offering (Part 1)," SpendMatter.com, September 9, 2009.

3. Figures reported in this discussion are found in *Statistical Abstract of the United States: 2012* (Washington, D.C.: U.S. Census Bureau, 2011).

4. "NASA Needs More Money for Lockheed Martin's Orion," *Denver Business Journal,* January 16, 2011.

5. *2002 NAICS United States Manual* (Washington, D.C.: Office of Management and Budget, 2002).

6. This listing and portions of the following discussion are based on F. Robert Dwyer and John F. Tanner, Jr., *Business Marketing,* 4th ed. (Burr Ridge, IL: McGraw-Hill/Irwin, 2009); Michael D. Hutt and Thomas W. Speh, *Business Marketing Management: B2B,* 10th ed. (Mason, OH: South-Western, 2010); and Frank G. Bingham, Jr., Roger Gomes, and Patricia A. Knowles, *Business Marketing,* 3rd ed. (Burr Ridge, IL: McGraw-Hill/Irwin, 2006).

7. "Siemens Awarded $28 Million Contract for JetBlue Airways's Baggage Handling System with Integrated Security," Siemens USA press release, July 12, 2006.

8. Adrienne Sieko, "The Business Case for Diversity," www.industryweek.com, September 1, 2008.

9. For a study of buying criteria used by industrial firms, see Daniel H. McQuiston and Rockney G. Walters, "The Evaluation Criteria of Industrial Buyers: Implications for Sales Training," *Journal of Business & Industrial Marketing,* Summer–Fall 1989, pp. 65–75.

10. "Machine Vision Looks well Beyond Inspection," *Packaging Digest,* August 2005, pp. 32–35.

11. This example is found in Sandy D. Jap and Jakki J. Mohr, "Leveraging Internet Technologies in B2B Relationships," *California Management Review,* Summer 2002, pp. 24–38.

12. Stephen C. Rogers, *The Supply-Based Advantage: How to Link Suppliers to Your Organization's Corporate Strategy* (New York: AMACOM, 2009); "America's Most Admired Companies," *Fortune,* March 8, 2008, pp. 80ff; Traci Parum, "Harley-Davidson: Earning Accolades, Posting Profits," www.industryweek.com, November 17, 2005; and Brian Milligan, "Medal of Excellence: Harley-Davidson Wins by Getting Suppliers on Board," *Purchasing,* September 2000, pp. 52–65.

13. "The Smartest Machines on Earth," *Fortune,* September 18, 2006, pp. 129–136.

14. "The Kraft/EDS Outsourcing Deal: One Year After," EDS news release, June 12, 2007; and "HP Finalizes $3 Billion Outsourcing Agreement to Manage Procter and Gamble's IT Infrastructure," Hewlett-Packard news release, May 6, 2003.

15. This discussion is based on James C. Anderson, James A. Narus, and Das Narayandas, *Business Market Management,* 3rd ed. (Upper Saddle River, NJ: Prentice Hall, 2009); and Jeffrey K. Liker and Thomas Y. Choi, "Building Deep Supplier Relationships," *Harvard Business Review,* December 2004, pp. 104–113.

16. Helen Walker and Wendy Phillips, "Sustainable Procurement: Emerging Issues," *International Journal of Procurement Management* 2, no. 1 (2009), pp. 41–61.

17. Thomas V. Bonoma, "Major Sales: Who Really Does the Buying?" *Harvard Business Review,* May–June 1982, pp. 11–19. Also see, Philip L. Dawes, Don Y. Lee, and Grahame R. Dowling, "Information Control and Influence in Emerging Buying Centers," *Journal of Marketing,* July 1998, pp. 55–68; and Thomas Tellefsen, "Antedents and Consequences of Buying Center Leadership: An Emergent Perspective," *Journal of Business-to-Business Marketing* 13, no. 1 (2006), pp. 53–59.

18. Allison Enright, "It Takes a Committee to Buy into B-to-B," *Marketing News,* February 15, 2006, pp. 11–13; and Bonoma, "Major Sales: Who Really Does the Buying?"

19. Jeffrey E. Lewin and Naveen Donthu, "The Influence of Purchase Situation on Buying Center Structure and Involvement: A Select Meta-Analysis of Organizational Buying Behavior Research," *Journal of Business Research,* October 2005, pp. 1381–1390. Representative studies on the buy-class framework that document its usefulness include Erin Anderson, Wujin Chu, and Barton Weitz, "Industrial Purchasing: An Empirical Exploration of the Buy-Class Framework," *Journal of Marketing,* July 1987, pp. 71–86; and Thomas W. Leigh and Arno J. Ethans, "A Script-Theoretic Analysis of Industrial Purchasing Behavior," *Journal of Marketing,* Fall 1984, pp. 22–32. Studies not supporting the buy-class framework include Donald W. Jackson, Janet E. Keith, and Richard K. Burdick, "Purchasing Agents' Perceptions of Industrial Buying Center Influences: A Situational Approach," *Journal of Marketing,* Fall 1984, pp. 75–83; R. Vekatesh, Ajay Kohli, and Gerald Zaltman, "Influence Strategies in Buying Centers," *Journal of Marketing,* October 1995, pp. 61–72; Gary L. Lilien and Anthony Wong, "An Exploratory Investigation of the Structure of the Buying Center in the Metal Working Industry," *Journal of Marketing Research,* February 1984, pp. 1–11; and Wesley J. Johnston and Thomas V. Bonoma, "The Buying Center: Structure and Interaction Patterns," *Journal of Marketing,* Summer 1981, pp. 143–56.

20. These definitions are adapted from Frederick E. Webster, Jr., and Yoram Wind, *Organizational Buying Behavior* (Englewood Cliffs, NJ: Prentice Hall, 1972), p. 6.

21. "Can Corning Find Its Optic Nerve?" *Fortune,* March 19, 2001, pp. 148–50.

22. This discussion is based on "B2B, Take 2," *Bloomberg Businessweek Online,* November 25, 2005; Jennifer Reinhold, "What We Learned in the New Economy," *Fast Company,* March 4, 2004, pp. 56ff; Mark Roberti, "General Electric's Spin Machine," *The Industry Standard,* January 22–29, 2001, pp. 74–83; "Grainger Lightens Its Digital Load," *Industrial Distribution,* March 2001, pp. 77–79; and www.boeing.com/procurement, downloaded March 10, 2007.

23. "Former eBay CEO Urges Action on Small Business," washingtonpost.com, June 11, 2008; "New Study Reveals 724,000 Americans Rely on eBay Sales for Income," eBay press release, July 21, 2005; Robyn Greenspan, "Net Drives Profits to Small Biz," www.clickz.com, downloaded March 25, 2006; "eBay Realizes Success in Small-Biz Arena," *Marketing News,* May 1, 2004, p. 11; and www.ebaybusiness.com.

24. agentrics.com, downloaded March 1, 2012.

25. ghx.com, downloaded March 1, 2012.

26. This discussion is based on Robert J. Dolan and Youngme Moon, "Pricing and Market Making on the Internet," *Journal of Interactive Marketing,* Spring 2000, pp. 56–73; Ajit Kambil and Eric van Heck, *Making Markets: How Firms Can Benefit from Online Auctions and Exchanges* (Boston: Harvard Business School Press, 2002); Shawn P. Daley and Prithwiraz Nath, "Reverse Auctions for Relationship Marketers," *Industrial Marketing Management,* February 2005, pp. 157–66; and Sandy Jap, "The Impact of Online Reverse Auction Design on Buyer–Seller Relationships," *Journal of Marketing,* January 2007, pp. 146–59.

27. Susan Avery, "Supply Management Is Core of Success at UTC," *Purchasing,* September 7, 2006, pp. 36–39.

Trek: This case was written by Steven Hartley. Sources: "Trek Bicycle Corporation," Hoovers, 2011; "Alliance Data Signs Long-Term Extension Agreement with Trek Bicycle Corporation," *PR Newswire,* November 22, 2010; Lou Massante, "Trek Bicycle Buys Villiger, A Leader in the Swiss Market," Bicycle Retailer & Industry News, January 1, 2003, p. 10; "Trek Bicycle Corporation," Wikipedia, accessed September 4, 2011; and Trek website, http://www.trekbikes.com/us/en/company/believe, accessed September 4, 2011.

Chapter 6

1. "Dell India 2011 Revenue Slows, Exceeds Global Growth Rate," wsj.com, February 22, 2012; "How Dell Conquered India," CNNMoney.com, February 10, 2011; "Dell Unveils New Computers Targeting Emerging Markets," *Marketing News,* September 15, 2008, p. 32; "Dell Wants to Sell Emerging Consumers Their First PC," Reuters.com, September 23, 2008; and "Dell Plans to Up Focus on India Biz," AdAge.com, October 24, 2008.

2. Dennis R. Appleyard, Alfred J. Field, Jr., and Steven Cobb, *International Economics,* 7th ed. (Burr Ridge, IL: McGraw-Hill/Irwin, 2010), chapter 15; Tansa Mesa, "Africa and Caribbean Fear EU Latam Banana Tariff Cuts," *International Herald Tribune,* August 26, 2008, p. 8; Yuri Kageyama, "Selling Rice to Japan? U.S. Plans to Try," msnbc.com, March 7, 2004; "Shot in the Foot," *The Wall Street Journal,* September 6–7, 2008, p. A10; and *Economic Report of the President* (Washington, DC: U.S. Government Printing Office, 2009).

3. This discussion is based on information provided by the World Trade Organization, www.wto.org, downloaded March 25, 2012.

4. This discussion on the European Union is based on information provided at www.europa.eu, downloaded April 19, 2012.

5. This discussion is based on "Probable Effect of Certain Modifications to the North American Free Trade Agreement Rules of Origin" (Washington, DC: U.S. International Trade Commission, 2006); and "Target Is Going Abroad to Canada," *The Wall Street Journal,* January 14, 2011, pp. B1, B2.

6. For an overview of different types of global companies and marketing strategies, see, for example, Massaki Kotabe and Kristiaan Helsen, *Global Marketing Management,* 4th ed. (New York: Wiley, 2008), p. 221; Warren J. Keegan and Mark C. Green, *Global Marketing,* 4th ed. (Upper Saddle River, NJ: Prentice Hall, 2005); and Michael Czinkota and Ilkka A. Ronkainen, *International Marketing,* 8th ed. (Mason, OH: South-Western, 2007).

7. Johnny K. Johansson and Ilkka A. Ronkainen, "The Brand Challenge," *Marketing Management,* March–April 2004, pp. 54–55.

8. Kevin Lane Keller, *Strategic Brand Management,* 3rd ed. (Upper Saddle River, NJ: Prentice Hall, 2008), p. 602; and Michael Fielding, "Global Brands Need Balance of Identity, Cultural Respect," *Marketing News,* September 1, 2006, pp. 8–10.

9. "Get Ready for the Middle-Class Boom," www.msnmoney.com, October 18, 2011; "Coca-Cola, Nike and Adidas Top Brands for Teens Globally, TRU Study Finds," teenresearch.com, March 2, 2009;

"Global Habbo Youth Survey," marketinginsight@sulake.com, downloaded March 20, 2009; mtv.com/company, downloaded January 10, 2011; Bay Fong, "Spending Spree," *U.S. News & World Report,* May 1, 2006, pp. 42–50; and "Burgeoning Bourgeoisie," *The Economist,* February 14, 2009 (special report on the new middle classes).

10. For comprehensive references on cross-cultural aspects of marketing, see Paul A. Herbig, *Handbook of Cross-Cultural Marketing* (New York: Halworth Press, 1998); Jean Claude Usunier, *Marketing Across Cultures,* 4th ed. (London: Prentice Hall Europe, 2005); and Philip K. Cateora, Mary Gilly, and John L. Graham, *International Marketing,* 15th ed. (Burr Ridge, IL: McGraw-Hill/Irwin, 2011). Unless otherwise indicated, examples found in this section appear in these excellent sources.

11. Michael Esterl and David Crawford, "Siemens Pays Record Fine in Probe," *The Wall Street Journal,* December 16, 2008, p. B2.

12. These examples appear in Del I. Hawkins and David L. Mothersbaugh, *Consumer Behavior,* 10th ed. (Burr Ridge, IL: McGraw-Hill/Irwin, 2010), chap. 2.

13. "Greeks Protest Coke's Use of Parthenon," *Dallas Morning News,* August 17, 1992, p. D4.

14. "How Did Kit Kat Become King of Candy in Japan?" cnnmoney .com, February 2, 2012.

15. Jennifer Reingold, "Can P&G Make Money in Places Where People Earn $2 a Day?" *Fortune,* January 17, 2011, pp. 86–91; Vijay Mahajan and Kamini Banga, *The 86 Percent Solution: How to Succeed in the Biggest Market Opportunity of the Next 50 Years* (Upper Saddle River, NJ: Pearson Education, 2006); C. K. Pralahad, *The Fortune at the Bottom of the Pyramid: Eradicating Poverty through Profits* (Upper Saddle River, NJ: Pearson Education, 2005); and www.unilever.com, downloaded April 1, 2012.

16. "Burgeoning Bourgeoisie," *The Economist.*

17. "Mattel Plans to Double Sales Abroad," *The Wall Street Journal,* February 11, 1998, pp. A3, A11.

18. Eric Clark, *The Real Toy Story* (New York: The Free Press, 2007); and Cateora, Gilly, and Graham, *International Marketing.*

19. For an extensive and recent examination of these market-entry options, see, for example, Johnny K. Johansson, *Global Marketing: Foreign Entry, Local Marketing, and Global Management,* 5th ed. (Burr Ridge, IL: McGraw-Hill/Irwin, 2008); A. Coskun Samli, *Entering & Succeeding in Emerging Countries: Marketing to the Forgotten Majority* (Mason, OH: South-Western, 2004); and Keegan and Green, *Global Marketing.*

20. Based on an interview with Pamela Viglielmo, director of international marketing, Fran Wilson Creative Cosmetics; and "Foreign Firms Think Their Way into Japan," www.successstories.com/nikkei, downloaded March 24, 2003.

21. *Small and Medium Sized Enterprises: Overview of Participation in U.S. Exports* (Washington, DC: International Trade Administration, October 2008).

22. *McDonald's 2010 Annual Report.*

23. "About Us," www.strauss-group.com, downloaded March 15, 2011.

24. "FedEx Expands Reach in China with Buyout of Joint Venture," *The Wall Street Journal,* January 25, 2006.

25. This discussion is based on Keller, *Strategic Brand Management,* pp. 709–10; Todd J. Gillman, "Chip Off the Old Block," *Dallas Morning News,* July 30, 2006, pp. 1A, 22A; "Machines for the Masses," *The Wall Street Journal,* December 9, 2003, pp. A19, A20; "The Color of Beauty," *Forbes,* November 22, 2000, pp. 170–76; "It's Goo, Goo, Goo, Goo Vibrations at the Gerber Lab," *The Wall Street Journal,* December 4, 1996, pp. A1, A6; Donald R. Graber, "How to Manage a Global Product Development Process," *Industrial Marketing Management,* November 1996, pp. 483–98; and Herbig, *Handbook of Cross-Cultural Marketing.*

26. Jagdish N. Sheth and Atul Parvatiyar, "The Antecedents and Consequences of Integrated Global Marketing," *International Marketing Review* 18, no. 1 (2001), pp. 16–29.

27. "With Profits Elusive, Wal-Mart to Exit Germany," *The Wall Street Journal,* July 29, 2006, pp. A1, A6.

28. "Rotten Apples," *Dallas Morning News,* April 7, 1998, p. 14A.

29. For an in-depth discussion on gray markets, see Kersi D. Antia, Mark Bergen, and Shantanu Dutta, "Competing with Gray Markets," *Sloan Management Review,* Fall 2004, pp. 63–69.

CNS Breathe Right strips: This case was prepared by Mary L. Brown based on interviews with Kevin McKenna, vice president, international, and Nick Naumann, senior marketing communications manager of CNS, Inc.

Chapter 7

1. " 'Hunger Games' One for the Record Books," *Star Tribune,* March 26, 2012, p. E8; and Michelle Tauber, "Game On," *People,* March 26, 2012, pp. 66–74.

2. John Horn, "Studios Play Name Games," *Star Tribune,* August 10, 1997, p. F11; and "Flunking Chemistry," *Star Tribune,* April 11, 2003, p. E13.

3. Tad Friend, "The Cobra," *The New Yorker,* January 19, 2009, pp. 41–49.

4. Willow Bay, "Test Audiences Have Profound Effect on Movies," *CNN Newsstand & Entertainment Weekly,* September 28, 1998. See www.cnn.com/SHOWBIZ/Movies/9809/28/screen.test.

5. Helene Diamond, "Lights, Camera . . . Research!" *Marketing News,* September 11, 1989, pp. 10–11; and "Killer!" *Time,* November 16, 1987, pp. 72–79.

6. Carl Diorio, "Tracking Projectings: Box Office Calculations an Inexact Science," *Variety,* May 24, 2001.

7. Ronald Grover, Tom Lowry, and Michael White, "King of the World (Again)," *Bloomberg Businessweek,* February 1 & 8, 2010, pp. 48–56; and Richard Corliss, "Avatar Ascendant," *Time,* February 8, 2010, pp. 50–51.

8. A lengthier, expanded definition from 2004 is found on the American Marketing Association's website at www.marketingpower.com. For a researcher's comments on this and other definitions of marketing research, see Lawrence D. Gibson, "Quo Vadis, Marketing Research?" *Marketing Research,* Spring 2000, pp. 36–41.

9. Etienne Benson, "Toy Stories," *Observer* 19, no. 12 (December 2006).

10. Lawrence D. Gibson, "Defining Marketing Problems," *Marketing Research,* Spring 1998, pp. 4–12.

11. David A. Aaker, V. Kumar, George S. Day, and Robert P. Leone, *Marketing Research,* 10th ed. (Hoboken, NJ: John Wiley & Sons, Inc., 2010), pp. 114–116.

12. Brian Stelter, "New Nielsen Ratings Measure TV and Online Ads Together," *The New York Times Media Decoder,* March 18, 2012; and Andrew Hamp, "Nielsen Adds Ratings for Away-from-Home TV Networks," *Advertising Age-Creativity,* June 14, 2010, p. 13.

13. Amanda Kondolojy, "TV Ratings Broadcast Top 25: TV by the Numbers," May 22, 2012 from Zap2It.com. See http://tvbythenumbers .zap2it.com/2012/05/22/tv-ratings-broadcast-top-25-american-idol-ncis-top-week-35-viewing/135326.

14. "U.S. Spending Totals by Medium: ZenithOptimedia Forecast 2012," *Advertising Age,* June 25, 2012, p. 22.

15. Jessica E. Vascellaro, "On TV, New Ways to Gauge the Ads," *The Wall Street Journal,* February 4, 2011, p. B10.

16. David Kiley, "Counting the Eyeballs," *BusinessWeek,* January 16, 2006, pp. 84–85; and "The Ultimate Marketing Machine," *The Economist,* July 8, 2006, pp. 61–64.

17. Colleen Moore-Mezler, "Mystery Shoppers Are an Important Resource," *Alert! Magazine,* Marketing Research Association 46, no. 4 (April 2008), pp. 10, 12; and Robert Frank, "How to Live Large and Largely for Free, Jennifer Voitle's Way," *The Wall Street Journal,* June 9, 2003, pp. A1, A8.

18. Sarah Ellison, "P&G Chief's Turnaround Recipe: Find Out What Women Want," *The Wall Street Journal,* June 1, 2005, p. A1; Mark

Maremont, "New Toothbrush Is Big-Ticket Item," *The Wall Street Journal,* October 27, 1998, pp. B1, B6; and Emily Nelson, "P&G Checks Out Real Life," *The Wall Street Journal,* May 17, 2001, pp. B1, B4.

19. Gavin Johnson and Melinda Rea-Holloway, "Ethnography: How to Know If It's Right for Your Study," *Alert! Magazine,* Marketing Research Association 47, no. 2 (February 2009), pp. 1–4. See www.mra-net.org/alert.

20. Kenneth Chang, "Enlisting Science's Lessons to Entice More Shoppers to Spend More," *The New York Times,* September 19, 2006, p. D3; and Janet Adamy, "Cooking Up Changes at Kraft Foods," *The Wall Street Journal,* February 20, 2007, p. B1.

21. Martin Lindstrom, *Buyology: Truth and Lies about Why We Buy* (New York: Doubleday, 2008), pp. 8–36; C. B. Whittemore, "Martin Lindstrom's Buyology," *Flooring the Consumer blogspot,* March 1, 2009; Seth Brown, "Buyology Offers a Peek Inside Buyers' Heads," *USA Today,* October 29, 2008; and Andrea Sachs, "Business Books," *Time,* October 23, 2008.

22. Ilan Brat, "The Emotional Quotient of Soup Shopping," *The Wall Street Journal,* February 17, 2010, p. B6.

23. For a more complete discussion of questionnaire methods, see Joseph F. Hair, Jr., Robert P. Bush, and David J. Ortinau, *Marketing Research,* 4th ed. (New York: McGraw-Hill/Irwin, 2009), Chaps. 6 and 13.

24. Constance Gustke, "Built to Last," *Sales & Marketing Management,* August 1997, pp. 78–83.

25. See www.trendhunter.com/about-trend-hunter.

26. "What Is Online Research?" Marketing Research Association, see http://www.mra-net.org/press/online.cfm; and see also www.markettools.com/pdfs/press_releases/release_20081204.pdf.

27. For more discussion on wording questions effectively, see Gilbert A. Churchill, Jr., Tom J. Brown, and Tracy A. Suter, *Basic Marketing Research,* 7th ed. (Mason, OH: South-Western, Cengage Learning, 2010), pp. 289–307.

28. Jeff Gerst of Bolin Marketing provided the Carmex example, with the permission of Carma Laboratories, Inc.

29. Mark Jeffarey, *Data-Driven Marketing: The 15 Metrics Everyone in Marketing Should Know* (Hoboken, NJ: John Wiley & Sons, Inc., 2010), pp. 156–86.

30. Douglas D. Bates, "The Future of Qualitative Research Is Online," *Alert! Magazine,* Marketing Research Association 47, no. 2 (February 2009); Jack Neff, "The End of Consumer Surveys?" *Advertising Age,* September 15, 2008; Jack Neff, "Marketing Execs: Researchers Could Use a Softer Touch," *Advertising Age,* January 27, 2009; Bruce Mendelsohn, "Social Networking: Interactive Marketing Lets Researchers Reach Consumers Where They Are," *Alert! Magazine,* Marketing Research Association 46, no. 4 (April 2008); Toby, "Social Media Research: Interview with Joel Rubinson of ARF: Part 1," *Diva Marketing Blog,* February 16, 2009; and Toby, "Social Media Research: Interview with Joel Rubinson of ARF: Part 2," *Diva Marketing Blog,* February 23, 2009.

31. Byron Acohido, "Online Tracking Takes a Scary Turn," *USA Today,* August 4, 2011, pp. B1, B2; "Data, Data Everywhere—A Special Report on Managing Information: A Different Game," *The Economist,* February 27, 2010, pp. 6–8.

32. Joel Stein, "Your Data, Yourself," *Time,* March 21, 2011, pp. 39–46; Ryan Flinn, "The Big Business of Sifting through Social Media Data," *Bloomberg Businessweek,* October 25–October 31, 2010, pp. 20–22; Michael Lev-Ram, "The Hot New Gig in Tech," *Fortune,* September 5, 2011, p. 29; and Geoffrey A. Fowler and Emily Steel, "Facebook Says User Data Sold to Broker," *The Wall Street Journal,* November 1, 2010, p. B3.

33. The step 4 discussion was written by David Ford and Don Rylander of Ford Consulting Group, Inc.; the Tony's Pizza example was provided by Teré Carral of Tony's Pizza.

34. http://www.newbalance.com/NB-Minimus/minimus,default,pg.html and http://www.goodformrunning.com.

Carmex: This case was written by Jeff Gerst of Bolin Marketing.

Chapter 8

1. Kimberly Weisal, "A Shine in Their Shoes," *BusinessWeek,* December 5, 2005, p, 84; and information from the "Executive Biographies," section of the Zappos.com website.

2. Jeffrey M. O'Brien, "Zappos Knows How to Kick It," *Fortune,* February 2, 2009, pp. 55–60; and Max Chafkin, "Get Happy," *Inc.,* May 2009, pp. 66–71.

3. Weisal, "A Shine in Their Shoes," p. 84.

4. Duff McDonald, "Zappos.com: Success through Simplicity," *CIO-Insight,* November 10, 2006.

5. Jena McGregor, "Zappos' Secret: It's an Open Book," *Bloomberg Businessweek,* March 23 and 30, 2009, p. 62; Jeffrey M. O'Brien, "The 10 Commandments of Zappos," *Fortune,* January 22, 2009; http://money.cnn.com/2009/01/21/news/companies/obrien_zappos10.fortune/; and Zappos.com.

6. Motoko Rich, "Why Is This Man Smiling?" *The New York Times,* April 10, 2011, pp. ST1, ST10; Christopher Palmeri, "Now for Sale, the Zappos Culture," *Bloomberg Businessweek,* January 11, 2010, p. 57.

7. Natalie Zmuda, "Marketer of the Year: Zappos," *Advertising Age,* October 20, 2008, p. 36.

8. Eric N. Berkowitz, Roger A. Kerin, and William Rudelius, *Marketing* (St. Louis, MO: Times Mirror/Mosby College Publishing, 1986), pp. 189–91; Sleep Research Institute, the National Sleep Foundation, and the International Sleep Products Association (March 20, 2007); and Frederick G. Crane, Roger A. Kerin, Steven W. Hartley, and William Rudelius, *Marketing* 8th Canadian ed. (Toronto, Canada: McGraw-Hill Ryerson Ltd., 2011), pp. 229–32.

9. Ellen Byron, "As Middle Class Shrinks, P&G Aims High and Low," *The Wall Street Journal,* September 12, 2011, pp. A1, A16; Ellen Byron, "P&G Puts Spotlight on Newer Products," *The Wall Street Journal,* October 21, 2010, pp. B1, B2; Anthony Bianco, "The Vanishing Mass Market," *BusinessWeek,* July 12, 2004, pp. 61–65; and Geoff Colvin, "Selling P&G," *Fortune,* September 17, 2007, pp. 163–69.

10. Jeffrey A. Trachtenberg and Ann Paul Sonne, "Rowling Casts E-Book Spell," *The Wall Street Journal,* June 24, 2011, pp. B1, B2; and Larry Neumeister, "Rowling to Testify against Fan in Bid to Block Publication of 'Harry Potter' Encyclopedia," StarTribune.com from an Associated Press article, April 13, 2008; www.startribune.com/entertainment/17761909.html.

11. James Cook, "Where's the Niche?" *Forbes,* September 24, 1984, p. 54.

12. J. P. Donlon, "The Road Ahead," *Chief Executive,* July/August, 2011, pp. 31–37; "Epiphany in Dearborn," *The Economist,* December 11, 2010, pp. 72–74; and Bill Saporito, "How to Make Cars and Make Money Too," *Time,* August 9, 2010, pp. 36–39.

13. *2010 Ann Taylor Annual Report* and selected press releases.

14. Miguel Bastillo, "Walmart Sees Small Stores in Big Cities," *The Wall Street Journal,* October 14, 2010, pp. B1, B6.

15. The relation of these criteria to implementation is discussed in Jacqueline Dawley, "Making Connections: Enhance the Implementation of Value of Attitude-Based Segmentation," *Marketing Research,* Summer 2006, pp. 16–22.

16. Ian Michiels, "Customer Analytics: Segmentation beyond Demographics," *The Aberdeen Group,* August 2008, p. 11.

17. The discussion of fast-food trends and market share is based on Experian Simmons Winter 2012 NHCS Full-Year Adult Survey 12 OneViewSM Crosstabulation Report © Experian Simmons 2012 (See http://www.experian.com/simmons).

18. Mariko Sanchanta and Yoree Kuh, "McDonald's in Japan Gives New Meaning to Supersize," *The Wall Street Journal,* January 12, 2011,

pp. B1, B2; and Julie Jargon, "On the McDonald's Menu: Variety, Caution," *The Wall Street Journal,* November 9, 2010, p. B5.

19. Burt Helm, "An Expensive Face-Lift on Burger King's Menu," *Bloomberg Businessweek,* October 11–17, 2010, pp. 21–22; and Julie Jargon and Gina Chon, "BK's Strategy: Play Catch Up," *The Wall Street Journal,* September 3, 2010, p. B1.

20. Josh Sanburn, "Fast-Casual Nation," *Time,* April 23, 2012, pp. 60–61; Don Jacobson, "Fast-Casual Restaurants Are Just What Landlords Ordered," *Star Tribune,* January 20, 2012, p. D5; and Tiffany Hsu, "Fast, Casual, Trendy," *Star Tribune,* January 5, 2012, pp. D1, D3; and Al Reis, "Viewpoint," *Advertising Age,* January 20, 2011, p. 16.

21. Keith O'Brien, "Supersize," *The New York Times Magazine,* May 6, 2012, pp. 44–48; and "A Look Ahead: 2011—Fast Food," *Advertising Age,* January 20, 2011, p. 4.

22. Julie Jargon, "Wendy's Stages a Palace Coup," *The Wall Street Journal,* December 21, 2011, pp. B1, B2.

23. "The 2009 Zagat Fast-Food Survey," June 8, 2009; www.zagat.com/fastfood.

24. The discussion of Apple's segmentation strategies through the years is based on information from its website, www.apple.com; and www.apple-history.com/history.html.

25. Much of the discussion about positioning and perceptual maps is based on Roger A. Kerin and Robert A. Peterson, *Strategic Marketing Problems: Cases and Comments,* 12th ed. (Upper Saddle River, NJ: Prentice Hall, 2010), pp. 146–47; and John M. Mullins, Orville C. Walker, Jr., and Harper W. Boyd, Jr., *Marketing Management: A Strategic Decision-Marketing Approach,* 7th ed. (New York: McGraw-Hill/Irwin, 2010), p. 202.

26. Nicholas Zamiska, "How Milk Got a Major Boost by Food Panel," *The Wall Street Journal,* August 30, 2004, pp. B1, B5; and Rebecca Winter, "Chocolate Milk," *Time,* April 30, 2001, p. 20.

Prince Sports: This case was written by William Rudelius and is based on personal interviews with Linda Glassel, Tyler Herring, and Nick Skally.

Chapter 9

1. Edward C. Baig, "On New iPad, Looks Are Everything," *USA Today,* March 16, 2012, p. B3; Walter Isaacson, "American Icon," *Time,* October 17, 2011, pp. 32–35; Lev Grossman and Harry McCracken, "The Inventor of the Future," *Time,* October 17, 2011, pp. 36–44; Brad Stone, "1997–2011: The Return," *Bloomberg Businessweek,* October 10–October 16, 2011, pp. 36–42; Sean Wilsey, "The Products," *Bloomberg Businessweek,* October 10–October 16, 2011, pp. 48–61; Beth Snyder Bulik, "Marketer of the Decade," *Advertising Age*, October 18, 2010, p. 14; Geoff Colvin, "The World's Most Admired Companies: 2011," *Fortune,* March 3, 2011, accessed online September 26, 2011. See http://money.cnn.com/2011/03/02/news/companies/most_admired_intro.fortune/index.htm; Adam Lashinsky, "The Decade of Steve," *Fortune,* November 23, 2009, pp. 92–100; and Michael Arndt and Bruce Einhorn, "The 50 Most Innovative Companies," *Bloomberg Businessweek,* April 25, 2010, pp. 34–40.

2. Apple Special Event, June 6, 2011. See http://www.apple.com/apple-events/wwdc-2011.

3. Jessica E. Vascellaro, "Apple Tries to Keep Edge," *The Wall Street Journal,* March 8, 2012, pp. B1, B4; Jessica E. Vascellaro, Erica Orden, and Sam Schechner, "Hollywood Studios Warm to Apple's iCloud Effort," *The Wall Street Journal,* March 12, 2012, pp. B1, B6; Lev Grossman, "Cloud Control. Apple's iCold Is a Great Service–and a Blow to the Power of the PC," *Time*, June 20, 2011, p. 51; and William J. Holstein, "Can Cloud Live Up to Its Promise?" Chief_Executive.Net, July/August, 2011, pp. 46–50.

4. Suzanne C. Makarem, Susan M. Mudambi, Jeffrey S. Podoshen, "Satisfaction in Technology-Enabled Service Encounters," *The Journal of Services Marketing* 3 (2009), p. 134; Peter C. Honebein and Roy F. Cammarano, "Customers at Work: Self-Service Customers Can Reduce Costs and Become Cocreators of Value," *Marketing Management,* January/February 2006, pp. 26–31; and Matthew L. Meuter, Amy L. Ostrom, Robert I. Roundtree, and Mary Jo Bittner, "Self-Service Technologies: Understanding Customer Satisfaction with Technology-Based Service Encounters," *Journal of Marketing,* July 2000, pp. 50–64.

5. John Ozment and Edward Morash, "The Augmented Service Offering for Perceived and Actual Service Quality," *Journal of the Academy of Marketing Science,* Fall 1994, pp. 352–63.

6. A. Parasuraman, Valerie A. Zeithaml, and Leonard L. Berry, "Reassessment of Expectations as a Comparison Standard in Measuring Service Quality: Implications for Further Research," *Journal of Marketing,* January 1994, pp. 111–24; and Leonard L. Berry, *On Great Service* (New York: Free Press, 1995).

7. Valerie A. Zeithaml, A. Parasuraman, and Leonard L. Berry, *Delivering Quality Service* (New York: Free Press, 1990); and Stephen W. Brown and Teresa Swartz, "A Gap Analysis of Professional Service Quality," *Journal of Marketing,* April 1989, pp. 92–98.

8. Anna S. Mattila, "Do Women Like Option More than Men? An Examination in the Context of Service Recovery," *Journal of Services Marketing,* 2010(7), pp. 499–508; Leslie M. Fine, "Service Marketing," *Business Horizons,* May–June 2008, pp. 163–168; and James G. Maxham III and Richard G. Netermeyer, "A Longitudinal Study of Complaining Customers' Evaluations of Multiple Service Failures and Recovery Efforts," *Journal of Marketing,* October 2002, pp. 57–71.

9. Barrett Sheridan, "Sony's Wii Avatar," *Bloomberg Businessweek,* September 27–October 3, 2010, p. 90.

10. Interview with Geek Squad founder Robert Stephens on *60 Minutes,* January 28, 2007, www.geeksquad.com; Debora Viana Thompson, Rebecca W. Hamilton, and Roland Rust, "Feature Fatigue: When Product Capabilities Become Too Much of a Good Thing," *Journal of Marketing Research,* November 2005, pp. 431–42; and Ronald T. Rust, Debora Viana Thompson, Rebecca W. Hamilton, "Defeating Feature Fatigue," *Harvard Business Review,* February 2006, pp. 98–107.

11. Youngme Moon, "Break Free from the Product Life Cycle," *Harvard Business Review,* May 2005, pp. 86–94.

12. See "The 25 Biggest Product Flops of All Time," www.walletpop.com/photos/top-25-biggest-product-flops-of-all-time; and Zac Frank and Tania Khadder, "The 20 Worst Product Failures," www.saleshq.monster.com/news/articles/2655-the-20-worst-product-failures.

13. Joan Schneider and Julie Hall, "Why Most Product Launches Fail," *Harvard Business Review,* April 2011, pp. 21–23.

14. Robert G. Cooper, "New Products: What Separates the Winners from the Losers?" in *The PDMA Handbook of New Product Development,* eds. M. D. Rosenau, A. Griffin, G. Castellion, and N. Ansch eutz (New York: Wiley and Sons, 1996), pp. 3–18; Robert G. Cooper, "The Impact of Product Innovativeness on Performance," *Journal of Product Innovation Management,* April 1999, pp. 115–33; Thomas D. Kuczmarski, "Measuring Your Return on Innovation," *Marketing Management,* Spring 2000, pp. 25–32; and Merle Crawford and Anthony D. Benedetto, *New Products Management,* 9th ed. (New York: McGraw-Hill/Irwin, 2008), pp. 61–71.

15. Julie Fortser, "The Lucky Charm of Steve Sanger," *BusinessWeek,* March 26, 2001, pp. 75–76.

16. The Avert Virucidal tissues, Hey! There's A Monster In My Room spray, and Garlic Cake examples are adapted from Robert M. McMath and Thom Forbes, *What Were They Thinking?* (New York: Random House, 1998); and Global New Products Database. See www.gnpd.com.

17. Schneider and Hall, "Why Most Product Launches Fail," p. 22.

18. Dan P. Lovallo and Olivier Sibony, "Distortions and Deceptions in Strategic Decisions," *The McKinsey Quarterly* 1 (2006), pp. 19–29; and Byron G. Augusto, Eric P. Harmon, and Vivek Pandit, "The

Right Service Strategies for Product Companies," *The McKinsey Quarterly* 1 (2006), pp. 41–51.

19. "The 25 Biggest Product Flops of All Time."

20. Isabelle Royer, "Why Bad Projects Are So Hard to Kill," *Harvard Business Review,* February 2003, pp. 48–56; John T. Morn, Dan P. Lovallo, and S. Patrick Viguerie, "Beating the Odds in Market Entry," *The McKinsey Quarterly* 4 (2005), pp. 35–45; Leslie Perlow and Stephanie Williams, "Is Silence Killing Your Company?" *Harvard Business Review,* May 2003, pp. 52–58; Beverly K. Brockman and Robert M. Morgan, "The Moderating Effect of Organizational Cohesiveness in Knowledge Use and New Product Development," *Journal of Marketing Science* 3 (Summer 2006), pp. 295–306; Eyal Biyalogorsky, William Boulding, and Richard Staelin, "Stuck in the Past: Why Managers Persist with New Product Failures," *Journal of Marketing,* April 2006, pp. 108–21; and Irwin L. Janis, *Groupthink* (New York: Free Press, 1988).

21. Robert G. Cooper, "What Leading Companies Are Doing to Reinvent Their NPD Process," *PDMA Visions Magazine,* September 2008, pp. 6–10; Robert G. Cooper, "The Stage-Gate Idea-to-Launch Process—Update: What's New and NexGen Systems," *Journal of Product Innovation Management,* May 2008, pp. 213–32; Leland D. Shaeffer and Michael Zirkle, "Beyond 'Phase Gate'—Why Not a Tailored Solution?" *PDMA Visions Magazine,* June 2008, pp. 21–25; and Gloria Barczak, Abbie Griffin, and Kenneth B. Kahn, "Perspective: Trends and Drivers of Success in NPD Practices: Results of the 2003 PDMA Best Practices Study," *Journal of Product Innovation Management,* January 2009, pp. 3–23.

22. Peter Erickson, "One Food Company's Foray into Open Innovation," *PDMA Visions Magazine,* June 2008, pp. 12–14; Benn Lawson, Kenneth J. Petersen, Paul D. Cousins, and Robert B. Handfield, "Knowledge Sharing in Interorganizational Product Development Teams: The Effect of Formal and Informal Socialization Mechanisms," *Journal of Product Innovation Management,* March 2009, pp. 156–72; and James I. Cash, Jr., Michael J. Earl, and Robert Morison, "Teaming Up to Crack Innovation and Enterprise Integration," *Harvard Business Review,* November 2008, pp. 90–100.

23. "Epiphany in Dearborn," *The Economist,* December 11, 2010, pp. 72–74; and Bill Saporito, "How to Make Cars and Make Money Too," *Time,* August 9, 2010, pp. 36–39.

24. Bryce G. Hoffman, "Inside Ford's Fight to Avoid Disaster," *The Wall Street Journal,* March 9, 2012, B1, B7; and J. P. Donlon, "CEO of the Year: The Road Ahead," *Chief Executive.Net,* July/August 2011, pp. 31–37.

25. Kimberly Judson, Denise D. Schoenabachler, Geoffrey L. Gordon, Rick E. Ridnour, and Dan C. Weilbaker, "The New Product Development Process: Let the Voice of the Salesperson Be Heard," *Journal of Product & Brand Management* 15, no. 3 (2006), pp. 194–202.

26. Morgan L. Swink and Vincent A. Mabert, "Product Development Partnerships: Balancing Needs of OEMs and Suppliers," *Business Horizons,* May–June 2000, pp. 59–68.

27. C. K. Prahalad and Venkat Ramswamy, *The Future of Competition* (Boston: Harvard Business School Press, 2004); Steve Hamm, "Adding Customers to the Design Team," *BusinessWeek,* March 1, 2004, pp. 22–23; and Anthony W. Ulwick, "Turn Customer Input into Innovation," *Harvard Business Review,* January 2002, pp. 91–97.

28. Sarah Ellison, "P & G Chief's Turnaround Recipe: Find Out What Women Want," *The Wall Street Journal,* June 1, 2005, pp. A1, A16.

29. Emily Glazer, "Tide Rides Convenience Wave," *The Wall Street Journal,* February 23, 2012, p. 138; Jack Neff, "P&G Reinvents Laundry with $150 Million Tide Pods Launch," *Advertising Age,* April 26, 2011, downloaded April 28, 2011; and Emily Glazer, "P&G to Alter Tide Pods Packaging," *The Wall Street Journal,* May 26–27, 2012, p. B3.

30. Elisabeth A. Sullivan, "A Group Effort," *Marketing News,* February 28, 2010, pp. 22–29.

31. Adam Lashinsky, "Inside Apple," *Fortune,* May 23, 2011, p. 128; Daniel Turner, "The Secret of Apple Design," *MIT Technology Review,* May/June 2007; Leander Kahney, "Silicon Valley Loves Transparency and Cooperation. Not Steve Jobs. How Apple Got Everything Right by Doing Everything Wrong," *Wired Business Trends,* April 2008, pp. 137–43; and Karl T. Ulrich and Stephen D. Eppinger, *Product Design and Development* 4th ed. (New York: McGraw-Hill/Irwin, 2008), Chap 10.

32. Joseph Weber, Stanley Holmes, and Christopher Palmeri, "'Mosh Pits' of Creativity," *BusinessWeek,* November 7, 2005, pp. 98–100.

33. Bruce Nussbaum, "The Best Global Design of 2008," *BusinessWeek,* July 28, 2008, pp. 44–46; and Tim Brown, "He Prizes Questions More Than Answers," *The New York Times,* October 25, 2009, p. BU2.

34. Bruce Nussbaum, "The Power of Design," *BusinessWeek,* May 17, 2004, pp. 86–94; the article gives many techniques for idea and concept generation, as do Appendixes A and B in Merle Crawford and Anthony Di Benedetto, *New Products Management,* 10th ed. (New York: McGraw-Hill/Irwin, 2011).

35. Erickson, "One Food Company's Foray into Open Innovation," p. 12.

36. Erickson, "One Food Company's Foray into Open Innovation," p. 13.

37. Simona Covel, "My Brain, Your Brawn," *The Wall Street Journal,* October 13, 2008, p. R12.

38. Steve Hoeffler, "Measuring Preferences for Really New Products," *Journal of Marketing Research,* November 2003, pp. 406–20.

39. Christopher Lovelock and Jochen Wirtz, *Services Marketing* (Englewood Cliffs, NJ: Prentice Hall, 2007), pp. 260–84.

40. Sheridan Prasso, "The Unlikely King of Yogurt," *Fortune,* December 12, 2011, pp. 43–46; "About Chobani," http://chobani.com/about, downloaded April 27, 2011; Stuart Elliott, "Chobani, Greek Yogurt Leader, Lets Its Fans Tell the Story," *The New York Times,* February 16, 2011, downloaded May 2, 2011; "Drinks, Snacks, Breakfast Solutions Are Top Product Launches," *Canadian Grocer,* March 30, 2011, downloaded April 23, 2011; "Using the Online Channel for CPG Product Launch: Yoplait Greek," http://blog.compete.om/2010/05/03, downloaded May 2, 2011; and Jenny Liu, "CPG Product Launches in the New Digital Age," *Google CPG Blog,* July 13, 2010, downloaded April 29, 2011.

41. Jessica Bennett, "Marissa Mayer on the Day She Broke the Internet," *Newsweek,* July 25, 2011, p. 74; Helen Walters, "Google Did," *Bloomberg Businessweek,* May 10–16, 2010; Laura M. Holson, "Putting a Bolder Face on Google," *The New York Times,* March 1, 2009, pp. BU1, BU8; and Julian Gutherie, "The Adventures of Marissa," *San Francisco,* March 2008.

42. Gilbert A. Churchill, Jr., Tom J. Brown, and Tracy A. Suter, *Basic Marketing Research,* 7th ed. (Mason, OH: South-Western, Cengage Learning, 2010), pp. 122–130.

43. "The French Fry Wars: Burger King Cooks Up a New Recipe," *The Miami Herald,* December 12, 2011; http:www.miamiherald .com/2011/12/07/2535291/the-french-fry-wars-burger-king .html; "New Fries at Burger King Restaurants," Burger King press release, November 30, 2011; http://www.bk.com/en/us/company-info/news-press/detail/new-fries-at-burger-king-restaurants-559.html; "Burger King Introduces Hotter, Crispier, Better-Tasting French Fries," PRNewswire, December 10, 2011; http://www2.prnewswire.com/cgi-bin/stories.pl?ACCT=104&STORY=www/story/12-10-97/375783&EDATE; and Jennifer Ordonez, "How Burger King Got Burned in Quest to Make the Perfect Fry," *The Wall Street Journal,* January 16, 2001, pp. A1, A8.

44. Kerry A. Dolan, "Speed: The New X Factor," *Forbes,* December 26, 2005, pp. 74–77.

Warm Delights: This case was prepared by David Ford based on interviews with Vivian Milroy Callaway.

1. "Gatorade's New Selling Point: We're Necessary Performance Gear," *Advertising Age,* January 2, 2012, p. 2ff; "The Best Goes On," *BrandWeek,* May 10, 2010, p. 22; "Gatorade: Before and After," *The Wall Street Journal,* April 23, 2010, p. B8; "Pepsi Turns to Innovation to Boost Gatorade," *The Wall Street Journal,* October 21, 2009, p. B7; "G2, Zyrtec Top New Product Sales in '08," *BrandWeek,* March 23, 2009; "Gatorade Refreshes Look," *BrandWeek,* January 15, 2009, p. 4; Darren Rovell, *First in Thirst: How Gatorade Turned the Science of Sweat into a Cultural Phenomenon* (New York: AMA-COM, 2005); and Gatorade.com.

2. For an extended discussion of the generalized product life cycle, see Donald R. Lehmann and Russell S. Winer, *Product Management,* (Burr Ridge, IL: McGraw-Hill, 2010).

3. "Gillette Fusion Case Study" (New York: Datamonitor, June 6, 2008). All subsequent references to Gillette Fusion are based on this case study.

4. John W. Mullins, Orville C. Walker, Jr., Harper W. Boyd, Jr., and Jean-Claude Larréché, *Marketing Management: A Strategic Decision-Making Approach,* 5th ed. (Burr Ridge, IL: McGraw-Hill/Irwin, 2005), p. 396.

5. Portions of this discussion on the fax machine product life cycle are based on Mike Elgan, "Tired Technologies That Should Die Off in 2010," pcworld.com, December 30, 2009; Karen Prema, "Faxes Are Evolving," Purchasing *Magazine Online,* March 16, 2006; and "Atlas Electronics Corporation," in Roger A. Kerin and Robert A. Peterson, *Strategic Marketing Problems: Cases and Comments,* 8th ed. (Upper Saddle River, NJ: Prentice Hall, 1998), pp. 494–506.

6. "Hosted Email Market, 2010–2014" (Palo Alto, CA: The Radicate Group, 2010); and "Why Are Faxes Still Around?" *Wired,* January 2009, p. 47.

7. Kate MacArthur, "Coke Energizes Tab, Neville Isdell's Fave," *Advertising Age,* August 29, 2005, pp. 3, 21.

8. "Hosiery Sales Hit Major Snag," *Dallas Morning News,* December 18, 2006, p. 50.

9. "How to Separate Trends from Fads," *BrandWeek,* October 23, 2000, pp. 30, 32.

10. Everett M. Rogers, *Diffusion of Innovations,* 5th ed. (New York: Free Press, 2003).

11. Jagdish N. Sheth and Banwasi Mitral, *Consumer Behavior: A Managerial Perspective,* 2nd ed. (Mason, OH: South-Western College Publishing, 2003).

12. "When Free Samples Become Saviors," *The Wall Street Journal,* August 14, 2001, pp. B1, B4.

13. "Downsized: More and More Products Lose Weight," *Consumer Reports,* February 2011, p. 32ff; "The Lowdown on Downsizing," *Consumer Reports,* October 2008, pp. 10–11; and Bruce Horovitz, "Shoppers Beware: Products Shrink but Prices Stay the Same," www.usatoday.com, June 11, 2008.

14. This discussion is based on Kevin Lane Keller, *Strategic Brand Management,* 3rd ed. (Upper Saddle River, NJ: Prentice Hall, 2008). Also see, Susan Fornier, "Building Brand Community on the Harley-Davidson Posse Ride," Harvard Business School Note #5-501-502 (Boston: Harvard Business School, 2001); and Tulin Erdem, Joffre Swait, and Ana Valenzuela, "Brands as Signals: A Cross-Country Validation Study," *Journal of Marketing,* January 2006, pp. 34–49.

15. Keller, *Strategic Brand Management.*

16. This discussion is based on John Deighton, "How Snapple Got Its Juice Back," *Harvard Business Review,* January 2002, pp. 47–53; and "Breakfast King Agrees to Sell Bagel Business," *The Wall Street Journal,* September 28, 1999, pp. B1, B6. Also see, Vithala R. Rao, Manj K. Agarwal, and Denise Dahlhoff, "How Is Manifest Branding Strategy Related to the Value of a Corporation?" *Journal of Marketing,* October 2004, pp. 125–41.

17. "As Playboy Bunny Logo Multiplies, Collectors Are Barely Interested in It," *The Wall Street Journal,* April 5, 2010, pp. A1, A6; "Judge Pooh-Poohs Lawsuit over Disney Licensing Fees," USATODAY.com, March 30, 2004; and Keller, *Strategic Brand Management.*

18. John Brodie, "The Many Faces of Ralph Lauren," Fortune.com, August 29, 2007; and "Polo Ralph Lauren Enters into Licensing Agreement with Luxottica Group, S.P.A.," www.thebusinessedition.com, February 28, 2006.

19. Beth Snyder Bulik, "What's in a (Good) Product Name? Sales," *Advertising Age,* February 2, 2009, p. 10; and Keller, *Strategic Brand Management.* Also see, Chiranjeev Kohli and Douglas W. LaBahn, "Creating Effective Brand Names: A Study of the Naming Process," *Journal of Advertising Research,* January–February 1997, pp. 67–75.

20. Jack Neff, "The End of the Line for Line Extensions?" *Advertising Age,* July 7, 2008, pp. 3, 28.

21. David Aaker, *Brand Portfolio Strategy* (New York: Free Press, 2004).

22. Mark Ritson, "Should You Launch a Fighter Brand?" *Harvard Business Review,* October 2009, pp. 87–94.

23. "Ribbons Roll Out on Rides," *Dallas Morning News,* September 30, 2005, p. 8D.

24. Nikhil Bahadur, "How to Slim Down a Brand Portfolio," *Strategy & Business,* Winter 2006, pp. 15–16.

25. "Walmart Spices Up Private Label," *The Wall Street Journal,* February 6–7, 2010, p. B16; "Consumers Flock to Private Labels," *Advertising Age,* February 2, 2009, p. 27; and Lien Lamey, Barbara Deleersnyder, Marnik G. Dekimpe, and Jan-Benedict E. M. Steenkamp, "How Business Cycles Contribute to Private-Label Success: Evidence from the United States and Europe," *Journal of Marketing,* January 2007, pp. 1–15.

26. "So Sweet: William and Kate PEZ Dispensers," today.msnbc.com, March 30, 2012; www.pez.com, downloaded February 1, 2012; David Welch, *Collecting Pez* (Murphysboro, IL: Bubba Scrubba Publications, 1995); and "Elements Design Adds Dimension to Perennial Favorite Pez Brand," *Package Design Magazine,* May 2006, pp. 37–38.

27. "Market Statistics," Packaging-Gateway.com downloaded March 25, 2008.

28. "Green Bean Casserole Turns 50," *Dallas Morning News,* November 19, 2005, p. 16D.

29. "L'eggs Hatches a New Hosiery Package," *BrandWeek,* January 1, 2001, p. 6.

30. Representative scholarly research on packaging and labeling perceptions include Priya Rgahubir and Eric A. Greenleaf, "Ratios in Proportion: What Should the Shape of the Package Be?" *Journal of Marketing,* April 2006, pp. 95–107; Peter H. Bloch, Frederic F. Brunel, and Todd Arnold, "Individual Differences in the Centrality of Visual Product Aesthetics: Concept and Measurement," *Journal of Consumer Research,* March 2003, pp. 551–65; and Pamela Anderson, Joan Giese, and Joseph A. Cote, "Impression Management Using Typeface Design," *Journal of Marketing,* October 2004, pp. 60–72.

31. Betsy McKay, "Pepsi's New Marketing Dance: Can Can," *The Wall Street Journal,* January 12, 2007, p. B3.

32. "Asian Brands Are Sprouting English Logos in Pursuit of Status, International Image," *The Wall Street Journal,* August 7, 2001, p. B7C.

33. Ilan Bray, "The Emotional Quotient of Soup Shopping," *The Wall Street Journal,* February 17, 2010, p. B6; Ellen Bryon, "Consumer Products Getting a Makeover," *The Wall Street Journal,* June 2, 2008, p. B9; and Susanna Hamner, "Packaging That Pays," *Business 2.0,* July 26, 2006, pp. 68–69.

34. "Walmart: Use Less Packaging," *Dallas Morning News,* September 23, 2006, p. 2D.

35. "Let It Rip: New Packaging on Rise," *Dallas Morning News,* March 18, 2012, p. 3D.

36. This discussion is based on Valerie A. Zeithaml, Mary Jo Bitner, and Dwayne D. Gremler, *Services Marketing: Integrating Customer Focus across the Firm,* 5th ed. (Burr Ridge, IL: McGraw-Hill/Irwin, 2009.

37. Thomas T. Nagle, John E. Hogan, and Joseph Zale, *The Strategy and Tactics of Pricing,* 5th ed. (Upper Saddle River, NJ: Prentice Hall, 2011).

38. Paula Andruss, "Delivering WOW through Service," *Marketing News,* October 15, 2008, p. 10.

39. Leonard L. Berry and Neeli Bedapudi, "Clueing in Customers," *Harvard Business Review,* February 2003, pp. 100–6.

Mary Kay, Inc.: This case was written by Roger A. Kerin based on company interviews and the following sources: "Mary Kay to Expand in India," cosmeticbusiness.com, March 15, 2010; "Mary Kay to Invest Rs 90 Cr in India in Next Five Years," economictimes.indiatimes.com, March 11, 2010; "Adkins-Green Eyes Mary Kay Growth," brandweek.com, March 30, 2009; David Barboza, "Direct Selling Flourishes in China," nytimes.com, December 26, 2009; Daniel Gross, "How Do You Say 'Pink Cadillac' in Mandarin," newsweek.com, November 17, 2009; and "Cosmetics and Toiletries-India," *Euromonitor International: Country Market Report,* June 2009.

Chapter 11

1. "Vizio Takes Home Entertainment Beyond TV," hdtvmagazine.com, downloaded, January 2012; "Vizio Extends Battle Plan," *The Wall Street Journal,* January 3, 2011, p. B3; "How Vizio Beat Sony in High-Def TV," businessweek.com, April 22, 2010; "U.S. Upstart Takes on TV Giants in Price War," *The Wall Street Journal,* April 15, 2008, pp. B1, B6; and "The VIZIO Story," vizio.com, downloaded March 10, 2012.

2. Eric Young, "Giants Strike Online Ticket Deal," *Silicon Valley/San Jose Business Journal,* February 9, 2009; and Scott McCartney, "Airfare Quotes That Lay Bare Hidden Fees," *The Wall Street Journal,* March 10, 2009, pp. D1, D3.

3. Aaron Robinson, 2011 Bugatti Veyron 16.4 Super Sport—First Drive Review, *Car and Driver,* October 2010. Accessed September 26, 2011. See http://www.caranddriver.com/reviews/car/10q4/ 2011_bugatti_veyron_16.4_super_sport-first_drive_review; and Rex Roy, First Drive: 2011 Bugatti Veyron Super Sport, *AutoBlog,* November 23, 2010. Accessed September 26, 2011. See http://www .autoblog.com/2010/11/23/2011-bugatti-veyron-super-sport-first-drive-review-road-test.

4. Numerous studies have examined the price-quality-value relationship. See, for example, Jacob Jacoby and Jerry C. Olsen, eds., *Perceived Quality* (Lexington, MA: Lexington Books, 1985); William D. Dodds, Kent B. Monroe, and Dhruv Grewal, "Effects of Price, Brand, and Store Information on Buyers' Product Evaluations," *Journal of Marketing Research,* August 1991, pp. 307–19; and Roger A. Kerin, Ambuj Jain, and Daniel Howard, "Store Shopping Experience and Consumer Price-Quality-Value Perceptions," *Journal of Retailing,* Winter 1992, pp. 235–45. For a thorough review of the price-quality-value relationship, see Valerie A. Zeithaml, "Consumer Perceptions of Price, Quality, and Value," *Journal of Marketing,* July 1988, pp. 2–22.

5. Roger A. Kerin and Robert A. Peterson, "Bates Manor Furniture, Inc. (A)," *Strategic Marketing Problems: Cases and Comments,* 12th ed. (Upper Saddle River, NJ: Prentice Hall, 2010), pp. 301–12.

6. The conditions favoring skimming versus penetration pricing are described in Kent B. Monroe, *Pricing: Making Profitable Decisions,* 3rd ed. (New York: McGraw-Hill/Irwin, 2003).

7. Jean-Noel Kapferer, *The New Strategic Brand Management: Advanced Insights and Strategic Thinking,* 5th ed. (London: Kogan Page Ltd, 2012).

8. "Premium AA Alkaline Batteries," *Consumer Reports,* March 21, 2002, p. 54; Kemp Powers, "Assault and Batteries," *Forbes,* September 4, 2000, pp. 54, 56; and "Razor Burn at Gillette," *BusinessWeek,* June 18, 2001, p. 37.

9. Thomas T. Nagle, John E. Hogan, and Joseph Zale, *The Strategy and Tactics of Pricing,* 5th ed. (Englewood Cliffs, NJ: Prentice Hall, 2011).

10. Robert J. Dolan and Hermann Simon, *Power Pricing: How Managing Price Transforms the Bottom Line* (New York: Free Press, 1996), p. 249; and Scott McCartney, "You Paid What for That Flight?" *The Wall Street Journal,* August 26, 2010, pp. D1, D2.

11. "What Popcorn Prices Mean for Movies," *Advertising Age,* May 19, 2008, p. 4.

12. "A New Beverage Attitude," *Convenience Store/Petroleum News,* May 2010, pp. 110–12.

13. "Is the Music Store Over?" *Business 2.0,* March 2004, pp. 115–19.

14. Frank Bruni, "Price of Newsweek: It Depends," *Dallas Times Herald,* August 14, 1986, pp. S1, S20. See also, Stephanie Clifford, "A Stress Test for Magazines: Raising Prices without Losing Readers," *The Wall Street Journal,* April 13, 2009, pp. B1, B5.

15. Thomas T. Nagle, John E. Hogan, and Joseph Zale, *The Strategy and Tactics of Pricing.*

16. Peter Coy, "Can't Stop Guzzling," *BusinessWeek,* July 31, 2006, pp. 26–29.

17. Christina Binkley, "How Can Jeans Cost $300?" *The Wall Street Journal,* July 7, 2011, pp. D1, D2.

18. Ken Belson, "Mets Going for the Gold on Tickets for More Games," *The New York Times,* April 8, 2009, p. B13.

19. "Samsung Edges Out TV Rivals," *The Wall Street Journal,* February 17, 2010, p. B4.

20. Ian Sheer, "Tablet War Is an Apple Rout," *The Wall Street Journal,* August 12, 2011, pp. B1, B2.

21. "Six Vitamin Firms Agree to Settle Price-Fixing Suit," *The Wall Street Journal,* October 11, 2000, p. B10.

22. "How Dell Fine-Tunes Its PC Pricing to Gain Edge in a Slow Market, *The Wall Street Journal,* June 8, 2001, pp. A1, A8.

23. "Are Minority Shoppers Treated Unfairly? An Expensive Reason to Care," www.diversity.com, downloaded May 18, 2003; Florian Zettelmeyer, Fiona Scott Morton, and Jorge Silva-Risso, "How the Internet Lowers Prices: Evidence from Matched Survey and Automobile Transaction Data," *Journal of Marketing Research,* May 2006, pp. 168–81; and Fiona Scott Morton, Florian Zettelmeyer, and Jorge Silva-Risso, "Consumer Information and Discrimination: Does the Internet Affect the Pricing of New Cars to Women and Minorities?" *Quantitative Marketing and Economics,* 1 (2003), pp. 65–92.

Washburn Guitar: This case was edited by Steven Hartley. Sources: Burkhard Bilger, "String Theory, Building a Better Guitar," *The New Yorker,* May 14, 2007, p. 79; and the Washburn Guitar website (www.washburn.com).

Chapter 12

1. www.callawaygolf.com, downloaded April 15, 2012; Stephanie Kang, "Callaway Will Use Retailers to Sell Goods Directly to Consumers Online," *The Wall Street Journal,* November 6, 2006, p. B5; and "Justin Timberlake Putting the 'Sexy' Back in Callaway Golf," www.sportinggoodsnewswire.com, November 19, 2008.

2. "Eddie Bauer's Banner Time of Year," *Advertising Age,* October 1, 2001, p. 55.

3. *Internet Retailer Top 500 Guide,* 2012 Edition. www .internetretailer.com, downloaded February 10, 2012.

4. "Second-Largest Cereal Producer Turns 20, with Style," General Mills Press Release, September 13, 2010.

5. For an overview of vertical marketing systems, see Lou Pelton, Martha Cooper, David Strutton, and James R. Lumpkin, *Marketing Channels,* 3rd ed. (Burr Ridge, IL: McGraw-Hill/Irwin, 2005).

6. "Saks to Add Exclusive Lines," *The Wall Street Journal,* February 25, 2010, p. B2.

7. "Dell Treads Carefully into Selling PCs in Stores," *The Wall Street Journal,* January 3, 2008, p. B1.

8. Rafi A. Mohammed, Robert J. Fisher, Bernard J. Jaworski, and Gordon J. Paddison, *Internet Marketing: Building Advantage in a Networked Economy,* 2nd ed. (Burr Ridge, IL: McGraw-Hill/Irwin, 2004).

9. "American Airlines Yanks Its Flights off Travel Sites," www .USAtoday.com, December 23, 2010; Ethan Smith, "Why a

Grand Plan to Cut CD Prices Went off the Track," *The Wall Street Journal,* June 4, 2004, pp. A1, A6; and "Feud with Seller Hurts Nike Sales, Shares," *Dallas Morning News,* June 28, 2003, p. 30.

10. For an extensive discussion on channel influence and power, see Anne T. Couglan, Erin Anderson, Louis W. Stern, and Adel I. El-Ansary, *Marketing Channels,* 7th ed. (Upper Saddle River, NJ: Prentice Hall, 2006), Chapters 6 and 7.

11. David Simchi-Levi, Philip Kaminsky, and Edith Simchi-Levi, *Designing and Managing the Supply Chain,* 4th ed. (Burr Ridge, IL: McGraw-Hill/Irwin, 2011).

12. *The Smarter Supply Chain of the Future: Industry Edition* (Somer, NY: IBM Corporation, 2009); and John Paul MacDuffie and Takahiro Fujimoto, "Why Dinosaurs Will Keep Ruling the Automobile Industry," *Harvard Business Review,* June 2010, pp. 23–25.

13. Major portions of this discussion are based on Sunil Chopra and Peter Meindl, *Supply Chain Management: Strategy, Planning, and Operations,* 4th ed. (Upper Saddle River, NJ: Prentice Hall, 2010), Chapters 1–3; and Hau L. Lee, "The Triple-A Supply Chain," *Harvard Business Review* (October 2004), pp. 102–12.

14. Jessi Hempel, "IBM's Super Second Act," *Fortune,* March 21, 2011, pp. 115 ff; Kevin O'Marah, "The AMR Supply Chain Top 25 for 2010," Gartner, Inc., June 2010; and Thomas A. Foster, "World's Best-Run Supply Chains Stay on Top Regardless of the Competition," *Global Logistics & Supply Chain Strategies,* February 2006, pp. 27–41.

15. This discussion is based on "The Gartner Supply Chain Top 25 for 2011," www.gartner.com, June 2011; "*Harvard Business Review,* on Managing Supply Chains," *Harvard Business Review*, June, 2011; "The Lessons from Dell's Supply Chain Transformation," www.supplychaindigest.com, March 18, 2011; Brett Booen, "Walmart's Supply Chain Acts as If Every Day Is Black Friday," *Supply Chain Digital,* November 19, 2010; and Chopra and Meindl, *Supply Chain Management.*

16. Christina Passariello, "Logistics Are in Vogue with Designers," *The Wall Street Journal,* June 27, 2008, p. B1; Bill Mongelluzzo, "Logistics Makeover at Saks: Retailer Says Changes in Supply Chain Practices Have Reduced Inventory and Costs," *The Journal of Commerce,* October 24, 2005; and Michael Levy and Barton A. Weitz, *Retailing Management,* 6th ed. (Burr Ridge, IL: McGraw-Hill/Irwin, 2008).

17. Jean Murphy, "Better Forecasting, S&OP Support Transformation at Campbell's Soup Co.," *Global Logistics & Supply Chain Strategies,* June 2004, pp. 28–30.

18. "Rewriting the Rules for E-Cycling," *Fortune,* March 22, 2010, Special Section; Steve Miller, "Recycling Becomes Electric for CE Brands," *BrandWeek,* May 13, 2008, p. 4; "Don't Toss Out That Old Gadget," *Newsweek,* November 3, 2008, p. E8; and Lorraine Woellert, "HP Wants Your Old PCs Back," *BusinessWeek,* April 10, 2006, pp. 82–83.

19. Brian Hindo, "Everything Old Is New Again," *BusinessWeek,* September 25, 2006, pp. 64–70.

20. Doug Bartholomew, "IT Delivers for UPS," *Industry Week,* August 2002, pp. 35–36.

Amazon.com: This case is based on material available on the company website and the following sources: Robert D. Hof and Heather Green, "How Amazon Cleared That Hurdle," *BusinessWeek,* February 4, 2002, p. 60; Heather Green, "How Hard Should Amazon Swing?" *BusinessWeek,* January 14, 2002, p. 38; Robert D. Hof, "We've Never Said We Had to Do It All," *BusinessWeek,* October 15, 2001, p. 53; and Bob Walter, "Amazon Leases Distribution Center from Sacramento, Calif., Development Firm," *Sacramento Bee,* July 19, 2001.

Chapter 13

1. "Marketers, It's Time to Figure Out Your Mobile Marketing Strategy,"* *Advertising Age,* February 14, 2011; Diane Brady, "Social Media's New Mantra: Location, Location, Location,"

Bloomberg Businessweek, May 10, 2010, pp. 34–36; Brad Stone and Barrett Sheridan, "The Retailer's Clever Little Helper," *Bloomberg Businessweek,* August 30, 2010, pp. 31–31; "Shopkick, Simon Properties Planning Location-Based Coupons," *Techweb,* August 13, 2010; Sherwin Loh, "Be a Mayor with Foursquare," *The Straits Times,* March 3, 2010; "Follow Me: Location-Based Service on Mobile Phones," *The Economist,* March 6, 2010; Maria Halkias, "Smart Phone Can Make You a Smarter Shopper," *The Dallas Morning News,* November 26, 2010, p. A1; Jessica Guynn, "Facebook Unveils Deals Program," *Los Angeles Times,* November 4, 2010, p. 3; and Ana-Marija Ozimec, Martin Natter, and Thomas Reutterer, "Geographical Information Systems–Based Marketing Decisions: Effects of Alternative Visualizations on Decision Quality," *Journal of Marketing* 74 (November 2010), pp. 94–110; "About Foursquare," https://foursquare.com, accessed June 19, 2012.

2. "The Fortune 500," *Fortune,* May 21, 2012, p. F-1; *The World Factbook* (Washington, DC: Central Intelligence Agency), www.cia.gov, accessed June 19, 2012; *Statistical Abstract of the United States: 2012,* 131st ed. (Washington, DC: U.S. Department of Commerce, Bureau of the Census, 2011), Table 20, Large Metropolitan Statistical Areas.

3. *Statistical Abstract of the United States: 2012,* Table 1051, Retail Trade and Food Services.

4. "The Global 2000," *Forbes,* April 18, 2012.

5. "About us," Wal-Mart Stores, Inc., Press Room, www.walmartstores .com, accessed June 19, 2012.

6. Natalie Zmuda and Andrew Hampp, "When It Comes to Commercials, Target and Others Keep It Green," *Advertising Age,* January 10, 2011, p. 1; "Can Green Marketing Work?" *Advertising Age,* November 8, 2010, p. 19; Nathalie Atkinson, "Green Army, Sure Companies Are Jumping on the Eco-Bandwagon but It's This Sort of Retailing We Should Encourage," *National Post,* April 17, 2010, p. TO4; "The Company of the Future: Fact Sheet," Wal-Mart, Inc., www .walmartfacts.com, accessed April 8, 2011; and "Research and Markets: Going Green Isn't Just Good for the Environment—It's Good for Business Too," *Business Wire,* February 20, 2009.

7. "Retail Trade—Establishments, Employees, and Payroll," *Statistical Abstract of the United States: 2012,* 131st ed. (Washington, DC: U.S. Department of Commerce, Bureau of the Census), Table 1048; "County Business Patterns," Bureau of the Census, www.censtats .census.gov/cgi-bin/cbpnaic/cbpdetl.pl, accessed April 8, 2011.

8. "2012 Franchise 500," *Entrepreneur,* http://www.entrepreneur .com/franchise500/index.html, accessed April 9, 2012.

9. Alana Semuels, "Self-Service Machines Replacing Retail Workers," *The Star-Ledger,* March 13, 2011, p. 1; Bridget Carey, "You Can Get Most Anything at a Kiosk," *The Miami Herald,* August 20, 2010; "Check This Out: Palm Beach County Library System Adds Self-Service Checkouts," *South Florida Sun-Sentinel,* February 17, 2009; "Research Shows Consumers Seek More Self-Service Options Due to Pressures of Price and Time," *Business Wire,* January 12, 2009; and Peter C. Honebein and Roy F. Cammarano, "Customers at Work," *Marketing Management,* January/February 2006, pp. 26–31.

10. Rachel Dodes, "Corporate News: Nordstrom Joins Fray, Buys 'Flash Sale' Site," *The Wall Street Journal,* February 18, 2011, p. B8; Peter King, "Personal Shoppers Find Clothes to Make the Man," *The Wall Street Journal,* August 12, 2010, p. D3; Will Ashworth, "Retail Customer Service Excellence Pays," *Investopedia Advisor,* December 9, 2010; and Michael A. Wiles, "The Effect of Customer Service on Retailers' Shareholder Wealth: The Role of Availability and Reputation Cues," *Journal of Retailing,* 2007, pp. 19–31.

11. Jackie Crosby, "Vending Machine Variety Goes Beyond Snack Food Offerings," *Los Angeles Times,* January 18, 2011, p. B2; Carlie Kollath, "Veggies in Vending Machines?" *Biz Buzz,* April 6, 2011; Joyce Smith, "New Vending Machines Have Thieves Covered," *The Star Phoenix,* April 16, 2011, p. B6; "2012 State of the Vending Industry Report," *Automatic Merchandiser,* June/July 2012; and

http://www.vending.org/industry/vending101.pdf. accessed June 19, 2012.

12. Ilan Brat, "U.S. News: Vending Machines Try Electronic Self-Defense," *The Wall Street Journal,* January 31, 2011, p. A2; Ilan Brat, "Business Technology: Restocking the Snack Machine—Sales Pinched, Vending-Machine Operators Add Touch Screen, Card Readers," *The Wall Street Journal,* August 3, 2010, p. B5; and Joe Astrouski, "Eastern Illinois U. Vending Machines Go Green," *University Wire,* November 21, 2008.

13. *Statistical Fact Book,* Direct Marketing Association (New York, 2012), pp. 36, 53–54 (with assistance from Dr. Yoram Wurmser); David Kaplan, "Catalogs Thinner but Still Carry Weight, Retailers Use Them to Draw Consumers to Stores, Web or Social Media Sites," *The Houston Chronicle,* November 28, 2010, p. 1; Mercedes Cardona, "Catalog Role Is Communications, Not Sales," *DM News,* November 1, 2010; and IKEA website, www.ikea.com, accessed June 19, 2012.

14. Ira Teinowitz and Nat Ives, "No Day Is a Good Day for No Mail," *Advertising Age,* February 9, 2009, p. 8; "A Zip-Code Screen for Catalog Customers," *The Wall Street Journal,* June 24, 2008, p. B1; and Richard H. Levey, "It's All about Me," *Direct,* November 1, 2008.

15. Liberty Interactive Reports Fourth Quarter and Year End 2011 Financial Results, February 23, 2012; accessed June 19, 2012. See http://ir.libertyinteractive.com/releasedetail.cfm?ReleaseID=650939. See also http://www.qvc.com/qic/qvcapp.aspx/main.html.file .%7Ccs%7Cfaq_aboutqvc,html, accessed June 19, 2012. "QVC Extends Global Reach to Italy," *PR Newswire,* September 26, 2008; and "Fact Sheet" from the QVC website, www.qvc.com/qic, accessed April 15, 2011.

16. "Queen of Rock 'n' Roll Priscilla Presley Schedules to Return to QVC to Debut New Pieces from the Priscilla Presley Jewelry Collection," *PR Newswire,* March 16, 2011; Elizabeth Holmes, "The Golden Age of TV Shopping," *The Wall Street Journal,* November 11, 2010, p. D1; Christine H. O'Toole, "Attention, QVC Shoppers. . ." *The Washington Post,* January 28, 2009, p. C2; "QVC Mulls Further Channel Developments," *Retail Week,* October 17, 2008; Richard Mullins and Michael Messano, "HSN's New Deal," *Tampa Tribune,* August 20, 2008, p. 1; Laura Petrecca, "QVC Shops for Ideas for Future Sales," *USA TODAY,* May 5, 2008, p. 1B; and Jon Fine, "Lights, Camera, Shop!" *BusinessWeek,* January 12, 2009, p. 62.

17. "Black Friday Boasts $816 Million in U.S. Online Holiday Spending, Up 26 Percent vs. Year Ago," comScore.com.; see http://www .comscore.com/Press_Events/Press_Releases/2011/11/Black_ Friday_Boasts_816_Million_in_U.S._Online_Holiday_Spending and "Cyber Monday Spending Hits $1.25 Billion to Rank as Heaviest U.S. Online Spending Day in History," comScore.com; see http://www.comscore.com/Press_Events/Press_ Releases/2011/11/Cyber_Monday_Spending_Hits_1.25_Billion; accessed June 19, 2012. Thad Rueter, "E-Retail Spending to Increase 62% by 2016," Internet Retailer.com (from a report from Forrester Research), February 27, 2012. See http://www.internetretailer. com/2012/02/27/e-retail-spending-increase-45-2016; and "Walmart Expands Its Multichannel Offering with National Rollout of 'Pick Up Today,' " Walmart website: http://walmartstores.com/ pressroom/news/10549.aspx, March 10, 2011.

18. "eBay Marketplaces Fast Facts At-A-Glance (Q1 2012)," accessed June 19, 2012. See http://www.ebayinc.com/assets/pdf/fact_ sheet/eBay_Marketplaces_Fact_Sheet_Q12012_v2.pdf.

19. Nicole Paitsel, "Use Web to Help Shop and Ship," *Richmond Times Dispatch,* December 7, 2008, p. J5; and Stephen Thompson, "Is Your Snazzy New Site Cloaked in Invisibility?" *Advertising Age,* October 13, 2008, p. 24.

20. "DM Driven Sales by Medium and Market," *Statistical Fact Book,* Direct Marketing Association (New York, NY, 2012), p. 6.

21. "FTC Issues the FY 2011 National Do Not Call Registry Data Book; Nearly 210 Million Phone Numbers on Do Not Call List," Federal Trade Commission, November 10, 2011; accessed June 19, 2012. See http://ftc.gov/opa/2011/11/dnc.shtm.

22. "Direct Selling USA—Pinpoint Growth Sectors and Identify Factors Driving Change," *M2 Press Wire,* April 12, 2011; "Fact Sheet: U.S. Direct Selling in 2011," Direct Selling Association; accessed June 19, 2012. See http://www.dsa.org/research/industry-statistics/11gofactsheet.pdf.

23. "Avon Reports Fisrt-Quarter 2012 Results," press release—Avon; accessed June 19, 2012. See http://media.avoncompany.com/ index.php?s=10922&item=126089. "Avon Announces Management Realignments," *PR Newswire,* February 24, 2011; and Chris Knape, "Alticor Reports Record Sales in 2010, Growth Fueled by Strong Results in China, Amway's Largest Market," *Grand Rapids Press,* February 18, 2011, p. A8.

24. About Us: Company Facts—Pampered Chef; accessed June 19, 2012. See http://new.pamperedchef.com/company-facts. Olivera Perkins, "Direct Sales Proves Attractive to Long-Term Jobless Workers: Companies Selling Retail Goods at Home Parties See Profits Climbing," *Plain Dealer,* February 6, 2011, p. D1; Carol Lewis, "Calling All Avon Ladies—Direct Selling Is Back," *The Times,* December 28, 2010, p. 40; "Company Facts," The Pampered Chef website, http://www.pamperedchef.com/company-facts .jsp, accessed April 29, 2011; and Morris Kaplan, "Direct Selling Grows on the Net," *Weekend Australian,* March 7, 2009, p. 32.

25. Francis J. Mulhern and Robert P. Leon, "Implicit Price Bundling of Retail Products: A Multiproduct Approach to Maximizing Store Profitability," *Journal of Marketing,* October 1991, pp. 63–76.

26. Marc Vanhuele and Xavier Dreze, "Measuring the Price Knowledge Shoppers Bring to the Store," *Journal of Marketing,* October 2002, p. 72–85.

27. "Wal-Mart Reducing CE Floor Space in Remodeling," *Consumer Electronics Daily,* April 13, 2011; and Gwen Ortmeyer, John A. Quelch, and Walter Salmon, "Restoring Credibility to Retail Pricing," *Sloan Management Review,* Fall 1991, pp. 55–66.

28. William B. Dodds, "In Search of Value: How Price and Store Name Information Influence Buyers' Product Perceptions," *Journal of Consumer Marketing,* Spring 1991, pp. 15–24.

29. "Q3 2011 Supervalu Inc. Earning Conference Call-Final," *FD Wire,* January 11, 2011; and Leonard L. Berry, "Old Pillars of New Retailing," *Harvard Business Review,* April 2001, pp. 131–37.

30. Eric Anderson and Duncan Simester, "Mind Your Pricing Cues," *Harvard Business Review,* September 2003, pp. 96–103.

31. Julie Baker, A. Parasuraman, Dhruv Grewal, and Glenn B. Voss, "The Influence of Multiple Store Environment Cues on Perceived Merchandise Value and Patronage Intentions," *Journal of Marketing,* April 2002, pp. 120–41.

32. Hyeong Min Kim, "Consumers' Responses to Price Presentation Formats in Rebate Advertisements," *Journal of Retailing,* no. 4 (2006), pp. 309–17.

33. Rita Koselka, "The Schottenstein Factor," *Forbes,* September 28, 1992, pp. 104, 106.

34. "About WEM," West Edmonton Mall website, www.westedmall .com, accessed April 29, 2011.

35. Ernesto Portillo, "Home Depot Part of Center Plan," *McClatchy-Tribune Business News,* November 20, 2008; and Lisa A. Bernard, "Anchor ID'd for 'Big Box' Power Center," *Dayton Daily News,* July 19, 2007.

36. Umut Konus, Peter C. Verhoef, and Scott A. Neslin, "Multichannel Shopper Segments and Their Covariates," *Journal of Retailing,* December 2008, p. 398; and Robert A. Peterson and Sridhar Balasubramanian, "Retailing in the 21st Century: Reflections and Prologue to Research," *Journal of Retailing,* Spring 2002, pp. 9–16.

37. Jim Carter and Norman Sheehan, "From Competition to Cooperation: E-Tailing's Integration with Retailing," *Business Horizons,* March–April 2004, pp. 71–8.

38. Pierre Martineau, "The Personality of the Retail Store,[5] *Harvard Business Review,* January–February 1958, p. 47.

39. Julie Baker, Dhruv Grewal, and A. Parasuraman, "The Influence of Store Environment on Quality Inferences and Store Image," *Journal of the Academy of Marketing Science,* Fall 1994, pp. 328–39; Howard Barich and Philip Kotler, "A Framework for Marketing Image Management," *Sloan Management Review,* Winter 1991, pp. 94–104; Susan M. Keaveney and Kenneth A. Hunt, "Conceptualization and Operationalization of Retail Store Image: A Case of Rival Middle-Level Theories," *Journal of the Academy of Marketing Science,* Spring 1992, pp. 165–75; James C. Ward, Mary Jo Bitner and John Barnes, "Measuring the Prototypicality and Meaning of Retail Environments," *Journal of Retailing,* Summer 1992, p. 194; and Dhruv Grewal, R. Krishnan, Julie Baker, and Norm Burin, "The Effect of Store Name, Brand Name and Price Discounts on Consumers' Evaluations and Purchase Intentions," *Journal of Retailing,* Fall 1998, pp. 331–52. For a review of the store image literature, see Mary R. Zimmer and Linda L. Golden, "Impressions of Retail Stores: A Content Analysis of Consumer Images," *Journal of Retailing,* Fall 1988, pp. 265–93.

40. Jack Neff, "Shopper Marketing's New Frontier: e-Commerce," *Advertising Age,* March 14, 2011, p. 14; Andrew Adam Newman, "Taking Pickles Out of the Afterthought Aisle," *The New York Times,* April 26, 2011, p. 3: Piet Levy, "Snack Attack," *Marketing News,* February 28, 2011, p. 12; Yong Jian Wang, Michael S. Minor, and Jie Wei, "Aesthetics and the Online Shopping Environment: Understanding Consumer Responses," *Journal of Retailing,* 87 no. 1 (2011), pp. 46–58; and Els Breugelmans and Katia Campo, "Effectiveness of In-Store Displays in a Virtual Store Environment," *Journal of Retailing,* 87 no. 1 (2011), pp. 75–89.

41. Jans-Benedict Steenkamp and Michel Wedel, "Segmenting Retail Markets on Store Image Using a Consumer-Based Methodology," *Journal of Retailing,* Fall 1991, p. 300; Philip Kotler, "Atmospherics as a Marketing Tool," *Journal of Retailing* 49 (Winter 1973–74), p. 61; and Roger A. Kerin, Ambuj Jain, and Daniel L. Howard, "Store Shopping Experience and Consumer Price-Quality-Value Perceptions," *Journal of Retailing,* Winter 1992, pp. 376–97.

42. Mary Jo Bitner, "Servicescapes: The Impact of Physical Surroundings on Customers and Employees," *Journal of Marketing,* April 1992, pp. 57–71.

43. Joseph M. Hall, Praveen K. Kopale, and Aradhna Krishna, "Retailer Dynamic Pricing and Ordering Decisions: Category Management versus Brand-by-Brand Approaches," *Journal of Retailing,* 86 no. 2 (2010), pp. 172–83; and "Category Management Professionals Can Benefit from Integration of Leading Category and Space Management Suite with Comprehensive and Accurate Product Information," *Business Wire,* April 28, 2011.

44. John Davis, *Measuring Marketing* (Singapore: Wiley and Sons, 2007), p. 46.

45. Tom Webb, "Retail Ramifications: Best Buy and Apple Seem a Perfect Pair—Except for Apple's Store Ambitions," *St. Paul Pioneer Press,* February 19, 2011; Paul W. Farris, Neil T. Bendle, Phillip E. Pfeifer, David J. Reibstein, *Marketing Metrics* (Philadelphia: Wharton School Publishing, 2006), p. 106; Jerry Useem, "Simply Irresistible," *Fortune,* March 19, 2007, pp. 107–12; "Apple 2.0," ww.blogs.business2.com; Steve Lohr, "Apple, a Success at Stores, Bets Big on Fifth Avenue," *The New York Times,* May 19, 2006; Jim Dalrymple, "Inside the Apple Stores," *MacWorld,* June 2007, pp. 16–17; John Davis, *Measuring Marketing* (Singapore: Wiley and Sons, 2007), pp. 280–81; and Retailsails 2011 Chain Store Productivity Report, September 23, 2011, http://retailsails.files .wordpress.com/2011/09/rs_spsf.pdf, accessed October 7, 2011; RetailSails Retailer Profiles at the end of 2011; accessed June 19, 2012. See http://retailsails.com/monthly-sales-summary.

46. The wheel of retailing theory was originally proposed by Malcolm P. McNair, "Significant Trends and Development in the Postwar Period," in *Competitive Distribution in a Free, High-Level Economy and Its Implications for the University,* ed. A. B. Smith, (Pittsburgh: University of Pittsburgh Press, 1958), pp. 1–25; also see Stephen Brown, "The Wheel of Retailing—Past and Future," *Journal of Retailing,* Summer 1990, pp. 143–49; and Malcolm P. McNair and Eleanor May, "The Next Revolution of the Retailing Wheel," *Harvard Business Review,* September–October 1978, pp. 81–91.

47. Emily Bryson York, "McDonald's Is Getting In on the Oatmeal Trend," *Los Angeles Times,* December 21, 2010, p. B7; Marissa, "Healthy Fast Food? The McDonald's Australia Oven-Baked Menu Rolls Out in 44 Locations," *CalorieLab,* March 20, 2011; and Kat Odell, "French McDonald's Test Table Service," *Eater LA,* February 14, 2011.

48. "Our Story," Checkers website, http://checkerscompany.com/ our_story, accessed April 29, 2011; and "About," Boston Market website, www.bostonmarket.com/newsroom/index .jsp?page=about, accessed April 29, 2011.

49. William R. Davidson, Albert D. Bates, and Stephen J. Bass, "Retail Life Cycle," *Harvard Business Review,* November–December 1976, pp. 89–96.

Mall of America: This case was written by David P. Brennan and is based on an interview with Maureen Cahill and materials provided by Mall of America.

Chapter 14

1. Michael Learmonth, "#Winning on Twitter: The Top 10 Promoted Tweets," *Advertising Age,* May 9, 2011, p. 4; Natalie Zmuda, "QR Codes Gaining Prominence Thanks to a Few Big Players," *Advertising Age,* March 21, 2011, p. 8; Natalie Zmuda, "For PepsiCo, Entertainment Is Part of Big Picture," *Advertising Age,* May 24, 2010, p. 16; Kunur Patel, "Will Growing Crop of TV Apps Engage Viewers, Advertisers?" *Advertising Age,* May 17, 2010, p. 3; and Alyssa S. Groom, "Integrated Marketing Communication Anticipating the 'Age of Engage,'" *Communication Research Trends,* December 1, 2008, p. 3.

2. Sita Mishra and Sushma Muralie, "Managing Dynamism of IMC—Anarchy to Order," *Journal of Marketing and Communication,* September 2010, pp. 29–37; Philip J. Kitchen, Ilchul Kim, and Don E. Schultz, "Integrated Marketing Communications: Practice Leads Theory," *Journal of Advertising Research,* December 2008, pp. 531–46; Bob Liodice, "Essentials for Integrated Marketing," *Advertising Age,* June 9, 2008, p. 26; and Shu-pei Tsai, *Journal of Advertising* 34 (Winter 2005), pp. 11–23.

3. Wilbur Schramm, "How Communication Works," in *The Process and Effects of Mass Communication,* Wilbur Schramm, ed., (Urbana, IL: University of Illinois Press, 1955), pp. 3–26.

4. E. Cooper and M. Jahoda, "The Evasion of Propaganda," *Journal of Psychology* 22 (1947), pp. 15–25; H. Hyman and P. Sheatsley, "Some Reasons Why Information Campaigns Fail," *Public Opinion Quarterly* 11 (1947), pp. 412–23; and J. T. Klapper, *The Effects of Mass Communication* (New York: Free Press, 1960), chap. VII.

5. "Mistakes in Advertising," on the Learn English website, http:// www.learnenglish.de/mistakes/HorrorMistakes.htm, accessed May 5, 2011; and Bianca Bartz, "Advertising Bloopers," Trend-Hunter Marketing website, http://www.trendhunter.com/trends/ advertising-bloopers-international-ads-lost-in-translation, accessed May 5, 2011.

6. Rik Pieters and Michel Wedel, "Attention Capture and Transfer in Advertising: Brand Pictorial, and Text-Size Effects," *Journal of Marketing,* April 2004, pp. 36–50.

7. Adapted from American Marketing Association, Resource Library, Dictionary, http://www.marketingpower.com/_layouts/ Dictionary.aspx?dLetter=P, accessed May 5, 2011.

8. Dave Folkens, "3 Ways Social Media Is Changing Public Relations," *Online Marketing Blog,* February 17, 2011; Michael Bush, "How

Social Media Is Helping the Public-Relations Sector Not Just Survive, but Thrive," *Advertising Age,* August 23, 2010, p. 1; David Robinson, "Public Relations Comes of Age," *Business Horizons* 49 (2006), pp. 247–56; and Dick Martin, "Gilded and Gelded: Hard-Won Lessons from the PR Wars," *Harvard Business Review,* October 2003, pp. 44–54.

9. Piet Levy, "CSR Take Responsibility," *Marketing News,* May 30, 2010, p. 20; "McDonald's Corporation Worldwide Corporate Social Responsibility 2010 Report," available at http://www.aboutmcdonalds.com/etc/medialib/csr/docs.Par.32488.File.tmp/mcd063_2010%20PDFreport_v9.pdf; and *Open for Discussion,* McDonald's Values in Practice Blog, http://www.aboutmcdonalds.com/mcd/csr/blog.10829.3047257.html, accessed May 5, 2011.

10. Jooyoung Kim, Hye Jin Yoon, and Sun Young Lee, "Integrating Advertising and Publicity: A Theoretical Examination of the Effects of Exposure Sequence, Publicity Valence, and Product Attribute Consistency," *Journal of Advertising,* Spring 2010, p. 97; and Marsha d. Loda and Barbara Carrick Coleman, "Sequence Matters: A More Effective Way to Use Advertising and Publicity," *Journal of Advertising Research* 45 (December 2005), pp. 362–71.

11. Kusum L. Ailawadi, Scott A. Neslin, and Karen Gedenk, "Pursuing the Value-Conscious Consumer: Store Brands versus National Brand Promotions," *Journal of Marketing,* January 2001, pp. 71–8.

12. Nikki Hopewell, "The Rules of Engagement: A Bevy of Rules and Best Practices Govern Promotions and Contests," *Marketing News,* June 1, 2008, p. 6; and Gerard Predergast, Yi-Zheng Shi, and Ka-Man Cheung, "Behavioural Response to Sales Promotion Tools," *International Journal of Advertising,* (2005), pp. 467–486.

13. Adapted from American Marketing Association, Resource Library, Dictionary, http://www.marketingpower.com/_layouts/Dictionary.aspx?dLetter=D, accessed May 27, 2011.

14. Edmund Lee, "How Social Media Stole Your Mind, Took Advertising with It," *Advertising Age,* February 28, 2011, p. 2; Antje Cockrill, Mark M. Goode, and Amy White, "The Bluetooth Enigma: Practicalities Impair Potential," *Journal of Advertising Research,* March 2011, pp. 298–312; Thomas Pardee, "Media-Savvy Gen Y Finds Smart and Funny Is 'New Rock-n-Roll,'" *Advertising Age,* October 11, 2010, p. 17; "5 Tips for Marketing to Millennials," *Advertising Age,* October 11, 2010, p. 17: Klint Finley, "U.S. Consumers Say They Now Spend as Much Time on the Internet as They Do Watching TV," *ReadWriteWeb,* December 13, 2010; Tac Anderson, "Global Trends in Youth Media Consumption and Increased Multitasking," *New Comm Bizz,* June 2, 2010; Andrew Rohm, Fareena Sultan, and Fleura Bardihi, "Multitasking Youth: To Engage Youth Consumers, You Must Understand the Paradox of Their Media Consumption," *Marketing Management,* November/December 2009, p. 20; "Mobile Metrics to Know before You Make the Call," *Marketing News,* April 30, 2010, p. 5; and Elizabeth Sullivan, "The Tao of Mobile Marketing," *Marketing News,* April 30, 2010, p. 16. "U.S. Wireless Quick Facts," CTIA: The Wireless Association, http://www.ctia.org/consumer_info/index.cfm/AID/10323, accessed June 19, 2012; Aaron Smith, "Nearly Half of American Adults are Smartphone Owners," Pew Interest and American Life Project, March 1, 2012, http://pewinternet.org/Reports/2012/Smartphone-Update-2012/Findings/Findings.aspx accessed June 19, 2012.

15. "Push vs. Pull Strategies," *Daily News,* May 3, 2011; "Question: Should B2B Be Focusing All Its Efforts on 'Pull' Marketing Therefore Turning Its Back on 'Push' Marketing Techniques?" *B2B Marketing Magazine,* September 2009; and Michael Levy, John Webster, and Roger Kerin, "Formulating Push Marketing Strategies: A Method and Application," *Journal of Marketing,* Winter 1983, pp. 25–34.

16. Jamie LaReau, "Ford Dealers Revamp Pay Plans; Some Efforts Resemble Stair-Step Programs," *Automotive News,* February 14, 2011, p. 10; Terry Box, "Pressure's Rising for Ford Dealers," *Dallas Morning News,* February 10, 2007; and Richard Truett, "Ford to Dealers: We'll Support Sales," *Automotive News,* June 18, 2007, p. 3.

17. Jeremy A. Greene and Aaron S. Kesselheim, "Pharmaceutical Marketing and the New Social Media," *PharmaGossip,* November 24, 2010; Sheng Yuan, "Public Response to Direct-to-Consumer Advertising of Prescription Drugs," *Journal of Advertising Research,* March 2008, pp. 30–41; and Fusun F. Gonul, Franklin Carter, Elina Petrova, and Kannan Srinivasan, "Promotion of Prescription Drugs and Its Impact on Physicians' Choice Behavior," *Journal of Marketing,* July 2001, pp. 79–90. John Mack, "Lipitor Holds Key to DTC Ad Spending in 2012," Pharma Marketing Blog, April 15, 2012, http://pharmamkting.blogspot.com/2012/04/lipitor-holds-key-to-dtc-ad-spending-in.html, accessed June 19, 2012.

18. Lauren Drell, "4 Ways Behavioral Targeting Is Changing the Web," *Mashable,* April 26, 2011; adapted from American Marketing Association, Resource Library, Dictionary, http://www.marketing-power.com/_layouts/Dictionary.aspx?dLetter=B, accessed May 28, 2011.

19. Robert J. Lavidge and Gary A. Steiner, "A Model for Predictive Measurement of Advertising Effectiveness," *Journal of Marketing,* October 1961, p. 61.

20. "100 Leading National Advertisers," *Advertising Age,* June 20, 2011, p. 10.

21. George S. Low and Jakki J. Mohr, "Setting Advertising and Promotion Budgets in Multi-Brand Companies," *Journal of Advertising Research,* January/February 1999, pp. 67–78; Don E. Schultz and Anders Gronstedt, "Making Marcom an Investment," *Marketing Management,* Fall 1997, pp. 41–49; and J. Enrique Bigne, "Advertising Budget Practices: A Review," *Journal of Current Issues and Research in Advertising,* Fall 1995, pp. 17–31.

22. John Philip Jones, "Ad Spending: Maintaining Market Share," *Harvard Business Review,* January–February 1990, pp. 38–42; and Charles H. Patti and Vincent Blasko, "Budgeting Practices of Big Advertisers," *Journal of Advertising Research* 21 (December 1981), pp. 23–30.

23. "Advertising as Percent of Sales," *Advertising Age,* June 21, 2010, p. 24.

24. Brenda Marlin, "Adding It Up: You Can Save Time by Trying One of Three Short-Cut Approaches to an Annual Budget," *ABA Banking,* October 1, 2007, p. 36; James A. Shroer, "Ad Spending: Growing Market Share," *Harvard Business Review,* January–February 1990, pp. 44–48; and Jeffrey A. Lowenhar and John L. Stanton, "Forecasting Competitive Advertising Expenditures," *Journal of Advertising Research* 16, no. 2 (April 1976), pp. 37–44.

25. Daniel Seligman, "How Much for Advertising?" *Fortune,* December 1956, p. 123.

26. James E. Lynch and Graham J. Hooley, "Increasing Sophistication in Advertising Budget Setting," *Journal of Advertising Research* 30 (February–March 1990), pp. 67–75.

27. Jimmy D. Barnes, Brenda J. Muscove, and Javad Rassouli, "An Objective and Task Media Selection Decision Model and Advertising Cost Formula to Determine International Advertising Budgets," *Journal of Advertising* 11, no. 4 (1982), pp. 68–75.

28. Graham Ruddock, "London Olympics Sponsors Are Already into Their Stride," *The Daily Telegraph,* May 6, 2011, p. 8; "The Olympics Come But Once Every Two Years," *Marketing News,* November 1, 2008, p. 12; "Olympics Will Bring Online Opportunities for Many Brands," *Revolution,* July 14, 2008, p. 13; and Don E. Schultz, "Olympics Get the Gold Medal in Integrating Marketing Event," *Marketing News,* April 27, 1998, pp. 5, 10.

29. "Integrated Marketing: One Message, Many Media," *Marketing Week,* September 18, 2008, p. 31; and Cornelia Pechman, Guangzhi Zhao, Marvin E. Goldberg, and Ellen Thomas Reibling, "What to Convey in Antismoking Advertisements for Adolescents: The Use of Protection Motivation Theory to Identify Effective Message Themes," *Journal of Marketing,* April 2003, pp. 1–18.

30. "Pic Promos Get Tactile," *Daily Variety,* May 26, 2011, p. 1; " Pirates' Plunder: A 3D Litmus Test?" *Daily Variety,* May 24, 2011, p. 1; "Free Lego Toy, Get Your Arr-Some Pirates of the Caribbean Freebie Mini Black Pearl Boat," *The Sun,* May 16, 2011, p. 18; and Will Freeman, "Review: Games: Lego Pirates of the Caribbean Xbox 360, PS3, Wii, PC, Disney," *The Observer,* May 15, 2011, p. 36.

31. Mike Reid, "Performance Auditing of Integrated Marketing Communication (IMC) Actions and Outcomes," *Journal of Advertising* 34 (Winter 2005), p. 41.

32. Michael Bush, "Agency A-List: Media Agency of the Year Horizon Media," *Advertising Age,* January 24, 2011, p. 25; and the Horizon Media website, www.horizonmedia.com, accessed May 30, 2011.

33. "Integrated Marketing: The Benefits of Integrated Marketing," *Marketing Week,* September 18, 2008, p. 33; and Tom Duncan, "Is Your Marketing Communications Integrated?" *Advertising Age,* January 24, 1994, p. 26.

34. Don E. Schultz, "The Media Circuits Evolution," *Marketing News,* March 30, 2011, p. 11; "Integrated Marketing: Digital Fuels Integration Boom," *Marketing Week,* December 11, 2008, p. 27; Don E. Schultz, "IMC Is Do or Die in New Pull Marketplace," *Marketing News,* August 15, 2006, p. 7; and Don E. Schultz, "Integration's New Role Focuses on Customers," *Marketing News,* September 15, 2006, p. 8.

35. *Statistical Fact Book 2011* (New York: Direct Marketing Association, 2011), p. 20; and "Which Media Are You Using?" Integrated Marketing Research, unpublished report, Direct Marketing Association, 2011. *Statistical Fact Book 2012,* (New York: Direct Marketing Association, 2012), pp. 4, 6, 16.

36. "Shoppers to Discover Elevated Gift Offering, Compelling Prices and Superior Shopping Experience," *Business Wire,* November 10, 2010; "JCPenney Kicks Off Christmas Gift Program," *Wireless News,* November 16, 2010; Alex Palmer, "JCPenney Launches Facebook e-Commerce Store," *DMNews,* December 15, 2010; Tim Peterson, "Porsche Launches Integrated Campaign to Shift Consumer Perception," *DMNews,* March 25, 2011; and *Statistical Fact Book 2011* (New York: Direct Marketing Association, 2011), p. 5.

37. *Statistical Fact Book 2011* (New York: Direct Marketing Association, 2011), p. 113; and "Six Ways Lands' End Makes Online Shopping a Joy," *PR Newswire,* November 21, 2007. *Statistical Fact Book 2012,* (New York: Direct Marketing Association, 2012), p. 24.

38. Theresa Howard, "E-mail Grows as Direct-Marketing Tool: They're Quicker to Make, Cheap to Send," *USA Today,* November 28, 2008, p. 5B.

39. Time Parry, "Fill-Mail Savings," *Catalog Age,* August 1, 2008, p. 35; and Christopher Hosford, "Database Face-to-Face," *B to B,* February 9, 2009, p. 21.

40. "China: New Media Blossoming as Business Models Revamp," BBC Monitoring World Media, December 9, 2008; "The Data Dilemma," *Marketing Direct,* February 6, 2007, p. 37; and Marc Nohr, "South Africa—A Worthy Contender," *Marketing Direct,* March 5, 2007, p. 20.

41. "Cell Phones Now Protected by the Do Not Call List," *States News Service,* May 16, 2011; Jonathan Brunt, "'Do Not Mail' Can't Gain Traction," *Spokesman Review,* May 5, 2010, p. 7; "DMA: 'Do Not Track Online Act' Is Unnecessary," *States News Service,* May 9, 2011; "DMA Updates Its 'Guidelines for Ethical Business Practice,'" *States News Service,* May 25, 2011; Martin Courtney and Tony Lock, "Keep It Safe, Keep It Legal," *Computing,* May 26, 2011; Siobhain Butterworth, "Cookie Law Shambles Really Takes the Biscuit," *Guardian Unlimited,* May 27, 2011; and Lara O'Reilly, "New Cookie Law: What You Need to Know," *Marketing Week,* May 26, 2011.

Mountain Dew: This case was written by Steven Hartley. Sources: "Dewmocracy Campaign Overview," www.dewmocracymediahub.com; "The Mountain Dew Dewmocracy 2 Campaign Empowers Brand Loyalists Nationwide to Create and Launch the Next New Dew," press release, http://www.dewmocracymediahub.com/images/press_release_041910.pdf; "Fresh Dew," *Prepared Foods,* June 2010, vol. 179, p. 39; "Montain

Dew Embraces the Spirit of 'Dewmocracy,' Most Memorable New Product Launch website, http://mmnpl.wordpress.com/?s=mountain; "Marketing Campaign: Winner: Dewmocracy 2," *Beverage World,* vol. 129, p. 35; "Program Overview and Dewmocracy 2–Campaign Statistics, www.dwmocracymediahub.com; Jessica E. Vascellaro and Suzanne Vranica, "Shaping Ads for Web-Connected TV—Software Offers New Real Estate to Tout Products, Ability to Target Messages," *The Wall Street Journal,* September 20, 2010, p. B9; and Natalie Zmuda, "Why Mtn Dew Let Skater Dudes Take Control of Its Marketing," *Advertising Age,* March 22, 2010, p. 30.

Chapter 15

1. Brian Steinberg, "12 Minutes, 10 Ideas That Tried to Change TV Ad Time Forever," *Advertising Age,* April 18, 2011, p. 12; Michael Learmonth, "Web TV? Xbox, Verizon and Others Appear to Be Up for the Challenge," *Advertising Age,* April 18, 2011, p. 6; Andrew Hampp, "The Next Big Thing in TV? Well, It's Not on TV," *Advertising Age,* May 16, 2011, p. 4; Michael Learmonth, "Beyond TV, Marketers Look to 'Earn' Love for Video Ads," *Advertising Age,* May 16, 2011, p. 14; and Kelty Logan, "Hulu.com or NBC? Streaming Video versus Traditional TV," *Journal of Advertising Research,* March 2011, pp. 276–85.

2. Karen V. Fernandez and Dennis L. Rosen, "The Effectiveness of Information and Color in Yellow Pages Advertising," *Journal of Advertising,* Summer 2000, p. 61; David A. Aaker and Donald Norris, "Characteristics of TV Commercials Perceived as Informative," *Journal of Advertising Research* 22, no. 2 (April–May 1982), pp. 61–70.

3. Larry D. Compeau and Dhruv Grewal, "Comparative Price Advertising: An Integrative Review," *Journal of Public Policy & Marketing,* Fall 1998, pp. 257–73; and William Wilkie and Paul W. Farris, "Comparison Advertising: Problems and Potentials," *Journal of Marketing,* October 1975, pp. 7–15.

4. Chingching Chang, "The Relative Effectiveness of Comparative and Noncomparative Advertising: Evidence for Gender Differences in Information-Processing Strategies," *Journal of Advertising,* Spring 2007, p. 21; Jerry Gotlieb and Dan Sorel, "The Influence of Type of Advertisement, Price, and Source Credibility on Perceived Quality," *Journal of the Academy of Marketing Science,* Summer 1992, pp. 253–60; and Cornelia Pechman and David Stewart, "The Effects of Comparative Advertising on Attention, Memory, and Purchase Intentions," *Journal of Consumer Research,* September 1990, pp. 180–92.

5. Kathy L. O'Malley, Jeffrey J. Bailey, Chong Leng Tan, and Carl S. Bozman, "Effects of Varying Web-Based Advertising-Substantiation Information on Attribute Beliefs and Perceived Product Quality," *Academy of Marketing Studies Journal,* 2007, p. 19; Bruce Buchanan and Doron Goldman, "Us vs. Them: The Minefield of Comparative Ads," *Harvard Business Review,* May–June 1989, pp. 38–50; Dorothy Cohen, "The FTC's Advertising Substantiation Program," *Journal of Marketing,* Winter 1980, pp. 26–35; and Michael Etger and Stephen A. Goodwin, "Planning for Comparative Advertising Requires Special Attention," *Journal of Advertising* 8, no. 1 (Winter 1979), pp. 26–32.

6. David W. Schumann, Jan M. Hathcote, and Susan West, "Corporate Advertising in America: A Review of Published Studies on Use, Measurement, and Effectiveness," *Journal of Advertising,* September 1991, p. 35; Lewis C. Winters, "Does It Pay to Advertise in Hostile Audiences with Corporate Advertising?" *Journal of Advertising Research,* June–July 1988, pp. 11–18; and Robert Selwitz, "The Selling of an Image," *Madison Avenue,* February 1985, pp. 61–69.

7. Natalie Zmuda, "Can Dr Pepper's Mid-Cal Soda Score a 10 with Men?" *Advertising Age,* February 21, 2011, p. 4; E. J. Schultz, "Strong Consumer Demand Pushes Greek Yogurt into a Dairy-Aisle Battlefield," *Advertising Age,* March 14, 2011, p. 8; Natalie Zmuda, "Another Gatorade Product Line," *Advertising Age,* May 2, 2011, p. 4; and Jeremy Mullman, "Nike: What Slowdown?" *Advertising Age,* October 20, 2008, p. 34.

8. Ira Teinowitz, "Self-Regulation Urged to Prevent Bias in Ad Buying," *Advertising Age,* January 18, 1999, p. 4.

9. See the Advertising Research Foundation website, http://www.thearf.org/assets/ad-effectiveness-council, accessed June 14, 2011.

10. "Super Bowl Ads Cost Average of 3.5M," *ESPN.com,* February 5, 2012; Bruce Horovitz, Laura Petrecca, and Gasy Strauss, "Super Bowl Ad Meter Winner: Score One for the Doritos Baby," *USA Today,* February 8, 2012; Bill Gorman, "Will Super Bowl TV Viewership Set Another Record?" *tvbythenumbers.com,* February 4, 2011; Bill Gorman, "Second-by-Second Super Bowl TV Viewing Revealed: 98.8% Stayed Tuned for the Ads," *tvbythenumbers.com,* February 9, 2011; "Advertising Champs! Volkswagen, Chrysler, E*Trade and Other Super Bowl Advertisers Score Big in Social Media," *PR Newswire,* February 14, 2011; and Rama Ylkur, Chuck Tomkovick, and Patty Traczyk, "Super Bowl Effectiveness: Hollywood Finds the Games Golden," *Journal of Advertising Research,* March 2004, pp. 143–59.

11. Ioni Lewis, Barry Watson, Richard Tay, and Katherine M. White, "The Role of Fear Appeals in Improving Driver Safety," *The International Journal of Behavioral Consultation and Therapy,* June 22, 2007, p. 203; Lenore Skenazy, "Take the Fat Out of Your Food," *Advertising Age,* January 14, 2008, p. 12; Cornelia Pechmann, Guangzhi Zhao, Marvin E. Goldberg, and Ellen Thomas Reibling, "What to Convey in Antismoking Advertisements for Adolescents: The Use of Protection Motivation Theory to Identify Effective Message Themes," *Journal of Marketing,* April 2003, pp. 1–18; Jeffrey D. Zbar, "Fear!" *Advertising Age,* November 14, 1994, pp. 18–19; and John F. Tanner, Jr., James B. Hunt, and David R. Eppright, "The Protection Motivation Model: A Normative Model of Fear Appeals," *Journal of Marketing,* July 1991, pp. 36–45.

12. "About Bebe," Bebe website, www.bebe.com, accessed June 16, 2011; and Sanjay Putrevu, "Consumer Responses toward Sexual and Nonsexual Appeals: The Influence of Involvement, Need for Cognition (NFC), and Gender," *Journal of Advertising,* Summer 2008, p. 57.

13. Rupal Parekh, "With Strong Work for Walmart and Geico, Martin Agency Is Creating a New Specialty: Making Marketers Recession-Proof," *Advertising Age,* January 19, 2009, p. 30; and Louis Llovio, "Geico Gecko's Viral Videos," *Richmond Times Dispatch,* March 28, 2009, p. B-9.

14. Thomas W. Cline and James J. Kellaris, "The Influence of Humor Strength and Humor-Message Relatedness on Ad Memorability: A Dual Process Model," *Journal of Advertising,* Spring 2007, p. 55; Yong Zhang and George M. Zinkham, "Responses to Humorous Ads," *Journal of Advertising,* Winter 2006, p. 113; and Yih Hwai Lee and Elison Ai Ching Lim, "What's Funny and What's Not: The Moderating Role of Cultural Orientation in Ad Humor," *Journal of Advertising,* Summer 2008, p. 71.

15. "4A's Costs Survey Shows Minimal Rise in Production, Larger Boost for Post," SourceCreative.com citing the *2010 Television Production Cost Survey* (New York: American Association of Advertising Agencies, 2011), http://www.sourceecreative.com/news.php?ID=6234, accessed June 19, 2012; and Jean Halliday, "Exotic Ads Get Noticed," *Advertising Age,* April 9, 2001, p. S4.

16. Rupal Parekh, "Ad Age's Agency of the Year," *Advertising Age,* January 24, 2011, p. 6; Teressa Iezzi, "Creativity's Agency of the Year: Wieden & Kennedy," *Advertising Age,* January 24, 2011, p. 7; and Megan O'Neill, "Old Spice Response Campaign Was More Popular than Obama," *socialtimes.com,* August 5, 2010.

17. "Advertising Expenditure Forecasts," ZenithOptimedia, June 2012, p. 191.

18. Vicki R. Lane, "The Impact of Ad Repetition and Ad Content on Consumer Perceptions of Incongruent Extensions," *Journal of Marketing,* April 2000, pp. 80–91.

19. Brian Steinberg, "American Idol, pro football duke it out for priciest TV spot," *Advertising Age,* October 24, 2011, p. 4; Jack Neff, "Killing Off 30-Second Spot Is Bad Medicine for OTC Drug Industry," *Advertising Age,* September 13, 2010, p. 1; and Kate Newstead and Jenni Romaniuk, "Cost per Second: The Relative Effectiveness of 15- and 30-Second Television Advertisements," *Journal of Advertising Research,* 2009, pp. 68–76.

20. "Other Industry Data," National Cable & Telecommunications Association, www.ncta.com, accessed June 17, 2011; and Brian Steinberg, "Turner Experiments with Building a Smarter Ad for Its Cable Networks," *Advertising Age,* April 11, 2011, p. 3.

21. "Broadcast Station Totals as of March 31, 2011," *FCC News,* Federal Communications Commission, May 16, 2011; "National Radio Format Shares and Station Counts," p. 13; and "Time Spent Listening," p. 105, in *Radio Today,* 2011 edition, Arbitron, accessed October 13, 2011. See http://www.arbitron.com/downloads/Radio_Today_2011.pdf.

22. "Corporate Overview," SiriusXM Radio Inc. website, http://www.siriusxm.com/corporate, accessed June 19, 2012; and "Hour-by-Hour Listening," in *Radio Today,* 2012 Edition, Arbitron, p. 89.

23. "A Magazine for Everyone," *Magazine Media Factbook 2011/12,* New York: The Association of Magazine Media, p. 64; "*Athlon Sports* and *Dash* Share the Top Spot for Mr. Magazine™ Most Notable Launch of 2010," http://mrmagazine.wordpress.com/, accessed June 19, 2011; John Barber, "The New Yorker: There Is Even an App for That," globeandmail.com, June 9, 2011; and Ben Dowell, "Media: Have Trade Magazines Got a Shelf Life?" *The Guardian,* April 25, 2011, p. 1.

24. "Number of Magazines by Category," American Society of Magazine Editors, http://www.magazine.org/ASME/EDITORIAL_TRENDS/1145.aspx, accessed October 13, 2011; and "Magazines Are the Medium of Engagement," *Magazine Media Factbook 2011/12,* New York: The Association of Magazine Media, p. 14.

25. Phil Rosenthal, "New Newspaper Circulation Figures beyond Compare, Thanks to New Metrics," *Chicago Tribune.com,* May 3, 2011; "Metro Newspaper Is the #1 Free Daily Newspaper in Boston," *Business Wire,* June 13, 2011; "General Advertising Rate Card," *The Wall Street Journal,* http://www.wsjmediakit.com/downloads/General_Rate_Card_2012.pdf?120621012107, accessed June 19, 2012; "2012 Advertising Rate Card," *USA Today,* http://i.usatoday.net/marketing/media_kit/images/2012_Advertising_Rate_Card.pdf, accessed June 19, 2012; and "About Metro," *Metro.* http://www.metro.us/newyork/aboutus accessed June 19, 2012.

26. "BIA/Kelsey's Global Yellow Pages Forecast: 2011–2015," December 21, 2011, p. 7, http://www.biakelsey.com/webinars/GlobalYellowPagesBIAKelseyGYPForecast2011–2015.pdf, accessed June 19, 2012; "As Media Habits Evolve, Yellow Pages and Search Engines Firmly Established as Go-To Sources for Consumer Shopping Locally," *PR Newswire,* June 13, 2011; "Yellow Pages Publishers Discuss Plans to Overturn Phone Book Ban," *Entertainment Close-Up,* May 30, 2011; Carol Krol, "Yellow Pages Bleeding Red Ink," *B to B,* August 11, 2008, p. 1; and "Extinction Threatens Yellow-Pages Publishers," *The Wall Street Journal,* November 17, 2008.

27. See "Examine Web Audiences by Site, Size, Demographic Profile and Behavior," at Nielsen Online website, www.nielsen-online.com/solutions, accessed April 23, 2009; and Abbey Klaassen, "Why the Click Is the Wrong Metric for Online Ads," *Advertising Age,* February 23, 2009, p. 4.

28. "Click Fraud Rate Drops to 19.1 Percent in Q4 2010," *Business Wire,* January 26, 2011; Sara Yin, "Click Fraud Skyrockets," *PC Magazine,* October 21, 2010; Alex Mindlin, "Click Fraud Climbs with Mobile Gear," *The New York Times,* November 1, 2010, p. 2; Gareth Jones, "Briefing-Paid Search-Advertisers Stung by Rising Click Fraud," *Revolution,* May 1, 2009, p. 18; "30 Seconds on Click Fraud," *Marketing Direct,* December 1, 2008, p. 42; Brian Grow and Ben Elgin, "Click Fraud," *BusinessWeek,* October 2, 2006, pp. 46–57; and Rob Hof, "Is Google Too Powerful?" *BusinessWeek,* April 9, 2007, p. 48.

29. Arch G. Woodside, "Outdoor Advertising as Experiments," *Journal of the Academy of Marketing Science* 18 (Summer 1990), pp. 229–37.

30. "Clear Channel Outdoor Holdings Releases 'Out-of-Home Advertising and the Retail Industry' Report," *Professional Services Close-Up,* January 25, 2011; Andrew Hampp, "What's New with Outdoor Ads, and What's This Digital Out-of-Home I Keep Hearing About?" *Advertising Age,* September 27, 2010, p. 48; "The Year Ahead for . . . Outdoor," *Campaign,* January 9, 2009, p. 28; Andrew Hampp, "Digital Out of Home. That's Those Pixilated Billboards, Right?" *Advertising Age,* March 30, 2009; Andrew Hampp, "Out of Home That Stood Out," *Advertising Age,* December 15, 2008, p. 22; and Daniel W. Baack, Rick T. Wilson, and Brian D. Till, "Creativity and Memory Effects," *Journal of Advertising,* Winter 2008, p. 85.

31. Schoon Park and Minhi Hahn, "Pulsing in a Discrete Model of Advertising Competition," *Journal of Marketing Research,* November 1991, pp. 297–405.

32. Peggy Masterson, "The Wearout Phenomenon," *Marketing Research,* Fall 1999, pp. 27–31; and Lawrence D. Gibson, "What Can One TV Exposure Do?" *Journal of Advertising Research,* March–April 1996, pp. 9–18.

33. Rik Pieters, Michel Wedel, and Rajeev Batra, "The Stopping Power of Advertising: Measure and Effects of Visual Complexity," *Journal of Marketing,* September 2010, pp. 48–60; Rob Norton, "How Uninformative Advertising Tells Consumers Quite a Bit," *Fortune,* December 26, 1994, p. 37; and "Professor Claims Corporations Waste Billions on Advertising," *Marketing News,* July 6, 1992, p. 5.

34. "ANA Survey Finds Fees Persist as Dominant Method of Agency Compensation, Even with the Emergence of Other Models," *Target News Service,* July 27, 2010; Rance Crain, "Why Agencies—and the Media—Are Reluctant to Bet It All on Value-Compensation Systems," *Advertising Age,* June 7, 2010, p. 31; Stephen Fajen, "The Agency Model Is Bent but Not Broken," *Advertising Age,* July 7, 2008, p. 17; Jeremy Mullman, "Anheuser-Busch Whacks Retainers for Its Agencies," *Advertising Age,* February 16, 2009, p. 1; and Jack Neff, "No One-Size-Fits-All Snuggie Model Exists for DRTV Shops," *Advertising Age,* March 23, 2009.

35. The discussion of posttesting is based on William F. Arens, Michael F. Weigold, and Christian Arens, *Contemporary Advertising,* 12th ed. (New York: McGraw-Hill Irwin, 2009), pp. 228–30.

36. "ROI Metric Available in MRI Starch Syndicated," Mediamark Research & Intelligence, www.mediamark.com, accessed April 23, 2009.

37. David A. Aaker and Douglas M. Stayman, "Measuring Audience Perceptions of Commercials and Relating Them to Ad Impact," *Journal of Advertising Research* 30 (August–September 1990), pp. 7–17; and Ernest Dichter, "A Psychological View of Advertising Effectiveness," *Marketing Management* 1, no. 3 (1992), pp. 60–62.

38. David Krugel, "Television Advertising Effectiveness and Research Innovation," *Journal of Consumer Marketing,* Summer 1988, pp. 43–51; and Laurence N. Gold, "The Evolution of Television Advertising Sales Measurement: Past, Present, and Future," *Journal of Advertising Research,* June–July 1988, pp. 19–24.

39. Patricia E. Odell, "Promo Lite," *Promo,* October 2008, p. 14; and Bradley Johnson, "100 Leading National Advertisers by Total U.S. Advertising Spending 2010: Zenith Optimedia Forecasts through 2012," *Advertising Age,* June 20, 2011, p. 18.

40. Tom Hansen, "Media Mash," *Promo,* February 1, 2007, p. 66; Magid M. Abraham and Leonard M. Lodish, "Getting the Most Out of Advertising and Promotion," *Harvard Business Review,* May–June 1990, pp. 50–60; Steven W. Hartley and James Cross, "How Sales Promotion Can Work for and against You," *Journal of Consumer Marketing,* Summer 1988, pp. 35–42; Robert D. Buzzell, John A. Quelch, and Walter J. Salmon, "The Costly Bargain of Trade Promotion," *Harvard Business Review,* March–April 1990, pp. 141–49; and Mary L. Nicastro, "Break-Even Analysis Determines Success of Sales Promotions," *Marketing News,* March 5, 1990, p. 11.

41. "Annual Coupon Facts," NCH Marketing Services, 2012, p. 3, 7–8, 10, 13, 31; Jessica Guynn and Nathan Olivarez-Giles, "Facebook Testing Daily Deals Service; and "The Social Network Enters a Fast-Growing Coupon Market in a Challenge to Groupon and LivingSocial," *Los Angeles Times,* April 27, 2011, p. B2.

42. "What Is Coupon Fraud?" The Coupon Information Corporation, http://www.couponinformationcenter.com, accessed June 20, 2011; Josh Elledge, "Coupon Fraud Hurts Us All," *Grand Rapids Press,* April 19, 2011, p. B1; and Amy Johannes, "Flying the Coup," *Promo,* July 1, 2008, p. 28.

43. Amy Johannes, "Premium Connections," *Promo,* October 2008, p. 34; and Gerard P. Prendergast, Alex S. L. Tsang, Derek T. Y. Poon, *Journal of Advertising Research,* June 2008, p. 287.

44. "Six Consumer-Created Doritos and Pepsi MAX Ads Crash the Super Bowl Advertising Stage, Now Compete for $5 Million in Prizes," *PR Newswire,* February 6, 2011; and "User Content Offers a New Perspective," *PR Week,* February 23, 2009, p. 21.

45. Sarah Firshein, "HGTV Dream Home Winner Revealed!: Here's a Warm 'n' Fuzzy Story. . ." *Curbed NY,* March 11, 2011; and Charlotte McEleny, "Social Media and Mobile Boost Participation for McDonald's Monopoly," *New Media Age Online,* April 18, 2011.

46. "Mars Chocolate North America Launches 5 Characters, 5 Cars Promotion," *Travel & Leisure Close-Up,* June 20, 2011; "Buy a Large Coke at Carl's Jr. and Win—Guaranteed; Guest Can Win Big with My Coke Rewards Point and Food Prizes," *Business Wire,* May 27, 2011; "Coca-Cola and Celebrity Cruises Beverage Package Sweepstakes," Celebrity Cruises website, http://pages.email.celebritycruises.com/SweepStakesMay/, accessed June 21, 2011.

47. Brian Quinton, "The Hands-On Experience," *Promo,* October 2008, p. 37; Larry Jaffee, "Try It," *Promo,* September 1, 2007, p. AR25; Lorin Cipolla, "Instant Gratification," *Promo,* April 1, 2004, p. 4; "Best Activity Generating Brand Awareness/Trial," *Promo,* September 2001, p. 51; and "Brand Handing," *Promo's 9th Annual Sourcebook* (2002), p. 32.

48. Kelly Hlavinka and Jim Sullivan, *The Billion Member March: The 2011 Colloquy Loyalty Census,* LoyaltyOne Colloquy, http://www.colloquy.com/files/2011-COLLOQUY-Census-Talk-White-Paper.pdf, 2011; Kara McGuire, "Retailers Work to Make Shopping Its Own Reward," *Star Tribune,* December 19, 2010, p. 1A; and "Loyalty Rewards Membership on the Rise," *Brandweek.com,* April 17, 2009.

49. "The Case for Rebates," *Chief Marketer,* July 1, 2011; and Marvin A. Jolson, Joshua L. Wiener, and Richard B. Rosecky, "Correlates of Rebate Proneness," *Journal of Advertising Research,* February–March 1987, pp. 33–43.

50. "Bond 23 Earns $45 Million as Product Placement Revenue," *Indiantelevision.com,* May 6, 2011; "FCC Examines Product Placement Rules," *Marketing News,* July 15, 2008, p. 8; Josh Halliday, "Product Placement: P Logo Stands for Puzzled Public," *Guardian Unlimited,* June 20, 2011; Kate Ward, "'American Idol' Product Placement: Does It Distract from the Show?" www.popwatch.com, April 19, 2011; Brandchannel.com website, http://www.brandchannel.com/brandcameo_films.asp?movie_year=2011#movie_list, accessed June 21, 2011; and Ecaterina V. Karniouchina, Can Uslay, and Grigori Erenburg, "Do Marketing Media Have Life Cycles? The Case of Product Placement in Movies," *Journal of Marketing,* May 2011, pp. 27–49.

51. This discussion is drawn particularly from John A. Quelch, *Trade Promotions by Grocery Manufacturers: A Management Perspective* (Cambridge, MA: Marketing Science Institute, August 1982).

52. Michael Chevalier and Ronald C. Curhan, "Retail Promotions as a Function of Trade Promotions: A Descriptive Analysis," *Sloan Management Review* 18 (Fall 1976), pp. 19–32.

53. G. A. Marken, "Firms Can Maintain Control over Creative Co-op Programs," *Marketing News,* September 28, 1992, pp. 7, 9.

Google, Inc.: This case was written by Steven Hartley. Sources: "Mobile Cellular Subscriptions: 2000–2010," International Telecommunication

Union, accessed October 15, 2011, http://www.itu.int/ITU-D/ict/material/FactsFigures2010.pdf; Jessica E. Vascellaro, "Google Decides to Find Its Creative Side," *The Wall Street Journal,* October 7, 2009; Robert D. Hof, "Google's New Ad Weapon," *BusinessWeek,* June 22, 2009, p. 52; Maria Bartiromo, "Eric Schmidt on Where Google Is Headed," *BusinessWeek,* August 17, 2009, p. 11; "Why Microsoft-Yahoo Deal Could Be Good for Google," *Advertising Age,* August 10, 2009, p. 10; Peter Burrow, "Apple and Google: Another Step Apart," *BusinessWeek,* August 17, 2009, p. 24; Jeff Jarvis, "How The Google Model Could Help," *BusinessWeek,* February 9, 2009, p. 32; Abbey Klaasen, "Google Says Print Ads Isn't the Answer for Newspapers," *Advertising Age,* January 26, 2009, p. 17; Matthew Creamer, "Recession Doesn't Dent Total Value of Top 100 Brands," *Advertising Age,* April 27, 2009; "The 500 Largest U.S. Corporations," *Fortune,* May 4, 2009, F-1; "ComScore Releases August 2009 U.S. Search Engine Rankings," www.comscore.com, October 10, 2009; interviews with Google personnel; and information contained on the Google website, (www.google.com).

Chapter 16

1. Natasha Singer, "On Campus, It's One Big Commercial," *The New York Times,* September 11, 2011, pp. BU1, BU4; Natalie Zmuda, "Marketers Hitting Campus Harder than Ever," *Advertising Age,* October 17, 2001, pp. 26, 28; and Bruce Horovitz, "Marketers Pull an Inside Job on College Campuses," *USA Today,* October 4, 2010, pp. 2A, 2B.
2. Ibid.
3. Ibid.
4. Andreas M. Kaplan and Michael Haenlein, "Users of the World, Unite! The Challenges and Opportunities of Social Media," *Business Horizons* 53, no. 1 (2010), pp. 59–68.
5. Dave Evans, *Social Media Marketing: An Hour a Day* (Indianapolis, IN: Wiley Publishing, Inc., 2009), pp. 57–59; Jason Miletsky, *Principles of Internet Marketing* (Boston, MA: Course Technology, Cengage Learning, 2010), pp. 75–76; Kristin Tillotson, "Blogging's Getting Old These Days," *Star Tribune,* December 22, 2010, p. E1; and Soumitra Dutta and Matthew Fraser, "Web 2.0: The ROI Case," *CEO Magazine,* May/June 2009, pp. 42–44.
6. "Participative Web and User-Created Content: Web 2.0, Wikis, and Social Networking" (Paris: Organization for Economic Co-operation and Development, 2007); and Jason Daley, "Tearing Down the Walls," *Entrepreneur,* December 2010, pp. 57–60.
7. Dave Evans, *Social Media Marketing: An Hour a Day,* pp. 31–37.
8. Kaplan and Haenlein, "Users of the World, Unite! The Challenges and Opportunities of Social Media," pp. 62–64.
9. Drake Bennett, "Ten Years of Inaccuracy and Remarkable Detail," *Bloomberg Businessweek,* January 10–January 16, 2011, pp. 57–61.
10. Starr Hall and Chadd Rosenberg, *Get Connected: The Social Networking Toolkit for Business* (Madison, WI: Entrepreneur Press, 2009), pp. 17–20.
11. Emily Steel and Geoffrey Fowler, "Facebook in Privacy Breach," *The Wall Street Journal,* October 18, 2010, pp. A1, A2; and Geoffrey Fowler and Emily Steel, "Facebook Says User Data Sold to Broker," *The Wall Street Journal,* November 1, 2010, p. B3.
12. This discussion of Facebook and Twitter uses material on the Ford Consulting Group website provided by David Ford; and Clara Shih, *The Facebook Era* (Boston, MA: Pearson Education, Inc., 2009), pp. 25–51.
13. "Facestagram's Photo Opportunity," *The Economist,* April 14, 2012, p. 71.
14. "Facebook Statistics," accessed October 13, 2011. See http://www.facebook.com/press/info.php?statistics; and Lev Grossman, "2010 Person of the Year: Mark Zuckerberg," *Time,* December 27, 2010–January 3, 2011, p. 59.
15. Lev Grossman, "2010 Person of the Year: Mark Zuckerberg," pp. 44–75; and Brad Stone, "Sell Your Friends," *Bloomberg Businessweek,* September 27–October 3, 2010, pp. 64–72.
16. "The Value of Friendship," *The Economist,* February 4, 2012, pp. 23–26.
17. Randall Stross, "Social Networks, Small and Smaller," *The New York Times,* April 15, 2012, p. BU3.
18. Ben Pickering, "How to Use Facebook Ads: An Introduction," Socialmediaexaminer.com, May 3, 2012; and Martin Peers, "Facebook Pokes Its Rivals," *The Wall Street Journal,* November 16, 2010, p. C12.
19. "Top 10 Ways to Engage Fans on Facebook," Buddy Media, Inc., 2010.
20. Figure 16–3 is adapted from "The CMO's Guide to the Social Landscape," prepared by 97th Floor, CMO.com, March 20, 2012. Site Profile: DoubleClick Ad Planner by Google for Facebook.com, U.S. Demographic Profile Data (Age, Gender, Education, and Household Income) for June 2012, accessed July 31, 2012. See https://accounts.google.com/ServiceLogin?service=branding&passive=1209600&continue=https://www.google.com/adplanner/site_profile&followup=https://www.google.com/adplanner/site_profile&ltmpl=adplanner (registration required).
21. Brad Stone, "Idiot Proof," *Bloomberg Businessweek,* March 5–March 11, 2012, pp. 62–67; and "What Is Twitter," accessed October 13, 2011. See http://business.twitter.com/basics/what-is-twitter; Mark Hachman, "Twitter Continues to Soar in Popularity, Site's Numbers Reveal," PC Magazine (online edition), September 8, 2011; accessed October 13, 2011. See http://www.pcmag.com/article2/0,2817,2392658,00.asp#fbid=mTJD8c71Z0C.
22. Jeff Herring and Maritza Parra, *The Wall Street Journal,* "Make the Most of Tweeting," *Star Tribune,* January 6, 2011, p. E4.
23. "About Us: LinkedIn Facts," accessed October 13, 2011. See http://press.linkedin.com/about.
24. Kristin Burnham, "5 LinkedIn Tips for Career Success in 2012," www.c10.com, January 5, 2012.
25. Lev Grossman, "The Beast with a Billion Eyes," *Time,* January 30, 2012, pp. 39–43.
26. Mike Hale, "Is YouTube's New Design a Sign of Things to Come?" *Star Tribune,* December 19, 2011, p. E2.
27. Alex Perry/0bo, "The Warlord vs. the Hipsters," *Time,* pp. 36–41; and Solomon Moore, "U.S. Plays a Bigger Part in Hunt for Kony," *The Wall Street Journal,* April 30, 2012, p. A16.
28. Brad Stone and Andy Fixmar, "MustSee YouTube," *Bloomberg Businessweek,* May 7–May 13, 2012, pp. 42–44; and Tanzina Vega, "Your Ad, as Seen on YouTube," *Media Decoder: The New York Times,* April 23, 2012.
29. Damian Kulash, Jr., "The New Rock Star Paradigm," *The Wall Street Journal,* December 17, 2010, p. D1; and "YouTube Press Room: Statistics," accessed October 13, 2011. See http://www.youtube.com/t/press_statistics.
30. Christa Toole, "Ten Tips for Those Who Still Aren't Using YouTube," *Advertising Age* (adage.com), October 19, 2010, downloaded January 11, 2011; and Felix Gillette, "On YouTube, Seven-Figure Views, Six-Figure Paychecks," *Bloomberg Businessweek,* September 27–October 3, 2010, pp. 35–36.
31. Unique Monthly Visitors: Facebook, Twitter, LinkedIn, and YouTube as of September 2011, Site Analytics: Compete.com, a Kantor Media Company, accessed October 17, 2011. See http://siteanalytics.compete.com/facebook.com.
32. Site Profile: DoubleClick Ad Planner by Google for Facebook.com, U.S. Demographic Profile Data (Age, Gender, Education, and Household Income) for September 2011, accessed October 17, 2011. See https://www.google.com/adplanner/planning/site_profile#siteDetails?uid=domain%253A%2520facebook.com&geo=US&lp=false.
33. This example and the section on measuring results were provided by Brian Stuckey and Amanda Axvig of AOI Marketing, Inc.
34. Suzanne Vranica and Shayne Raice, "The Big Doubt Over Facebook," *The Wall Street Journal,* May 2, 2012, pp. B1, B5; Matthew Creamer, "Study: Only 1% of Facebook 'Fans' Engage With Brands," *Digital-Advertising Age,* January 27, 2012; and April Dembosky and Tim Bradshaw, "Advertisers Uneasy With Facebook," *Financial Times,* May 6, 2012.

35. Dale Buss, "Pepsi Kicks Off 'Live for Now' Global Campaign with Nicki Minaj," *Brandchannel*, April 30, 2012. See http://brandchannel.com/home/post/2012/04/30/Pepsi-Live-for-Now-Campaign-043012.aspx; Natalie Zmuda, "Pepsi Debuts First Global Campaign," *Advertising Age*, April 30, 2012. See http://adage.com/article/cmo-strategy/pepsi-debuts-global-campaign-live/234379; Natalie Zmuda, "Pepsi Tackles Identify Crisis," *Advertising Age*, May 7, 2012. See http://adage.com/article/news/pepsi-tackles-identity-crisis/234586; Brian Anthony Hernandez, "Pepsi Unwraps 'Pulse' Digital Dashboard for Pop Culture," *Mashable Entertainment*, April 30, 2012. See http://mashable.com/2012/04/30/pepsi-pulse-live-for-now; Mike Snider, "Social Media Is Latest Front of Cola Wars, "*USA Today*, April 30, 2012. See http://www.usatoday.com/tech/news/story/2012-04-30/pepsicoke-social-media/54631902/1; Joe Berkowitz, "Pepsi Launches First Global Campaign 'Live For Now' with New Social Platform, Pulse," Fastcocreate.com blog post. See http://www.fastcocreate.com/1680713/pepsi-launches-first-global-campaign-live-for-now-with-new-social-platform-pulse.

36. See http://www.huffingtonpost.com/2012/04/06/pinterest-traffic-growth_n_1408088.html.

37. The Greenpeace-Nestlé example uses material on the Ford Consulting Group website provided by David Ford.

38. ComScore Reports August 2011 U.S. Mobile Subscriber Market Share, ComScore.com, October 5, 2011, accessed October 13, 2011. See http://www.comscore.com/Press_Events/Press_Releases/2011/10/comScore_Reports_August_20_11_U.S._Mobile_Subscriber_Market_Share. "Living in a See-Through World," *The Economist*, November 6, 2010, p. 21.

39. Alex Konrad, "Romancing the App Developer," *Fortune*, April 30, 2012, p. 38; and Adam Satariano, "Anarchy in the App Store," *Bloomberg Businessweek*, March 19–March 25, 2012, pp. 47–49.

40. Keith Wagstaff, "Drawsome," *Time*, April 9, 2012, p. 55; Cliff Edwards and Douglas MacMillan, "Game Makers Place Their Bets," *Bloomberg Businessweek*, April 2–April 8, 2012, pp. 43–44; and Robert Klara, "Foul Play" *Adweek*, May 30–June 5, 2011, pp. 32–33.

41. Andreas M. Kaplan, "If You Love Something, Let It Go Mobile: Mobile Marketing and Mobile Social Media 4×4," *Business Horizons* 55, no. 2, pp. 129–139.

42. Geoffrey A. Fowler, "A High-Tech Edge on Black Friday," *The Wall Street Journal*, November 24, 2010, pp. D1, D3.

43. Geoffrey A. Fowler and Vauhini Vara, "Using 'Likes' for Gift Ideas," *The Wall Street Journal*, December 22, 2010, p. B1.

44. Dave Evans, *Social Media Marketing: An Hour a Day*, pp. 127–149.

45. Kara McGuire, "Shoppers Hunt Bargains via Their Smart Phones," *Star Tribune*, November 28, 2010, pp. D1, D10; Michelle Higgins, "Smart Phone Apps Can Help You Avoid Holiday Travel Headaches," *Star Tribune*, December 19, 2010, p. 63; Sue Stock, "Code Alert for Smart Phones," *Star Tribune*, November 17, 2010, p. D8; Miguel Bustillo and Ann Zimmerman, "Phone-Wielding Shoppers Strike Fear into Retailers," *The Wall Street Journal*, December 16, 2010, pp. A1, A19; and Roger Cheng, "The Phone Delivers Gift Cards," *The Wall Street Journal*, November 24, 2010, p. D3.

46. Mike Swift, "Smart Phones Ring Up a Bigger Slice of Holiday Sales," *Star Tribune*, December 30, 2010, pp. A1, A10; Evan Ramsted, "TV Makers Turn Their Hopes to Apps," *The Wall Street Journal*, January 4, 2011, pp. A1, A2; Randall Stross, "Someday, Store Coupons May Tap You on the Shoulder," *The New York Times*, December 26, 2010, p. BU3; and Jackie Crosby, "Just Call It V-Commerce," *Star Tribune*, January 2, 2011, p. D1.

47. Gordon Fairclough and Leos Rousek, "'Brusli?' No. Chuck Norris," *The Wall Street Journal*, December 29, 2010, p. B6.

Bitter Girls: This case was written by Jennifer Katz, Amanda Axvig, and Brian Stuckey of AOI Marketing, Inc., with appreciation for permissions granted by Bitter Girls®.

Chapter 17

1. Interview with Lindsey Smith, GE Healthcare, May 17, 2011.

2. Jessi Hempel, "IBM's All-Star Salesman," cnnmoney.com, September 26, 2008.

3. "Surgical Visits," *Business 2.0*, April 2006, p. 94.

4. Mark W. Johnston and Greg W. Marshall, *Relationship Selling*, 3rd ed. (Burr Ridge, IL: McGraw-Hill/Irwin, 2010).

5. Gerhard Gschwandtner, "How Much Time Do Your Salespeople Spend Selling?" *Selling Power*, March/April 2011, p. 8.

6. Scott Sterns, "Cold Calls Have Yet to Breathe Their Last Gasp," *The Wall Street Journal*, December 14, 2006, p. D2.

7. Jim Edwards, "Dinner, Interrupted," *BrandWeek*, May 26, 2003, pp. 28–32.

8. Christopher Conkey, "Record Fine Levied for Telemarketing," *The Wall Street Journal*, December 14, 2005, pp. D1, D4.

9. Philip R. Cateora, Mary C. Gilly, and John L. Graham, *International Marketing*, 15th ed. (Burr Ridge, IL: McGraw-Hill/Irwin, 2011).

10. This discussion is based on Johnston and Marshall, *Relationship Selling*.

11. Kapil R. Tuli, Ajay K. Kohli, and Sundar G. Bharadwaj, "Rethinking Customer Solutions: From Product Bundles to Relational Processes," *Journal of Marketing*, July 2007, pp. 1–17.

12. For an extensive discussion of objections, see Charles M. Futrell, *Fundamentals of Selling*, 10th ed. (Burr Ridge, IL: McGraw-Hill/Irwin, 2010), chap. 12.

13. Theodore Levitt, *The Marketing Imagination* (New York: Free Press, 1983), p. 111.

14. Barton A. Weitz, Stephen B. Castleberry, and John F. Tanner, Jr., *Selling: Building Partnerships*, 6th ed. (Burr Ridge, IL: McGraw-Hill/Irwin, 2010).

15. *Management Briefing: Sales and Marketing* (New York: Conference Board, October 1996), pp. 3–4.

16. "Group Dynamics," *Sales & Marketing Management*, January/February 2007, p. 8; and Steve Atlas and Elise Atlas, "Team Approach," *Selling Power*, May 2000, pp. 126–28.

17. William L. Cron and David W. Cravens, "Sales Force Strategy," in Robert A. Peterson and Roger A. Kerin, eds., *Wiley International Encyclopedia of Marketing: Volume 1—Marketing Strategy* (West Sussex, UK: John Wiley & Sons, Ltd., 2011), pp. 197–207.

18. This discussion is based on William L. Cron and Thomas E. DeCarlo, *Dalrymple's Sales Management*, 10th ed. (Hoboken, NJ: John Wiley & Sons, Inc., 2009).

19. Rosann L. Spiro, Gregory A. Rich, and William J. Stanton, *Management of the Sales Force*, 12th ed. (Burr Ridge, IL: McGraw-Hill/Irwin, 2008), chap. 7.

20. Spiro et al., *Management of the Sales Force*, chap. 8. Also see, Thomas Steenbargh and Michael Ahearne, "Motivating Salespeople: What Really Works," *Harvard Business Review*, July–August, 2012, pp. 71–75; Julia Chang, "Wholly Motivated," *Sales & Marketing Management*, March 2007, pp. 24ff.

21. This discussion is based on Johnson and Marshall, *Sales Force Management*, chap. 11; and Andris Zoltner, Prabhakant Sinha, and Sally E. Lorimer, *The Complete Guide to Sales Force Incentive Compensation* (New York: AMACOM, 2006).

22. www.marykay.com, downloaded April 20, 2012.

23. Dina Bass, "Microsoft Turns Attention to Customer Satisfaction," www.seattlepi, accessed January 5, 2005.

24. Mark Cotteleer, Edward Inderrieden, and Felissa Lee, "Selling the Sales Force on Automation," *Harvard Business Review*, July–August 2006, pp. 18–22.

25. "Corporate America's New Sales Force," *Fortune*, August 11, 2003, special advertising section; and www.toshiba.com/technology, downloaded May 15, 2006.

Xerox: This case was written by Steven Hartley and Roger Kerin. Sources: Joseph Kornik, "Table Talk: A Sales Leaders Roundtable," *Sales &*

Marketing Management, February 2007; Philip Chadwick, "Xerox Global Service," *Printweek,* October 11, 2007, p. 32; Kevin Maney, "Mulcahy Traces Steps of Xerox's Comeback," *USA Today,* September 11, 2006, p. 48; Sarah Campbell, "What It's Like Working for Xerox," *The Times,* September 14, 2006, p. 9; "Anne Mulcahy: How I Compete," *BusinessWeek,* August 21, 2006, p. 55; Simon Avery, "CEO's HR Skills Turn Xerox Fortunes," *The Globe and Mail,* June 2, 2006, p. B3; Julia Chang, "Ultimate Motivation Guide: Happy Sales Force, Happy Returns," *Sales & Marketing Management,* March 2006; "The World's Most Powerful Women," www.forbes.com, August 27, 2008; and resources available on the Xerox website, www.xerox.com, including About Xerox, Executive Biographies, the Xerox 2007 Fact Sheet, the Online Fact Book: Historical Highlights, and the Online Fact Book: How Xerox Sells.

Chapter 18

1. Interview with Mattison Crowe, Director of Marketing at Seven Cycles, Inc., May 1, 2011; and www.sevencycles.com, May 2, 2011.
2. "U.S. Online Retail Forecast: 2010–2015," www.forrester.com, February 27, 2012.
3. Rafl A. Mohammed, Robert J. Fisher, Bernard J. Jaworski, and Gordon J. Paddison, *Internet Marketing: Building Advantage in a Networked Economy,* 2nd ed. (Burr Ridge, IL: McGraw-Hill/Irwin, 2004).
4. Ward A. Hanson and Kirthi Kalyanam, *Internet Marketing & Electronic Commerce* (Mason, OH: Thompson Higher Education, 2007).
5. Hanson and Kalyanam, *Internet Marketing & Electronic Commerce.*
6. Judy Strauss, Adel El-Ansary, and Raymond Frost, *E-Marketing,* 5th ed. (Upper Saddle River, NJ: Prentice Hall, 2009).
7. Piet Levy, "The Delta Dilemma," *Marketing News,* January 30, 2011, pp. 20–21.
8. This discussion is drawn from Jeffrey F. Rayport and Bernard J. Jaworski, *e-Commerce,* 2nd ed. (Burr Ridge, IL: McGraw-Hill/Irwin, 2004); and *The Essential Guide to Best Practices in eCommerce* (Portland, OR: Webtrends, Inc., 2006).
9. Mylene Mangalindan, "Websites Want You to Stick Around," *The Wall Street Journal,* April 15, 2008, p. B5.
10. "Demographics of Internet Users," www.pewinternet.org, downloaded October 7, 2011.
11. "Statistics: U.S. Online Shoppers," www.pewinternet.org, downloaded October 7, 2010.
12. "Moms Spend 24 Hours a Week Online, According to Just Released Study by Disney Online," *prnewswire,* October 27, 2011; "Internet Moms," www.newsmediatrend.com, April 28, 2011.
13. "U.S. Online Retail Forecast: 2010–2015."
14. Jerry Wind and Arvind Ranaswamy, "Customerization: The Next Wave in Mass Customization," *Journal of Interactive Marketing,* Winter 2001, pp. 13–32.
15. Valerie Bauerkin, "Gatorade's Mission: Sell More Drinks," *The Wall Street Journal,* September 14, 2010, p. B6; and Tom Hayes and Michael S. Malone, "Marketing in the World of the Web," *The Wall Street Journal,* November 29–30, 2008, p. A13. Also see, Kate Fitzgerald, "Blogs Fascinate, Frighten Marketers," *Advertising Age,* March 5, 2007, p. S-4.
16. Quoted in Strauss et al., *E-Marketing,* p. 357.
17. Victoria Taylor, "The Best-Ever Social Media Campaigns," www.forbes.com, August 17, 2010.
18. Ethan Smith, "Tying Price to Tickets, Demand," *The Wall Street Journal,* April 19, 2011, p. B8.
19. "Buying a Car Online?" www.msnmoney.com, February 28, 2012.
20. "Cookies Cause Bitter Backlash," *The Wall Street Journal,* September 20, 2010, pp. B1, B2.
21. "Sites Are Accused of Privacy Failings," *The Wall Street Journal,* February 13, 2012, pp. B1, B8; "Ad Industry Takes Another Look at 'Do Not Track' in Browsers," *The Wall Street Journal,* March 31, 2011, p. B5; Edmund Lee, "Online Self-Regulation May Not Satisfy

Administration," *Advertising Age,* March 21, 2011, p. 3; *2010 Internet Crime Report,* www.ic3.gov; Joel Stein, "Your Data, Yourself," *Time,* March 21, 2011, pp. 40–46; and "Online Privacy: A World with No Secrets," *The Wall Street Journal,* November 15, 2011, pp. B5–B11.
22. "More Offices Block Online Shopping," *Dollar Morning News,* December 4, 2011, p. 3D; "Survey: Many Admit to Online Shopping at Work," www.moneycentral.msn.com, December 2, 2008; and Susan Adams et al., "This Time It Is Personal: Employee Online Shopping at Work," *Interactive Marketing,* April 2005, pp. 326–36.
23. This discussion is based on "Attention Shoppers: Online Product Research," www.pewresearch.org, September 29, 2010; "Online Research Drives Offline Sales," www.emarketer.com, February 26, 2008; "Study: More Consumers Do Research Online, Shop Offline," *Brandweek,* November 3, 2008, p. 8; and Tamera Mendelsohn, "The State of Multichannel Consumers in the U.S. and Europe," www.forresterresearch.com, June 25, 2007.
24. "Retailers' Panty Raid on Victoria's Secret," *The Wall Street Journal,* June 20, 2007, pp. B1, B12.
25. www.callaway.com, May 5, 2011; Stephanie Kang, "Callaway Will Use Retailers to Sell Goods Directly to Consumers Online," *The Wall Street Journal,* November 6, 2006, p. B5.
26. Erik Hauser and Max Lenderman, "Experiential Marketing," *BrandWeek,* September 20, 2008: Special Section; and Timothy J. Mullaney, "E-Biz Strikes Again," *BusinessWeek,* May 10, 2004, pp. 80–90.
27. "Attention Shoppers: Online Product Research."

Pizza Hut: This case was prepared by Pizza Hut and imc² executives for exclusive use in this text.

Appendix B

1. Catherine Kaputa, *You Are a Brand!: How Smart People Brand Themselves for Business Success* (Nicholas Brealey Publishing, Boston: MA, 2010); Diane Brady, "Creating Brand You," *BusinessWeek,* August 22, 2007, pp. 72–73; and Denny E. McCorkle, Joe F. Alexander, and Memo F. Diriker, "Developing Self-Marketing Skills for Student Career Success," *Journal of Marketing Education,* Spring, 1992, pp. 57–67.
2. Linda J. Popky, *Marketing Your Career: Positioning, Packaging and Promoting Yourself for Success* (Woodside Business Press, 2009); Marianne E. Green, "Marketing Yourself: From Student to Professional," *Job Choices for Business & Liberal Arts Students,* 50th ed., 2007, pp. 30–31; and Joanne Cleaver, "Find a Job through Self-Promotion," *Marketing News,* January 31, 2000, pp. 12, 16.
3. Kevin Cochrane, "The 21st Century Marketer," *Marketing News,* March 30, 2011, p. 22; and John N. Frank, "Stand Out from the Crowd, Landing a Marketing Job Today Means Touting Your Specialty and Staying Positive," *Marketing News,* January 30, 2009, p. 22.
4. Jonathan Harper and Frank Birkel, "From CMO to CEO: The Route to the Top," *Research & Insight,* Spencer Stuart, December 2009, http://www.spencerstuart.com/research/articles/1329/, accessed June 25, 2011; and "Leading CEO's: A Statistical Snapshot of S&P 500 Leaders," *Research & Insight, Spencer Stuart,* December 2008, www.spencerstuart.com/research/ceo/975/, accessed June 14, 2009.
5. "Starting Salary by Academic Major," *Salary Survey* (Bethlehem, PA: National Association of Colleges and Employers, April 2012), pp. 9-10.
6. "Advertising, Marketing, Promotions, Public Relations, and Sales Managers," *Occupational Outlook Handbook,* 2010–11 Edition (Washington, DC: U.S. Department of Labor, 2010), www.bls.gov/oco/ocos020.htm, accessed June 25, 2011.
7. Matthew Creamer, "P&G Primes Its Pinpoint Marketing," *Advertising Age,* May 7, 2007.
8. "Wholesale Trade," *Occupational Handbook,* 2010–11 Edition (Washington, DC: U.S. Department of Labor, 2010), www.bls.gov/oco/cg/cgs026.htm, accessed June 25, 2010.

9. S. William Pattis, *Careers in Advertising* (New York: McGraw-Hill, 2004).

10. Roslyn Dolber, *Opportunities in Retailing Careers* (New York: McGraw-Hill, 2008).

11. Peter Coy, "Help Wanted," *Businessweek,* May 11, 2009, pp. 40–46; and "The Way We'll Work," *Time,* May 25, 2009, pp. 39–50.

12. Rebecca Aronaur, "Shaping the Profession of Sales," *Sales & Marketing Management,* July 1, 2006.

13. Jack and Suzy Welch, "Dear Graduate . . . To Stand Out among Your Peers, You Have to Overdeliver," *Businessweek,* June 19, 2006, p. 100.

14. Piet Levy, "10 Minutes with Stan Sthanunathan, Vice President of Marketing Strategy and Insights, The Coca-Cola Co.," *Marketing News,* February 28, 2011, p. 34; and Edmund Hershberger and Madhav N. Segal, "Ads for MR Positions Reveal Desired Skills," *Marketing News,* February 1, 2007, p. 28.

15. "Market Research Analyst," in Les Krantz, ed., *Jobs Rated Almanac,* 6th ed. (New York: St. Martin's Press, 2002).

16. Deborah L. Vence, "In an Instant, More Researchers Use IM for Fast, Reliable Results," *Marketing News,* March 1, 2006, p. 53; and Joshua Grossnickle and Oliver Raskin, "What's Ahead on the Internet," *Marketing Research,* Summer 2001, pp. 9–13.

17. "2011 Franchise 500," *Entrepreneur* website, at www.entrepreneur.com, accessed June 26, 2011.

18. Lisa Bertagnoli, "Marketing Overseas Excellent for Career," *Marketing News,* June 4, 2001, p. 4.

19. Barbara Flood, "Turbo Charge Your Job Search, Job Searching and Career Development Tips," *Information Outlook,* May 1, 2007, p. 40.

20. Barbara Flood, "Turbo Charge Your Job Search, Job Searching and Career Development Tips," *Information Outlook,* May 1, 2007, p. 40.

21. Barbara Kiviat, "The New Rules of Web Hiring," *Time,* November 24, 2003, p. 57; Karen Epper Hoffman, "Recruitment Sites Changing Their Focus," *Internet World,* March 15, 1999; Pamela Mendels, "Now That's Casting a Wide Net," *Businessweek,* May 25, 1998: and James C. Gonyea, *The Online Job Search Companion* (New York: McGraw-Hill, 1995).

22. Ronald B. Marks, *Personal Selling: A Relationship Approach,* 6th ed. (New York: Pearson, 1996).

23. Sima Dahl, "A New Job Is No Excuse to Ease Up on Networking," *Marketing News,* February 28, 2011, p. 4; Leonard Felson, "Undergrad Marketers Must Get Jump on Networking Skills," *Marketing News,* April 8, 2001, p. 14; Wayne E. Baker, *Networking Smart* (New York: McGraw-Hill, 1994); and Piet Levy, "AMA Chapters across the Country Are Increasingly Using Job Boards, Networking Events and Other Techniques to Help Members in This Economy," *Marketing News,* March 15, 2009, p. 14.

24. Tim Post, "New Graduates Use Social Media to Look for Jobs," *St. Paul Pioneer Press,* June 3, 2011; Susan Berfield, "Dueling Your Facebook Friends for a New Job," *Bloomberg Businessweek,* March 7, 2011, p. 35; and Dan Schawbel, "Top 10 Social Sites for Finding a Job," *Mashable,* February 24, 2009.

25. Amy Diepenbrock, "Will Your Resume Open the Door to an Interview?" *Job Choices for Business & Liberal Arts Students, 2011,* National Association of Colleges and Employers, p. 31; and Marianne E. Green, "Marketing Yourself: From Student to Professional," *Job Choices for Business & Liberal Arts Students: 2009* (Bethlehem, PA: National Association of Colleges and Employers, 2008), pp. 28–29.

26. Marianne E. Green, "Resume Writing: Sell Your Skills to Get the Interview!" *Job Choices for Business & Liberal Arts Students,* 50th ed., 2007, pp. 39–47.

27. C. Randall Powell, "Secrets of Selling a Résumé," in Peggy Schmidt, ed., *The Honda How to Get a Job Guide* (New York: McGraw-Hill, 1984), pp. 4–9.

28. "Post with Caution: Your Online Profile and Our Job Search," *Job Choices for Business & Liberal Arts Students: 2009* (Bethlehem, PA: National Association of Colleges and Employers, 2008), p. 30; "If I 'Google' You, What Will I Find?" *Job Choices for Business and Liberal Arts Students,* 50th ed., 2007, p. 16; Joyce Lain Kennedy, "Computer-Friendly Résumé Tips," Planning Job Choices: 1999, 42nd ed. (Bethlehem, PA: National Association of Colleges and Employers, 1998), p. 49; and Joyce Lain Kennedy and Thomas J. Morrow, *Electronic Résumé Revolution* (New York: Wiley and Sons, 1994).

29. William J. Banis, "The Art of Writing Job-Search Letters," *Job Choices for Business and Liberal Arts Students,* 50th ed., 2007, pp. 32–38; and Arthur G. Sharp, "The Art of the Cover Letter," *Career Futures* 4, no. 1 (1992), pp. 50–51.

30. Lindsey Pollak, "The 10 Commandments of Social Media Job Seeking," *Job Choices for Business & Liberal Arts Students, 2011,* National Association of Colleges and Employers, p. 20; Alison Damast, "Recruiters' Top 10 Complaints," *Businessweek,* April 26, 2007; and Marilyn Moats Kennedy, "'Don't List' Offers Important Tips for Job Interviews," *Marketing News,* March 15, 2007, p. 26.

31. Sima Dahl, "Where Do You See Yourself in Five Years?" *Marketing News,* November 15, 2010, p. 4; and Dana James, "A Day in the Life of a Corporate Recruiter," *Marketing News,* April 10, 2000, pp. 1, 11.

32. Robert M. Greenberg, "The Company Visit—Revisited," *NACE Journal,* Winter 2003, pp. 21–27.

33. Mary E. Scott, "High-Touch vs. High-Tech Recruitment," *NACE Journal,* Fall 2002, pp. 33–39.

CREDITS

New Product Works. P. 205, © GfK Custom Research, LLC. P. 208, Courtesy Ford Motor Company. P. 208, © M. Hruby. P. 209, Courtesy of IDEO. P. 209, Courtesy Gary Schwarzberg. P. 210, © M. Hruby. P. 211, Jim Wilson/The New York Times/Redux. P. 211, Jose Azel/Aurora. P. 212, Courtesy General Mills; Photo: Bolin Marketing. P. 213, © M. Hruby. P. 216, Courtesy General Mills; Photo: Bolin Marketing. P. 216, Courtesy General Mills.

CHAPTER 10

P. 218, Photo by Rob Tringali/SportsChrome/Getty Images. P. 220, Photo by J. Meric/Getty Images. P. 222, Getty Images. P. 223, AP Photo/Mary Altaffer. P. 223, Courtesy Amazon.com Inc. P. 229, © 2009 Blue Moon. P. 230, Copyright 2011 by Consumers Union of U.S., Inc. Yonkers, NY 10703-1057, a non-profit organization. P. 230, Courtesy Lowe Worldwide; Photo: Brian Kuhlman; Talent: Cameo Amato. P. 232, DR. PEPPER is a registered trademark of Dr. Pepper/Seven Up, Inc. Used with permission. P. 233, *No credit.* P. 235, © M. Hruby. P. 236, Courtesy QPG Sherpa. P. 237, © M. Hruby. P. 238, © M. Hruby. P. 239, Used with permission from McDonald's Corporation. P. 240, Trademarks and copyrights used herein are properties of the United States Postal Service and are used under license to McGraw-Hill. All Rights Reserved. P. 244, Courtesy Mary Kay, Inc.

CHAPTER 11

P. 246, Courtesy Vizio, Inc. P. 248, *No credit.* P. 251, © Terry McElroy. P. 252, © M. Hruby. P. 253, Courtesy of Rock & Roll Hall of Fame. P. 254, © M. Hruby. P. 256, © M. Hruby. P. 263, Courtesy Panasonic Consumer Electronics Company. P. 265, Courtesy Payless ShoeSource, Inc. P. 268, Photo by Neil Lupi/Redferns/Getty Images.

CHAPTER 12

P. 270, Courtesy Callaway Golf; Photo by Sam Greenwood/Getty Images. P. 277, Photo by James Leynse/Corbis. P. 278, Courtesy Nestle SA. P. 281, Courtesy Jiffy Lube International, Inc. P. 281, © Amy Etra. P. 283, © Joe & Kathy Heiner. P. 285, *All photos:* © M. Hruby. P. 287, Courtesy IBM Corporation. P. 287, Courtesy Dell, Inc. P. 287, Courtesy Wal-Mart Stores, Inc. P. 290, Courtesy Hewlett-Packard Company. P. 292, Courtesy Amazon.com Inc.

CHAPTER 13

P. 294, Handout/MCT/Newscom. P. 294, *Both:* Courtesy Foursquare. P. 297, © Daniel Hambury/Corbis. P. 298, Courtesy Green Retail Association. P. 298, © 2012 macys.com. P. 299, Courtesy Doctor's Associates, Inc. P. 300, Courtesy Staples, Inc. P. 301, Courtesy Healtht You Vending. P. 302, © M. Hruby. P. 302, © M. Hruby. P. 302, Courtesy L.L.Bean, Inc. P. 303, Scott Lewis/Bloomberg via Getty Images. P. 303, Courtesy MySimon, Inc. P. 304, © 2007-2012 Mary Kay Inc. P. 305, Photographer: Jin Lee/Bloomberg via Getty Images. P. 306, Courtesy TJX Companies, Inc. P. 306, AP Photo/Paul Sakuma. P. 310, Supplied by: Checkers Drive-In Restaurants, Inc. P. 314, *Both:* Courtesy Mall of America.

CHAPTER 14

P. 316, Courtesy Brian Solis, www.briansolis.com. P. 319, Courtesy VF Outdoors. P. 322, Courtesy Alpargatas USA. P. 322, © M. Hruby. P. 322, Courtesy Ford Motor Company. P. 324, Courtesy of Restaurant Business Magazines. P. 324, Courtesy Purina Incredible Dog Challenge. P. 325, *No credit.* P. 326, Artwork supplied by Merck-Schering/Plough Pharmaceuticals. P. 328, © 2012 Procter & Gamble. P. 328, © 2012 Verizon Wireless. P. 329, Franck Fife/AFP/Getty Images/Newscom. P. 330, © M. Hruby. P. 332, *No credit* P. 333, Created for Target by CatalystStudios.com. P. 334, *No credit.* P. 336, © M. Hruby.

CHAPTER 15

P. 338, Bloomberg via Getty Images. P. 338, Hamin Lee Photography/ BELL MOBILITY/Newscom. P. 340, Courtesy Campbell Soup Company. P. 340, Courtesy 1&1 Internet, Inc. P. 340, Courtesy Red Bull North America. P. 341, Copyright © Bayer AG. P. 341, Ad developed by McCann Worldgroup on behalf of the U.S. Army. P. 342, © 2012 Dr. Pepper/Seven Up, Inc. P. 342, *No credit.* P. 342, © M. Hruby. P. 343, Courtesy Iconix Brand. P. 347, Courtesy Oxygen Media, LLC. P. 347, © M. Hruby. P. 348, © 2012 USA TODAY, a division of Gannett Satellite Information Network, Inc. P. 348, Courtesy USA Today. P. 348, © M. Hruby. P. 349, Spike Mafford/Getty Images. P. 349, Courtesy 24/7 Real Media Inc. P. 350, Courtesy Nationwide Insurance. P. 350, Courtesy Wieden + Kennedy/New York. P. 352, Courtesy MRI Starch. P. 353, Courtesy of Valpak Direct Marketing Systems, Inc. P. 354, © M. Hruby. P. 355, *No credit.* P. 355, © Geffen Pictures/Zuma Press. P. 355, Photo by Michael Becker/Fox/Picture Group via AP Images. P. 355, © Rex USA. P. 359, © Google.

CHAPTER 16

P. 362, Courtesy AOI Marketing/Minneapolis. P. 362, *No credit.* P. 362, © Jeremy M. Lange. P. 362, Courtesy Carma Laboratories. P. 362, P. 364, © Ford Consulting Group. P. 365, © Ford Consulting Group. P. 366, © K. Rousonelos. P. 367, AP Photo/Marcio Jose Sanchez. P. 368, Courtesy AOI Marketing/Minneapolis. P. 369, Facebook © 2012. P. 369, © 2012 Twitter. P. 369, LinkedIn Corporation © 2012. P. 369, Courtesy YouTube LLC. P. 370, Courtesy Carma Laboratories. P. 370, *No credit.* P. 371, *Both photos: No credit.* P. 372, Copyright © 2012 Yahoo, Inc. P. 372, *No credit.* P. 372, *No credit.* P. 372, © Google. P. 372, four-square © 2012. P. 372, *No credit.* P. 372, *No credit.* P. 372, © 2012 Tumblr. P. 372, *No credit.* P. 372, *No credit.* P. 375, Courtesy Pepsi-Cola Company. P. 376, Courtesy YouTube LLC. P. 376, *No credit.* P. 377, AP Photo/KEYSTONE/Laurent Gillieron. P. 377, AP Photo/ Irwin Fedriansyah. P. 379, *No credit.* P. 379, *No credit.* P. 379, *No credit.* P. 379, *No credit.* P 379, *No credit.* P. 379, *No credit.* P. 379, © 2012 Rovio Entertainment Ltd. P. 380, Courtesy Tesco PLC; Agency Cheil Worldwide/Korea. P. 381, T-Mobile Christmas Campaign 2010 with Chuck Norris produced by Saatchi & Saatchi Prague, Czech Republic. P. 383, Courtesy AOI Marketing/Minneapolis. P. 384, *All:* Courtesy AOI Marketing/Minneapolis. P. 384, *All:* Courtesy AOI Marketing/Minneapolis.

CHAPTER 17

P. 386, Courtesy General Electric Company. P. 389, Courtesy Medtronic. P. 390, © Mitch Kezar/Windigo Images. P. 391, Asia Images/Getty Images. P. 391, Tetra Images/Getty Images. P. 391, © Royalty-Free/Corbis. P. 391, © Susan Van Etten/PhotoEdit, Inc. P. 393, © Einzig Photography. P. 394, © Image Source/Corbis. P. 395, © Richard Pasley/Stock Boston, LLC. P. 396, Frank Herholdt/Stone/Getty Images. P. 397, Purestock/ GettyImages. P. 399, Courtesy Xerox Corporation. P. 401, Comstock Images/Getty Images. P. 401, Courtesy Mary Kay, Inc. P. 404, *Both* Courtesy of Toshiba Medical Systems & Interactive Media. P. 407, Courtesy Xerox Corporation.

CHAPTER 18

P. 408, *Both* Courtesy Seven Cycles, Inc. P. 412, © Kainaz Amaria. P. 413, Courtesy Reebok International Ltd. P. 414, *No credit.* P. 415, Courtesy Travelocity. P. 417, © Paul Barton/Corbis. P. 418, © Tom Grill/Corbis. P. 419, © 2008 Zappos.com., Inc. P. 420, © Clayton Hauck Photography. P. 421, Courtesy Career Builder.com. P. 422, © Joe Zeff Design. P. 423, PeskyMonkey/Vetta/Getty Images. P. 426, Courtesy Pizza Hut, Inc. P. 427, Coutesy Pizza Hut, Inc. P. 428, Courtesy Pizza Hut, Inc.

NAME INDEX

COMPANY INDEX

A

A. C. E. S. Flight Simulation, 314
AA Direct Connect, 283
Abbott Laboratories, 117
ABC, 154, 339
Aberdeen Group, 180
Accenture, 434
Accountancy Age, 347
Accutron, 233
Ace Hardware, 279
ACNielsen, 115
Acura ZDZ, 335
Adidas, 17, 128, 129, 229, 300
Advil, 90
Aeon, 297
AFLAC, 343
Aflac, 368
Agentrics, 117
Aldi, 177
Amazing Mirror Maze, 314
Amazon.com, 26, 66, 223, 251, 272,
    276, 302, 303, 339, 419, 425
    supply chain and logistics
        management, 292–293
Amazon Living Social, 102
Amazon Outdoor Recreation store, 293
Ambassador brand cards, 277
American Airlines, 61, 75, 252, 283
American Eagle Outfitters, 363
American Enterprise Institute, 116
American Express, 239, 389
American Express Centurian Card, 87
American Hospital Supply, 284
American Idol, 354, 355, 374
American Lung Association, 77
American Red Cross, 27, 106, 198,
    341, 357
    mission, 25
America Online, 96
Ameritrade, 61
Amway, 304
Anacin, 233
Android, 378
Angry Birds app, 378–379
Anheuser-Busch, 95, 99, 342
Ann Taylor Corporation, 177
Ann Taylor LOFT stores, 177
AOI Marketing, Inc., launch of Bitter
    girls, 383–385
Apple II computer, 7, 187, 195, 201, 203
Apple Inc., 4, 7, 26, 27, 66, 81, 82, 83,
    97, 128, 129, 140, 177, 204, 208,
    215, 231, 232, 262, 278, 281,
    339, 355, 363, 378
    changing segmentation strategy,
        187–188
    new product innovations, 195–196
Apple Industrial Design Group, 208
Apple Macintosh, 187
Apple Stores, 308
Arby's, 95
Arm & Hammer, 234, 235
Armani Exchange, 314
Arrow shirts, 254
Associated Grocers, 279, 299
Athenos yogurt, 211, 342
Athlon Sports, 347
AT&T, 66, 82, 132, 138, 328, 348, 350,
    354, 355, 395

Audi, 344
Aurora Foods, 232
Autobytel.com, 276
Avatar, 147
Avert Virucidal, 204
Avis Rent-A-Car, 188, 279
Avon Products, Inc., 16, 73, 127,
    304, 388
Axe, 233, 234

B

Babies "R" Us, 200
Bagel-Fuls, 209
Banana Republic, 177
Barbie doll, 135, 136, 211
Barnes & Noble, 26, 73, 300, 307,
    416, 425
Barnesandnoble.com, 303, 416
Baseball magazine, 176
Batman, 147
Bausch and Lomb, 355, 359
Bayer, 341
Bebe, 343
Bell bicycle helmets, 7
Ben & Jerry's, 24, 25, 30, 33, 35, 41
    marketing dashboard, 28
    mission, 20, 21
Benetton, 129
Ben Franklin stores, 279
Best Buy, 117, 202, 254, 281, 300, 301,
    306, 308, 317, 355
Best Foods, 98
Be Tough, 220
Betty Crocker, 166
Betty Crocker Dessert Bowls, 216
BettyCrocker Warm Delights, 215–217
Bic pens, 234
Bic perfume, 233
Biggest Loser, 356
Bitter Girls, 367, 368, 380
    Facebook for launch of, 383–385
BJ's Wholesale, 247
Black & Decker, 126, 140, 215,
    235, 399
BlackBerry, 81
Blistex, 160
Bloomingdale's, 254, 284, 298, 306,
    314, 432
Bloomspot, 102
Blue-Cross-Blue Shield, 335
Bluetooth, 325
BluFarm Group, 144
BMW, 213, 304, 335
BMX bikes, 119
Boeing Company, 67, 116, 137,
    167, 262
Bold detergent, 234, 432
Bolin Digital, 170–171
Bolin Marketing, 170–171
Bontrager, 120
Booyah, 295
Bose audio systems, 231, 418
Boston Market, 309
Boucheron, 280
Brawny paper towels, 230
Breathe Right strips, 143–145
Bridgestone, 230, 341
Brighter Girls, 385

Brightkite, 295
Brillo pads, 15
Bring It, 220
Brita, 63
British Airways, 82
Broadview Security, 198
Brooks Brothers Clothiers, 87
Brookstone, 333
Brother, 224
Buckle, 433
Buddy Media, 368
Bugatti Veyron, 248–249, 262
Buick, 83, 283, 402
Burger Chef, 310
Burger King, 180, 181, 186, 189,
    405, 420
    complexities of commercialization, 213
Burlington Coat Factory, 306
Business Talk Radio, 347
BuyWithMe, 102
BzzAgent, 94
    operations and clients, 95

C

Cadbury Schweppes, 232
Cadillac, 402
Calistoga, 230
Callaway Diablo Edge Driver, 270
Callaway Golf Company, 423
    marketing channels, 271
Callbookstores.com, 303
Camay, 235
Campbell Soup Company, 89, 98, 117,
    156, 179, 229, 234, 237, 340
Campbell's V-8, 85
Candie's, 343
Canon, 242, 262
CareerBuilder.com, 342, 420,
    421, 435
Carma Laboratories, Inc.,
    160, 369
CarMax, 264, 296, 297
Carmex, 161, 362, 369, 370
    marketing dashboard, 160
    use of Facebook, 170–171
Carnation Instant Breakfast, 17
Carrefour, 297
Cartier, 251
Casera brand, 98
Catalyst Paper, Inc., 105
Caterpillar, 128, 275, 290
CBS, 154
Celanese Chemical Company, 291
Celebrity Apprentice, 356
Celebrity Cruises, 354
Celestial Seasonings, 237, 238, 272
Cereal Partners Worldwide, 278
CGCT, 154
Champion heart pacemaker, 35–37
Chanel, 128, 142, 251, 281
Chaps, 233
Chapstick, 160
Charlesburg Furniture, 282, 283
Charles Schwab, 405, 412, 419
Chatter Telephone, 149–151
Checkers Drive-In Restaurants, 309, 310
Cheer, 234, 432
Cheerios, 161, 212, 238

Cheese Nips, 237
Cheetos, 138
Chevrolet, 266
Chevron, 273, 341
Chevy Volt, 63, 233
Chicago Symphony Orchestra, 240
Chicken of the Sea, 237
Chips Ahoy, 238
Chobani's Greek Yogurt, 210–211
Chop Chop, 347
Christie's, 128
Chrysler Corporation, 342, 344
Church & Dwight, 234
Cirque du Soleil, 315
Cirrus system, 240
Citibank, 355
CityDeal, 103
Clairol, 90
Cling-Free, 233
Clinique, 424
Clorox Company, 89, 234
CNN, 203
CNS, Inc.
    going global, 143–145
    local partners, 144–145
    managing growth, 145
Coca-Cola Company, 69, 73, 82, 127,
    128, 129, 133, 134, 140, 224,
    231, 237, 238, 273, 280, 299,
    342, 354, 355, 419, 426, 433
    advertising mistakes, 131–132
Coca-Cola C2, 8
Coke, 305
Colgate-Palmolive Company, 91, 92,
    126, 203
Collegester, 59
ColorMatch Custom Makeup
    Selector, 227
Columbia House, 416
Computer Weekly, 347
ConAgra, 103
Consumer Reports, 81
Corning, Inc., 106, 114
Costco, 117, 236, 247, 297, 299
Cost Cutters Family Hair Care, 240
Coupon.com, 353
Coupon Information Corporation, 353
Courtyard Hotels, 235
Cover Girl, 227
Craftsman tools, 96, 234, 251
Craigslist, 436
Crate & Barrel, 302
Cray Inc., 200
Crest Neat Squeeze toothpaste, 208
Crest toothpaste, 200, 284
Croma, 123
Crowdsaver, 103
Cub Foods, 299
Cunard Cruise Line, 64

D

Dannon, 211
Darberry, 103
DeBeers, 128
Deere & Company, 111
Deli Creations, 155
Dell Asia-Pacific and Japan, 123
Dell.com, 276, 416

SUBJECT INDEX

Note: Boldface entries indicate key terms and the page numbers where they are defined.

Want an online, **searchable version** of your textbook?

Wish your textbook could be **available online** while you're doing your assignments?

Connect™ Plus Marketing eBook

If you choose to use *Connect™ Plus Marketing*, you have an affordable and searchable online version of your book integrated with your other online tools.

Connect™ Plus Marketing eBook offers features like:

- Topic search
- Direct links from assignments
- Adjustable text size
- Jump to page number
- Print by section

Want to get more **value** from your textbook purchase?

Think learning marketing should be a bit more **interesting**?

Check out the **STUDENT RESOURCES** section under the *Connect™* Library tab.

Here you'll find a wealth of resources designed to help you achieve your goals in the course. You'll find things like **quizzes, PowerPoints, and Internet activities** to help you study. Every student has different needs, so explore the STUDENT RESOURCES to find the materials best suited to you.